SPSS/PC+
Advanced Statistics ™ *4.0*
for the IBM PC/XT/AT and PS/2

D0933149

```
          2      1 2
          2      1 2
         21     11222  2   2
         21     11222  2   2
         11     11222 2 2   2
         11     1111222     2
     11 211    11111222222
     11 211    11111222222
     11 2111   11111222222          22
     11 2111   11111222222          22
     11 1111   111112211222  2 22  12
     11 1111   111112211222  2 22  12
     11 1111   111112211222  2122  12
     11 1111   111112211222  2122  12
  -2.0    -1.0      0.0      1.0    2.0
```

SPSS

Marija J. Norušis/SPSS Inc.

SPSS Inc.
444 N. Michigan Avenue
Chicago, Illinois 60611
Tel: (312) 329-2400
Fax: (312) 329-3668

For more information about SPSS/PC+™ software products, please write or call

Marketing Department
SPSS Inc.
444 North Michigan Avenue
Chicago, IL 60611
Tel: (312) 329-2400
Fax: (312) 329-3668

SPSS/PC+™ Advanced Statistics™ 4.0
Copyright © 1990 bySPSS Inc.
All rights reserved.
Printed in the United States of America.

4 5 6 7 8 9 0   93 92

ISBN 0-923967-13-3

Library of Congress Catalog Card Number: 90-070750

Preface

SPSS/PC+ is a powerful software package for microcomputer data management and analysis. The Advanced Statistics option for SPSS/PC+ 4.0 is an add-on enhancement that enables you to perform sophisticated multivariate statistical analyses. The procedures in Advanced Statistics must be used with the SPSS/PC+ base system and are completely integrated into that system. The Advanced Statistics option does not require the Statistics option.

Advanced Statistics includes procedures for discriminant analysis, hierarchical and general log-linear analysis, multivariate analysis of variance, reliability analysis of additive scales, nonlinear regression, probit analysis, and survival analysis. These procedures bring most of the power of mainframe statistical software to the personal computer. The algorithms and much of the programming are identical to those used in SPSS on mainframe computers. Although the size of the problems you can analyze may be limited by the amount of memory installed on your PC, statistical results you obtain from SPSS/PC+ will be as accurate as those computed on a mainframe.

SPSS/PC+ with Advanced Statistics will enable you to perform many analyses on your PC that were previously possible only on much larger machines. We hope that this new statistical power will make SPSS/PC+ an even more useful tool in your work.

Compatibility

SPSS Inc. warrants that SPSS/PC+ and enhancements are designed for personal computers in the IBM PC and IBM PS/2™ lines with a 10MB or larger hard disk. These products also function on most closely IBM-compatible machines. Contact SPSS Inc. for details about specific IBM-compatible hardware.

Serial Numbers

Your serial number is your identification number with SPSS Inc. You will need this serial number when you call SPSS Inc. for information regarding support, payment, a defective diskette, or an upgraded system.

The serial number can be found on the diskette labeled U1 that came with your base system. Before using the system, please copy this number to the **registration card.**

Registration Card

STOP! Before continuing on, *fill out and send us your registration card.* Until we receive your registration card, you have an unregistered system. Even if you have previously sent a card to us, please fill out and return the card enclosed in your SPSS/PC+ Advanced Statistics package.

Registering your system entitles you to

- Technical support on our customer hotline.
- Favored customer status.
- *Keywords*—the SPSS user newsletter.
- New product announcements.

Of course, unregistered systems receive none of the above, so *don't put it off—send your registration card now!*

Replacement Policy   Call the Micro Software Department at 312/329-3300 to report a defective diskette. You must provide us with the serial number of your system. (The normal installation procedure will detect any damaged diskettes.) SPSS Inc. will ship replacement diskettes the same day we receive notification from you. Please return the defective diskettes to the Micro Software Department, SPSS Inc., 444 North Michigan Avenue, Chicago, IL 60611.

Shipping List   The shipping list for SPSS/PC+ Advanced Statistics 4.0 is on a separate sheet in the package.

Training Seminars   SPSS Inc. provides both public and onsite training seminars for SPSS/PC+. There is a two-day introductory course to familiarize users with the basics of SPSS/PC+. In addition there is an advanced course, also two days, that deals with more sophisticated aspects of the program. Additional seminars treat specialized topics such as data entry, graphics, report writing, and time series analysis. All seminars feature hands-on workshops.

SPSS/PC+ seminars will be offered in major U.S. and European cities on a regular basis. For further information on these seminars or to schedule an onsite seminar, call the SPSS Inc. Training Department at 312/329-3557.

Additional Documentation   Additional copies of all SPSS product manuals may be purchased separately. To order additional manuals, just fill out the Documentation Card included with your system and send it to SPSS Inc. Documentation Sales, 444 N. Michigan Avenue, Chicago, IL, 60611.

Note: In Europe, additional copies of documentation can be purchased by site-licensed customers only. Please contact the European office at the address listed on the copyright page for more information.

Technical Support   The SPSS technical hotline is available to registered customers of SPSS/PC+. Customers may call the Techline for assistance in using SPSS products or for installation help for one of the warranted hardware environments.

To reach an SPSS technical support consultant, call 312/329-3410, 9:00 a.m. to 5:00 p.m. CST. Be prepared to identify yourself, your organization, and the serial number of your system.

If you are a Value Plus or Customer EXPress customer, use the priority 800 number you received with your materials. For information on subscribing to the Value Plus or Customer EXPress plan, call SPSS Inc. at 312/329-3313.

Lend Us Your Thoughts   Your comments are important. So send us a letter and let us know about your experiences with SPSS products. We especially like to hear about new and interesting applications using the SPSS/PC+ system. Write to SPSS Inc. Marketing Department, Attn: Micro Software Products Manager, 444 N. Michigan Avenue, Chicago, IL, 60611.

Contacting SPSS Inc.   If you would like to be on our mailing list, write to us at one of the addresses below. We will send you a copy of our newsletter and let you know about SPSS Inc. activities in your area.

SPSS Inc.
444 North Michigan Ave.
Chicago, IL 60611
Tel: (312) 329-2400
Fax: (312) 329-3668

SPSS Federal Systems
12030 Sunrise Valley Dr.
Suite 300
Reston, VA 22091
Tel: (703) 391-6020
Fax (703) 391-6002

SPSS Latin America
444 North Michigan Ave.
Chicago, IL 60611
Tel: (312) 329-3556
Fax: (312) 329-3668

SPSS Benelux BV
P.O. Box 115
4200 AC Gorinchem
The Netherlands
Tel: +31.1830.36711
Fax: +31.1830.35839

SPSS UK Ltd.
SPSS House
5 London Street
Chertsey
Surrey KT16 8AP
United Kingdom
Tel: +44.932.566262
Fax: +44.932.567020

SPSS UK Ltd., New Delhi
c/o Ashok Business Centre
Ashok Hotel
50B Chanakyapuri
New Delhi 110 021
India
Tel: +91.11.600121 x1029
Fax: +91.11.6873216

SPSS GmbH Software
Steinsdorfstrasse 19
D-8000 Munich 22
Germany
Tel:+49.89.2283008
Fax: +49.89.2285413

SPSS Scandinavia AB
Sjöängsvägen 21
S-191 72 Sollentuna
Sweden
Tel: +46.8.7549450
Fax: +46.8.7548816

SPSS Asia Pacific Pte. Ltd.
10 Anson Road, #34-07
International Plaza
Singapore 0207
Singapore
Tel: +65.221.2577
Fax: +65.221.9920

SPSS Japan Inc.
Gyoen Sky Bldg.
2-1-11, Shinjuku
Shinjuku-ku
Tokyo 160
Japan
Tel: +81.3.33505261
Fax: +81.3.33505245

SPSS Australasia Pty. Ltd.
121 Walker Street
North Sydney, NSW 2060
Australia
Tel: +61.2.954.5660
Fax: +61.2.954.5616

Contents

Introduction

About This Manual

This manual documents the additional statistical procedures available in SPSS/PC+ Advanced Statistics™. The manual is organized similarly to the *SPSS/PC+ Base Manual* in that there are different parts designed to meet the needs of different users. For those who have limited experience with statistics, statistical overviews are available. For those who are already familiar with statistical computing, a reference section presents the procedures in SPSS/PC+ Advanced Statistics without extensive examples. You are likely to find different parts of the manual most valuable as your experience with SPSS/PC+ grows.

To use SPSS/PC+ Advanced Statistics, you should be familiar with the SPSS/PC+ language as described in the *SPSS/PC+ Base Manual*. In addition, this manual assumes that you know how to run the SPSS/PC+ system and that you are familiar with basic data entry and manipulation. If you are unfamiliar with SPSS/PC+, consult the base manual for further information.

If you have just received SPSS/PC+ Advanced Statistics, you may want to turn first to the installation instructions, which are in a separate booklet. You need to install SPSS/PC+ Advanced Statistics only once, unless you remove it from your system. (You can, however, remove and reinstall portions of the SPSS/PC+ system: see the section on SPSS MANAGER in the *SPSS/PC+ Base Manual*.)

The three basic parts to this manual are described below.

Statistics Guide. The Statistics Guide (Part B) contains overviews of the statistics and operations for the eight procedures contained in SPSS/PC+ Advanced Statistics. The SPSS/PC+ input used to create the sample output in these chapters is shown to help you understand each procedure's operation.

Command Reference. The Command Reference (Part C) is a detailed reference to the syntax and operations of the eight procedures contained in SPSS/PC+ Advanced Statistics. The individual procedures are presented in alphabetical order. For each procedure, the Command Reference provides complete syntax rules plus details of operations.

Examples. The examples presented in Part D illustrate typical uses of the eight analytical procedures contained in SPSS/PC+ Advanced Statistics. The annotated input and output are arranged not to imitate an interactive SPSS/PC+ session but to demonstrate a set of commands that carry out a complete data analysis task. You may find that these examples, with their interpretative commentary, extend your understanding of the logic of SPSS/PC+ command structure.

Statistics Guide

Contents

1 Discriminant Analysis: Procedure DSCRIMINANT

Gazing into crystal balls is not the exclusive domain of soothsayers. Judges, college admissions counselors, bankers, and many other professionals must foretell outcomes such as parole violation, success in college, and creditworthiness.

An intuitive strategy is to compare the characteristics of a potential student or credit applicant to those of cases whose success or failure is already known. Based on similarities and differences a prediction can be made. Often this is done subjectively, using only the experience and wisdom of the decision maker. However, as problems grow more complex and the consequences of bad decisions become more severe, a more objective procedure for predicting outcomes is often desirable.

Before considering statistical techniques, let's summarize the problem. Based on a collection of variables, such as yearly income, age, marital status, and total worth, we wish to distinguish among several mutually exclusive groups, such as good credit risks and bad credit risks. The available data are the values of the variables for cases whose group membership is known, that is, cases who have proven to be good or bad credit risks. We also wish to identify the variables that are important for distinguishing among the groups and to develop a procedure for predicting group membership for new cases whose group membership is undetermined.

Discriminant analysis, first introduced by Sir Ronald Fisher, is the statistical technique most commonly used to investigate this set of problems. The concept underlying discriminant analysis is fairly simple. Linear combinations of the independent, sometimes called predictor, variables are formed and serve as the basis for classifying cases into one of the groups.

For the linear discriminant function to be "optimal," that is, to provide a classification rule that minimizes the probability of misclassification, certain assumptions about the data must be met. Each group must be a sample from a multivariate normal population, and the population covariance matrices must all be equal. Section 1.42 discusses tests for violations of the assumptions and the performance of linear discriminant analysis when assumptions are violated.

Sections 1.2 through 1.34 cover the basics of discriminant analysis and the output from SPSS/PC+ DSCRIMINANT, using a two-group example. Extending this type of analysis to include more than two groups is discussed beginning in Section 1.35.

1.1
INVESTIGATING RESPIRATORY DISTRESS SYNDROME

Respiratory Distress Syndrome (RDS) is one of the leading causes of death in premature infants. Although intensive research has failed to uncover its causes, a variety of physiological disturbances, such as insufficient oxygen uptake and high blood acidity, are characteristic of RDS. These are usually treated by administering oxygen and buffers to decrease acidity. However, a substantial proportion of RDS infants fail to survive.

P. K. J. van Vliet and J. M. Gupta (1973) studied 50 infants with a diagnosis of RDS based on clinical signs and symptoms and confirmed by chest x-ray. For each case they report the infant's outcome—whether the infant died or survived—as well as values for eight variables that might be predictors of outcome. Table 1.1 gives the SPSS/PC+ names and descriptions of these variables.

Table 1.1 Possible predictors of survival

Variable name	Description
SURVIVAL	Infant's outcome. Coded 1 if infant died, 2 if survived.
SEX	Infant's sex. Coded 0 for females, 1 for males.
APGAR	Score on the APGAR test, which measures infant's responsiveness. Scores range from 0 to 10.
AGE	The gestational age of the infant measured in weeks. Values of 36 to 38 are obtained for full-term infants.
TIME	Time, measured in minutes, that it took the infant to begin breathing spontaneously.
WEIGHT	Birthweight measured in kilograms.
PH	The acidity level of the blood, measured on a scale from 0 to 14.
TREATMNT	Type of buffer administered (buffer neutralizes acidity). Coded 1 for THAM, 0 for sodium carbonate.
RESP	Indicates whether respiratory therapy was initiated. Coded 0 for no, 1 for yes.

Some dichotomous variables such as SEX are included among the predictor variables. Although, as previously indicated, the linear discriminant function requires that the predictor variables have a multivariate normal distribution, the function has been shown to perform fairly well in a variety of other situations (see Section 1.42).

In this example, we will use discriminant analysis to determine whether the variables listed in Table 1.1 distinguish between infants who recover from RDS and those who do not. If high-risk infants can be identified early, special monitoring and treatment procedures may be instituted for them. It is also of interest to determine which variables contribute most to the separation of infants who survive from those who do not.

1.2
Selecting Cases for the Analysis

The first step in discriminant analysis is to select cases to be included in the computations. A case is excluded from the analysis if it contains missing information for the variable that defines the groups or for any of the predictor variables.

If many cases have missing values for at least one variable, the actual analysis will be based on a small subset of cases. This may be troublesome for two reasons. First, estimates based on small samples are usually quite variable. Second, if the cases with missing values differ from those without missing values, the resulting estimates may be too biased. For example, if highly educated people are more likely to provide information on the variables used in the analysis, selecting cases with complete data will result in a sample that is highly educated. Results obtained from such a sample might differ from those that would be obtained if people at all educational levels were included. Therefore, it is usually a good strategy to examine cases with missing values to see whether there is evidence that missing values are associated with some particular characteristics of the cases. If there are many missing values for some variables, you should consider the possibility of eliminating those variables from the analysis.

Figure 1.2 shows the entire SPSS/PC+ session and the output produced by DSCRIMINANT after all the data have been processed. The first line of the output indicates how many cases are eligible for inclusion. The second line indicates the number of cases excluded from analysis because of missing values for the predictor variables or the variable that defines the groups. In this example, two cases with missing values are excluded from the analysis. If you use the WEIGHT command, DSCRIMINANT displays the sum of the weights in each group and the actual number of cases.

Figure 1.2 Case summary

```
TITLE 'INFANT SURVIVAL EXAMPLE--2-GROUP DISCRIMINANT'.
DATA LIST  /CASEID 1-2 SURVIVAL 4 TREATMNT 6
   TIME 8-10(1)  WEIGHT 12-15(3) APGAR 17-18
   SEX 20  AGE 22-23 PH 33-35(2) RESP 37.
VARIABLE LABELS SURVIVAL 'INFANT SURVIVAL'
   TREATMNT 'TREATMNT ADMINISTERED'
   TIME 'TIME TO SPONTANEOUS RESPIRATION'
   WEIGHT 'BIRTHWEIGHT IN KILOGRAMS'
   APGAR 'APGAR SCORE'
   SEX 'SEX OF INFANT'
   PH 'PH LEVEL'
   RESP 'RESPIRATORY THERAPY'.
MISSING VALUES RESP(9).
VALUE LABELS TREATMNT 1'THAM' 0'SODIUM BICARBONATE'/
   SEX 0'FEMALE' 1'MALE'/
   RESP 1'YES' 0'NO' 9'NO ANSWER'/
   SURVIVAL 2'SURVIVE' 1'DIE'.
DSCRIMINANT GROUPS=SURVIVAL(1,2)
   /VARIABLES=TREATMNT TO RESP.
```

```
On groups defined by SURVIVAL  INFANT SURVIVAL

           50 (unweighted) cases were processed.
            2 of these were excluded from the analysis.
              0 had missing or out-of-range group codes.
              2 had at least one missing discriminating variable.
           48 (unweighted) cases will be used in the analysis.


Number of Cases by Group

                    Number of Cases
   SURVIVAL  Unweighted    Weighted  Label

         1         26         26.0  DIE
         2         22         22.0  SURVIVE

   Total           48         48.0
```

1.3
Analyzing Group Differences

Although the variables are interrelated and we will need to employ statistical techniques that incorporate these dependencies, it is often helpful to begin analyzing the differences between groups by examining univariate statistics.

Figure 1.3a contains the means for the eight independent variables for infants who died (Group 1) and who survived (Group 2), along with the corresponding standard deviations. The last row of each table, labeled **Total**, contains the means and standard deviations calculated when all cases are combined into a single sample.

Figure 1.3a Group means and standard deviations

```
DSCRIMINANT GROUPS=SURVIVAL(1,2)
   /VARIABLES=TREATMNT TO RESP
   /STATISTICS=1 2.
```

Group means

SURVIVAL	TREATMNT	TIME	WEIGHT	APGAR	SEX	AGE	PH	RESP
1	0.38462	2.88462	1.70950	5.50000	0.65385	32.38462	7.17962	0.65385
2	0.59091	2.31818	2.36091	6.31818	0.68182	34.63636	7.34636	0.27273
Total	0.47917	2.62500	2.00806	5.87500	0.66667	33.41667	7.25604	0.47917

Group Standard Deviations

SURVIVAL	TREATMNT	TIME	WEIGHT	APGAR	SEX	AGE	PH	RESP
1	0.49614	3.48513	0.51944	2.77489	0.48516	3.11226	0.08502	0.48516
2	0.50324	3.70503	0.62760	2.69720	0.47673	2.71759	0.60478	0.45584
Total	0.50485	3.56027	0.65353	2.74152	0.47639	3.12051	0.41751	0.50485

From Figure 1.3a you can see that 38% of the infants who died were treated with THAM, 65% were male, and 65% received respiratory therapy. (When a variable is coded 0 or 1, the mean of the variable is the proportion of cases with a value of 1.) Infants who died took longer to breathe spontaneously, weighed less, and had lower APGAR scores than infants who survived.

Figure 1.3b shows significance tests for the equality of group means for each variable. The *F* values and their significance, shown in columns 3 and 4, are the same as those calculated from a one-way analysis of variance with survival as the grouping variable. For example, the *F* value in Figure 1.3c, which is an analysis of variance table for WEIGHT from procedure ONEWAY, is 15.49, the same as shown for WEIGHT in Figure 1.3b. (When there are two groups, the *F* value is just the square of the *t* value from the two-sample t-test.) The significance level is 0.0003. If the observed significance level is small (less than 0.05), the hypothesis that all group means are equal is rejected.

Figure 1.3b Tests for univariate equality of group means

```
DSCRIMINANT GROUPS=SURVIVAL(1,2)
  /VARIABLES=TREATMNT TO RESP
  /STATISTICS=1 2 6.
```

```
Wilks' Lambda (U-statistic) and univariate F-ratio
with   1 and        46 degrees of freedom

  Variable   Wilks' Lambda          F          Significance

  TREATMNT     0.95766           2.034           0.1606
  TIME         0.99358            .2971          0.5883
  WEIGHT       0.74810           15.49           0.0003
  APGAR        0.97742            1.063          0.3080
  SEX          0.99913            .4024D-01      0.8419
  AGE          0.86798            6.997          0.0111
  PH           0.95956            1.939          0.1705
  RESP         0.85551            7.769          0.0077
```

Figure 1.3c ONEWAY analysis of variance table for WEIGHT

```
ONEWAY WEIGHT BY SURVIVAL(1,2)
  /OPTIONS=2.
```

```
- - - - - - - - - - - - - - O N E W A Y - - - - - - - - - - - - - - -

      Variable  WEIGHT    BIRTHWEIGHT IN KILOGRAMS
    By Variable SURVIVAL  INFANT SURVIVAL

                            Analysis of Variance

                             Sum of        Mean          F      F
          Source      D.F.   Squares      Squares     Ratio   Prob.

  Between Groups        1     5.0566       5.0566    15.4894   .0003

  Within Groups        46    15.0171        .3265

  Total                47    20.0737
```

1.4
Wilks' Lambda

Another statistic displayed in Figure 1.3b is Wilks' lambda, sometimes called the *U* statistic (see Section 1.17). When variables are considered individually, lambda is the ratio of the within-groups sum of squares to the total sum of squares. For example, Figure 1.3c shows the sums of squares for variable WEIGHT. The ratio of the within-groups sum of squares (15.02) to the total sum of squares (20.07) is 0.748, the value for Wilks' lambda for WEIGHT in Figure 1.3b.

A lambda of 1 occurs when all observed group means are equal. Values close to 0 occur when within-groups variability is small compared to the total variability, that is, when most of the total variability is attributable to differences between the means of the groups. Thus, large values of lambda indicate that group means do not appear to be different, while small values indicate that group means do appear to be different. From Figure 1.3b, WEIGHT, AGE, and RESP are the variables whose means are most different for survivors and nonsurvivors.

1.5
Correlations

Since interdependencies among the variables affect most multivariate analyses, it is worth examining the correlation matrix of the predictor variables. Figure 1.5a is the pooled within-groups correlation matrix. WEIGHT and AGE have the largest correlation coefficient, 0.84. This is to be expected, since weight increases with gestational age. Section 1.19 discusses some of the possible consequences of including highly correlated variables in the analysis.

A *pooled within-groups* correlation matrix is obtained by averaging the separate covariance matrices for all groups and then computing the correlation matrix. A *total* correlation matrix is obtained when all cases are treated as if they are from a single sample.

Figure 1.5a   Pooled within-groups correlation matrix

```
DSCRIMINANT GROUPS=SURVIVAL(1,2)
  /VARIABLES=TREATMNT TO RESP
  /STATISTICS=1 2 6 4.
```

```
Pooled Within-Groups Correlation Matrix

              TREATMNT TIME     WEIGHT   APGAR    SEX      AGE      PH       RESP

   TREATMNT   1.00000
   TIME        .01841  1.00000
   WEIGHT      .09091  -.21244  1.00000
   APGAR      -.03394  -.50152   .22161  1.00000
   SEX        -.03637  -.12982   .19500  -.02098  1.00000
   AGE         .05749  -.20066   .84040   .36329  -.00129  1.00000
   PH         -.08307   .09102   .12436  -.07197  -.03156   .00205  1.00000
   RESP       -.00774  -.06994  -.02394   .16123   .26732  -.06828   .03770  1.00000

Correlations which cannot be computed are printed as '.'
```

The total and pooled within-groups correlation matrices can be quite different. For example, Figure 1.5b shows a plot of two hypothetical variables for three groups. When each group is considered individually, the correlation coefficient is close to 0. Averaging, or pooling, these individual estimates also results in a coefficient close to 0. However, the correlation coefficient computed for all cases combined (total) is 0.97, since groups with larger X values also have larger Y values.

Figure 1.5b   Hypothetical variable plot for three groups

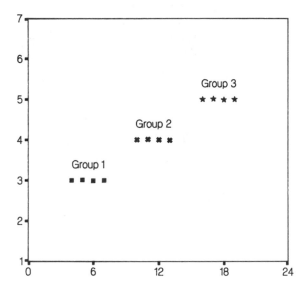

1.6
Estimating the Coefficients

Descriptive statistics and univariate tests of significance provide basic information about the distributions of the variables in the groups and help identify some differences among the groups. However, in discriminant analysis and other multivariate statistical procedures, the emphasis is on analyzing the variables together, not one at a time. By considering the variables simultaneously, we are able to incorporate important information about their relationships.

In discriminant analysis, a linear combination of the independent variables is formed and serves as the basis for assigning cases to groups. Thus, information contained in multiple independent variables is summarized in a single index. For example, by finding a weighted average of variables such as age, weight, and APGAR score, you can obtain a score that distinguishes infants who survive from those who do not. In discriminant analysis, the weights are estimated so that they result in the "best" separation between the groups.

The linear discriminant equation

$$D = B_0 + B_1X_1 + B_2X_2 + \ldots + B_pX_p \qquad \text{Equation 1.6a}$$

is similar to the multiple linear regression equation. The X's are the values of the independent variables and the B's are coefficients estimated from the data. If a linear discriminant function is to distinguish infants who die from those who survive, the two groups must differ in their D values.

Therefore, the B's are chosen so that the values of the discriminant function differ as much as possible between the groups, or that for the discriminant scores the ratio

$$\frac{\text{between-groups sum of squares}}{\text{within-groups sum of squares}} \qquad \text{Equation 1.6b}$$

is a maximum. Any other linear combination of the variables will have a smaller ratio.

The actual mechanics of computing the coefficients, especially if there are more than two groups, is somewhat involved (see Morrison, 1967; Tatsuoka, 1971).

The coefficients for the eight variables listed in Table 1.1 are shown in Figure 1.6. Small and large values are sometimes displayed in scientific notation. For example, the number 0.006998343 might be displayed as 0.6998343D−02.

Figure 1.6   Unstandardized discriminant function coefficients

```
DSCRIMINANT GROUPS=SURVIVAL(1,2)
  /VARIABLES=TREATMNT TO RESP
  /STATISTICS=1 2 6 4 11.
```

```
Unstandardized Canonical Discriminant Function Coefficients

                 FUNC  1

TREATMNT      .4311545
TIME          .3671274D-01
WEIGHT       2.044035
APGAR         .1264302
SEX           .6998343D-02
AGE          -.2180711
PH            .4078705
RESP        -1.244539
(constant)   -.2309344
```

1.7
Calculating the Discriminant Score

Based on the coefficients in Figure 1.6, it is possible to calculate the discriminant score for each case. For example, Figure 1.7a contains the value of each variable for the first five cases in the data file. The discriminant score for Case 1 is obtained by multiplying the unstandardized coefficients by the values of the variables, summing these products, and adding the constant. For Case 1, the discriminant score is

$$D_1 = 0.431(1) + 0.0367(2) + 2.044(1.05) + 0.126(5)$$

$$+ 0.007(0) - 0.218(28) + 0.408(7.09) - 1.244(0) - 0.231 = -0.16$$

Equation 1.7

Figure 1.7a   Values of the variables for the first five cases

```
COMPUTE SCORE=.431*TREATMNT + .0367*TIME + 2.04*WEIGHT + .126*APGAR
              + .007*SEX - .218*AGE + .408*PH - 1.24*RESP - .231.
FORMAT SCORE(F6.3).
LIST CASES=5 /VARIABLES=TREATMNT TO RESP SURVIVAL SCORE
   /FORMAT=NUMBERED.
```

```
C TREATMNT TIME WEIGHT APGAR SEX AGE   PH RESP SURVIVAL  SCORE

1      1    2.0  1.050    5   0  28 7.09   0        1  -.166
2      1    2.0  1.175    4   0  28 7.11   1        1 -1.269
3      1     .5  1.230    7   0  29 7.24   9        1
4      1    4.0  1.310    4   1  29 7.13   1        1 -1.123
5      1     .5  1.500    8   1  32 7.23   1        1  -.973


Number of cases read =     5    Number of cases listed =      5
```

Figure 1.7b contains basic descriptive statistics for the discriminant scores in the two groups. The mean score for all cases combined is 0 and the pooled within-groups variance is 1. This is always true for discriminant scores calculated by SPSS/PC+.

Figure 1.7b   Descriptive statistics from procedure MEANS

```
DSCRIMINANT GROUPS=SURVIVAL(1,2)
   /VARIABLES=TREATMNT TO RESP
   /SAVE=SCORES=DISCORE.
VARIABLE LABELS DISCORE1 'DISCRIMINANT SCORE'.
MEANS TABLES=DISCORE1 BY SURVIVAL
   /STATISTICS=1.
```

```
Summaries of   DISCORE1   DISCRIMINANT SCORE
By levels of   SURVIVAL   INFANT SURVIVAL

    Value Label                  Sum       Mean    Std Dev  Sum of Sq    Cases

      1 DIE            -18.525394  -.7125152  .9055960 20.5026022       26
      2 SURVIVE         18.5253943  .8420634 1.1018901 25.4973978       22
Within Groups Total    0.00000000 0.00000000 1.0000000 46.0000000       48
```

1.8
Bayes' Rule

Using the discriminant score, it is possible to obtain a rule for classifying cases into one of the two groups. The technique used in SPSS/PC+ DSCRIMINANT is based on Bayes' rule. The probability that a case with a discriminant score of D belongs to group i is estimated by

$$P(G_i | D) = \frac{P(D | G_i) P(G_i)}{\sum_{i=1}^{g} P(D | G_i) P(G_i)}$$

Equation 1.8

Sections 1.9 through 1.11 describe the various components of this equation and their relationships.

1.9
Prior Probability

The *prior probability,* represented by $P(G_i)$, is an estimate of the likelihood that a case belongs to a particular group when no information about it is available. For example, if 30% of infants with RDS die, the probability that an infant with RDS will die is 0.3.

The prior probability can be estimated in several ways. If the sample is considered representative of the population, the observed proportions of cases in each group can serve as estimates of the prior probabilities. In this example, 26 out of 48 cases for whom all information is available, or 54%, belong to Group 1 (nonsurvivors), and 22 (46%) belong to Group 2 (survivors). The prior probability of belonging to Group 1, then, is 0.54, and the prior probability of belonging to Group 2 is 0.46.

Often samples are chosen so that they include a fixed number of observations per group. For example, if deaths from RDS were rare, say occurring once per 100 RDS births, even reasonably large samples of RDS births would result in a small number of cases in the nonsurvivor group. Therefore, an investigator might include the same number of survivors and nonsurvivors in the study. In such situations, the prior probability of group membership can be estimated from other sources, such as hospital discharge records.

When all groups are equally likely, or when no information about the probability of group membership is known, equal prior probabilities for all groups may be selected. Since each case must belong to one of the groups, the prior probabilities must sum to 1.

Although prior probabilities convey some information about the likelihood of group membership, they ignore the attributes of the particular case. For example, an infant who is known to be very sick based on various criteria is assigned the same probability of dying as is an infant known to be healthier.

1.10
Conditional Probability

To take advantage of the additional information available for a case in developing a classification scheme, we need to assess the likelihood of the additional information under different circumstances. For example, if the discriminant function scores are normally distributed for each of two groups and the parameters of the distributions can be estimated, it is possible to calculate the probability of obtaining a particular discriminant function value of D if the case is a member of Group 1 or Group 2.

This probability is called the *conditional probability* of D given the group and is denoted by $P(D|G_i)$. To calculate this probability, the case is assumed to belong to a particular group and the probability of the observed score given membership in the group is estimated.

1.11
Posterior Probability

The conditional probability of D given the group gives an idea of how likely the score is for members of a particular group. However, when group membership is unknown, what is really needed is an estimate of how likely membership in the various groups is, given the available information. This is called the *posterior probability* and is denoted by $P(G_i|D)$. It can be estimated from $P(D|G_i)$ and $P(G_i)$ using Bayes' rule. A case is classified, based on its discriminant score D, in the group for which the posterior probability is the largest. That is, it is assigned to the most likely group based on its discriminant score (see Tatsuoka, 1971, for further information).

1.12
Classification Output

Figure 1.12 is an excerpt from the SPSS/PC+ output that lists classification information for each case for a group of cases whose membership is known. The first column, labeled **Case Number**, is the sequence number of the case in the file. The next column, **Mis Val**, contains the number of variables with missing values for that case. Cases with missing values are not used in estimating the coefficients and are not included in the output shown in Figure 1.12 (note the absence of cases 3 and 28). However, those two cases with missing values could have been classified and included in the table by substituting group means for missing values. The third column (Sel) indicates whether a case has been excluded from the computations using the SELECT subcommand.

Figure 1.12 Classification output

```
DSCRIMINANT GROUPS=SURVIVAL(1,2)
  /VARIABLES=TREATMNT TO RESP
  /STATISTICS=1 2 6 4 11 14.
```

Case Number	Mis Val	Sel	Actual Group		Highest Group	Probability P(D/G) P(G/D)	2nd Highest Group P(G/D)	Discrim Scores
1			1		1	0.5821 0.5873	2 0.4127	-0.1622
2			1		1	0.5776 0.8884	2 0.1116	-1.2695
4			1		1	0.6814 0.8637	2 0.1363	-1.1230
5			1		1	0.7962 0.8334	2 0.1666	-0.9708
6			1		1	0.9080 0.7367	2 0.2633	-0.5970
7			1	**	2	0.4623 0.5164	1 0.4836	0.1070
8			1		1	0.8433 0.7112	2 0.2888	-0.5149
9			1		1	0.6581 0.8695	2 0.1305	-1.1551
10			1		1	0.4577 0.5134	2 0.4866	0.0302
11			1		1	0.6087 0.6017	2 0.3983	-0.2006
12			1		1	0.1722 0.9655	2 0.0345	-2.0775
13			1		1	0.1140 0.9750	2 0.0250	-2.2930
14			1		1	0.3430 0.9360	2 0.0640	-1.6607
15			1		1	0.7983 0.6923	2 0.3077	-0.4569
16			1		1	0.7008 0.6482	2 0.3518	-0.3283
17			1		1	0.2090 0.9593	2 0.0407	-1.9687
18			1		1	0.1128 0.9752	2 0.0248	-2.2982
19			1		1	0.4383 0.9178	2 0.0822	-1.4875
20			1	**	2	0.9418 0.7493	1 0.2507	0.7690
21			1		1	0.7384 0.6658	2 0.3342	-0.3786
22			1	**	2	0.5161 0.5495	1 0.4505	0.1927
23			1		1	0.5399 0.8967	2 0.1033	-1.3255
24			1		1	0.4409 0.5026	2 0.4974	0.0582
25			1	**	2	0.8126 0.8288	1 0.1712	1.0791
26			1		1	0.7050 0.6502	2 0.3498	-0.3339
27			1		1	0.5804 0.5864	2 0.4136	-0.1597
29			2	**	1	0.4595 0.5146	2 0.4854	0.0272
30			2		2	0.8552 0.7160	1 0.2840	0.6596
31			2		2	0.6172 0.6062	1 0.3938	0.3423
32			2		2	0.6928 0.6443	1 0.3557	0.4469
33			2		2	0.8887 0.8063	1 0.1937	0.9820
34			2		2	0.6169 0.8793	1 0.1207	1.3423
35			2		2	0.6823 0.8635	1 0.1365	1.2514
36			2		2	0.7755 0.6824	1 0.3176	0.5568
37			2		2	0.6368 0.8746	1 0.1254	1.3143
38			2		2	0.0874 0.9795	1 0.0205	2.5512
39			2		2	0.1236 0.9735	1 0.0265	2.3821
40			2		2	0.0181 0.9925	1 0.0075	3.2050
41			2		2	0.9033 0.7349	1 0.2651	0.7206
42			2	**	1	0.5613 0.8920	2 0.1080	-1.2934
43			2	**	1	0.5270 0.5560	2 0.4440	-0.0799
44			2	**	1	0.3851 0.9281	2 0.0719	-1.5810
45			2		2	0.5574 0.5735	1 0.4265	0.2553
46			2		2	0.7718 0.8401	1 0.1599	1.1321
47			2		2	0.6792 0.6377	1 0.3623	0.4286
48			2		2	0.9649 0.7819	1 0.2181	0.8861
49			2		2	0.5742 0.8891	1 0.1109	1.4040
50			2		2	0.4533 0.9148	1 0.0852	1.5920

For cases included in the computation of the discriminant function, actual group membership is known and can be compared to that predicted using the discriminant function. The group to which a case actually belongs is listed in the column labeled **Actual Group.** The most-likely group for a case based on the discriminant analysis (the group with the largest posterior probability) is listed in the column labeled **Highest Group.** Cases that are misclassified using the discriminant function are flagged with asterisks next to the actual group number.

The next value listed is the probability of a case's discriminant score, or one more extreme, if the case is a member of the most-likely group.

The larger posterior probabilities of membership in the two groups $P(G|D)$ follow in Figure 1.12. When there are only two groups, both probabilities are given since one is the highest and the other the second highest. The probabilities 0.5873 and 0.4127 sum to 1, since a case must be a member of one of the two groups.

1.13
Classification Summary

You can obtain the number of misclassified cases by counting the number of cases with asterisks in Figure 1.12. In this example, 9 cases out of 50 are classified incorrectly.

More detailed information on the results of the classification phase is available from the output in Figure 1.13, sometimes called the "Confusion Matrix." For each group, this output shows the numbers of correct and incorrect classifications. In this example only the cases with complete information for all predictor variables are included in the classification results table. Correctly classified cases appear on the diagonal of the table since the predicted and actual groups are the same. For example, of 26 cases in Group 1, 22 were predicted correctly to be members of Group 1 (84.6%), while 4 (15.4%) were assigned incorrectly to Group 2. Similarly, 18 out of 22 (81.8%) of the Group 2 cases were identified correctly, and 4 (18.2%) were misclassified. The overall percentage of cases classified correctly is 83.3% (40 out of 48).

Figure 1.13   Classification results

```
DSCRIMINANT GROUPS=SURVIVAL(1,2)
  /VARIABLES=TREATMNT TO RESP
  /STATISTICS=1 2 6 4 11 14 13.
```

```
Classification Results -

                              No. of     Predicted Group Membership
            Actual Group      Cases         1           2
                                         _____    _____
Group        1                  26          22           4
DIE                                       84.6%        15.4%

Group        2                  22           4          18
SURVIVE                                   18.2%        81.8%

Percent of "grouped" cases correctly classified:  83.33%
```

1.14
Histograms of Discriminant Scores

To see how much the two groups overlap and to examine the distribution of the discriminant scores, it is often useful to plot the discriminant function scores for the groups. Figure 1.14a is a histogram of the scores for each group separately. Four symbols (either 1's or 2's) represent one case. (The number of cases represented by a symbol depends on the number of cases used in an analysis.) The row of 1's and 2's underneath the plot denote to which group scores are assigned. We note that four Group 1 cases fall into the Group 2 classification region, and four Group 2 cases fall into the Group 1 region.

The average score for a group is called the group centroid and is indicated on each plot as well as in Figure 1.14b. These values are the same as the means in Figure 1.7b. On the average, infants who died have smaller discriminant function scores than infants who survived. The average value for Group 1 infants who died is −0.71, whereas the average value for those who survived is 0.84.

Figure 1.14a   Histograms of discriminant scores

```
DSCRIMINANT GROUPS=SURVIVAL(1,2)
  /VARIABLES=TREATMNT TO RESP
  /STATISTICS=1 2 6 4 11 14 13 16.
```

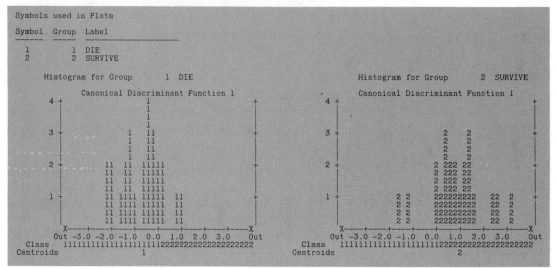

Figure 1.14b   Discriminant functions evaluated at group means

```
DSCRIMINANT GROUPS=SURVIVAL(1,2)
  /VARIABLES=TREATMNT TO RESP
  /STATISTICS=1 2 6 4 11 14 13 16.
```

```
Canonical Discriminant Functions evaluated at Group Means (Group Centroids)

   Group     FUNC   1

      1      -0.71252
      2       0.84206
```

The combined distribution of the scores for the two groups is shown in Figure 1.14c. Again, four symbols represent a case, and you can see the amount of overlap between the two groups. For example, the interval with midpoint -1.25 has four cases, three from Group 1 and one from Group 2.

**Figure 1.14c   All-groups stacked histogram
canonical discriminant function**

```
DSCRIMINANT GROUPS=SURVIVAL(1,2)
  /VARIABLES=TREATMNT TO RESP
  /STATISTICS=1 2 6 4 11 14 13 16 15.
```

```
              All-groups stacked Histogram

             Canonical Discriminant Function 1
         4 +            2    1 2                        +
           |            2    1 2
           |            2    1 2
           |            2    1 2
         3 +            1    11222 2   2                +
           |            1    11222 2   2
           |            1    11222 2   2
           |            1    11222 2   2
         2 +        11 211   11111222222                +
           |        11 211   11111222222
           |        11 211   11111222222
           |        11 211   11111222222
         1 +        11 1111  111112211222    22  2      +
           |        11 1111  111112211222    22  2
           |        11 1111  111112211222    22  2
           |        11 1111  111112211222    22  2
           X----+----+----+----+----+----+----+----X
         Out -3.0 -2.0 -1.0  0.0  1.0  2.0  3.0    Out
   Class  11111111111111111111111122222222222222222222
Centroids              1            2
```

1.15
Estimating Misclassification Rates

A model usually fits the sample from which it is derived better than it will fit another sample from the same population. Thus, the percentage of cases classified correctly by the discriminant function is an inflated estimate of the true performance in the population, just as R^2 is an overly optimistic estimate of a model's fit in regression.

There are several ways to obtain a better estimate of the true misclassification rate. If the sample is large enough to be randomly split into two parts, you can use one to derive the discriminant function and the other to test it. Since the same cases are not used for both estimating the function and testing it, the observed error rate in the "test" sample should better reflect the function's effectiveness. However, this method requires large sample sizes and does not make good use of all of the available information.

Another technique for obtaining an improved estimate of the misclassification rate is the "jackknife," sometimes called the leaving-one-out method. It involves leaving out each of the cases in turn, calculating the function based on the remaining n-1 cases, and then classifying the left-out case. Again, since the case which is being classified is not included in the calculation of the function, the observed (or apparent) misclassification rate is a less-biased estimate of the true one.

When one of the groups is much smaller than the other, a highly correct classification rate can occur even when most of the "minority" group cases are misclassified. The smaller group—adopters of a new product, diseased individuals, or parole violators—are, however, often of particular interest, and their correct classification is of paramount importance. The desired result is not to minimize the overall misclassification rate but to identify most cases of the smaller group. For example, by judging everyone to be disease-free in a cancer-screening program, the error rate will be very small, since few people actually have the disease. However, the results are useless since the goal is to identify the diseased individuals.

The result of different classification rules for identifying "minority" cases can be examined by ranking all cases on the value of their discriminant score, and determining how many "minority" cases are in the various deciles. If most of the cases of interest are at the extremes of the distribution, a good rule for identifying them can be obtained at the expense of increasing the number of misclassified cases from the larger group. If the intent of the discriminant analysis is to identify persons to receive promotional materials for a new product, or undergo further screening procedures, this is a fairly reasonable tactic. Unequal costs for misclassification can also be incorporated into the classification rule by adjusting the prior probabilities to reflect them. For further discussion, see Lachenbruch (1975).

1.16
The Expected Misclassification Rate

The percentage of cases classified correctly is often taken as an index of the effectiveness of the discriminant function. When evaluating this measure it is important to compare the observed misclassification rate to that expected by chance alone. For example, if there are two groups with equal prior probabilities, assigning cases to groups based on the outcome of a flip of a fair coin, that is, heads allocate to Group 1 and tails allocate to Group 2, results in an expected misclassification rate of 50%. A discriminant function with an observed misclassification rate of 50% is performing no better than chance. In fact, if the rate is based on the sample used for deriving the function, it is probably doing worse.

As the number of groups with equal prior probabilities increases, the percentage of cases that can be classified correctly by chance alone decreases. If there are 10 groups, only 10% of the cases would be expected to be classified correctly by chance. Observed misclassification rates should always be viewed in light of results expected by chance.

1.17
Other Discriminant Function Statistics

The percentage of cases classified correctly is one indicator of the effectiveness of the discriminant function. Another indicator of effectiveness of the function is the actual discriminant scores in the groups. A "good" discriminant function is one that has much between-groups variability when compared to within-groups variability. In fact, the coefficients of the discriminant function are chosen so that the ratio of the between-groups sum of squares to the within-groups sum of squares is as large as possible. Any other linear combination of the predictor variables will have a smaller ratio.

Figure 1.17a   Analysis of variance table from MEANS for discriminant score

```
DSCRIMINANT GROUPS=SURVIVAL(1,2)
  /VARIABLES=TREATMNT TO RESP
  /SAVE=SCORES=DISCORE.
VARIABLE LABELS DISCORE1 'DISCRIMINANT SCORE'.
MEANS TABLES=DISCORE1 BY SURVIVAL
  /STATISTICS=1.
```

```
Criterion Variable DISCORE1


                              Analysis of Variance
                      Sum of                   Mean
 Source               Squares      D.F.        Square        F       Sig.

 Between Groups       28.7992        1         28.7992     28.7992    .0000

 Within Groups        46.0000       46          1.0000

                        Eta =  .6205    Eta Squared =  .3850
```

Figure 1.17a is an analysis of variance table from procedure MEANS using the discriminant scores as the dependent variable and the group variable as the independent or classification variable. Figure 1.17a shows a variety of statistics based on the analysis of variance table. For example, the eigenvalue in Figure 1.17b is simply the ratio of the between-groups to within-groups sums of squares. Thus, from Figure 1.17a, it is

$$\text{eigenvalue} = \frac{\text{between-groups ss}}{\text{within-groups ss}} = \frac{28.8}{46.0} = 0.626 \qquad \textbf{Equation 1.17a}$$

Large eigenvalues are associated with "good" functions. The next two entries in Figure 1.17b, percent of variance and cumulative percent, are always 100 for the two-group situation (see Section 1.38 for further explanation).

Figure 1.17b   Canonical discriminant functions

```
DSCRIMINANT GROUPS=SURVIVAL(1,2)
  /VARIABLES=TREATMNT TO RESP.
```

```
                                Canonical Discriminant Functions

                     Percent of  Cumulative   Canonical  :  After
Function  Eigenvalue  Variance     Percent    Correlation : Function  Wilks' Lambda  Chi-squared  D.F.  Significance
                                                          :     0       0.6149800      20.419        8     0.0089
  1*       0.62607    100.00       100.00      0.6204998  :
 * marks the   1 canonical discriminant functions remaining in the analysis.
```

The *canonical correlation* is a measure of the degree of association between the discriminant scores and the groups. It is equivalent to eta from the oneway analysis of variance, in which the discriminant score is the dependent variable and group is the independent variable. Remember, eta^2 is the ratio of the between-groups sum of squares to the total sum of squares and represents the proportion of the total variance attributable to differences among the groups. Thus, from Figure 1.17a, eta is

$$eta = \sqrt{\frac{28.8}{74.8}} = 0.6205 \qquad \textbf{Equation 1.17b}$$

In the two-group situation, the canonical correlation is simply the usual Pearson correlation coefficient between the discriminant score and the group variable, which is coded 0 and 1.

Statistics Guide

For the two-group case, Wilks' lambda is the ratio of the within-groups sum of squares to the total sum of squares. It is the proportion of the total variance in the discriminant scores not explained by differences among groups (lambda plus eta^2 sum to 1). From Figure 1.17a, lambda is

$$\lambda = \frac{46}{74.8} = 0.615 \qquad \text{Equation 1.17c}$$

As indicated in Section 1.38, small values of lambda are associated with functions that have much variability between groups and little variability within groups. A lambda of 1 occurs when the mean of the discriminant scores is the same in all groups and there is no between-groups variability.

A test of the null hypothesis that in the populations from which the samples are drawn there is no difference between the group means can be based on Wilks' lambda. Lambda is transformed to a variable which has approximately a chi-square distribution. Figure 1.17b shows that a lambda of 0.615 is transformed to a chi-square value of 20.42 with 8 degrees of freedom. The observed significance level is 0.0089. Thus, it appears unlikely that infants who die from RDS and those who survive have the same means on the discriminant function.

It is important to remember that even though Wilks' lambda may be statistically significant, it provides little information about the effectiveness of the discriminant function in classification. It only provides a test of the null hypothesis that the population means are equal. Small differences may be statistically significant but still not permit good discrimination among the groups. If the means and covariance matrices are equal, of course, discrimination is not possible.

1.18
Interpreting the Discriminant Function Coefficients

Table 1.18 contains the standardized and unstandardized discriminant function coefficients for the RDS example. The unstandardized coefficients are the multipliers of the variables when they are expressed in the original units. As in multiple regression, the standardized coefficients are used when the variables are standardized to a mean of 0 and a standard deviation of 1.

Table 1.18   Standardized and unstandardized discriminant function coefficients

Variable	Unstandardized	Standardized
TREATMNT	0.43115	0.21531
TIME	0.03671	0.13170
WEIGHT	2.04404	1.16789
APGAR	0.12643	0.34638
SEX	0.00700	0.00337
AGE	−0.21807	−0.64084
PH	0.40787	0.16862
RESP	−1.24454	−0.58743
(CONSTANT)	−0.23093	

The interpretation of the coefficients is also similar to that in multiple regression. Since the variables are correlated, it is not possible to assess the importance of an individual variable. The value of the coefficient for a particular variable depends on the other variables included in the function.

It is sometimes tempting to interpret the magnitudes of the coefficients as indicators of the relative importance of variables. Variables with large coefficients are thought to contribute more to the overall discriminant function. However, the magnitude of the unstandardized coefficients is not a good index of relative importance when the variables differ in the units in which they are measured. For example, the gestational age (variable AGE) is measured in weeks and ranges from 28 to 39 weeks, while the pH level ranges from 6.85 to 7.37. When the absolute values of the unstandardized coefficients are ranked from largest to smallest, age

(−0.22) has a rank of 5. However, when the coefficients are standardized to adjust for the unequal means and standard deviations of the independent variables, the coefficient for age (−0.64) is the second largest.

The actual signs of the coefficients are arbitrary. The negative coefficients for age and respiratory therapy could just as well be positive if the signs of the other coefficients were reversed.

By looking at the groups of variables which have coefficients of different signs, we can determine which variable values result in large and small function values. For example, since respiratory therapy is usually initiated for infants who are in considerable distress, it is a bad omen for survival. Values of 1 for the RESP variable will decrease the function value. Infants who weigh more usually have better-developed lungs and are more likely to survive. Thus, larger weights increase the function. Large function values are associated with survival, while small function values are associated with death.

1.19
Function-Variable Correlations

Another way to assess the contribution of a variable to the discriminant function is to examine the correlations between the values of the function and the values of the variables. The computation of the coefficients is straightforward. For each case the value of the discriminant function is computed, and the Pearson correlation coefficients between it and the original variables are obtained.

Separate correlation matrices can be calculated for each group and the results combined to obtain a *pooled within-groups* correlation matrix like that in Figure 1.19. Or all of the cases can be considered together and a *total* correlation matrix calculated. The total correlation coefficients are larger than the corresponding within-groups correlations. However, the relative magnitudes will be similar. Variables with high total correlations will also have high pooled within-groups correlations.

Figure 1.19 Pooled within-groups correlations

```
Structure Matrix:

Pooled-within-groups correlations between discriminating variables
                                    and canonical discriminant functions
(Variables ordered by size of correlation within function)

                FUNC  1
WEIGHT         0.73338
RESP          -0.51940
AGE            0.49290
TREATMNT       0.26572
PH             0.25946
APGAR          0.19210
TIME          -0.10157
SEX            0.03738
```

Figure 1.19 indicates that variable WEIGHT has the highest correlation with the discriminant function. RESP has the second largest correlation in absolute value. The negative sign indicates that small function values are associated with the presence of respiratory therapy (coded 1) and larger values are associated with the absence of respiratory therapy. These results are similar to those obtained from the standardized coefficients.

However, if you compare Table 1.18 and Figure 1.19, you will notice that AGE, which has a negative standardized coefficient, is positively correlated with the discriminant function. Similarly, TIME, which has a positive standardized coefficient, has a negative correlation with the discriminant score. This occurs because WEIGHT and AGE, as expected, are highly correlated. The correlation coefficient is 0.84 from Figure 1.5a. Thus, the contribution of AGE and WEIGHT is shared and the individual coefficients are not meaningful. You should exercise care when attempting to interpret the coefficients, since correlations between variables affect the magnitudes and signs of the coefficients.

1.20
Fisher's Classification Function Coefficients

In Table 1.18, the linear discriminant function coefficients are those that maximize the ratio of between-groups to within-groups sums of squares. These coefficients are sometimes called the canonical discriminant function coefficients, since they are identical to those obtained from canonical correlation analysis when maximally correlated linear combinations of the group membership variables and predictor variables are formed (see Tatsuoka, 1971).

Another set of coefficients, sometimes called Fisher's linear discriminant function coefficients or classification coefficients, can be used directly for classification. A set of coefficients is obtained for each group and a case is assigned to the group for which it has the largest discriminant score. The classification results are identical for both methods if all canonical discriminant functions are used (see Kshirsagar & Arseven, 1975; Green, 1979).

1.21
Relationship to Multiple Regression Analysis

Two-group linear discriminant analysis is closely related to multiple linear regression analysis. If the binary grouping variable is considered the dependent variable and the predictor variables are the independent variables, the multiple regression coefficients in Table 1.21 are obtained. Comparison of these coefficients to the discriminant function coefficients shows that the two sets of coefficients are proportional. The discriminant coefficients can be obtained by multiplying the regression coefficients by 4.04. The exact constant of proportionality varies from data set to data set, but the two sets of coefficients are always proportional. This is true only for two-group discriminant analysis.

Table 1.21 Regression and discriminant coefficients

Variable	B Regression	B Discriminant	Ratio
RESP	−0.3082	−1.2445	4.04
TIME	0.0091	0.0367	4.04
PH	0.1010	0.4079	4.04
TREATMNT	0.1068	0.4311	4.04
SEX	0.0017	0.0070	4.04
AGE	−0.0540	−0.2180	4.04
APGAR	0.0313	0.1264	4.04
WEIGHT	0.5062	2.0040	4.04

1.22
VARIABLE SELECTION METHODS

In many situations, discriminant analysis, like multiple regression analysis, is used as an exploratory tool. In order to arrive at a good model, a variety of potentially useful variables are included in the data set. It is not known in advance which of these variables are important for group separation and which are, more or less, extraneous. One of the desired end-products of the analysis is identification of the "good" predictor variables. All of the caveats for variable selection procedures in multiple regression (see *SPSS/PC+ Statistics*) apply to discriminant analysis as well.

The three most commonly used algorithms for variable selection—forward entry, stepwise selection, and backward elimination—are available in DSCRIMINANT. The principles are the same as in multiple regression. What differs are the actual criteria for variable selection. In the following example, only minimization of Wilks' lambda will be considered. Some others are discussed in Sections 1.30 through 1.34.

1.23
A Stepwise Selection Example

Since stepwise variable selection algorithms combine the features of forward selection and backward elimination, output from the stepwise method will be discussed. Remember that in a stepwise method the first variable included in the analysis has the largest acceptable value for the selection criterion. After the first variable is entered, the value of the criterion is reevaluated for all variables not in the model, and the variable with the largest acceptable criterion value is entered next. At this point, the variable entered first is reevaluated to determine whether it meets the removal criterion. If it does, it is removed from the model.

The next step is to examine the variables not in the equation for entry, followed by examination of the variables in the equation for removal. Variables are removed until none remain that meet the removal criterion. Variable selection terminates when no more variables meet entry or removal criteria.

1.24
Variable Selection Criteria

Figure 1.24 is output from the beginning of a stepwise variable selection session, listing the criteria in effect. As mentioned previously, several criteria are available for variable selection (see Section 1.22). This example uses minimization of Wilks' lambda. Thus, at each step the variable that results in the smallest Wilks' lambda for the discriminant function is selected for entry.

Figure 1.24 Stepwise variable selection

```
DSCRIMINANT GROUPS=SURVIVAL(1,2)
   /VARIABLES=TREATMNT TO RESP
   /METHOD=WILKS.
```

```
Stepwise variable selection

   Selection rule:  Minimize Wilks' Lambda
   Maximum number of steps...................       16
   Minimum Tolerance Level................... 0.00100
   Minimum F to enter.......................  1.0000
   Maximum F to remove......................  1.0000
```

Each entry or removal of a variable is considered a step. The maximum number of steps permitted in an analysis is either twice the number of independent variables (the default) or a user-specified value.

As in multiple regression, if there are independent variables that are linear combinations of other independent variables, a unique solution is not possible. To prevent computational difficulties the tolerance of a variable is checked before it is entered into a model. The tolerance is a measure of the degree of linear association between the independent variables. For the ith independent variable, it is $1 - R_i^2$, where R_i^2 is the squared multiple correlation coefficient when the ith independent variable is considered the dependent variable and the regression equation between it and the other independent variables is calculated. Small values for the tolerance indicate that the ith independent variable is almost a linear combination of the other independent variables. Variables with small tolerances (by default, less than 0.001) are not permitted to enter the analysis. Also, if entry of a variable would cause the tolerance of a variable already in the model to drop to an unacceptable level (0.001 by default), the variable is not entered. The smallest acceptable tolerance for a particular analysis is shown in Figure 1.24.

The significance of the change in Wilks' lambda when a variable is entered or removed from the model can be based on an F statistic. Either the actual value of F or its significance level can be used as the criterion for variable entry and removal. These two criteria are not necessarily equivalent, since a fixed F value has different significance levels depending on the number of variables in the model at any step. The actual significance levels associated with the F-to-enter and F-to-remove statistics are not those usually obtained from the F distribution, since many variables are examined and the largest and smallest F values selected. The true significance level is difficult to compute since it depends on many factors, including the correlations between the independent variables.

1.25
The First Step   Before the stepwise selection algorithm begins, at Step 0, basic information about the variables is displayed, as shown in Figure 1.25a. The tolerance and minimum tolerance are 1, since there are no variables in the model. (The tolerance is based only on the independent variables in the model. The minimum tolerance, which is the smallest tolerance for any variable in the equation if the variable under consideration is entered, is also based only on the variables in the equation.) The F-to-enter in Figure 1.25a is equal to the F test for equality of group means in Figure 1.3b. The univariate Wilks' lambda is also the same.

Figure 1.25a   Output at Step 0

```
DSCRIMINANT GROUPS=SURVIVAL(1,2)
  /VARIABLES=TREATMNT TO RESP
  /METHOD=WILKS
  /STATISTICS=5.


----------------- Variables not in the analysis after step    0 ----------------

                        Minimum
Variable  Tolerance   Tolerance   F to enter   Wilks' Lambda

TREATMNT  1.0000000   1.0000000     2.0335        0.95766
TIME      1.0000000   1.0000000      .29713       0.99358
WEIGHT    1.0000000   1.0000000    15.489         0.74810
APGAR     1.0000000   1.0000000     1.0628        0.97742
SEX       1.0000000   1.0000000      .40245D-01   0.99913
AGE       1.0000000   1.0000000     6.9967        0.86798
PH        1.0000000   1.0000000     1.9388        0.95956
RESP      1.0000000   1.0000000     7.7693        0.85551
```

The WEIGHT variable has the smallest Wilks' lambda, and correspondingly the largest F-to-enter, so it is the first variable entered into the equation. When WEIGHT is entered, as shown in Figure 1.25b, the Wilks' lambda and corresponding F are the same as in Figures 1.3b and 1.25a. The degrees of freedom for the Wilks' lambda displayed in Figure 1.25b are for its untransformed (not converted to an F) distribution.

After each step, SPSS/PC+ displays a table showing the variables in the model (see Figure 1.25c). When only one variable is in the model, this table contains no new information. The F-to-remove corresponds to that in Figure 1.25b since it represents the change in Wilks' lambda if WEIGHT is removed. The last column usually contains the value of Wilks' lambda if the variable is removed. However, since removal of WEIGHT results in a model with no variables, no value is displayed at the first step.

Figure 1.25b   Summary statistics for Step 1

```
At step    1, WEIGHT   was included in the analysis.

                                   Degrees of Freedom Signif.    Between Groups
Wilks' Lambda        0.74810       1    1        46.0
Equivalent F        15.4894             1        46.0  0.0003
```

Figure 1.25c   Variables in the analysis after Step 1

```
----------------- Variables in the analysis after step    1 ----------------

Variable  Tolerance  F to remove   Wilks' Lambda

WEIGHT    1.0000000     15.489
```

SPSS/PC+ also displays a test of differences between pairs of groups after each step. When there are only two groups, the F value displayed is the same as that for Wilks' lambda for the overall model, as shown in Figures 1.25c and 1.25d.

Figure 1.25d *F* values and significance at Step 1

```
F statistics and significances between pairs of groups after step   1
Each F statistic has   1 and        46.0 degrees of freedom.

                   Group        1
                            DIE
     Group

         2  SURVIVE        15.489
                            0.0003
```

1.26
Statistics for Variables Not in the Model

Also displayed at each step is a set of summary statistics for variables not yet in the model. From Figure 1.26, RESP is the variable which results in the smallest Wilks' lambda for the model if it is entered next. Note that the Wilks' lambda calculated is for the variables WEIGHT and RESP jointly. Its *F*-test is a multivariate significance test for group differences.

The *F* value for the change in Wilks' lambda when a variable is added to a model which contains *p* independent variables is

$$F_{change} = \left(\frac{n - g - p}{g - 1}\right) \left(\frac{(1 - \lambda_{p+1}/\lambda_p)}{\lambda_{p+1}/\lambda_p}\right)$$

Equation 1.26a

where *n* is the total number of cases, *g* is the number of groups, λ_p is Wilks' lambda before adding the variable, and λ_{p+1} is Wilks' lambda after inclusion.

If variable RESP is entered into the model containing variable WEIGHT, Wilks' lambda is 0.669. The lambda for WEIGHT alone is 0.748 (see Figure 1.25b). The *F* value for the change, called *F*-to-enter, is from Equation 1.26a:

$$F = \frac{(48 - 2 - 1)(1 - 0.669/0.748)}{(2 - 1)(0.669/0.748)} = 5.31$$

Equation 1.26b

This is the value for RESP in Figure 1.26.

Figure 1.26 Variables not in the analysis after Step 1

```
--------------- Variables not in the analysis after step   1 ---------------

                          Minimum
Variable   Tolerance   Tolerance   F to enter    Wilks' Lambda

TREATMNT   0.9917361   0.9917361     .84207         0.73435
TIME       0.9548707   0.9548707     .64894D-01     0.74702
APGAR      0.9508910   0.9508910     .19398D-01     0.74777
SEX        0.9619762   0.9619762     .24443         0.74406
AGE        0.2937327   0.2937327    1.0931          0.73035
PH         0.9845349   0.9845349     .60606         0.73816
RESP       0.9994270   0.9994270    5.3111          0.66912
```

1.27
The Second Step

Figure 1.27 shows the output when RESP is entered into the model. Wilks' lambda for the model is the same as Wilks' lambda for RESP in Figure 1.26. If WEIGHT is removed from the current model, leaving only RESP, the resulting Wilks' lambda is 0.855, the entry for WEIGHT in the second part of Figure 1.27. The *F* value associated with the change in lambda, *F*-to-remove, is 12.5, which is also displayed in Figure 1.27.

$$F\text{-to-remove} = \frac{(48 - 2 - 1)(1 - 0.669/0.855)}{(1)(0.669/0.855)} = 12.5$$

Equation 1.27

Since the *F*-to-remove for all the variables in the model is larger than the default value of 1, none are removed.

Figure 1.27 RESP included in analysis at Step 2

```
At step    2, RESP       was included in the analysis.

                                    Degrees of Freedom  Signif.   Between Groups
Wilks' Lambda          0.66912          2    1      46.0
Equivalent F          11.1260                2      45.0  0.0001


------------------ Variables in the analysis after step    2 ------------------


Variable  Tolerance  F to remove   Wilks' Lambda

WEIGHT    0.9994270    12.535         0.85551
RESP      0.9994270     5.3111        0.74810


---------------- Variables not in the analysis after step    2 ----------------

                    Minimum
Variable  Tolerance  Tolerance   F to enter    Wilks' Lambda

TREATMNT  0.9917051  0.9911962    .71594        0.65841
TIME      0.9492383  0.9492383    .53176D-02    0.66904
APGAR     0.9231403  0.9231403    .25589        0.66526
SEX       0.8879566  0.8879566    .19884D-01    0.66882
AGE       0.2914116  0.2914116   1.3783         0.64880
PH        0.9828797  0.9828797    .66764        0.65912


F statistics and significances between pairs of groups after step    2
Each F statistic has    2 and       45.0 degrees of freedom.
```

After WEIGHT and RESP have both been included in the model, the next variable that would result in the smallest Wilks' lambda if entered is AGE. Its F-to-enter is 1.38, and the resulting model lambda is 0.649. Thus, AGE is entered in Step 3.

1.28
The Last Step

After AGE is entered, all F-to-remove values are still greater than 1, so no variables are removed. All variables not in the model after Step 3 have F-to-enter values less than 1, so none are eligible for inclusion and variable selection stops (see Figure 1.28).

Figure 1.28 Output for Step 3

```
At step    3. AGE       was included in the analysis.

                                    Degrees of Freedom  Signif.   Between Groups
Wilks' Lambda          0.64880          3    1      46.0
Equivalent F           7.93913                3      44.0  0.0002

------------------ Variables in the analysis after step    3 ------------------


Variable  Tolerance  F to remove   Wilks' Lambda

WEIGHT    0.2926088    8.1466         0.76893
AGE       0.2914116    1.3783         0.66912
RESP      0.9915294    5.5307         0.73035


---------------- Variables not in the analysis after step    3 ----------------

                    Minimum
Variable  Tolerance  Tolerance   F to enter    Wilks' Lambda

TREATMNT  0.9904436  0.2907779    .61371        0.63967
TIME      0.9469645  0.2907135    .22714D-03    0.64880
APGAR     0.8055887  0.2543036    .92868        0.63509
SEX       0.8086141  0.2548962    .45854D-01    0.64811
PH        0.9482218  0.2778589    .34965        0.64357


F statistics and significances between pairs of groups after step    3
Each F statistic has    3 and       44.0 degrees of freedom.
```

1.29
Summary Tables

After the last step, SPSS/PC+ displays a summary table (see Figure 1.29). For each step this table lists the action taken (entry or removal) and the resulting Wilks' lambda and its significance level. Note that although inclusion of additional variables results in a decrease in Wilks' lambda, the observed significance level does not necessarily decrease since it depends both on the value of lambda and on the number of independent variables in the model.

Figure 1.29 Summary table

```
                        Summary Table

              Action      Vars  Wilks'
   Step Entered Removed    In    Lambda   Sig.   Label
     1   WEIGHT            1    .74810   .0003  BIRTHWEIGHT IN KILOGRAMS
     2   RESP             2    .66912   .0001  RESPIRATORY LEVEL
     3   AGE              3    .64880   .0002  GESTATION AGE
```

Table 1.29 shows the percentage of cases classified correctly at each step of the analysis. The model with variables WEIGHT, RESP, and AGE classifies almost 80% of the cases correctly, while the complete model with eight variables classifies 83% of the cases correctly. Including additional variables does not substantially improve classification. In fact, sometimes the percentage of cases classified correctly actually decreases if poor predictors are included in the model.

Table 1.29 Cases correctly classified by step

Variables included	Percent correctly classified
WEIGHT	68.00
WEIGHT, RESP	75.00
WEIGHT, RESP, AGE	79.17
All eight variables	83.33

1.30
Other Criteria for Variable Selection

In previous sections, variables were included in the model based on Wilks' lambda. At each step, the variable that resulted in the smallest Wilks' lambda was selected. Other criteria besides Wilks' lambda are sometimes used for variable selection.

1.31
Rao's V

Rao's V, also known as the Lawley-Hotelling trace, is defined as

$$V = (n - g) \sum_{i=1}^{p} \sum_{j=1}^{p} w_{ij} * \sum_{k=1}^{g} n_k (\overline{X}_{ik} - \overline{X}_i)(\overline{X}_{jk} - \overline{X}_j)$$

Equation 1.31

where p is the number of variables in the model, g is the number of groups, n_k is the sample size in the kth group, $\overline{X}_{ik}$ is the mean of the ith variable for the kth group, $\overline{X}_i$ is the mean of the ith variable for all groups combined, and $w_{ij}*$ is an element of the inverse of the within-groups covariance matrix. The larger the differences between group means, the larger Rao's V.

One way to evaluate the contribution of a variable is to see how much it increases Rao's V when it is added to the model. The sampling distribution of V is approximately a chi-square with $p(g - 1)$ degrees of freedom. A test of the significance of the change in Rao's V when a variable is included can also be based on the chi-square distribution. It is possible for a variable to actually decrease Rao's V when it is added to a model.

1.32
Mahalanobis' Distance

Mahalanobis' distance, D^2, is a generalized measure of the distance between two groups. The distance between groups a and b is defined as

$$D_{ab}^2 = (n - g) \sum_{i=1}^{p} \sum_{j=1}^{p} w_{ij} * (\overline{X}_{ia} - \overline{X}_{ib})(\overline{X}_{ja} - \overline{X}_{jb})$$

Equation 1.32

where p is the number of variables in the model, $\overline{X}_{ia}$ is the mean for the ith variable in group a, and $w_{ij}*$ is an element from the inverse of the within-groups covariance matrix.

When Mahalanobis' distance is the criterion for variable selection, the Mahalanobis' distances between all pairs of groups are calculated first. The variable that has the largest D^2 for the two groups that are closest (have the smallest D^2 initially) is selected for inclusion.

1.33
Between-Groups F

A test of the null hypothesis that the two sets of population means are equal can be based on Mahalanobis' distance. The corresponding F statistic is

$$F = \frac{(n-1-p)n_1 n_2}{p(n-2)(n_1+n_2)}\ D^2_{ab} \qquad \text{Equation 1.33}$$

This F value can also be used for variable selection. At each step the variable chosen for inclusion is the one with the largest F value. Since the Mahalanobis' distance is weighted by the sample sizes when the between-groups F is used as the criterion for stepwise selection, the results from the two methods may differ.

1.34
Sum of Unexplained Variance

As mentioned previously, two-group discriminant analysis is analogous to multiple regression in which the dependent variable is either 0 or 1, depending on the group to which a case belongs. In fact, the Mahalanobis' distance and R^2 are proportional. Thus,

$$R^2 = cD^2 \qquad \text{Equation 1.34}$$

For each pair of groups, a and b, the unexplained variation from the regression is 1 $- R^2_{ab}$, where R^2_{ab} is the square of the multiple correlation coefficient when a variable coded as 0 or 1 (depending on whether the case is a member of a or b) is considered the dependent variable.

The sum of the unexplained variation for all pairs of groups can also be used as a criterion for variable selection. The variable chosen for inclusion is the one that minimizes the sum of the unexplained variation.

1.35
THREE-GROUP DISCRIMINANT ANALYSIS

The previous example used discriminant analysis to distinguish between members of two groups. This section presents a three-group discriminant example. The basics are the same as in two-group discriminant analysis, although there are several additional considerations.

One of the early applications of discriminant analysis in business was for credit-granting decisions. Many different models for extending credit based on a variety of predictor variables have been proposed. Churchill (1979) describes the case of the Consumer Finance Company, which must screen credit applicants. It has available for analysis 30 cases known to be poor, equivocal, and good credit risks. For each case, the annual income (in thousands of dollars), the number of credit cards, the number of children, and the age of the household head are known. The task is to use discriminant analysis to derive a classification scheme for new cases based on the available data.

1.36
The Number of Functions

With two groups, it is possible to derive one discriminant function that maximizes the ratio of between- to within-groups sums of squares. When there are three groups, two discriminant functions can be calculated. The first function, as in the two-group case, has the largest ratio of between-groups to within-groups sums of squares. The second function is uncorrelated with the first and has the next largest ratio. In general, if there are k groups, $k - 1$ discriminant functions can be computed. They are all uncorrelated with each other and maximize the ratio of between-groups to within-groups sums of squares, subject to the constraint of being uncorrelated.

Figure 1.36a contains the two sets of unstandardized discriminant function coefficients for the credit risk example. Based on these coefficients it is possible to compute two scores for each case, one for each function. Consider, for example, the first case in the file with an annual income of $9,200, 2 credit cards, 3 children, and a 27-year-old head of household. For Function 1, the discriminant score is

$$D_{11} = -14.47 + 0.33(9.2) + 0.13(2) + 0.24(27) + 0.15(3) = -4.2 \quad \textbf{Equation 1.36}$$

The discriminant score for Function 2 is obtained the same way, using the coefficients for the second function. Figure 1.36b shows the discriminant scores and other classification information.

Figure 1.36a   Unstandardized canonical discriminant function coefficients

```
DSCRIMINANT GROUPS=RISK(1,3)
  /VARIABLES=INCOME TO CHILDREN
  /STATISTICS=11.
```

```
Unstandardized Canonical Discriminant Function Coefficients

                FUNC 1          FUNC 2

INCOME          .3257077        -.2251991
CREDIT          .1344126        -.5564818D-02
AGEHEAD         .2444825         .1497008
CHILDREN        .1497964         .1778159
(constant)    -14.46811        -2.540298
```

Figure 1.36b   Classification output

```
DSCRIMINANT GROUPS=RISK(1,3)
  /VARIABLES=INCOME TO CHILDREN
  /STATISTICS=11 14.
```

Case Number	Mis Val	Sel	Actual Group	Highest Probability Group	P(D/G)	P(G/D)	2nd Highest Group	P(G/D)	Discriminant Scores...	
1			1	1	0.8229	0.9993	2	0.0007	-4.1524	-0.0479
2			1	1	0.2100	0.9999	2	0.0001	-4.7122	-1.3738
3			1	1	0.7864	0.9885	2	0.0115	-3.3119	0.5959
4			1	1	0.8673	0.9718	2	0.0282	-2.9966	-0.0155
5			1	1	0.7610	0.9646	2	0.0354	-2.9464	0.3933
6			1	1	0.8797	0.9865	2	0.0135	-3.2056	-0.4530
7			1	1	0.7589	0.9995	2	0.0005	-4.2685	-0.1243
8			1	1	0.5684	0.9812	2	0.0188	-3.1762	0.9402
9			1	1	0.8191	0.9980	2	0.0020	-3.7851	-0.6398
10			1	1	0.7160	0.9336	2	0.0664	-2.7267	0.0973
11			2	2	0.9923	0.9938	1	0.0060	-0.3287	-0.0043
12			2	2	0.7764	0.9922	1	0.0076	-0.3718	-0.5939
13			2	2	0.6003	0.9938	3	0.0059	0.5383	0.6958
14			2	2	0.2482	0.6334	1	0.3666	-1.7833	0.8513
15			2	2	0.5867	0.9856	3	0.0143	0.7262	-0.0908
16			2	2	0.5199	0.9770	3	0.0229	0.8454	-0.0539
17			2	2	0.5355	0.9788	3	0.0211	0.8312	0.1126
18			2	2	0.3812	0.7845	1	0.2155	-1.5451	0.6993
19			2	2	0.9734	0.9961	1	0.0036	-0.1879	0.3225
20			2	2	0.2789	0.7086	1	0.2914	-1.5878	-0.8148
21			3	3	0.8476	0.9977	2	0.0023	3.2486	0.0529
22			3	3	0.3037	1.0000	2	0.0000	4.2453	1.4329
23			3	3	0.4273	0.9996	2	0.0004	3.6041	-1.3365
24			3	3	0.0973	0.9997	2	0.0003	3.6535	-2.2021
25			3	3	0.5946	0.9861	2	0.0139	2.7974	-0.1220
26			3	3	0.2355	0.9988	2	0.0012	3.4655	1.6148
27		**	3	2	0.0585	0.7055	3	0.2945	1.6111	1.5539
28			3	3	0.2221	1.0000	2	0.0000	5.5428	0.0977
29			3	3	0.0510	1.0000	2	0.0000	4.2979	-2.4410
30			3	3	0.1170	1.0000	2	0.0000	5.6787	0.8533

1.37
Classification

When there is one discriminant function, classification of cases into groups is based on the values for the single function. When there are several groups, a case's values on all functions must be considered simultaneously.

Figure 1.37a contains group means for the two functions. Group 1 has negative means for both functions, Group 2 has a negative mean for Function 1 and a positive mean for Function 2, while Group 3 has a positive mean on Function 1 and a slightly negative mean on Function 2.

Figure 1.37a   Canonical discriminant function—group means

```
Canonical Discriminant Functions evaluated at Group Means (Group Centroids)

   Group      FUNC   1     FUNC   2

     1        -3.52816     -0.06276
     2        -0.28634      0.11238
     3         3.81449     -0.04962
```

Figure 1.37b shows the territorial map for the three groups on the two functions. The mean for each group is indicated by an asterisk (*). The numbered boundaries mark off the combination of function values that result in the classification of the cases into the three groups. All cases with values that fall into the region bordered by the 3's are classified into the third group, those that fall into the region bordered by 2's are assigned to the second group, and so on.

Figure 1.37b   Territorial map

```
DSCRIMINANT GROUPS=RISK(1,3)
  /VARIABLES=INCOME TO CHILDREN
  /STATISTICS=11 14 10.
```

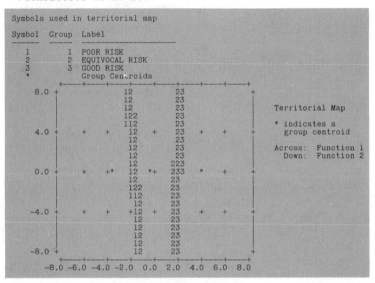

Figure 1.37c is a plot of the values of the two discriminant scores for each case. Cases are identified by their group number. When several cases fall into the same plotting location, only the symbol of the last case is displayed.

Figure 1.37c   All-groups scatterplot

```
DSCRIMINANT GROUPS=RISK(1,3)
  /VARIABLES=INCOME TO CHILDREN
  /STATISTICS=11 14 10 15.
```

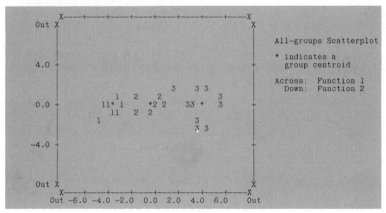

From Figures 1.36b and 1.37c you can see approximately how many cases are misclassified. For example, the case at the (1.6, 1.6) coordinates is denoted by a 3 but falls into the Group 2 region.

Figure 1.37d is the summary of the classification results. The diagonal elements are the number of cases classified correctly into the groups. For example, all poor and equivocal risks are classified correctly (10 out of 10 in each group). One of the good risks is misclassified as an equivocal risk. The overall percentage of cases classified correctly is the sum of the number of cases classified correctly in each group divided by the total number of cases. In this example, 29 out of 30 cases (96.7%) are classified correctly. These results may differ slightly from those obtained by counting plotted points in Figure 1.37c, since a single point in the plot may represent multiple cases.

Figure 1.37d   Classification table

```
DSCRIMINANT GROUPS=RISK(1,3)
  /VARIABLES=INCOME TO CHILDREN
  /STATISTICS=11 14 10 15 13.
```

```
Classification Results -

                           No. of   Predicted Group Membership
          Actual Group     Cases       1        2        3

Group       1               10         10        0        0
POOR RISK                           100.0%     0.0%     0.0%

Group       2               10          0       10        0
EQUIVOCAL RISK                        0.0%   100.0%     0.0%

Group       3               10          0        1        9
GOOD RISK                             0.0%    10.0%    90.0%

Percent of "grouped" cases correctly classified:  96.67%


Classification Processing Summary

     30 Cases were processed.
      0 Cases were excluded for missing or out-of-range group codes.
      0 Cases had at least one missing discriminating variable.
     30 Cases were used for printed output.
```

1.38
Additional Statistics

When more than one discriminant function is derived, several statistics other than those discussed in Section 1.17 are of interest. Consider Figure 1.38a. For each function, the eigenvalue is the ratio of between-groups to within-groups sums of squares. From Figure 1.38b (the analysis of variance tables for the two functions), the eigenvalue for Function 1 is 10.03 (270.8/27). For Function 2, it is 0.007 (0.19/27).

Figure 1.38a   Additional statistics

```
DSCRIMINANT GROUPS=RISK(1,3)
  /VARIABLES=INCOME TO CHILDREN.
```

					Canonical Discriminant Functions				
Function	Eigenvalue	Percent of Variance	Cumulative Percent	Canonical Correlation	: After Function	Wilks' Lambda	Chi-squared	D.F.	Significance
					: 0	0.0900296	61.394	8	0.0000
1*	10.02971	99.93	99.93	0.9535910	: 1	0.9930012	.17910	3	0.9809
2*	0.00705	0.07	100.00	0.0836587	:				

```
* marks the  2 canonical discriminant functions remaining in the analysis.
```

Figure 1.38b   ONEWAY analysis of variance for the two functions

```
DSCRIMINANT GROUPS=RISK(1,3)
  /VARIABLES=INCOME TO CHILDREN
  /SAVE=SCORES=DISCORE.
ONEWAY DISCORE1 DISCORE2 BY RISK(1,3).
```

```
- - - - - - - - - - - - - - O N E W A Y - - - - - - - - - - - - - - - - -

      Variable  DISCORE1   FIRST DISCRIMINANT SCORE
   By Variable  RISK

                              Analysis of Variance

                          Sum of          Mean           F       F
       Source       D.F.   Squares        Squares       Ratio   Prob.

Between Groups        2    270.8023       135.4011      135.4011 0.0

Within Groups        27     27.0000         1.0000

Total                29    297.8023
- - - - - - - - - - - - - - O N E W A Y - - - - - - - - - - - - - - - - -

      Variable  DISCORE2   SECOND DISCRIMINANT SCORE
   By Variable  RISK

                              Analysis of Variance

                          Sum of          Mean           F       F
       Source       D.F.   Squares        Squares       Ratio   Prob.

Between Groups        2      .1903          .0951         .0951   .9095

Within Groups        27    27.0000         1.0000

Total                29    27.1903
```

The canonical correlation for a function is the square root of the between-groups to total sums of squares. When squared, it is the proportion of total variability explained by differences between groups. For example, for Function 1 the canonical correlation is

$$\sqrt{\frac{270.8}{297.8}} = 0.953$$

Equation 1.38a

When two or more functions are derived, it may be of interest to compare their merits. One frequently encountered criterion is the percentage of the total between-groups variability attributable to each function. Remember from the two-group example that the canonical discriminant functions are derived so that the pooled within-groups variance is 1. (This is seen in Figure 1.38b by the value of 1 for the within-groups mean square.) Thus, each function differs only in the between-groups sum of squares.

The first function always has the largest between-groups variability. The remaining functions have successively less between-groups variability. From Figure 1.38a, Function 1 accounts for 99.93% of the total between-groups variability:

Equation 1.38b

$$\frac{\text{Between Groups SS for Function 1}}{\text{Between Groups SS for Function 1} + \text{Between Groups SS for Function 2}} = 0.9993$$

Function 2 accounts for the remaining 0.07% of the between-groups variability. These values are listed in the column labeled **Percent of Variance** in Figure 1.38a. The next column, labeled **Cumulative Percent**, is simply the sum of the percentage of variance of that function and the preceding ones.

1.39
Testing the Significance of the Discriminant Functions

When there are no differences among the populations from which the samples are selected, the discriminant functions reflect only sampling variability. A test of the null hypothesis that, in the population, the means of all discriminant functions in all groups are really equal and 0 can be based on Wilks' lambda. Since several functions must be considered simultaneously, Wilks' lambda is not just the ratio of the between-groups to within-groups sums of squares but is the product of the univariate Wilks' lambda for each function. For example, the Wilks' lambda for both functions considered simultaneously is, from Figure 1.38b:

$$\Lambda = \left(\frac{27}{297.8}\right)\left(\frac{27}{27.19}\right) = 0.09$$

Equation 1.39

The significance level of the observed Wilks' lambda can be based on a chi-square transformation of the statistic. The value of lambda and its associated chi-square value, the degrees of freedom, and the significance level are shown in the second half of Figure 1.38a in the first row. Since the observed significance level is less than 0.00005, the null hypothesis that the means of both functions are equal in the three populations can be rejected.

When more than one function is derived, you can successively test the means of the functions by first testing all means simultaneously and then excluding one function at a time, testing the means of the remaining functions at each step. Using such successive tests, it is possible to find that a subset of discriminant functions accounts for all differences and that additional functions do not reflect true population differences, only random variation.

As shown in Figure 1.38a, DSCRIMINANT displays Wilks' lambda and the associated statistics as functions are removed successively. The column labeled **After Function** contains the number of the last function removed. The 0 indicates that no functions are removed, while a value of 2 indicates that the first two functions have been removed. For this example, the Wilks' lambda associated with Function 2 after Function 1 has been removed is 0.993. Since it is the last remaining function, the Wilks' lambda obtained is just the univariate value from Figure 1.38b. The significance level associated with the second function is 0.981, indicating that it does not contribute substantially to group differences. This can also be seen in Figure 1.37c, since only the first function determines the classification boundaries. All three groups have similar values for Function 2.

Figure 1.39 is a classification map that illustrates the situation in which both functions contribute to group separation. In other words, a case's values on both functions are important for classification. For example, a case with a value of -2 for the first discriminant function will be classified into Group 2 if the second function is negative and into Group 1 if the second function is positive.

Figure 1.39   Territorial map

```
TITLE INFANT SURVIVAL EXAMPLE--3-GROUP DISCRIMINANT.
COMPUTE CASE=$CASENUM.
RECODE CASE(1,2,3,4,5,6,18,22,23=2)(ELSE=1).
IF (CASE EQ 2) SURVIVAL=2.
RECODE SURVIVAL (2=2) (1=3) (0=1).
VALUE LABELS SURVIVAL 3'SURVIVE' 1'DIE' 2'DIE LATER'.
DSCRIMINANT GROUPS=SURVIVAL(1,3)
  /VARIABLES=TREATMNT TO RESP
  /STATISTICS=10.
```

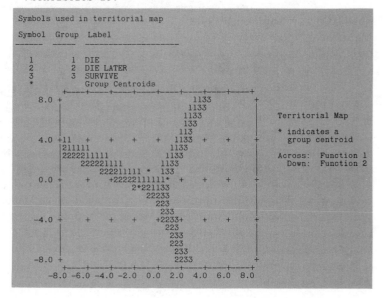

1.40
Classification with One Function

Instead of using all available functions to classify cases into groups, you can restrict the functions to the subset that has substantial between-groups variability. Eliminating weak functions should result in a more stable classification rule, since some of the sampling variability is removed.

When only one discriminant function is used to classify the credit risk cases, 96.67% of the cases are still classified correctly, as shown in Figure 1.40a.

Figure 1.40a   Classification table

```
DSCRIMINANT GROUPS=RISK(1,3)
  /VARIABLES=INCOME TO CHILDREN
  /FUNCTIONS= 1
  /STATISTICS=11 14 10 15 13.
```

```
Classification Results -

                        No. of    Predicted Group Membership
       Actual Group      Cases       1           2          3
                                  _____    _____   _____
Group        1            10        10           0          0
POOR RISK                         100.0%        0.0%       0.0%

Group        2            10         0          10          0
EQUIVOCAL RISK                      0.0%       100.0%       0.0%

Group        3            10         0           1          9
GOOD RISK                           0.0%        10.0%      90.0%

Percent of "grouped" cases correctly classified:  96.67%
```

Figure 1.40b shows the all-groups histogram for the single discriminant function. Large negative values are associated with poor risks, large positive values with good risks, and small positive and negative values with equivocal risks.

Figure 1.40b   All-groups histogram

```
DSCRIMINANT GROUPS=RISK(1,3)
  /VARIABLES=INCOME TO CHILDREN
  /FUNCTIONS=1.0
  /STATISTICS=11 14 10 15 13.
```

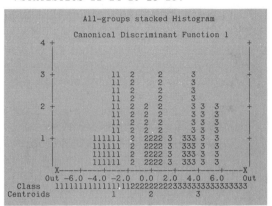

1.41
The Variables

To assess the contribution of each variable to the discriminant functions, you can compute standardized coefficients. From Figure 1.41a, income and age of the household head appear to be the variables with the largest standardized coefficients.

Figure 1.41a   Standardized canonical discriminant functions

```
DSCRIMINANT GROUPS=RISK(1,3)
  /VARIABLES=INCOME TO CHILDREN.
```

Standardized Canonical Discriminant Function Coefficients

	FUNC 1	FUNC 2
INCOME	0.89487	-0.61872
CREDIT	0.31363	-0.01298
AGEHEAD	0.84508	0.51746
CHILDREN	0.22936	0.27226

Another way to examine the contributions of the variables is to examine the correlation coefficients between the variables and the functions, as shown in Figure 1.41b. To help you interpret the functions, variables with large coefficients for a particular function are grouped together. These groupings are indicated with asterisks.

Figure 1.41b   Pooled within-groups correlation matrix

```
DSCRIMINANT GROUPS=RISK(1,3)
  /VARIABLES=INCOME TO CHILDREN
  /STATISTICS=11 14 10 15 13 4.
```

Structure Matrix:

Pooled-within-groups correlations between discriminating variables
                              and canonical discriminant functions
(Variables ordered by size of correlation within function)

	FUNC 1	FUNC 2
CREDIT	0.22728*	0.19774
INCOME	0.48482	-0.84832*
AGEHEAD	0.58577	0.72023*
CHILDREN	-0.00069	0.38568*

1.42
WHEN ASSUMPTIONS
ARE VIOLATED

As previously indicated, the linear discriminant function minimizes the probability of misclassification if in each group the variables are from multivariate normal distributions and the covariance matrices for all groups are equal. A variety of tests for multivariate normality are available (see Andrews, 1973). A simple tactic is to examine first the distributions of each of the variables individually. If the variables are jointly distributed as a multivariate normal, it follows that each is individually distributed normally. Therefore, if any of the variables have markedly non-normal distributions, there is reason to suspect that the multivariate normality assumption is violated. However, if all variables are normally distributed, the joint distribution is not necessarily multivariate normal.

There are several ways to test equality of the group covariance matrices. DSCRIMINANT displays Box's M test, which is based on the determinants of the group covariance matrices. As shown in Figure 1.42, the significance probability is based on an F transformation. A small probability might lead us to reject the null hypothesis that the covariance matrices are equal. However, when sample sizes in the groups are large, the significance probability may be small even if the group covariance matrices are not too dissimilar. The test is also sensitive to departures from multivariate normality. That is, it tends to call matrices unequal if the normality assumption is violated.

Figure 1.42   Test of equality of group covariance matrices

```
DSCRIMINANT GROUPS=SURVIVAL(1,2)
  /VARIABLES=TREATMNT TO RESP
  /MAXSTEPS=1
  /METHOD=WILKS
  /STATISTICS=7.
```

```
Test of equality of group covariance matrices using Box's M

   The ranks and natural logarithms of determinants printed are those
   of the group covariance matrices.

      Group Label                 Rank   Log Determinant

          1 DIE                     3       -1.722152
          2 SURVIVE                 3       -1.902866
     Pooled Within-Groups
     Covariance Matrix             3       -1.698666

   Box's M        Approximate F  Degrees of freedom   Significance
   4.8753            .75422      6,       14168.3        0.6058
```

If the covariance matrices are unequal but the joint distribution of the variables is multivariate normal, the optimum classification rule is the quadratic discriminant function. However, if the covariance matrices are not too dissimilar the linear discriminant function performs quite well, especially if the sample sizes are small (Wahl & Kronmal, 1977). Simulation studies suggest that with small sample sizes the quadratic rule can perform quite poorly. Since DSCRIMINANT uses the discriminant function values to classify cases, not the original variables, it is not possible to obtain the optimum quadratic rule. (When covariance matrices are assumed identical, classification based on the original variables and all canonical functions are equivalent.) However, results obtained using the functions and their covariance matrices might not be too different from those obtained using covariance matrices for the original variables (Tatsuoka, 1971).

In situations where the independent variables are all binary (yes-no, male-female) or a mixture of continuous and discrete variables, the linear discriminant function is not optimal. A variety of nonparametric procedures as well as special procedures for binary variables are available (see Hand, 1981; Goldstein & Dillon, 1978). In the case of dichotomous variables, most evidence suggests that the linear discriminant function often performs reasonably well (Gilbert, 1981; Moore, 1973).

1.43
RUNNING
PROCEDURE
DSCRIMINANT

DSCRIMINANT provides six methods for obtaining discriminant functions: forced entry and five stepwise procedures. You can use the discriminant functions to classify cases, and you can assess the accuracy of these classifications by examining classification results tables, plots of classified cases, and other statistical output provided by DSCRIMINANT.

Only two subcommands are required to obtain discriminant functions using the forced-entry method: the GROUPS subcommand, which specifies the grouping variable; and the VARIABLES subcommand, which specifies the predictor variables. These subcommands produce the eigenvalue and Wilks' lambda for each function, the standardized discriminant-function coefficients, the pooled within-groups correlations between the discriminant scores and the predictor variables, and the group centroids. To obtain unstandardized discriminant functions and coefficients, you must use the STATISTICS subcommand (see Section 1.56).

1.44
Specifying the Groups

Use the GROUPS subcommand to specify the grouping variable and its range of values. For example, the subcommand

```
/GROUPS=RISK(1,3)
```

indicates that RISK is the grouping variable, with integer values from 1 to 3. This subcommand produces a three-group analysis. If there were no cases for one of the specified RISK values, DSCRIMINANT would perform a two-group analysis.

Cases with values outside the range specified for the grouping variable are not used to obtain the discriminant functions. However, such cases are classified into one of the existing groups if classification is requested.

You can specify only one GROUPS subcommand per DSCRIMINANT command.

1.45
Specifying the Variables

List all variables to be used as predictor variables on the VARIABLES subcommand. You can specify only numeric variables, and you can use only one VARIABLES subcommand per DSCRIMINANT command. For example, the command

```
DSCRIMINANT GROUPS=SURVIVAL(1,2)
  /VARIABLES=TREATMNT SEX APGAR AGE TIME WEIGHT PH RESP.
```

produces the output in Figures 1.2 and 1.17b.

1.46
Specifying the Analyses

The ANALYSIS subcommand is useful when you want several discriminant analyses, each with the same grouping variable but different predictor variables. Name all variables to be used in your analysis on the VARIABLES subcommand, and then use the ANALYSIS subcommand to specify subsets of these variables for particular analyses. In this way, you can specify several analyses on a single DSCRIMINANT command.

The variable list on ANALYSIS follows the usual SPSS/PC+ conventions for variable lists with one exception: the TO keyword refers to the order of variables on the VARIABLES subcommand, not their order on the active file. You can use the keyword ALL to refer to all variables listed on the VARIABLES subcommand. A maximum of ten ANALYSIS subcommands are allowed in any one execution of the DSCRIMINANT procedure.

The following command produces two discriminant analyses, both with RISK as the grouping variable:

```
DSCRIMINANT GROUPS=RISK(1,3)
  /VARIABLES=INCOME CREDIT AGEHEAD CHILDREN
  /ANALYSIS=INCOME CREDIT
  /ANALYSIS=INCOME TO CHILDREN.
```

The first analysis uses INCOME and CREDIT as the predictor variables. The second analysis uses INCOME, CREDIT, AGEHEAD, and CHILDREN as the predictor variables.

1.47
Specifying the Selection Method

Use the METHOD subcommand to specify the method for selecting variables for inclusion in the discriminant analysis. Specify METHOD after the ANALYSIS subcommand (or after the VARIABLES subcommand if ANALYSIS is not used). Each METHOD subcommand applies only to the previous ANALYSIS subcommand when multiple ANALYSIS subcommands are used.

DIRECT *Forced entry.* All variables in the VARIABLES or ANALYSIS subcommand are entered simultaneously (if they satisfy tolerance criteria). This is the default. (See Sections 1.1 through 1.21.)

WILKS *Stepwise analysis based on minimizing the overall Wilks' lambda.* (See Sections 1.24 through 1.29.)

RAO *Stepwise analysis based on maximizing the increase in Rao's V.* (See Section 1.31.)

MAHAL *Stepwise analysis based on maximizing Mahalanobis' distance between the two closest groups.* (See Section 1.32.)

MAXMINF *Stepwise analysis based on maximizing the smallest F ratio for pairs of groups.* (See Section 1.33.)

MINRESID *Stepwise analysis based on minimizing the sum of unexplained variation between groups.* (See Section 1.34.)

To obtain forced entry, do not specify a METHOD subcommand, or specify

```
DSCRIMINANT GROUPS=SURVIVAL(1,2)
  /VARIABLES=SEX APGAR AGE TIME WEIGHT PH TREATMNT RESP
  /METHOD=DIRECT.
```

The following command produces a stepwise analysis based on Wilks' lambda:

```
DSCRIMINANT GROUPS=RISK(1,3)
  /VARIABLES=INCOME CREDIT AGEHEAD CHILDREN
  /METHOD=WILKS.
```

1.48
Inclusion Levels

When you specify a stepwise method, you can use the ANALYSIS subcommand to control the order in which variables are considered for entry. By default, variables are examined for entry or removal on the basis of their partial F values. To control the order in which sets of variables are examined, specify an inclusion level in parentheses following the sets of variables on the ANALYSIS subcommand. The inclusion level can be any integer between 0 and 99, as in

```
DSCRIMINANT GROUPS=SURVIVAL(1,2)
  /VARIABLES=SEX APGAR AGE TIME WEIGHT PH TREATMNT RESP
  /ANALYSIS=SEX APGAR TIME PH(2) WEIGHT AGE RESP TREATMNT(1)
  /METHOD=WILKS.
```

The inclusion level controls the order in which variables are entered, the way in which they are entered, and whether or not they should be considered for removal, according to the rules outlined below. All variables must still pass the tolerance criterion to be entered.

- Variables with higher inclusion levels are considered for entry before variables with lower levels. Variables do not have to be ordered by their inclusion level on the subcommand itself.
- Variables with even inclusion levels are entered together.
- Variables with odd inclusion levels are entered one variable at a time according to the stepwise method specified on the METHOD subcommand.
- Only variables with an inclusion level of 1 may be considered for removal. To make a variable with a higher inclusion level eligible for removal, name it twice on the ANALYSIS subcommand, first specifying the desired inclusion level and then an inclusion level of 1.

- An inclusion level of 0 prevents a variable from being entered, although an entry criterion is computed and displayed.
- The default inclusion level is 1.

Example of Backwards Elimination and Forward Selection. For example, to perform backward elimination of variables, all variables must first be entered. Those meeting criteria for removal can then be eliminated. The command

```
DSCRIMINANT GROUPS=SURVIVAL(1,2)
  /VARIABLES=SEX TP RESP
  /ANALYSIS SEX TO RESP(2)
          SEX TO RESP(1)
  /METHOD=WILKS.
```

enters all variables meeting the tolerance criteria and then removes those meeting removal criteria.

1.49
Specifying the Number of Steps

By default, the maximum number of steps in a stepwise analysis is twice the number of variables with inclusion level of 1 (the default), plus the number of variables with inclusion level greater than 1. Use the MAXSTEPS subcommand to decrease the maximum. Specify MAXSTEPS after the METHOD subcommand. The form of MAXSTEPS is MAXSTEPS=n where n is the maximum number of steps desired. MAXSTEPS applies only to the previous ANALYSIS subcommand.

1.50
Setting Statistical Criteria

Several subcommands are available to override the default statistical criteria for discriminant analysis. Specify these subcommands, in any order, after the METHOD subcommand. These subcommands apply only to the previous ANALYSIS subcommand.

TOLERANCE=n *Tolerance level.* The default tolerance level is 0.001. You can reset it to any decimal number between 0 and 1. This sets the minimum tolerance as well as the tolerance for individual variables. (See Section 1.24.)

FIN=n *F-to-enter.* The default *F*-to-enter is 1.0. You may reset it to any nonnegative number. (See Section 1.24.)

FOUT=n *F-to-remove.* The default *F*-to-remove is 1.0. You may reset it to any nonnegative number. (See Section 1.24.)

PIN=n *Probability of* F-*to-enter.* There is no default value, since *F*-to-enter is the default criterion used for selection. Use PIN to maintain a fixed significance level as the entry criterion. You can specify any number between 0 and 1. (See Section 1.24.)

POUT=n *Probability of* F-*to-remove.* There is no default value, since *F*-to-remove is the default criterion used for selection. Use POUT to maintain a fixed significance level as the removal criterion. You can specify any number between 0 and 1. (See Section 1.24.)

VIN=n *Rao's* V-*to-enter.* The default value is 0. (See Section 1.31.)

For example, the following command requests two discriminant analyses:

```
DSCRIMINANT GROUPS=RISK(1,3)
  /VARIABLES=INCOME CREDIT AGEHEAD CHILDREN
  /ANALYSIS=INCOME CREDIT
  /TOLERANCE=.01
  /ANALYSIS=INCOME TO CHILDREN
  /METHOD=RAO
  /VIN=.01.
```

The first requests a forced entry with the tolerance criterion reset to 0.01, and the second requests a stepwise analysis based on Rao's V, with the increase in Rao's V required to be at least 0.01 for entry.

1.51
Specifying the Number of Functions

By default, DSCRIMINANT calculates all discriminant functions available. To reduce the number of functions obtained, specify FUNCTIONS=*nf,* where *nf* is the number of functions desired. FUNCTIONS applies only to the previous ANALYSIS subcommand.

1.52
Selecting Cases

Use the SELECT subcommand to select a subset of cases for computing basic statistics and coefficients. You can then use these coefficients to classify either all the cases or only the unselected cases.

The specification for the SELECT subcommand is a variable name followed by a value in parentheses. Only cases with the specified value on the selection variable are used during the analysis phase. The value must be an integer, as in

```
DSCRIMINANT GROUPS=TYPE(1,5) /VARIABLES=A TO H
  /SELECT=LASTYEAR(81).
```

This command limits the analysis phase to cases containing the value 81 for variable LASTYEAR. The SELECT subcommand must precede the first ANALYSIS subcommand. It remains in effect for all analyses.

When you use the SELECT subcommand, DSCRIMINANT by default reports classification statistics separately for selected and unselected cases. To limit classification to unselected cases, use the options described in Section 1.55.

1.53
Specifying the Prior Probabilities

By default, DSCRIMINANT assumes the prior probabilities of group membership to be equal. You can specify other prior probabilities with the PRIORS subcommand. It follows the ANALYSIS subcommand and applies only to the previous ANALYSIS subcommand. You can specify any of the following:

EQUAL   *Equal prior probabilities.* This is the default specification.

SIZE   *Sample proportion of cases actually falling into each group.*

value list *User-specified list of probabilities.* These must sum to 1, and there must be as many probabilities as there are groups.

For example, the command

```
DSCRIMINANT GROUPS=RISK(1,3)
  /VARIABLES=INCOME CREDIT AGEHEAD CHILDREN
  /PRIORS=.2 .4 .4.
```

specifies a prior probability of 0.2 for the first RISK group and 0.4 for the second and third groups.

1.54
Saving Discriminant Statistics

Much of the casewise information produced by Statistic 14 (Section 1.36) can be added to the active file. The SAVE subcommand specifies the type of information to be saved and the variable names assigned to each piece of information. Three different types of variables can be saved using the following keywords:

CLASS   *Save a variable containing the predicted group value.*

PROBS   *Save posterior probabilities of group membership for each case.* For example, if you have three groups, the first probability is the probability of the case being in Group 1 given its discriminant scores, the second probability is its probability of being in Group 2, and the third probability is its probability of being in Group 3. Since DSCRIMINANT produces more than one probability, a *rootname* used to create a set of variables of the form alpha1 to alpha*n* must be supplied. The rootname cannot exceed seven characters.

SCORES   *Save the discriminant scores.* The number of scores equals the number of functions derived. As with the PROBS parameter, the designated rootname is used to create a set of variables.

Consider the following example:

```
DSCRIMINANT GROUPS=RISK(1,3)
  /VARIABLES=INCOME CREDIT AGEHEAD CHILDREN
  /SAVE=CLASS=PRDCLAS SCORES=SCORE PROBS=PRB.
```

Since the number of groups is 3, DSCRIMINANT adds the 6 variables illustrated in Table 1.54 to the active file.

Table 1.54 Saved casewise results

Name	Description
PRDCLAS	Predicted Group
SCORE1	Discriminant score for Function 1
SCORE2	Discriminant score for Function 2
PRB1	Probability of being in Risk Group 1
PRB2	Probability of being in Risk Group 2
PRB3	Probability of being in Risk Group 3

Only the types of variables specified are saved. You can specify the keywords in any order, but the order in which the variables are added to the file is fixed. The group variable (CLASS) is always written first, followed by discriminant scores (SCORES) and probabilities (PROBS). Variable labels are provided automatically for the newly saved variables. Any value labels defined for the group variable are also saved for the predicted-group variable.

The SAVE subcommand applies only to the previous ANALYSIS subcommand. If there are multiple analyses and you want to save casewise materials from each, use multiple SAVE subcommands. Be sure to use different rootnames.

1.55
Specifying Options

You can request the following options by using the OPTIONS subcommand with the DSCRIMINANT command:

Missing Values. By default, cases missing on any of the variables named on the VARIABLES subcommand and cases out of range or missing on the GROUPS subcommand are not used during the analysis phase. Cases missing or out of range on the GROUPS variable are used during the classification phase.

Option 1 *Include missing values.* User-missing values are treated as valid values. Only the system-missing value is treated as missing.

Option 8 *Substitute means for missing values during classification.* Cases with missing values are not used during analysis. During classification, means are substituted for missing values and cases containing missing values are classified.

Display Options. Two options are available to reduce the amount of output produced during stepwise analysis.

Option 4 *Suppress display of step-by-step output.*
Option 5 *Suppress display of the summary table.*

These two options only affect display, not the computation of intermediate results.

Rotation Options. The pattern and structure matrices displayed during the analysis phase can be rotated to facilitate interpretation of results.

Option 6 *Rotate pattern matrix.*
Option 7 *Rotate structure matrix.*

Neither Option 6 nor Option 7 affects the classification of cases since the rotation is orthogonal.

Classification Options. Three options related to the classification phase are available via the associated OPTIONS subcommand.

Option 9 *Classify only unselected cases.* If you use the SELECT subcommand, by default DSCRIMINANT classifies all nonmissing cases. Two sets of classification results are produced, one for the selected cases and one for the nonselected cases. Option 9 suppresses the classification phase for cases selected via the SELECT subcommand.

Option 10 *Classify only unclassified cases.* Cases whose values on the grouping variable fall outside the range specified on the GROUPS subcommand are considered initially unclassified. During classification, these ungrouped cases are classified as a separate entry in the classification results table. Option 10 suppresses classification of cases that fall into the range specified on the GROUPS subcommand and classifies only cases falling outside the range.

Option 11 *Use separate-group covariance matrices of the discriminant functions for classification.* By default, DSCRIMINANT uses the pooled within-groups covariance matrix to classify cases. Option 11 uses the separate-group covariance matrices for classification. However, since classification is based on the discriminant functions and not the original variables, this option is not equivalent to quadratic discrimination (Tatsuoka, 1971).

1.56
Specifying Optional Statistics

You can request the following optional statistics by using the STATISTICS subcommand with the DSCRIMINANT command:

Statistic 1 *Means.* Requests total and group means for all variables named on the ANALYSIS subcommand. (See Section 1.3.)

Statistic 2 *Standard deviations.* Requests total and group standard deviations for all variables named on the ANALYSIS subcommand. (See Section 1.3.)

Statistic 3 *Pooled within-groups covariance matrix.*

Statistic 4 *Pooled within-groups correlation matrix.* (See Sections 1.5 and 1.41.)

Statistic 5 *Matrix of pairwise F ratios.* Requests the F ratio for each pair of groups. The F's are for significance tests for the Mahalanobis' distances between groups. This statistic is available only with stepwise methods. (See Section 1.25.)

Statistic 6 *Univariate F ratios.* Requests F for each variable. This is a one-way analysis of variance test for equality of group means for a single predictor variable. (See Section 1.3.)

Statistic 7 *Box's M test.* Tests the equality of group covariance matrices. (See Section 1.42.)

Statistic 8 *Group covariance matrices.*

Statistic 9 *Total covariance matrix.*

Statistic 11 *Unstandardized discriminant functions and coefficients.* (See Sections 1.6 and 1.36.)

Statistic 12 *Classification function coefficients.*

1.57
Classification Tables and Plots

To obtain the classification results table, specify Statistic 13 on the STATISTICS subcommand. For example, the following commands request the classification table shown in Figure 1.13:

```
DSCRIMINANT GROUPS=SURVIVAL(1,2)
  /VARIABLES=TREATMNT SEX APGAR AGE TIME WEIGHT PH RESP
  /STATISTICS=13.
```

Two types of classification plots are available, and a territorial map is available when there is more than one discriminant function (see Sections 1.37 and 1.39). If you have at least two functions, you can obtain separate-groups and all-groups scatterplots with the axes defined by the first two functions (see Section 1.37). If you have only one function, separate-groups and all-groups histograms are available (see Section 1.14).

To obtain any of these plots, use the STATISTICS subcommand:

Statistic 10 *Territorial map.* (See Sections 1.37 and 1.46.)

Statistic 13 *Classification results table.*

Statistic 15 *All-groups scatterplot or histogram.* (See Sections 1.14, 1.37, and 1.40.)

Statistic 16 *Separate-groups scatterplot or histogram.* (See Section 1.14.)

1.58
Discriminant Scores and Membership Probabilities

Use Statistic 14 to obtain casewise information that includes the observed group, the classified group, group membership probabilities, and discriminant scores (see Figures 1.12 and 1.36b).

Statistic 14 *Discriminant scores and classification information.* (See Sections 1.12 and 1.36.)

1.59
Annotated Example

The following commands produce the output in Figures 1.24, 1.25a, 1.25b, 1.25c, 1.25d, 1.26, 1.27, 1.28, and 1.29:

```
DATA LIST   /CASEID 1-2 SURVIVAL 4 TREATMNT 6 TIME 8-10(1)
    WEIGHT 12-15(3) APGAR 17-18 SEX 20 AGE 22-23 PH 33-35(2) RESP 37.
VARIABLE LABELS  SURVIVAL 'INFANT SURVIVAL'
    TREATMNT 'TREATMENT ADMINISTERED'
    TIME 'TIME TO SPONTANEOUS RESPIRATION'
    WEIGHT 'BIRTHWEIGHT IN KILOGRAMS'
    APGAR 'APGAR SCORE'
    SEX 'SEX OF RESPONDENT'
    AGE 'GESTATION AGE'
    PH 'PH LEVEL'
    RESP 'RESPIRATORY LEVEL'.
VALUE LABELS SURVIVAL 1'DIE' 2'SURVIVE'/
    TREATMNT 1'THAM' 0'SODIUM BICARBONATE'/
    SEX 1'MALE' 0'FEMALE'/
    RESP 1'YES' 0'NO' 9'NO ANSWER'.
RECODE SURVIVAL (0=1)(1=2).
MISSING VALUES  RESP(9).
BEGIN DATA.
data records
END DATA.
DSCRIMINANT GROUPS=SURVIVAL(1,2)
    /VARIABLES=TREATMNT TO RESP
    /METHOD=WILKS
    /STATISTICS=5
    /OPTIONS=6 7.
```

- The DATA LIST command gives the variable names and column locations for the variables in the analysis.

- The VARIABLE LABELS and VALUE LABELS commands provide descriptive labels to be used in the output.

- The RECODE command recodes the values of SURVIVAL.

- The MISSING VALUES command assigns the value 9 as a user-missing value for RESP.

- The DSCRIMINANT command requests the WILKS method for entering the variables into the analysis phase. It also requests a matrix of pairwise F ratios (Statistic 5) and a varimax rotation of both the function matrix and stucture matrix (Options 6 and 7).

B

Statistics Guide

Contents

2 Logistic Regression Analysis: Procedure LOGISTIC REGRESSION

Predicting whether an event will or will not occur, as well as identifying the variables useful in making the prediction, is important in most academic disciplines as well as the "real" world. Why do some citizens vote and others not? Why do some people develop coronary heart disease and others not? Why do some businesses succeed while others fail?

There is a variety of multivariate statistical techniques that can be used to predict a binary dependent variable from a set of independent variables. Multiple regression analysis and discriminant analysis are two related techniques that quickly come to mind. However, these techniques pose difficulties when the dependent variable can have only two values—an event occurring or not occurring.

When the dependent variable can have only two values, the assumptions necessary for hypothesis testing in regression analysis are necessarily violated. For example, it is unreasonable to assume that the distribution of errors is normal. Another difficulty with multiple regression analysis is that predicted values cannot be interpreted as probabilities. They are not constrained to fall in the interval between 0 and 1.

Linear discriminant analysis does allow direct prediction of group membership, but the assumption of multivariate normality of the independent variables, as well as equal variance-covariance matrices in the two groups, is required for the prediction rule to be optimal.

In this chapter we will consider another multivariate technique for estimating the probability that an event occurs: the logistic regression model. This model requires far fewer assumptions than discriminant analysis; and even when the assumptions required for discriminant analysis are satisfied, logistic regression still performs well. (See Hosmer & Lemeshow, 1989, for an introduction to logistic regression.)

2.1 THE LOGISTIC REGRESSION MODEL

In logistic regression you directly estimate the probability of an event occurring. For the case of a single independent variable, the logistic regression model can be written as

$$Prob\,(event) = \frac{e^{B_0 + B_1 X}}{1 + e^{B_0 + B_1 X}}$$

Equation 2.1a

or equivalently

$$Prob\,(event) = \frac{1}{1 + e^{-(B_0 + B_1 X)}}$$

Equation 2.1b

where B_0 and B_1 are coefficients estimated from the data, X is the independent variable, and e is the base of the natural logarithms, approximately 2.718.

For more than one independent variable the model can be written as

$$Prob(event) = \frac{e^Z}{1 + e^Z}$$

Equation 2.1c

or equivalently,

$$Prob(event) = \frac{1}{1 + e^{-Z}}$$

Equation 2.1d

where Z is the linear combination

$$Z = B_0 + B_1X_1 + B_2X_2 + \dots + B_pX_p$$

Equation 2.1e

The probability of the event not occurring is estimated as

$$Prob(no\ event) = 1 - Prob(event)$$

Equation 2.1f

Figure 2.1 is a plot of a logistic regression curve when the values of Z are between -3 and $+3$. As you can see, the curve is S-shaped. It closely resembles the curve obtained when the cumulative probability of the normal distribution is plotted. The relationship between the independent variable and the probability is nonlinear. The probability estimates will always be between 0 and 1, regardless of the value of Z.

Figure 2.1   Plot of logistic regression curve

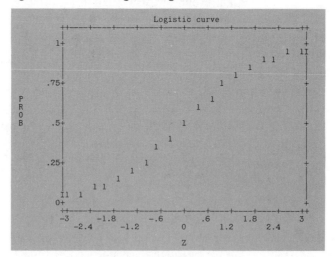

In linear regression we estimate the parameters of the model using the method of least squares. That is, we select regression coefficients that result in the smallest sums of squared distances between the observed and the predicted values of the dependent variable.

In logistic regression the parameters of the model are estimated using the maximum-likelihood method. That is, the coefficients that make our observed results most "likely" are selected. Since the logistic regression model is nonlinear, an iterative algorithm is necessary for parameter estimation.

2.2
An Example

The treatment and prognosis of cancer depends on how much the disease has spread. One of the regions to which a cancer may spread is the lymph nodes. If the lymph nodes are involved, the prognosis is generally poorer than if they are not. That's why it's desirable to establish as early as possible whether the lymph nodes are cancerous. For certain cancers, exploratory surgery is done just to determine whether the nodes are cancerous, since this will determine what treatment is needed. If we could predict whether the nodes are affected on the basis of data that indicate no surgery required, considerable discomfort and expense could be avoided.

For this chapter we will use data presented by Brown (1980) for 53 men with prostate cancer. For each patient he reports the age, serum acid phosphatase (a laboratory value that is elevated if the tumor has spread to certain areas), the stage of the disease (an indication of how advanced the disease is), the grade of the tumor (an indication of malignancy), and x-ray results, as well as whether the cancer had spread to the regional lymph nodes at the time of surgery. The problem is to predict whether the nodes are positive for cancer based on the values of the variables that can be measured without surgery.

2.3
Coefficients for the
Logistic Model

Figure 2.3 contains the estimated coefficients (under column heading **B**) and related statistics from the logistic regression model that predicts nodal involvement from a constant and the variables AGE, ACID, XRAY, STAGE, and GRADE. The last three of these variables (XRAY, STAGE, and GRADE) are *indicator* variables, coded 0 or 1. The value of 1 for XRAY indicates positive x-ray findings, the value of 1 for STAGE indicates advanced stage, and the value of 1 for GRADE indicates a malignant tumor.

Figure 2.3   Parameter estimates for the logistic regression model

```
LOGISTIC REGRESSION NODES WITH AGE ACID XRAY GRADE STAGE.

------------------- Variables in the Equation -------------------

Variable         B        S.E.     Wald     df     Sig      R      Exp(B)

AGE          -.0693      .0579    1.4320     1    .2314    .0000    .9331
ACID          .0243      .0132    3.4229     1    .0643    .1423   1.0246
XRAY         2.0453      .8072    6.4207     1    .0113    .2509   7.7317
GRADE         .7614      .7708     .9758     1    .3232    .0000   2.1413
STAGE        1.5641      .7740    4.0835     1    .0433    .1722   4.7783
Constant      .0618     3.4599     .0003     1    .9857
```

Given these coefficients, the logistic regression equation for the probability of nodal involvement can be written as

$$Prob(nodal\ involvement) = \frac{1}{1+e^{-Z}}$$

Equation 2.3a

where

$$Z = 0.0618 - 0.0693(AGE) + 0.0243(ACID)$$
$$+ 2.0453(XRAY) + 1.5641(STAGE) + 0.7614(GRADE)$$

Equation 2.3b

Applying this to a man who is 66 years old, with a serum phosphatase level of 48 and values of 0 for the remaining independent variables, we find

$$Z = 0.0618 - 0.0693(66) + 0.0243(48) = -3.346$$

Equation 2.3c

The probability of nodal involvement is then estimated to be

$$Prob(nodal\ involvement) = \frac{1}{1+e^{-(-3.346)}} = 0.0340$$

Equation 2.3d

Based on this estimate we would predict that the nodes are unlikely to be malignant. In general, if the estimated probability of the event is less than 0.5, we predict that the event will not occur. If the probability is greater than 0.5, we predict that the event will occur. (In the unlikely event that the probability is exactly 0.5, we can flip a coin for our prediction!)

2.4
Testing Hypotheses about the Coefficients

For large sample sizes, the test that a coefficient is 0 can be based on the Wald statistic, which has a chi-square distribution. When a variable has a single degree of freedom, the Wald statistic is just the square of the ratio of the coefficient to its standard error. For categorical variables the Wald statistic has degrees of freedom equal to one less than the number of categories.

For example, the coefficient for age is −0.0693 and its standard error is 0.0579. (The standard errors for the logistic regression coefficients are shown in the column labeled **S.E.** in Figure 2.3.) The Wald statistic is $(-0.0693/0.0579)^2$, or about 1.432. The significance level for the Wald statistic is shown in the column labeled **Sig.** In this example, only the coefficients for XRAY and STAGE appear to be significantly different from 0, using a significance level of 0.05.

Unfortunately, the Wald statistic has a very undesirable property. When the absolute value of the regression coefficient becomes large, the estimated standard error is too large. This produces a Wald statistic that is too small, leading you to fail to reject the null hypothesis that the coefficient is 0, when in fact you should. Therefore, whenever you have a large coefficient, you should not rely on the Wald statistic for hypothesis testing. Instead, you should build a model with and without that variable and base your hypothesis test on the difference between the two likelihood-ratio chi-squares (Hauck & Donner, 1977).

2.5
Partial Correlation

As is the case with multiple regression, the contribution of individual variables in logistic regression is difficult to determine. The contribution of each variable depends on the other variables in the model. This is a problem particularly when independent variables are highly correlated.

A statistic that is used to look at the partial correlation between the dependent variable and each of the independent variables is the R statistic, shown in Figure 2.3. R can range in value from −1 to +1. A positive value indicates that as the variable increases in value, so does the likelihood of the event occurring. If R is negative, the opposite is true. Small values for R indicate that the variable has a small partial contribution to the model.

The equation for the R statistic is

$$R = \sqrt{\left(\frac{WALD\ STATISTIC - 2K}{-2\,LL_{(0)}}\right)}$$

Equation 2.5

(Atkinson, 1980). The denominator is −2 times the log likelihood of a base model that contains only the intercept, or a model with no variables if there is no intercept. (If you have several METHOD subcommands, the base model for each subcommand is the result of the previous subcommands.) The sign of the corresponding coefficient is attached to R. The value of 2 in Equation 2.5 is an adjustment for the number of parameters estimated. If the Wald statistic is less than 2, R is set to 0.

2.6
Interpreting the Regression Coefficients

In multiple linear regression the interpretation of the regression coefficient is straightforward. It tells you the amount of change in the dependent variable for a one-unit change in the independent variable.

To understand the interpretation of the logistic coefficients, consider a rearrangement of the equation for the logistic model. The logistic model can be rewritten in terms of the odds of an event occurring. (The *odds* of an event occurring are defined as the ratio of the probability that it will occur to the probability that it will not. For example, the odds of getting a head on a single flip of a fair coin are 0.5/0.5 = 1. Similarly, the odds of getting a diamond on a single draw from a card deck is 0.25/0.75 = 1/3. Don't confuse this technical meaning of odds with its informal usage to mean simply the probability.)

First let's write the logistic model in terms of the log of the odds, which is called a *logit*.

$$log \left(\frac{Prob(event)}{Prob(no\ event)} \right) = B_0 + B_1 X_1 + ... + B_p X_p \qquad \text{Equation 2.6a}$$

From Equation 2.6a, you see that the logistic coefficient can be interpreted as the change in the log odds associated with a one-unit change in the independent variable. For example, from Figure 2.3, you see that the coefficient for GRADE is 0.76. This tells you that when the grade changes from 0 to 1, and the values of the other independent variables remain the same, the log odds of the nodes being malignant increase by 0.76.

Since it's easier to think of odds, rather than log odds, the logistic equation can be written in terms of odds as

$$\frac{Prob\,(event)}{Prob\,(no\ event)} = e^{B_0 + B_1 X_1 + ... + B_p X_p} = e^{B_0} e^{B_1 X_1} ... e^{B_p X_p} \qquad \text{Equation 2.6b}$$

Then e raised to the power B_i is the factor by which the odds change when the ith independent variable increases by one unit. If B_i is positive this factor will be greater than 1, which means that the odds are increased; if B_i is negative the factor will be less than 1, which means that the odds are decreased. When B_i is 0 the factor equals 1, which leaves the odds unchanged. For example, when the GRADE changes from 0 to 1, the odds are increased by a factor of 2.14, as is shown in the **Exp(B)** column in Figure 2.3.

As a further example, let's calculate the odds of having malignant nodes for a 60-year-old man with a serum acid phosphatase level of 62, a value of 1 for x-ray results, and values of 0 for stage and grade of tumor. First, calculate the probability that the nodes are malignant:

$$Estimated\ prob(malignant\ nodes) = \frac{1}{1 + e^{-Z}} \qquad \text{Equation 2.6c}$$

where

$$Z = 0.0618 - 0.0693(60) + 0.0243(62) + 2.0453(1) \qquad \text{Equation 2.6d}$$
$$+ 0.7614(0) + 1.5641(0) = -0.54$$

The estimated probability of malignant nodes is therefore 0.37. The probability of not having malignant nodes is 0.63 (that is, 1 - 0.37). The *odds* of having a malignant node are then estimated as

$$Odds = prob(event)/prob(no\ event) = \frac{0.37}{1 - 0.37} = 0.59 \qquad \text{Equation 2.6e}$$

and the log odds are -0.53.

What would be the probability of malignant nodes if instead of 0, the case had a value of 1 for grade? Following the same procedure as before, but using a value of 1 for grade, the estimated probability of malignant nodes is 0.554. Similarly, the estimated odds are 1.24, and the log odds are 0.22.

By increasing the value of grade by one unit we have increased the log odds by about 0.75, the value of the coefficient for grade. (Since we didn't use many digits in our hand calculations, our value of 0.75 isn't exactly equal to the 0.76 value for grade shown in Figure 2.3. If we carried the computations out with enough precision, we would arrive at exactly the value of the coefficient.)

By increasing the value of grade from 0 to 1, the odds changed from 0.59 to 1.24. That is, they increased by a factor of about 2.1. This is the value of "Exp(B)" for GRADE in Figure 2.3.

2.7
Assessing the Goodness of Fit of the Model

There are various ways to assess whether or not the model fits the data. Sections 2.8 through 2.11 discuss the goodness of fit of the model.

2.8
The Classification Table

One way to assess how well our model fits is to compare our predictions to the observed outcomes. Figure 2.8 is the classification table for this example.

Figure 2.8 Classification table

LOGISTIC REGRESSION NODES WITH AGE ACID XRAY GRADE STAGE.

```
Classification Table for NODES
                         Predicted
                   Negative  Positive     Percent Correct
                      N         P
Observed         +---------+---------+
    Negative   N  |   28    |    5    |    84.85%
                 +---------+---------+
    Positive   P  |    7    |   13    |    65.00%
                 +---------+---------+
                            Overall   77.36%
```

From the table, you see that 28 patients without malignant nodes were correctly predicted by the model not to have malignant nodes. Similarly, 13 men with positive nodes were correctly predicted to have positive nodes. The off-diagonal entries of the table tell you how many men were incorrectly classified. A total of 12 men were misclassified in this example—5 men with negative nodes and 7 men with positive nodes. Of the men without diseased nodes, 84.85% were correctly classified. Of the men with diseased nodes, 65% were correctly classified. Overall, 77.36% of the 53 men were correctly classified.

The classification table doesn't reveal the distribution of estimated probabilities for men in the two groups. For each predicted group, all the table shows is whether the estimated probability is greater or less than one-half. For example, you cannot tell from the table whether the 7 patients who had false-negative results had predicted probabilities near 50%, or low predicted probabilities. Ideally, you would like the two groups to have very different estimated probabilities. That is, you would like to see small estimated probabilities of positive nodes for all men without malignant nodes and large estimated probabilities for all men with malignant nodes.

2.9
Histogram of Estimated Probabilities

Figure 2.9 is a histogram of the estimated probabilities of cancerous nodes. The symbol used for each case designates the group to which the case actually belongs. If you have a model that successfully distinguishes the two groups, the cases for whom the event has occurred should be to the right of 0.5, while those cases who have not had the event should be to the left of 0.5. The more the two groups cluster at their respective ends of the plot, the better.

Figure 2.9   Histogram of estimated probabilities

LOGISTIC REGRESSION NODES WITH AGE ACID XRAY GRADE STAGE
   /CLASSPLOT.

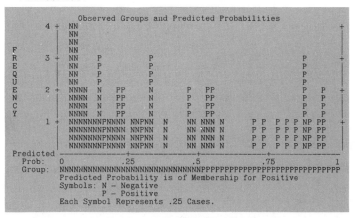

From Figure 2.9, you see that there is only one noncancerous case with a high estimated probability of having positive nodes. (The case identified with the symbol "N" at a probability value of about 0.88.) However, there are four diseased cases with estimated probabilities less than 0.25.

By looking at this histogram of predicted probabilities you can see whether a different rule for assigning cases to groups might be useful. For example, if most of the misclassifications occur in the region about 0.5, you might decide to withhold judgment for cases with values in this region. In this example, that would mean that you would predict nodal involvement only for cases for which you were reasonably sure the logistic prediction would be correct. You might decide to operate on all questionable cases.

If the consequences of misclassification are not the same in both directions (for example, calling nodes negative when they are really positive is worse than calling nodes positive when they are really negative), the classification rule can be altered to decrease the possibility of making the more severe error. For example, you might decide to call cases "negative" only if their estimated probability is less than 0.3. By looking at the histogram of the estimated probabilities you can get some idea of how different classification rules might perform. (Of course, when you apply the model to new cases, you can't expect the classification rule to behave exactly the same.)

2.10
Goodness of Fit of the Model

Seeing how well the model classifies the observed data is one way of determining how well the logistic model performs. Another way of assessing the goodness of fit of the model is to actually examine how likely the sample results are, given the parameter estimates. (Recall that we chose parameter estimates which would make our observed results as likely as possible.)

The probability of the observed results given the parameter estimates is known as the *likelihood*. Since the likelihood is a small number less than 1, it is customary to use -2 times the log of the likelihood (-2 LL) as a measure of how well the estimated model fits the data. A good model is one that results in a high likelihood of the observed results. This translates to a small value for -2 LL. (If a model fits perfectly, the likelihood is 1, and -2 times the log likelihood is 0.)

For the logistic regression model that contains only the constant, -2 LL is 70.25, as shown in Figure 2.10. The results for a model containing all the independent variables are shown in Figure 2.11.

Figure 2.10   −2 LL for model containing only the constant

LOGISTIC REGRESSION NODES WITH AGE ACID XRAY GRADE STAGE.

```
Dependent Variable..   NODES
Beginning Block Number  0.  Initial Log Likelihood Function
−2 Log Likelihood   70.252153
* Constant is included in the model.
```

To test the null hypothesis that the observed likelihood does not differ from 1 (the value of the likelihood for a model that fits perfectly), you can use the value of −2 LL. Under the null hypothesis that the model fits perfectly, −2 LL has a chi-square distribution with $N - p$ degrees of freedom, where N is the number of cases and p is the number of parameters estimated. (This statistic is sometimes called the *deviance.*) Since there are 53 observations and 6 parameters estimated, the degrees of freedom are 47. Since the observed significance level is large, you do not reject the hypothesis that the model fits.

Another statistic that can be used to test how well the model fits is the goodness-of-fit statistic. It compares the observed probabilities to those predicted by the model. The goodness-of-fit statistic is defined as

$$Z^2 = \sum \frac{Residual_i^2}{P_i(1 - P_i)}$$

Equation 2.10

where the residual is the difference between the observed value, Y_i, and the predicted value, P_i. This statistic also has a chi-square distribution, if the model fit is the correct one, with approximately $N - p$ degrees of freedom (see McCullagh & Nelder, 1983, and Hosmer & Lemeshow, 1989). In Figure 2.11, you see that the goodness-of-fit statistic leads to the same conclusion as the −2 LL.

If you have groups of cases with the same values for the independent variables, the previous tests can be modified to reflect this grouping (see Hosmer & Lemeshow, 1989).

2.11
Goodness of Fit with All Variables

Figure 2.11 shows the goodness-of-fit statistics for the model with all of the independent variables. As discussed in Section 2.11, the first row of the table compares the present model to a "perfect" model. The chi-square value is 48.126, the value of -2 LL for the current model. The large observed significance level indicates that this model does not differ significantly from the "perfect" model. The goodness-of-fit statistic in the last row of the table leads to a similar conclusion.

Figure 2.11   Statistics for model containing the independent variables

LOGISTIC REGRESSION NODES WITH AGE ACID XRAY GRADE STAGE.

	Chi-Square	df	Significance
−2 Log Likelihood	48.126	47	.4270
Model Chi-Square	22.126	5	.0005
Improvement	22.126	5	.0005
Goodness of Fit	46.790	47	.4812

There are two additional entries in Figure 2.11. They are labeled **Model Chi-square** and **Improvement**. In this example, the model chi-square is the difference between −2 LL for the model with only a constant and −2 LL for the current model. (If a constant is not included in the model, the likelihood for the model without any variables is used for comparison. If variables are already in the equation when variable selection begins, the model with these variables is used as the base model.) Thus, the model chi-square tests the null hypothesis that the coefficients for all of the terms in the current model, except the constant, are 0. This is comparable to the overall F test for regression.

In this example, -2 LL for the model with only the constant is 70.25 (from Figure 2.10) while for the complete model it is 48.126. The model chi-square, 22.126, is the difference between these two values. The degrees of freedom for the model chi-square are the difference between the degrees of freedom for the two models being compared. In this example, the degrees of freedom for the constant-only model are 52, while the degrees of freedom for the model with the five independent variables and constant are 47. The model chi-square has $52 - 47$, or 5, degrees of freedom.

The entry labeled **Improvement** is the change in -2 LL between successive steps of building a model. It tests the null hypothesis that the coefficients for the variables added at the last step are 0. In this example, we considered only two models: the constant-only model and the model with the constant and the five independent variables. Thus, the model chi-square and the improvement chi-square values are the same. If you sequentially consider more than just these two models, using either forward or backward variable selection, the model chi-square and improvement chi-square will differ. The improvement chi-square test is comparable to the F-change test in multiple regression.

2.12
Categorical Variables

In logistic regression, just as in linear regression, the codes for the independent variables must be meaningful. You cannot take a nominal variable like religion, assign arbitrary codes from 1 to 35, and then use the resulting variable in the model. In this situation you must recode the values of the independent variable by creating a new set of variables that correspond, in some way, to the original categories.

If you have a two-category variable like sex, you can code each case as 0 or 1 to indicate either female or not female. Or you could code it as being male or not male. This is called *dummy variable* or *indicator variable* coding. GRADE, STAGE and XRAY are all examples of two-category variables that have been coded as 0 and 1. The code of 1 indicates that the poorer outcome is present. The interpretation of the resulting coefficients for GRADE, STAGE and XRAY is straightforward. It tells you the difference between the log odds when a case is a member of the "poor" category and when it is not.

When you have a variable with more than two categories, you must create new variables to represent the categories. The number of new variables required to represent a categorical variable is one less than the number of categories. For example, if instead of the actual values for serum acid phosphatase, you had values of 1, 2, or 3, depending on whether the value was low, medium, or high, you would have to create two new variables to represent the serum phosphatase effect. Sections 2.13 and 2.14 show two alternative coding schemes.

2.13
Indicator-Variable Coding Scheme

One of the ways you can create two new variables for serum acid phosphatase is to use indicator variables to represent the categories. With this method, one variable would represent the low value, coded 1 if the value is low and 0 otherwise. The second variable would represent the medium value, coded 1 if the value is average and 0 otherwise. The value "high" would be represented by codes of 0 for both of these variables. The choice of the category to be coded as 0 for both variables is arbitrary. You can select any of the categories as the reference category.

With categorical variables, the only statement you can make about the effect of a particular category is in comparison with some other category. For example, if you have a variable that represents type of cancer, you can only make statements such as "lung cancer compared to bladder cancer decreases your chance of survival." Or you might say that "lung cancer compared to all the cancer types in the study decreases your chance of survival." You can't make a statement about lung cancer without relating it to the other types of cancer.

If you use indicator variables for coding, the coefficients for the new variables represent the effect of each category compared to a reference category. The coefficient for the reference category is 0. As an example, consider Figure 2.13a. The variable CATACID1 is the indicator variable for low serum acid phosphatase, coded 1 for low levels and 0 otherwise. Similarly, the variable CATACID2 is the indicator variable for medium serum acid phosphatase. The reference category is high levels.

Figure 2.13a   Indicator variables

```
COMPUTE CATACID1=0.
COMPUTE CATACID2=0.
IF (ACID LE 50) CATACID1=1.
IF (ACID GT 50 AND ACID LT 75) CATACID2=1.
LOGISTIC REGRESSION NODES WITH AGE CATACID1 CATACID2
    XRAY GRADE STAGE.
```

```
--------------------- Variables in the Equation ---------------------

Variable           B        S.E.      Wald     df      Sig        R     Exp(B)

AGE            -.0522      .0630     .6862      1     .4075    .0000    .9492
CATACID1      -2.0079     1.0520    3.6427      1     .0563   -.1529    .1343
CATACID2      -1.0923      .9264    1.3903      1     .2384    .0000    .3355
XRAY           2.0348      .8375    5.9033      1     .0151    .2357   7.6503
GRADE           .8076      .8233     .9623      1     .3266    .0000   2.2426
STAGE          1.4571      .7683    3.5968      1     .0579    .1508   4.2934
Constant       1.7698     3.8088     .2159      1     .6422
```

The coefficient for CATACID1 is the change in log odds when you have a low value compared to a high value. Similarly, CATACID2 is the change in log odds when you have a medium value compared to a high value. The coefficient for the high value is necessarily 0, since it does not differ from itself. In Figure 2.13a, you see that the coefficients for both of the indicator variables are negative. This means that, compared to high values for serum acid phosphatase, low and medium values are associated with decreased log odds of malignant nodes. The low category decreases the log odds more than the medium category.

The LOGISTIC REGRESSION procedure will automatically create new variables for categorical variables, if you have declared them as categorical on the CATEGORICAL subcommand. You can choose the coding scheme you want to use for the new variables on the CONTRAST subcommand.

Figure 2.13b shows the table that is displayed for each categorical variable. The rows of the table correspond to the categories of the variable. The actual value is given in the column labeled **Value.** The number of cases with each value is displayed in the column labeled **Freq.** Subsequent columns correspond to new variables created by the program. The number in parentheses indicates the suffix used to identify the variable on the output. The codes that represent each original category using the new variables are listed under the corresponding new-variable column.

Figure 2.13b   Indicator-variable coding scheme

```
LOGISTIC REGRESSION NODES WITH AGE CATACID XRAY GRADE STAGE
    /CATEGORICAL CATACID
    /CONTRAST(CATACID)=IND.
```

	Value	Freq	Parameter Coding (1)	(2)
CATACID				
	1.00	15	1.000	.000
	2.00	20	.000	1.000
	3.00	18	.000	.000

From Figure 2.13b, you see that there are 20 cases with a value of 2 for CATACID. Each of these cases will be assigned a code of 0 for the new variable CATACID(1) and a code of 1 for the new variable CATACID(2). Similarly, cases with a value of 3 for CATACID will be given the code of 0 for both CATACID(1) and CATACID(2).

2.14
Another Coding Scheme

The statement you can make based on the logistic regression coefficients depends on how you have created the new variables used to represent the categorical variable. As shown in the previous section, when you use indicator variables for coding, the coefficients for the new variables represent the effect of each category compared to a reference category. If, on the other hand, you wanted to compare the effect of each category to the average effect of all of the categories, you could have selected the default DEVIATION coding scheme shown in Figure 2.14a. This differs from indicator-variable coding only in that the last category is coded as -1 for each of the new variables.

With this coding scheme, the logistic regression coefficients tell you how much better or worse each category is compared to the average effect of all categories, as shown in Figure 2.14b. For each new variable, the coefficients now represent the difference from the average effect over all categories. The value of the coefficient for the last category is not displayed, but it is no longer 0. Instead, it is the negative of the sum of the displayed coefficients. From Figure 2.14b, the coefficient for "high" level is calculated as $-(-0.9745 - 0.0589) = 1.0334$.

Figure 2.14a Another coding scheme

```
LOGISTIC REGRESSION NODES WITH AGE CATACID XRAY GRADE STAGE
    /CATEGORICAL CATACID
    /CONTRAST(CATACID)=DEV.
```

	Value	Freq	Parameter Coding (1)	(2)
CATACID				
	1.00	15	1.000	.000
	2.00	20	.000	1.000
	3.00	18	-1.000	-1.000

Figure 2.14b New coefficients

Variable	B	S.E.	Wald	df	Sig	R	Exp(B)
AGE	-.0522	.0630	.6862	1	.4075	.0000	.9492
CATACID			3.8361	2	.1469	.0000	
CATACID(1)	-.9745	.6410	2.3116	1	.1284	-.0666	.3774
CATACID(2)	-.0589	.5727	.0106	1	.9181	.0000	.9428
XRAY	2.0348	.8375	5.9033	1	.0151	.2357	7.6503
GRADE	.8076	.8233	.9623	1	.3266	.0000	2.2426
STAGE	1.4571	.7683	3.5968	1	.0579	.1508	4.2934
Constant	.7364	3.7352	.0389	1	.8437		

Different coding schemes result in different logistic regression coefficients, but not in different conclusions. That is, even though the actual values of the coefficients differ between Figures 2.13a and 2.14b, they tell you the same thing. Figure 2.13a tells you the effect of category 1 compared to category 3, while Figure 2.14b tells you the effect of category 1 compared to the average effect of all of the categories. You can select the coding scheme to match the type of comparisons you want to make.

2.15
Interaction Terms

Just as in linear regression, you can include terms in the model that are products of single terms. For example, if it made sense, you could include a term for the ACID by AGE interaction in your model. (The LOGISTIC REGRESSION procedure will automatically create interaction terms for you.)

Interaction terms for categorical variables can also be computed. They are created as products of the values of the new variables. For categorical variables, make sure that the interaction terms created are those of interest. If you are using categorical variables with indicator coding, the interaction terms generated as the product of the variables are generally not those that you are interested in. Consider, for example, the interaction term between two indicator variables. If you just multiply the variables together you will obtain a value of 1 only if both of the variables are coded "present." What you would probably like is a code of 1 if both of the variables are present or both are absent. You will obtain this if you use the default coding scheme for category variables instead of specifying the scheme as indicator variables.

2.16
Selecting Predictor Variables

In logistic regression, as in other multivariate statistical techniques, you may want to identify subsets of independent variables that are good predictors of the dependent variable. All of the problems associated with variable selection algorithms in regression and discriminant analysis are found in logistic regression as well. None of the algorithms result in a "best" model in any statistical sense. Different algorithms for variable selection may result in different models. It is a good idea to examine several possible models and choose among them on the basis of interpretability, parsimony, and ease of variable acquisition.

As always, the model is selected to fit a particular sample well, so there is no assurance that the same model will be selected if another sample from the same population is taken. The model will always fit the sample better than the population from which it is selected.

The LOGISTIC REGRESSION procedure has several methods available for model selection. You can enter variables into the model at will with the ENTER subcommand. You can also use forward stepwise selection and backward stepwise elimination for automated model building. The score statistic is always used for entering variables into a model. Either the Wald statistic or the change in likelihood can be used for removing variables from a model. All variables that are used to represent the same categorical variable are entered or removed from the model together.

2.17
Forward Stepwise Selection

Forward stepwise variable selection in logistic regression proceeds the same way as in multiple linear regression. You start out with a model that contains only the constant, unless the option to omit the constant term from the model is selected. At each step, the variable with the smallest significance level for the score statistic, provided it is less than the chosen cutoff value (by default 0.05), is entered into the model. All variables in the model that were listed on the FSTEP keyword are then examined to see if they meet removal criteria. If the default Wald statistic is used for deleting variables, the Wald statistics for all variables in the model are examined and the variable with the largest significance level for the Wald statistic, provided it exceeds the chosen cutoff value (by default 0.1), is removed from the model. If no variables meet removal criteria, the next eligible variable is entered into the model.

If a variable is selected for removal and it results in a model that has already been considered, variable selection stops. Otherwise, the model is estimated without the deleted variable and the variables are again examined for removal. This continues until no more variables are eligible for removal. Then variables are again examined for entry into the model. The process continues either until a previously considered model is encountered (which means the algorithm is cycling) or no variables meet entry or removal criteria.

2.18
The Likelihood-Ratio Test

A better, but computationally more intensive, criterion for determining variables to be removed from the model is the likelihood-ratio (LR) test. This involves estimating the model with each variable eliminated in turn and looking at the change in the log likelihood when each variable is deleted. The likelihood-ratio test for the null hypothesis that the coefficients of the terms removed are 0 is obtained by dividing the likelihood for the complete model by the likelihood for the reduced model.

If the null hypothesis is true and the sample size is sufficiently large, the quantity -2 times the log of the likelihood-ratio statistic has a chi-square distribution with r degrees of freedom, where r is the difference between the number of terms in the full model and the reduced model. (The model chi-square and the improvement chi-square are both likelihood-ratio tests.)

When the likelihood-ratio test is used for removing terms from a model, its significance level is compared to the cutoff value. The algorithm proceeds as previously described but with the likelihood-ratio statistic, instead of the Wald statistic, being evaluated for removing variables.

2.19
An Example of Forward Selection

To see what the output looks like for forward selection, consider Figure 2.19a, which contains part of the summary statistics for the model when the constant is the only term included. First you see the previously described statistics for the constant. Then you see statistics for variables not in the equation. (The R for variables not in the equation is calculated using the score statistic instead of the Wald statistic.)

Figure 2.19a   Variables not in the equation

```
LOGISTIC REGRESSION NODES WITH AGE ACID XRAY GRADE STAGE
    /FSTEP.
```

```
----------------------- Variables in the Equation -----------------------

Variable          B        S.E.      Wald      df       Sig        R     Exp(B)

Constant       -.5008     .2834     3.1227      1      .0772


------------- Variables not in the Equation -------------
Residual Chi Square      19.451 with        5 df      Sig =  .0016

Variable            Score      df       Sig        R

AGE               1.0945      1      .2955     .0000
ACID              3.1168      1      .0775     .1261
XRAY             11.2829      1      .0008     .3635
GRADE             4.0745      1      .0435     .1718
STAGE             7.4381      1      .0064     .2782
```

The residual chi-square statistic tests the null hypothesis that the coefficients for all variables not in the model are 0. (The residual chi-square statistic is calculated from the score statistics, so it is not exactly the same value as the improvement chi-square value that you see in Figure 2.11. However, in general the two statistics should be similar in value.) If the observed significance level for the residual chi-square statistic is small (that is, if you have reason to reject the hypothesis that all of the coefficients are 0), it is sensible to proceed with variable selection. If you can't reject the hypothesis that the coefficients are 0, you should consider terminating variable selection. If you continue to build a model, there is a reasonable chance that your resulting model will not be useful for other samples from the same population.

In this example, the significance level for the residual chi-square is small, so we can proceed with variable selection. For each variable not in the model, the score statistic and its significance level, if the variable were entered next into the model, is shown. The score statistic is an efficient alternative to the Wald statistic for testing the hypothesis that a coefficient is 0. Unlike the Wald statistic, it does not require the explicit computation of parameter estimates, so it is useful in situations where recalculating parameter estimates for many different models would be computationally prohibitive. The likelihood-ratio statistic, the Wald statistic, and Rao's efficient score statistic are all equivalent in large samples, when the null hypothesis is true (Rao, 1973).

From Figure 2.19a, you see that XRAY has the largest score statistic and its observed significance level is smaller than 0.05, the default value for entry, so it is entered into the model. Statistics for variables not in the model at this step are shown in Figure 2.19b. You see that the STAGE variable has the largest score statistic and meets entry criteria, so it is entered next. Figure 2.19c contains logistic coefficients when STAGE is included in the model. Since the observed significance levels of the coefficients for both variables in the model are less than 0.1, the default criterion for removal, neither variable is removed from the model.

Figure 2.19b   Variables not in the equation

```
LOGISTIC REGRESSION NODES WITH AGE ACID XRAY GRADE STAGE
    /FSTEP.
```

—————————— Variables not in the Equation ——————————				
Residual Chi Square	10.360 with		4 df	Sig = .0348
Variable	Score	df	Sig	R
AGE	1.3524	1	.2449	.0000
ACID	2.0732	1	.1499	.0323
GRADE	2.3710	1	.1236	.0727
STAGE	5.6393	1	.0176	.2276

Figure 2.19c   Logistic coefficients with STAGE and XRAY

```
LOGISTIC REGRESSION NODES WITH AGE ACID XRAY GRADE STAGE
    /FSTEP.
```

——————— Variables in the Equation ———————						
Variable	B	S.E.	Wald	df	Sig	R	Exp(B)
XRAY	2.1194	.7468	8.0537	1	.0045	.2935	8.3265
STAGE	1.5883	.7000	5.1479	1	.0233	.2117	4.8953
Constant	−2.0446	.6100	11.2360	1	.0008		

The goodness-of-fit statistics for the model with XRAY and STAGE are shown in Figure 2.19d. Both the −2 log likelihood and the goodness-of-fit tests indicate that the model fits the data reasonably well. The model chi-square, the difference between −2 LL when only the constant is in the model and −2 LL when the constant, XRAY, and STAGE are in the model (70.25 − 53.35 = 16.90), indicates that there has been a significant change in the model. The improvement chi-square is the change in −2 LL when STAGE is added to a model containing XRAY and the constant. The small observed significance level indicates that the addition of STAGE significantly improved the model. −2 LL for the model with only the constant and XRAY is 59.001, so the improvement chi-square is 59.00 − 53.35 = 5.65.

Figure 2.19d   Goodness-of-fit statistics with STAGE and XRAY

```
LOGISTIC REGRESSION NODES WITH AGE ACID XRAY GRADE STAGE
    /FSTEP.
```

	Chi-Square	df	Significance
−2 Log Likelihood	53.353	50	.3466
Model Chi-Square	16.899	2	.0002
Improvement	5.647	1	.0175
Goodness of Fit	54.018	50	.3235

The statistics for variables not in the model after STAGE is entered are shown in Figure 2.19e. All three of the observed significance levels are greater than 0.05, so no additional variables are included in the model.

Figure 2.19e   Variables not in the model after STAGE

```
LOGISTIC REGRESSION NODES WITH AGE ACID XRAY GRADE STAGE
    /FSTEP.
```

—————————— Variables not in the Equation ——————————				
Residual Chi Square	5.422 with		3 df	Sig = .1434
Variable	Score	df	Sig	R
AGE	1.2678	1	.2602	.0000
ACID	3.0917	1	.0787	.1247
GRADE	.5839	1	.4448	.0000

2.20
Forward Selection with the Likelihood-Ratio Criterion

If you select the likelihood-ratio statistic instead of the Wald statistic for deleting variables, the output will look slightly different from that previously described. For variables in the equation at a particular step, output similar to that shown in Figure 2.20 is produced, in addition to the usual coefficients and Wald statistics.

Figure 2.20 Variables not in the model after STAGE

```
LOGISTIC REGRESSION NODES WITH AGE ACID XRAY GRADE STAGE
    /FSTEP(LR).
```

Term Removed	Log Likelihood	-2 Log LR	df	Significance of Log LR
XRAY	-31.276	9.199	1	.0024
STAGE	-29.500	5.647	1	.0175

(— Model if Term Removed —)

For each variable in the model, Figure 2.20 contains the log likelihood for the model if the variable is removed from the model; $-2LR$, which tests the null hypothesis that the coefficient of the term is 0; and the observed significance level. If the observed significance level is greater than the cutoff value for remaining in the model, the term is removed from the model and the model statistics recalculated to see if any other variables are eligible for removal.

2.21
Backward Elimination

Forward selection starts without any variables in the model. Backward elimination starts with all of the variables in the model. Then, at each step, variables are evaluated for entry and removal. The score statistic is always used for determining whether variables should be added to the model. Just as in forward selection, either the Wald statistic or the likelihood-ratio statistic can be used to select variables for removal.

2.22
Diagnostic Methods

Whenever you build a statistical model, it is important to examine the adequacy of the resulting model. In linear regression we look at a variety of residuals, measures of influence, and indicators of collinearity. These are valuable tools for identifying points for which the model does not fit well, points that exert a strong influence on the coefficient estimates, and variables that are highly related to each other.

In logistic regression there are comparable diagnostics that should be used to look for problems. The LOGISTIC REGRESSION procedure provides a variety of such statistics.

The *residual* is the difference between the observed probability of the event and the predicted probability of the event based on the model. For example, if we predict the probability of malignant nodes to be 0.80 for a man who has malignant nodes, the residual is $1 - 0.80 = 0.20$.

The *standardized residual* is the residual divided by an estimate of its standard deviation. In this case:

$$Z_i = \frac{Residual_i}{\sqrt{(Pred.\,Prob._i)(1 - Pred.\,Prob._i)}}$$

Equation 2.22a

For each case the standardized residual can also be considered a component of the chi-square goodness-of-fit statistic. If the sample size is large, the standardized residuals should be approximately normally distributed with a mean of 0 and a standard deviation of 1.

For each case, the *deviance* compares the predicted probability of being in the correct group based on the model to the perfect prediction of 1. It can be viewed as a component of -2 LL, which compares a model to the "perfect" model (see Section 2.10).

The deviance can be written in the form of a likelihood-ratio test as

$$-2 \times log(L0/L1)$$

Equation 2.22b

where $L1$ is always 1, since the likelihood of the correct prediction in a perfect model is 1, and $L0$ is the predicted probability of membership in the correct group. This simplifies to

$$-2 \times log(predicted\ probability\ of\ the\ correct\ group)$$

Equation 2.22c

The deviance is calculated by taking the square root of the above statistic and attaching a negative sign if the event did not occur for that case. For example, the deviance for a man without malignant nodes and a predicted probability of 0.8 for nonmalignant nodes is

$$Deviance = -\sqrt{-2 \log(0.8)} = -0.668$$

Equation 2.22d

Large values for deviance indicate that the model does not fit the case well. For large sample sizes the deviance is approximately normally distributed.

The *studentized residual* for a case is the change in the model deviance if the case is excluded. Discrepancies between the deviance and the studentized residual may identify unusual cases. Normal probability plots of the studentized residuals may be useful.

The *logit residual* is the residual for the model if it is predicted in the logit scale. That is,

$$Logit\ residual = \frac{residual}{P_i(1 - P_i)}$$

Equation 2.22e

The *leverage* in logistic regression is in many respects analogous to the leverage in least-squares regression. Leverage values are often used for detecting observations that have a large impact on the predicted values. Unlike linear regression, the leverage values in logistic regression depend on both the dependent variable scores and the design matrix. Leverage values are bounded by 0 and 1. Their average value is p/n, where p is the number of estimated parameters in the model, including the constant, and n is the sample size.

Cook's distance is a measure of the influence of a case. It tells you how much deleting a case affects not only the residual for that case, but also the residuals of the remaining cases. Cook's distance depends on the standardized residual for a case, as well as its leverage. It is defined as

$$Cook's\ D = \frac{Z_i^2 \times h_i}{(1 - h_i)^2}$$

Equation 2.22f

where Z_i is the standardized residual and h_i is the leverage.

Another useful diagnostic measure is the *change in the logistic coefficients* when a case is deleted from the model, or DFBETA. You can compute this change for each coefficient, including the constant. For example, the change in the first coefficient when case i is deleted is

$$DFBETA(B_1^{(i)}) = B_1 - B_1^{(i)}$$

Equation 2.22g

where B_1 is the value of the coefficient when all cases are included and $B_1^{(i)}$ is the value of the coefficient when the ith case is excluded. Large values for change identify observations which should be examined.

2.23
Plotting Diagnostics

All of the diagnostic statistics described in this chapter can be listed for each case or a subset of cases using the CASEWISE subcommand or saved for further analysis using the SAVE subcommand. If you save the values for the diagnostics, you can, when appropriate, obtain normal probability plots using the EXAMINE procedure and plot the diagnostics using the PLOT procedure.

Figure 2.23a is a normal probability of the deviances. As you can see, the deviances do not appear to be normally distributed. That's because there are cases for which the model just doesn't fit well. In Figure 2.9, you see cases that have high probabilities for being in the incorrect group.

Figure 2.23a   Normal probability of the deviances

```
LOGISTIC REGRESSION NODES WITH AGE ACID XRAY GRADE STAGE
   /SAVE DEV LEVER DFBETA ZRESID.
EXAMINE DEV_1/PLOT NPPLOT.
```

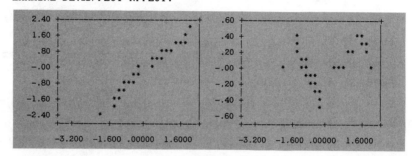

A plot of the standardized residuals against the case sequence numbers is shown in Figure 2.23b. Again you see cases with large values for the standardized residuals. In particular, the circled point, Case 37, has a very large standardized residual. Figure 2.23c shows that there is one case with a leverage value that is much larger than the rest. Similarly, Figure 2.23d shows that there is a case that has substantial impact on the estimation of the coefficient for ACID (Case 24). Examination of the data reveals that this case has the largest value for serum acid phosphatase and yet does not have malignant nodes. Since serum acid phosphatase was positively related to malignant nodes, as shown in Figure 2.3, this case is quite unusual. If we remove Case 24 from the analysis, the coefficient for serum acid phosphatase changes from 0.0243 to 0.0490. A variable that was a very marginal predictor, at best, becomes much more important.

Figure 2.23b   Plot of standardized residual with ID

```
PLOT PLOT=ZRE_1 LEV_1 DFB2_1 WITH ID.
```

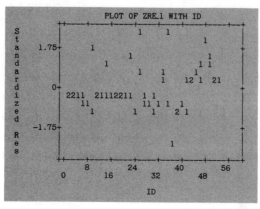

Figure 2.23c   Plot of leverage with ID

PLOT PLOT=ZRE_1 **LEV_1** DFB2_1 WITH ID.

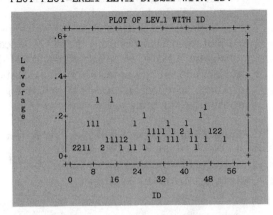

Figure 2.23d   Plot of change in ACID coefficient with ID

PLOT PLOT=ZRE_1 LEV_1 **DFB2_1** WITH ID.

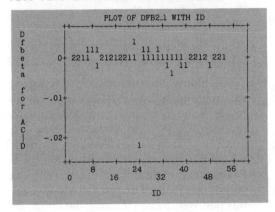

2.24
RUNNING PROCEDURE LOGISTIC REGRESSION

The LOGISTIC REGRESSION procedure builds logistic regression models, which are used to estimate the probability that an event occurs. It allows user-specified entry of variables into the equation as well as both forward and backward stepwise entry. It also has facilities for automatically converting categorical variables into sets of contrast variables, using any of seven contrast types or any user-specified contrast. The subcommands for residual analysis help detect influential data points, outliers, and violations of the model assumptions.

2.25
Building the Equation

To build a simple logistic regression model, you specify the equation on a VARIABLES subcommand. The format of the VARIABLES subcommand is

LOGISTIC REGRESSION VARIABLES=dependent WITH independents.

The dependent variable is dichotomous. If some of the independent variables are categorical and you want the program to transform them, name them on the CATEGORICAL subcommand (see Section 2.27).

2.26
VARIABLES
Subcommand

The VARIABLES subcommand provides, at minimum, the name of the dichotomous dependent variable. You can also provide the names of the independent variables, using the keyword WITH to separate them from the dependent variable. The actual keyword VARIABLES is optional; you can enter the variables specification immediately after LOGISTIC REGRESSION, as in:

```
LOGISTIC REGRESSION NODES WITH AGE, ACID, XRAY, STAGE, GRADE.
```

This command produces the default output: a classification table and regression statistics for all of the independent variables.

Variable lists on the LOGISTIC REGRESSION command cannot use the TO keyword. Each variable must be named separately.

You can include interaction terms in the model using the form *variable BY variable.* Simply include the interaction term among the independent variables:

```
LOGISTIC REGRESSION NODES WITH AGE, ACID, XRAY, STAGE, GRADE,
   GRADE BY STAGE.
```

This command calculates the interaction term GRADE BY STAGE and includes it in the model along with the five independent variables. The components of the interaction (here GRADE and STAGE) do not need to be individually included among the independent variables.

2.27
CATEGORICAL
Subcommand

One of the most convenient features of the LOGISTIC REGRESSION procedure is the ease with which it handles categorical independent variables. If you supply a CATEGORICAL subcommand with the name of one or more of the independent variables, LOGISTIC REGRESSION automatically converts the categorical variable(s) into a group of contrasts. They are entered or removed from the equation as a group. For example, to use a categorical variable CATACID, specify:

```
LOGISTIC REGRESSION NODES WITH AGE, CATACID, XRAY, STAGE, GRADE
   /CATEGORICAL=CATACID.
```

Note that the default treatment of categorical variables uses deviation contrasts, which do not give the same results as indicator-variable analysis. If your categorical variables are already indicator variables and you declare them as categorical, by default they will be transformed using deviation contrasts. If you wish to keep them as indicator variables, do not list them on the CATEGORICAL subcommand, or specify INDICATOR contrasts on the CONTRAST subcommand (see Section 2.28).

2.28
CONTRAST
Subcommand

When you name a variable with n categories on the CATEGORICAL subcommand, LOGISTIC REGRESSION converts it into a group of $n-1$ variables and displays a table showing the values assigned to these variables for each category of the original variable. The variables can be calculated in many different ways, corresponding to different contrasts of the parameters. The choice of contrast type has no effect on the significance of the variable taken as a whole, but it does affect the coefficients and significance levels of the individual parameters.

By default, LOGISTIC REGRESSION uses deviation contrasts. To specify a different contrast type for a categorical variable, use the CONTRAST subcommand, followed by the name of the categorical variable in parentheses, an equals sign, and one of the following keywords:

DEVIATION(refcat)   *Deviations from the overall effect.* This is the default. The effect for each category of the independent variable except one is compared to the overall effect. The optional reference category (refcat) is the category for which parameter estimates are not displayed. By default, it is the last category. To omit a category other than the last, specify the sequential number of the omitted category in parentheses after the DEVIATION keyword.

INDICATOR(refcat) *Indicator variables.* Contrasts indicate the presence or absence of category membership. This contrast is equivalent to the traditional group of "dummy variables." By default, the reference category is the last one. To omit a category other than the last, specify the sequence number of the omitted category in parentheses after the INDICATOR keyword.

SIMPLE(refcat) *Simple contrasts.* By default, each category of the independent variable except the last is compared to the last category. To use a category other than the last as the omitted reference category, specify its sequential number in parentheses following keyword SIMPLE.

DIFFERENCE *Difference or reverse Helmert contrasts.* The effects for each category of the independent variable except the first are compared to the mean effect of the previous categories.

HELMERT *Helmert contrasts.* The effects for each category of the independent variable except the last is compared to the mean effects of subsequent categories.

POLYNOMIAL(metric) *Polynomial contrasts.* The first degree of freedom contains the linear effect across the categories of the independent variable; the second contains the quadratic effect; and so on. By default, the categories are assumed to be equally spaced; unequal spacing can be specified by entering a metric consisting of one integer for each category of the independent variable in parentheses after the keyword POLYNOMIAL. For example, CONTRAST(STIMULUS) = POLYNOMIAL(1,2,4) indicates that the three levels of STIMULUS are actually in the proportion 1:2:4. The default metric is always $(1,2,...,k)$, where k is the number of categories.

REPEATED *Comparison of adjacent categories.* Each category of the independent variable except the first is compared to the previous category.

SPECIAL(matrix) *User-defined contrast.* After this keyword a matrix is entered in parentheses with $k-1$ rows and k columns (where k is the number of categories of the independent variable).

To obtain indicator contrasts for the above example, specify:

```
LOGISTIC REGRESSION NODES WITH AGE, CATACID, XRAY, STAGE, GRADE
  /CATEGORICAL=CATACID
  /CONTRAST(CATACID)=INDICATOR.
```

2.29
METHOD Subcommand

If you specify the independent variables after the keyword WITH on the VARIABLES subcommand, the METHOD subcommand is optional. If you do not specify them on VARIABLES, you must use a METHOD subcommand to indicate what variables are in the model. Note that the actual keyword METHOD is optional.

You can use more than one METHOD subcommand, in which case each method is applied to the equation as it stands at the end of the processing of the previous METHOD subcommand.

The METHOD subcommand consists of one of the following keywords, followed by an optional list of independent variables. If you omit the variable list, the method uses all of the independent variables from the VARIABLES subcommand.

ENTER *Forced entry.* All variables are entered in a single step. This is the default if you omit the METHOD subcommand.

FSTEP *Forward stepwise.* The independent variables specified in the variable list are tested for entry into the model one by one, based on the significance level of the score statistic. The variable with the smallest significance less than PIN is entered into the model. Next, variables that are already in the model at each step are tested for possible removal, on the basis of the significance level of the

Wald statistic. (To use the likelihood-ratio statistic as the test for removal from the equation instead, specify LR in parentheses after the keyword FSTEP.) If the significance level is greater than POUT the variable is removed. Once no more variables satisfy the removal criterion, variables not in the model are evaluated for entry. The algorithm stops when no more variables can be entered or removed.

BSTEP *Backward stepwise.* On the first step, all variables specified on the BSTEP variable list are entered into the model. Selection then proceeds as with the FSTEP method, with the initial search being for variables to remove from the equation. To use the likelihood-ratio statistic instead of the Wald statistic as the test for removal from the equation, specify LR in parentheses after the keyword BSTEP. The algorithm stops when no more variables can be entered or removed.

You can combine METHOD subcommands to specify the exact sequence in which equation-building proceeds. To start with an equation containing AGE and STAGE and then continue to build it using the forward-stepwise algorithm, you would use the command:

```
LOGISTIC REGRESSION NODES WITH AGE, ACID, XRAY, STAGE, GRADE
    /ENTER AGE STAGE
    /FSTEP.
```

By default, both AGE and STAGE are on the FSTEP variable list and are thus eligible for removal. To prevent them from being removed, supply a variable list for FSTEP that does not include them, as in:

```
/FSTEP ACID XRAY GRADE.
```

2.30
CRITERIA Subcommand

You can control the criteria by which LOGISTIC REGRESSION enters and removes independent variables from the equation, the criteria that determine when the iterative search for a solution terminates, and the criterion used in redundancy checking with the CRITERIA subcommand. After CRITERIA, enter one or more of the following keywords:

BCON(value) *Change in parameter estimates to terminate iteration.* Iteration terminates when the parameters change by less than this value, unless the ITERATE or LCON criterion is met first. The default is 0.001.

ITERATE(value) *Maximum number of iterations.* Iteration terminates after this many iterations, unless the BCON or LCON criterion is met first. The default is 20.

LCON(value) *Percent change in the log-likelihood ratio for termination of iterations.* Iteration terminates when the log-likelihood ratio decreases by less than this value, unless the BCON or ITERATE criterion is met first. The default is 0.0001.

PIN(value) *Probability of score statistic for variable entry.* Larger probabilities make it easier for variables to enter the model. The default is 0.05.

POUT(value) *Probability of Wald or LR statistic to remove a variable.* Larger probabilities make it easier for variables to remain in the model. The default is 0.10.

EPS(value) *Epsilon value used for redundancy checking.* The specified value must be less than or equal to 0.05 and greater than or equal to 10^{-12}. Larger values make it more likely that variables will be removed from the model as redundant. The default is 0.00000001.

2.31
ORIGIN Subcommand

The logistic regression model contains a constant term. Specify the ORIGIN subcommand to force the constant term to equal 0. ORIGIN has no additional specifications.

You cannot compare parameter estimates or goodness-of-fit statistics obtained with the ORIGIN subcommand with those obtained without it.

2.32
SELECT Subcommand

Use the SELECT subcommand to select a subset of cases for computing the equation. Classification results are reported for both selected and unselected cases. The form of the SELECT subcommand is

```
/SELECT=variable  relation  value
```

where the *relation* is EQ, NE, LT, LE, GT, or GE.

For example, to generate predicted probabilities and residuals for all patients based on a model estimated for patients with values less than 5 for variable GROUP, specify:

```
LOGISTIC REGRESSION NODES WITH AGE, ACID, XRAY, STAGE, GRADE
  /SELECT=GROUP LT 5
  /CASEWISE=PRED RESID.
```

2.33
PRINT Subcommand

You can obtain additional output or you can suppress the default output displayed after each step by using the PRINT subcommand. If you enter one or more of the following keywords after PRINT, only the specified output is displayed.

DEFAULT   *Classification tables and statistics for variables in and not in the equation after each step.* Separate output is displayed for each split file and each METHOD subcommand.

SUMMARY   *Classification tables and statistics for variables in and not in the equation for the final model.*

CORR   *Correlation matrix of parameter estimates for all parameters estimated in the model.*

ITER(value)   *Parameter estimates reported after each nth iteration during the solution.* Specify the iteration count for reporting parameter estimates in parentheses after ITER. If you omit the iteration count and parentheses, estimates are reported after each iteration.

ALL   *All available output.*

For example, to obtain parameter estimates after every third iteration, plus a correlation matrix of the final parameter estimates, specify

```
LOGISTIC REGRESSION NODES WITH AGE, CATACID, XRAY, STAGE, GRADE
  /CATEGORICAL=CATACID /CONTRAST(CATACID)=INDICATOR.
  /PRINT=ITER(3) CORR.
```

2.34
CLASSPLOT
Subcommand

To obtain a classification plot of the actual and predicted values of the dependent variable at each step, specify the CLASSPLOT subcommand. CLASSPLOT has no additional specifications.

```
LOGISTIC REGRESSION NODES WITH AGE, ACID, XRAY, STAGE, GRADE
  /CLASSPLOT.
```

2.35
MISSING Subcommand

Use the MISSING subcommand to include user-missing values in the analysis. After MISSING, specify one of the following:

EXCLUDE   *Exclude cases with user- or system-missing values for any variable named in the procedure from the analysis.* Predicted values are still calculated if only the dependent variable is missing. This is the default.

INCLUDE   *Include cases with user-missing values.* System-missing values are excluded from analysis.

2.36
EXTERNAL Subcommand

Use the EXTERNAL subcommand when you are analyzing large data files to indicate that results should be held in temporary files rather than in memory. This makes it possible to analyze larger problems but increases processing time. There are no additional specifications on EXTERNAL.

2.37
Analyzing Residuals

Once you have built a model, you can display any of the following diagnostic statistics or add them to your file as new variables. These keywords are used on both the CASEWISE and SAVE subcommands. See Section 2.22 for discussion of these statistics.

PRED   *Predicted probability.*

PGROUP *Predicted group.*

RESID   *Difference between observed and predicted probability.*

DEV   *Deviance values.*

LRESID   *Logit residual.*

SRESID   *Studentized residual.*

ZRESID   *Normalized residual.*

LEVER   *Leverage value.*

COOK   *Analog of Cook's influence statistic.*

DFBETA *Difference in beta.* One value for DFBETA is produced for each coefficient in the model, including the constant.

2.38
CASEWISE Subcommand

Use the CASEWISE subcommand to obtain listings of any of the above statistics for each case in your file or for outliers only. After CASEWISE, enter one or more of the keywords listed in Section 2.37 to display that statistic for all cases.

To obtain a casewise listing for outliers only, enter the following keyword along with one or more of the above:

OUTLIER(value) *Display only cases for which the absolute value of SRESID, the Studentized residual, is greater than the specified value.* If you omit the value and the parentheses, a value of 2 is used.

For example, for each case with a Studentized residual greater than 2.5, the following command displays the predicted probability of being in the second category of NODES; the residual; and the difference in each of the six regression coefficients if the case were omitted:

```
LOGISTIC REGRESSION NODES WITH AGE, ACID, XRAY, STAGE, GRADE
  /CASEWISE=PRED RESID DFBETA OUTLIER(2.5).
```

2.39
SAVE Subcommand

Use the SAVE subcommand to add any of the statistics listed in Section 2.37 to your file as new variables. LOGISTIC REGRESSION generates and reports names for the new variables and adds them to your file. To specify your own new variable names, include the name in parentheses after the corresponding statistics keyword. For the DFBETA keyword, which yields several variables, include a *root name* of seven characters or less in the parentheses.

For example, the following command adds eight new variables to the active system file:

```
LOGISTIC REGRESSION NODES WITH AGE, ACID, XRAY, STAGE, GRADE
  /SAVE=PRED(NODEPROB) SRESID(RESID) DFBETA(INFL).
```

NODEPROB contains the estimated probability of the case having the second value for NODE; RESID contains the case's Studentized residual; and the six variables INFL0 to INFL5 contain the differences in the constant and the five regression coefficients if the case were omitted.

2.40
ID Subcommand

Case listings produced by the CASEWISE subcommand are normally identified by case number. You can label the listing with the values or value labels of a variable in the file by using the ID subcommand. After ID, specify the name of a variable in the active system file. LOGISTIC REGRESSION will label its casewise listing with the first eight characters of the value labels of that variable, if they are defined, or with the actual values of the variable otherwise.

Contents

3 Multivariate Analysis of Variance: Procedure MANOVA

"Tilted" houses featured in amusement parks capitalize on the challenge of navigating one's way in the presence of misleading visual cues. It's difficult to maintain balance when walls are no longer parallel and rooms assume strange shapes. We are all dependent on visual information to guide movement, but the extent of this dependence has been found to vary considerably.

Based on a series of experiments, Witkin (1954) classified individuals into two categories: those who can ignore misleading visual cues, termed field independent, and those who cannot, termed field dependent. Field dependence has been linked to a variety of psychological characteristics such as self-image and intelligence. Psychologists theorize that it derives from childhood socialization patterns—field-dependent children learn to depend on highly structured environments while field independent children learn to cope with ambiguous situations.

In this chapter, the relationship between field dependence, sex, and various motor abilities is examined, using data reported by Barnard (1973). Students (63 female and 71 male) from the College of Southern Idaho were administered a test of field independence, the rod and frame test. On the basis of this test, subjects were classified as field dependent, field independent, or intermediate. Four tests of motor ability were also conducted: two tests of balance, a test of gross motor skills, and a test of fine motor skills.

For the balance test, subjects were required to maintain balance while standing on one foot on a rail. Two trials for each of two conditions, eyes open and eyes closed, were administered and the average number of seconds a subject maintained balance under each condition was recorded. Gross motor coordination was assessed with the side-stepping test. For this test, three parallel lines are drawn four feet apart on the floor and a subject stands on the middle line. At the start signal the subject must sidestep to the left until the left foot crosses the left line. He or she then sidesteps to the right until the right line is crossed. A subject's score is the average number of lines crossed in three ten-second trials. The Purdue Pegboard Test was used to quantify fine motor skills. Subjects are required to place small pegs into pegholes using only the left hand, only the right hand, and then both hands simultaneously. The number of pegs placed in two 30-second trials for each condition was recorded and the average over six trials calculated.

The experiment described above is fairly typical of many investigations. There are several "classification" or independent variables, sex and field independence in this case, and a dependent variable. The goal of the experiment is to examine the relationship between the classification variables and the dependent variable. For example, is motor ability related to field dependence? Does the relationship differ for men and women? Analysis of variance techniques are usually used to answer these questions.

In this experiment, however, the dependent variable is not a single measure but four different scores obtained for each student. Although ANOVA tests can be computed separately for each of the dependent variables, this approach ignores the interrelation among the dependent variables. As explained in the previous chapters, substantial information may be lost when correlations between variables are ignored. For example, several bivariate regression analyses cannot substitute for a multiple regression model which considers the independent variables jointly. Only when the independent variables are uncorrelated with each other are the bivariate and multivariate regression results equivalent. Similarly, analyzing multiple two-dimensional tables cannot substitute for an analysis that considers the variables simultaneously.

3.1
MULTIVARIATE ANALYSIS OF VARIANCE

The extension of univariate analysis of variance to the case of multiple dependent variables is termed *multivariate analysis of variance,* abbreviated as MANOVA. Univariate analysis of variance is just a special case of MANOVA, the case with a single dependent variable. The hypotheses tested with MANOVA are similar to those tested with ANOVA. The difference is that sets (sometimes called a vector) of means replace the individual means specified in ANOVA. In a one-way design, for example, the hypothesis tested is that the populations from which the groups are selected have the same means for all dependent variables. Thus, the hypothesis might be that the population means for the four motor-ability variables are the same for the three field dependence categories.

3.2
Assumptions

For the case of a single dependent variable, two assumptions are necessary for the proper application of the ANOVA test: the groups must be random samples from normal populations with the same variance. Similar assumptions are necessary for MANOVA. Since we are dealing with several dependent variables, however, we must make assumptions about their joint distribution, that is, the distribution of the variables considered together. The extension of the ANOVA assumptions to MANOVA requires that the dependent variables have a multivariate normal distribution with the same variance-covariance matrix in each group. A variance-covariance matrix, as its name indicates, is a square arrangement of elements, with the variances of the variables on the diagonal, and the covariances of pairs of variables off the diagonal. A variance-covariance matrix can be transformed into a correlation matrix by dividing each covariance by the standard deviations of the two variables. Later sections of the chapter will present tests for these assumptions.

3.3
One-Sample Hotelling's T^2

Before considering more complex generalizations of ANOVA techniques, let's consider the simple one-sample t-test and its extension to the case of multiple dependent variables. As you will recall, the one-sample t-test is used to test the hypothesis that the sample originates from a population with a known mean. For example, you might want to test the hypothesis that schizophrenics do not differ in mean IQ from the general population, which is assumed to have a mean IQ of 100. If additional variables such as reading comprehension, mathematical aptitude, and motor dexterity are also to be considered, a test that allows comparison of several observed means to a set of constants is required.

A test developed by Hotelling, called Hotelling's T^2, is often used for this purpose. It is the simplest example of MANOVA. To illustrate this test and introduce some of the SPSS/PC+ MANOVA output, we will use the field-dependence and motor-ability data to test the hypothesis that the observed sample comes from a population with specified values for the means of the four tests. That is, we will assume that normative data are available for the four tests and we will test the hypothesis that our sample is from a population having the normative means.

For illustrative purposes, the standard values are taken to be 13 seconds for balancing with eyes open, 3 seconds for balancing with eyes closed, 18 lines for the side-stepping test, and 10 pegs for the pegboard test. Since SPSS/PC+ MANOVA automatically tests the hypothesis that a set of means is equal to 0, the normative values must be subtracted from the observed scores and the hypothesis that the differences are 0 is tested.

Figure 3.3 contains the message displayed by SPSS/PC+ MANOVA when the cases are processed. It indicates the number of cases to be used in the analysis as well as the number of cases to be excluded. In this example, 134 cases will be included in the analysis. SPSS/PC+ also indicates whether any cases contain missing values for the variables being analyzed or have independent-variable (factor) values outside of the designated range. Such cases are excluded from the analysis.

Since the hypothesis being tested involves only a test of a single sample, all observations are members of one "cell," in ANOVA terminology. If two independent samples, for example males and females, were compared, two "cells" would exist. The last line of Figure 3.3 indicates how many different MANOVA models have been specified.

Figure 3.3   Case information

```
COMPUTE BALOMEAN=((TEST1+TEST2)/2)-13.
COMPUTE BALCMEAN=((TEST3+TEST4)/2)-3.
COMPUTE SSTMEAN=((TEST5+TEST6)/2)-18.
COMPUTE PP=((TEST7+TEST8)/2)-10.
MANOVA BALOMEAN BALCMEAN SSTMEAN PP
  /DESIGN.
```

```
134 cases accepted.
  0 cases rejected because of out-of-range factor values.
  0 cases rejected because of missing data.
  1 non-empty cells.

  1 design will be processed.
```

3.4
Descriptive Statistics

One of the first steps in any statistical analysis, regardless of how simple or complex it may be, is examination of the individual variables. This preliminary screening provides information about a variable's distribution and permits identification of unusual or outlying values.

Of course, when multivariate analyses are undertaken, it is not sufficient just to look at the characteristics of the variables individually. Information about their joint distribution must also be obtained. Similarly, identification of outliers must be based on the joint distribution of variables. For example, a height of six feet is not very unusual, and neither is a weight of 100 pounds, nor being a man. A six-foot-tall male who weighs 100 pounds, however, is fairly atypical and needs to be identified, not for any humanitarian reasons, but to ascertain that the values have been correctly recorded, and if so to gauge the effect of such a lean physique on subsequent analyses.

Figure 3.4 contains means, standard deviations, and confidence intervals for each of the four motor-ability variables after the normative values have been subtracted. The sample exceeds the norm for balancing with eyes closed and peg insertion and is poorer than the norm for balancing with eyes open and side-stepping. The only confidence interval that includes 0 is for the balancing-with-eyes-closed variable.

Figure 3.4   Cell means and standard deviations

```
SET WIDTH=WIDE.
MANOVA BALOMEAN BALCMEAN SSTMEAN PP
   /PRINT=CELLINFO(MEANS)
   /DESIGN.
```

```
Cell Means and Standard Deviations
Variable .. BALOMEAN
                                    Mean    Std. Dev.        N    95 percent Conf. Interval

For entire sample                 -1.540      5.860        134      -2.541      -.539
 _ _ _ _ _ _ _ _ _

Variable .. BALCMEAN
                                    Mean    Std. Dev.        N    95 percent Conf. Interval

For entire sample                   .143      1.405        134      -.097       .383
 _ _ _ _ _ _ _ _ _

Variable .. SSTMEAN
                                    Mean    Std. Dev.        N    95 percent Conf. Interval

For entire sample                 -2.597      2.681        134      -3.055     -2.139
 _ _ _ _ _ _ _ _ _

Variable .. PP
                                    Mean    Std. Dev.        N    95 percent Conf. Interval

For entire sample                  4.973      1.495        134       4.717      5.228
```

The 95% confidence intervals that are displayed are individual confidence intervals. This means that no adjustment has been made for the fact that the confidence intervals for several variables have been computed. We have 95% confidence that each of the individual intervals contains the unknown parameter value. We do not have 95% confidence that *all* intervals considered jointly contain the unknown parameters. The distinction here is closely related to the problem of multiple comparisons in ANOVA.

When many tests are done, the chance that some observed differences appear to be statistically significant when there are no true differences in the populations increases with the number of comparisons made. To protect against calling too many differences "real" when in fact they are not, the criterion for how large a difference must be before it is considered "significant" is made more stringent. That is, larger differences are required, depending on the number of comparisons made. The larger the number of comparisons, the greater the observed difference must be. Similarly, if a confidence region that simultaneously contains values of observed population parameters with a specified overall confidence level is to be constructed, the confidence interval for each variable must be wider than that needed if only one variable is considered.

3.5
Further Displays for Checking Assumptions

Although the summary statistics presented in Figure 3.4 provide some information about the distributions of the dependent variables, more detailed information is often desirable. Figure 3.5 is a stem-and-leaf plot of the pegboard variable after the normative values have been subtracted. Stem-and-leaf plots provide a convenient way to examine the distribution of a variable.

In Figure 3.5, the numbers to the left of the dotted line are called the *stem,* while those to the right are the *leaves.* Each case is represented by a leaf. For example, the first line of the plot is for a case with a value of 1.2 and a case with a value of 1.3. The stem, 1, is the same for both cases while the values of the leaves (2 and 3) differ. When there are several cases with the same values, the leaf value is repeated. For example, there are two cases with a value of 2.7 and four cases with a value of 2.8. In this example, each stem value occurs twice, once for cases with leaves 0 through 4, and once for cases with leaves 5 through 9. This is not always the case, since the stem values depends on the actual data. In this example, the decimal point for each case occurs between the value of the stem and the leaf. This also is not always the case. SPSS/PC+ MANOVA scales the variables so that the stem-and-leaf plot is based on the number of significant digits. Since the purpose of the plot is to display the distribution of the variable, the actual scale is not important.

Figure 3.5   Stem-and-leaf plot—pegboard test

```
MANOVA BALOMEAN BALCMEAN SSTMEAN PP
  /PLOT=STEMLEAF
  /DESIGN.
```

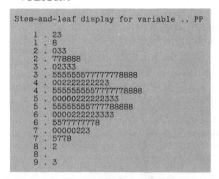

```
Stem-and-leaf display for variable .. PP
    1 . 23
    1 . 8
    2 . 033
    2 . 778888
    3 . 02333
    3 . 555555577777778888
    4 . 002222222223
    4 . 5555555557777778888
    5 . 00000222222333
    5 . 55555555777788888
    6 . 0000222223333
    6 . 5577777778
    7 . 00000223
    7 . 5778
    8 . 2
    8 .
    9 . 3
```

One assumption needed for hypothesis testing in MANOVA is the assumption that the dependent variables have a multivariate normal distribution. If variables have a multivariate normal distribution, each one taken individually must be normally distributed. (However, variables that are normally distributed individually will not necessarily have a multivariate normal distribution when considered together.) The stem-and-leaf plot for each variable allows us to assess the reasonableness of the normality assumption, since if any distribution appears to be markedly nonnormal, the assumption of multivariate normality is likely to be violated.

3.6
Normal Plots

Although the stem-and-leaf plot gives a rough idea of the normality of the distribution of a variable, other plots that are especially designed for assessing normality can also be obtained. For example, we can assess normality using a normal probability plot, which is obtained by ranking the observed values of a variable from smallest to largest and then pairing each value with an expected normal value for a sample of that size from a standard normal distribution.

Figure 3.6a is a normal probability plot of the pegboard variable. The symbols represent the number of cases that fall in the same position on the plot. If the observed scores are from a normal distribution, the plot in should be approximately a straight line. Since the distribution of the pegboard scores appeared fairly normal in the stem-and-leaf plot (Figure 3.5a), the normal probability plot should be fairly linear, and it is.

Figure 3.6a   Normal probability plot—pegboard test

```
MANOVA BALOMEAN BALCMEAN SSTMEAN PP
  /PLOT=NORMAL
  /DESIGN.
```

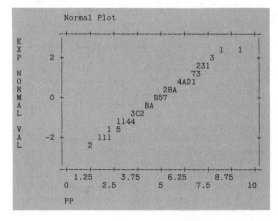

To further assess the linearity of the normal probability plot, we can calculate the difference between the observed point and the expected point under the assumption of normality and plot this difference for each case. If the observed sample is from a normal distribution, these differences should be fairly close to 0 and be randomly distributed.

Figure 3.6b is a plot of the differences for the normal probability plot shown in Figure 3.6a. This plot is called a detrended normal plot since the trend in Figure 3.6a, the straight line, has been removed. Note that the values fall roughly in a horizontal band about 0, though there appears to be some pattern. Also notice the two outliers, one in the lower-right corner and the other in the upper-left corner. These correspond to the smallest and largest observations in the sample and indicate that the observed distribution doesn't have quite as much spread in the tails as expected. For the smallest value, the deviation from the expected line is positive, indicating that the smallest value is not quite as small as would be expected. For the largest value, the value is not as large as would be expected. Since most of the points cluster nicely around 0, this small deviation is probably not of too much concern. Nonetheless, it is usually a good idea to check outlying points to ascertain that they have been correctly recorded and entered. If the distribution of a variable appears markedly nonnormal, transformation of the data should be considered.

Figure 3.6b Detrended normal plot—pegboard test

```
            Detrended Normal Plot
        -+-----+----+----+----+-----+----+----+-----+-
         |                                         |
      .2 +  1                                      +
         |                    3 2 1          11 1 1
    D    |              1 1   3 233            1
    E    |            1 1 1  232324221       2111
    V    |                  1 11 122232412  21   1
    I   0 +        1    1 2 111 22 143413 11       +
    A    |                1 22        2123211
    T    |                1 11          1 1
    I    |                              1
    O    |
    N  -.2 +                                       +
         |
         |                                      1
        -+-----+----+----+----+-----+----+----+-----+-
           1.25     3.75     6.25     8.75
         0      2.5      5      7.5       10
        PP
```

3.7
Another Plot

To get a little more practice in interpreting the previously described plots, consider Figure 3.7a, which is the plot for the balancing-with-eyes-closed variable. From this stem-and-leaf plot, you can see that the distribution of the data is skewed to the right. That is, there are several large values that are quite removed from the rest.

Figure 3.7a Stem-and-leaf plot—balance variable

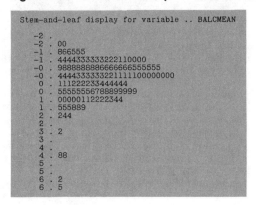

```
Stem-and-leaf display for variable .. BALCMEAN
 -2 .
 -2 . 00
 -1 . 866555
 -1 . 4444333333222110000
 -0 . 9888888886666666555555
 -0 . 444433333221111100000000
  0 . 111222233444444
  0 . 55555556788899999
  1 . 00000112222344
  1 . 555889
  2 . 244
  2 .
  3 . 2
  3 .
  4 .
  4 . 88
  5 .
  5 .
  6 . 2
  6 . 5
```

Figure 3.7b is the corresponding normal probability plot. Note that the plot is no longer linear but is curved, especially for larger values of the variable. This downward curve indicates that the observed values are larger than predicted by the corresponding expected normal values. This is also seen in the stem-and-leaf plot. The detrended normal plot for this variable is shown in Figure 3.7c, which shows that there is a definite pattern to the deviations. The values no longer cluster in a horizontal band about 0. A transformation might be considered.

Figure 3.7b   Normal probability plot—balance variable

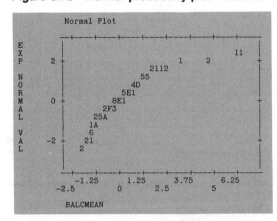

Figure 3.7c   Detrended normal plot—balance variable

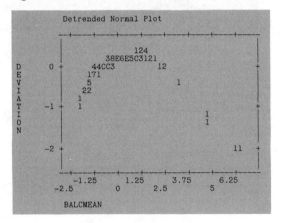

3.8
Bartlett's Test of Sphericity

Since there is no reason to use the multivariate analysis of variance procedure if the dependent variables are not correlated, it is useful to examine the correlation matrix of the dependent variables. If the variables are independent, the observed correlation matrix is expected to have small off-diagonal elements. Bartlett's test of sphericity can be used to test the hypothesis that the population correlation matrix is an identity matrix, that is, all diagonal terms are 1 and all off-diagonal terms are 0.

The test is based on the determinant of the within-cells correlation matrix. A determinant that is close in value to 0 indicates that one or more of the variables can almost be expressed as a linear function of the other dependent variables. Thus, the hypothesis that the variables are independent is rejected if the determinant is small. Figure 3.8a contains output from Bartlett's test of sphericity. The determinant is displayed first, followed by a transformation of the determinant (which has a chi-square distribution). Since the observed significance level is small (less than 0.0005), the hypothesis that the population correlation matrix is an identity matrix is rejected.

Figure 3.8a   Bartlett's test of sphericity

```
MANOVA BALOMEAN BALCMEAN SSTMEAN PP
  /PRINT=ERROR(COR)
  /DESIGN.
```

```
Statistics for WITHIN CELLS correlations

Determinant =                       .82942
Bartlett test of sphericity =   24.46993 with 6 D. F.
Significance =                      .000
```

A graphical test of the hypothesis that the correlation matrix is an identity matrix is described by Everitt (1978). The observed correlation coefficients are transformed using Fisher's Z-transform, and then a half-normal plot of the transformed coefficients is obtained. A half-normal plot is very similar to the normal plot described above. The only difference is that both positive and negative values are treated identically. If the population correlation matrix is an identity matrix, the plot should be fairly linear and the line should pass through the origin.

Figure 3.8b is the plot of the transformed correlation coefficients for the correlation matrix in Figure 3.4. The plot shows deviations from linearity, suggesting that the dependent variables are not independent, a result also indicated by Bartlett's test.

Figure 3.8b   A half-normal plot of the correlation coefficients

```
MANOVA BALOMEAN BALCMEAN SSTMEAN PP
  /PLOT=ZCORR
  /DESIGN.
```

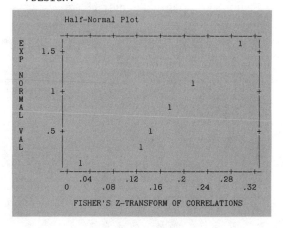

3.9
Testing Hypotheses

Once the distributions of the variables have been examined, we are ready to test the hypothesis that there is no difference between the population means and the hypothesized values. To test the various hypotheses of interest, SPSS/PC+ MANOVA computes a design matrix whose columns correspond to the various effects in the model (see Section 3.16). Figure 3.9a shows the table displayed by SPSS/PC+ MANOVA containing the names of the effects to be tested and their corresponding columns in the design matrix. In the one-sample MANOVA design, there is only one effect, labeled **CONSTANT.**

Figure 3.9a   The effects matrix

```
MANOVA BALOMEAN BALCMEAN SSTMEAN PP
  /PRINT=ERROR(SSCP)
  /DESIGN.
```

```
Correspondence between Effects and Columns of BETWEEN-Subjects DESIGN 1

Starting  Ending
 Column   Column   Effect Name

    1        1       CONSTANT
```

To understand how the statistic for testing the hypothesis that all differences are 0 is constructed, recall the one-sample t-test. The statistic for testing the hypothesis that the population mean is some known constant, which we will call μ_0, is

$$t = \frac{\overline{X} - \mu_0}{S/\sqrt{N}}$$

Equation 3.9a

where $\overline{X}$ is the sample mean and S is the standard deviation. The numerator of the *t* value is a measure of how much the sample mean differs from the hypothesized value, while the denominator is a measure of how variable the sample mean is.

When you simultaneously test the hypothesis that several population means do not differ from a specified set of constants, a statistic that considers all variables together is required. Hotelling's T^2 statistic is usually used for this purpose. It is computed as

$$T^2 = N(\overline{\underset{\sim}{X}} - \mu_0)' S^{-1} (\overline{\underset{\sim}{X}} - \mu_0)$$

Equation 3.9b

where S^{-1} is the inverse of the variance-covariance matrix of the dependent variables and $\overline{X} - \mu_0$ is the vector of differences between the sample means and the hypothesized constants. The two matrices upon which Hotelling's T^2 is based can be displayed by SPSS/PC+ MANOVA. The matrix that contains the differences between the observed sample means and the hypothesized values is shown in Figure 3.9b.

Figure 3.9b The hypothesis sum of squares and cross-products matrix

```
MANOVA BALOMEAN BALCMEAN SSTMEAN PP
  /PRINT=SIGNIF(HYPOTH)
  /DESIGN.
```

```
EFFECT .. CONSTANT
Adjusted Hypothesis Sum-of-Squares and Cross-Products

            BALOMEAN    BALCMEAN    SSTMEAN         PP

BALOMEAN     317.764
BALCMEAN     -29.490       2.737
SSTMEAN      535.894     -49.733    903.761
PP         -1026.104      95.226  -1730.478    3313.434
```

The diagonal elements are just the squares of the sample means minus the hypothesized values, multiplied by the sample size. For example, from Figure 3.4, the difference between the eyes-open balance score and the hypothesized value is −1.54. Squaring this difference and multiplying it by the sample size of 134, we get 317.76, the entry for BALOMEAN in Figure 3.9b. The off-diagonal elements are the product of the differences for the two variables, multiplied by the sample size. For example, the cross-products entry for the BALOMEAN and BALCMEAN is, from Figure 3.4, $-1.54 \times 0.14 \times 134 = -29.49$. For a fixed sample size, as the magnitude of the differences between the sample means and hypothesized values increases, so do the entries of this sums-of-squares and cross-products matrix.

The matrix whose entries indicate how much variability there is in the dependent variables is called the within-cells sums-of-squares and cross-products matrix. It is designated as S in the previous formula and is shown in Figure 3.9c. The diagonal entries are (N−1) times the variance of the dependent variables. For example, the entry for the pegboard variable is, from Figure 3.4, $1.49^2 \times (133) = 297.12$. The off-diagonal entries are the sums of the cross-products for the two variables. For example, for variables X and Y the cross-product is

$$CPSS_{xy} = \sum_{i=1}^{N} (X_i - \overline{X})(Y_i - \overline{Y})$$

Equation 3.9c

To compute Hotelling's T^2, the inverse of this within-cells sums-of-squares matrix is required, as well as the hypothesis sums-of-squares matrix in Figure 3.9b. The significance level associated with T^2 can be obtained from the F distribution. Figure 3.9d contains the value of Hotelling's T^2 divided by $(N-1)$, its transformation to a variable that has an F distribution, and the degrees of freedom associated with the F statistic. Since there are four dependent variables in this example, the hypothesis degrees of freedom are 4, while the remaining degrees of freedom, 130, are associated with the error sums of squares. Since the observed significance level is small (less than 0.0005), the null hypothesis that the population means do not differ from the hypothesized constants is rejected.

Figure 3.9c   Within-cells sums-of-squares and cross-products matrix

```
MANOVA BALOMEAN BALCMEAN SSTMEAN PP
   /PRINT=ERROR(SSCP)
   /DESIGN.
```

```
WITHIN CELLS Sum-of-Squares and Cross-Products

                BALOMEAN    BALCMEAN    SSTMEAN          PP

BALOMEAN        4567.274
BALCMEAN         311.080     262.501
SSTMEAN          459.656      94.833    956.239
PP                26.795      40.782     70.422     297.122
```

Figure 3.9d   Hotelling's statistic

```
MANOVA BALOMEAN BALCMEAN SSTMEAN PP
   /DESIGN.
```

```
Multivariate Tests of Significance (S = 1, M = 1 , N = 64 )

Test Name      Value  Approx. F Hypoth. DF   Error DF  Sig. of F

Hotellings   13.20587  429.19091       4.00    130.00        0.0
```

3.10
Univariate Tests

When the hypothesis of no difference is rejected, it is often informative to examine the univariate test results to get some idea of where the differences may be. Figure 3.10 contains the univariate results for the four dependent variables. The hypothesis and error sums of squares are the diagonal terms in Figures 3.9b and 3.9c. The mean squares are obtained by dividing the sums of squares by their degrees of freedom, 1 for the hypothesis sums of squares and 133 for the error sums of squares. The ratio of the two mean squares is displayed in the column labeled F. These F values are nothing more than the squares of one-sample t values. Thus, from Figure 3.4, the mean difference for the BALOMEAN variable is -1.54 and the standard deviation is 5.86. The corresponding t value is

$$t = \frac{-1.54}{5.86/\sqrt{134}} = -3.04$$

Equation 3.10

Squaring this produces the value 9.25, which is the entry in Figure 3.10. From Figure 3.10, we can see that the balancing-with-eyes-closed variable is the only one whose t value is not significant. This is to be expected, since it has a 95% confidence interval that includes 0. The significance levels for the univariate statistics are not adjusted for the fact that several comparisons are being made and thus should be used with a certain amount of caution. For a discussion of the problem of multiple comparisons, see Miller (1981) or Burns (1984).

Figure 3.10 Univariate F tests

```
MANOVA BALOMEAN BALCMEAN SSTMEAN PP
  /PRINT=SIGNIF(UNIV)
  /DESIGN.
```

```
Univariate F-tests with (1,133) D. F.

Variable   Hypoth. SS   Error SS  Hypoth. MS    Error MS              F  Sig. of F

BALOMEAN    317.76355 4567.27368   317.76355    34.34040        9.25334       .003
BALCMEAN      2.73673  262.50070     2.73673     1.97369        1.38661       .241
SSTMEAN     903.76111  956.23869   903.76111     7.18976      125.70107       0.0
PP         3313.43322  297.12189  3313.43322     2.23400     1483.18463       0.0
```

3.11
The Two-Sample Multivariate T-Test

In the previous sections, we were concerned with testing the hypothesis that the sample was drawn from a population with a particular set of means. There was only one sample involved, though there were several dependent variables. In this section, we will consider the multivariate generalization of the two-sample t-test. The hypothesis that men and women do not differ on the four motor-ability variables will be tested.

Figure 3.11a contains descriptive statistics for each variable according to sex. The female subjects are coded as *1*'s, and the males are coded as *2*'s. Males appear to maintain balance with eyes open longer than females and cross more lines in the stepping test.

Figure 3.11a Cell means and standard deviations

```
SET WIDTH=WIDE.
MANOVA BALOMEAN BALCMEAN SSTMEAN PP BY SEX(1,2)
     /PRINT=CELLINFO(MEANS)
     /DESIGN.
```

```
Cell Means and Standard Deviations
Variable .. BALOMEAN
     FACTOR          CODE             Mean  Std. Dev.          N  95 percent Conf. Interval

SEX                  1              9.748      5.707         63     8.311     11.186
SEX                  2             12.979      5.605         71    11.652     14.306
For entire sample                  11.460      5.860        134    10.459     12.461

- - - - - - - - -
Variable .. BALCMEAN
     FACTOR          CODE             Mean  Std. Dev.          N  95 percent Conf. Interval

SEX                  1              3.191      1.518         63     2.809      3.574
SEX                  2              3.100      1.306         71     2.791      3.409
For entire sample                   3.143      1.405        134     2.903      3.383

- - - - - - - - -
Variable .. SSTMEAN
     FACTOR          CODE             Mean  Std. Dev.          N  95 percent Conf. Interval

SEX                  1             14.095      2.255         63    13.527     14.663
SEX                  2             16.563      2.501         71    15.972     17.155
For entire sample                  15.403      2.681        134    14.945     15.861

- - - - - - - - -
Variable .. PP
     FACTOR          CODE             Mean  Std. Dev.          N  95 percent Conf. Interval

SEX                  1             15.466      1.453         63    15.100     15.831
SEX                  2             14.535      1.401         71    14.204     14.867
For entire sample                  14.973      1.495        134    14.717     15.228
```

Another way to visualize the distribution of scores in each of the groups is with box-and-whisker plots, as shown in Figure 3.11b for the two balance variables. The upper and lower boundaries of the boxes are the upper and lower quartiles. The box length is the interquartile distance and the box contains the middle 50% of values in a group. The asterisk (*) inside the box identifies the group median. The larger the box, the greater the spread of the observations. The lines emanating from each box (the whiskers) extend to the smallest and largest observations in a group that are less than one interquartile range from the end of the box. These are marked with an *X*. Any points outside of this range but less than one-and-a-half interquartile ranges from the end of the box are marked with *O*'s for outlying. Points more than 1.5 interquartile distances away are marked with *E*'s for extreme. If there are multiple points at a single position, the number of points is also displayed.

Figure 3.11b   Box-and-whisker plots

```
MANOVA BALOMEAN BALCMEAN SSTMEAN PP BY SEX(1,2)
   /PLOT=BOXPLOTS
   /DESIGN.
```

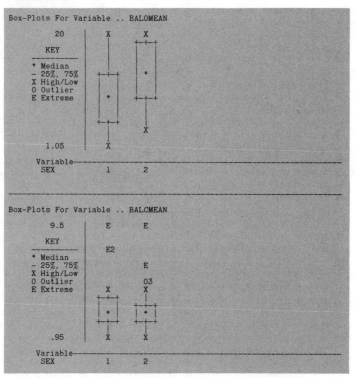

3.12
Tests of Homogeneity of Variance

In the one-sample Hotelling's T^2 test, there was no need to worry about the homogeneity of the variance-covariance matrices since there was only one matrix. In the two-sample test, there are two matrices (one for each group) and tests for their equality are necessary.

The variance-covariance matrices are shown in Figure 3.12a. They are computed for each group using the means of the variables within that group. Thus, each matrix indicates how much variability there is in a group. Combining these individual matrices into a common variance-covariance matrix results in the pooled matrix displayed in Figure 3.12b.

Figure 3.12a   Variance-covariance matrices for BALOMEAN and BALCMEAN

```
SET WIDTH=WIDE.
MANOVA BALOMEAN BALCMEAN SSTMEAN PP BY SEX(1,2)
   /PRINT=CELLINFO(COV)
   /DESIGN.
```

```
Cell Number .. 1
Variance-Covariance matrix

                  BALOMEAN    BALCMEAN     SSTMEAN          PP

BALOMEAN          32.57185
BALCMEAN           3.39103     2.30400
SSTMEAN             .42704      .55622     5.08397
PP                 1.43677      .36703     1.30888     2.11036


- - - - - - - - -

Cell Number .. 2
Variance-Covariance matrix

                  BALOMEAN    BALCMEAN     SSTMEAN          PP

BALOMEAN          31.42090
BALCMEAN           1.58111     1.70536
SSTMEAN            2.38612      .96952     6.25267
PP                  .54349      .21702      .94178     1.96263
```

Figure 3.12b   Pooled matrix

```
Pooled within-cells Variance-Covariance matrix

                  BALOMEAN    BALCMEAN     SSTMEAN          PP

BALOMEAN          31.96150
BALCMEAN           2.43122     1.98654
SSTMEAN            1.46594      .77540     5.70374
PP                  .96306      .28748     1.11421     2.03202
```

Figure 3.12c contains two homogeneity-of-variance tests *(Cochran's C* and the Bartlett-Box *F)* for each variable individually. The significance levels indicate that there is no reason to reject the hypotheses that the variances in the two groups are equal. Although these univariate tests are a convenient starting point for examining the equality of the covariance matrices, they are not sufficient. A test that simultaneously considers both the variances and covariances is required.

Box's *M* test, which is based on the determinants of the variance-covariance matrices in each cell as well as of the pooled variance-covariance matrix, provides a multivariate test for the homogeneity of the matrices. However, Box's *M* test is very sensitive to departures from normality. The significance level can be based on either an *F* or a χ^2 statistic, and both approximations are given in the output, as shown in Figure 3.12d. Given the result of Box's *M* test, there appears to be no reason to suspect the homogeneity-of-dispersion-matrices assumption.

Figure 3.12c   Univariate homogeneity of variance tests

```
MANOVA BALOMEAN BALCMEAN SSTMEAN PP BY SEX(1,2)
   /PRINT=HOMOGENEITY(COCHRAN BARTLETT)
   /DESIGN.
```

```
Univariate Homogeneity of Variance Tests

Variable .. BALOMEAN

      Cochrans C(66,2) =                          .50899, P =  .884 (approx.)
      Bartlett-Box F(1,51762) =                   .02113, P =  .884

Variable .. BALCMEAN

      Cochrans C(66,2) =                          .57466, P =  .224 (approx.)
      Bartlett-Box F(1,51762) =                  1.48033, P =  .224

Variable .. SSTMEAN

      Cochrans C(66,2) =                          .55155, P =  .403 (approx.)
      Bartlett-Box F(1,51762) =                   .69438, P =  .405

Variable .. PP

      Cochrans C(66,2) =                          .51813, P =  .769 (approx.)
      Bartlett-Box F(1,51762) =                   .08603, P =  .769
```

Figure 3.12d Homogeneity of dispersion matrices

```
MANOVA BALOMEAN BALCMEAN SSTMEAN PP BY SEX(1,2)
  /PRINT=HOMOGENEITY(COCHRAN BARTLETT BOXM)
  /DESIGN.
```

```
Cell Number .. 1
Determinant of Variance-Covariance matrix =          538.89601
LOG(Determinant) =                                     6.28952

- - - - - - - - - -

Cell Number .. 2
Determinant of Variance-Covariance matrix =          522.34684
LOG(Determinant) =                                     6.25833

- - - - - - - - - -


Determinant of pooled Variance-Covariance matrix     557.40536
LOG(Determinant) =                                     6.32329


- - - - - - - - - -

Multivariate test for Homogeneity of Dispersion matrices


Boxs M =                               6.64101
F WITH (10,80608) DF =                  .64228, P =    .779 (Approx.)
Chi-Square with 10 DF =                6.42361, P =    .779 (Approx.)
```

3.13
Hotelling's T^2 for Two Independent Samples

The actual statistic for testing the equality of several means with two independent samples is also based on Hotelling's T^2. The formula is

$$T^2 = \frac{N_1 N_2}{N_1 + N_2} (\overline{X}_1 - \overline{X}_2)' \, S^{-1} \, (\overline{X}_1 - \overline{X}_2)$$

Equation 3.13a

where $\overline{X}_1$ is the vector of means for the first group (females), $\overline{X}_2$ is the vector for the second group (males), and S^{-1} is the inverse of the pooled within-groups covariance matrix. The statistic is somewhat similar to the one described for the one-sample test in Section 3.9.

Again, two matrices are used in the computation of the statistic. The pooled within-groups covariance matrix has been described previously and is displayed in Figure 3.12b. The second matrix is the adjusted hypothesis sums-of-squares and cross-products matrix. It is displayed under the heading EFFECT.. SEX and in Figure 3.13a. The entries in this matrix are the weighted squared differences of the group means from the combined mean. For example, the entry for the balancing-with-eyes-open variable is

$$SS = 63(9.75 - 11.46)^2 + 71(12.98 - 11.46)^2 = 348.36$$

Equation 3.13b

where, from Figure 3.11a, 9.75 is the mean value for the 63 females, 12.98 is the value for the 71 males, and 11.46 is the mean for the entire sample. The first off-diagonal term for balancing with eyes open (BALOMEAN) and eyes closed (BALCMEAN) is similarly

$$SS = (9.75 - 11.46)(3.19 - 3.14)63 + (12.98 - 11.46)(3.10 - 3.14)71$$

Equation 3.13c

$$= -9.84$$

The diagonal terms should be recognizable to anyone familiar with analysis of variance methodology. They are the sums of squares due to groups for each variable.

Figure 3.13a   Adjusted hypothesis sums of squares and cross-products matrix

```
SET WIDTH=WIDE.
MANOVA BALOMEAN BALCMEAN SSTMEAN PP BY SEX(1,2)
  /PRINT=SIGNIF(HYPOTH)
  /DESIGN.
```

```
EFFECT .. SEX
Adjusted Hypothesis Sum-of-Squares and Cross-Products

                 BALOMEAN     BALCMEAN      SSTMEAN           PP

BALOMEAN       348.35572
BALCMEAN        -9.84205       .27807
SSTMEAN        266.15115     -7.51953    203.34512
PP            -100.32892      2.83458    -76.65342     28.89544
```

Figure 3.13b contains the value of Hotelling's T^2 statistic divided by $N-2$ for the test of the hypothesis that men and women do not differ on the motor-ability test scores. The significance level is based on the F distribution with 4 and 129 degrees of freedom. The observed significance level is small (less than 0.0005), so the null hypothesis that men and women perform equally well on the motor-ability tests is rejected.

Figure 3.13b   Hotelling's T^2 statistic

```
MANOVA BALOMEAN BALCMEAN SSTMEAN PP BY SEX(1,2)
  /PRINT=SIGNIF(HYPOTH MULTIV)
  /DESIGN.
```

```
Multivariate Tests of Significance (S = 1, M = 1 , N = 63 1/2)

Test Name          Value  Approx. F Hypoth. DF   Error DF  Sig. of F

Hotellings        .66953   21.59224       4.00     129.00       .000
```

3.14
Univariate Tests

To get some idea of where the differences between men's and women's scores occur, the univariate tests for the individual variables may be examined. These are the same as the F values from one-way analyses of variance. In the case of two groups, the F values are just the squares of the two-sample t values.

Figure 3.14   Univariate F tests

```
MANOVA BALOMEAN BALCMEAN SSTMEAN PP BY SEX(1,2)
  /PRINT=SIGNIF(HYPOTH MULTIV UNIV)
  /DESIGN.
```

```
EFFECT .. SEX (CONT.)
Univariate F-tests with (1,132) D. F.

Variable   Hypoth. SS    Error SS Hypoth. MS     Error MS          F  Sig. of F

BALOMEAN    348.35572  4218.91817  348.35572     31.96150   10.89923       .001
BALCMEAN       .27807   262.22270     .27807      1.98654     .13998       .709
SSTMEAN     203.34512   752.89249  203.34512      5.70373   35.65125       .000
PP           28.89544   268.22570   28.89544      2.03201   14.22011       .000
```

From Figure 3.14, we can see that there are significant univariate tests for all variables except balancing with eyes closed. Again, the significance levels are not adjusted for the fact that four tests, rather than one, are being performed.

**3.15
Discriminant Analysis**

In Chapter 1, we considered the problem of finding the best linear combination of variables for distinguishing among several groups. Coefficients for the variables are chosen so that the ratio of between-groups sums of squares to total sums of squares is as large as possible. Although the equality of means hypotheses tested in MANOVA may initially appear quite unrelated to the discriminant problem, the two procedures are closely related. In fact, MANOVA can be viewed as a problem of first finding linear combinations of the dependent variables that best separate the groups and then testing whether these new variables are significantly different for the groups. For this reason, the usual discriminant analysis statistics can be obtained as part of the SPSS/PC+ MANOVA output.

Figure 3.15a contains the eigenvalues and canonical correlation for the canonical discriminant function that separates males and females. Remember that the eigenvalue is the ratio of the between-groups sum of squares to the within-groups sum of squares, while the square of the canonical correlation is the ratio of the between-groups sums of squares to the total sum of squares. Thus, about 40% of the variability in the discriminant scores is attributable to between-group differences ($0.633^2 = 0.401$).

Figure 3.15a Eigenvalue and canonical correlation

```
SET WIDTH=WIDE.
MANOVA BALOMEAN BALCMEAN SSTMEAN PP BY SEX(1,2)
  /PRINT=SIGNIF(HYPOTH MULTIV UNIV EIGEN)
  /DESIGN.
```

Eigenvalues and Canonical Correlations				
Root No.	Eigenvalue	Pct.	Cum. Pct.	Canon Cor.
1	.66953	100.00000	100.00000	.63327

As discussed in Chapter 1, when there are two groups, Wilks' lambda can be interpreted as a measure of the proportion of total variability not explained by group differences. As shown in Figure 3.15b, almost 60% of the observed variability is not explained by the group differences. The hypothesis that in the population there are no differences between the group means can be tested using Wilks' lambda. Lambda is transformed to a variable that has an F distribution. For the two-group situation, the F value for Wilks' lambda is identical to that given for Hotelling's T^2 (Figure 3.13b).

Figure 3.15b Wilks' lambda

```
MANOVA BALOMEAN BALCMEAN SSTMEAN PP BY SEX(1,2)
  /DESIGN.
```

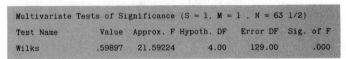

Multivariate Tests of Significance (S = 1, M = 1 , N = 63 1/2)					
Test Name	Value	Approx. F	Hypoth. DF	Error DF	Sig. of F
Wilks	.59897	21.59224	4.00	129.00	.000

Both raw and standardized discriminant function coefficients can be displayed by SPSS/PC+ MANOVA. The raw coefficents are the multipliers of the dependent variables in their original units, while the standardized coefficients are the multipliers of the dependent variables when the latter have been standardized to a mean of 0 and a standard deviation of 1. Both sets of coefficients are displayed in Figure 3.15c.

Figure 3.15c   Raw and standardized discriminant function coefficients

```
SET WIDTH=WIDE.
MANOVA BALOMEAN BALCMEAN SSTMEAN PP BY SEX(1,2)
  /DISCRIM=RAW STAN
  /DESIGN.
```

```
EFFECT .. SEX (CONT.)
Raw discriminant function coefficients
          Function No.

Variable               1

BALOMEAN         -.07465
BALCMEAN          .19245
SSTMEAN          -.36901
PP                .49189

- - - - - - - - -

Standardized discriminant function coefficients
          Function No.

Variable               1

BALOMEAN         -.42205
BALCMEAN          .27125
SSTMEAN          -.88128
PP                .70118
```

The side-stepping and pegboard scores have the largest standardized coefficients and, as you will recall from Figure 3.9a, they also have the largest univariate *F*'s, suggesting that they are important for separating the two groups. Of course, when variables are correlated, the discriminant function coefficients must be interpreted with care, since highly correlated variables share the discriminant weights.

The correlation coefficients for the discriminant scores and each dependent variable are somewhat less likely to be strongly influenced by the correlations between the variables. These coefficients, sometimes called *structure coefficients,* are displayed in Figure 3.15d. Once again, the side-stepping test and the pegboard test are most highly correlated with the discriminant function, while the correlation coefficient between balancing with eyes closed and the discriminant function is near 0. Again, balancing with eyes closed had a nonsignificant univariate *F*.

Figure 3.15d   Correlations between dependent variables and canonical variables

```
SET WIDTH=WIDE.
MANOVA BALOMEAN BALCMEAN SSTMEAN PP BY SEX(1,2)
  /DISCRIM=RAW STAN CORR
  /DESIGN.
```

```
Correlations between DEPENDENT and canonical variables
          Canonical Variable

Variable               1

BALOMEAN         -.35118
BALCMEAN          .03980
SSTMEAN          -.63514
PP                .40113
```

An additional statistic displayed as part of the discriminant output in MANOVA is an estimate of the effect for the canonical variable. Consider Figure 3.15e (from procedure DSCRIMINANT), which gives the average canonical function scores for the two groups. We can estimate the effect of a canonical variable by measuring its average distance from 0 across all groups. In this example the average distance is $(0.862 + 0.765)/2 = 0.814$, as shown in Figure 3.15f. Canonical variables with small effects do not contribute much to separation between groups.

Figure 3.15e   Average canonical function scores from DSCRIMINANT

```
DSCRIMINANT GROUPS=SEX(1,2)
  /VARIABLES=BALOMEAN SSTMEAN BALCMEAN PP
  /METHOD=DIRECT
  /DESIGN.
```

```
Canonical Discriminant Functions evaluated at Group Means (Group Centroids)

   Group     FUNC  1
     1       -.86214
     2        .76500
```

Figure 3.15f   Estimates of effects for canonical variables

```
SET WIDTH=WIDE.
MANOVA BALOMEAN BALCMEAN SSTMEAN PP BY SEX(1,2)
  /DISCRIM=RAW STAN CORR ESTIM
  /DESIGN.
```

```
Estimates of effects for canonical variables
          Canonical Variable

  Parameter          1

       2          .81357
```

3.16
Parameter Estimates

As for most other statistical techniques, there is for MANOVA a mathematical model that expresses the relationship between the dependent variable and the independent variables. Recall, for example, that in a univariate analysis of variance model with four groups, the mean for each group can be expressed as

$$Y_{.1} = \mu + \alpha_1 \qquad\qquad\quad + E_{.1}$$

$$Y_{.2} = \mu \quad + \alpha_2 \qquad\qquad + E_{.2}$$

$$Y_{.3} = \mu \qquad\quad + \alpha_3 \qquad + E_{.3}$$

$$Y_{.4} = \mu \qquad\qquad\qquad + \alpha_4 + E_{.4}$$

Equation 3.16a

In matrix form this can be written as

$$
\begin{bmatrix} Y_{.1} \\ Y_{.2} \\ Y_{.3} \\ Y_{.4} \end{bmatrix}
=
\begin{bmatrix} 1 & 1 & 0 & 0 & 0 \\ 1 & 0 & 1 & 0 & 0 \\ 1 & 0 & 0 & 1 & 0 \\ 1 & 0 & 0 & 0 & 1 \end{bmatrix}
\begin{bmatrix} \mu \\ \alpha_1 \\ \alpha_2 \\ \alpha_3 \\ \alpha_4 \end{bmatrix}
+
\begin{bmatrix} E_{.1} \\ E_{.2} \\ E_{.3} \\ E_{.4} \end{bmatrix}
$$

Equation 3.16b

or

$$Y_. = A\Theta^* + E$$

Equation 3.16c

Since the Θ matrix has more columns than rows, it does not have a unique inverse. We are unable to estimate five parameters (μ and α_1 to α_4) on the basis of four sample means. Instead we can estimate four linear combinations, termed contrasts, of the parameters (see Finn, 1974).

Several types of contrasts are available in SPSS/PC+ MANOVA, resulting in different types of parameter estimates. Deviation contrasts, the default, estimate each parameter as its difference from the overall average for that parameter. This results in parameter estimates of the form $\mu_j - \mu$. Deviation contrasts do not require any particular ordering of the factor levels.

Simple contrasts are useful when one of the factor levels is a comparison or control group. All parameter estimates are then expressed as a deviation from the value of the control group. When factor levels have an underlying metric, orthogonal polynomial contrasts may be used to determine whether group means are related to the values of the factor level. For example, if three doses of an agent are administered (10 units, 20 units, and 30 units), you can test whether response is related to dose in a linear or quadratic fashion.

Figure 3.16 contains parameter estimates corresponding to the default deviation contrasts. For each dependent variable, the entry under CONSTANT is just the unweighted average of the means in the two groups. For example, from Figure 3.11a, we see that the mean for balancing with eyes open is 9.748 for females and 12.979 for males. The estimate for the average time balanced with eyes open, the constant term in Figure 3.16, is 11.364, the average of 12.979 and 9.748.

Figure 3.16 Parameter estimates

```
Estimates for BALOMEAN
CONSTANT

    Parameter      Coeff.   Std. Err.     t-Value    Sig. t  Lower -95% CL- Upper

          1    11.3636425     .48926    23.22635       0.0     10.39584    12.33144
SEX

    Parameter      Coeff.   Std. Err.     t-Value    Sig. t  Lower -95% CL- Upper

          2    -1.6152302     .48926    -3.30140      .001     -2.58303     -.64743

- - - - - - - - -

Estimates for BALCMEAN
CONSTANT

    Parameter      Coeff.   Std. Err.     t-Value    Sig. t  Lower -95% CL- Upper

          1     3.14563447    .12198    25.78916       0.0      2.90436     3.38691
SEX

    Parameter      Coeff.   Std. Err.     t-Value    Sig. t  Lower -95% CL- Upper

          2     .045634894    .12198      .37413      .709      -.19564      .28691

- - - - - - - - -

Estimates for SSTMEAN
CONSTANT

    Parameter      Coeff.   Std. Err.     t-Value    Sig. t  Lower -95% CL- Upper

          1    15.3293074     .20668    74.16860       0.0     14.92047    15.73814
SEX

    Parameter      Coeff.   Std. Err.     t-Value    Sig. t  Lower -95% CL- Upper

          2    -1.2340701     .20668    -5.97087      .000     -1.64291     -.82523

- - - - - - - - -

Estimates for PP
CONSTANT

    Parameter      Coeff.   Std. Err.     t-Value    Sig. t  Lower -95% CL- Upper

          1    15.0004080     .12336   121.59533       0.0     14.75638    15.24443
SEX

    Parameter      Coeff.   Std. Err.     t-Value    Sig. t  Lower -95% CL- Upper

          2     .465197766    .12336     3.77096      .000      .22117      .70922
```

There are two estimates for the sex parameter, one for females and one for males. The output includes only values for the first parameter (females), since the value for the second parameter is just the negative of the value for the first. The sex effect for females is estimated as the difference between the mean score of females and the overall unweighted mean. For balancing with eyes open it is $9.75 - 11.36 = -1.61$, the value displayed in Figure 3.16. Confidence intervals and t tests for the null hypothesis that a parameter value is 0 can also be calculated. Again, these are calculated on a parameter-by-parameter basis and do not offer an overall protection level against Type 1 errors. Note that the t values displayed for each parameter are equal to the square root of the F values displayed for the univariate F tests in Figure 3.14.

3.17
A Multivariate Factorial
Design

So far we have considered two very simple multivariate designs, generalizations of the one- and two-sample *t* tests to the case of multiple dependent variables. We are now ready to examine a more complex design. Recall that in the experiment conducted by Barnard, the hypothesis of interest concerned the relationship among field dependence, sex, and motor abilities. Since subjects are classified into one of three field-dependence categories—low, intermediate, and high—we have a two-way factorial design with three levels of field dependence and two categories of sex.

Figure 3.17a contains the location of the effects in the design matrix. The number of columns required by each effect equals its degrees of freedom. Thus, there is one column for sex, two for field-dependence, and two for the sex-by-field-dependence interaction.

Figure 3.17a   Correspondence table

```
MANOVA BALCMEAN BY SEX(1,2) FIELD(1,3) WITH BALOMEAN
   /DESIGN.
```

```
Correspondence between Effects and Columns of BETWEEN-Subjects DESIGN 1

   Starting   Ending
   Column     Column     Effect Name
      1          1        CONSTANT
      2          2        SEX
      3          4        FIELD
      5          6        SEX BY FIELD
```

When orthogonal contrasts are requested for a factor; that is, when the sum of the products of corresponding coefficients for any two contrasts is 0, the numbers in the columns of the design matrix are the coefficients of the contrasts, except for scaling. When nonorthogonal contrasts, such as "deviation" or "simple," are requested for a factor, the columns of the matrix are not the contrast coefficients but are the basis for the contrast requested (see Bock, 1975; Finn, 1974). The actual parameter estimates always correspond to the contrast requested.

Descriptive statistics are available for each cell in the design. Some additional plots may also be useful. Plotting the mean of a variable for all the cells in the design, as shown in Figure 3.17b, gives an idea of the spread of the means. The top row of numbers indicates how many cell means there are in each interval. You can see from the plot that there are two cells with means close to 14 seconds, three cells with means less than 10 seconds, and 1 cell with a mean in between.

Figure 3.17b   Distribution of cell means for BALOMEAN

```
SET WIDTH=WIDE.
MANOVA BALCMEAN BY SEX(1,2) FIELD(1,3) WITH BALOMEAN
   /PLOT=CELLPLOTS
   /DESIGN.
```

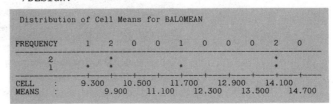

```
Distribution of Cell Means for BALOMEAN

FREQUENCY     1    2    0    0    1    0    0    0    2    0
     2             *                             *
     1        *    *              *              *
          ---+----+----+----+----+----+----+----+----+----+----
CELL  :   9.300    10.500   11.700   12.900   14.100
MEANS :       9.900    11.100   12.300   13.500   14.700
```

Although both univariate and multivariate analyses of variance require equal variances in the cells, there are many situations in which cell means and standard deviations, or cell means and variances, are proportional. Figure 3.17c shows plots of cell means versus cell variances and cell standard deviations. There appears to be no relationship between the means and the measures of variability. If patterns were evident, transformations of the dependent variables might be used to stabilize the variances.

Figure 3.17c   Plots of cell means, cell variances, and cell standard deviations

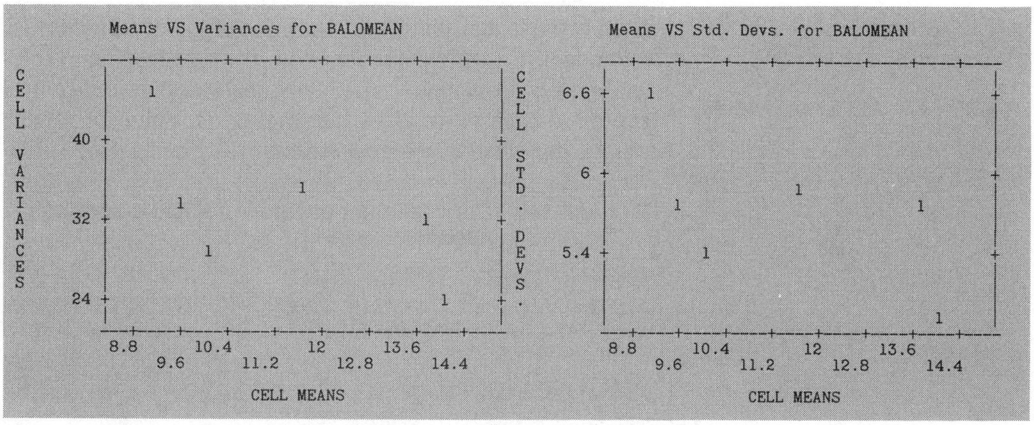

3.18
Principal Components Analysis

Bartlett's test of sphericity provides information about the correlations among the dependent variables by testing the hypothesis that the correlation matrix is an identity matrix. Another way to examine dependencies among the dependent variables is to perform a principal components analysis of their within-cells correlation or covariance matrix (for a discussion of principal components analysis, see *SPSS/PC+ Statistics*). If principal components analysis reveals that one of the variables can be expressed as a linear combination of the others, the error sums-of-squares and cross-products matrix will be singular and a unique inverse cannot be obtained.

Figure 3.18a contains the within-cells correlation matrix for the two-way factorial design. The eigenvalues and percent of variance explained by each are shown in Figure 3.18b. The first two principal components account for about two-thirds of the total variance, and the remaining two components account for the rest. None of the eigenvalues is close enough to 0 to cause concern about the error matrix being singular.

Figure 3.18a   Within-cells correlation matrix

```
SET WIDTH=WIDE.
MANOVA BALOMEAN BALCMEAN SSTMEAN PP BY SEX(1,2) FIELD(1,3)
   /PRINT=ERROR(COR)
   /DESIGN.
```

```
WITHIN CELLS Correlations with Std. Devs. on Diagonal

              BALOMEAN     BALCMEAN     SSTMEAN          PP

BALOMEAN       5.67488
BALCMEAN        .30019     1.41485
SSTMEAN         .11506      .24341     2.39327
PP              .11100      .14334      .34698     1.43842
```

Figure 3.18b   Eigenvalues and percent of variance

```
SET WIDTH=WIDE.
MANOVA BALOMEAN BALCMEAN SSTMEAN PP BY SEX(1,2) FIELD(1,3)
   /PCOMPS=CORR
   /DESIGN.
```

```
Eigenvalues of WITHIN CELLS correlation matrix

        Eigenvalue  Pct of Var    Cum Pct

    1      1.63610    40.90258    40.90258
    2      1.02780    25.69499    66.59757
    3       .72258    18.06447    84.66204
    4       .61352    15.33796   100.00000
```

Figure 3.18c contains the loadings, which in this case are equivalent to correlations, between the principal components and dependent variables. The components can be rotated, as shown in Figure 3.18d, to increase interpretability. Each variable loads highly on only one of the components, suggesting that none is redundant or highly correlated with the others. When there are many dependent variables, a principal components analysis may indicate how the variables are related to each other. This information is useful for establishing the number of unique dimensions being measured by the dependent variables.

Figure 3.18c   Correlations between principal components and dependent variable

```
SET WIDTH=WIDE.
MANOVA BALOMEAN BALCMEAN SSTMEAN PP BY SEX(1,2) FIELD(1,3)
   /PCOMPS=CORR ROTATE(VARIMAX)
   /DESIGN.
```

Normalized principal components Components				
Variables	1	2	3	4
BALOMEAN	-.55200	-.63056	-.48683	.24635
BALCMEAN	-.66950	-.41517	.49417	-.36770
SSTMEAN	-.69880	.41598	.27636	.51212
PP	-.62837	.53366	-.40619	-.39416

Figure 3.18d   Rotated correlations between components and dependent variable

VARIMAX rotated correlations between components and DEPENDENT variable Can. Var.				
DEP. VAR.	1	2	3	4
BALOMEAN	.98696	.04774	.14699	.04503
BALCMEAN	.15005	.05958	.98016	.11501
SSTMEAN	.04632	.17390	.11606	.97680
PP	.04835	.98230	.05905	.17104

3.19
Tests of Multivariate Differences

Once the preliminary steps of examining the distribution of the variables for outliers, nonnormality, and inequality of variances have been taken and no significant violations have been found, hypothesis testing can begin. In the one- and two-sample test, Hotelling's T^2, a multivariate generalization of the univariate t value, is used. For more complicated designs, an extension of the familiar analysis of variance F test to the multivariate case is needed.

The univariate F tests in ANOVA are the ratios of the hypothesis mean squares to the error mean squares. When there is more than one dependent variable, there is no longer a single number that represents the hypothesis and error sums of squares. Instead, as shown in Section 3.9, there are matrices for the hypothesis and error sums of squares and cross-products. These matrices must be combined into some type of test statistic.

Most multivariate test statistics are based on the determinant of HE^{-1}, where H is the hypothesis sums-of-squares and cross-products matrix and E^{-1} is the inverse of the error sums-of-squares and cross-products matrix. The determinant is a measure of the generalized variance, or dispersion, of a matrix. This determinant can be calculated as the product of the eigenvalues of a matrix, since each eigenvalue represents a portion of the generalized variance. In fact, the process of extracting eigenvalues can be viewed as a principal components analysis on the HE^{-1} matrix.

Various test statistics are available for evaluating multivariate differences based on the eigenvalues of HE^{-1}. Four of the most commonly used tests are displayed by SPSS/PC+ MANOVA:

• Pillai's Trace

$$V = \sum_{i=1}^{s} \frac{1}{1 + \lambda_i}$$

Equation 3.19a

• Wilks' Lambda

$$W = \prod_{i=1}^{s} \frac{1}{1 + \lambda_i}$$

Equation 3.19b

• Hotelling's Trace

$$T = \Sigma \lambda_i$$

Equation 3.19c

• Roy's Largest Root

Equation 3.19d

$$R = \frac{\lambda_{MAX}}{1 + \lambda_{MAX}}$$

where λ_{max} is the largest eigenvalue, λ_i is the ith eigenvalue, and s is the number of nonzero eigenvalues of HE^{-1}.

Although the exact distributions of the four criteria differ, they can be transformed into statistics that have approximately an F distribution. Tables of the exact distributions of the statistics are also available.

When there is a single dependent variable, all four criteria are equivalent to the ordinary ANOVA F statistic. When there is a single sample or two independent samples with multiple dependent variables, they are all equivalent to Hotelling's T^2. In both situations, the transformed statistics are distributed exactly as F's.

Two concerns dictate the choice of the multivariate criterion—power and robustness. That is, the test statistic should detect differences when they exist and not be much affected by departures from the assumptions. For most practical situations, when differences among groups are spread along several dimensions, the ordering of the test criteria in terms of decreasing power is Pillai's, Wilks', Hotelling's, and Roy's. Pillai's trace is also the most robust criterion. That is, the significance level based on it is reasonably correct even when the assumptions are violated. This is important since a test that results in distorted significance levels in the presence of mild violations of homogeneity of covariance matrices or multivariate normality is of limited use (Olson, 1976).

3.20
Testing the Effects

Since our design is a two-by-three factorial (two sexes and three categories of field dependence), there are three effects to be tested: the sex and field-dependence main effects and the sex-by-field-dependence interaction. As in univariate analysis of variance, the terms are tested in reverse order. That is, higher-order effects are tested before lower-order ones, since it is difficult to interpret lower-order effects in the presence of higher-order interactions. For example, if there is a sex-by-field-dependence interaction, testing for sex and field-dependence main effects is not particularly useful and can be misleading.

SPSS/PC+ MANOVA displays separate output for each effect. Figure 3.20a shows the label displayed on each page to identify the effect being tested. The hypothesis sums-of-squares and cross-products matrix can be displayed for each effect. The same error matrix (the pooled within-cells sums-of-squares and cross-products matrix) is used to test all effects and is displayed only once before the effect-by-effect output. Figure 3.20b contains the error matrix for the factorial design. Figure 3.20c is the hypothesis sums-of-squares and cross-product matrix. These two matrices are the ones involved in the computation of the test statistic displayed in Figure 3.20d.

Figure 3.20a   Label for effect being tested

```
EFFECT .. SEX BY FIELD
```

Figure 3.20b   Error sums-of-squares and cross-products matrix

```
SET WIDTH=WIDE.
MANOVA BALOMEAN BALCMEAN SSTMEAN PP BY SEX(1,2) FIELD(1,3)
  /PRINT=ERROR(SSCP)
  /DESIGN.
```

WITHIN CELLS Sum-of-Squares and Cross-Products

	BALOMEAN	BALCMEAN	SSTMEAN	PP
BALOMEAN	4122.15198			
BALCMEAN	308.51396	256.22940		
SSTMEAN	200.02101	105.49892	733.14820	
PP	115.98110	37.33887	152.89478	264.83723

Figure 3.20c   Hypothesis sums-of-squares and cross-products matrix

```
SET WIDTH=WIDE.
MANOVA BALOMEAN BALCMEAN SSTMEAN PP BY SEX(1,2) FIELD(1,3)
  /PRINT=SIGNIF(HYPOTH)
  /DESIGN.
```

Adjusted Hypothesis Sum-of-Squares and Cross-Products

	BALOMEAN	BALCMEAN	SSTMEAN	PP
BALOMEAN	18.10216			
BALCMEAN	8.23621	3.77316		
SSTMEAN	2.49484	.55197	13.52285	
PP	-.00369	.21322	-4.85733	1.78987

Figure 3.20d   Multivariate tests of significance

```
MANOVA BALOMEAN BALCMEAN SSTMEAN PP BY SEX(1,2) FIELD(1,3)
  /PRINT=SIGNIF(HYPOTH MULTIV)
  /DESIGN.
```

Multivariate Tests of Significance (S = 2, M = 1/2, N = 61 1/2)

Test Name	Value	Approx. F	Hypoth. DF	Error DF	Sig. of F
Pillais	.05245	.84827	8.00	252.00	.561
Hotellings	.05410	.83848	8.00	248.00	.570
Wilks	.94813	.84339	8.00	250.00	.565
Roys	.03668				

The first line of Figure 3.20d contains the values of the parameters (S, M, N) used to find significance levels in tables of the exact distributions of the statistics. For the first three tests, the value of the test statistic is given, followed by its transformation to a statistic that has approximately an F distribution. The next two columns contain the numerator (hypothesis) and denominator (error) degrees of freedom for the F statistic. The observed significance level (the probability of observing a difference at least as large as the one found in the sample when there is no difference in the populations) is given in the last column. All of the observed significance levels are large, causing us not to reject the hypothesis that the sex-by-field-dependence interaction is 0. There is no straightforward transformation for Roy's largest root criterion to a statistic with a known distribution, so only the value of the largest root is displayed.

Since the multivariate results are not statistically significant, there is no reason to examine the univariate results shown in Figure 3.20e. When the multivariate results are significant, however, the univariate statistics may help determine which variables contribute to the overall differences. The univariate F tests for the SEX by FIELD interaction are the same as the F's for SEX by FIELD in a two-way ANOVA. Figure 3.20f contains a two-way analysis of variance for the balancing-with-eyes-open (BALOMEAN) variable. The within-cells sum of squares is identical to the diagonal entry for BALOMEAN in Figure 3.20b. Similarly, the SEX by FIELD sum of squares is identical to the diagonal entry for BALOMEAN in Figure 3.20c. The *F* value for the interaction term, 0.281, is the same as in the first line of Figure 3.20e.

Figure 3.20e Univariate *F* tests

```
MANOVA BALOMEAN BALCMEAN SSTMEAN PP BY SEX(1,2) FIELD(1,3)
   /PRINT=SIGNIF(HYPOTH MULTIV UNIV)
   /DESIGN.
```

```
EFFECT .. SEX BY CAT (CONT.)
Univariate F-tests with (2,128) D. F.

Variable   Hypoth. SS   Error SS  Hypoth. MS   Error MS          F  Sig. of F

BALOMEAN     18.10216  4122.15198    9.05108   32.20431     .28105       .755
BALCMEAN      3.77316   256.22940    1.88658    2.00179     .94244       .392
SSTMEAN      13.52285   733.14820    6.76143    5.72772    1.18047       .310
PP            1.78987   264.83723     .89493    2.06904     .43254       .650
```

Figure 3.20f Two-way analysis of variance

```
MANOVA BALOMEAN BY SEX(1,2) FIELD(1,3)
   /DESIGN.
```

```
Tests of Significance for BALOMEAN using UNIQUE sums of squares
Source of Variation         SS      DF         MS         F  Sig of F

WITHIN CELLS           4122.15     128      32.20
CONSTANT              16042.05       1   16042.05    498.13      .000
SEX                     389.33       1     389.33     12.09      .001
CAT                      55.19       2      27.59       .86      .427
SEX BY CAT               18.10       2       9.05       .28      .755
```

3.21
Discriminant Analysis

As discussed in Section 3.15 for the two-group situation, the MANOVA problem can also be viewed as one of finding the linear combinations of the dependent variables that best separate the categories of the independent variables. For main effects, the analogy with discriminant analysis is clear: What combinations of the variables distinguish men from women and what combinations distinguish the three categories of field dependence? When interaction terms are considered, we must distinguish among the six (two sex and three field-dependence) categories jointly. This is done by finding the linear combination of variables that maximizes the ratio of the hypothesis to error sums-of-squares. Since the interaction effect is not significant, there is no particular reason to examine the discriminant analysis results. However, we will consider them for illustrative purposes.

Figure 3.21a contains the standardized discriminant function coefficients for the interaction term. The number of functions that can be derived is equal to the degrees of freedom for that term if it is less than the number of dependent variables. The two variables that have the largest standardized coefficients are the side-stepping test and the Purdue Pegboard Test. All warnings concerning the interpretation of coefficients when variables are correlated apply in this situation as well. However, the magnitude of the coefficients may give us some idea of the variables contributing most to group differences.

Figure 3.21a Standardized discriminant function coefficients

```
SET WIDTH=WIDE.
MANOVA BALOMEAN BALCMEAN SSTMEAN PP BY SEX(1,2) FIELD(1,3)
   /DISCRIM=STAN ALPHA(1)
   /DESIGN.
```

```
EFFECT .. SEX BY FIELD (CONT.)
Standardized discriminant function coefficients
        Function No.

Variable         1           2

BALOMEAN     .02621     -.27281
BALCMEAN    -.19519     -.90129
SSTMEAN      .98773      .02421
PP          -.73895      .15295
```

As discussed in Chapter 1, a measure of the strength of the association between the discriminant functions and the grouping variables is the canonical correlation coefficient. Its square is the proportion of variability in the discriminant function scores explained by the independent variables. All multivariate significance tests, which were expressed as functions of the eigenvalues in Section 3.19, can also be expressed as functions of the canonical correlations.

Figure 3.21b contains several sets of statistics for the discriminant functions. The entry under eigenvalues is the dispersion associated with each function. The next column is the percentage of the total dispersion associated with each function. (It is obtained by dividing each eigenvalue by the sum of all eigenvalues and multiplying by 100.) The last column contains the canonical correlation coefficients. The results in Figure 3.21b are consistent with the results of the multivariate significance tests. Both the eigenvalues and canonical correlation coefficients are small, indicating that there is no interaction effect.

Figure 3.21b Eigenvalues and canonical correlations

```
SET WIDTH=WIDE.
MANOVA BALOMEAN BALCMEAN SSTMEAN PP BY SEX(1,2) FIELD(1,3)
  /PRINT=SIGNIF(EIGEN)
  /DESIGN.
```

Root No.	Eigenvalue	Pct.	Cum. Pct.	Canon Cor.
1	.03808	70.39068	70.39068	.19152
2	.01602	29.60932	100.00000	.12556

EFFECT .. SEX BY FIELD (CONT.)
Eigenvalues and Canonical Correlations

When more than one discriminant function can be derived, you should examine how many functions contribute to group differences. The same tests for successive eigenvalues described in Chapter 1 can be obtained from SPSS/PC+ MANOVA. The first line in Figure 3.21c is a test of the hypothesis that all eigenvalues are equal to 0. The value for Wilks' lambda in the first line of Figure 3.21c is equal to the test of multivariate differences in Figure 3.20d. Successive lines in Figure 3.21c correspond to tests of the hypothesis that all remaining functions are equal in the groups. These tests allow you to assess the number of dimensions on which the groups differ.

Figure 3.21c Dimension reduction analysis

```
MANOVA BALOMEAN BALCMEAN SSTMEAN PP BY SEX(1,2) FIELD(1,3)
  /PRINT=SIGNIF(EIGEN DIMENR)
  /DESIGN.
```

EFFECT .. SEX BY FIELD (CONT.)

Dimension Reduction Analysis

Roots	Wilks L.	F	Hypoth. DF	Error DF	Sig. of F
1 TO 2	.94813	.84339	8.00	250.00	.565
2 TO 2	.98424	.67273	3.00	126.00	.570

**3.22
Testing for Differences among Field Dependence and Sex Categories**

Since the field-dependence-by-sex interaction term is not significant, the main effects can be tested. Figure 3.22a contains the multivariate tests of significance for the field-dependence variable. All four criteria indicate that there is not sufficient evidence to reject the null hypothesis that the means of the motor-ability variables do not differ for the three categories of field dependence.

Figure 3.22a   Multivariate tests of significance for FIELD

```
MANOVA BALOMEAN BALCMEAN SSTMEAN PP BY SEX(1,2) FIELD(1,3)
  /PRINT=SIGNIF(EIGEN DIMENR MULTIV)
  /DESIGN.
```

```
EFFECT .. FIELD
- - - - - - - - -
Multivariate Tests of Significance (S = 2, M = 1/2, N = 61 1/2)

Test Name        Value   Approx. F Hypoth. DF   Error DF  Sig. of F

Pillais         .04152    .66780      8.00       252.00     .720
Hotellings      .04244    .65789      8.00       248.00     .728
Wilks           .95889    .66285      8.00       250.00     .724
Roys            .02533
```

The multivariate tests of significance for the sex variable are shown in Figure 3.22b. All four criteria indicate that there are significant differences between men and women on the motor-ability variables. Compare Figure 3.22b with Figure 3.13b, which contains Hotelling's statistic for the two-group situation. Note that although the two statistics are close in value—0.669 when SEX is considered alone and 0.609 when SEX is included in a model containing field dependence and the sex-by-field-dependence interaction—they are not identical. The reason is that in the second model the sex effect is adjusted for the other effects in the model (see Section 3.24).

Figure 3.22b   Multivariate tests of significance for SEX

```
EFFECT .. SEX
- - - - - - - - -
Multivariate Tests of Significance (S = 1, M = 1 , N = 61 1/2)

Test Name        Value   Approx. F Hypoth. DF   Error DF  Sig. of F

Pillais         .37871  19.04870      4.00       125.00     .000
Hotellings      .60956  19.04870      4.00       125.00     .000
Wilks           .62129  19.04870      4.00       125.00     .000
Roys            .37871
```

3.23
Stepdown *F* Tests

If the dependent variables are ordered in some fashion, it is possible to test for group differences of variables adjusting for effects of other variables. This is termed a *stepdown* procedure. Consider Figure 3.23a, which contains the stepdown tests for the motor-ability variables. The first line is just a univariate *F* test for the balancing-with-eyes-open variable. The value is the same as that displayed in Figure 3.23b, which contains the univariate *F* tests. The next line in Figure 3.23a is the univariate *F* test for balancing with eyes closed when balancing with eyes open is taken to be a covariate. That is, differences in balancing with eyes open are eliminated from the comparison of balancing with eyes closed. Figure 3.23c is the ANOVA table for the BALCMEAN variable when BALOMEAN is treated as the covariate. Note that the *F* value of 1.76 for SEX in Figure 3.23c is identical to that for BALCMEAN in Figure 3.23a.

Figure 3.23a   Stepdown tests

```
MANOVA BALOMEAN BALCMEAN SSTMEAN PP BY SEX(1,2) FIELD(1,3)
  /PRINT=SIGNIF(EIGEN DIMENR MULTIV STEPDOWN)
  /DESIGN.
```

```
EFFECT .. SEX (CONT.)
- - - - - - - - -
Roy-Bargman Stepdown F - tests

Variable    Hypoth. MS    Error MS StepDown F Hypoth. DF   Error DF  Sig. of F

BALOMEAN     389.32559    32.20431  12.08924       1          128      .001
BALCMEAN       3.24111     1.83574   1.76556       1          127      .186
SSTMEAN      149.80319     5.46262  27.42333       1          126      .000
PP            44.19749     1.84899  23.90357       1          125      .000
```

Figure 3.23b   Univariate F tests

```
MANOVA BALOMEAN BALCMEAN SSTMEAN PP BY SEX(1,2) FIELD(1,3)
  /PRINT=SIGNIF(EIGEN DIMENR MULTIV STEPDOWN UNIV)
  /DESIGN.
```

```
EFFECT .. SEX (CONT.)
- - - - - - - - -
Univariate F-tests with (1,128) D. F.

Variable   Hypoth. SS   Error SS Hypoth. MS   Error MS         F  Sig. of F

BALOMEAN    389.32559 4122.15198  389.32559   32.20431  12.08924      .001
BALCMEAN      .16537  256.22940     .16537    2.00179    .08261      .774
SSTMEAN     172.11227  733.14820  172.11227    5.72772  30.04900      .000
PP           23.56111  264.83723   23.56111    2.06904  11.38746      .001
```

Figure 3.23c   ANOVA table for BALCMEAN with BALOMEAN as the covariate

```
MANOVA BALOMEAN BALCMEAN SSTMEAN PP BY SEX(1,2) FIELD(1,3)
  /ANALYSIS=BALCMEAN WITH BALOMEAN
  /DESIGN.
```

```
Tests of Significance for BALCMEAN using UNIQUE sums of squares
Source of Variation        SS       DF        MS         F  Sig of F

WITHIN CELLS           233.14      127      1.84
REGRESSION              23.09        1     23.09     12.58      .001
CONSTANT               135.46        1    135.46     73.79      .000
SEX                      3.24        1      3.24      1.77      .186
CAT                      2.40        2      1.20       .65      .522
SEX BY CAT               2.63        2      1.32       .72      .490
```

The third line of Figure 3.23a, the test for the side-stepping variable, is adjusted for both the balancing-with-eyes-open variable and the balancing-with-eyes-closed variable. Similarly, the last line, the Purdue Pegboard Test score, has balancing with eyes open, balancing with eyes closed, and the side-stepping test as covariates. Thus, each variable in Figure 3.23a is adjusted for variables that precede it in the table.

The order in which variables are displayed on the stepdown tests in MANOVA output depends only on the order in which the variables are specified for the procedure. If this order is not meaningful, the stepdown tests that result will not be readily interpretable or meaningful.

3.24
Different Types of Sums of Squares

When there is more than one factor and unequal numbers of cases in each cell in univariate analysis of variance, the total sums of squares cannot be partitioned into additive components for each effect. That is, the sums of squares for all effects do not add up to the total sums of squares. Differences between factor means are "contaminated" by the effects of the other factors.

There are many different algorithms for calculating the sums of squares for unbalanced data. Different types of sums of squares correspond to tests of different hypotheses. Two frequently used methods for calculating the sums of squares are the regression method, in which an effect is adjusted for all other effects in the model, and the sequential method, in which an effect is adjusted only for effects that precede it in the model.

In multivariate analysis of variance, unequal sample sizes in the cells lead to similar problems. Again, different procedures for calculating the requisite statistics are available. SPSS/PC+ MANOVA offers two options—the regression solution (requested by keyword UNIQUE) and the sequential solution (requested by keyword SEQUENTIAL). All output displayed in this chapter is obtained from the regression solution, the default (see Milliken & Johnson, 1984).

For any connected design, the hypotheses associated with the sequential sums of squares are weighted functions of the population cell means, with weights depending on the cell frequencies (see Searle, 1971). For designs in which every cell is filled, it can be shown that the hypotheses corresponding to the regression model sums of squares are the hypotheses about the unweighted cell means. With empty cells, the hypotheses will depend on the pattern of missingness. In such cases, you can display the solution matrix, which contains the coefficients of the linear combinations of the cell means being tested.

3.25
Problems with Empty Cells

When there are no observations in one or more cells in a design, the analysis is greatly complicated. This is true for both univariate and multivariate designs. Empty cells result in the inability to estimate uniquely all of the necessary parameters. Hypotheses that involve parameters corresponding to the empty cells usually cannot be tested. Thus, the output from an analysis involving empty cells should be treated with caution (see Freund, 1980; Milliken & Johnson, 1984).

3.26
Examining Residuals

Residuals—the differences between observed values and those predicted from a model—provide information about the adequacy of fit of the model and the assumptions. Previous chapters have discussed residual analysis for regression and log-linear models. The same techniques are appropriate for analysis of variance models as well.

In the two-factor model with interactions, the equation is

$$\hat{Y}_{ij} = \hat{\mu} + \hat{\alpha}_i + \hat{\beta}_j + \hat{\delta}_{ij} \qquad \text{Equation 3.26a}$$

where $\hat{Y}_{ij}$ is the predicted value for the cases in the ith category of the first variable and the jth category of the second. As before, $\hat{\mu}$ is the grand mean, $\hat{\alpha}_i$ the effect of the ith category of the first variable, $\hat{\beta}_j$ is the effect of the jth category of the second variable, and $\hat{\delta}_{ij}$ is their interaction.

Consider Figure 3.26a, which contains deviation parameter estimates for the balancing-with-eyes-open variable. From this table, the predicted value for females in the low field-dependence category is

$$\hat{Y}_{11} = 11.42 - 1.78 - 0.97 + 0.51 = 9.18 \qquad \text{Equation 3.26b}$$

Similarly, the predicted value for males in the high field-dependence category is

$$\hat{Y}_{23} = 11.42 + 1.78 + 0.53 + 0.09 = 13.82 \qquad \text{Equation 3.26c}$$

Note that only independent parameter estimates are displayed and the other estimates must be derived from these. (For the main effects these can be requested with the keyword NEGSUM.) For example, the parameter estimate displayed for the sex variable is for the first category, females. The estimate for males is the negative of the estimate for females, since the two values must sum to 0. The value for the third category of field dependence is 0.53, the negative of the sum of the values for the first two categories. The two parameter estimates displayed for the interaction effects are for females with low field dependence and females with medium field dependence. The remaining estimates can be easily calculated. For example, the value for males in the low field-dependence category is -0.51, the negative of that for females. Similarly, the value for females in the high field-dependence category is -0.087, the negative of the sum of the values for females in low and medium field-dependence categories.

Figure 3.26a   Parameter estimates

```
MANOVA BALOMEAN BALCMEAN SSTMEAN PP BY SEX(1,2) FIELD(1,3)
  /PRINT=PARAMETERS(ESTIM)
  /ANALYSIS=BALOMEAN
  /DESIGN.
```

Estimates for BALOMEAN
CONSTANT

Parameter	Coeff.	Std. Err.	t-Value	Sig. t	Lower -95% CL- Upper	
1	11.4196871	.51166	22.31890	0.0	10.40728	12.43209

SEX

Parameter	Coeff.	Std. Err.	t-Value	Sig. t	Lower -95% CL- Upper	
2	-1.7790199	.51166	-3.47696	.001	-2.79143	-.76661

CAT

Parameter	Coeff.	Std. Err.	t-Value	Sig. t	Lower -95% CL- Upper	
3	-.97446433	.74485	-1.30827	.193	-2.44828	.49935
4	.445727366	.70743	.63006	.530	-.95405	1.84551

SEX BY CAT

Parameter	Coeff.	Std. Err.	t-Value	Sig. t	Lower -95% CL- Upper	
5	.514565980	.74485	.69083	.491	-.95925	1.98838
6	-.42730430	.70743	-.60402	.547	-1.82709	.97248

Figure 3.26b contains an excerpt of some cases in the study and their observed and predicted values for the balancing-with-eyes-open variable. The fourth column is the residual, the difference between the observed and predicted values. The residuals can be standardized by dividing each one by the error standard deviation (Column 5).

Figure 3.26b   Observed and predicted values

```
SET WIDTH=WIDE.
MANOVA BALOMEAN BALCMEAN SSTMEAN PP BY SEX(1,2) FIELD(1,3)
  /RESIDUALS=CASEWISE PLOT
  /ANALYSIS=BALOMEAN
  /DESIGN.
```

Observed and Predicted Values for Each Case
Dependent Variable.. BALOMEAN

Case No.	Observed	Predicted	Raw Resid.	Std Resid.
1	4.00000	10.08214	-6.08214	-1.07176
2	8.85000	9.18077	-.33077	-.05829
3	10.00000	9.65909	.34091	.06007
4	3.55000	10.08214	-6.53214	-1.15106
5	2.80000	9.65909	-6.85909	-1.20867
6	14.50000	9.65909	4.84091	.85304
.	.	.	.	.
.	.	.	.	.
.	.	.	.	.
127	5.00000	13.81470	-8.81470	-1.55328
128	20.00000	11.70968	8.29032	1.46088
129	20.00000	13.81470	6.18530	1.08994
130	19.00000	11.70968	7.29032	1.28466
131	16.14999	14.07174	2.07826	.36622
132	20.00000	14.07174	5.92826	1.04465
.	.	.	.	.
.	.	.	.	.
.	.	.	.	.

As in regression analysis, a variety of plots are useful for checking the assumptions. Figure 3.26c is a plot of the observed and predicted values for the BALOMEAN variable. The cases fall into six rows for the predicted values, since all cases in the same cell have the same predicted value. Residuals are plotted against the predicted values in Figure 3.26d and against the case numbers in Figure 3.26e. The plot against the case numbers is useful if the data are gathered and entered into the file sequentially. Any patterns in this plot lead to suspicions that the data are not independent of each other. Of course, if the data have been sorted before being entered, a pattern is to be expected.

Figure 3.26c   Plot of observed and predicted values

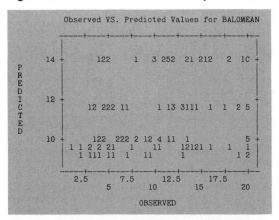

Figure 3.26d   Plot of predicted and residual values

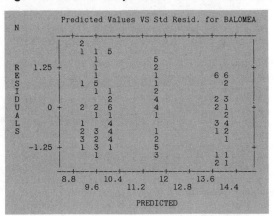

Figure 3.26e   Plot of case numbers and residuals

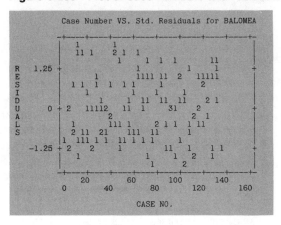

If the assumption of multivariate normality is met, the distribution of the residuals for each variable should be approximately normal. Figure 3.26f is a normal plot of the residuals for the balancing-with-eyes-open variable, while Figure 3.26g is the detrended normal plot of the same variable. Both of these plots suggest that there may be reason to suspect that the distribution of the residuals is not normal.

Figure 3.26f   Normal plot of residuals

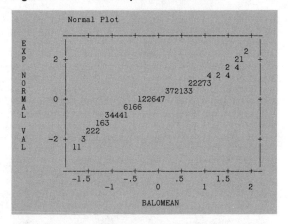

Figure 3.26g   Detrended normal plot

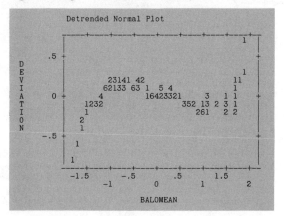

3.27
Predicted Means

Figure 3.27a shows a table that contains observed and predicted means for all cells in the design, as well as residuals, for the balancing-with-eyes-open variable. The first column of the table, labeled **Obs. Mean**, is the observed mean for that cell. The next value, labeled **Adj. Mean**, is the mean predicted from the model adjusted for the covariates. The column labeled **Est. Mean** contains the predicted means without correcting for covariates. When covariates are present, the differences between the adjusted and estimated means provide an indication of the effectiveness of the covariate adjustment (see Finn, 1974). For a complete factorial design without covariates, the observed, adjusted and estimated means will always be equal. The difference between them, the residual, will also be equal to 0.

If the design is not a full-factorial model, the observed means and those predicted using the parameter estimates will differ. Consider Figure 3.27b, which contains a table of means for the main-effects-only model. The observed cell means are no longer equal to those predicted by the model. The difference between the observed and estimated mean is shown in the column labeled **Raw Resid**. The residual divided by the error standard deviation is shown in the column labeled **Std. Resid.** From this table it is possible to identify cells for which the model does not fit well.

Figure 3.27a   Table of predicted means

```
MANOVA BALOMEAN BALCMEAN SSTMEAN PP BY SEX (1,2) FIELD (1,3)
   /PMEANS=TABLES(SEX BY FIELD)
   /DESIGN.
```

```
Adjusted and Estimated Means
Variable .. BALOMEAN
   CELL      Obs. Mean    Adj. Mean    Est. Mean   Raw Resid. Std. Resid.

      1         9.181        9.181        9.181        0.0        0.0
      2         9.659        9.659        9.659        0.0        0.0
      3        10.082       10.082       10.082        0.0        0.0
      4        11.710       11.710       11.710        0.0        0.0
      5        14.072       14.072       14.072        0.0        0.0
      6        13.815       13.815       13.815        0.0        0.0
```

It is also possible to obtain various combinations of the adjusted means. For example, Figure 3.27b contains the combined adjusted means for the SEX and FIELD variables for the main effects design. The means are labeled as unweighted, since the sample sizes in the cells are not used when means are combined over the categories of a variable.

Figure 3.27b   Table of predicted means

```
MANOVA BALOMEAN BALCMEAN SSTMEAN PP BY SEX (1,2) FIELD (1,3)
   /PMEANS=TABLES(SEX,FIELD)
   /DESIGN SEX FIELD.
```

```
Adjusted and Estimated Means
Variable .. BALOMEAN
   CELL      Obs. Mean    Adj. Mean    Est. Mean   Raw Resid. Std. Resid.

      1         9.181        8.410        8.410       .771       .136
      2         9.659       10.062       10.062      -.403      -.071
      3        10.082       10.123       10.123      -.041      -.007
      4        11.710       12.033       12.033      -.323      -.057
      5        14.072       13.686       13.686       .386       .068
      6        13.815       13.747       13.747       .068       .012

Combined Adjusted Means for SEX
Variable .. BALOMEAN
         SEX
           1       UNWGT.      9.53176
           2       UNWGT.     13.15531

Combined Adjusted Means for FIELD
Variable .. BALOMEAN
         FIELD
           1       UNWGT.     10.22132
           2       UNWGT.     11.87418
           3       UNWGT.     11.93510
```

3.28
Some Final Comments

In this chapter, only the most basic aspects of multivariate analysis of variance have been covered. The MANOVA procedure is capable of testing more elaborate models of several types. Chapter 4 considers a special class of designs called repeated measures designs. In such designs, the same variable or variables are measured on several occassions. For further discussion about multivariate analysis of variance, consult Morrison (1967) and Tatsuoka (1971).

3.29
RUNNING
PROCEDURE MANOVA

MANOVA is a generalized analysis of variance and covariance program that performs both univariate and multivariate procedures. You can analyze such designs as block, split-plot, nested, and repeated measures designs. (Repeated measures designs and the MANOVA commands needed to analyze them are discussed in Chapter 4.) MANOVA can also be used to obtain multivariate regression coefficients, principal components, discriminant function coefficients, canonical correlations, and other statistics.

A program with so many facilities naturally has a large number of subcommands available. This section concentrates on the most commonly used subcommands and briefly describes the rest. The repeated measures subcommands WSFACTORS, WSDESIGN, and RENAME are discussed in Chapter 4. For further information and examples, see Command Reference: MANOVA.

3.30
Specifying Factors and the Structure of the Data

To run MANOVA, you must indicate which variables are dependent variables, which (if any) are factors, and which (if any) are covariates. You also need to specify the design to be used.

The simplest MANOVA specification is a list of variables. If no other subcommands or keywords are used, all variables listed are treated as dependent variables and a one-sample Hotelling's T^2 is calculated. Thus, the output in Figure 3.9d was produced by specifying

```
MANOVA BALOMEAN BALCMEAN SSTMEAN PP.
```

3.31
The Dependent Variable List

The first variables specified are the dependent variables in the analysis. By default, MANOVA treats a list of dependent variables as jointly dependent and therefore uses a multivariate design. This default can be changed by using the ANALYSIS subcommand (see Section 3.34).

3.32
The Factor List

If factors are to be used in the analysis, they are specified following the dependent variable list and the keyword BY. Each factor is followed by two integer values enclosed in parentheses and separated by a comma, specifying the lowest and highest values for the factor. For example,

```
MANOVA BALOMEAN BALCMEAN SSTMEAN PP BY SEX(1,2) FIELD(1,3).
```

indicates that there are two factors: SEX with possible values 1 and 2, and FIELD with possible values 1, 2, and 3. Cases with values outside the range specified are excluded from the analysis. Since MANOVA requires factor levels to be integer, you need to recode any noninteger factor values. Factors with empty categories must also be recoded, since MANOVA expects the levels of a factor to be adjacent.

If several factors have the same value range, you can specify a list of factors followed by a single value range, in parentheses, as in the command

```
MANOVA SALES BY TVAD RADIOAD MAGAD NEWSPAD(2,5).
```

Certain analyses, such as regression, canonical correlation, and the one-sample Hotelling's T^2, do not require a factor specification. For these analyses, the factor list and the keyword BY should be omitted.

3.33
The Covariate List

The covariate list specifies any covariates to be used in the analysis. It follows the factor list and is separated from it by the keyword WITH, as in

```
MANOVA BALOMEAN BALCMEAN SSTMEAN PP BY SEX(1,2) FIELD(1,3) WITH IQ.
```

3.34
Specifying the Model

Use the ANALYSIS subcommand to specify a model based on a subset of variables in the variable list. You can also use ANALYSIS to change the model specified in the variable list by changing dependent variables to covariates or covariates to dependent variables. When ANALYSIS is specified, it completely overrides the dependent variable list and covariate list in the MANOVA specification, but it does not affect the factors. Only variables in the original MANOVA variable list (or covariate list) can be specified on the ANALYSIS subcommand, as in

```
MANOVA BALOMEAN BALCMEAN SSTMEAN PP BY SEX(1,2) FIELD(1,3) WITH IQ
    /ANALYSIS=BALOMEAN BALCMEAN PP WITH SSTMEAN.
```

This command changes SSTMEAN from a dependent variable to a covariate. The command

```
MANOVA BALOMEAN BALCMEAN SSTMEAN BY SEX(1,2) FIELD(1,3) WITH IQ PP
    /ANALYSIS=BALOMEAN BALCMEAN SSTMEAN PP WITH IQ.
```

changes PP from a covariate to a dependent variable. The factors SEX and FIELD are still used in the analysis (unless eliminated with a DESIGN subcommand; see Section 3.35).

Dependent variables or covariates can be eliminated from the analysis, as in

```
MANOVA SALES OPINION BY TVAD RADIOAD NEWSPAD(2,5) WITH PCTBUSNS
   /ANALYSIS=OPINION.
```

which deletes the variables SALES and PCTBUSNS from the analysis.

Although only one ANALYSIS subcommand can be specified per DESIGN subcommand, a single ANALYSIS subcommand can be used to obtain multiple analyses, as long as the lists of dependent variables do not overlap. For example, the command

```
MANOVA BALOMEAN BALCMEAN SSTMEAN PP BY SEX(1,2) FIELD (1,3)
     WITH EDUC IQ
   /ANALYSIS=(BALOMEAN BALCMEAN /SSTMEAN /PP WITH IQ).
```

specifies three analyses. The first has BALOMEAN and BALCMEAN as dependent variables and no covariates, the second has SSTMEAN as the dependent variable and no covariates, and the third has PP as the dependent variable and IQ as a covariate. (Note that none of the variable lists overlap.) Although three separate ANALYSIS and DESIGN subcommands could be used to get the same results, this would increase processing time.

To request three separate analyses with EDUC as the covariate for all of them, specify

```
MANOVA BALOMEAN BALCMEAN SSTMEAN PP BY SEX (1,2) FIELD(1,3)
     WITH EDUC IQ
   /ANALYSIS=(BALOMEAN BALCMEAN /SSTMEAN /PP WITH IQ) WITH EDUC
   /DESIGN.
```

This is equivalent to

```
MANOVA BALOMEAN BALCMEAN SSTMEAN PP BY SEX(1,2) FIELD(1,3)
     WITH EDUC IQ
   /ANALYSIS=BALOMEAN BALCMEAN WITH EDUC
   /DESIGN
   /ANALYSIS=SSTMEAN WITH EDUC
   /DESIGN
   /ANALYSIS=PP WITH IQ EDUC
   /DESIGN.
```

When specifying multiple analyses in this fashion, you may sometimes find the keywords CONDITIONAL and UNCONDITIONAL useful. CONDITIONAL indicates that subsequent variable lists should include as covariates all previous dependent variables on that ANALYSIS subcommand. UNCONDITIONAL (the default) indicates that each list should be used as is, independent of the others. For example, the command

```
MANOVA SALES LEADS OPINIONS CONTRACT BY TVAD RADIOAD MAGAD
NEWSPAD(2,5)
     WITH PCTHOMES PCTBUSNS
   /ANALYSIS(CONDITIONAL)=(LEADS OPINIONS CONTRACT/SALES) WITH
PCTBUSNS
   /DESIGN.
```

is equivalent to

```
MANOVA SALES LEADS OPINIONS CONTRACT BY TVAD RADIOAD MAGAD
NEWSPAD(2,5)
     WITH PCTHOMES PCTBUSNS
   /ANALYSIS=LEADS OPINIONS CONTRACT WITH PCTBUSNS
   /DESIGN
   /ANALYSIS=SALES WITH LEADS OPINIONS CONTRACT PCTBUSNS
   /DESIGN.
```

3.35
Specifying the Design

Use the DESIGN subcommand to specify the structure of the model. DESIGN must be the *last* subcommand for any given model, and it can be used more than once to specify different models. The default model (obtained when DESIGN is used without further specification) is the full-factorial model.

Because of its importance the DESIGN subcommand is discussed at this point in the chapter. Remember that the other subcommands discussed later on must *precede* the DESIGN subcommand(s) to which they apply.

3.36
Specifying Effects

When a full-factorial model is not desired, the DESIGN subcommand can be used to specify the effects in the model. The format is simply

```
/DESIGN=list of effects
```

with the effects separated by blanks or commas. For example, a model with only main effects is specified by the command

```
MANOVA BALOMEAN BALCMEAN SSTMEAN PP BY SEX(1,2) FIELD(1,3)
  /DESIGN=SEX FIELD.
```

Interaction terms are indicated with the keyword BY, so that the command

```
MANOVA SALES BY TVAD RADIOAD MAGAD NEWSPAD(2,5)
  /DESIGN=TVAD RADIOAD MAGAD NEWSPAD TVAD BY RADIOAD TVAD BY RADIOAD
        BY NEWSPAD.
```

specifies a model with all main effects, the two-way interaction between TVAD and RADIOAD, and the three-way interaction between TVAD, RADIOAD, and NEWSPAD.

If single-degree-of-freedom effects are to be included, a PARTITION subcommand may be used before specifying these effects in the DESIGN subcommand, as in

```
MANOVA RELIEF BY DRUG(1,4)
  /CONTRAST(DRUG)=SPECIAL(1 1 1 1, 1 -1 0 0, 4 4 -8 0, 4 4 1 -9)
  /PARTITION(DRUG)
  /DESIGN=DRUG(1) DRUG(2) DRUG(3).
```

The above command is equivalent to

```
MANOVA RELIEF BY DRUG(1,4)
  /CONTRAST(DRUG)=SPECIAL(1 1 1 1, 1 -1 0 0, 4 4 -8 0, 4 4 1 -9)
  /DESIGN=DRUG(1) DRUG(2) DRUG(3).
```

For further information about the PARTITION subcommand, see Section 3.46. For the CONTRAST subcommand, see Section 3.47.

The keyword POOL is used with DESIGN to incorporate continuous variables into a single effect. The variables to be incorporated must not have been specified in the previous ANALYSIS subcommand as dependent variables or covariates. When you use POOL on DESIGN, dependent variables must be defined with an ANALYSIS subcommand. For example, the command

```
MANOVA SALES TEST1 TEST2 TEST3 BY TVAD RADIOAD MAGAD NEWSPAD(2,5)
        WITH PCTBUSNS
  /ANALYSIS=SALES WITH PCTBUSNS
  /DESIGN=POOL(TEST1 TEST2 TEST3).
```

incorporates TEST1, TEST2, and TEST3 into a single effect with three degrees of freedom. See Command Reference: MANOVA for further information about POOL.

To specify interactions between factors and continuous variables, simply list these interaction effects on the DESIGN subcommand using keyword BY. You cannot specify interactions between two continuous variables (including covariates), and you cannot use variables that are included in the model by an ANALYSIS subcommand.

Effects can be pooled together into a single effect by using a plus sign. For example,

```
/DESIGN=TVAD + TVAD BY RADIOAD
```

combines the effects of TVAD and TVAD BY RADIOAD into a single effect. (The BY keyword is evaluated before the plus sign.)

To obtain estimates that consist of the sum of the constant term and the parameter values, use the MUPLUS keyword. The constant term μ is then combined with the parameter following the MUPLUS keyword. For example, if the subcommand

```
/DESIGN=MUPLUS SEX
```

is specified, the mean of each dependent variable is added to the SEX parameters for that variable. This produces conditional means or "marginals" for each dependent variable. Since these means are adjusted for any covariates in the model, they are also the usual adjusted means when covariates are present. When the adjusted means cannot be estimated, MUPLUS produces estimates of the constant plus the requested effect. These are no longer the predicted means.

The MUPLUS approach is the only way you can obtain the standard errors of the conditional means. (However, conditional and adjusted means can be obtained by using the OMEANS and PMEANS subcommands; see Section 3.48). You can obtain unweighted conditional means for a main effect by specifying the full factorial model and specifying MUPLUS before the effect whose means are to be found. (For an interaction effect, the DESIGN should not include any lower-order effects contained in it.) For example, the subcommand

```
/DESIGN=MUPLUS SEX FIELD SEX BY FIELD
```

obtains the unweighted marginal means for SEX in a two-factor design. Only one MUPLUS keyword may be used per DESIGN subcommand.

Although MANOVA automatically includes the constant term (the correction for the mean), it will not be included if you specify NOCONSTANT on a METHOD subcommand. You can override NOCONSTANT by specifying CONSTANT on the DESIGN subcommand. A variable named CONSTANT is not recognized on DESIGN.

3.37
Specifying Nested Designs

The WITHIN keyword, or W, indicates that the term to its left is nested in the term to its right. For example, the subcommand

```
/DESIGN=TREATMNT WITHIN TESTCAT
```

indicates that TREATMNT is nested within TESTCAT, while the subcommand

```
/DESIGN=TREATMNT WITHIN TESTCAT BY EDUC BY MOTIVTN
```

indicates that TREATMNT is nested within the interaction TESTCAT by EDUC by MOTIVTN.

3.38
Specifying Error Terms

Error terms for individual effects are specified on the DESIGN subcommand with the following keywords:

WITHIN   *Within-cells error terms.* Alias W.
RESIDUAL   *Residual error terms.* Alias R.
WITHIN+RESIDUAL   *Combined within-cells and residual error terms.* Alias WR or RW.

To test a term against one of these error terms, specify the term to be tested, followed by the VS keyword and the error-term keyword. For example, to test the SEX BY FIELD term against the residual error term, specify

```
/DESIGN=SEX BY FIELD VS RESIDUAL
```

You can also create up to ten user-defined error terms by declaring any term in the model as an error term. To create such a term, specify the term followed by an equals sign and an integer from 1 to 10 on the DESIGN subcommand, as in

```
/DESIGN=SEX BY FIELD=1 FIELD VS 1 SEX VS 1
```

This command designates the SEX by FIELD term as error term 1, which is then used to test the sex and field main effects. To use a special error term in a test of significance, specify

```
term=n  VS  error-term keyword
```

or

```
term  VS  term=n
```

Any term present in the design but not specified on DESIGN is lumped into the residual error term. The default error term for all tests is WITHIN.

3.39
Specifying the Error Term

To specify the default error term for each between-subjects effect in subsequent designs, use the ERROR subcommand with the following keywords:

WITHIN   *Within-cells error term.* Alias W.
RESIDUAL   *Residual error term.* Alias R.
WITHIN+RESIDUAL *Pooled within-class and residual error terms.* Alias WR or RW.
n   *Model term.*

You can designate a model term *(n)* as the default error term only if you explicitly define error term numbers on the DESIGN subcommand. If the specified error term number is not defined for a particular design, MANOVA does not carry out the significance tests involving that error term, although the parameter estimates and hypothesis sums of squares will be computed. For example, if the command

```
MANOVA BALOMEAN BALCMEAN SSTMEAN PP BY SEX(1,2) FIELD(1,3)
    /ERROR=1
    /DESIGN=SEX FIELD SEX BY FIELD=1
    /DESIGN=SEX FIELD.
```

is specified, no significance tests for SEX or FIELD are displayed for the second design, which contains no term defined as error term 1.

3.40
Specifying Within-Subjects Factors

The WSFACTORS subcommand is used for repeated measures analysis (see Chapter 4). It provides the names and number of levels for within-subjects factors when you use the multivariate data setup. For example, to supply a within-subjects factor name for DRUG1 to DRUG4, specify

```
MANOVA DRUG1 TO DRUG4
    /WSFACTORS=TRIAL(4).
```

Each name follows the naming conventions of SPSS/PC+, and each name must be unique. That is, a within-subjects factor name cannot be the same as that of any dependent variable, between-subjects factor, or covariate in the MANOVA job. The within-subjects factors exist only during the MANOVA analysis.

WSFACTORS must be the first subcommand after the MANOVA specification, and it can be specified only once per MANOVA command. You can specify up to 20 within-subjects and grouping factors altogether. Presence of a WSFACTORS subcommand invokes special repeated-measures processing. See Chapter 4 for a complete discussion of the WSFACTORS subcommand.

3.41
Specifying a Within-Subjects Model

The WSDESIGN subcommand specifies a within-subjects model and a within-subjects transformation matrix based on the ordering of the continuous variables and the levels of the within-subjects factors. See Chapter 4 for a complete discussion of the WSDESIGN subcommand.

3.42
Analyzing Doubly Multivariate Designs

You can use SPSS/PC+ MANOVA to analyze doubly multivariate repeated measures designs, in which subjects are measured on two or more responses on two or more occasions. When the data are entered using the multivariate setup, you can use the MEASURE subcommand to name the multivariate pooled results, as in

```
MANOVA TEMP1 TO TEMP6, WEIGHT1 TO WEIGHT6 BY GROUP(1,4)
  /WSFACTOR=AMPM(2), DAYS(3)
  /MEASURE=TEMP WEIGHT
  /WSDESIGN=AMPM DAYS, AMPM BY DAYS.
```

See Chapter 4 for a discussion of the MEASURE subcommand.

3.43
Specifying Linear Transformations

To specify linear transformations of the dependent variables and covariates, use the TRANSFORM subcommand. The first specification on TRANSFORM is the list of variables to be transformed in parentheses. Multiple variable lists can be used if they are separated by slashes and each list contains the same number of variables. MANOVA then applies the indicated transformation to each list. By default, MANOVA transforms all dependent variables and covariates. If a list is specified, however, only variables included in the list are transformed.

Any number of TRANSFORM subcommands may be specified in a MANOVA command. A TRANSFORM subcommand remains in effect until MANOVA encounters another one. Transformations are *not* cumulative; each transformation applies to the original variables.

Transformed variables should be renamed to avoid possible confusion with the original variables. If you use TRANSFORM but do not supply a RENAME subcommand, MANOVA names the transformed variables T1, T2, and so on. You must use the new names for the continuous variables in all subsequent subcommands except OMEANS.

Seven types of transformations are available. These are

DEVIATIONS(refcat) *Compare a dependent variable to the means of the dependent variables in the list.* By default, MANOVA omits the comparison of the last variable to the list of variables. You can omit a variable other than the last by specifying the number of the omitted variable in parentheses.

DIFFERENCE *Compare a dependent variable with the mean of the previous dependent variables in the list.* Also known as reverse Helmert.

HELMERT *Compare a dependent variable to the means of the subsequent dependent variables in the list.*

SIMPLE(refcat) *Compare each dependent variable with the last.* You can specify a variable other than the last as the reference variable by giving the number of the variable in parentheses.

REPEATED *Compare contiguous variable pairs, thereby producing difference scores.*

POLYNOMIAL(metric) *Fit orthogonal polynomials to the variables in the transformation list.* The default metric is equal spacing, but you can specify your own metric.

SPECIAL(matrix) *Fit your own transformation matrix reflecting combinations of interest.* The matrix must be square, with the number of rows and columns equal to the number of variables being transformed.

For example, the subcommand

```
/TRANSFORM(SALES LEADS OPINIONS CONTRACT)=POLYNOMIAL
```

fits orthogonal polynomials to variables SALES, LEADS, OPINIONS, and CONTRACT, with equal spacing assumed.

B

Statistics Guide

The type of transformation can be preceded by the keywords CONTRAST, BASIS, or ORTHONORM. CONTRAST and BASIS are alternatives; ORTHO-NORM may be used with either CONTRAST or BASIS, or alone, which implies CONTRAST.

CONTRAST *Generate the transformation matrix directly from the contrast matrix of the given type.* This is the default.

BASIS *Generate the transformation matrix from the one-way basis corresponding to the specified CONTRAST.*

ORTHONORM *Orthonormalize the transformation matrix by rows before use.* MANOVA does not, by default, orthonormalize rows.

CONTRAST or BASIS can be used with any of the available methods for defining contrasts on the CONTRAST subcommand (see Section 3.47). On the TRANS-FORM subcommand, keywords CONTRAST and BASIS are used to generate the transformed variables for later analysis, rather than simply to specify the contrasts on which significance testing and parameter estimation will be based.

For further information on the TRANSFORM subcommand, see Command Reference: MANOVA.

3.44
Renaming Transformed Variables

Use the RENAME subcommand to rename dependent variables and covariates after they have been transformed using TRANSFORM or WSFACTORS. The format is

```
/RENAME=newname1 newname2 ... newnamek
```

The number of new names must be equal to the number of dependent variables and covariates. For further information about RENAME, see Command Reference: MANOVA.

3.45
Specifying the Method

The METHOD subcommand is used to control some of the computational aspects of MANOVA. The following keywords are available:

MODELTYPE *The model for parameter estimation.*
ESTIMATION *The method for estimating parameters.*
SSTYPE *The method of partitioning sums of squares.*

Each keyword has associated options as listed below. These options are specified in parentheses after the keyword.

The options available on **MODELTYPE** are

MEANS *Use the cell-means model for parameter estimation.*
OBSERVATIONS *Use the observations model for parameter estimation.*

If continuous variables are specified on the DESIGN subcommand, MANOVA automatically uses the observations model. Otherwise, MEANS is the default. Since the observations model is computationally less efficient than the means model and the same estimates are obtained, the observations model should be used only when it is appropriate.

Up to four keywords, one from each of the following pairs, may be specified on **ESTIMATION**. The first keyword in each pair is the default.

QR/CHOLESKY QR estimates parameters using the Householder transformations to effect an orthogonal decomposition of the design matrix. A less expensive (and sometimes less accurate) procedure is the Cholesky method, selected by specifying the alternative CHOLESKY keyword.

NOBALANCED/BALANCED NOBALANCED assumes that the design is unbalanced. If your design is balanced and orthogonal, request balanced processing by specifying the alternative BAL-ANCED keyword. BALANCED should be specified only when no cell is empty, the cell-means model applies, all cell sizes are equal, and the contrast type for each factor is orthogonal.

NOLASTRES/LASTRES   NOLASTRES calculates sums of squares for all effects. The alternative LASTRES keyword computes the last effect in the design by subtracting the between-groups sums of squares and cross-products from the total sums of squares and cross-products. When applicable, LASTRES can significantly decrease processing costs. Parameter estimates will not be available for the effect whose sum of squares was computed by subtraction. If LASTRES is specified, you may not use the POOL specification on DESIGN to include continuous variables in the last effect (see Section 3.36). Do not use LASTRES unless you have specified SEQUENTIAL for the SSTYPE parameter (see below). It should not be used with UNIQUE (the default) since component sums of squares do not add up to the total sum of squares in a UNIQUE decomposition.

CONSTANT/NOCONSTANT   CONSTANT requests that the model contain a constant term. The alternative keyword NOCONSTANT suppresses the constant term. NOCONSTANT can be overridden on a subsequent DESIGN subcommand (see Section 3.36).

The following options may be specified on **SSTYPE**:

UNIQUE   *Requests sums of squares corresponding to unweighted combinations of means* (the regression approach). These sums of squares are not orthogonal unless the design is balanced. SSTYPE(UNIQUE) is the default.

SEQUENTIAL *Requests an orthogonal decomposition of the sums of squares.* A term is corrected for all terms to its left in a given DESIGN specification, and confounded with all terms to its right.

For example, the subcommand

```
/METHOD=ESTIMATION(CHOLESKY,LASTRES) SSTYPE(SEQUENTIAL)
```

requests the less-expensive CHOLESKY estimation method, with the sums of squares for the last effect calculated by subtraction. SEQUENTIAL decomposition is requested, as is required for LASTRES. We assume that parameter estimates are not needed for the last effect and that the POOL keyword will not appear in the last effect on a DESIGN statement for this METHOD subcommand.

3.46
Subdividing the Degrees of Freedom

The degrees of freedom associated with a factor can be subdivided by using a PARTITION subcommand. Specify the factor name in parentheses, an equals sign, and a list of integers in parentheses indicating the degrees of freedom for each partition. For example, if EDUCATN has six values (five degrees of freedom), it can be partitioned into single degrees of freedom by specifying

```
/PARTITION(EDUCATN)=(1,1,1,1,1)
```

or, more briefly, by specifying

```
/PARTITION(EDUCATN)=(5*1)
```

Since the default degrees-of-freedom partition consists of the single degrees-of-freedom partition, these subcommands are equivalent to

```
/PARTITION(EDUCATN)
```

The subcommand

```
/PARTITION(EDUCATN)=(2,2,1)
```

partitions EDUCATN into three subdivisions, the first two with 2 degrees of freedom and the third with 1 degree of freedom. This subcommand can also be specified as

```
/PARTITION(EDUCATN)=(2,2)
```

since MANOVA automatically generates a final partition with the remaining degree(s) of freedom (1 in this case). If you were to then specify ED(1) on the DESIGN subcommand, it would refer to the first partition, which in this case has 2 degrees of freedom.

3.47
Specifying the Contrasts

The contrasts desired for a factor are specified by the CONTRAST subcommand. Specify the factor name in parentheses, followed by an equals sign and a contrast keyword. The contrast keyword can be any of the following:

DEVIATION   *The deviations from the grand mean.* This is the default.

DIFFERENCE   *Difference or reverse Helmert contrast.* Compare levels of a factor with the mean of the previous levels of the factor.

SIMPLE   *Simple contrasts.* Compare each level of a factor to the last level.

HELMERT   *Helmert contrasts.* Compare levels of a factor with the mean of the subsequent levels of the factor.

POLYNOMIAL   *Orthogonal polynomial contrasts.*

REPEATED   *Adjacent levels of a factor.*

SPECIAL   *A user-defined contrast.* See the example in Section 3.36.

If you want to see the parameter estimates of the specified contrast, use PRINT=PARAM(ESTIM).

3.48
Specifying Printed Output

The PRINT and NOPRINT subcommands control the output produced by MANOVA. PRINT requests specified output, while NOPRINT suppresses it. On both PRINT and NOPRINT, you specify keywords followed by the keyword options in parentheses. For example, the command

```
MANOVA SALES BY TVAD RADIOAD MAGAD NEWSPAD(2,5)
  /PRINT=CELLINFO(MEANS).
```

requests the display of cell means of SALES for all combinations of values of TVAD, RADIOAD, MAGAD, and NEWSPAD.

The specifications available on PRINT and NOPRINT are listed below, followed by the options available for each.

CELLINFO   *Cells information.*

HOMOGENEITY   *Homogeneity of variance tests.*

DESIGN   *Design information.*

ERROR   *Error matrices.*

SIGNIF   *Significance tests.*

PARAMETERS   *Estimated parameters.*

TRANSFORM   *Transformation matrix.*

The options for **CELLINFO** are

MEANS   *Cell means, standard deviations, and counts.*

SSCP   *Cell sums-of-squares and cross-products matrices.*

COV   *Cell variance-covariance matrices.*

COR   *Cell correlation matrices.*

The options for **HOMOGENEITY** are

BARTLETT   *Bartlett-Box F test.*

COCHRAN   *Cochran's C.*

BOXM   *Box's M (multivariate case only).*

The options for **DESIGN** are

ONEWAY	*The one-way basis for each factor.*
OVERALL	*The overall reduced-model basis (design matrix).*
DECOMP	*The QR/CHOLESKY decomposition of the design.*
BIAS	*Contamination coefficients displaying the bias present in the design.*
SOLUTION	*Coefficients of the linear combination of the cell means being tested.*

The options available for **ERROR** are

SSCP	*Error sums-of-squares and cross-product matrix.*
COV	*Error variance-covariance matrix.*
COR	*Error correlation matrix and standard deviations.*
STDDEV	*Error standard deviations (univariate case).*

If ERROR(COR) is specified in the multivariate case, MANOVA automatically displays the determinant and Bartlett's test of sphericity.

The options for **SIGNIF** are

MULTIV	*Multivariate* F *tests for group differences* (default display).
EIGEN	*Eigenvalues of $S_h S_e^{-1}$.*
DIMENR	*A dimension-reduction analysis.*
UNIV	*Univariate* F *tests* (default display).
HYPOTH	*The hypothesis SSCP matrix.*
STEPDOWN	*Roy-Bargmann step-down* F *tests.*
AVERF	*An averaged* F *test.* Use with repeated measures (default display for repeated measures).
BRIEF	*A shortened multivariate output.* BRIEF overrides any of the preceding SIGNIF keywords.
AVONLY	*Averaged results only.* Use with repeated measures (overrides other SIGNIF keywords).
SINGLEDF	*Single-degree-of-freedom listings of effects.*

When BRIEF is used, the output consists of a table similar in appearance to a univariate ANOVA table, but with the generalized *F* and Wilks' lambda replacing the univariate *F*.

The options available for **PARAMETERS** are

ESTIM	*The estimates themselves, along with their standard errors, t-tests, and confidence intervals.*
ORTHO	*The orthogonal estimates of parameters used to produce the sums of squares.*
COR	*Correlations between the parameters.*
NEGSUM	*For main effects, the negative sum of the other parameters* (representing the parameter for the omitted category).

Parameters are not displayed by default.

TRANSFORM produces the transformation matrix, which shows how MANOVA transforms variables when a multivariate repeated measures design and a WSFACTORS subcommand are used (see Chapter 4). There are no subspecifications for PRINT=TRANSFORM.

3.49
Specifying Principal Components Analysis

The PCOMPS subcommand produces a principal components analysis of the error sums-of-squares and cross-products matrices in a multivariate design. The options for the PCOMPS subcommand are

COR	*Principal components analysis of the error correlation matrix.*
COV	*Principal components analysis of the error variance-covariance matrix.*
ROTATE(rottype)	*Rotation of the principal component loadings.* For rottype, substitute VARIMAX, EQUAMAX, QUARTIMAX, or NOROTATE.

NCOMP(n)   *The number of principal components to be rotated.* Specify *n*, or let *n* default to all components extracted.

MINEIGEN(eigcut)   *The eigenvalue cutoff value for principal components extraction.*

3.50
Specifying Canonical Analyses

The DISCRIM subcommand requests a canonical analysis of dependent and independent variables in multivariate analyses. If the independent variables are continuous, MANOVA produces a canonical correlation analysis; if they are categorical, MANOVA produces a canonical discriminant analysis. Available options are

RAW   *Raw discriminant function coefficients.*

STAN   *Standardized discriminant function coefficients.*

ESTIM   *Effect estimates in discriminant function space.*

COR   *Correlations between the dependent and canonical variables defined by the discriminant functions.*

ROTATE(rottyp) *Rotation of the matrix of correlations between dependent and canonical variates.* For rottype, specify VARIMAX, EQUAMAX, or QUARTIMAX.

ALPHA(alpha)   *The significance level for the canonical variate.* The default is 0.15.

MANOVA does not perform rotation unless there are at least two significant canonical variates.

3.51
Producing Tables of Combined Observed Means

OMEANS produces tables of combined observed means. The specifications on OMEANS may consist of the keywords VARIABLES, TABLES, or both. With no specifications, the OMEANS subcommand produces a table of observed means for all of the continuous variables. The keyword VARIABLES allows you to enter, in parentheses, names of the dependent variables and covariates for which means are desired. When you explicitly specify variables on the OMEANS subcommand, you must also enter a TABLES specification as described below, as in

```
MANOVA BALOMEAN BALCMEAN SSTMEAN PP BY SEX(1,2) FIELD(1,3)
  /OMEANS VARIABLES(BALOMEAN) TABLES(SEX BY FIELD).
```

If the variable list is omitted, MANOVA displays combined means for all variables. MANOVA also displays both weighted and unweighted means. Tables of observed means are displayed if the keyword TABLES is used, with a list of *factors* by which the tables should be displayed. The subcommand

```
 /OMEANS TABLES(SEX,FIELD,SEX BY FIELD)
```

results in three tables, one collapsed over SEX, one collapsed over FIELD, and one showing the observed means themselves.

When a transformation has been requested with TRANSFORM or with WSFACTORS (described in repeated-measures MANOVA), OMEANS produces means of the original, untransformed variables. Always use the original variable names in the VARIABLES specification on OMEANS.

3.52
Computing Predicted and Adjusted Means

PMEANS computes predicted and adjusted (for covariates) means, which are displayed for each error term in each design. VARIABLES and TABLES are two specifications that can be used; the format is the same as that for OMEANS. For designs with covariates and multiple error terms, use the ERROR(error) specification to indicate which error term's regression coefficients to use in calculating the predicted means. The format for specifying an error term with ERROR is the same as for the ERROR subcommand (see Section 3.39). If no error term is given when one is needed, MANOVA will not calculate predicted means. Predicted means are also suppressed if the last term is being calculated by subtraction (METHOD=

ESTIM(LASTRES)) or if the design contains the MUPLUS keyword (see Section 3.36).

If the WSFACTORS subcommand is used to specify a repeated measures design (see Chapter 4), the means of the orthonormalized variables are displayed when PMEANS is used. If the TRANSFORM or WSFACTORS subcommands are used for a design, PMEANS displays the means of the transformed variables. Therefore the VARIABLES specification on PMEANS, unlike that on OMEANS, uses the names of the *transformed* variables in analyses which use the WSFACTORS or TRANSFORM subcommand. These are either the names you specify on the RENAME subcommand, or the names supplied by SPSS/PC+ if there is no RENAME subcommand (T1, T2, etc.). The keyword PLOT on the PMEANS subcommand produces a group-order plot of the estimated, adjusted, and observed means for each dependent variable, and a group-order plot of the mean residuals for each dependent variable. When there is more than one factor in the analysis, the rightmost factor changes most quickly.

3.53
Producing Residual Listings and Plots

The RESIDUALS subcommand produces listings or plots of predicted values and residuals. Casewise listings of residuals are produced by the keyword CASEWISE. This output includes, for each case, the observed and predicted value of each dependent variable, the residual, and the standardized residual. Like PMEANS, RESIDUALS requires an ERROR specification for designs with covariates and multiple error terms, as in

```
MANOVA SALES BY TVAD RADIOAD(2,5) WITH PCTBUSNS
  /RESIDUALS=CASEWISE ERROR(WITHIN)
  /DESIGN TVAD VS 1,RADIOAD VS 1, TVAD BY RADIOAD = 1 VS WITHIN.
```

There will be no output if the error term is not specified when needed. Predicted observations will be suppressed if the last term is calculated by subtraction (METHOD=ESTIM(LASTRES)) or if the DESIGN subcommand contains the MUPLUS keyword. If the designated error term does not exist for a given design, no predicted values or residuals are calculated.

The keyword PLOT on the RESIDUALS subcommand displays the following plots: observed values vs. standardized residuals, predicted values vs. standardized residuals, case number vs. standardized residuals, a normal probability plot, and a detrended normal probability plot for the standardized residuals.

3.54
Producing Plots

Plots are requested with the PLOT subcommand. The following keywords are available:

CELLPLOTS   *Plot cell statistics,* including a plot of cell means vs. cell variances, a plot of cell means vs. cell standard deviations, and a histogram of cell means, for each of the continuous variables (dependent variables and covariates) defined in the MANOVA specification.

BOXPLOTS   *Plot a boxplot for each continuous variable.*

NORMAL   *Plot a normal plot and a detrended normal plot* for each continuous variable.

STEMLEAF   *Plot a stem-and-leaf display* for each continuous variable.

ZCORR   *Plot a half-normal plot* of the within-cells correlations between the dependent variables in a multivariate analysis.

If there is not enough memory to produce a plot, MANOVA displays a warning and does not produce the plot.

3.55
Reading and Writing Matrix Materials

MANOVA can write out a set of matrix materials, which it can then use for subsequent jobs. The WRITE subcommand is used to write these materials and the READ subcommand to read them. The WRITE subcommand has the format

```
/WRITE
```

This sends results to the "resulting file," which by default is named SPSS.PRC.

The READ subcommand reads the materials written by using WRITE and has the format

```
/READ
```

READ is used in conjunction with the DATA LIST MATRIX statement. For details, see Command Reference: DATA LIST Matrix Materials.

3.56
Missing Value Treatment

By default, missing values for any of the variables named in the MANOVA specification are excluded from the analysis. To include user-missing values in the analysis, enter the subcommand MISSING=INCLUDE. The alternative specification, MISSING=LISTWISE, is the default. The missing subcommand can be used only once.

The missing values for factors must be within the ranges specified on the MANOVA variables specification in order to be included in the analysis.

3.57
Annotated Example

The following SPSS/PC+ commands produced the output in Figures 3.15b, 3.15c, 3.15d, 3.15f, and 3.16.

```
DATA LIST FREE/X1 TO X22.
IF    (X1 LT 200) SEX=1.
IF    (X1 GE 200) SEX=2.
COMPUTE BALOMEAN=(X10+X11)/2.
COMPUTE  BALCMEAN=(X12+X13)/2.
COMPUTE SSTMEAN=(X14+X15+X16)/3.
COMPUTE PP=(X17+X18+X19+X20+X21+X22)/6.
BEGIN DATA.
data records
END DATA.
MANOVA BALOMEAN BALCMEAN SSTMEAN PP BY SEX(1,2)
  /DISCRIM=RAW STAN CORR ESTIM
   /PRINT=SIGNIF(DIMENR) PARAMETERS(ESTIM)
   /DESIGN.
FINISH.
```

- The DATA LIST command reads in the variables in freefield format.
- The IF commands set up the variable SEX.
- The COMPUTE statements compute the dependent variables as averages of the original variables.
- The MANOVA command begins by specifying BALOMEAN, BALCMEAN, SSTMEAN and PP as the dependent variables and SEX as a factor. The DISCRIM subcommand requests a canonical analysis of the dependent and independent variables. The PRINT subcommand requests parameter estimates and a dimension-reduction analysis.

Contents _____

4 Repeated Measures Analysis of Variance: More on Procedure MANOVA

Anyone who experiences difficulties sorting through piles of output, stacks of bills, or assorted journals must be awed by the brain's ability to organize, update, and maintain the memories of a lifetime. It seems incredible that someone can instantly recall the name of his first-grade teacher. On the other hand, that same person might spend an entire morning searching for a misplaced shoe.

Memory has two components—storage and retrieval. Many different theories explaining its magical operation have been proposed (for example, see Eysenck, 1977). In this chapter, an experiment concerned with latency—the length of time required to search a list of items in memory—is examined.

Bacon (1980) conducted an experiment in which subjects were instructed to memorize a number. They were then given a "probe" digit and told to indicate whether it was included in the memorized number. One hypothesis of interest is the relationship between the number of digits in the memorized number and the latency. Is more time required to search through a longer number than a shorter one? Twenty-four subjects were tested on 60 memorized numbers, 20 each of two, three, and four digits in random order. The average latencies, in milliseconds, were calculated for each subject on the two-, three-, and four-digit numbers. Thus, three scores are recorded for each subject, one for each of the number lengths. The probe digit was included in the memorized number in a random position.

4.1
REPEATED MEASURES

When the same variable is measured on several occasions for each subject, it is a *repeated measures* design. The simplest repeated measures design is one in which two measurements are obtained for each subject—such as pre- and post-test scores. These type of data are usually analyzed with a paired t-test.

The advantages of repeated measurements are obvious. Besides requiring fewer experimental units (in this study, human subjects), they provide a control on their differences. That is, variability due to differences between subjects can be eliminated from the experimental error. Less attention has been focused on some of the difficulties that may be encountered with repeated measurements. Broadly, these problems can be classified as the carry-over effect, the latent effect, and the order or learning effect.

The carry-over effect occurs when a new treatment is administered before the effect of a previous treatment has worn off. For example, Drug B is given while Drug A still has an effect. The carry-over effect can usually be controlled by increasing the time between treatments. In addition, special designs that allow one to assess directly the carry-over effects are available (Cochran & Cox, 1957).

The latent effect—when one treatment may activate the dormant effect of the previous treatment, or interact with the previous treatment—is not so easily countered. This effect is especially problematic in drug trials and should be considered before using a repeated measures experimental design. Usually, if a latency effect is suspected, a repeated measures design should not be used.

The learning effect occurs when the response may improve merely by repetition of a task, independent of any treatment. For example, subjects' scores on a test may improve each time they take the test. Thus, treatments that are administered later may appear to improve performance, even though they have no effect. In such situations it is important to pay particular attention to the sequencing of treatments. Learning effects can be assessed by including a control group that performs the same tasks repeatedly without receiving any treatment.

4.2
Describing the Data

In a repeated measures experiment, as well as any other, the first step is to obtain descriptive statistics. These provide some idea of the distributions of the variables as well as their average values and dispersions. Figure 4.2a contains cell means and standard deviations, as well as individual confidence intervals, for the variables P2DIGIT, P3DIGIT, and P4DIGIT. The shortest average latency time (520 milliseconds) was observed for the two-digit numbers (P2DIGIT). The longest (581 milliseconds) was observed for the four-digit numbers. A plot of the mean latency times against the number of digits is shown in Figure 4.2b. Note that there appears to be a linear relationship between the latency time and the number of digits in the memorized number.

Figure 4.2a Means and standard deviations

```
SET WIDTH=WIDE.
MANOVA P2DIGIT P3DIGIT P4DIGIT
   /PRINT=CELLINFO(MEANS)
   /DESIGN.
```

```
Cell Means and Standard Deviations
Variable .. P2DIGIT
                                    Mean    Std. Dev.        N    95 percent Conf. Interval

For entire sample                 520.583    131.366         24     465.112    576.054

 - - - - - - - - - -
Variable .. P3DIGIT
                                    Mean    Std. Dev.        N    95 percent Conf. Interval

For entire sample                 560.000    118.776         24     509.845    610.155

 - - - - - - - - - -
Variable .. P4DIGIT
                                    Mean    Std. Dev.        N    95 percent Conf. Interval

For entire sample                 581.250    117.325         24     531.708    630.792

 - - - - - - - - - -
```

Figure 4.2b Plot of means from procedure PLOT

```
COMPUTE CONS=1.
AGGREGATE OUTFILE=*
   /BREAK=CONS
   /MPDIG2 MPDIG3 MPDIG4=MEAN(P2DIGIT P3DIGIT P4DIGIT).
COMPUTE C2=2.
COMPUTE C3=3.
COMPUTE C4=4.
PLOT SYMBOLS='***'/VSIZE=15/HSIZE=30
   /FORMAT=OVERLAY
   /TITLE 'MEAN LATENCY TIMES'
   /HORIZONTAL 'NUMBER OF DIGITS'/VERTICAL 'MEAN LATENCY'
   /PLOT=MPDIG2 WITH C2;MPDIG3 WITH C3;MPDIG4 WITH C4.
```

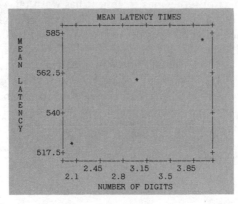

The stem-and-leaf plot of latencies for the P4DIGIT is shown in Figure 4.2c. The corresponding normal probability plot is shown in Figure 4.2d. From this, it appears that the values are somewhat more "bunched" than one would expect if they were normally distributed. The bunching of the data might occur because of limitations in the accuracy of the measurements. Similar plots can be obtained for the other two variables.

Figure 4.2c   Stem-and-leaf plot for P4DIGIT

```
MANOVA P2DIGIT P3DIGIT P4DIGIT
  /PLOT=STEMLEAF
  /DESIGN.
```

```
Stem-and-leaf display for variable .. P4DIGIT

    3 . 9
    4 . 347
    5 . 01111225558
    6 . 2889
    7 . 0125
    8 . 6
```

Figure 4.2d   Normal probability plot for P4DIGIT

```
MANOVA P2DIGIT P3DIGIT P4DIGIT
  /PLOT=NORMAL
  /DESIGN.
```

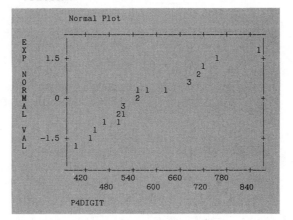

4.3
Analyzing Differences

Since multiple observations are made on the same experimental unit in a repeated measures design, special procedures that incorporate dependencies within an experimental unit must be used. For example, in the paired t-test design, instead of analyzing each score separately, we analyze the difference between the two scores. When there are more than two scores for a subject, the analysis becomes somewhat more complicated. For example, if each subject receives three treatments, there are three pairwise differences: the difference between the first two treatments, the difference between the second two treatments, and the difference between the first and third treatments.

Performing three paired t-tests of the differences may seem to be the simplest analysis, but it is not, for several reasons, the best strategy. First, the three t-tests are not statistically independent, since they involve the same means in overlapping combinations. Some overall protection against calling too many differences significant is needed, especially as the number of treatments increases. Second, since there are three separate t-tests, a single test of the hypothesis that there is no difference between the treatments is not available.

There are several approaches for circumventing such problems in the analysis of data from repeated measures experiments. These approaches are described in the remainder of this chapter.

4.4
Transforming the Variables

To test the null hypothesis that the mean latencies are the same for the three digit lengths, the original three variables must be "transformed." That is, instead of analyzing the original three variables, we analyze linear combinations of their differences. (In the paired t-test, the transformation is the difference between the values for each subject or pair.) For certain methods of analysis, these linear combinations, sometimes called *contrasts,* must be chosen so that they are statistically independent (orthogonal) and so that the sum of the squared coefficients is 1 (normalized). Such contrasts are termed *orthonormalized.* The number of statistically independent contrasts that can be formed for a factor is one less than the number of levels of the factor. In addition, a contrast corresponding to the overall mean (the constant term in the model) is always formed. For this example, this contrast is

CONTRAST 1 = P2DIGIT + P3DIGIT + P4DIGIT   **Equation 4.4a**

There are many types of transformations available. One is the difference contrast, which compares each level of a factor to the average of the levels that precede it. (Another transformation, orthogonal polynomials, is discussed in Section 4.12.)

The first difference contrast for the DIGIT factor is

CONTRAST 2 = P3DIGIT − P2DIGIT   **Equation 4.4b**

and the second difference contrast is divided by

CONTRAST 3 = 2 × P4DIGIT − P3DIGIT − P2DIGIT   **Equation 4.4c**

The contrasts can be normalized by dividing each contrast by the square root of the sum of the coefficients squared. The contrast for the overall mean is divided by

$$\sqrt{1^2 + 1^2 + 1^2} = \sqrt{3}$$

Equation 4.4d

and the second difference constrast is divided by

$$\sqrt{2^2 + 1^2 + 1^2} = \sqrt{6}$$

Equation 4.4e

Figure 4.4 shows the orthonormalized transformation matrix from MANOVA for creating new variables from P2DIGIT, P3DIGIT, and P4DIGIT with the difference transformation. A column contains the coefficients for a particular contrast. Each row corresponds to one of the original variables. Thus, the first linear combination is

CONSTANT = 0.57735(P2DIGIT + P3DIGIT + P4DIGIT)   **Equation 4.4f**

This new variable is, for each case, the sum of the values of the three original variables, multiplied by 0.57735. Again, the coefficients are chosen so that the sum of their squared values is 1. The next two variables are the normalized difference contrasts for the DIGIT effect.

Figure 4.4   Orthonormalized transformation matrix for difference contrasts

```
SET WIDTH=WIDE.
MANOVA P2DIGIT P3DIGIT P4DIGIT
  /WSFACTORS=DIGIT(3)
  /CONTRAST(DIGIT)=DIFFERENCE
  /RENAME=CONS DIF12 DIF12V3
  /WSDESIGN
  /PRINT=TRANSFORM
  /DESIGN.
```

```
Orthonormalized Transformation Matrix (Transposed)

                    CONS        DIF12       DIF12V3

P2DIGIT            .57735      -.70711      -.40825
P3DIGIT            .57735       .70711      -.40825
P4DIGIT            .57735       0.0          .81650
```

What do these new variables represent? The first variable, the sum of the original variables, is the average response over all treatments. It measures latency times over all digit lengths. The hypothesis that the average response, the constant, is equal to 0 is based on this variable. The second two contrasts together represent the treatment (DIGIT) effect. These two contrasts are used to test hypotheses about differences in latencies for the three digit lengths.

4.5
Testing for Differences

In Chapter 3, analysis of variance models with more than one dependent variable are described. The same techniques can be used for repeated measures data. For example, we can use the single-sample tests to test whether particular sets of the transformed variables in the Bacon experiment have means of 0. If the number of digits does not affect latency times, the mean values of the two contrasts for the DIGIT effect are expected to be 0. Different hypotheses are tested using different transformed variables.

4.6
Testing the Constant Effect

When a repeated measures design is specified in SPSS/PC+ MANOVA, several hypotheses are automatically tested. The first hypothesis is that the overall mean latency time is 0. It is based on the first transformed variable, which corresponds to the CONSTANT effect.

To help identify results, MANOVA displays the names of the transformed variables used to test a hypothesis. In this example, we assigned new names to the transformed variables within the MANOVA procedure (see Figure 4.4). These new names will appear on the output. The first transformed variable is renamed to CONS, the second to DIF12, and the third to DIF12V3. If new names are not assigned to the transformed variables, MANOVA assigns the names T1, T2, and so on, to the transformed variables.

Figure 4.6 shows the explanation displayed when the CONSTANT effect is tested. The column labeled **Variates** indicates which transformed variables are involved in the test of a particular effect. Since the test for the constant is based only on variable CONS, its name appears in that column. When there are no covariates in the analysis, the column labeled **Covariates** is empty, as shown. The note below the table is a reminder that analyses are based on the transformed variables, and that the particular analysis is for the CONSTANT effect.

B

Statistics Guide

Figure 4.6   Renamed variables used in the analysis

```
MANOVA P2DIGIT P3DIGIT P4DIGIT
  /WSFACTORS=DIGIT(3)
  /CONTRAST(DIGIT)=DIFFERENCE
  /RENAME=CONS DIF12 DIF12V3
  /WSDESIGN
  /PRINT=TRANSFORM
  /DESIGN.
```

```
Order of Variables for Analysis

  Variates      Covariates

   CONS

   1 Dependent Variable
   0 Covariates
 _ _ _ _ _ _ _ _ _
Note..  TRANSFORMED variables are in the variates column.
        These TRANSFORMED variables correspond to the
        Between-subject effects.
```

4.7
The Analysis of Variance
Table

Since the test for the constant is based on a single variable, the results are displayed in the usual univariate analysis of variance table (Figure 4.7a). The large F value and the small observed significance level indicate that the hypothesis that the constant is 0 is rejected. This finding is of limited importance here, since we do not expect the time required to search a number to be 0. Tests about the constant might be of interest if the original variables are difference scores—change from baseline, for example—since the test of the constant would then correspond to the test that there has been no overall change from baseline.

Figure 4.7a   Analysis of variance table

```
MANOVA P2DIGIT P3DIGIT P4DIGIT
  /WSFACTORS=DIGIT(3)
  /CONTRAST(DIGIT)=DIFFERENCE
  /RENAME=CONS DIF12 DIF12V3
  /WSDESIGN
  /PRINT=PARAMETERS(ESTIM)
  /DESIGN.
```

```
Tests of Significance for CONS using UNIQUE sums of squares
Source of Variation        SS        DF      MS           F    Sig of F

WITHIN CELLS          995411.11      23   43278.74
CONSTANT            22093520.22       1   22093520     510.49     .000
```

After the ANOVA table, SPSS/PC+ MANOVA displays parameter estimates and tests of the hypotheses that the individual transformed variables have means of 0. These are shown in Figure 4.7b. For the CONSTANT effect, the parameter estimate is nothing more than

$$0.57735 \times (520.58 + 560.00 + 581.25)$$ **Equation 4.7**

where the numbers within the parentheses are just the means of the original three variables shown in Figure 4.2a. The 0.57735 is the value used to normalize the contrast from Figure 4.4. The test of the hypothesis that the true value of the first parameter is 0 is equivalent to the test of the hypothesis that the constant is 0. Therefore, the t value displayed for the test is the square root of the F value from the ANOVA table (the square root of 510.49 = 22.59). (When the t statistic is squared it is equal to an F statistic with one degree of freedom for the numerator and the same degrees of freedom for the denominator as the t statistic.)

Figure 4.7b Parameter estimates

```
Estimates for CONS
CONSTANT

  Parameter      Coeff.   Std. Err.    t-Value   Sig. t  Lower -95% CL- Upper

        1     959.459922   42.46506   22.59410      0.0   871.61426 1047.30558
```

4.8
Testing the Digit Effect

The hypothesis of interest in this study is whether latency time depends on the number of digits in the memorized number. As shown in Figure 4.8a, this test is based on the two transformed variables, labeled **DIF12** and **DIF12V3**. Figure 4.8b contains the multivariate tests of the hypothesis that the means of these two variables are 0. In this situation, all multivariate criteria are equivalent and lead to rejection of the hypothesis that the number of digits does not affect latency time.

Figure 4.8a Transformed variables used

```
MANOVA P2DIGIT P3DIGIT P4DIGIT
  /WSFACTORS=DIGIT(3)
  /CONTRAST(DIGIT)=DIFFERENCE
  /RENAME=CONS DIF12 DIF12V3
  /WSDESIGN
  /PRINT=TRANSFORM
  /DESIGN.
```

```
Order of Variables for Analysis

   Variates      Covariates

   DIF12
   DIF12V3

   2 Dependent Variables
   0 Covariates

_ _ _ _ _ _ _ _
Note.. TRANSFORMED variables are in the variates column.
       These TRANSFORMED variables correspond to the
       'DIGIT' WITHIN-SUBJECT effect.
```

Figure 4.8b Multivariate hypothesis tests

```
EFFECT .. DIGIT
Multivariate Tests of Significance (S = 1, M = 0, N = 10 )

Test Name        Value   Approx. F Hypoth. DF    Error DF  Sig. of F

Pillais         .60452   16.81439      2.00        22.00      .000
Hotellings     1.52858   16.81439      2.00        22.00      .000
Wilks           .39548   16.81439      2.00        22.00      .000
Roys            .60452
```

Univariate F tests for the individual transformed variables are shown in Figure 4.8c. The first row corresponds to a test of the hypothesis that there is no difference in average latency times for numbers consisting of two digits and those consisting of three. (This is equivalent to a one-sample t-test that the mean of the second transformed variable DIF12 is 0.) The second row of Figure 4.8c provides a test of the hypothesis that there is no difference between the average response to numbers with two and three digits and numbers with four digits. The average value of this contrast is also significantly different from 0, since the observed significance level is less than 0.0005. (See Section 4.12 for an example of a different contrast type.)

Figure 4.8c   Univariate hypothesis tests

```
MANOVA P2DIGIT P3DIGIT P4DIGIT
  /WSFACTORS=DIGIT(3)
  /CONTRAST(DIGIT)=DIFFERENCE
  /RENAME=CONS DIF12 DIF12V3
  /WSDESIGN
  /PRINT=SIGNIF(UNIV)
  /DESIGN.
```

Variable	Hypoth. SS	Error SS	Hypoth. MS	Error MS	F	Sig. of F
DIF12	18644.0833	19800.9167	18644.0833	860.90942	21.65627	.000
DIF12V3	26841.3611	22774.3056	26841.3611	990.18720	27.10736	.000

Univariate F-tests with (1,23) D. F.

To estimate the magnitudes of differences among the digit lengths, we can examine the values of each contrast. These are shown in Figure 4.8d. The column labeled **Coeff** is the average value for the normalized contrast. As shown in Section 4.4, the second contrast is 0.707 times the difference between two- and three-digit numbers, which is $0.707 \times (520.58 - 560.00) = 27.87$, the value shown in Figure 4.8d. To obtain an estimate of the absolute difference between mean response to two and three digits, the parameter estimate must be divided by 0.707. This value is 39.42. Again, the t value for the hypothesis that the contrast is 0 is equivalent to the square root of the F value from the univariate analysis of variance table.

Figure 4.8d   Estimates for contrasts

Estimates for DIF12
DIGIT

Parameter	Coeff.	Std. Err.	t-Value	Sig. t	Lower –95% CL– Upper
1	27.8717923	5.98926	4.65363	.000	15.48207 40.26152

Estimates for DIF12V3
DIGIT

Parameter	Coeff.	Std. Err.	t-Value	Sig. t	Lower –95% CL– Upper
1	33.4423391	6.42322	5.20647	.000	20.15489 46.72979

Similarly, the parameter estimate for the third contrast, the normalized difference between the average of two and three digits and four digits, is 33.44. The actual value of the difference is 40.96 (33.44 divided by 0.8165). The t value, the ratio of the parameter estimate to its standard error, is 5.206, which when squared equals the F value in Figure 4.8c. The t-values are the same for normalized and nonnormalized contrasts.

The parameter estimates and univariate F tests help identify which individual contrasts contribute to overall differences. However, the observed significance levels for the individual parameters are not adjusted for the fact that several comparisons are being made (see Miller, 1981; Burns, 1984). Thus, the significance levels should serve only as guides for identifying potentially important differences.

4.9
Averaged Univariate Results

The individual univariate tests can be "pooled" to obtain the averaged F test shown in Figure 4.9. The entries in Figure 4.9 are obtained from Figure 4.8c by summing the hypothesis and error sums of squares and the associated degrees of freedom. In this example, the averaged F test also leads us to reject the hypothesis that average latency times do not differ for numbers of different lengths. This is the same F statistic obtained by specifying a repeated measures design as a "mixed-model" univariate analysis of variance (Winer, 1971).

Figure 4.9   Averaged univariate hypothesis tests

AVERAGED Tests of Significance for MEAS.1 using UNIQUE sums of squares

Source of Variation	SS	DF	MS	F	Sig of F
WITHIN CELLS	42575.22	46	925.55		
DIGIT	45485.44	2	22742.72	24.57	.000

4.10
Choosing Multivariate or Univariate Results

In the previous section, we saw that hypothesis tests for the DIGIT effect could be based on multivariate criteria such as Wilks' lambda, or on the averaged univariate F tests. When both approaches lead to similar results, choosing between them is not of much importance. However, there are situations in which the multivariate and univariate approaches lead to different results and the question of which is appropriate arises.

The multivariate approach considers the measurements on a subject to be a sample from a multivariate normal distribution, and makes no assumption about the characteristics of the variance-covariance matrix. The univariate (sometimes called *mixed-model*) approach requires certain assumptions about the variance-covariance matrix. If these conditions are met, especially for small sample sizes, the univariate approach is more powerful than the multivariate approach. That is, it is more likely to detect differences when they exist.

Modifications of the univariate results when the assumptions are violated have also been proposed. These corrected results are approximate and are based on the adjustment of the degrees of freedom of the F ratio (Greenhouse-Geisser, 1959; Huynh & Feldt, 1976). The significance levels for the corrected tests will always be larger than for the uncorrected. Thus, if the uncorrected test is not significant, there is no need to calculate corrected values.

4.11
Assumptions Needed for the Univariate Approach

Since subjects in the current example are not subdivided by any grouping characteristics, the only assumption required for using the univariate results is that the variances of all the transformed variables for an effect be equal and that their covariances be 0. (Assumptions required for more complicated designs are described in Section 4.22.)

Mauchly's test of sphericity is available in MANOVA for testing the hypothesis that the covariance matrix of the transformed variables has a constant variance on the diagonal and zeros off the diagonal (Morrison, 1976). For small sample sizes this test is not very powerful. For large sample sizes the test may be significant even when the impact of the departure on the analysis of variance results may be small.

Figure 4.11 contains Mauchly's test of sphericity and the observed significance level based on a chi-square approximation. The observed significance level is 0.149, so the hypothesis of sphericity is not rejected. If the observed significance level is small and the sphericity assumption appears to be violated, an adjustment to the numerator and denominator degrees of freedom can be made. Two estimates of this adjustment, called epsilon, are available in MANOVA. These are also shown in Figure 4.11. Both the numerator and denominator degrees of freedom must be multiplied by epsilon, and the significance of the F ratio evaluated with the new degrees of freedom. The Huynh-Feldt epsilon is an attempt to correct the Greenhouser-Geisser epsilon, which tends to be overly conservative, especially for small sample sizes. The lowest value possible for epsilon is also displayed. The Huynh-Feldt epsilon sometimes exceeds the value of one. When this occurs, MANOVA displays a value of one.

Figure 4.11 Within-cells correlation

```
MANOVA P2DIGIT P3DIGIT P4DIGIT
  /WSFACTORS=DIGIT(3)
  /CONTRAST(DIGIT)=DIFFERENCE
  /RENAME=CONS DIF12 DIF12V3
  /DESIGN.
```

```
Tests involving 'DIGIT' Within-Subject Effect.


Mauchly sphericity test, W =         .84103
Chi-square approx. =                3.80873 with 2 D. F.
Significance =                        .149

Greenhouse-Geisser Epsilon =         .86284
Huynh-Feldt Epsilon =                .92638
Lower-bound Epsilon =                .50000
```

4.12
Selecting Other Contrasts

Based on the orthonormalized transformation matrix shown in Figure 4.4 and the corresponding parameter estimates in Figure 4.8d, hypotheses about particular combinations of the means were tested. Remember, the second contrast compared differences between the two- and three-digit numbers, while the third contrast compared the average of the two- and three-digit numbers to the four-digit numbers. A variety of other hypotheses can be tested by selecting different orthogonal contrasts.

For example, to test the hypothesis that latency time increases linearly with the number of digits in the memorized number, orthogonal polynomial contrasts can be used. (In fact, polynomial contrasts should have been the first choice for data of this type. Difference contrasts were used for illustrative purposes.) When polynomial contrasts are used, the first contrast for the DIGIT effect represents the linear component, and the second contrast represents the quadratic component. Figure 4.12 contains parameter estimates corresponding to the polynomial contrasts. You can see that there is a significant linear trend, but the quadratic trend is not significant. This is also shown in the plot in Figure 4.2b, since the means fall more or less on a straight line, which does not appear to curve upward or downward.

Figure 4.12   Parameter estimates for polynomial contrasts

```
MANOVA P2DIGIT P3DIGIT P4DIGIT
  /WSFACTORS=DIGIT(3)
  /CONTRAST(DIGIT)=POLYNOMIAL
  /RENAME=CONS LIN QUAD
  /WSDESIGN
  /PRINT=PARAMETERS(ESTIM)
  /DESIGN.
```

```
Estimates for LIN
DIGIT

  Parameter      Coeff.   Std. Err.    t-Value   Sig. t  Lower -95% CL- Upper

         1   42.8683486     7.28780    5.88221     .000   27.79239   57.94430

- - - - - - - - - -
Estimates for QUAD
DIGIT

  Parameter      Coeff.   Std. Err.    t-Value   Sig. t  Lower -95% CL- Upper

         1   -7.3995003     4.91598   -1.50519     .146  -17.56898    2.76998
```

The requirement that contrasts be orthonormalized is necessary for the averaged F tests. It is not required for the multivariate approach. The SPSS/PC+ MANOVA procedure, however, requires all contrasts for the within-subjects factors to be orthonormal. If nonorthogonal contrasts such as simple or deviation are requested, they are orthonormalized prior to the actual analysis. The transformation matrix should always be displayed so that the parameter estimates and univariate F ratios can be properly interpreted.

4.13
Adding Another Factor

The experimental design discussed so far is a very simple one. Responses to all levels of one factor (number of digits) were measured for all subjects. However, repeated measures designs can be considerably more complicated. Any factorial design can be applied to a single subject. For example, we can administer several different types of medication at varying dosages and times of day. Such a design has three factors (medication, dosage, and time) applied to each subject.

All of the usual analysis of variance hypotheses for factorial designs can be tested when each subject is treated as a complete replicate of the design. However, since observations from the same subject are not independent, the usual ANOVA method is inappropriate. Instead, we need to extend the previously described approach to analyzing repeated measures experiments.

To illustrate the analysis of a two-factor repeated measures design, consider the Bacon data again. The experiment was actually more involved than first described. The single "probe" digit was not always present in the memorized number. Instead, each subject was tested under two conditions—probe digit present and probe digit absent. Presence and absence of the probe digit was randomized. The two conditions were included to test the hypothesis that it takes longer to search through numbers when the probe digit is not present than when it is present. If memory searches are performed sequentially, one would expect that when the probe digit is encountered, searching stops. When the probe digit is not present in a number, searching must continue through all digits of the memorized number.

Thus, each subject has in fact six observations: latency times for the three number lengths when the probe is present, and times for the numbers when the probe is absent. This design has two factors—number of digits, and the probe presence/absence condition. The DIGIT factor has three levels (two, three, and four digits) and the CONDITION factor has two levels (probe present and probe absent).

4.14
Testing a Two-Factor Model

The analysis of this modified experiment proceeds similarly to the analysis described for the single-factor design. However, instead of testing only the DIGIT effect, tests for the DIGIT effect, the CONDITION effect, and the DIGIT by CONDITION interaction are required. Figure 4.14 is the orthonormalized transformation matrix for the two-factor design.

Figure 4.14   Orthonormalized transformation matrix for the two-factor design

```
SET WIDTH=WIDE.
MANOVA P2DIGIT P3DIGIT P4DIGIT NP2DIGIT NP3DIGIT NP4DIGIT
  /WSFACTORS=COND(2) DIGIT(3)
  /CONTRAST(DIGIT)=DIFFERENCE
  /RENAME=CONS TCONDIF TDIGIT1 TDIGIT2 TINT1 TINT2
  /WSDESIGN
  /PRINT=TRANSFORM PARAM(ESTIM) SIGNIF(AVERF)
  /DESIGN.
```

Orthonormalized Transformation Matrix (Transposed)

	CONS	TCONDIF	TDIGIT1	TDIGIT2	TINT1	TINT2
P2DIGIT	.40825	.40825	-.50000	-.28868	-.50000	-.28868
P3DIGIT	.40825	.40825	.50000	-.28868	.50000	-.28868
P4DIGIT	.40825	.40825	0.0	.57735	0.0	.57735
NP2DIGIT	.40825	-.40825	-.50000	-.28868	.50000	.28868
NP3DIGIT	.40825	-.40825	.50000	-.28868	-.50000	.28868
NP4DIGIT	.40825	-.40825	0.0	.57735	0.0	-.57735

4.15
The Transformed Variables

The coefficients of the transformation matrix indicate that the first contrast is an average of all six variables. The second contrast is the average response under the "present" condition compared to the average response under the "absent" condition. The third contrast is the difference between two and three digits averaged over the two conditions. The fourth contrast is the average of two and three digits compared to four digits, averaged over both conditions. As before, these two contrasts jointly provide a test of the DIGIT effect. The last two contrasts are used for the test of interaction. If there is no interaction effect, the difference between the two- and three-digit numbers should be the same for the two probe conditions. The contrast labeled **TINT1** is the difference between two and three digits for Condition 1, minus two and three digits for Condition 2. Similarly, if there is no interaction between probe presence and the number of digits, the average of two and three digits compared to four should not differ for the two probe conditions. The contrast labeled **TINT2** is used to test this hypothesis.

4.16
Testing Hypotheses

Hypothesis testing for this design proceeds similarly to the single factor design. Each effect is tested individually. Both multivariate and univariate results can be obtained for tests of each effect. (When a factor has only two levels, there is one contrast for the effect and the multivariate and univariate results are identical.) Since the test of the constant is not of interest, we will proceed to the test of the CONDITION effect.

4.17
The CONDITION Effect

The table in Figure 4.17a explains that variable TCONDIF is being used in the analysis of the CONDITION effect. The analysis of variance table in Figure 4.17b indicates that the CONDITION effect is significant. The F value of 52 has an observed significance level of less than 0.0005. The parameter estimate for the difference between the two conditions is -75 as shown in Figure 4.17c. The estimate of the actual difference between mean response under the two conditions is obtained by dividing -75 by 0.408, since the contrast is actually

$$\text{contrast} = 0.408 \times (\text{mean present} - \text{mean absent})$$ **Equation 4.17**

Since the contrast value is negative, the latency times for the absent condition are larger than the latency times for the present condition. This supports the notion that memory searching may be sequential, terminating when an item is found rather than continuing until all items are examined.

Figure 4.17a   Test of the CONDITION effect

```
Order of Variables for Analysis

  Variates      Covariates

  TCONDIF

   1 Dependent Variable
   0 Covariates

 ─ ─ ─ ─ ─ ─ ─ ─ ─ ─
Note..  TRANSFORMED variables are in the variates column.
        These TRANSFORMED variables correspond to the
        'COND' WITHIN-SUBJECT effect.
```

Figure 4.17b   Analysis of variance table for the CONDITION effect

```
Tests of Significance for TCONDIF using UNIQUE sums of squares
Source of Variation        SS        DF        MS        F   Sig of F

WITHIN CELLS          58810.08        23   2556.96
COND                 134322.25         1 134322.25     52.53     .000
```

Figure 4.17c   Parameter estimates for the CONDITION effect

```
Estimates for TCONDIF
COND

  Parameter      Coeff.   Std. Err.    t-Value    Sig. t  Lower -95% CL- Upper

        1    -74.811499   10.32182    -7.24790      .000  -96.16381  -53.45918
```

4.18
The Number of Digits

The next effect to be tested is the number of digits in the memorized number. As shown in Figure 4.18a, the test is based on the two contrasts labeled **TDIGIT1** and **TDIGIT2**. To use the univariate approach, the assumption of sphericity is necessary.

Figure 4.18a   Test of the DIGIT effect

```
Order of Variables for Analysis

  Variates      Covariates

   TDIGIT1
   TDIGIT2

  2 Dependent Variables
  0 Covariates

_ _ _ _ _ _ _ _ _
Note..  TRANSFORMED variables are in the variates column.
        These TRANSFORMED variables correspond to the
        'DIGIT' WITHIN-SUBJECT effect.
```

Based on the multivariate criteria in Figure 4.18b, the hypothesis that there is no DIGIT effect should be rejected. From Figure 4.18c, we see that both of the contrasts are also individually different from 0. This can also be seen from Figure 4.18d, which contains the parameter estimates for the contrasts. Note that the tests that the parameter values are 0 are identical to the corresponding univariate F tests. The averaged tests of significance for the DIGIT effect, as shown in Figure 4.18e, lead to the same conclusion as the multivariate results in Figure 4.18b.

Figure 4.18b   Multivariate tests of significance

```
EFFECT .. DIGIT
Multivariate Tests of Significance (S = 1, M = 0, N = 10 )

Test Name         Value  Approx. F Hypoth. DF   Error DF  Sig. of F

Pillais          .64216  19.73989      2.00      22.00      .000
Hotellings      1.79454  19.73989      2.00      22.00      .000
Wilks            .35784  19.73989      2.00      22.00      .000
Roys             .64216
```

Figure 4.18c   Univariate tests of significance

```
Univariate F-tests with (1,23) D. F.

Variable  Hypoth. SS   Error SS Hypoth. MS    Error MS          F  Sig. of F

TDIGIT1  41002.6667 34710.8333 41002.6667 1509.16667   27.16908      .000
TDIGIT2  53682.7222 30821.4444 53682.7222 1340.06280   40.05986      .000
```

Figure 4.18d   Parameter estimates for the DIGIT contrasts

```
Estimates for TDIGIT1
DIGIT

Parameter      Coeff.   Std. Err.     t-Value    Sig. t  Lower -95% CL- Upper

        1   41.3333333    7.92981     5.21240      .000   24.92926   57.73740

_ _ _ _ _ _ _ _ _ _
Estimates for TDIGIT2
DIGIT

Parameter      Coeff.   Std. Err.     t-Value    Sig. t  Lower -95% CL- Upper

        1   47.2946096    7.47235     6.32929      .000   31.83688   62.75233
```

Figure 4.18e   Averaged tests of significance

```
AVERAGED Tests of Significance for MEAS.1 using UNIQUE sums of squares
Source of Variation        SS       DF        MS          F  Sig of F

WITHIN CELLS          65532.28       46   1424.61
DIGIT                 94685.39        2  47342.69      33.23      .000
```

4.19
The Interaction

The interaction between the number of digits in the memorized number and the presence or absence of the probe digit is based on the last two contrasts, labeled **TINT1** and **TINT2**, as indicated in Figure 4.19a. Based on the multivariate criteria shown in Figure 4.19b and the averaged univariate results in Figure 4.19c, the hypothesis that there is no interaction is not rejected.

Figure 4.19a Test of the interaction effect

```
Order of Variables for Analysis

  Variates      Covariates

   TINT1
   TINT2

   2 Dependent Variables
   0 Covariates

 - - - - - - - - -
Note..  TRANSFORMED variables are in the variates column.
        These TRANSFORMED variables correspond to the
        'COND BY DIGIT' WITHIN-SUBJECT effect.
```

Figure 4.19b Multivariate tests of significance

```
EFFECT .. COND BY DIGIT
Multivariate Tests of Significance (S = 1, M = 0, N = 10 )

Test Name        Value  Approx. F Hypoth. DF   Error DF  Sig. of F

Pillais         .00890    .09873      2.00       22.00      .906
Hotellings      .00898    .09873      2.00       22.00      .906
Wilks           .99110    .09873      2.00       22.00      .906
Roys            .00890
```

Figure 4.19c Averaged tests of significance

```
AVERAGED Tests of Significance for MEAS.1 using UNIQUE sums of squares
Source of Variation        SS        DF        MS         F  Sig of F

WITHIN CELLS           20751.50      46      451.12
COND BY DIGIT             88.17       2       44.08       .10     .907
```

4.20
Putting it Together

Consider Figure 4.20a, which contains a plot of the average latencies for each of the three number lengths and conditions. Means and standard deviations are shown in Figure 4.20b. Note that the average latency times for the absent condition are always higher than those for the present condition. The test for the statistical significance of this observation is based on the CONDITION factor. Figure 4.20a shows that as the number of digits in a number increases, so does the average latency time. The test of the hypothesis that latency time is the same regardless of the number of digits is based on the DIGIT factor. Again, the hypothesis that there is no DIGIT effect is rejected. The relationship between latency time and the number of digits appears to be fairly similar for the two probe conditions. This is tested by the CONDITION by DIGIT interaction, which was not found to be statistically significant. If there is a significant interaction, the relationship between latency time and the number of digits would differ for the two probe conditions.

Figure 4.20a   Plot of average latencies from procedure PLOT

```
COMPUTE CONS=1.
AGGREGATE OUTFILE=*/BREAK=CONS/MPDIG2 MPDIG3 MPDIG4
   MNPDIG2 MNPDIG3 MNPDIG4=MEAN(P2DIGIT P3DIGIT P4DIGIT
   NP2DIGIT NP3DIGIT NP4DIGIT).
COMPUTE C2=2.
COMPUTE C3=3.
COMPUTE C4=4.
PLOT SYMBOLS='PPPAAA'
   /VSIZE=45
   /HSIZE=45
   /TITLE 'LATENCY TIMES (P=PROBE PRESENT A=PROBE ABSENT)'
   /FORMAT=OVERLAY
   /HORIZONTAL 'NUMBER OF DIGITS' /VERTICAL 'MEAN LATENCY TIME'
   /PLOT=MPDIG2 WITH C2;MPDIG3 WITH C3;MPDIG4 WITH C4;
    MNPDIG2 WITH C2;MNPDIG3 WITH C3;MNPDIG4 WITH C4.
```

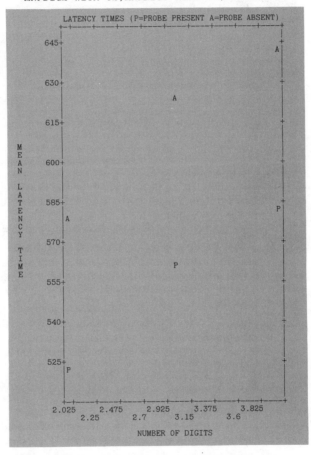

Figure 4.20b Means and standard deviations from TABLES

```
COMPUTE DUMMY1=1.
COMPUTE DUMMY2=1.
VARIABLE LABEL DUMMY1 'PRESENT'/DUMMY2 'ABSENT'
   /P2DIGIT '2 DIGIT'/P3DIGIT '3 DIGIT' /P4DIGIT '4 DIGIT'
   /NP2DIGIT '2 DIGIT'/NP3DIGIT '3 DIGIT' /NP4DIGIT '4 DIGIT'.
VALUE LABEL DUMMY1 DUMMY2 1 ''.
TABLES OBSERV=P2DIGIT TO NP4DIGIT
  /TABLE DUMMY1 BY P2DIGIT+P3DIGIT+P4DIGIT
  /STATISTICS MEAN STDDEV
  /TABLE DUMMY2 BY NP2DIGIT+NP3DIGIT+NP4DIGIT
  /STATISTICS MEAN STDDEV.
```

	2 DIGIT		3 DIGIT		4 DIGIT	
	Mean	Standard Deviation	Mean	Standard Deviation	Mean	Standard Deviation
PRESENT 1.00	520.58	131.37	560.00	118.78	581.25	117.32

	2 DIGIT		3 DIGIT		4 DIGIT	
	Mean	Standard Deviation	Mean	Standard Deviation	Mean	Standard Deviation
ABSENT 1.00	579.75	132.17	623.00	135.14	642.33	144.81

4.21
Within-Subjects and Between-Subjects Factors

Both number of digits and probe status are called "within-subjects" factors since all combinations occur within each of the subjects. It is also possible to have "between-subjects" factors in repeated measures designs. Between-subjects factors subdivide the sample into discrete subgroups. Each subject has only one value for a between-subjects factor. For example, if cases in the previously described study are subdivided into males and females, sex is a between-subjects factor. Similarly, if cases are classified as those who received "memory enhancers" and those who did not, the memory enhancement factor is a between-subjects factor. If the same subject is tested with and without memory enhancers, memory enhancement would be a within-subjects factor. Thus, the same factor can be either a within-subjects or between-subjects factor, depending on the experimental design. Some factors, such as sex and race, can only be between-subjects factors since the same subject can be of only one sex or race.

4.22
Additional Univariate Assumptions

In a within-subjects design, a sufficient condition for the univariate model approach to be valid is that, for each effect, the variance-covariance matrix of the transformed variables used to test the effect has covariances of 0 and equal variances. Including between-subjects factors in a design necessitates an additional assumption. The variance-covariance matrices for the transformed variables for a particular effect must be equal for all levels of the between-subjects factors. These two assumptions are often called the "symmetry conditions." If they are not tenable, the F ratios from the averaged univariate results may not be correct.

4.23
Back to Memory

In addition to the two within-subjects factors, Bacon's experiment also included a between-subjects factor—the hand subjects used to press the instrument that signaled the presence or absence of the probe digit. All subjects were right-handed, but half were required to signal with the right hand and half with the left. (If a subject had been tested under both conditions, right hand and left hand, hand would be a within-subjects factor.) The hypothesis of interest was whether latency would increase for subjects using the left hand.

The hypothesis that the variance-covariance matrices are equal across all levels of the between-subjects factor can be examined using the multivariate generalization of Box's *M* test. It is based on the determinants of the variance-covariance matrices for all between-subjects cells in the design. Figure 4.23a contains the multivariate test for equality of the variance-covariance matrices for the two levels of the HAND factor (which hand the subject used). Note that in SPSS/PC+ MANOVA, this test is based on all the original variables for the within-subjects effects.

Figure 4.23a   Box's *M*

```
MANOVA P2DIGIT P3DIGIT P4DIGIT NP2DIGIT NP3DIGIT NP4DIGIT
  BY HAND(1,2)
  /WSFACTORS=COND(2) DIGIT(3)
  /CONTRAST(DIGIT)=DIFFERENCE
  /RENAME=CONS TCONDIF TDIGIT1 TDIGIT2 TINT1 TINT2
  /WSDESIGN
  /PRINT=HOMOGENEITY(BOXM) PARAM(ESTIM)
  /DESIGN.
```

```
Multivariate test for Homogeneity of Dispersion matrices


Boxs M =                            25.92434
F WITH (21,1780) DF =                .86321, P =   .641 (Approx.)
Chi-Square with 21 DF =            18.43322, P =   .621 (Approx.)
```

Adding a between-subjects factor to the experiment introduces more terms into the analysis of variance model. Besides the DIGIT, CONDITION, and CONDITION by DIGIT effects, the model includes the main effect HAND and the interaction terms HAND by DIGIT, HAND by CONDITION, and HAND by DIGIT by CONDITION.

The analysis proceeds as before. Variables corresponding to the within-subjects factors are again transformed using the transformation matrix shown in Figure 4.23b. The between-subjects factors are not transformed.

Figure 4.23b   Transformation matrix

```
SET WIDTH=WIDE.
MANOVA P2DIGIT P3DIGIT P4DIGIT NP2DIGIT NP3DIGIT NP4DIGIT
  BY HAND(1,2)
  /WSFACTORS=COND(2) DIGIT(3)
  /CONTRAST(DIGIT)=DIFFERENCE
  /RENAME=CONS TCONDIF TDIGIT1 TDIGIT2 TINT1 TINT2
  /WSDESIGN
  /PRINT=HOMOGENEITY(BOXM) TRANSFORM
  /DESIGN.
```

```
Orthonormalized Transformation Matrix (Transposed)

                 CONS     TCONDIF    TDIGIT1    TDIGIT2     TINT1      TINT2

P2DIGIT         .40825     .40825    -.50000    -.28868    -.50000    -.28868
P3DIGIT         .40825     .40825     .50000    -.28868     .50000    -.28868
P4DIGIT         .40825     .40825     0.0        .57735     0.0        .57735
NP2DIGIT        .40825    -.40825    -.50000    -.28868     .50000     .28868
NP3DIGIT        .40825    -.40825     .50000    -.28868    -.50000     .28868
NP4DIGIT        .40825    -.40825     0.0        .57735     0.0       -.57735
```

The within-subjects factors and their interactions are tested as when there were no between-subjects factors in the design. Tests of the between-subjects factors and the interactions of the between- and within-subjects factors treat the transformed within-subjects variables as dependent variables. For example, the test of the HAND effect is identical to a two-sample t-test, with the transformed variable corresponding to the constant as the dependent variable. The test of the CONDITION by HAND interaction treats the transformed variable corresponding to the CONDITION effect as the dependent variable. Similarly, the DIGIT by HAND interaction considers the two transformed variables for the DIGIT effect as dependent variables. The test of the three-way interaction HAND by DIGIT by

CONDITION treats the two variables corresponding to the interaction of DIGIT by CONDITION as the dependent variables. HAND is always the grouping variable.

The SPSS/PC+ output for a design with both within- and between-subjects factors looks much like before. The variables used for each analysis are first identified, as shown for the CONSTANT effect in Figure 4.23c.

Figure 4.23c   Test of the HAND effect

```
Order of Variables for Analysis

  Variates      Covariates

  CONS

  1 Dependent Variable
  0 Covariates

- - - - - - - - -
Note..  TRANSFORMED variables are in the variates column.
        These TRANSFORMED variables correspond to the
        Between-subject effects.
```

All tests based on the same transformed variables are presented together. Since the test of the HAND effect is based on the same variable as the test for the CONSTANT effect, the tests are displayed together, as shown in Figure 4.23d. The table is the usual analysis of variance table since there is only one dependent variable in the analyses. From the ANOVA table, it appears that the CONSTANT is significantly different from 0, an uninteresting finding we have made before. The HAND effect, however, is not statistically significant since its observed significance level is very close to 1. This means that there is not sufficient evidence to reject the null hypothesis that there is no difference in average latency times for subjects who used their right hand and subjects who used their left.

Figure 4.23d   Tests of significance using unique sums of squares

```
Tests of Significance for CONS using UNIQUE sums of squares
Source of Variation            SS       DF        MS         F  Sig of F

WITHIN CELLS              2196663.86    22   99848.36
CONSTANT                 49193858.03     1   49193858    492.69      .000
HAND                          300.44     1     300.44       .00      .957
```

For the transformed variable used to test the HAND effect, the overall mean is 1,432. The mean for the right-hand subjects is 1435 and for the left-hand subjects is 1,428. The parameter estimates in Figure 4.23e are based on these means. The parameter estimate for CONSTANT is the unweighted grand mean, while the parameter estimate for HAND is the deviation of the right-hand group from the overall mean. (For between-subjects variables such as HAND, deviation parameter estimates are the default.)

Figure 4.23e   Parameter estimates for the HAND contrasts

```
Estimates for CONS
CONSTANT

  Parameter      Coeff.   Std. Err.    t-Value    Sig. t  Lower -95% CL- Upper

        1    1431.69273   64.50076   22.19652       0.0  1297.92634 1565.45913
HAND

  Parameter      Coeff.   Std. Err.    t-Value    Sig. t  Lower -95% CL- Upper

        2     3.53815185   64.50076     .05485      .957 -130.22824  137.30454
```

Figure 4.23f is the ANOVA table based on the transformed variable for the CONDITION effect. Again there is a significant effect for CONDITION, but the HAND by CONDITION effect is not significant.

Figure 4.23f   Analysis of variance for the interaction

```
Tests of Significance for TCONDIF using UNIQUE sums of squares
Source of Variation          SS        DF        MS           F  Sig of F

WITHIN CELLS            57889.97        22    2631.36
COND                   134322.25         1  134322.25       51.05      .000
HAND BY COND              920.11         1     920.11         .35      .560
```

Since the DIGIT effect has two degrees of freedom, its test is based on two transformed variables, and both univariate and multivariate results are displayed for hypotheses involving DIGIT. The multivariate results for the HAND by DIGIT interaction are shown in Figure 4.23g. It appears that there is no interaction between number of digits and the hand used to signal the response. The multivariate results for the DIGIT effect are shown in Figure 4.23h. Again, they are highly significant. Figure 4.23i shows the averaged univariate results for terms involving the DIGIT effect.

Figure 4.23g   Multivariate tests of significance for the HAND by DIGIT interaction

```
EFFECT .. HAND BY DIGIT
Multivariate Tests of Significance (S = 1, M = 0, N = 9 1/2)

Test Name      Value    Approx. F  Hypoth. DF   Error DF  Sig. of F

Pillais       .08477      .97258       2.00       21.00      .394
Hotellings    .09263      .97258       2.00       21.00      .394
Wilks         .91523      .97258       2.00       21.00      .394
Roys          .08477
```

Figure 4.23h   Multivariate tests of significance for DIGIT effect

```
EFFECT .. DIGIT
Multivariate Tests of Significance (S = 1, M = 0, N = 9 1/2)

Test Name      Value    Approx. F  Hypoth. DF   Error DF  Sig. of F

Pillais       .64219     18.84488      2.00       21.00      .000
Hotellings   1.79475     18.84488      2.00       21.00      .000
Wilks         .35781     18.84488      2.00       21.00      .000
Roys          .64219
```

Figure 4.23i   Averaged tests of significance

```
MANOVA P2DIGIT P3DIGIT P4DIGIT NP2DIGIT NP3DIGIT NP4DIGIT
  BY HAND(1,2)
  /WSFACTORS=COND(2) DIGIT(3)
  /CONTRAST(DIGIT)=DIFFERENCE
  /RENAME=CONS TCONDIF TDIGIT1 TDIGIT2 TINT1 TINT2
  /WSDESIGN
  /PRINT=HOMOGENEITY(BOXM) TRANSFORM ERROR(COR) SIGNIF(AVERF)
  /DESIGN.
```

```
AVERAGED Tests of Significance for MEAS.1 using UNIQUE sums of squares
Source of Variation          SS        DF        MS           F  Sig of F

WITHIN CELLS            64376.89        44    1463.11
DIGIT                   94685.39         2   47342.69       32.36      .000
HAND BY DIGIT            1155.39         2     577.69         .39      .676
```

Figure 4.23j shows the multivariate results for the HAND by CONDITION by DIGIT effect. Again these are not significant. The univariate tests, shown in Figure 4.23k, agree with the multivariate results.

Figure 4.23j   Multivariate tests of significance for the three-way interaction

```
EFFECT .. HAND BY COND BY DIGIT
Multivariate Tests of Significance (S = 1, M = 0, N = 9 1/2)

Test Name      Value    Approx. F  Hypoth. DF   Error DF  Sig. of F

Pillais       .07632      .86760       2.00       21.00      .434
Hotellings    .08263      .86760       2.00       21.00      .434
Wilks         .92368      .86760       2.00       21.00      .434
Roys          .07632
```

Figure 4.23k Averaged tests of significance for the three-way interaction

```
AVERAGED Tests of Significance for MEAS.1 using UNIQUE sums of squares
Source of Variation          SS        DF        MS         F   Sig of F

WITHIN CELLS              20138.11     44      457.68
COND BY DIGIT                88.17      2       44.08       .10     .908
HAND BY COND BY DIGI       613.39      2      306.69       .67     .517
T
```

4.24
Summarizing the Results

The hand used by the subject to signal the response does not seem to affect overall latency times. It also does not appear to interact with the number of digits in the memorized number, nor the presence or absence of the probe digit. This is an interesting finding, since it was conceivable that using a nonpreferred hand would increase the time required to signal. Or subjects using their right hands might have had shorter latency times because of the way different activities are governed by the hemispheres of the brain. Memory is thought to be a function of the left hemisphere, which also governs the activity of the right hand. Thus, using the right hand would not necessitate a "switch" of hemispheres and might result in shorter latency times.

4.25
Analysis of Covariance with a Constant Covariate

The speed with which a subject signals that the probe digit is or is not present in the memorized number may depend on various characteristics of the subject. For example, some subjects may generally respond more quickly to stimuli than others. The reaction time or "speed" of a subject may influence performance in the memory experiments. To control for differences in responsiveness, we might administer a reaction-time test to each subject. This time can then be used as a covariate in the analysis. If subjects responding with the right hand are generally slower than subjects responding with their left, we may be able to account for the fact that no differences between the two groups were found.

To adjust for differences in covariates, the regression between the dependent variable and the covariate is calculated. For each subject, the response that would have been obtained if they had the same average "speed" is then calculated. Further analyses are based on these corrected values.

In a repeated measures design, the general idea is the same. The between-subjects effects are adjusted for the covariates. There is no need to adjust the within-subjects effects for covariates whose values do not change during the course of an experiment, since within-subjects factor differences are obtained from the same subject. That is, a subject's "quickness" or "slowness" is the same for all within-subjects factors.

To see how this is done, consider a hypothetical extension of Bacon's experiment. Let's assume that prior to the memory tests, each subject was given a series of trials in which he or she pressed a bar as soon as a light appeared. The interval between the time the light appeared and the time the subject pressed the bar will be termed the reaction time. For each subject, the average reaction time over a series of trials is calculated. This reaction time will be considered a covariate in the analysis.

As in the previous examples, all analyses are based on the transformed within-subjects variables. Figure 4.25a shows the orthonormalized transformation matrix. It is similar to the one used before, except that there are now six additional rows and columns that are used to transform the covariates. Although there is only one covariate in this example, the MANOVA procedure requires you to specify a covariate for each within-subjects variable, which is done by repeating the same covariate. The transformation applied to the covariates is the same as the transformation for the within-subjects factors.

Figure 4.25a   Transformation matrix with covariates

```
COMPUTE C1=REACT.
COMPUTE C2=REACT.
COMPUTE C3=REACT.
COMPUTE C4=REACT.
COMPUTE C5=REACT.
COMPUTE C6=REACT.
SET WIDTH=WIDE.
MANOVA P2DIGIT P3DIGIT P4DIGIT NP2DIGIT NP3DIGIT NP4DIGIT
  BY HAND(1,2)
  WITH C1 C2 C3 C4 C5 C6
  /WSFACTORS=COND(2) DIGIT(3)
  /CONTRAST(DIGIT)=DIFFERENCE
  /RENAME=CONS TCONDIF TDIGIT1 TDIGIT2 TINT1 TINT2
   TC1 TC2 TC3 TC4 TC5 TC6
  /WSDESIGN
  /PRINT=TRANSFORM
  /DESIGN.
```

Orthonormalized Transformation Matrix (Transposed)

	CONS	TCONDIF	TDIGIT1	TDIGIT2	TINT1	TINT2	TC1	TC2	TC3	TC4	TC5
P2DIGIT	.40825	.40825	−.50000	−.28868	−.50000	−.28868	0.0	0.0	0.0	0.0	0.0
P3DIGIT	.40825	.40825	.50000	−.28868	.50000	−.28868	0.0	0.0	0.0	0.0	0.0
P4DIGIT	.40825	.40825	0.0	.57735	0.0	.57735	0.0	0.0	0.0	0.0	0.0
NP2DIGIT	.40825	−.40825	−.50000	−.28868	.50000	.28868	0.0	0.0	0.0	0.0	0.0
NP3DIGIT	.40825	−.40825	.50000	−.28868	−.50000	.28868	0.0	0.0	0.0	0.0	0.0
NP4DIGIT	.40825	−.40825	0.0	.57735	0.0	−.57735	0.0	0.0	0.0	0.0	0.0
C1	0.0	0.0	0.0	0.0	0.0	0.0	.40825	.40825	−.50000	−.28868	−.50000
C2	0.0	0.0	0.0	0.0	0.0	0.0	.40825	.40825	.50000	−.28868	.50000
C3	0.0	0.0	0.0	0.0	0.0	0.0	.40825	.40825	0.0	.57735	0.0
C4	0.0	0.0	0.0	0.0	0.0	0.0	.40825	−.40825	−.50000	−.28868	.50000
C5	0.0	0.0	0.0	0.0	0.0	0.0	.40825	−.40825	.50000	−.28868	−.50000
C6	0.0	0.0	0.0	0.0	0.0	0.0	.40825	−.40825	0.0	.57735	0.0

	TC6
P2DIGIT	0.0
P3DIGIT	0.0
P4DIGIT	0.0
NP2DIGIT	0.0
NP3DIGIT	0.0
NP4DIGIT	0.0
C1	−.28868
C2	−.28868
C3	.57735
C4	.28868
C5	.28868
C6	−.57735

Figure 4.25b is a description of the variables used in the analysis of the constant and the between-subjects variable. The dependent variable is CONSTANT, the covariate TC1. All of the other variables, including the five transformed replicates of the same covariate labeled **TC2** to **TC6**, are not used for this analysis.

Figure 4.25b   Test of the constant effect

```
Order of Variables for Analysis

   Variates      Covariates

   CONS          TC1

   1 Dependent Variable
   1 Covariate

- - - - - - - - -
Note..  TRANSFORMED variables are in the variates column.
        These TRANSFORMED variables correspond to the
        Between-subject effects.
```

The analysis of variance table for the HAND and CONSTANT effects is shown in Figure 4.25c. Note how the table has changed from Figure 4.23d, the corresponding table without the reaction-time covariate. In Figure 4.25c, the within-cells error term is subdivided into two components—error sums of squares and sums of squares due to the regression. In an analysis of covariance model, we are able to explain some of the variability within a cell of the design by the fact that cases have different values for the covariates. The regression sum of squares is the variability attributable to the covariate. If one were to calculate a regression between the transformed constant term and the transformed covariate, the regression sums of squares would be identical to those in Figure 4.25c. The test for the HAND effect is thus no longer based on the CONSTANT, but on the CONSTANT adjusted for the covariate. Thus, differences between the groups in overall reaction time are eliminated. The HAND effect is still not significant, however. The sums of squares attributable to the CONSTANT have also changed. This is because the hypothesis tested is no longer that the overall mean is 0, but that the intercept in the regression equation for the constant and the reaction time is 0.

Figure 4.25c   Analysis of covariance

```
Tests of Significance for CONS using UNIQUE sums of squares
Source of Variation              SS        DF        MS           F    Sig of F

WITHIN CELLS                656243.80      21    31249.70
REGRESSION                 1540420.06       1  1540420.1       49.29      .000
CONSTANT                       126.81       1      126.81         .00      .950
HAND                          3745.90       1     3745.90         .12      .733
```

Figure 4.25d shows that the regression coefficient for the transformed reaction time is 97.5746. The test of the hypothesis that the coefficient is 0 is identical to the test of the regression effect in the ANOVA table.

Figure 4.25d   Regression coefficient for reaction time

```
Regression analysis for WITHIN CELLS error term
Dependent variable .. CONS

COVARIATE              B          Beta      Std. Err.      t-Value      Sig. of t      Lower -95%      CL- Upper

TC1        97.5746661658    .8374092999    13.89762       7.02096          .000        68.67298      126.47635
```

When constant covariates are specified, messages such as that shown in Figure 4.25e are displayed. All the message says is that since all the covariates are identical, they are linearly dependent. You can simply ignore this message.

Figure 4.25e   Linear dependency warning message

```
*    W A R N I N G    * For WITHIN CELLS error matrix, these covariates
*                     * appear LINEARLY DEPENDENT on preceding
*                     * variables ...
                        TC2
                      1 D.F. will be returned to this error term.
```

4.26
Doubly Multivariate Repeated Measures Designs

There is only one dependent variable in Bacon's experiment, latency time, which was measured for all subjects. In some situations, more than one dependent variable may be measured for each factor combination. For example, to test the effect of different medications on blood pressure, both systolic and diastolic blood pressures may be recorded for each treatment. This is sometimes called a doubly multivariate repeated measures design, since each subject has multiple variables measured at multiple times.

Analysis of doubly multivariate repeated measures data is similar to the analyses above. Each dependent variable is transformed using the same orthonormalized transformation. All subsequent analyses are based on these transformed variables. The tests for each effect are based on the appropriate variables for all dependent variables. For example, in the memory experiment, if two dependent variables had been measured for the three number lengths, the test of the DIGIT effect would be based on four transformed variables, two for the first dependent variable and two for the second. Similarly, the test for CONSTANT would have been based on two variables corresponding to averages for each dependent variable.

4.27
RUNNING MANOVA FOR REPEATED MEASURES DESIGNS

The operation of the MANOVA procedure is more fully documented in Chapter 3. Most of the subcommands described there can be used with repeated measures designs as well. This chapter covers only the subcommands needed to specify repeated measures designs.

4.28
Specifying the Variables

The first MANOVA specification is the list of variables to be used in the analyses. Dependent variables are named first, followed by the keyword BY and factor names and ranges. If there are covariates, list them last following keyword WITH. In a repeated measures design, list all variables that correspond to within-subjects factors as dependent variables. Between-subjects variables are considered factors.

For example, the command

```
MANOVA P2DIGIT P3DIGIT P4DIGIT.
```

specifies the three variables corresponding to number length when the probe digit is present as the dependent variable. To include the present/absent condition in the analysis as well, specify

```
MANOVA P2DIGIT P3DIGIT P4DIGIT NP2DIGIT NP3DIGIT NP4DIGIT.
```

To include the between-groups factor HAND with two levels coded as 1 and 2, specify

```
MANOVA P2DIGIT P3DIGIT P4DIGIT NP2DIGIT NP3DIGIT NP4DIGIT
  BY HAND(1,2).
```

When there are additional between-subjects factors, list them all after the BY keyword. Additional rules for specifying variables are given in Chapter 3.

4.29
Specifying a Constant Covariate

In a repeated measures design, you must specify as many covariate names as there are dependent variables on the MANOVA command. If there is a single covariate that is measured only once, for example before the experiment was conducted, use the COMPUTE command to replicate the covariate values. (A covariate that is measured once is called a *constant covariate*.) For example, the analysis of covariance described in Section 4.25, where REACT is the value of the reaction time, can be specified as

```
COMPUTE C1=REACT.
COMPUTE C2=REACT.
COMPUTE C3=REACT.
COMPUTE C4=REACT.
COMPUTE C5=REACT.
COMPUTE C6=REACT.
MANOVA P2DIGIT P3DIGIT P4DIGIT NP2DIGIT NP3DIGIT NP4DIGIT
  BY HAND(1,2)
    WITH C1 C2 C3 C4 C5 C6.
```

4.30
Specifying the Within-Subjects Factors

For a repeated measures design, you must also specify the structure of the design. For example, if there are six variables in the dependent variable list, they may have originated from a variety of repeated measures designs. There may be one within-subjects factor, say TREATMENT, which has six values representing six different agents administered to the same subject. Or there may be two within-subjects factors such as TREATMENT and DOSE, one having three levels and the other having two, e.g., each subject receives three different treatments at two dosage levels. Or perhaps two treatments at each of three dosage levels are given.

The WSFACTORS subcommand identifies the correspondence between the variable list and the within-subjects factors. WSFACTORS supplies the name of each factor, followed by the number of levels in parentheses. The product of the number of levels of the factors must equal the number of dependent variables (except in doubly multivariate repeated measures; see Section 4.32). WSFACTOR must be the first subcommand after the variable list.

For example, to indicate that the three variables P2DIGIT, P3DIGIT, and P4DIGIT correspond to three levels of a within-subjects factor which is to be assigned the name DIGIT, specify

```
MANOVA P2DIGIT P3DIGIT P4DIGIT
  /WSFACTORS=DIGIT(3).
```

The names assigned to the within-subjects factors must follow the SPSS/PC+ variable-naming conventions. Each within-subjects factor name must be unique. The within-subjects factor names exist only during the MANOVA analysis in which they are defined.

A name must be assigned to each within-subjects factor. For example, to define the two within-subjects factors for number length and presence/absence condition, specify

```
MANOVA P2DIGIT P3DIGIT P4DIGIT NP2DIGIT NP3DIGIT NP4DIGIT
  /WSFACTORS=COND(2) DIGIT(3).
```

Each variable named on the variable list corresponds to a particular combination of within-subjects factor levels. For example, variable P2DIGIT is the latency time for a two-digit number when the probe digit is present.

The order in which factors are named on WSFACTORS must correspond to the sequence of variables on the variable list. The first factor named on WSFACTORS changes most slowly. Thus, in the example above, values of the DIGIT factor change faster than values of the COND factor. For example, P2DIGIT is the response at the first level of CONDITION and the first level of DIGIT, and P3DIGIT is the response at the first level of CONDITION and the second level of DIGIT. If the order of the variables on the MANOVA command is changed, the order of factor names on the WSFACTORS subcommand must also be changed, as in

```
MANOVA P2DIGIT NP2DIGIT P3DIGIT NP3DIGIT P4DIGIT NP4DIGIT
  /WSFACTORS=DIGIT(3) COND(2).
```

In general, the variables must be arranged in the variable list in such a way that their structure can be represented on a WSFACTORS subcommand. For example, it is not possible to represent the following list of variables on a WSFACTORS subcommand, since the variables are not arranged in a predictable sequence:

```
MANOVA P2DIGIT P3DIGIT NP2DIGIT NP3DIGIT P4DIGIT NP4DIGIT
```

4.31
Renaming the
Transformed Variables

When a repeated measures design is specified, the original variables are transformed using an orthonormal transformation matrix, and the transformed variables are then analyzed. To make the SPSS/PC+ MANOVA output easier to interpret, it is a good idea to assign names to the new variables. This is done with the RENAME subcommand.

For example, the following command created the output shown in Figure 4.23c:

```
MANOVA P2DIGIT P3DIGIT P4DIGIT NP2DIGIT NP3DIGIT NP4DIGIT
  BY HAND(1,2)
  /WSFACTORS=COND(2) DIGIT(3)
  /RENAME=CONS TCONDIF TDIGIT1 TDIGIT2 TINT1 TINT2.
```

The name CONS is assigned to the CONSTANT effect, the name TCONDIF to the CONDITION effect, the names TDIGIT1 and TDIGIT2 to the two transformed variables for the DIGIT effect, and TINT1 and TINT2 to the two transformed variables that represent the interaction of condition and digit length.

The number of names listed on the RENAME subcommand must equal the number of dependent variables and covariates on the variable list. To retain a variable's original name, specify either the original name or an asterisk. For example, to retain the names of the covariates in the following command, specify:

```
MANOVA P2DIGIT P3DIGIT P4DIGIT NP2DIGIT NP3DIGIT NP4DIGIT
  BY HAND(1,2)
  WITH C1 C2 C3 C4 C5 C6
  /WSFACTORS=COND(2) DIGIT(3)
  /RENAME=CONS TCONDIF TDIGIT1 TDIGIT2 TINT1 TINT2 * * * * * *.
```

If you do not supply a RENAME subcommand in a situation where the variables are being transformed, as in repeated-measures analysis, MANOVA automatically assigns the names T1, T2, and so on, to the transformed variables. You must use the new names in all subsequent subcommands, whether you assigned them yourself or MANOVA supplied them. (The exception is the OMEANS subcommand, which uses the original variable names and produces tables of observed means of the untransformed variables.)

4.32
Labeling the Display of Averaged Results

In a doubly multivariate repeated measures design (when more than one variable is measured at each combination of the factor levels), you can use the MEASURE subcommand to differentiate sets of dependent variables. In a doubly multivariate design, the arrangement of the within-subjects factors must be the same for all sets of variables. For example, if both systolic and diastolic blood pressure are measured at three points in time, you could specify

```
MANOVA SYS1 SYS2 SYS3 DIAS1 DIAS2 DIAS3
  /WSFACTORS=TIME(3)
  /MEASURE=SYSTOL DIASTOL.
```

This command names one factor, TIME, which has three levels for two sets of dependent variables. Variables SYS1, SYS2, and SYS3 are in the SYSTOL set, and DIAS1, DIAS2, and DIAS3 are DIASTOL. Note that the product of the number of variables named on MEASURE times the product of the levels of factors named on WSFACTORS equals the number of dependent variables on the variable list.

If you omit MEASURE from the above command, SPSS/PC+ MANOVA will automatically generate a doubly multivariate design based on the three levels of the TIME factor. The advantage of using MEASURE is that the display of averaged results (produced by SIGNIF(AVERF) on the PRINT subcommand) will be labeled with the names you specify on MEASURE. If you do not use MEASURE, MANOVA displays the results but uses its own labeling. Thus, the MEASURE subcommand is optional, but it is recommended for clarity.

4.33
Specifying the Contrasts

All of the CONTRASTS described in Chapter 3 can also be used for between-subjects factors in repeated measures designs. In the case of within-subjects factors, nonorthogonal contrasts such as deviation and simple are orthonormalized prior to the repeated measures analysis. If the contrast requested is not orthogonal, the parameter estimates obtained for terms involving the within-subjects factors will not correspond to the contrast requested. Therefore, it is recommended that only orthogonal contrasts be specified on the CONTRAST subcommand for within-subjects factors. Orthogonal contrast types are DIFFERENCE, HELMERT, and POLYNOMIAL.

If nonorthogonal contrasts are requested, the transformation matrix should always be displayed to ascertain what orthonormalized contrasts are used. Since the default contrasts are deviation, they produce parameter estimates that are not easily interpreted.

4.34
Specifying the Design for Within-Subjects Factors

The WSDESIGN subcommand specifies the design for the within-subjects factors. Its specification is similar to the DESIGN subcommand discussed in Chapter 3. For example, to specify a complete factorial design for the DIGIT and COND within-subjects factors, specify

```
MANOVA P2DIGIT P3DIGIT P4DIGIT NP2DIGIT NP3DIGIT NP4DIGIT
  /WSFACTORS=COND(2) DIGIT(3)
  /WSDESIGN=COND DIGIT COND BY DIGIT.
```

As is the case for between-subjects factors, the complete factorial design is the default, and can be obtained by omitting the WSDESIGN command altogether, or by entering it with no specifications. To suppress estimation of the CONDITION by DIGIT interaction and specify a main-effects model, specify

```
MANOVA P2DIGIT P3DIGIT P4DIGIT NP2DIGIT NP3DIGIT NP4DIGIT
  /WSFACTORS=COND(2) DIGIT(3)
  /WSDESIGN=COND DIGIT.
```

The following specifications, which can be used on the DESIGN subcommand, are not permitted on the WSDESIGN subcommand:

- Error term references and definitions.
- The MUPLUS and CONSTANT keywords.
- Continuous variables.
- Between-subjects factors.

The WSDESIGN specification signals the beginning of within-subjects design processing, so if you explicitly enter a WSDESIGN subcommand, all other subcommands that affect the within-subjects design must appear before it. For example, if a POLYNOMIAL contrast is to be used for the DIGIT effect, this must be indicated prior to the WSDESIGN subcommand, as in

```
MANOVA P2DIGIT P3DIGIT P4DIGIT NP2DIGIT NP3DIGIT NP4DIGIT
  /WSFACTORS=COND(2) DIGIT(3)
  /CONTRAST(DIGIT)=POLY(1,2)
  /WSDESIGN COND DIGIT.
```

4.35
Repeated-Measures Processing

In a repeated measures analysis of variance, all dependent variables are not tested together as is usually done in MANOVA. Instead, sets of transformed variables that correspond to particular effects are tested. For example, in the memory experiment, the constant is tested first, then the variable that represents the CONDITION effect, then the two variables that represent the DIGIT effect, and finally the two variables that represent the DIGIT by CONDITION interaction. The cycling through the dependent variables is automatically accomplished when you enter a WSFACTORS subcommand.

For example, to obtain a test of the full-factorial within-subjects design, specify

```
MANOVA P2DIGIT P3DIGIT P4DIGIT NP2DIGIT NP3DIGIT NP4DIGIT
  /WSFACTORS=COND(2) DIGIT(3)
  /RENAME=CONS TCONDIF TDIGIT1 TDIGIT2 TINT1 TINT2.
```

4.36
Specifying the Between-Subjects Factors

Use the DESIGN subcommand according to the rules defined in Chapter 3 to list between-subjects effects to be tested. If no effects are listed on the DESIGN subcommand, the default is a full-factorial design. Thus, the complete memory experiment can be analyzed with the commands

```
MANOVA P2DIGIT P3DIGIT P4DIGIT NP2DIGIT NP3DIGIT NP4DIGIT
  BY HAND(1,2)
  /WSFACTORS=COND(2) DIGIT(3)
  /RENAME=CONS TCONDIF TDIGIT1 TDIGIT2 TINT1 TINT2
  /WSDESIGN=COND DIGIT COND BY DIGIT
  /DESIGN=HAND.
```

Here both the WSDESIGN and the DESIGN subcommands are optional, since complete factorial designs are the default.

4.37
Specifying Optional Output

All statistics and plots described in Chapter 3 are also available for repeated measures designs. However, some output is particularly useful for repeated measures designs. The orthonormalized transformation matrix used to generate the transformed variables is requested with the keyword TRANSFORM. The averaged univariate F tests are displayed by default but can be explicitly requested with the keywords SIGNIF(AVERF).

For example, to display the transformation matrix specify

```
/PRINT=TRANSFORM
```

Homogeneity of variance tests and Mauchly's test of sphericity may be used to analyze departures from the symmetry assumptions necessary for a univariate (averaged F test) analysis. Use keyword HOMOGENEITY (BARTLETT, COCHRAN, and/or BOXM) to request the homogeneity tests, as in

```
/PRINT=TRANSFORM SIGNIF(AVERF) HOMOGENEITY(BARTLETT BOXM)
```

Mauchly's test is always displayed for a repeated measures analysis.

4.38
Annotated Example

The following SPSS/PC+ commands produced the output in Figures 4.7a, 4.7b, 4.8a, 4.8b, 4.8c, and 4.8d:

```
DATA LIST FREE
  /HAND P2DIGIT P3DIGIT P4DIGIT NP2DIGIT NP3DIGIT NP4DIGIT REACT.
BEGIN DATA.
data records
END DATA.
MANOVA P2DIGIT P3DIGIT P4DIGIT
  /WSFACTORS=DIGIT(3)
  /CONTRAST(DIGIT)=DIFFERENCE
  /RENAME=CONS DIF12 DIF12V3
  /WSDESIGN
  /PRINT=PARAMETERS(ESTIM) TRANSFORM
  /DESIGN.
FINISH.
```

- The DATA LIST command gives the variable names and tells SPSS/PC+ that the data will be found in freefield format.

- The MANOVA command specifies the three variables corresponding to number length when the probe digit is present as the dependent variables. The WSFACTORS subcommand indicates that the three variables P2DIGIT, P3DIGIT, and P4DIGIT correspond to three levels of a within-subjects factor assigned the name DIGIT. The CONTRAST subcommand requests DIFFERENCE orthogonal contrasts. The RENAME subcommand gives new names to the transformed variables. The WSDESIGN requests a complete factorial design. The PRINT subcommand requests the parameter estimates and the transformation matrix as part of the display.

B

Statistics Guide

Contents _____

5 Hierarchical Log-Linear Models: Procedure HILOGLINEAR

There is only one way to achieve
happiness on this terrestrial ball,
And that is to have either a clear
conscience or, none at all.

Ogden Nash

Ignoring Nash's warning, many of us continue to search for happiness in terrestrial institutions and possessions. Marriage, wealth, and health are all hypothesized to contribute to happiness. But do they really? And how would one investigate possible associations?

Consider Figure 5.0, which is a two-way classification of marital status and score on a happiness scale. The data are from the 1982 General Social Survey conducted by the National Opinion Research Center. Of the 854 currently married respondents, 92% indicated that they were very happy or pretty happy, while only 79% of the 383 divorced, separated, or widowed people classified themselves as happy.

Figure 5.0   Output from procedure CROSSTABS

```
CROSSTABS TABLES=HAPPY BY MARITAL
   /OPTIONS=4.
```

Crosstabulation:	HAPPY By MARITAL			
MARITAL->	Count Col Pct	MARRIED 1	SINGLE 2	SPLIT 3	Row Total
HAPPY					
YES	1	787 92.2	221 82.5	301 78.6	1309 87.0
NO	2	67 7.8	47 17.5	82 21.4	196 13.0
	Column Total	854 56.7	268 17.8	383 25.4	1505 100.0

Number of Missing Observations =   1

Although the results in Figure 5.0 are interesting, they suggest many new questions. What role does income play in happiness? Are poor married couples happier than affluent singles? What about health? Determining the relationship among such variables is potentially complicated. If family income is recorded in three categories and condition of health in two, a separate two-way table of happiness score and marital status is obtained for each of the six possible combinations of health and income. As additional variables are included in the cross-classification tables, the number of cells rapidly increases and it is difficult, if not impossible, to unravel the associations among the variables by examining only the cell entries.

The usual response of researchers faced with crosstabulated data is to compute a chi-square test of independence for each subtable. This strategy is fraught with problems and usually does not result in a systematic evaluation of the relationship among the variables. The classical chi-square approach also does not provide estimates of the effects of the variables on each other, and its application to tables with more than two variables is complicated.

5.1
LOG-LINEAR MODELS

The advantages of statistical models that summarize data and test hypotheses are well recognized. Regression analysis, for example, examines the relationship between a dependent variable and a set of independent variables. Analysis of variance techniques provide tests for the effects of various factors on a dependent variable. But neither technique is appropriate for categorical data, where the observations are not from populations that are normally distributed with constant variance.

A special class of statistical techniques, called log-linear models, has been formulated for the analysis of categorical data (Haberman, 1978; Bishop, Feinberg, & Holland, 1975). These models are useful for uncovering the potentially complex relationships among the variables in a multiway crosstabulation. Log-linear models are similar to multiple regression models. In log-linear models, all variables that are used for classification are independent variables, and the dependent variable is the number of cases in a cell of the crosstabulation.

5.2
A Fully Saturated Model

Consider Figure 5.0 again. Using a log-linear model, the number of cases in each cell can be expressed as a function of marital status, degree of happiness, and the interaction between degree of happiness and marital status. To obtain a linear model, the natural logs of the cell frequencies, rather than the actual counts, are used. The natural logs of the cell frequencies in Figure 5.0 are shown in Table 5.2a. (Recall that the natural log of a number is the power to which the number e (2.718) is raised to give that number.) For example, the natural log of the first cell entry in Figure 5.0 is 6.668, since $e^{6.668} = 787$.)

Table 5.2a   Natural logs

Happy	Married	Single	Split	Average
Yes	6.668	5.398	5.707	5.924
No	4.205	3.850	4.407	4.154
Average	5.436	4.624	5.057	5.039

The log-linear model for the first cell in Figure 5.0 is

$$\log(787) = \mu + \lambda_{yes}^{happy} + \lambda_{married}^{marital} + \lambda_{yes\ married}^{happy\ marital}$$

Equation 5.2a

The term denoted as μ is comparable to the grand mean in the analysis of variance. It is the average of the logs of the frequencies in all table cells. The lambda parameters represent the increments or decrements from the base value (μ) for particular combinations of values of the row and column variables.

Each individual category of the row and column variables has an associated lambda. The term $\lambda_{married}^{marital}$ indicates the effect of being in the married category of the marital-status variable, and similarly, λ_{yes}^{happy} is the effect of being in the very happy category. The term $\lambda_{yes\ married}^{happy\ marital}$ represents the interaction of being very happy and married. Thus, the number of cases in a cell is a function of the values of the row and column variables and their interactions.

In general, the model for the log of the observed frequency in the ith row and the jth column is given by

$$\ln F_{ij} = \mu + \lambda_i^H + \lambda_j^S + \lambda_{ij}^{HS}$$

Equation 5.2b

where F_{ij} is the observed frequency in the cell, λ_i^H is the effect of the ith happiness category, λ_j^S is the effect of the jth marital-status category, and λ_{ij}^{HS} is the interaction effect for the ith value of the happiness category, and the jth value of the marital status variable.

The lambda parameters and μ are estimated from the data. The estimate for μ is simply the average of the logs of the frequencies in all table cells. From Table 5.2a, the estimated value of μ is 5.039. Estimates for the lambda parameters are obtained in a manner similar to analysis of variance. For example, the effect of the very-happy category is estimated as

$$\lambda_{yes}^{happy} = 5.924 - 5.039 = 0.885$$

Equation 5.2c

where 5.924 is the average of the logs of the observed counts in the happy cells. The lambda parameter is just the average log of the frequencies in a particular category minus the grand mean. In general, the effect of the ith category of a variable, called a main effect, is estimated as

$$\lambda_i^{VAR} = \mu_i - \mu$$

Equation 5.2d

where μ_i is the mean of the logs in the ith category and μ is the grand mean. Positive values of lambda occur when the average number of cases in a row or a column is larger than the overall average. For example, since there are more married people in the sample than single or separated, the lambda for married is positive. Similarly, since there are fewer unhappy people than happy people, the lambda for not happy is negative.

The interaction parameters indicate how much difference there is between the sums of the effects of the variables taken individually and collectively. They represent the "boost" or "interference" associated with particular combinations of the values. For example, if marriage does result in bliss, the number of cases in the happy and married cell would be larger than the number expected based only on the frequency of married people ($\lambda_{married}^{marital}$) and the frequency of happy people (λ_{yes}^{happy}). This excess would be represented by a positive value for $\lambda_{yes\ married}^{happy\ marital}$. If marriage decreases happiness, the value for the interaction parameter would be negative. If marriage neither increases nor decreases happiness, the interaction parameter would be 0.

The estimate for the interaction parameter is the difference between the log of the observed frequency in a particular cell and the log of the predicted frequency using only the lambda parameters for the row and column variables. For example,

$$\lambda_{yes\ married}^{happy\ marital} = \ln F_{11} - (\mu + \lambda_{yes}^{happy} + \lambda_{married}^{marital})$$
$$= 6.668 - (5.039 + 0.885 + 0.397) = 0.347$$

Equation 5.2e

where F_{11} is the observed frequency in the married and happy cell. Table 5.2b contains the estimates of the λ parameters for the main effects (marital status and happiness) and their interactions.

Table 5.2b Estimates of lambda parameters

$$\lambda_{\text{yes}}^{\text{happy}}=5.924-5.039=0.885$$

$$\lambda_{\text{no}}^{\text{happy}}=4.154-5.039=-0.885$$

$$\lambda_{\text{married}}^{\text{marital}}=5.436-5.039=0.397$$

$$\lambda_{\text{single}}^{\text{marital}}=4.624-5.039=-0.415$$

$$\lambda_{\text{split}}^{\text{marital}}=5.057-5.039=0.018$$

$$\lambda_{\text{YM}}^{\text{HM}}\ =6.668-(5.039+0.885+0.397)=0.346$$

$$\lambda_{\text{NM}}^{\text{HM}}\ =4.205-(5.039-0.885+0.397)=-0.346$$

$$\lambda_{\text{YSi}}^{\text{HM}}\ =5.398-(5.039+0.885-0.415)=-0.111$$

$$\lambda_{\text{NSi}}^{\text{HM}}\ =3.850-(5.039-0.885-0.415)=0.111$$

$$\lambda_{\text{YSp}}^{\text{HM}}\ =5.707-(5.039+0.885+0.018)=-0.235$$

$$\lambda_{\text{NSp}}^{\text{HM}}\ =4.407-(5.039-0.885+0.018)=0.235$$

To uniquely estimate the lambda parameters, we need to impose certain constraints on them. The lambdas must sum to 0 across the categories of a variable. For example, the sum of the lambdas for marital status is $0.397 + (-0.415)$ $+0.018 =0$. Similar constraints are imposed on the interaction terms. They must sum to 0 over all categories of a variable.

Each of the observed cell frequencies is reproduced exactly by a model that contains all main-effect and interaction terms. This type of model is called a *saturated* model. For example, the observed log frequency in Cell 1 of Figure 5.0 is given by

$$\ln F_{11}=\mu+\lambda_{\text{yes}}^{\text{happy}}\ +\lambda_{\text{married}}^{\text{marital}}+\ \lambda_{\text{yes}\ \text{married}}^{\text{happy}\ \text{marital}} \qquad \text{Equation 5.2f}$$
$$=5.039+0.885+0.397+0.346=6.67$$

All other observed cell frequencies can be similarly expressed as a function of the lambdas and the grand mean.

5.3
Output for the Cells

Consider Figure 5.3, which contains the observed and expected (predicted from the model) counts for the data shown in Figure 5.0. The first column gives the names of the variables used in the analysis, and the second contains the value labels for the cells in the table. The next column indicates the number of cases in each of the cells. For example, 787 people who classify themselves as happy are married, which is 52.29% of all respondents in the survey (787 out of 1505). This percentage is listed in the next column. Since the number of cases in each cell is expressed as a percentage of the total cases, the sum of all the percentages is 100. The saturated model reproduces the observed cell frequencies exactly, so the expected and observed cell counts and percentages are equal. For the same reason the next two columns, which compare the observed and expected counts, are all zeros. (Models that do not exactly reproduce the observed cells counts are examined later.)

Figure 5.3 Observed and expected frequencies for saturated model

```
HILOGLINEAR HAPPY(1,2) MARITAL(1,3)
    /DESIGN=HAPPY*MARITAL.
```

```
Observed, Expected Frequencies and Residuals.
       Factor          Code       OBS. count  & PCT.    EXP. count  & PCT.    Residual   Std. Resid.

   HAPPY           YES
      MARITAL         MARRIED      787.00 (52.29)        787.00 (52.29)          0.0          0.0
      MARITAL         SINGLE       221.00 (14.68)        221.00 (14.68)          0.0          0.0
      MARITAL         SPLIT        301.00 (20.00)        301.00 (20.00)          0.0          0.0

   HAPPY           NO
      MARITAL         MARRIED       67.00 ( 4.45)         67.00 ( 4.45)          0.0          0.0
      MARITAL         SINGLE        47.00 ( 3.12)         47.00 ( 3.12)          0.0          0.0
      MARITAL         SPLIT         82.00 ( 5.45)         82.00 ( 5.45)          0.0          0.0
```

5.4
Parameter Estimates

The estimates of the log-linear model parameters are also displayed as part of the HILOGLINEAR output. Figure 5.4 contains parameter estimates for the data in Figure 5.0. The parameter estimates are displayed in blocks for each effect.

Parameter estimates for the interaction effects are displayed first. Because estimates must sum to 0 across the categories of each variable, only two parameter estimates need to be displayed for the interaction effects: those for $\lambda_{yes\ married}^{happy\ marital}$ and for $\lambda_{yes\ single}^{happy\ marital}$. All other interaction parameter estimates can be derived from these.

After the interaction terms, parameter estimates for the main effects of the variables are displayed. The first estimate is for λ_{yes}^{happy} and is identical to the value given in Table 5.2b (0.885). Again, only one parameter estimate is displayed, since we can infer that the parameter estimate for λ_{no}^{happy} is -0.885 (the two estimates must sum to 0). Two parameter estimates and associated statistics are displayed for the marital variable, since it has three categories. The estimate for the third parameter $\lambda_{split}^{marital}$ is the negative of the sum of the estimates for $\lambda_{married}^{marital}$ and $\lambda_{single}^{marital}$. Thus, $\lambda_{split}^{marital}$ is estimated to be 0.0178, as shown in Figure 5.2b.

Since the individual parameter estimates in Figure 5.4 are not labeled, the following rules for identifying the categories to which they correspond may be helpful. For main effects, the parameter estimates correspond to the first $K-1$ categories of the variable, where K is the total number of categories. For interaction parameters, the number of estimates displayed is the product of the number of categories, minus one, of each variable in the interaction, multiplied together. For example, marital status has three categories and happiness has two, so the number of estimates displayed is $(3-1) \times (2-1) = 2$.

To identify individual parameters, first look at the order in which the variable labels are listed in the heading. In this case the heading is HAPPY*MARITAL. The first estimate corresponds to the first category of both variables, which is happy-yes and marital-married. The next estimate corresponds to the first category of the first variable (HAPPY) and the second category of the second variable (MARITAL). In general, the categories of the last variable rotate most quickly and those of the first variable most slowly. Terms involving the last categories of the variables are omitted.

Figure 5.4 also displays the standard error for each estimate. For the λ_{yes}^{happy} parameter, the standard error is 0.03997. The ratio of the parameter estimate to its standard error is given in the column labeled **Z-Value**. For sufficiently large sample sizes, the test of the null hypothesis that lambda is 0 can be based on this Z value, since the standardized lambda is approximately normally distributed with a mean of 0 and a standard deviation of 1 if the model fits the data. Lambdas with Z values greater than 1.96 in absolute value can be considered significant at the 0.05 level. When tests for many lambdas are calculated, however, the usual problem of multiple comparisons arises. That is, when many comparisons are made, the probability that some are found to be significant when there is no effect increases rapidly. Special multiple-comparison procedures for testing the lambdas are discussed in Goodman (1964).

Figure 5.4 Estimates for parameters

```
HILOGLINEAR HAPPY(1,2) MARITAL(1,3)
  /PRINT=ESTIM
  /DESIGN=HAPPY*MARITAL.
```

Estimates for Parameters.

HAPPY*MARITAL

Parameter	Coeff.	Std. Err.	Z-Value	Lower 95 CI	Upper 95 CI
1	.3464441901	.05429	6.38147	.24004	.45285
2	-.1113160745	.06122	-1.81833	-.23131	.00867

HAPPY

Parameter	Coeff.	Std. Err.	Z-Value	Lower 95 CI	Upper 95 CI
1	.8853236244	.03997	22.14946	.80698	.96367

MARITAL

Parameter	Coeff.	Std. Err.	Z-Value	Lower 95 CI	Upper 95 CI
1	.3972836534	.05429	7.31793	.29088	.50369
2	-.4150216289	.06122	-6.77930	-.53501	-.29503

Individual confidence intervals can be constructed for each lambda. The 95% confidence interval for λ_{yes}^{happy} is $0.885 \pm (1.96 \times 0.03997)$, which results in a lower limit of 0.80698 and an upper limit of 0.96367. Since the confidence interval does not include 0, the hypothesis that the population value is 0 can be rejected. These values are displayed in the last two columns of Figure 5.4.

5.5
The Independence Model

Representing an observed-frequency table with a log-linear model that contains as many parameters as there are cells (a saturated model) does not result in a parsimonious description of the relationship between the variables. It may, however, serve as a good starting point for exploring other models that could be used to represent the data. Parameters that have small values can be excluded from subsequent models.

To illustrate the general procedure for fitting a model that does not contain all possible parameters (an unsaturated model), consider the familiar independence hypothesis for a two-way table. If variables are independent they can be represented by a log-linear model that does not have any interaction terms. For example, if happiness and marital status are independent

$$\log \widehat{F}_{ij} = \mu + \lambda_i^{happy} + \lambda_j^{marital}$$

Equation 5.5a

Note that $\widehat{F}_{ij}$ is no longer the observed frequency in the (i,j)th cell, but is now the expected frequency based on the model. The estimates of the lambda parameters are obtained using an iterative algorithm (the previously described formulas, which provide direct estimates, apply only to saturated models). That is, the λ's are repeatedly estimated until successive estimates do not differ from each other by more than a preset amount. Each time an estimate is obtained it is called an iteration, while the preset amount is called the convergence criterion.

The message in Figure 5.5a gives the number of iterations required for convergence. For this example, two iterations were required for convergence. The observed and expected counts in each of the cells of the table are shown in Figure 5.5b.

**Figure 5.5a   HILOGLINEAR message:
iterations required for convergence**

```
HILOGLINEAR HAPPY(1,2) MARITAL(1,3)
  /DESIGN=MARITAL HAPPY.
```

```
DESIGN 1 has generating class

    MARITAL
    HAPPY

The Iterative Proportional Fit algorithm converged at iteration 2.
The maximum difference between observed and fitted marginal totals is     .000
and the convergence criterion is     .250
```

**Figure 5.5b   Observed and expected frequencies
for unsaturated model**

```
Observed, Expected Frequencies and Residuals.

        Factor            Code          OBS. count  & PCT.    EXP. count  & PCT.     Residual   Std. Resid.

HAPPY            YES
  MARITAL        MARRIED               787.00 (52.29)         742.78 (49.35)          44.219        1.622
  MARITAL        SINGLE                221.00 (14.68)         233.10 (15.49)         -12.098        -.792
  MARITAL        SPLIT                 301.00 (20.00)         333.12 (22.13)         -32.121       -1.760

HAPPY            NO
  MARITAL        MARRIED                67.00 ( 4.45)         111.22 ( 7.39)         -44.219       -4.193
  MARITAL        SINGLE                 47.00 ( 3.12)          34.90 ( 2.32)          12.098        2.048
  MARITAL        SPLIT                  82.00 ( 5.45)          49.88 ( 3.31)          32.121        4.548
```

The expected values are identical to those obtained from the usual formulas for expected values in a two-way crosstabulation, as shown in Figure 5.5c. For example, from Figure 5.0, the estimated probability of an individual being happy is 1309/1505, and the estimated probability of an individual being married is 854/1505. If marital status and happiness are independent, the probability of a happy, married person is estimated to be

$$1309/1505 \times 854/1505 = 0.4935$$ **Equation 5.5b**

The expected number of happy, married people in a sample of 1505 is then

$$0.4935 \times 1505 = 742.78$$ **Equation 5.5c**

This is the value displayed in the expected-count column in Figure 5.5b. Since the independence model is not saturated, the observed and expected counts are no longer equal, as was the case in Figure 5.3.

Figure 5.5c   Crosstabulation of happiness by marital status

```
CROSSTABS TABLE=HAPPY BY MARITAL
  /OPTIONS=14
  /STATISTICS=1.
```

```
Crosstabulation:      HAPPY
                   By MARITAL


                  Count  |MARRIED |SINGLE  |SPLIT   |
MARITAL->         Exp Val|        |        |        |   Row
                         |     1  |    2   |    3   |  Total
HAPPY            --------+--------+--------+--------+
                     1   |  787   |  221   |  301   |  1309
  YES                    |  742.8 |  233.1 |  333.1 |  87.0%
                  -------+--------+--------+--------+
                     2   |   67   |   47   |   82   |   196
  NO                     |  111.2 |  34.9  |  49.9  |  13.0%
                  -------+--------+--------+--------+
                   Column    854     268      383     1505
                   Total    56.7%   17.8%    25.4%   100.0%


Chi-Square     D.F.      Significance        Min E.F.      Cells with E.F.< 5
---------      ----      ------------        --------      ------------------

 48.81639        2         0.0000             34.902             None

Number of Missing Observations =       1
```

5.6
Chi-square Goodness-of-Fit Tests

The test of the hypothesis that a particular model fits the observed data can be based on the familiar Pearson chi-square statistic, which is calculated as

$$\chi^2 = \sum_i \sum_j \frac{(F_{ij} - \hat{F}_{ij})^2}{\hat{F}_{ij}}$$

Equation 5.6a

where the subscripts i and j include all cells in the table. An alternative statistic is the likelihood-ratio chi-square, which is calculated as

$$L^2 = 2 \sum_i \sum_j F_{ij} \ln \frac{F_{ij}}{\hat{F}_{ij}}$$

Equation 5.6b

For large sample sizes these statistics are equivalent. The advantage of the likelihood-ratio chi-square statistic is that it, like the total sums of squares in analysis of variance, can be subdivided into interpretable parts that add up to the total (see Section 5.10).

Figure 5.6 shows that the value of the Pearson chi-square statistic is 48.82 and the likelihood-ratio chi-square is 48.01. The degrees of freedom associated with a particular model are the number of cells in the table minus the number of independent parameters in the model. In this example, there are six cells and four independent parameters to be estimated (the grand mean, λ_{yes}^{happy}, $\lambda^{married}$, λ^{split}), so there are two degrees of freedom. (There are only four independent parameters because of the constraint that parameter estimates must sum to 0 over the categories of a variable. Therefore, the value for one of the categories is determined by the values of the others and is not, in a statistical sense, independent.)

The observed significance level associated with both chi-square statistics is very small (less than 0.0005), and the independence model is rejected. Note that the Pearson chi-square statistic displayed for independence model is identical to the chi-square value displayed by procedure CROSSTABS, as shown in Figure 5.5c.

Figure 5.6   Chi-square goodness-of-fit test

```
Goodness-of-fit test statistics

    Likelihood ratio chi square =      48.01198    DF = 2   P =   .000
              Pearson chi square =      48.81638    DF = 2   P =   .000
```

5.7
Residuals

Another way to assess how well a model fits the data is to examine the differences between the observed and expected cell counts based on the model. If the model fits the observed data well, these differences, called residuals, should be fairly small in value and not have any discernible pattern. The column labeled **Residual** in Figure 5.5b shows the differences between the observed and expected counts in each cell. For example, since 787 individuals were found to be very happy and married, while 742.78 are expected to fall into this category if the independence model is correct, the residual is $787 - 742.78 = 44.22$.

As in regression analysis, it is useful to standardize the residuals by dividing them by their standard error, in this case the square root of the expected cell count. For example, the standardized residual for the first cell in Figure 5.5b is

$$\frac{Standardized}{Residual} = \frac{Observed\,Count - Expected\,Count}{\sqrt{Expected\,Count}} = 1.62$$

Equation 5.7

This value is displayed in the column labeled **Std. Resid.** in Figure 5.5b. If the model is adequate, the standardized residuals are approximately normally distributed with a mean of 0 and standard deviation of one. Standardized residuals greater than 1.96 or less than -1.96 suggest important discrepancies, since they are unlikely to occur if the model is adequate. Particular combinations of cells with large standardized residuals may suggest which other models might be more appropriate.

The same types of diagnostics for residuals used in regression analysis can be used in log-linear models. Figures 5.7a and 5.7b are plots of the standardized residuals against the observed and expected cell frequencies, respectively. If the model is adequate, there should be no discernible pattern in the plots. Patterns suggest that the chosen log-linear model, or the log-linear representation in general, may not be appropriate for the data.

Figure 5.7a Plot of standardized residuals vs. observed (left) and expected (right) cell frequencies

```
HILOGLINEAR HAPPY(1,2) MARITAL(1,3)
  /PLOT=RESID
  /DESIGN=MARITAL HAPPY.
```

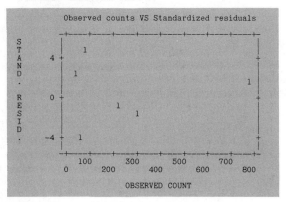

Figure 5.7b

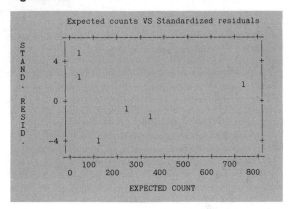

If the standardized residuals are normally distributed, the normal probability plot (Figure 5.7c) should be approximately linear. In this plot, the standardized residuals are plotted against expected residuals from a normal distribution.

Figure 5.7c   Plot of standardized residuals against expected residuals

```
HILOGLINEAR HAPPY(1,2) MARITAL(1,3)
  /PLOT=NORMPROB
  /DESIGN=MARITAL HAPPY.
```

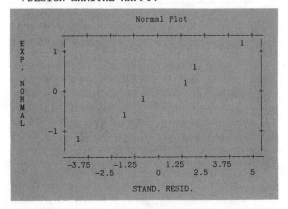

5.8
Hierarchical Models

A saturated log-linear model contains all possible effects. For example, a saturated model for a two-way table contains terms for the row main effects, the column main effects, and their interaction. Different models can be obtained by deleting terms from a saturated model. The independence model is derived by deleting the interaction effect. Although it is possible to delete any particular term from a model, in log-linear analysis attention is often focused on a special class of models which are termed *hierarchical*.

In a hierarchical model, if a term exists for the interaction of a set of variables, then there must be lower-order terms for all possible combinations of these variables. For a two-variable model, this means that the interaction term can only be included if both main effects are present. For a three-variable model, if the term λ^{ABC} is included in a model, then the terms λ^A, λ^B, λ^C, λ^{AB}, λ^{BC}, and λ^{AC} must also be included.

To describe a hierarchical model, it is sufficient to list the highest-order terms in which variables appear. This is called the *generating class* of a model. For example, the specification *ABC* indicates that a model contains the term λ^{ABC} and all its lower-order relations. (Terms are "relatives" if all variables that are included in one term are also included in the other. For example, the term λ^{ABCD} is a higher-order relative of the terms λ^{ABC}, λ^{BCD}, λ^{ACD}, λ^{BAD}, as well as all other lower-order terms involving variables *A, B, C,* or *D*. Similarly, λ^{AB} is a lower-order relative of both λ^{ABC} and λ^{ABD}.) The model

$$\ln F_{ijk} = \mu + \lambda_i^A + \lambda_j^B + \lambda_k^C + \lambda_{ij}^{AB}$$

Equation 5.8

can be represented by the generating class $(AB)(C)$, since *AB* is the highest-order term in which *A* and *B* occur, and *C* is included in the model only as a main effect.

5.9
Model Selection

Even if attention is restricted to hierarchical models, many different models are possible for a set of variables. How do you choose among them? The same guidelines used for model selection in regression analysis apply to log-linear models. A model should fit the data and be substantively interpretable and as simple (parsimonious) as possible. For example, if models with and without higher-order interaction terms fit the data well, the simpler models are usually preferable since higher-order interaction terms are difficult to interpret.

A first step in determining a suitable model might be to fit a saturated model and examine the standardized values for the parameter estimates. Effects with small estimated values can usually be deleted from a model. Another strategy is to systematically test the contribution to a model made by terms of a particular order. For example, you might fit a model with interaction terms and then a model with main effects only. The change in the chi-square value between the two models is attributable to the interaction effects.

5.10
Partitioning the Chi-Square Statistic

In regression analysis, the change in multiple R^2 when a variable is added to a model indicates the additional information conveyed by the variable. Similarly, in log-linear analysis the decrease in the value of the likelihood-ratio chi-square statistic when terms are added to the model signals their contribution to the model. (Remember, R^2 increases when additional variables are added to a model, since large values of R^2 are associated with good models. Chi-square decreases when terms are added, since small values of chi-square are associated with good models.)

As an example, consider the happiness and marital-status data when two additional variables, total income in 1982 and the condition of one's health, are included. Figure 5.10a contains goodness-of-fit statistics for three different models. Design 3 contains all terms except the four-way interaction of HAPPY, MARITAL, INCOME82, and HEALTH. Design 2 contains main effects and second-order interactions only, and Design 1 is a main-effects-only model.

Design 1 has a large chi-square value and an observed significance level less than 0.0005, so it definitely does not fit well. To judge the adequacy of Designs 2 and 3, consider the changes in the chi-square goodness-of-fit statistic as terms are removed from the model.

For a saturated model, the value of the chi-square statistic is always 0. Eliminating the fourth-order interaction (Design 3) results in a likelihood-ratio chi-square value of 3.99. The change in chi-square from 0 to 3.99 is attributable to the fourth-order interaction. The change in the degrees of freedom between the two models equals 4, since a saturated model has 0 degrees of freedom and the third-order interaction model has four. The change in the chi-square value can be used to test the hypothesis that the fourth-order interaction term is 0. If the observed significance level for the change is small, the hypothesis that the fourth-order term is 0 is rejected, since this indicates that the model without the fourth-order term does not fit well. A chi-square value of 3.99 has an observed significance of 0.41, so the hypothesis that the fourth-order term is 0 is not rejected.

Figure 5.10a   Goodness-of-fit statistics for three models

```
HILOGLINEAR HAPPY(1,2) MARITAL(1,3) INCOME82(1,3) HEALTH(1,2)
  /PRINT=ESTIM
  /DESIGN=HAPPY MARITAL INCOME82 HEALTH
  /PRINT=ESTIM
  /DESIGN=HAPPY*MARITAL  HAPPY*INCOME82  HAPPY*HEALTH
MARITAL*INCOME82
          MARITAL*HEALTH  INCOME82*HEALTH
  /PRINT=ESTIM
  /DESIGN=HAPPY*MARITAL*INCOME82  HAPPY*MARITAL*HEALTH
          MARITAL*INCOME82*HEALTH  HAPPY*INCOME82*HEALTH.
```

```
DESIGN 1 has generating class

   HAPPY
   MARITAL
   INCOME82
   HEALTH

The Iterative Proportional Fit algorithm converged at iteration 2.

  Goodness-of-fit test statistics

     Likelihood ratio chi square =    404.06381    DF = 29  P = 0.0
                 Pearson chi square =    592.88247    DF = 29  P = 0.0


DESIGN 2 has generating class

   HAPPY*MARITAL
   HAPPY*INCOME82
   HAPPY*HEALTH
   MARITAL*INCOME82
   MARITAL*HEALTH
   INCOME82*HEALTH

The Iterative Proportional Fit algorithm converged at iteration 6.

  Goodness-of-fit test statistics

     Likelihood ratio chi square =     12.60130    DF = 16  P =  .702
                 Pearson chi square =     12.31572    DF = 16  P =  .722


DESIGN 3 has generating class

   HAPPY*MARITAL*INCOME82
   HAPPY*MARITAL*HEALTH
   MARITAL*INCOME82*HEALTH
   HAPPY*INCOME82*HEALTH

The Iterative Proportional Fit algorithm converged at iteration 3.

  Goodness-of-fit test statistics

     Likelihood ratio chi square =      3.99256    DF = 4  P =  .407
                 Pearson chi square =      3.97332    DF = 4  P =  .410
```

The likelihood-ratio chi-square value for Design 2, the second-order interaction model, is 12.60. This value provides a test of the hypothesis that all third- and fourth-order interaction terms are 0. The difference between 12.60 and 3.99 (8.61) provides a test of the hypothesis that all third-order terms are 0. In general, the test of the hypothesis that the kth-order terms are 0 is based on

$$\chi^2 = \chi^2_{k-1} - \chi^2_k$$

Equation 5.10

where χ^2_k is the value for the model that includes the kth-order effect or effects, and χ^2_{k-1} is the chi-square value for the model without the kth-order effects.

The SPSS/PC+ HILOGLINEAR (hierarchical log-linear) procedure automatically calculates tests of two types of hypotheses: the hypothesis that all kth- and higher-order effects are 0 and the hypothesis that the kth-order effects are 0. Figure 5.10b contains the test for the hypothesis that k- and higher-order effects are 0.

Figure 5.10b   Tests that *k*-way and higher-order effects are 0

```
HILOGLINEAR HAPPY(1,2) MARITAL(1,3) INCOME82(1,3) HEALTH(1,2)
  /PRINT=ASSOCIATION
  /DESIGN.
```

Tests that K-way and higher order effects are zero.

K	DF	L.R. Chisq	Prob	Pearson Chisq	Prob	Iteration
4	4	3.994	.4069	3.973	.4097	3
3	16	12.602	.7016	12.316	.7220	6
2	29	404.064	0.0	592.882	0.0	2
1	35	2037.779	.0000	2938.738	.0000	0

The first line of Figure 5.10b is a test of the hypothesis that the fourth-order interaction is 0. Note that the likelihood-ratio chi-square value of 3.99 is identical to the value displayed for Design 3 in Figure 5.10a. This is the goodness-of-fit statistic for a model without the fourth-order interaction. Similarly, the entry for the *k* of 3 is the goodness-of-fit test for a model without third- and fourth-order effects, like Design 2 in Figure 5.11. The last line, *k*=1, corresponds to a model that has no effects except the grand mean. That is, the expected value for all cells is the same—the average of the logs of the observed frequencies in all cells.

The column labeled **Prob** in Figure 5.10b gives the observed significance levels for the tests that *k*- and higher-order effects are 0. Small observed significance levels indicate that the hypothesis that terms of particular orders are 0 should be rejected. Note in Figure 5.10b that the hypotheses that all effects are 0 and that second-order and higher effects are 0 should be rejected. Since the observed significance level for the test that third- and higher-order terms are 0 is large (0.72), the hypothesis that third- and fourth-order interactions are 0 should not be rejected. Thus, it appears that a model with first- and second-order effects is adequate to represent the data.

It is sometimes also of interest to test whether interaction terms of a *particular* order are 0. For example, rather than asking if all effects greater than two-way are 0, the question is whether two-way effects are 0. Figure 5.10c gives the tests for the hypothesis that *k*-way effects are 0.

Figure 5.10c   Tests that *k*-way effects are 0

Tests that K-way effects are zero.

K	DF	L.R. Chisq	Prob	Pearson Chisq	Prob	Iteration
1	6	1633.715	0.0	2345.856	0.0	0
2	13	391.462	0.0	580.567	0.0	0
3	12	8.608	.7360	8.343	.7578	0
4	4	3.994	.4069	3.973	.4097	0

From Figure 5.10b the likelihood-ratio chi-square for a model with only the mean is 2037.779. The value for a model with first-order effects is 404.064. The difference between these two values, 1633.715, is displayed on the first line of Figure 5.10c. The difference is an indication of how much the model improves when first-order effects are included. The observed significance level for a chi-square value of 1634 with six degrees of freedom (35−29) is small, less than 0.00005, so the hypothesis that first-order effects are 0 is rejected. The remaining entries in Figure 5.10c are obtained in a similar fashion. The test that third-order effects are 0 is the difference between a model without third-order terms ($\chi^2_{LR}=12.602$) and a model with third-order terms ($\chi^2_{LR}=3.994$). The resulting chi-square value of 8.608 with 12 degrees of freedom has a large observed significance level (0.736), so the hypothesis that third-order terms are 0 is not rejected.

5.11
Testing Individual Terms in the Model

The two tests described in Section 5.10 provide an indication of the collective importance of effects of various orders. They do not, however, test the individual terms. That is, although the overall hypothesis that second-order terms are 0 may be rejected, that does not mean that every second-order effect is present.

One strategy for testing individual terms is to fit two models differing only in the presence of the effect to be tested. The difference between the two likelihood-ratio chi-square values, sometimes called the partial chi-square, also has a chi-square distribution and can be used to test the hypothesis that the effect is 0. For example, to test that the HAPPY by MARITAL by INCOME effect is 0, a model with all three-way interactions can be fit. From Figure 5.10a, the likelihood-ratio chi-square value for this model is 3.99. When a model without the HAPPY by MARITAL by INCOME effect is fit (Figure 5.11a), the likelihood ratio is 7.363. Thus, the partial chi-square value with four (8−4) degrees of freedom is 3.37 (7.36−3.99).

Figure 5.11a   Model without HAPPY by MARITAL by INCOME

```
HILOGLINEAR HAPPY(1,2) MARITAL(1,3) INCOME82(1,3) HEALTH(1,2)
  /PRINT=ESTIM
  /DESIGN=HAPPY*MARITAL*HEALTH
          MARITAL*INCOME82*HEALTH
          HAPPY*INCOME82*HEALTH.
```

```
DESIGN 1 has generating class

    HAPPY*MARITAL*HEALTH
    MARITAL*INCOME82*HEALTH
    HAPPY*INCOME82*HEALTH

The Iterative Proportional Fit algorithm converged at iteration 4.

Goodness-of-fit test statistics

    Likelihood ratio chi square =        7.36257    DF = 8  P =  .498
               Pearson chi square =        7.50541    DF = 8  P =  .483
```

Figure 5.11b contains the partial chi-square values and their observed significance levels for all effects in the HAPPY by MARITAL by HEALTH by INCOME table. Note that the observed significance levels are large for all three-way effects, confirming that first- and second-order effects are sufficient to represent the data. The last column indicates the number of iterations required to achieve convergence.

Figure 5.11b   Partial chi-squares
for HAPPY by MARITAL by HEALTH by INCOME

```
HILOGLINEAR HAPPY(1,2) MARITAL(1,3) INCOME82(1,3) HEALTH(1,2)
  /PRINT=ASSOCIATION
  /DESIGN=HAPPY*MARITAL*HEALTH*INCOME82.
```

```
Tests of PARTIAL associations.

Effect Name                        DF   Partial Chisq    Prob   Iter

HAPPY*MARITAL*INCOME82              4          3.370     .4979    4
HAPPY*MARITAL*HEALTH               2           .458     .7954    4
HAPPY*INCOME82*HEALTH              2           .955     .6203    3
MARITAL*INCOME82*HEALTH            4          3.652     .4552    5
HAPPY*MARITAL                      2         15.050     .0005    5
HAPPY*INCOME82                     2         16.120     .0003    5
MARITAL*INCOME82                   4        160.739    0.0       4
HAPPY*HEALTH                       1         55.696     .0000    5
MARITAL*HEALTH                     2          8.391     .0151    5
INCOME82*HEALTH                    2         35.602     .0000    5
HAPPY                              1        849.539    0.0       2
MARITAL                           2        343.394    0.0       2
INCOME82                          2         86.114     .0000    2
HEALTH                            1        354.661    0.0       2
```

5.12
Model Selection Using Backward Elimination

As in regression analysis, another way to arrive at a "best" model is by using variable-selection algorithms. Forward selection adds effects to a model, while backward elimination starts with all effects in a model and then removes those that do not satisfy the criterion for remaining in the model. Since backward elimination appears to be the better procedure for model selection (Benedetti & Brown, 1978), it is the only procedure described here.

The initial model for backward elimination need not be saturated but can be any hierarchical model. At the first step, the effect whose removal results in the least-significant change in the likelihood-ratio chi-square is eligible for elimination, provided that the observed significance level is larger than the criterion for remaining in the model. To ensure a hierarchical model, only effects corresponding to the generating class are examined at each step. For example, if the generating class is MARITAL*HAPPY*INCOME*HEALTH, the first step examines only the fourth-order interaction.

Figure 5.12a shows output at the first step. Elimination of the fourth-order interaction results in a chi-square change of 3.994, which has an associated significance level of 0.4069. Since this significance level is not less than 0.05 (the default HILOGLINEAR criterion for remaining in the model), the effect is removed. The new model has all three-way interactions as its generating class.

Figure 5.12a First step in backward elimination

```
HILOGLINEAR HAPPY(1,2) MARITAL(1,3) INCOME82(1,3) HEALTH(1,2)
  /METHOD=BACKWARD
  /MAXSTEPS=6
  /DESIGN=HAPPY*MARITAL*INCOME82*HEALTH.
```

```
Backward Elimination for DESIGN 1 with generating class

  HAPPY*MARITAL*INCOME82*HEALTH

Likelihood ratio chi square =      0.0        DF = 0  P = 1.000


If Deleted Simple Effect is               DF  L.R. Chisq Change   Prob  Iter

HAPPY*MARITAL*INCOME82*HEALTH              4               3.994  .4069    3

Step 1

  The best model has generating class

      HAPPY*MARITAL*INCOME82
      HAPPY*MARITAL*HEALTH
      HAPPY*INCOME82*HEALTH
      MARITAL*INCOME82*HEALTH

  Likelihood ratio chi square =     3.99354   DF = 4  P =  .407
```

Figure 5.12b contains the statistics for the second step. The effects eligible for removal are all three-way interactions. The HAPPY*MARITAL*HEALTH interaction has the largest observed significance level for the change in the chi-square if it is removed, so it is eliminated from the model. The likelihood-ratio chi-square for the resulting model is 4.45.

Figure 5.12b Statistics used to eliminate second effect

```
If Deleted Simple Effect is               DF  L.R. Chisq Change   Prob  Iter

HAPPY*MARITAL*INCOME82                     4               3.370  .4979    4
HAPPY*MARITAL*HEALTH                       2                .458  .7954    4
HAPPY*INCOME82*HEALTH                      2                .955  .6203    3
MARITAL*INCOME82*HEALTH                    4               3.652  .4552    5

Step 2

  The best model has generating class

      HAPPY*MARITAL*INCOME82
      HAPPY*INCOME82*HEALTH
      MARITAL*INCOME82*HEALTH

  Likelihood ratio chi square =     4.45127   DF = 6  P =  .616
```

At the next three steps the remaining third-order interactions are removed from the model. The sixth step begins with all second-order items in the model, as shown in Figure 5.12c.

Figure 5.12c   Sixth step in backward elimination

```
If Deleted Simple Effect is                        DF   L.R. Chisq Change    Prob   Iter

  HAPPY*HEALTH                                       1            55.697     .0000     5
  HAPPY*MARITAL                                      2            15.052     .0005     5
  HAPPY*INCOME82                                     2            16.121     .0003     5
  MARITAL*INCOME82                                   4           160.739   0.0         5
  MARITAL*HEALTH                                     2             8.392     .0151     5
  INCOME82*HEALTH                                    2            35.603     .0000     4

Step 6

  The best model has generating class

      HAPPY*HEALTH
      HAPPY*MARITAL
      HAPPY*INCOME82
      MARITAL*INCOME82
      MARITAL*HEALTH
      INCOME82*HEALTH

  Likelihood ratio chi square =     12.60116    DF = 16  P =  .702


The final model has generating class

    HAPPY*HEALTH
    HAPPY*MARITAL
    HAPPY*INCOME82
    MARITAL*INCOME82
    MARITAL*HEALTH
    INCOME82*HEALTH

The Iterative Proportional Fit algorithm converged at iteration 0.
```

Since the observed significance level for removal of any of the two-way interactions is smaller than 0.05, no more effects are removed from the model. The final model contains all second-order interactions and has a chi-square value of 12.60. This is the same model suggested by the partial-association table.

At this point it is a good idea to examine the residuals to see if any anomalies are apparent. The largest standardized residual is 1.34, which suggests that the model fits well. The residual plots also show nothing suspicious.

5.13
RUNNING PROCEDURE HILOGLINEAR

The SPSS/PC+ HILOGLINEAR procedure allows you to fit, test, and estimate parameters of hierarchical log-linear models. Using HILOGLINEAR, you can examine and compare a variety of hierarchical models, either by specifying tests of partial association or by requesting backward elimination. HILOGLINEAR also provides estimates of the parameters for saturated models.

HILOGLINEAR operates via a variable list and subcommands. None of the subcommands are required; the minimum specification on HILOGLINEAR is simply the variable list. The output for the minimum specification includes observed and expected frequencies for a *k*-way table and parameter estimates for the saturated model.

5.14
Specifying the Variables

The variable list identifies the categorical variables used in the model or models you fit. Variables must be numeric and integer. Each variable in the list must be accompanied by minimum and maximum values in parentheses, as in the command

```
HILOGLINEAR SEX(1,2) RACE(1,2) HAPPY(1,2) MARITAL(1,3)
INCOME82(1,3).
```

If several consecutive variables in the variable list have the same ranges, the minimum and maximum values can be listed after the last variable with these values. Thus, the command

```
HILOGLINEAR SEX RACE HAPPY(1,2) MARITAL INCOME82(1,3).
```

is equivalent to the previous command.

The values of the variables should be consecutive positive integers because HILOGLINEAR assumes there is a category for every value in the specified range. For example, the values 1, 2, and 3 are preferable to the values 5, 10, and 15. If necessary, you can recode variables using the RECODE command prior to the HILOGLINEAR command.

5.15
Specifying the Generating Class

Use the DESIGN subcommand to specify the generating class for the terms in a model. Asterisks are used to specify the highest-order interactions in a generating class. For example, the command

```
HILOGLINEAR SEX RACE HAPPY(1,2) MARITAL INCOME82(1,3)
  /DESIGN=HAPPY*MARITAL*INCOME82 SEX.
```

specifies a hierarchical model with the main effects HAPPY, MARITAL, INCOME82, and SEX; all second-order effects involving HAPPY, MARITAL, and INCOME82; and the third-order interaction term HAPPY *MARITAL* INCOME82. The command

```
HILOGLINEAR HAPPY(1,2) MARITAL(1,3)
  /DESIGN=HAPPY*MARITAL.
```

specifies a hierarchical model with the main effects HAPPY and MARITAL and the second-order interaction of HAPPY and MARITAL, producing the output in Figures 5.3 and 5.4.

You can use multiple DESIGN subcommands on a HILOGLINEAR command. If you omit the DESIGN subcommand or use it without specifications, a default model is fit. SPSS/PC+ produces parameter estimates only if the saturated model is specified. If you request an unsaturated model, the output will contain only the goodness-of-fit test for the model, the observed and expected frequencies, and the residuals and standardized residuals.

5.16
Building a Model

Use the MAXORDER, CRITERIA, METHOD, and CWEIGHT subcommands to control computational and design aspects of a model and to perform model selection. Each of these subcommands remains in effect for any subsequent DESIGN subcommands unless overridden by new subcommand specifications.

5.17
Specifying the Order of the Model

The MAXORDER subcommand specifies the maximum order of terms in a model. If you specify MAXORDER=k, HILOGLINEAR fits a model with all terms of order k or less. Thus, MAXORDER provides an abbreviated way of specifying models. For example, the command

```
HILOGLINEAR MARITAL(1,3) HAPPY RACE SEX(1,2)
  /MAXORDER=2.
```

is equivalent to

```
HILOGLINEAR MARITAL(1,3) HAPPY RACE SEX(1,2)
  /DESIGN=MARITAL*HAPPY
          MARITAL*RACE
          MARITAL*SEX
          HAPPY*RACE
          HAPPY*SEX
          RACE*SEX.
```

If both MAXORDER and DESIGN are used, the MAXORDER subcommand restricts the model stated on the DESIGN subcommand. If MAXORDER specifies an order less than the total number of variables (i.e., if an unsaturated model is fit), HILOGLINEAR does not display parameter estimates but does produce a goodness-of-fit test and the observed and expected frequencies for the model.

B

Statistics Guide

5.18
Specifying the Estimation Criteria

HILOGLINEAR uses an iterative procedure to fit models. Use the CRITERIA subcommand to specify the values of constants in the iterative proportional-fitting and model-selection routines. The keywords available for CRITERIA are

CONVERGE(n) *Convergence criterion.* The default is 0.25. Iterations stop when the change in fitted frequencies is less than the specified value.
ITERATE(n) *Maximum number of iterations.* The default is 20.
P(p) *Probability of chi-square for removal.* The default value is 0.05.
MAXSTEPS(n) *Maximum number of steps.* The default is 10.
DEFAULT *Default values.* Use DEFAULT to restore defaults altered by a previous CRITERIA subcommand.

The value for each keyword must be enclosed in parentheses. You can specify more than one keyword on a CRITERIA subcommand. Only those criteria specifically altered are changed. The keywords P and MAXSTEPS apply only to model selection and, therefore, must be used with an accompanying METHOD subcommand.

5.19
Requesting Backward Elimination

The METHOD subcommand requests a search for the best model through backward elimination of terms from the model. Use the subcommand METHOD alone or with the BACKWARD keyword.

If you omit the METHOD subcommand, HILOGLINEAR tests the model requested on the DESIGN subcommand but does not perform any model selection.

You can use the METHOD subcommand with DESIGN specifications (Section 5.15) or MAXORDER (Section 5.16) to obtain backward elimination that begins with the specified hierarchical model. For example, the command

```
HILOGLINEAR RACE SEX HAPPY(1,2) MARITAL INCOME82(1,3)
    /MAXORDER=3
    /METHOD=BACKWARD.
```

requests backward elimination beginning with a hierarchical model that contains all three-way interactions and excludes all four- and five-way interactions.

You can use the CRITERIA subcommand with METHOD to specify the removal criterion and maximum number of steps for a backward-elimination analysis. Thus, the command

```
HILOGLINEAR MARITAL INCOME(1,3) SEX HAPPY(1,2)
    /METHOD=BACKWARD
    /CRITERIA=P(.01) MAXSTEPS(25).
```

specifies a removal probability criterion of 0.01 and a maximum of 25 steps. The command

```
HILOGLINEAR HAPPY(1,2) MARITAL (1,3) INCOME82 (1,3) HEALTH (1,2)
    /METHOD=BACKWARD
    /CRITERIA=MAXSTEPS(6)
    /DESIGN=HAPPY*MARITAL*INCOME82*HEALTH.
```

requests a backward elimination of terms with a maximum of six steps. These commands produce the output in Figures 5.12a, 5.12b, and 5.12c.

5.20
Setting Structural Zeros

Use the CWEIGHT subcommand to specify cell weights for a model. Do not use CWEIGHT to weight aggregated input data (use the SPSS/PC+ WEIGHT command instead). CWEIGHT allows you to impose structural zeros on a model. HILOGLINEAR ignores the CWEIGHT subcommand with a saturated model.

There are two ways to specify cell weights. First, you can specify a numeric variable whose values are the cell weights. The command

```
HILOGLINEAR MARITAL(1,3) SEX HAPPY(1,2)
    /CWEIGHT=CELLWGT
    /DESIGN=MARITAL*SEX SEX*HAPPY MARITAL*HAPPY.
```

weights a cell by the value of the variable CELLWGT when a case containing the frequency for that cell is read.

Alternatively, you can specify a matrix of weights enclosed in parentheses on the CWEIGHT subcommand. You can use the prefix $n*$ to indicate that a cell weight is repeated n times in the matrix. The command

```
HILOGLINEAR MARITAL(1,3) INCOME(1,3)
  /CWEIGHT=(0 1 1 1 0 1 1 1 0)
  /DESIGN=MARITAL INCOME.
```

is equivalent to

```
HILOGLINEAR MARITAL(1,3) INCOME(1,3)
  /CWEIGHT=(0 3*1 0 3*1 0)
  /DESIGN=MARITAL INCOME.
```

You must specify a weight for every cell in the table. Cell weights are indexed by the levels of the variables in the order they are specified in the variable list. The index values of the rightmost variable change the most quickly.

5.21
Producing Optional Output

By default, HILOGLINEAR displays observed and expected cell frequencies, residuals and standardized residuals, and, for saturated models, parameter estimates. Use the following keywords on the PRINT command to obtain additional output:

FREQ   *Observed and expected cell frequencies.*

RESID   *Residuals and standardized residuals.*

ESTIM   *Parameter estimates, standard errors of estimates, and confidence intervals for parameters.* These are calculated only for saturated models.

ASSOCIATION *Tests of partial association.* These are calculated only for saturated models.

DEFAULT   *Default display.* FREQ and RESID for all models plus ESTIM for saturated models.

ALL   *All available output.*

If you specify PRINT, only output explicitly requested is displayed. The PRINT subcommand affects all subsequent DESIGN subcommands unless a new PRINT subcommand is specified.

For example, the command

```
HILOGLINEAR HAPPY(1,2) MARITAL (1,3)
  /PRINT=ESTIM
  /DESIGN=HAPPY*MARITAL.
```

limits the display to parameter estimates, standard errors of estimates, and confidence intervals for the saturated model. This command produces the output in Figure 5.4.

5.22
Requesting Plots

To obtain plots of residuals, you must specify the PLOT subcommand. The following keywords are available on PLOT:

RESID   *Plot of standardized residuals against observed and expected counts.*

NORMPLOT   *Normal and detrended normal probability plots of the standardized residuals.*

NONE   *No plots.* Suppresses any plots requested on a previous PLOT subcommand. This is the default if the subcommand is omitted.

DEFAULT   *Default plots.* RESID and NORMPLOT are plotted when PLOT is used without keyword specifications or with keyword DEFAULT. No plots are produced if the subcommand is omitted entirely.

ALL   *All available plots.*

The PLOT subcommand affects all subsequent DESIGN subcommands unless a new PLOT subcommand is specified.

5.23
Missing Values

By default, HILOGLINEAR deletes cases with missing values for any variable named on the variable list from the analysis. Use the MISSING subcommand to include cases with user-missing values or to specify the default explicitly. The keywords are

LISTWISE *Delete cases with missing values listwise. This is the default.*
INCLUDE *Include cases with user-missing values.*
DEFAULT *Same as LISTWISE.*

The MISSING subcommand can be specified only once on each HILOGLINEAR command and applies to all the designs specified on that command.

5.24
Annotated Example

The following SPSS/PC+ commands produced the output in Figures 5.10b, 5.10c, 5.12a, 5.12b, and 5.12c:

```
DATA LIST /
     MARITAL 8 AGE 15-16 RACE 24 INCOME82 31-32
     SEX 40 HAPPY 48 HEALTH 56.
RECODE MARITAL (1=1)(5=2)(2 THRU 4=3)(ELSE=SYSMIS)/
     INCOME82 (1 THRU 10=1)(11 THRU 14=2)(15 THRU
17=3)(ELSE=SYSMIS)/
     SEX (1=2)(2=1)/HAPPY (1 THRU 2=1)(3=2)(ELSE=SYSMIS)/
     HEALTH (1 THRU 2=1)(3 THRU 4=2)(ELSE=SYSMIS).
VALUE LABELS MARITAL 1 'MARRIED' 2 'SINGLE' 3 'SPLIT'/
          INCOME82 1 'LOW' 2 'MIDDLE' 3 'HIGH'/
          SEX 1 'FEMALE' 2 'MALE'/
          HAPPY 1 'YES' 2 'NO'/
          HEALTH 1 'GOOD+' 2 'FAIR-'.
BEGIN DATA.
data records
END DATA.
HILOGLINEAR HAPPY(1,2) MARITAL (1,3) INCOME82 (1,3) HEALTH (1,2)
  /PLOT=ALL
  /METHOD=BACKWARD
  /MAXSTEPS=6
  /DESIGN=HAPPY*MARITAL*INCOME82*HEALTH.
FINISH.
```

- The DATA LIST command gives the variable names and column locations of the variables used in the analysis.
- The RECODE command recodes the variables into consecutive integers to assure efficient processing.
- The VALUE LABELS command assigns descriptive labels to the recoded values of variables MARITAL, INCOME82, SEX, HAPPY, and HEALTH.
- The HILOGLINEAR command requests a backward elimination of the model with a maximum number of six steps. It also requests plots of the standardized residuals against observed and expected counts, as well as the normal and detrended normal probability plots of the standardized residuals.

Contents_____

6 Log-Linear Models: Procedure LOGLINEAR

Why do some people slip on banana peels while others glide through life unscathed? Why are some people Pollyannas while others are Ebenezer Scrooges? Throughout history, many theories have been proposed to explain such differences. The ancient Greeks believed that the human body was composed of four humors: phlegm, blood, yellow bile, and black bile. The predominant humor determined the personality. For example, black bile is associated with melancholia, and phlegm with a phlegmatic disposition.

The Babylonians and Egyptians looked to the positions of the stars and planets to explain differences among people. The position of the sun and planets at the time of one's birth determined destiny. Though the four-humors theory has few followers today, astrology continues to intrigue many. Even the most serious scientist may on occasion sneak a look at the horoscope page, just for fun, of course...

The ultimate test of any theory is how well it withstands the rigors of scientific testing. The General Social Survey in 1984 recorded the zodiac signs of 1,462 persons, along with a variety of other information, ranging from views on the afterlife to mother's employment status when the respondent was 16 years old. In this chapter, the LOGLINEAR procedure is used to test a variety of hypotheses about zodiac signs and their relationships to other variables.

6.1
LOG-LINEAR MODELS

Chapter 7 of *SPSS/PC+ Advanced Statistics V2.0* describes the HILOGLINEAR procedure for testing hypotheses about hierarchical log-linear models. In this chapter, additional types of models, including nonhierarchical models, produced by the LOGLINEAR procedure are examined. Section 6.23 describes additional differences between HILOGLINEAR and LOGLINEAR. This chapter assumes familiarity with the hierarchical log-linear models described in Chapter 5.

6.2
Frequency Table Models

One of the first hypotheses you might want to test is whether all twelve zodiac signs appear to be equally likely in the population from which the General Social Survey draws its sample. Figure 6.2 contains the observed and expected cell counts under the model of *equiprobability*. For example, there are 113 Ariens, which is (113/1,462) or 7.73% of the sample. These values are shown in the column labeled **OBS. count & PCT**. If all zodiac signs are equally likely, 8.33% of the sample (1/12), or 121.83 (1,462/12) respondents, are expected in each cell. These values are shown in the column labeled **EXP. count & PCT**. The differences between the observed and expected counts are in the column labeled **Residual**.

Figure 6.2 Frequencies and residuals for the equiprobability model

```
COMPUTE X=1.
SET WIDTH=WIDE.
LOGLINEAR ZODIAC(1,12) WITH X
    /DESIGN=X.
```

Observed, Expected Frequencies and Residuals

Factor	Code	OBS. count & PCT.	EXP. count & PCT.	Residual	Std. Resid.	Adj. Resid.
ZODIAC	ARIES	113.00 (7.73)	121.83 (8.33)	-8.8333	-.8003	-.8359
ZODIAC	TAURUS	115.00 (7.87)	121.83 (8.33)	-6.8333	-.6191	-.6466
ZODIAC	GEMINI	137.00 (9.37)	121.83 (8.33)	15.1667	1.3741	1.4352
ZODIAC	CANCER	121.00 (8.28)	121.83 (8.33)	-.8333	-.0755	-.0789
ZODIAC	LEO	122.00 (8.34)	121.83 (8.33)	.1667	.0151	.0158
ZODIAC	VIRGO	133.00 (9.10)	121.83 (8.33)	11.1667	1.0117	1.0567
ZODIAC	LIBRA	144.00 (9.85)	121.83 (8.33)	22.1667	2.0082	2.0975
ZODIAC	SCORPIO	114.00 (7.80)	121.83 (8.33)	-7.8333	-.7097	-.7412
ZODIAC	SAGITTAR	116.00 (7.93)	121.83 (8.33)	-5.8333	-.5285	-.5520
ZODIAC	CAPRICOR	131.00 (8.96)	121.83 (8.33)	9.1667	.8305	.8674
ZODIAC	AQUARIUS	93.00 (6.36)	121.83 (8.33)	-28.8333	-2.6122	-2.7284
ZODIAC	PISCES	123.00 (8.41)	121.83 (8.33)	1.1667	.1057	.1104

Goodness-of-Fit test statistics

```
    Likelihood Ratio Chi Square =    16.58881    DF = 11   P =  .121
               Pearson Chi Square =    16.28181    DF = 11   P =  .131
```

As in regression analysis, it is useful to normalize the residuals by dividing them by their standard deviations. Both standardized and adjusted residuals are calculated by LOGLINEAR. Standardized residuals are obtained by dividing each residual by the square root of the expected count. Adjusted residuals are calculated by dividing each standardized residual by an estimate of its standard error. If the number of cells in the table is large when compared to the number of estimated parameters for a model, the adjusted and standardized residuals should be similar. For large sample sizes, the distribution of the adjusted residuals is approximately standard normal.

By examining residuals we can identify patterns of deviation from the model. In this example, the standardized and adjusted residuals are fairly comparable. The only noticeable deviations from the equiprobability model occur for the Librans and Aquarians. Both of these zodiac signs have adjusted residuals greater than 2 in absolute value. The value 2 is a rule of thumb for "suspiciousness" since, in a standard normal distribution, only 5% of the absolute values exceed 1.96.

From the chi-square goodness-of-fit statistics shown in Figure 6.2, it appears that there is not sufficient evidence to reject the hypothesis that all zodiac signs are equally likely. The likelihood ratio chi-square value is 16.59 with 11 degrees of freedom. The observed significance level is 0.12.

6.3
Generalized Residuals

Figure 6.2 shows the results for each zodiac sign individually. It might be interesting to collapse the signs into four categories based on seasons of the year and see whether a seasonal effect may be present. This can be done by forming a linear combination of observed and expected values corresponding to each season. The goodness-of-fit of the equiprobability model does not change since the model remains the same.

Figure 6.3 contains results for the four seasons of the year. The first contrast corresponds to the spring zodiac signs (Aries, Taurus and Gemini), the second to the summer signs, the third to the fall signs, and the fourth to the winter signs. Spring comes very close to the expected number of births, summer and fall have a few more births than expected, while winter has the fewest number of births. Residuals corresponding to linear combinations of the cells are called *generalized residuals* (Haberman, 1979).

Figure 6.3   Generalized residuals

```
COMPUTE X=1.
LOGLINEAR ZODIAC(1,12) WITH X
  /GRESID=(3*1 9*0) /GRESID=(3*0 3*1 6*0)
  /GRESID=(6*0 3*1 3*0) /GRESID=(9*0 3*1)
  /DESIGN=X.
```

```
Goodness-of-Fit test statistics

    Likelihood Ratio Chi Square =      16.58881   DF = 11  P =  .121
                Pearson Chi Square =      16.28181   DF = 11  P =  .131

- - - - - - - - - - - - - - - - - - - - - - - - - - - - - - - - - - - - - -

Generalized Residual

Contrast      OBS count    EXP count    Residual  Std Resid.  Adj Resid.

     1         365.0       365.50       -.500       -.026       -.030
     2         376.0       365.50       10.500       .549        .634
     3         374.0       365.50        8.500       .445        .513
     4         347.0       365.50      -18.500       -.968      -1.117
```

6.4
Fitting a Quadratic Function

Instead of assuming an equiprobability model, let's see if some other relationship exists between seasons and number of births. For example, if the number of births steadily increases from spring to winter, we might consider a linear relationship. From Figure 6.3, one can see the relationship between the number of births and the seasons does not appear linear. Instead, a function that peaks and then decreases again is needed. (Note: in the previous analysis, the original twelve zodiac signs are analyzed and the results of this analysis grouped into seasons for display. In this analysis, the data are the number of births in each season.)

Let's consider a quadratic function. Figure 6.4a contains the observed and expected frequencies for each of the seasons when the expected number of cases for a season is expressed as a quadratic function.

Figure 6.4a   Frequencies and residuals for the quadratic model

```
COMPUTE SEASON=ZODIAC.
RECODE SEASON(1,2,3=1) (4,5,6=2) (7,8,9=3) (10,11,12=4).
VALUE LABELS SEASON 1'SPRING' 2'SUMMER' 3'FALL' 4'WINTER'.
COMPUTE LIN=SEASON.
COMPUTE LIN2=SEASON*SEASON.
SET WIDTH=WIDE.
LOGLINEAR SEASON(1,4) WITH LIN LIN2
  /DESIGN=LIN LIN2.
```

```
Observed, Expected Frequencies and Residuals
    Factor         Code         OBS. count & PCT.   EXP. count & PCT.    Residual  Std. Resid.  Adj. Resid.

SEASON          SPRING          365.00 (24.97)      364.36 (24.92)        .6447       .0338       .1493
SEASON          SUMMER          376.00 (25.72)      377.93 (25.85)      -1.9342      -.0995      -.1493
SEASON          FALL            374.00 (25.58)      372.07 (25.45)       1.9342       .1003       .1493
SEASON          WINTER          347.00 (23.73)      347.64 (23.78)       -.6447      -.0346      -.1493
```

Note that the expected values are no longer equal for each season. Summer has the largest expected frequency, 377.93, while winter has the smallest. This is true for the observed frequencies as well. The observed and expected values are closer than in an equiprobability model. The statistics for the overall fit of the quadratic model are shown in Figure 6.4b. Note that the chi-squared value is very small (0.02229), indicating that the model fits quite well. Figure 6.4c shows that the coefficients for the linear and quadratic terms for the log frequencies are small. In addition, both 95% confidence intervals include 0.

Figure 6.4b   Goodness-of-fit for the quadratic model

```
Goodness-of-Fit test statistics

    Likelihood Ratio Chi Square =      .02229   DF = 1  P =  .881
                Pearson Chi Square =      .02229   DF = 1  P =  .881
```

Figure 6.4c Parameter estimates for the linear and quadratic terms

```
COMPUTE SEASON=ZODIAC.
RECODE SEASON(1,2,3=1) (4,5,6=2) (7,8,9=3) (10,11,12=4).
COMPUTE LIN=SEASON.
COMPUTE LIN2=SEASON*SEASON.
LOGLINEAR SEASON(1,4) WITH LIN LIN2
  /PRINT=ESTIM
  /DESIGN=LIN LIN2.
```

```
Estimates for Parameters

LIN

  Parameter        Coeff.        Std. Err.        Z-Value        Lower 95 CI        Upper 95 CI

       1         .1149510016        .13261          .86681          -.14497            .37487

LIN2

  Parameter        Coeff.        Std. Err.        Z-Value        Lower 95 CI        Upper 95 CI

       2       -.0261200872        .02616         -.99829          -.07740            .02516
```

An equiprobability model also fits the data reasonably well, as shown in Figure 6.4d. It has an observed significance level for goodness-of-fit of 0.694. Note that the goodness-of-fit statistics for this are not the same as for the individual zodiac signs. However, the generalized residuals for the seasons (Figure 6.3) are equal to the residuals in Figure 6.4d.

Including additional terms in the model improves the fit, but not by much. The additional parameters decrease the degrees of freedom and should be used only if they substantially improve the fit. In other words, a good model should fit the data well and be as simple as possible.

Figure 6.4d Statistics for the equiprobability model

```
COMPUTE SEASON=ZODIAC.
RECODE SEASON(1,2,3=1) (4,5,6=2) (7,8,9=3) (10,11,12=4).
VALUE LABELS SEASON 1'SPRING' 2'SUMMER' 3'FALL' 4'WINTER'.
COMPUTE X=1.
SET WIDTH=WIDE.
LOGLINEAR SEASON(1,4) WITH X
  /DESIGN=X.
```

```
Observed, Expected Frequencies and Residuals

      Factor        Code        OBS. count & PCT.    EXP. count & PCT.    Residual    Std. Resid.    Adj. Resid.

  SEASON        SPRING        365.00 (24.97)      365.50 (25.00)       -.5000        -.0262        -.0302
  SEASON        SUMMER        376.00 (25.72)      365.50 (25.00)      10.5000         .5492         .6342
  SEASON        FALL          374.00 (25.58)      365.50 (25.00)       8.5000         .4446         .5134
  SEASON        WINTER        347.00 (23.73)      365.50 (25.00)     -18.5000        -.9677       -1.1174

- - - - - - - - - - - - - - - - - - - - - - - - - - - - - - - - - - - - - - - - - - - - - - - - - - - - - - - -

Goodness-of-Fit test statistics

    Likelihood Ratio Chi Square =      1.44824    DF = 3   P =   .694
             Pearson Chi Square =      1.43639    DF = 3   P =   .697
```

6.5
The Zodiac and Job Satisfaction

Now that we've established that there is no reason to disbelieve that all zodiac signs are equally likely (Figure 6.2), let's consider the possible relationship of zodiac signs to various aspects of life. Since a zodiac sign is thought to influence everything from love to numerical aptitude, it might be associated with characteristics such as income, education, happiness, and job satisfaction.

Consider Figure 6.5, which is a crosstabulation of zodiac signs and responses to a question about job satisfaction. Respondents are grouped into two categories: those who are very satisfied with their jobs and those who are less enthusiastic. The row percentages show quite a bit of variability among the signs. The irrepressible Aquarians are most likely to be satisfied with their jobs, while Virgos are the least likely to be content.

Figure 6.5 Zodiac sign by job satisfaction from CROSSTABS

```
RECODE SATJOB(1=1) (2,3,4=2) (ELSE=SYSMIS).
VALUE LABELS SATJOB 1 'VERY SAT' 2 'NOT VERY SAT'.
CROSSTABS ZODIAC BY SATJOB
  /OPTIONS 3.
```

```
- - - - - - -  C R O S S T A B U L A T I O N  O F  - - - -
     ZODIAC   RESPONDENT'S ASTROLOGICAL SIGN
BY  SATJOB   JOB OR HOUSEWORK
- - - - - - - - - - - - - - - - - - - - - - - - - - - - - -
```

	COUNT ROW PCT	SATJOB VERY SAT 1	NOT VERY SAT 2	ROW TOTAL
ZODIAC				
ARIES	1	45 / 49.5	46 / 50.5	91 / 7.6
TAURUS	2	42 / 43.3	55 / 56.7	97 / 8.1
GEMINI	3	61 / 53.0	54 / 47.0	115 / 9.6
CANCER	4	48 / 48.5	51 / 51.5	99 / 8.2
LEO	5	48 / 48.0	52 / 52.0	100 / 8.3
VIRGO	6	41 / 38.0	67 / 62.0	108 / 9.0
LIBRA	7	51 / 42.5	69 / 57.5	120 / 10.0
SCORPIO	8	37 / 38.9	58 / 61.1	95 / 7.9
SAGITTARIUS	9	46 / 47.9	50 / 52.1	96 / 8.0
CAPRICORN	10	46 / 42.2	63 / 57.8	109 / 9.1
AQUARIUS	11	49 / 63.6	28 / 36.4	77 / 6.4
PISCES	12	37 / 38.9	58 / 61.1	95 / 7.9
COLUMN TOTAL		551 / 45.8	651 / 54.2	1202 / 100.0

```
NUMBER OF MISSING OBSERVATIONS =     271
```

6.6
Fitting a Logit Model

To test whether zodiac sign and job satisfaction are independent, a log-linear model can be fit to the data in Figure 6.5. If the two variables are independent, a model without the interaction term should be sufficient. In such models, no distinction is made between independent and dependent variables. Zodiac sign and job satisfaction are both used to estimate the expected number of cases in each cell.

When one variable is thought to depend on the others, a special class of log-linear models, called *logit models*, can be used to examine the relationship between the dichotomous dependent variable, such as job satisfaction, and one or more independent variables. Let's examine the relationship between job satisfaction and zodiac sign, considering job satisfaction as the dependent variable and zodiac sign as independent.

In many statistical procedures, a dichotomous dependent variable is coded as having values of 0 or 1, and subsequent calculations are based on these values. In a logit model, the dependent variable is not the actual value of the variable but the log odds. An odds is the ratio of the frequency of occurrence and the frequency of nonoccurrence. For example, from Figure 6.5 the observed frequency of an Arien's being very satisfied with his job is 45, while the observed frequency of an Arien's being not very satisfied with his job is 46. The estimated odds that an Arien is very satisfied are 45 to 46, or 0.98. This means that an Arien is about equally likely to be very satisfied or not very satisfied. Similarly, the odds for an Aquarian being very satisfied are 1.25 (49/28), indicating that Aquarians are somewhat more likely to be very satisfied than unsatisfied. The odds can also be interpreted as the ratio of two probabilities—the probability that an Arien is very satisfied and the probability that an Arien is not very satisfied.

Let's consider how a logit model can be derived from the usual log-linear model. In a saturated log-linear model, the log of the number of very satisfied Ariens can be expressed as

$$\ln F_{11} = \mu + \lambda^{\text{very satisfied}} + \lambda^{\text{Ariens}} + \lambda^{\text{very satisfied—Ariens}} \qquad \textbf{Equation 6.6a}$$

Similarly, the log of the number of unsatisfied Ariens is

$$\ln F_{12} = \mu + \lambda^{\text{unsatisfied}} + \lambda^{\text{Ariens}} + \lambda^{\text{unsatisfied—Arien}} \qquad \textbf{Equation 6.6b}$$

The log of the ratio of the two frequencies is called a "logit." Recalling that the log of the ratio is

$$\ln (F_{11}/F_{12}) = \ln F_{11} - \ln F_{12} \qquad \textbf{Equation 6.6c}$$

we can compute the logit for Ariens as

$$\ln (F_{11}/F_{12}) = (\mu - \mu) + (\lambda^{\text{very satisfied}} - \lambda^{\text{unsatisfied}}) + (\lambda^{\text{Ariens}} - \lambda^{\text{Ariens}}) \qquad \textbf{Equation 6.6d}$$
$$+ (\lambda^{\text{very satisfied—Arien}} - \lambda^{\text{unsatisfied—Arien}})$$

Equation 6.6d can be considerably simplified. Note first that all the μ and λ^{Arien} terms cancel. Next, remember that the lambda terms must sum to 0 over all categories of a variable. For a variable that has two categories, this means that the values of the lambda parameters are equal in absolute value but opposite in sign. Thus, $\lambda^{\text{very satisfied}} = -\lambda^{\text{unsatisfied}}$, and $\lambda^{\text{very satisfied—Arien}} = -\lambda^{\text{unsatisfied—Arien}}$. Using these observations, the previous equation can be expressed as

$$\ln (F_{11}/F_{12}) = 2 (\lambda^{\text{very satisfied}} + \lambda^{\text{very satisfied—Arien}}) \qquad \textbf{Equation 6.6e}$$

Thus, the logit is a function of the same lambda parameters that appear in the general log-linear model.

The output for a logit model differs somewhat from the usual log-linear model. As shown in Figure 6.6, the percentages are not based on the total table count but on the counts in each category of the independent variable. Thus, the percentages sum to 100 for each zodiac sign. For example, 49.5% of all Ariens are very satisfied with their jobs, while 50.5% are not. Since the logit model is saturated, the observed and expected frequencies are equal and all of the residuals are 0.

Figure 6.6 Observed and expected frequencies for the saturated logit model

```
SET WIDTH=WIDE.
LOGLINEAR SATJOB(1,2) BY ZODIAC(1,12)
  /DESIGN SATJOB SATJOB BY ZODIAC.
```

```
Observed, Expected Frequencies and Residuals

      Factor          Code           OBS. count & PCT.    EXP. count & PCT.    Residual    Std. Resid.    Adj. Resid.


SATJOB            VERY SAT
  ZODIAC          ARIES               45.50 (49.46)        45.50 (49.46)        .0000         .0000          .0000
  ZODIAC          TAURUS              42.50 (43.37)        42.50 (43.37)        .0000         .0000          .0000
  ZODIAC          GEMINI              61.50 (53.02)        61.50 (53.02)        .0000         .0000          .0000
  ZODIAC          CANCER              48.50 (48.50)        48.50 (48.50)        .0000         .0000          .0000
  ZODIAC          LEO                 48.50 (48.02)        48.50 (48.02)        .0000         .0000          .0000
  ZODIAC          VIRGO               41.50 (38.07)        41.50 (38.07)        .0000         .0000          .0000
  ZODIAC          LIBRA               51.50 (42.56)        51.50 (42.56)        .0000         .0000          .0000
  ZODIAC          SCORPIO             37.50 (39.06)        37.50 (39.06)        .0000         .0000          .0000
  ZODIAC          SAGITTAR            46.50 (47.94)        46.50 (47.94)        .0000         .0000          .0000
  ZODIAC          CAPRICOR            46.50 (42.27)        46.50 (42.27)        .0000         .0000          .0000
  ZODIAC          AQUARIUS            49.50 (63.46)        49.50 (63.46)        .0000         .0000          .0000
  ZODIAC          PISCES              37.50 (39.06)        37.50 (39.06)        .0000         .0000          .0000

SATJOB            NOT VERY
  ZODIAC          ARIES               46.50 (50.54)        46.50 (50.54)        .0000         .0000          .0000
  ZODIAC          TAURUS              55.50 (56.63)        55.50 (56.63)        .0000         .0000          .0000
  ZODIAC          GEMINI              54.50 (46.98)        54.50 (46.98)        .0000         .0000          .0000
  ZODIAC          CANCER              51.50 (51.50)        51.50 (51.50)        .0000         .0000          .0000
  ZODIAC          LEO                 52.50 (51.98)        52.50 (51.98)        .0000         .0000          .0000
  ZODIAC          VIRGO               67.50 (61.93)        67.50 (61.93)        .0000         .0000          .0000
  ZODIAC          LIBRA               69.50 (57.44)        69.50 (57.44)        .0000         .0000          .0000
  ZODIAC          SCORPIO             58.50 (60.94)        58.50 (60.94)        .0000         .0000          .0000
  ZODIAC          SAGITTAR            50.50 (52.06)        50.50 (52.06)        .0000         .0000          .0000
  ZODIAC          CAPRICOR            63.50 (57.73)        63.50 (57.73)        .0000         .0000          .0000
  ZODIAC          AQUARIUS            28.50 (36.54)        28.50 (36.54)        .0000         .0000          .0000
  ZODIAC          PISCES              58.50 (60.94)        58.50 (60.94)        .0000         .0000          .0000
```

6.7
Parameter Estimates

In the logit model, the parameter estimates displayed (Figure 6.7) are the actual lambdas, not twice lambda. Thus, the values are identical to those obtained in the log-linear model. No coefficient is displayed for the zodiac variable since it does not directly appear in the logit model (see Equation 6.6e).

Figure 6.7 Parameter estimates for the logit model

```
LOGLINEAR SATJOB(1,2) BY ZODIAC(1,12)
  /PRINT=ESTIM
  /DESIGN.
```

```
Estimates for Parameters

SATJOB

Parameter       Coeff.       Std. Err.      Z-Value  Lower 95 CI  Upper 95 CI

        1    -.0760266930       .02927      -2.59755     -.13339      -.01866

SATJOB BY ZODIAC

Parameter       Coeff.       Std. Err.      Z-Value  Lower 95 CI  Upper 95 CI

        2     .0651566997       .09958       .65433      -.13002       .26033
        3    -.0574127794       .09753      -.58866      -.24857       .13375
        4     .1364449296       .08982      1.51917      -.03959       .31248
        5     .0460176882       .09590       .47983      -.14195       .23399
        6     .0364020072       .09550       .38117      -.15078       .22358
        7    -.1671903923       .09467     -1.76596      -.35275       .01837
        8    -.0738457794       .08888      -.83085      -.24805       .10036
        9    -.1463162176       .09987     -1.46511      -.34206       .04942
       10     .0347661812       .09727       .35740      -.15589       .22542
       11    -.0797671036       .09283      -.85926      -.26172       .10218
       12     .3520609842       .11124      3.16475       .13402       .57010
```

As in the general log-linear model, the deviation parameter estimates (the default) can be used to predict the expected cell frequencies. However, in a logit model, instead of predicting individual cell frequencies, the log odds are predicted. For example, the predicted log odds for the Ariens is

$$\ln(F_{11}/F_{12}) = 2 \times (\lambda^{\text{satjob}} + \lambda^{\text{satjob}-\text{Arien}}) = 2\,(-0.0760 + 0.0652)$$
$$= -0.022 \ F_{11}/F_{12} = e^{-0.022} = 0.98$$

Equation 6.7

Since this is a saturated model, the predicted odds equal the observed odds, the ratio of satisfied to dissatisfied Ariens (45.5/46.5).

B

Statistics Guide

6.8
Measures of Dispersion and Association

When a model is formulated with one classification variable considered as dependent, it is possible to analyze the dispersion or spread in the dependent variable. Two statistics that are used to measure the spread of a nominal variable are Shannon's entropy measure:

$$H = - \Sigma p_j \log p_j \qquad \text{Equation 6.8a}$$

and Gini's concentration measure:

$$C = 1 - \Sigma p_j^2 \qquad \text{Equation 6.8b}$$

Using either of these measures, it is possible to subdivide the total dispersion of the dependent variable into that explained by the model and the residual, or unexplained, variance. Figure 6.8 contains the analysis of dispersion for the satisfaction and zodiac sign when a saturated logit model is fit.

Figure 6.8 Analysis of dispersion

```
Analysis of Dispersion

                                    Dispersion
      Source of Variation      Entropy  Concentration      DF

          Due to Model          10.452       10.341
          Due to Residual      826.905      592.540
          Total                837.357      602.881      1213

- - - - - - - - - - - - - - - - - - - - - - - - - - - - - - - - - -

Measures of Association

            Entropy =    .012482
      Concentration =    .017153
```

Based on the analysis of dispersion, it is possible to calculate statistics similar to R^2 in regression that indicate what proportion of the total dispersion in the dependent variable is attributable to the model. In Figure 6.8, when dispersion is measured by the entropy criterion, the ratio of the dispersion explained by the model to the total dispersion is 0.0125. When measured by the concentration criterion it is 0.0172. These values can be interpreted as measures of association. Although it is tempting to interpret the magnitudes of these measures similarly to R^2 in regression, this may be misleading since the coefficients may be small even when the variables are strongly related (Haberman, 1982). It appears that the coefficients are best interpreted in the light of experience.

6.9
Fitting an Unsaturated Logit Model

As discussed in Chapter 5, a saturated model exactly fits the data. This is also true for a logit model, which contains all interaction terms between the dependent variable and all combinations of the independent variables. Alternative models can be formed by deleting some terms from the saturated logit model. For example, to ascertain whether job satisfaction and zodiac sign are independent, we need to fit a logit model without the interaction term between job satisfaction and zodiac sign. Figure 6.9a contains the statistics for the cells and the chi-square values when the interaction term is eliminated.

Figure 6.9a   Statistics for the unsaturated model

```
SET WIDTH=WIDE.
LOGLINEAR SATJOB(1,2) BY ZODIAC(1,12)
   /DESIGN=SATJOB.
```

```
Observed, Expected Frequencies and Residuals

         Factor          Code         OBS. count & PCT.    EXP. count & PCT.    Residual   Std. Resid.   Adj. Resid.

SATJOB              VERY SAT
   ZODIAC           ARIES            45.00  (49.45)        41.71  (45.84)        3.2854       .5087          .7189
   ZODIAC           TAURUS           42.00  (43.30)        44.47  (45.84)       -2.4651      -.3697         -.5239
   ZODIAC           GEMINI           61.00  (53.04)        52.72  (45.84)        8.2837      1.1409         1.6302
   ZODIAC           CANCER           48.00  (48.48)        45.38  (45.84)        2.6181       .3886          .5513
   ZODIAC           LEO              48.00  (48.00)        45.84  (45.84)        2.1597       .3190          .4527
   ZODIAC           VIRGO            41.00  (37.96)        49.51  (45.84)       -8.5075     -1.2091        -1.7222
   ZODIAC           LIBRA            51.00  (42.50)        55.01  (45.84)       -4.0083      -.5404         -.7740
   ZODIAC           SCORPIO          37.00  (38.95)        43.55  (45.84)       -6.5483      -.9923        -1.4050
   ZODIAC           SAGITTAR         46.00  (47.92)        44.01  (45.84)        1.9933       .3005          .4257
   ZODIAC           CAPRICOR         46.00  (42.20)        49.97  (45.84)       -3.9659      -.5611         -.7995
   ZODIAC           AQUARIUS         49.00  (63.64)        35.30  (45.84)       13.7030      2.3065         3.2395
   ZODIAC           PISCES           37.00  (38.95)        43.55  (45.84)       -6.5483      -.9923        -1.4050

SATJOB              NOT VERY
   ZODIAC           ARIES            46.00  (50.55)        49.29  (54.16)       -3.2854      -.4680         -.7189
   ZODIAC           TAURUS           55.00  (56.70)        52.53  (54.16)        2.4651       .3401          .5239
   ZODIAC           GEMINI           54.00  (46.96)        62.28  (54.16)       -8.2837     -1.0496        -1.6302
   ZODIAC           CANCER           51.00  (51.52)        53.62  (54.16)       -2.6181      -.3575         -.5513
   ZODIAC           LEO              52.00  (52.00)        54.16  (54.16)       -2.1597      -.2935         -.4527
   ZODIAC           VIRGO            67.00  (62.04)        58.49  (54.16)        8.5075      1.1124         1.7222
   ZODIAC           LIBRA            69.00  (57.50)        64.99  (54.16)        4.0083       .4972          .7740
   ZODIAC           SCORPIO          58.00  (61.05)        51.45  (54.16)        6.5483       .9129         1.4050
   ZODIAC           SAGITTAR         50.00  (52.08)        51.99  (54.16)       -1.9933      -.2764         -.4257
   ZODIAC           CAPRICOR         63.00  (57.80)        59.03  (54.16)        3.9659       .5162          .7995
   ZODIAC           AQUARIUS         28.00  (36.36)        41.70  (54.16)      -13.7030     -2.1219        -3.2395
   ZODIAC           PISCES           58.00  (61.05)        51.45  (54.16)        6.5483       .9129         1.4050


Goodness-of-Fit test statistics

    Likelihood Ratio Chi Square =    21.12888    DF = 11    P =   .032
             Pearson Chi Square =    21.04523    DF = 11    P =   .033
```

The chi-square values indicate that an independence model does not fit the data well. The observed significance level is about 0.03. The adjusted residuals for the Aquarians are particularly large, so the model fits very poorly for this zodiac sign. The proportion of very satisfied Aquarians is substantially larger than expected.

Figure 6.9b is a plot of the observed values against the adjusted residuals. Two residuals are large in absolute value, and there may be a linear trend.

Figure 6.9b   Plot of observed counts and adjusted residuals

```
LOGLINEAR SATJOB(1,2) BY ZODIAC(1,12)
   /PLOT=RESID
   /DESIGN=SATJOB.
```

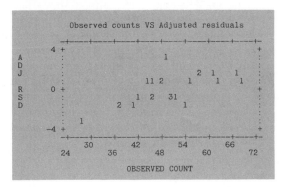

The results obtained from fitting a logit model without the interaction term are exactly identical to those that would be obtained if the usual log-linear model of independence were fit. The only difference is that, in the logit model, the parameter estimates for the zodiac values are not displayed, since they do not appear directly in the model. (The LOGLINEAR procedure, unlike HILOGLINEAR, produces parameter estimates for unsaturated models.)

6.10
Fitting a More Complicated Logit Model

Since earning money is usually an important reason for working, it is interesting to see what happens when income is included in the logit model of job satisfaction.

For the analysis, respondents' income is grouped into four categories, each containing roughly the same number of cases. Figure 6.10a contains the observed frequencies for the crosstabulation of job satisfaction with zodiac sign and income level.

Figure 6.10a   Three-way crosstabulation from TABLES

```
SET WIDTH=WIDE.
SET LENGTH 65.
TABLES /FORMAT=CWIDTH(15,7)
  /FTOTAL=T1'COLUMN TOTAL' T2'ROW TOTAL'
  /TABLE=ZODIAC + T1 BY SATJOB > (RINCOME+ T2)
  /STATISTICS=COUNT(ZODIAC'') CPCT(ZODIAC' ':ZODIAC SATJOB).
PRINT TABLES DEVICE=HPLASER /COMPRESSED.

Insert table from Xerox 9700.
(PICK UP FROM p. B-58, PC+ UPDATE MANUAL.)
```

Consider a logit model that includes only the effects of job satisfaction, job satisfaction by income, and job satisfaction by zodiac. Based on the statistics displayed in Figure 6.10b, it appears that the logit model without the three-way interaction of job satisfaction, income, and zodiac sign fits the data well. The observed significance level for the goodness-of-fit statistic is about 0.5. The diagnostic plots of adjusted residuals give no indication that there are suspicious departures from the model.

Figure 6.10b   Goodness-of-fit for the expanded logit model

```
LOGLINEAR SATJOB(1,2) BY ZODIAC(1,12) RINCOME(1,4)
  /DESIGN=SATJOB, SATJOB BY ZODIAC, SATJOB BY RINCOME.
```

```
Goodness-of-Fit test statistics

   Likelihood Ratio Chi Square =    31.62898    DF = 33  P =  .535
              Pearson Chi Square =    30.67426    DF = 33  P =  .583
```

Deviation parameter estimates for the logit model are shown in Figure 6.10c. The SATJOB parameter estimate is negative, indicating that overall the proportion of people highly satisfied with their jobs is less than the proportion that are dissatisfied. The coefficients corresponding to the RINCOME by SATJOB effect show the increase or decrease in the log-odds ratio associated with each income category. The parameter estimate shows that there is a progression from a fairly large negative value, -0.145, to a fairly large positive value, 0.166. (The estimate for the last income category is not displayed. It is obtained as the negative of the sum of the previous estimates.) Thus, it appears that lower income categories are associated with less job satisfaction than higher income categories. The parameter estimates for the ZODIAC by SATJOB interaction give the contribution of each zodiac sign to job satisfaction. Again, negative values are associated with dissatisfied zodiac signs while positive values are associated with more content signs. The largest positive parameter estimate (parameter 12) is for the Aquarians, who as a group are the most satisfied.

Figure 6.10c   Parameter estimates for the expanded logit model

```
LOGLINEAR SATJOB(1,2) BY ZODIAC(1,12) RINCOME(1,4)
  /PRINT=ESTIM
  /DESIGN=SATJOB, SATJOB BY ZODIAC, SATJOB BY RINCOME.
```

```
Estimates for Parameters
SATJOB

Parameter        Coeff.        Std. Err.      Z-Value      Lower 95 CI     Upper 95 CI

      1        -.0704541613      .03499       -2.01344        -.13904         -.00187

SATJOB BY ZODIAC

Parameter        Coeff.        Std. Err.      Z-Value      Lower 95 CI     Upper 95 CI

      2         .0564737768      .12811         .44083        -.19462         .30757
      3        -.1279033527      .11635       -1.09932        -.35594         .10014
      4         .1140066820      .10289        1.10807        -.08765         .31567
      5         .1178086027      .10963        1.07465        -.09706         .33267
      6         .0689561722      .11512         .59900        -.15667         .29459
      7        -.0802959724      .10761        -.74615        -.29122         .13063
      8        -.2077153468      .10751       -1.93201        -.41844         .00301
      9        -.1492020965      .11786       -1.26593        -.38021         .08180
     10         .0683122274      .11222         .60873        -.15164         .28826
     11        -.0634811554      .11004        -.57688        -.27916         .15220
     12         .3845323775      .12723        3.02224         .13515         .63391

SATJOB BY RINCOME

Parameter        Coeff.        Std. Err.      Z-Value      Lower 95 CI     Upper 95 CI

     13        -.1451090801      .06216       -2.33441        -.26694         -.02327
     14        -.0643412033      .05513       -1.16708        -.17240         .04371
     15         .0435190304      .05889         .73898        -.07191         .15894
```

Note that the logit is calculated as the log of the ratio of the number of cases in the first category to the number of cases in the second category. If SATJOB had been coded so that the first value was for the dissatisfied category, positive parameter estimates would occur for dissatisfied signs.

The expected log odds for each combination of income and zodiac sign can be obtained from the coefficients in Figure 6.10c. For example, the predicted log odds for Ariens with incomes of less than $6,000 is

$$2(-0.0704 - 0.145 + 0.0565) = -.318 \qquad \text{Equation 6.10}$$

The expected odds are $e^{-0.318}$, or 0.728. Thus, Ariens in low income categories are less likely to be highly satisfied than dissatisfied. Predicted odds values for the other cells are found in a similar fashion.

6.11
The Equivalent Log-Linear Model

As previously discussed, logit models can also be formulated as log-linear models. However, not all terms that are in the log-linear model appear in the logit model, since logit models do not include relationships among the independent variables. When the log odds ratios are formed, terms involving only the independent variables cancel, since for a particular combination of values of the independent variables, the effects are the same for both categories of the dependent variable.

Thus, the log-linear representation of a logit model contains additional terms for the independent variables. For example, the log-linear model that corresponds to the logit model described above has three additional terms: the main effect for zodiac, the main effect for income category, and the interaction between zodiac sign and income category (see Figure 6.11).

Figure 6.11   Goodness-of-fit statistics for the equivalent log-linear model

```
LOGLINEAR SATJOB(1,2) ZODIAC(1,12) RINCOME(1,4)
  /DESIGN SATJOB ZODIAC RINCOME SATJOB BY ZODIAC
          SATJOB BY RINCOME ZODIAC BY RINCOME.
```

```
Goodness-of-Fit test statistics
     Likelihood Ratio Chi Square =    31.62898   DF = 33   P =  .535
                Pearson Chi Square =    30.67426   DF = 33   P =  .583
```

6.12
MODELS FOR
ORDINAL DATA

In many situations, the categorical variables used in log-linear models are ordinal in nature. For example, income levels range from low to high, as does interest in a product, or severity of a disease. Ordinal variables may result from grouping values of interval variables such as income or education, or they may arise when ordering, but not distance, between categories can be established. Happiness, interest, and opinions on various issues are measured on ordinal scales. Although "a lot" is more than "some," the actual distance between the two response categories cannot be determined. The additional information contained in the ordering of the categories can be incorporated into log-linear models, which may result in a more parsimonious representation of the data (Agresti, 1984).

Let's consider some common models for ordinal data using the job satisfaction and income variables. Although only two categories of job satisfaction were used to illustrate logit models, there were actually four possible responses to the question: very satisfied, moderately satisfied, a little dissatisfied, and very dissatisfied. Figure 6.12 is the crosstabulation of job satisfaction and income categories. You can see that as salary increases, so does job satisfaction, especially at the ends of the salary scale. Almost 10% of people earning less than $6,000 are very dissatisfied with their jobs, while only 4% of those earning $25,000 or more are very dissatisfied with theirs. Similarly, almost 54% of those earning over $25,000 are very satisfied with their jobs, while only 40% of those earning less than $6,000 are very satisfied.

Figure 6.12   Job satisfaction by income level from CROSSTABS

```
RECODE SATJOB (1=4) (2=3) (3=2) (4=1) (ELSE=SYSMIS)
VALUE LABELS SATJOB 1 'VERY DIS' 2 'A LITTLE' 3 'MOD SAT' 4 'VER
SAT'/
           RINCOME 1 'LT 6000' 2 '6-15' 3 '15-25' 4 '25+'
CROSSTABS SATJOB BY RINCOME
  /OPTIONS 4
  /STATISTICS 1.
```

```
- - - - - - - - - - -  C R O S S T A B U L A T I O N  O F  - - - - - - - - - -
      SATJOB    JOB OR HOUSEWORK
BY   RINCOME    RESPONDENT'S INCOME
- - - - - - - - - - - - - - - - - - - - - - - - - - - - - - -  PAGE  1 OF 1
                     RINCOME
               COUNT
               COL PCT   LT 6000   6-15      15-25     25+        ROW
                                                                 TOTAL
                            1|        2|        3|        4|
SATJOB
           1        20        22        13         7          62
  VERY DIS          9.7       7.6       5.5       4.1         6.9

           2        24        38        28        18         108
  A LITTLE          11.7      13.1      11.9      10.5        12.0

           3        80       104        81        54         319
  MOD SAT           38.8      36.0      34.5      31.6        35.4

           4        82       125       113        92         412
  VER SAT           39.8      43.3      48.1      53.8        45.7

           COLUMN   206       289       235       171         901
           TOTAL    22.9      32.1      26.1      19.0        100.0


CHI-SQUARE     D.F.      SIGNIFICANCE        MIN E.F.      CELLS WITH E.F.< 5

  11.98857       9          0.2140            11.767            NONE

NUMBER OF MISSING OBSERVATIONS =        572
```

A variety of log-linear models that use the ordering of the job satisfaction and income variables can be entertained. Some of the models depend on the scores assigned to each category of response. Sometimes these may be arbitrary, since the actual distances between the categories are unknown. In this example, scores from 1 to 4 are assigned to both the income and job satisfaction categories. Other scores, such as the midpoints of the salary categories, might also be considered.

Three types of models will be considered for these data. One is the linear-by-linear association model, which uses the ordering of both variables. Another is the row effects model, which uses only the ordering of the column variable. The third is the column-effects model, which uses the ordering of the row variable.

6.13
The Linear-by-Linear Association Model

The linear-by-linear association model for two variables can be expressed as

$$\ln \widehat{F}_{ij} = \mu + \lambda_i^X + \lambda_j^Y + B(U_i - \overline{U})(V_j - \overline{V}) \qquad \text{Equation 6.13}$$

where the scores U_i and V_j are assigned to rows and columns. In this model, μ and the two lambda parameters are the usual log-linear terms for the overall mean and the main effects of income and job satisfaction. What differs is the inclusion of the term involving B. The coefficient B is essentially a regression coefficient that, for a particular cell, is multiplied by the scores assigned to that cell for income and job satisfaction. If the two variables are independent, the coefficient should be close to 0. (However, a coefficient of 0 does not necessarily imply independence since the association between the two variables may be nonlinear.) If the coefficient is positive, more cases are expected to fall in cells with large scores or small scores for both variables than would be expected if the two variables are independent. If the coefficient is negative, an excess of cases is expected in cells that have small values for one variable and large for the other.

Consider Figure 6.13a, which contains the deviation parameter estimates for the linear-by-linear association model for job satisfaction and income. The coefficient labeled **B** is the regression coefficient. It is positive and large when compared to its standard error, indicating that there is a positive association between income and job satisfaction. That is, as income increases or decreases, so does job satisfaction. The goodness-of-fit statistics displayed in Figure 6.13b indicate that the linear-by-linear interaction model fits the data very well. Inclusion of one additional parameter in the model has changed the observed significance level from 0.21 for the independence model (see Figure 6.12) to 0.97 for the linear-by-linear interaction model (see Figure 6.13b).

Figure 6.13a   Parameter estimates for the linear-by-linear model

```
COMPUTE B=RINCOME*SATJOB.
LOGLINEAR SATJOB(1,4) RINCOME(1,4) WITH B
  /PRINT=ESTIM
  /DESIGN=SATJOB RINCOME B.
```

Estimates for Parameters					
SATJOB					
Parameter	Coeff.	Std. Err.	Z-Value	Lower 95 CI	Upper 95 CI
1	-.6373902979	.15514	-4.10855	-.94146	-.33332
2	-.3298650538	.09273	-3.55723	-.51162	-.14811
3	.4926713610	.06961	7.07754	.35623	.62911
RINCOME					
Parameter	Coeff.	Std. Err.	Z-Value	Lower 95 CI	Upper 95 CI
4	.4628350833	.18277	2.53232	.10460	.82107
5	.4523050202	.08199	5.51637	.29160	.61301
6	-.1140864252	.07981	-1.42945	-.27052	.04234
B					
Parameter	Coeff.	Std. Err.	Z-Value	Lower 95 CI	Upper 95 CI
7	.1119394092	.03641	3.07462	.04058	.18330

Figure 6.13b   Goodness-of-fit for the linear-by-linear model

```
Goodness-of-Fit test statistics

    Likelihood Ratio Chi Square =      2.38592    DF = 8  P =  .967
                Pearson Chi Square =      2.32965    DF = 8  P =  .969
```

6.14
Row- and Column-Effects Models

In a row-effects model, only the ordinal nature of the column variable is used. For each row, a separate slope based on the values of the column variables is estimated. The magnitude and sign of the coefficient indicates whether cases are more or less likely to fall in a column with a high or low score, as compared to the independence model.

Consider the row-effects model when job satisfaction is the row variable. The coefficients for each row are displayed in Figure 6.14a under the heading SATJOB BY COV. The first coefficient is negative, indicating that very dissatisfied people are less likely to be in high income categories than the independence model would predict. The next two coefficients are positive but small, indicating that there is not much difference from the independence model in these rows. The fourth coefficient, which is not displayed, is the negative of the sum of the previous three coefficients (see Section 6.21). Its value is 0.17, indicating that there is an excess of respondents in the high income category who classify themselves as very satisfied. Overall, the row-effects model fits quite well, as shown in the goodness-of-fit statistics in Figure 6.14b. The observed significance level, 0.998, is quite large.

Figure 6.14a   Parameter estimates for the row-effects model

```
COMPUTE COV=RINCOME.
LOGLINEAR SATJOB(1,4) RINCOME(1,4) WITH COV
  /PRINT=ESTIM
  /DESIGN=SATJOB, RINCOME, SATJOB BY COV.
```

```
Estimates for Parameters

SATJOB

Parameter      Coeff.      Std. Err.     Z-Value Lower 95 CI Upper 95 CI

        1    -.5315173884      .23757     -2.23727    -.99716    -.06587
        2    -.5365551858      .20123     -2.66635    -.93097    -.14214
        3     .6100166132      .14540      4.19540     .32503     .89500

RINCOME

Parameter      Coeff.      Std. Err.     Z-Value Lower 95 CI Upper 95 CI

        4     .0324159194      .07298       .44420    -.11062     .17545
        5     .3101582155      .05654      5.48563     .19934     .42098
        6     .0299955391      .05864       .51154    -.08493     .14493

SATJOB BY COV

Parameter      Coeff.      Std. Err.     Z-Value Lower 95 CI Upper 95 CI

        7    -.2159732482      .10077     -2.14329    -.41348    -.01847
        8     .0340580646      .07897       .43129    -.12072     .18884
        9     .0071007552      .05807       .12228    -.10671     .12092
```

Figure 6.14b   Goodness-of-fit for the row-effects model

```
Goodness-of-Fit test statistics

   Likelihood Ratio Chi Square =        .52562    DF = 6  P =  .998
            Pearson Chi Square =        .52573    DF = 6  P =  .998
```

The column-effects model, which treats job satisfaction as an ordinal variable and ignores the ranking of the income categories, also fits the data reasonably well, as shown in Figure 6.14c. The observed significance level is 0.91. In fact, all three models that incorporate the ordinal nature of the classification variables result in good fit. Of the three, the linear-by-linear model is the most parsimonious since, when compared to the independence model, it estimates only one additional parameter. The row- and column-effects models are particularly useful when only one classification variable is ordinal or when both variables are ordinal but a linear trend across categories exists only for one.

Figure 6.14c   Goodness-of-fit for the column-effects model

```
COMPUTE COV=SATJOB.
LOGLINEAR SATJOB(1,4) RINCOME(1,4) WITH COV
   /DESIGN=SATJOB, RINCOME, COV BY RINCOME.
```

```
Goodness-of-Fit test statistics

   Likelihood Ratio Chi Square =       2.13725    DF = 6  P =  .907
            Pearson Chi Square =       2.11052    DF = 6  P =  .909
```

6.15
INCOMPLETE TABLES

All models examined so far have been based on complete tables. That is, all cells of the crosstabulation tables can have nonzero observed frequencies. This is not necessarily the case. For example, if you are studying the association between types of surgery and sex of the patient, the cell corresponding to Cesarian sections for males must be 0. This is termed a *fixed-zero cell,* since no cases can ever fall into it. Also, certain types of models ignore cells by treating them as if they were fixed zeros. Fixed-zero cells lead to incomplete tables, and special provisions must be made during analysis.

Cells in which the observed frequency is 0 but in which it is *possible* to have cases are sometimes called *random zeros.* For example, in a cross-classification of occupation and ethnic origin, the cell corresponding to Lithuanian sword-swallowers would probably be a random 0.

If a table has many cells with small expected values (say, less than 5), the chi-squared approximation for the goodness-of-fit statistics may be inadequate. In this case, pooling of categories should be considered.

There are many types of models for analyzing incomplete tables. In the next section, we will consider one of the simplest, the quasi-independence model, which considers the diagonal entries of a square table to be fixed zeros.

6.16
Testing Real against Ideal

What is the ideal number of children? The answer to the question is obviously influenced by various factors, including the size of the family in which one was raised. The 1982 General Social Survey asked respondents how many siblings they have as well as how many children should be in the ideal family. Figure 6.16 contains the crosstabulation of the number of children in the respondent's family and the number of children perceived as "ideal."

Figure 6.16   Actual children by ideal number of children from CROSSTABS

```
CROSSTABS IDEAL BY REAL
  /OPTIONS 4
  /STATISTICS 1.
```

```
- - - - - - - - - -  C R O S S T A B U L A T I O N   O F  - -
      IDEAL       IDEAL NUMBER OF CHILDREN
  BY  REAL        ACTUAL NUMBER OF CHILDREN
- - - - - - - - - - - - - - - - - - - - - - - - - - - - - - - -

                    REAL
           COUNT
           COL PCT  0-1       2       3-4      5 +       ROW
                                                        TOTAL
                    1.00|   2.00|   3.00|   4.00|
  IDEAL    --------+-------+-------+-------+-------+
             1        2       6      20      26       54
  0-1                2.7     3.0     4.5     3.9      3.9
           --------+-------+-------+-------+-------+
             2       55     138     278     335      806
  2                 74.3    68.7    62.3    49.7     57.8
           --------+-------+-------+-------+-------+
             3       16      48     139     287      490
  3-4               21.6    23.9    31.2    42.6     35.1
           --------+-------+-------+-------+-------+
             4        1       9       9      26       45
  5 +                1.4     4.5     2.0     3.9      3.2
           --------+-------+-------+-------+-------+
           COLUMN    74     201     446     674     1395
           TOTAL    5.3    14.4    32.0    48.3    100.0


  CHI-SQUARE    D.F.      SIGNIFICANCE        MIN E.F.        CELLS WITH E.F.< 5


   46.30171      9          0.0000            2.387          2 OF    16 ( 12.5%)

  NUMBER OF MISSING OBSERVATIONS =       111
```

To test the hypothesis that the "real" number of children and the "ideal" number are independent, the chi-squared test of independence can be used. From Figure 6.16, the chi-squared value is 46 with 9 degrees of freedom. The observed significance level is very small, indicating that it is unlikely that the numbers of real children and ideal children are independent.

6.17
Quasi-Independence

There are many reasons why the independence model may not fit the data. One possible explanation is that, in fact, the real and ideal sizes are fairly close to one another. However, if we ignore the diagonal entries of the table, we may find that the remaining cells are independent, in other words, that there is no tendency for children from small families to want large families or children from large families to want small families.

This hypothesis may be tested by ignoring the diagonal entries of the table and testing independence for the remaining cells, using the test of *quasi-independence*. Figure 6.17 contains the observed and expected cell frequencies for this model. Note that all diagonal entries have values of 0 for observed and expected cell frequencies. However, the residuals and goodness-of-fit statistics indicate that the quasi-independence model does not fit well either.

Figure 6.17   Statistics for the quasi-independence model

```
COMPUTE WEIGHT=1.
IF (IDEAL EQ REAL) WEIGHT=0.
SET WIDTH=WIDE.
LOGLINEAR REAL IDEAL(1,4)
  /CWEIGHT=WEIGHT
  /DESIGN=REAL IDEAL.
```

```
Observed, Expected Frequencies and Residuals

        Factor          Code        OBS. count & PCT.    EXP. count & PCT.    Residual    Std. Resid.    Adj. Resid.

REAL            0-1
    IDEAL       0-1                    .00  (  .00)          .00  (  .00)       .0000         .0000          .0000
    IDEAL       2                    55.00  ( 5.05)        39.97  ( 3.67)     15.0308        2.3775         3.7476
    IDEAL       3-4                  16.00  ( 1.47)        30.06  ( 2.76)    -14.0590       -2.5643        -3.5402
    IDEAL       5 +                   1.00  (  .09)         1.97  (  .18)      -.9718        -.6921         -.7423

REAL            2
    IDEAL       0-1                   6.00  (  .55)         5.34  (  .49)       .6554         .2835          .3143
    IDEAL       2                      .00  (  .00)          .00  (  .00)       .0000         .0000          .0000
    IDEAL       3-4                  48.00  ( 4.40)        54.11  ( 4.96)     -6.1061        -.8301        -2.3969
    IDEAL       5 +                   9.00  (  .83)         3.55  (  .33)      5.4508        2.8933         3.3175

REAL            3-4
    IDEAL       0-1                  20.00  ( 1.83)        20.30  ( 1.86)      -.2973        -.0660         -.0879
    IDEAL       2                   278.00  (25.50)       273.22  (25.07)      4.7763         .2890         1.2556
    IDEAL       3-4                   .00  (  .00)          .00  (  .00)       .0000         .0000          .0000
    IDEAL       5 +                   9.00  (  .83)        13.48  ( 1.24)     -4.4790       -1.2200        -2.3296

REAL            5 +
    IDEAL       0-1                  26.00  ( 2.39)        26.36  ( 2.42)      -.3580        -.0697         -.1025
    IDEAL       2                   335.00  (30.73)       354.81  (32.55)    -19.8071       -1.0515        -3.7838
    IDEAL       3-4                 287.00  (26.33)       266.83  (24.48)     20.1652        1.2345         4.4107
    IDEAL       5 +                   .00  (  .00)          .00  (  .00)       .0000         .0000          .0000

- - - - - - - - - - - - - - - - - - - - - - - - - - - - - - - - - - - - - - - - - - - - - - - - - - -

Goodness-of-Fit test statistics

    Likelihood Ratio Chi Square =    24.61341    DF = 5   P =   .000
              Pearson Chi Square =    26.05831    DF = 5   P =   .000
```

6.18
Symmetry Models

If the diagonal terms of Figure 6.16 are ignored, the table can be viewed as consisting of two triangles. The lower triangle consists of cells in which the ideal number of children is larger than the actual number of children. The upper triangle consists of cells in which the ideal number is smaller than the actual number. A three-variable representation of the data using the two lower triangles (the upper triangle is rotated around the diagonal) and the triangle number as a third variable is shown in Table 6.18.

Table 6.18   Two triangles for the symmetry model

```
  1   2   3   4      1   2    3    4
1                  1
2  55              2   6
3  16  48          3  20  278
4   1   9   9      4  26  335  287
```

Lower-left   Upper-right (rotated)
Triangle 1 (real > ideal)   Triangle 2 (real < ideal)

Several hypotheses about the two triangles may be of interest. One is the symmetry hypothesis. That is, are the corresponding entries of the two triangles equal? In a log-linear model framework, this implies that the main effects for the row and column variables, as well as their interaction, are the same for the two

$$\ln(\widehat{F}_{ijk}) = \mu + \lambda_i^{Real} + \lambda_j^{Ideal} + \lambda_{ij}^{RealIdeal}$$

Equation 6.18a

Figure 6.18a contains the LOGLINEAR output for this hypothesis. The expected values are simply the average of the observed frequencies for the two cells. Thus, the expected values for corresponding cells are always equal. For example, the first expected frequency, 30.5, is the average of 55 and 6. Note also that the second triangle has been "rotated" into lower-triangular form without changing the variable names, so that the variables are mislabeled in Triangle 2. For example, the entry labeled **TRIANGLE 2, IDEAL 2, SIBS 1** is really the entry for an ideal number of children of 0 or 1 and an actual number of 2.

Figure 6.18a Statistics for the symmetry model

```
COMPUTE TRIANGLE=2.
IF (IDEAL GE REAL)TRIANGLE=1.
* FLIP VARIABLES WHEN IDEAL LESS THAN REAL.
COMPUTE TEMP=IDEAL.
IF (TRIANGLE EQ 2) IDEAL=REAL.
IF (TRIANGLE EQ 2) REAL=TEMP.
SET WIDTH=WIDE.
LOGLINEAR TRIANGLE(1,2) IDEAL(2,4) REAL(1,3)
   /CWEIGHT=(1 0 0
            1 1 0
            1 1 1
            1 0 0
            1 1 0
            1 1 1)
        /DESIGN=REAL, IDEAL, REAL BY IDEAL.
```

```
Observed, Expected Frequencies and Residuals

    Factor          Code        OBS. count & PCT.   EXP. count & PCT.   Residual   Std. Resid.   Adj. Resid.


TRIANGLE          1
  IDEAL       2
    REAL      0-1              55.00 ( 5.05)       30.50 ( 2.80)      24.5000      4.4363       6.2738
    REAL      2                 .00 (  .00)         .00 (  .00)       .0000        .0000        .0000
    REAL      3-4               .00 (  .00)         .00 (  .00)       .0000        .0000        .0000
  IDEAL       3-4
    REAL      0-1              16.00 ( 1.47)       18.00 ( 1.65)      -2.0000     -.4714       -.6667
    REAL      2                48.00 ( 4.40)      163.00 (14.95)    -115.0000    -9.0075      -12.7385
    REAL      3-4               .00 (  .00)         .00 (  .00)       .0000        .0000        .0000
  IDEAL       5 +
    REAL      0-1               1.00 (  .09)       13.50 ( 1.24)     -12.5000     -3.4021      -4.8113
    REAL      2                 9.00 (  .83)      172.00 (15.78)    -163.0000    -12.4286     -17.5767
    REAL      3-4               9.00 (  .83)      148.00 (13.58)    -139.0000    -11.4257     -16.1584

TRIANGLE          2
  IDEAL       2
    REAL      0-1               6.00 (  .55)       30.50 ( 2.80)     -24.5000     -4.4363      -6.2738
    REAL      2                 .00 (  .00)         .00 (  .00)       .0000        .0000        .0000
    REAL      3-4               .00 (  .00)         .00 (  .00)       .0000        .0000        .0000
  IDEAL       3-4
    REAL      0-1              20.00 ( 1.83)       18.00 ( 1.65)      2.0000       .4714        .6667
    REAL      2               278.00 (25.50)      163.00 (14.95)     115.0000     9.0075       12.7385
    REAL      3-4               .00 (  .00)         .00 (  .00)       .0000        .0000        .0000
  IDEAL       5 +
    REAL      0-1              26.00 ( 2.39)       13.50 ( 1.24)      12.5000      3.4021       4.8113
    REAL      2               335.00 (30.73)      172.00 (15.78)     163.0000     12.4286      17.5767
    REAL      3-4             287.00 (26.33)      148.00 (13.58)     139.0000     11.4257      16.1584

- - - - - - - - - - - - - - - - - - - - - - - - - - - - - - - - - - - - - - - - - - - - - - -

Goodness-of-Fit test statistics

    Likelihood Ratio Chi Square =   977.41822    DF = 6   P =  .000
              Pearson Chi Square =   795.25964    DF = 6   P =  .000
```

The goodness-of-fit statistics, as well as the large residuals, indicate that the symmetry model fits poorly. This is not very surprising, since examination of Table 6.18 shows that the number of cases in each triangle is quite disparate.

The symmetry model provides a test of whether the probability of falling into cell (i,j) of Triangle 1 is the same as the probability of falling into cell (i,j) of Triangle 2. It does not take into account the fact that the overall observed probability of membership in Triangle 2 is much greater than the probability of membership in Triangle 1.

Since the triangle totals are so disparate, a more reasonable hypothesis to test is whether the probability of falling into corresponding cells in the two triangles is equal, adjusting for the observed totals in the two triangles. In other words, we test whether the probability of falling in cell (i,j) is the same for Triangle 1 and Triangle 2, assuming that the probability of membership in the two triangles is equal. The expected value for each cell is no longer the average of the observed frequencies for the two triangles but is a weighted average. The weights are the proportion of cases in each triangle. The expected value is the product of the expected probability and the sample size in the triangle.

The symmetry model that preserves triangle totals is represented by the following log-linear model:

$$\ln \widehat{F}_{ijk}) = \mu + \lambda_i^{\text{Real}} + \lambda_j^{\text{Ideal}} + \lambda_k^{\text{Triangle}} + \lambda_{i\ j}^{\text{RealIdeal}}$$

Equation 6.18b

This differs from the previous symmetry model in that the term λ^k, which preserves triangle totals, is included.

Figure 6.18b shows part of the LOGLINEAR output as a symmetry model that preserves triangle totals. Note that the expected number of cases in the first cell is 7.72. This is 5.59% of the total number of cases in Triangle 1. Similarly for Triangle 2, the expected number of cases in the first cell is 53.28. This is 5.59% of the cases in Triangle 2. Thus, the estimated probabilities are the same for the two triangles, although the actual numbers differ. The residuals and goodness-of-fit tests, however, suggest that a symmetry model preserving the observed totals in the two triangles does not fit the data well either.

Figure 6.18b   Statistics for the symmetry model preserving observed totals

```
SET WIDTH=WIDE.
LOGLINEAR TRIANGLE(1,2) IDEAL(2,4) REAL(1,3)
   /CWEIGHT=(1 0 0
             1 1 0
             1 1 1
             1 0 0
             1 1 0
             1 1 1)
   /DESIGN=TRIANGLE, IDEAL, REAL, IDEAL BY REAL.
```

```
Observed, Expected Frequencies and Residuals

     Factor          Code      OBS. count & PCT.   EXP. count & PCT.    Residual   Std. Resid.   Adj. Resid.

TRIANGLE         1
  IDEAL          2
    REAL         0-1            55.00 ( 5.05)        7.72 (  .71)       47.2771     17.0122       18.7353
    REAL         2                .00 (  .00)         .00 (  .00)        .0000        .0000         .0000
    REAL         3-4              .00 (  .00)         .00 (  .00)        .0000        .0000         .0000
  IDEAL          3-4
    REAL         0-1            16.00 ( 1.47)        4.56 (  .42)       11.4422      5.3596        5.8320
    REAL         2             48.00 ( 4.40)       41.27 ( 3.79)        6.7266      1.0470        1.3382
    REAL         3-4              .00 (  .00)         .00 (  .00)        .0000        .0000         .0000
  IDEAL          5 +
    REAL         0-1             1.00 (  .09)        3.42 (  .31)       -2.4183     -1.3080       -1.4173
    REAL         2              9.00 (  .83)       43.55 ( 4.00)      -34.5523     -5.2357       -6.7719
    REAL         3-4            9.00 (  .83)       37.48 ( 3.44)      -28.4752     -4.6515       -5.8317

TRIANGLE         2
  IDEAL          2
    REAL         0-1             6.00 (  .55)       53.28 ( 4.89)      -47.2771     -6.4771      -18.7353
    REAL         2                .00 (  .00)         .00 (  .00)        .0000        .0000         .0000
    REAL         3-4              .00 (  .00)         .00 (  .00)        .0000        .0000         .0000
  IDEAL          3-4
    REAL         0-1            20.00 ( 1.83)       31.44 ( 2.88)      -11.4422     -2.0406       -5.8320
    REAL         2            278.00 (25.50)      284.73 (26.12)       -6.7266      -.3986       -1.3382
    REAL         3-4              .00 (  .00)         .00 (  .00)        .0000        .0000         .0000
  IDEAL          5 +
    REAL         0-1            26.00 ( 2.39)       23.58 ( 2.16)        2.4183       .4980        1.4173
    REAL         2            335.00 (30.73)      300.45 (27.56)       34.5523      1.9934        6.7719
    REAL         3-4          287.00 (26.33)      258.52 (23.72)       28.4752      1.7710        5.8317

- - - - - - - - - - - - - - - - - - - - - - - - - - - - - - - - - - - - - - - - - - - - - - - - - - -

Goodness-of-Fit test statistics

     Likelihood Ratio Chi Square =    294.50141    DF = 5   P =   .000
              Pearson Chi Square =    423.62825    DF = 5   P =   .000
```

6.19
Adjusted Quasi-Symmetry

The previously described symmetry model preserves only totals in each triangle. It does not require that the row and column sums for the expected values equal the observed row and column sums. The original crosstabulation table shows that the marginal distributions of real and ideal children are quite different. The *adjusted quasi-symmetry model* can be used to test whether the pattern of association in the two triangles is similar when row and column totals are preserved in each triangle.

The log-linear model for adjusted quasi-symmetry is

$$\ln \hat{F}_{ijk}) = \mu + \lambda_i^{Real} + \lambda_j^{Ideal} + \lambda_k^{Triangle} + \lambda_{i\ j}^{RealIdeal} + \lambda_{i\ k}^{RealTriangle} + \lambda_{j\ k}^{IdealTriangle}$$

Equation 6.19

This model differs from the completely saturated model for the three variables only in that it does not contain the three-way interaction among number of real children, number of ideal children, and triangle number. Thus, the adjusted quasi-symmetry model tests whether the three-way interaction is significantly different from 0.

Figure 6.19 contains the goodness-of-fit statistics for the quasi-symmetry model. The small chi-squared value suggests that there is no reason to believe that the model does not fit well. However, there is only one degree of freedom for the model, since many parameters have been estimated.

Figure 6.19   Statistics for the adjusted quasi-symmetry model

```
SET WIDTH=WIDE.
LOGLINEAR TRIANGLE(1,2) IDEAL(2,4) REAL(1,3)
   /CWEIGHT=(1 0 0
            1 1 0
            1 1 1
            1 0 0
            1 1 0
            1 1 1)
   /DESIGN=IDEAL, REAL, TRIANGLE, IDEAL BY REAL,
           TRIANGLE BY REAL, TRIANGLE BY IDEAL.
```

```
Observed, Expected Frequencies and Residuals

       Factor           Code        OBS. count & PCT.   EXP. count & PCT.    Residual    Std. Resid.   Adj. Resid.


TRIANGLE           1
  IDEAL            2
    REAL           0-1              55.00 ( 5.05)      55.00 ( 5.05)        .0000        .0000         .0000
    REAL           2                  .00 (  .00)        .00 (  .00)        .0000        .0000         .0000
    REAL           3-4                .00 (  .00)        .00 (  .00)        .0000        .0000         .0000
  IDEAL            3-4
    REAL           0-1              16.00 ( 1.47)      14.76 ( 1.35)       1.2352        .3215        1.0756
    REAL           2                48.00 ( 4.40)      49.24 ( 4.52)      -1.2352       -.1760       -1.0756
    REAL           3-4                .00 (  .00)        .00 (  .00)        .0000        .0000         .0000
  IDEAL            5 +
    REAL           0-1               1.00 (  .09)       2.24 (  .21)      -1.2352       -.8262       -1.0756
    REAL           2                 9.00 (  .83)       7.76 (  .71)       1.2352        .4433        1.0756
    REAL           3-4               9.00 (  .83)       9.00 (  .83)        .0000        .0000         .0000

TRIANGLE           2
  IDEAL            2
    REAL           0-1               6.00 (  .55)       6.00 (  .55)        .0000        .0000         .0000
    REAL           2                  .00 (  .00)        .00 (  .00)        .0000        .0000         .0000
    REAL           3-4                .00 (  .00)        .00 (  .00)        .0000        .0000         .0000
  IDEAL            3-4
    REAL           0-1              20.00 ( 1.83)      21.24 ( 1.95)      -1.2352       -.2681       -1.0756
    REAL           2               278.00 (25.50)     276.76 (25.39)       1.2352        .0742        1.0756
    REAL           3-4                .00 (  .00)        .00 (  .00)        .0000        .0000         .0000
  IDEAL            5 +
    REAL           0-1              26.00 ( 2.39)      24.76 ( 2.27)       1.2352        .2482        1.0756
    REAL           2               335.00 (30.73)     336.24 (30.85)      -1.2352       -.0674       -1.0756
    REAL           3-4             287.00 (26.33)     287.00 (26.33)        .0000        .0000         .0000

- - - - - - - - - - - - - - - - - - - - - - - - - - - - - - - - - - - - - - - - - - - - - - - - - - - -

Goodness-of-Fit test statistics

     Likelihood Ratio Chi Square =    1.32440    DF = 1   P =  .250
              Pearson Chi Square =    1.15697    DF = 1   P =  .282
```

6.20
AN ORDINAL MODEL FOR REAL VERSUS IDEAL

Although the various symmetry models provide information about the relationship between the two triangles of a square table, we might wish to develop a more general model for the association between number of siblings in a family and one's view on the ideal number of children. The ordinal models considered in Sections 6.12 through 6.19 might be a good place to start.

Figure 6.16 reveals that two children seems to be the most popular number. However, as the number of real children in a family increases, so does the tendency toward a larger family size. For example, only 21.6% of only children consider 3 to

4 children to be ideal. Almost 43% of those from families of 5 or more children consider 3 or 4 children to be optimal. Thus, we might consider a row-effects model that incorporates the ordinal nature of the real number of children. Figure 6.20 contains the statistics for the row-effects model. The large observed significance level and small residuals indicate that the model fits reasonably well.

Figure 6.20   Statistics for the row-effects ordinal model

```
COMPUTE COV=REAL.
SET WIDTH=WIDE.
LOGLINEAR IDEAL REAL(1,4) WITH COV
     /DESIGN=IDEAL, REAL, COV BY IDEAL.
```

```
Observed, Expected Frequencies and Residuals
      Factor          Code        OBS. count & PCT.   EXP. count & PCT.   Residual   Std. Resid.   Adj. Resid.

IDEAL          0-1
   REAL          0-1               2.00 (  .14)         2.26 (  .16)       -.2621      -.1742       -.2196
   REAL          2                 6.00 (  .43)         7.02 (  .50)      -1.0168      -.3838       -.5189
   REAL          3-4              20.00 ( 1.43)        17.18 ( 1.23)       2.8197       .6803        .8651
   REAL          5 +              26.00 ( 1.86)        27.54 ( 1.97)      -1.5409      -.2936       -.8027

IDEAL          2
   REAL          0-1              55.00 ( 3.94)        56.98 ( 4.08)      -1.9848      -.2629       -.6737
   REAL          2               138.00 ( 9.89)       139.41 ( 9.99)      -1.4129      -.1197       -.2885
   REAL          3-4             278.00 (19.93)       269.22 (19.30)       8.7801       .5351       1.0663
   REAL          5 +             335.00 (24.01)       340.38 (24.40)      -5.3824      -.2917      -1.1155

IDEAL          3-4
   REAL          0-1              16.00 ( 1.15)        13.08 (  .94)       2.9156       .8060       1.0759
   REAL          2                48.00 ( 3.44)        49.11 ( 3.52)      -1.1141      -.1590       -.2443
   REAL          3-4             139.00 ( 9.96)       145.52 (10.43)      -6.5184      -.5404       -.8302
   REAL          5 +             287.00 (20.57)       282.28 (20.24)       4.7170       .2808       1.0304

IDEAL          5 +
   REAL          0-1               1.00 (  .07)         1.67 (  .12)       -.6687      -.5177       -.6410
   REAL          2                 9.00 (  .65)         5.46 (  .39)       3.5438      1.5172       2.0459
   REAL          3-4               9.00 (  .65)        14.08 ( 1.01)      -5.0814     -1.3541      -1.7244
   REAL          5 +              26.00 ( 1.86)        23.79 ( 1.71)       2.2063       .4523       1.2775

- - - - - - - - - - - - - - - - - - - - - - - - - - - - - - - - - - - - - - - - - - - - -

Goodness-of-Fit test statistics

    Likelihood Ratio Chi Square =    6.71177    DF = 6   P =  .348
              Pearson Chi Square =    6.83537    DF = 6   P =  .336
```

6.21
Parameter Estimates

Once an adequate model has been identified, you can examine the parameter estimates to assess the effects of the individual categories of the variables. Several different types of parameter estimates, corresponding to different types of contrasts, can be obtained. Consider Table 6.21a, which contains the expected cell frequencies for the row-effects model previously described. The natural logs of the expected cell frequencies are in Table 6.21b.

Table 6.21a   Expected cell frequencies for the row-effect model

	Real			
Ideal	1	2	3	4
1	2.26	7.02	17.18	27.54
2	56.98	139.41	269.22	340.38
3	13.08	49.11	145.52	282.28
4	1.67	5.46	14.08	23.79

Table 6.21b   Natural logs of the expected cell frequencies

	1	2	3	4	Average
1	0.815	1.949	2.844	3.316	
2	4.043	4.937	5.595	5.830	
3	2.571	3.894	4.980	5.643	
4	0.513	1.697	2.645	3.169	
Average	1.986	3.119	4.016	4.4895	3.403

From Table 6.21b, parameter estimates can be obtained for both variables. We will restrict our attention to estimates for the REAL variable, since they can be obtained from the column averages and the grand mean. Estimates for the IDEAL variable are a little more complicated to obtain, since the covariate effect must be eliminated from the row entries.

Often it is desirable to compare each effect to the grand mean. The parameter estimate for a category is its difference from the overall mean. These types of estimates are called deviation parameter estimates. (They are included in the default LOGLINEAR output if parameter estimates are requested.) For the first category of the REAL variable the value of the deviation parameter estimate is $1.986 - 3.403 = -1.417$. Similarly, for the second category it is $3.119 - 3.403 = -0.284$. These values are shown in the output displayed in Figure 6.21a. The value for the last category is not displayed and must be estimated as the negative of the sum of the previous values, since the sum of deviations about the mean is 0.

Figure 6.21a   Deviation parameter estimates

```
COMPUTE COV=REAL.
LOGLINEAR IDEAL REAL(1,4) WITH COV
  /CONTRAST(REAL)=DEV/PRINT=ESTIM/DESIGN=IDEAL REAL COV BY IDEAL.
```

REAL Parameter	Coeff.	Std. Err.	Z-Value	Lower 95 CI	Upper 95 CI
4	-1.4169683119	.12503	-11.33288	-1.66203	-1.17191
5	-.2834476028	.06767	-4.18893	-.41607	-.15082
6	.6135052404	.05876	10.44092	.49834	.72867

Difference contrasts are obtained by comparing the levels of a factor with the average effects of the previous levels of the factor. For example, the first parameter estimate in Figure 6.21b is just the difference between the mean of the second category and the mean of the first category, or $3.119 - 1.986 = 1.133$. Similarly, the second parameter estimate is obtained by comparing the third category of the REAL variable to the average of the first two categories. Thus, the difference parameter estimate for the third level of the REAL variable is calculated as

$$-0.5 \times 1.986 - 0.5 \times 3.119 + 4.016 = 1.463 \qquad \text{Equation 6.21a}$$

This value is displayed in Figure 6.21b as the fifth parameter estimate. For the fourth category, the value is

$$-0.33 \times 1.986 - 0.33 \times 3.119 - 0.33 \times 4.016 + 4.4895 = 1.449 \quad \text{Equation 6.21b}$$

Note that difference parameter estimates, unlike deviation parameter estimates, do not sum to 0 over all categories of a variable.

Figure 6.21b   Difference parameter estimates

```
LOGLINEAR IDEAL REAL(1,4) WITH COV
  /CONTRAST(REAL)=DIFF/PRINT=ESTIM/DESIGN=IDEAL REAL COV BY IDEAL.
```

REAL Parameter	Coeff.	Std. Err.	Z-Value	Lower 95 CI	Upper 95 CI
4	1.1335207090	.14907	7.60383	.84134	1.42570
5	1.4637131978	.11986	12.21180	1.22879	1.69864
6	1.4492142324	.12597	11.50452	1.20231	1.69611

When the last category of a variable is considered a reference category—for example, when it corresponds to a control group—all parameter estimates can be expressed as deviations from it. These are called simple contrasts. For example, for the first category of the REAL variable, the parameter estimate corresponding to a simple contrast is $1.986 - 4.490 = -2.504$. Similarly, for the second category it is $3.119 - 4.490 = -1.370$. The value for the fourth category, which is not displayed, is 0, since this category is the comparison category (see Figure 6.21c).

Figure 6.21c   Simple parameter estimates

```
LOGLINEAR IDEAL REAL(1,4) WITH COV
  /CONTRAST(REAL)=SIMPLE/PRINT=ESTIM/DESIGN=IDEAL REAL COV BY IDEAL.
```

REAL

Parameter	Coeff.	Std. Err.	Z-Value	Lower 95 CI	Upper 95 CI
4	-2.5038789861	.20842	-12.01359	-2.91238	-2.09537
5	-1.3703582771	.13527	-10.13055	-1.63549	-1.10523
6	-.4734054338	.08097	-5.84648	-.63211	-.31470

When the categories of a variable are ordered, parameter estimates corresponding to linear, quadratic, and higher-order polynomial effects can be obtained, as shown in Figure 6.21d. The first coefficient is for the linear effect, the second for the quadratic, and the third for the cubic. From the large Z values it appears that there is a significant linear and quadratic component.

Figure 6.21d   Polynomial parameter estimates

```
LOGLINEAR IDEAL REAL(1,4) WITH COV
  /CONTRAST(REAL)=POLY/PRINT=ESTIM/DESIGN=IDEAL REAL COV BY IDEAL.
```

Parameter	Coeff.	Std. Err.	Z-Value	Lower 95 CI	Upper 95 CI
4	1.8802178391	.15137	12.42113	1.58353	2.17691
5	-.3300576376	.07536	-4.38000	-.47775	-.18236
6	-.0418098970	.06323	-.66123	-.16574	.08212

6.22
The Design Matrix

LOGLINEAR also displays a "design" matrix, as shown in Figure 6.22. The columns of the matrix correspond to the parameter estimates for an effect. The number of columns for an effect is equal to its degrees of freedom. As indicated in the table labeled **Correspondence between effects and columns of design,** the first three columns of Figure 6.22 are for the IDEAL variable, the next three are for the REAL variable, and the last three are for the IDEAL-by-cell covariate effect.

Figure 6.22   Design matrix

```
SET WIDTH=WIDE.
COMPUTE COV=REAL.
LOGLINEAR IDEAL REAL(1,4) WITH COV/CONTRAST (IDEAL)=SIMPLE
  /CONTRAST(REAL)=POLY/PRINT=ALL/DESIGN=IDEAL REAL COV BY IDEAL.
```

Correspondence Between Effects and Columns of Design/Model 1

Starting Column	Ending Column	Effect Name
1	3	IDEAL
4	6	REAL
7	9	COV BY IDEAL

- -

Design Matrix

1-IDEAL 2-REAL

Factor 1	2	Parameter 1	2	3	4	5	6	7	8	9
1	1	.75000	-.25000	-.25000	-.67082	.50000	-.22361	.75000	-.25000	-.25000
1	2	.75000	-.25000	-.25000	-.22361	-.50000	.67082	1.50000	-.50000	-.50000
1	3	.75000	-.25000	-.25000	.22361	-.50000	-.67082	2.25000	-.75000	-.75000
1	4	.75000	-.25000	-.25000	.67082	.50000	.22361	3.00000	-1.00000	-1.00000
2	1	-.25000	.75000	-.25000	-.67082	.50000	-.22361	-.25000	.75000	-.25000
2	2	-.25000	.75000	-.25000	-.22361	-.50000	.67082	-.50000	1.50000	-.50000
2	3	-.25000	.75000	-.25000	.22361	-.50000	-.67082	-.75000	2.25000	-.75000
2	4	-.25000	.75000	-.25000	.67082	.50000	.22361	-1.00000	3.00000	-1.00000
3	1	-.25000	-.25000	.75000	-.67082	.50000	-.22361	-.25000	-.25000	.75000
3	2	-.25000	-.25000	.75000	-.22361	-.50000	.67082	-.50000	-.50000	1.50000
3	3	-.25000	-.25000	.75000	.22361	-.50000	-.67082	-.75000	-.75000	2.25000
3	4	-.25000	-.25000	.75000	.67082	.50000	.22361	-1.00000	-1.00000	3.00000
4	1	-.25000	-.25000	-.25000	-.67082	.50000	-.22361	-.25000	-.25000	-.25000
4	2	-.25000	-.25000	-.25000	-.22361	-.50000	.67082	-.50000	-.50000	-.50000
4	3	-.25000	-.25000	-.25000	.22361	-.50000	-.67082	-.75000	-.75000	-.75000
4	4	-.25000	-.25000	-.25000	.67082	.50000	.22361	-1.00000	-1.00000	-1.00000

B

Statistics Guide

When orthogonal contrasts are requested for a variable (when the sum of the product of corresponding coefficients for any two contrasts is 0), the numbers in the columns are the coefficients of the linear combinations of the logs of the predicted cell frequencies. For example, since polynomial contrasts are requested in Figure 6.22 for the REAL variable and they are orthogonal, Column 4 contains the coefficients for the linear effect, Column 5 for the quadratic effect, and Column 6 for the cubic effect. The parameter estimate for the quadratic effect is calculated as

$$(0.5(.815 + 3.316 + 4.043 + 5.830 + 2.571 + 5.643 + 0.513 + 3.169)$$
$$- 0.5(1.949 + 2.844 + 4.937 + 5.595 + 3.894 + 4.980 + 1.697$$
$$+ 2.645))/4 = -0.33.$$

Equation 6.22

The linear combination of the cell means is divided by the sum of all of the coefficients squared. In this example, that sum is $16 \times 0.5^2 = 4$. The value of -0.33 corresponds to the parameter estimate for the quadratic effect displayed in Figure 6.21d. The estimates for the linear and cubic effects can be obtained in a similar fashion using the coefficients in Columns 4 and 6.

LOGLINEAR uses a "reparameterized" model. When nonorthogonal contrasts such as deviation and simple are requested for an effect, the columns of the "design" matrix for that effect are not the contrast coefficients. Instead, they are the "basis" for the requested contrasts (see Bock, 1975; Finn, 1974). For example, in Figure 6.22, the three columns for the IDEAL effect contain coefficients for simple contrasts, the basis for deviation contrasts. The parameter estimates displayed correspond to those requested in the LOGLINEAR CONTRAST specification; in this case, SIMPLE for the IDEAL variable and POLYNOMIAL for the REAL variable.

When covariates are included in a model, they also occur in the design matrix. In this example the covariate values are just the scores from 1 to 4. For each cell these scores are multiplied by the corresponding entries of the first three columns to obtain the entries for the covariate by IDEAL interaction effects in Figure 6.22. Covariates in LOGLINEAR are treated as cell covariates. That is, all cases in the cell are assumed to have the same value for the covariate. If all cases in the cell do not have the same covariate value, the cell average is used to represent all cases in that cell. This will, in general, give different results from models that adjust for covariates on a case-by-case basis.

6.23
RUNNING
PROCEDURE
LOGLINEAR

The LOGLINEAR procedure can be used to fit many different types of models, including logit models and non-hierarchical log-linear models. Parameter estimates can be obtained for all types of models. For hierarchical models, the HILOGLINEAR procedure, which uses an iterative proportional fitting algorithm, may require less computing time. However, parameter estimates for unsaturated models cannot be obtained in HILOGLINEAR.

The LOGLINEAR command must begin with a list of variables, optionally followed by one or more subcommands. One model is produced for each DESIGN subcommand. All subcommands can be used more than once and, with the exception of the DESIGN subcommand, are carried from model to model unless explicitly overridden. The subcommands that affect a DESIGN subcommand should be placed before that DESIGN subcommand. If subcommands are placed after the last DESIGN subcommand, LOGLINEAR generates a saturated model as the last design.

6.24
The Variable List

The only required specification for LOGLINEAR is a list of all variables used in the models specified on the command. LOGLINEAR analyzes two classes of variables: categorical and continuous. Categorical variables are used to define the cells of the table. Continuous variables can be used as covariates.

Categorical variables must be numeric and integer. Specify a range in parentheses indicating the minimum and maximum values, as in

```
LOGLINEAR ZODIAC(1,12) RINCOME(1,4).
```

This command builds a 12 × 4 frequency table for analysis. The model produced is a general log-linear model since no BY keyword appears. The design defaults to a saturated model in which all main effects and interaction effects are fitted.

Cases with values outside the specified range are excluded from the analysis, and noninteger values within the range are truncated for purposes of building the table. The value range specified must match the values in the data. That is, if the range specified for a variable is 1 and 4, there should be cases for values 1, 2, 3, and 4. Empty categories are not allowed. Use the RECODE command to assign successive integer values to factor levels.

If several variables have the same range, you can specify the range following the last variable in the list, as in

```
LOGLINEAR ZODIAC(1,12) REAL IDEAL(1,4).
```

ZODIAC has twelve values ranging from 1 to 12, and both REAL and IDEAL have four values ranging from 1 to 4.

BY Keyword. Use the BY keyword to segregate the independent variables from the dependent variables in a logit model, as in

```
LOGLINEAR SATJOB(1,2) BY ZODIAC(1,12).
```

Categorical variables preceding the keyword BY are the dependent variables; categorical variables following the keyword BY are the independent variables. Usually you also specify a DESIGN subcommand to request the desired logit model (see Section 6.25).

WITH Keyword. Specify cell covariates at the end of the variables specification following the keyword WITH, as in

```
LOGLINEAR ZODIAC(1,12) SATJOB(1,2) WITH B.
```

To enter cell covariates into the model, you must specify them on the DESIGN subcommand (see Section 6.25). Section 6.22 discusses computations involving covariates in LOGLINEAR.

6.25
DESIGN Subcommand

The DESIGN subcommand specifies the model or models to be fit. If you do not specify the DESIGN subcommand or if you specify it without naming any variables on it, the default is a saturated model, in which all interaction effects are fit.

You can use multiple DESIGN subcommands, each specifying one model. Variables named on DESIGN must have been specified on the initial list of variables (see Section 6.24).

Main-Effects Models. To test for independence, a model with only main effects is fit. For example, to test that ZODIAC and SATJOB are independent, specify

```
LOGLINEAR ZODIAC(1,12) SATJOB(1,2)
  /DESIGN=ZODIAC SATJOB.
```

Interactions. Use the BY keyword to specify interaction terms. For example, to fit the saturated model that consists of the ZODIAC main effect, the SATJOB main effect, and the interaction of ZODIAC and SATJOB, specify

```
LOGLINEAR ZODIAC(1,12) SATJOB(1,2)
  /DESIGN=ZODIAC, SATJOB, ZODIAC BY SATJOB.
```

For the general log-linear model, this DESIGN specification is the same as the default model. Thus, the specification

```
LOGLINEAR ZODIAC(1,12) SATJOB(1,2)
  /DESIGN.
```

is equivalent to the preceding one.

Covariates. To include covariates, you must first identify them on the LOGLINEAR variable list by naming them after the keyword WITH. Then, simply specify the covariate on the DESIGN subcommand, as in

```
LOGLINEAR ZODIAC(1,12) SATJOB(1,2) WITH COV
  /DESIGN=ZODIAC SATJOB COV.
```

You can specify an interaction of a covariate and an independent variable. However, a covariate-by-covariate interaction is not allowed. Instead, use the COMPUTE command to create interaction variables (see Section 6.13). For example, for a linear-by-linear association model, specify

```
COMPUTE B=SATJOB*RINCOME.
LOGLINEAR SATJOB(1,2) RINCOME(1,4) WITH B
  /DESIGN=SATJOB RINCOME B.
```

To specify an equiprobability model, use a covariate that is actually a constant of 1 on the DESIGN subcommand, as in

```
COMPUTE X=1.
LOGLINEAR ZODIAC(1,12) WITH X
  /DESIGN=X.
```

This model tests whether the frequencies in the 12-cell table are equal (see Section 6.3).

Single-Degree-of-Freedom Partitions. A variable followed by an integer in parentheses refers to a single-degree-of-freedom partition of a specified contrast. For example, you can specify the row-effects model described in Section 6.14 as

```
LOGLINEAR SATJOB(1,4) RINCOME(1,4)
  /CONTRAST(RINCOME)=POLYNOMIAL
  /DESIGN=SATJOB, RINCOME, SATJOB BY RINCOME(1).
```

RINCOME(1) refers to the first partition of RINCOME, which is the linear effect of RINCOME since a polynomial contrast is specified.

Similarly, to fit the quadratic model for the season data (Section 6.4), specify

```
LOGLINEAR SEASON(1,4)
  /CONTRAST(SEASON)=POLYNOMIAL
  /DESIGN=SEASON(1) SEASON(2).
```

The actual parameter estimates for SEASON(1) and SEASON(2) will differ from those displayed in Figure 6.4c since the polynomial contrasts are orthonormalized. The ratio of the estimate to the standard error and other statistics will be the same for the two specifications.

6.26
CWEIGHT Subcommand

Use the CWEIGHT subcommand to specify cell weights for the model. By default, cell weights are equal to 1. You can specify either a matrix of weights or a numeric variable, as in

```
LOGLINEAR REAL IDEAL(1,4)
  /CWEIGHT=CWT.
```

This is useful for specifying structural zeros. Only one variable can be named as a weight variable. You can specify multiple CWEIGHT subcommands per LOGLINEAR command, but if you do you cannot name a weight variable. The CWEIGHT commands must all specify matrices of weights.

If you specify a matrix of weights, the matrix is enclosed in parentheses and its elements are separated by blanks and/or commas. The matrix must contain the same number of elements as the product of the levels of the categorical variables. If you specify weights for a multiple-variable model, the index value of the rightmost variable increases most rapidly. For example, the CWEIGHT subcommand

```
LOGLINEAR TRIANGLE(1,2) IDEAL(2,4) REAL(1,3)
  /CWEIGHT=(1 0 0
            1 1 0
            1 1 1
            1 0 0
            1 1 0
            1 1 1).
```

assigns cell weights as follows:

TRIANGLE	IDEAL	REAL	Weight	TRIANGLE	IDEAL	REAL	Weight
1	2	1	1	2	2	1	1
1	2	2	0	2	2	2	0
1	2	3	0	2	2	3	0
1	3	1	1	2	3	1	1
1	3	2	1	2	3	2	1
1	3	3	0	2	3	3	0
1	4	1	1	2	4	1	1
1	4	2	1	2	4	2	1
1	4	3	1	2	4	3	1

You can use the notation $n*c$ to indicate that value c is repeated n times, as in

```
LOGLINEAR TRIANGLE(1,2) IDEAL(2,4) REAL(1,3)
  /CWEIGHT=(1 0 0 1 1 0 3*1 1 0 0 1 1 0 3*1).
```

The CWEIGHT specification remains in effect until explicitly overridden with another CWEIGHT subcommand. For example,

```
LOGLINEAR A B (1,4)
  /CWEIGHT=(0 4*1 0 4*1 0 4*1 0)
  /DESIGN=A B
  /CWEIGHT=(16*1)
  /DESIGN=A B.
```

uses a second CWEIGHT subcommand to return to the default cell weights.

You can use CWEIGHT to impose fixed zeros on the model (see Section 6.15). This feature is useful in the analysis of incomplete tables. For example, to impose fixed zeros on the diagonal of a symmetric crosstabulation table, specify

```
COMPUTE CWT=1.
IF (REAL EQ IDEAL) CWT=0.
LOGLINEAR REAL IDEAL(1,4)
  /CWEIGHT=CWT.
```

CWT equals 0 when REAL equals IDEAL. Alternatively, you can specify a CWEIGHT matrix, as in

```
  /CWEIGHT=(0 4*1 0 4*1 0 4*1 0)
```

6.27
GRESID Subcommand

The GRESID subcommand calculates linear combinations of observed cell frequencies, expected cell frequencies, and adjusted residuals. Specify a variable or variables, or a matrix whose contents are the coefficients of the desired linear combinations. The matrix specification for GRESID is the same as for CWEIGHT (see Section 6.26). You can specify multiple GRESID subcommands, only one of which can specify a variable name. If you specify a matrix, it must contain as many elements as the number of cells implied by the variables specification, as in

```
LOGLINEAR ZODIAC(1,12)
  /GRESID=(3*1 9*0)
  /GRESID=(3*0 3*1 6*0)          .
  /GRESID=(6*0 3*1 3*0)
  /GRESID=(9*0 3*1).
```

The first GRESID subcommand combines the first three signs into a spring effect, the second subcommand combines the second three signs into a summer effect, and the last two subcommands form the fall and winter effects. For each effect, LOGLINEAR displays the observed and expected count, the residual, the standardized residual, and the adjusted residual (see Section 6.3).

6.28
PRINT and NOPRINT Subcommands

Use the PRINT and NOPRINT subcommands to control the statistical output. PRINT will display the named statistics, and NOPRINT suppresses statistics. You can use the following keywords on both the PRINT and NOPRINT subcommands:

FREQ *Observed and expected cell frequencies and percentages.* This is produced by default.

RESID *Raw, standardized, and adjusted residuals.* This is produced by default.

DESIGN *The design matrix of the model, showing the contrasts used.*

ESTIM *The parameter estimates of the model.* If you do not specify a design on the DESIGN subcommand, LOGLINEAR generates a saturated model and displays the parameter estimates for the saturated model by default.

COR *The correlation matrix of the parameter estimates.*

ALL *All available output.*

DEFAULT *FREQ and RESID.* ESTIM is also displayed by default if the DESIGN subcommand is not used.

NONE *PRINT=NONE suppresses all statistics except goodness-of-fit.* NOPRINT= NONE is the same as PRINT=ALL.

You can specify multiple PRINT and NOPRINT subcommands. Specifications are cumulative. For example,

```
LOGLINEAR SATJOB(1,2) RINCOME(1,4)
  /PRINT=ESTIM
  /DESIGN=SATJOB, RINCOME, SATJOB BY RINCOME
  /PRINT=ALL
  /DESIGN=SATJOB RINCOME.
```

specifies two designs. The first design is the saturated model. Since it fits the data exactly, you do not want to see the frequencies and residuals. Instead, you want to see parameter estimates, as specified by PRINT=ESTIM. The second design is the main-effects model, which implicitly tests the hypothesis of no association. The PRINT subcommand displays all available display output for this model.

6.29
PLOT Subcommand

The PLOT subcommand produces optional plots. No plots are displayed if PLOT is not specified.

RESID *Plots of adjusted residuals against observed and expected counts.*

NORMPROB *Normal and detrended normal plots of the adjusted residuals.*

NONE *No plots.* This is the default if the PLOT subcommand is omitted.

DEFAULT *RESID and NORMPROB.* These are the defaults if you specify PLOT without keywords.

You can use multiple PLOT subcommands on one LOGLINEAR command. The specifications are cumulative. For example,

```
LOGLINEAR RESPONSE(1,2) BY TIME(1,4)
  /CONTRAST(TIME)=SPECIAL(4*1 7 14 27 51 8*1)
  /PLOT=RESID NORMPROB
  /DESIGN=RESPONSE TIME(1) BY RESPONSE
  /PLOT=NONE
  /DESIGN.
```

displays RESID and NORMPROB plots for the first design and no plots for the second design.

6.30
CONTRAST Subcommand

The CONTRAST subcommand indicates the type of contrast for a categorical variable. Specify the variable name in parentheses after the CONTRAST subcommand, followed by the name of the contrast. For example,

```
LOGLINEAR SATJOB(1,2) RINCOME(1,4)
  /CONTRAST(RINCOME)=POLYNOMIAL.
```

applies a polynomial contrast to RINCOME.

In LOGLINEAR, contrasts do not have to sum to 0 or be orthogonal. The following contrasts are available:

DEVIATION(refcat)	*Deviations from the overall effect.* These are the default parameter estimates in LOGLINEAR. Refcat is the category for which parameter estimates are not displayed (they must be obtained as the negative of the sum of the others). By default, refcat is the last category of the variable.
DIFFERENCE	*Levels of a variable with the average effect of previous levels of a variable.* Also known as *reverse Helmert* contrasts.
HELMERT	*Levels of a variable with the average effect of subsequent levels of a variable.*
SIMPLE(refcat)	*Each level of a variable to the last level.* You can specify a value for refcat enclosed in parentheses after the keyword SIMPLE. By default, refcat is the last category of the variable as the reference category.
REPEATED	*Adjacent comparisons across levels of a variable.*
POLYNOMIAL(metric)	*Orthogonal polynomial contrasts.* The default metric is equal spacing (see Sections 6.21 and 6.22). Optionally, you can specify the coefficients of the linear polynomial in parentheses, indicating the spacing between levels of the treatment measured by the given variable.
(BASIS)SPECIAL(matrix)	*User-defined contrast.* You must specify as many elements as the number of categories squared. If BASIS is specified, a basis matrix is generated for the special contrast. Otherwise, the matrix specified is the basis matrix.

Only one contrast is in effect for each variable for a DESIGN subcommand. If you do not use the CONTRAST subcommand, the contrast defaults to DEVIATION. You must use separate CONTRAST subcommands for each variable for which you specify contrasts. A contrast specification remains in effect for subsequent designs until explicitly overridden with another CONTRAST subcommand, as in

```
LOGLINEAR SATJOB(1,2) RINCOME(1,4)
  /CONTRAST(RINCOME)=POLYNOMIAL
  /DESIGN=SATJOB, RINCOME, SATJOB BY RINCOME(1)
  /CONTRAST(RINCOME)=SIMPLE
  /DESIGN=SATJOB, RINCOME.
```

The first CONTRAST subcommand requests polynomial contrasts of RINCOME for the first design. The second CONTRAST subcommand requests SIMPLE contrasts of RINCOME, with the last category (value 4) used as the reference category for the second DESIGN subcommand.

You can display the design matrix used for the contrasts by specifying the DESIGN keyword on the PRINT subcommand (see Section 6.22).

6.31
CRITERIA Subcommand

The CRITERIA subcommand specifies the values of some constants in the Newton-Raphson algorithm, the estimation algorithm in LOGLINEAR.

CONVERGE(eps)   *Convergence criterion.* Specify *eps* as the convergence criterion. The default is 0.001.

ITERATION(n)   *Maximum number of iterations.* Specify *n* as the maximum number of iterations for the algorithm. The default is 20.

DELTA(d)   *Cell delta value.* The value *d* is added to each cell frequency before analysis. The default value is 0.5.

DEFAULT   *Default values.* Use DEFAULT to reset the parameters to the default.

For example, to increase the maximum number of iterations to 50, specify

```
LOGLINEAR DPREF(2,3) BY RACE ORIGIN CAMP(1,2)
  /CRITERIA=ITERATION(50).
```

Defaults or specifications remain in effect until overridden with another CRITERIA subcommand.

6.32
WIDTH Subcommand

By default, the display width is the width specified on the SET command. Use the WIDTH subcommand to specify a different display width. For example, you can specify a width of 132 to obtain the wide format output if you have a 132-character printer. Only one width can be in effect at a time and it controls all display. The WIDTH subcommand can be placed anywhere after the variables specification, as in

```
LOGLINEAR ZODIAC(1,12) SATJOB(1,2)
  /WIDTH=72.
```

A narrow format suppresses the display of percentages and standardized residuals in frequencies tables.

6.33
MISSING Subcommand

By default, LOGLINEAR deletes cases with missing values on any variable listed on the variables specification. To include cases with user-missing values, specify INCLUDE on the MISSING subcommand. Cases with system-missing values are always deleted from the analysis. If you specify MISSING=INCLUDE, you must also include the missing values in the value range specification for the variables.

INCLUDE   *Include missing values.*

Contents

7 Nonlinear Regression: Procedure NLR

Many real-world relationships are approximated with linear models, especially in the absence of theoretical models which can serve as guides. We would be unwise to model the relationship between speed of a vehicle and stopping time with a linear model, since the laws of physics dictate otherwise. However, nothing deters us from modeling salary as a linear function of variables such as age, education, and experience. In general, we choose the simplest model which fits an observed relationship. Another reason which explains our affinity to linear models is the accompanying simplicity of statistical estimation and hypothesis testing. Algorithms for estimating parameters of linear models are straightforward; direct solutions are available; iteration is not required. There are, however, situations in which it is necessary to fit nonlinear models. Before considering the steps involved in nonlinear model estimation, let's consider what makes a model "nonlinear."

7.1 WHAT IS A NONLINEAR MODEL?

There is often confusion about the characteristics of a nonlinear model. Consider the following equation:

$$Y = B_0 + B_1 X_1^2$$

Is this a linear or nonlinear model? The equation is certainly not that of a straight line—it is the equation for a parabola. However, the word *linear*, in this context, does not refer to whether the equation is that of a straight line or a curve. It refers to the functional form of the equation. That is, can the dependent variable be expressed as a linear combination of parameter values times values of the independent variables? The parameters must be linear. The independent variables can be transformed in any fashion. They can be raised to various powers, logged, and so on. The transformation cannot involve the parameters in any way, however.

The previous model is a linear model since it is nonlinear in only the independent variable X. It is linear in the parameters B_0 and B_1. In fact, we can write the model as

$$Y = B_0 + B_1 X'$$

where X' is the square of X_1. The parameters in the model can be estimated using the usual linear model techniques.

7.2 Transforming Nonlinear Models

Consider the model

$$Y = e^{B0 + B1X1 + B2X2 + E}$$

The model, as it stands, is not of the form

$$Y = B_0 + B_1 Z_1 + B_2 Z_2 + \ldots + B_P Z_{P + E}$$

where the B's are the parameters and the Z's are functions of the independent variables, so it is a nonlinear model. However, if we take natural logs of both sides of the equation we get the model

$$\ln Y = B_0 + B_1 X_1 + B_2 X_2 + E$$

The transformed equation is linear in the parameters and we can use the usual techniques for estimating them. Models which initially appear to be nonlinear but can be transformed to a linear form are sometimes called *intrinsically linear* models. It is a good idea to examine what appears to be a nonlinear model to see if it can be transformed to a linear one. Transformation to linearity makes estimation much easier.

Another example of a transformable nonlinear model is

$$Y = e^B X + E$$

The transformation $B' = e^B$ results in the model

$$Y = B'X + E$$

We can use the usual methods to estimate B' and then take its natural log to get the values of B.

7.3
Error Terms in Transformed Models

In both linear and nonlinear models we assume that the error term is additive. When we transform a model to linearity, we must make sure that the transformed error term satisfies the requisite assumptions. For example, if our original model is

$$Y = e^{BX} + E$$

taking natural logs does not result in a model that has an additive error term. To have an additive error term in the transformed model, our original model would have had to be

$$Y = e^{BX+E} = e^{BX}e^E.$$

7.4
Intrinsically Nonlinear Models

A model such as

$$Y = B_0 + e^{B_1 X_1} + e^{B_2 X_2} + e^{B_3 X_3} + E$$

is intrinsically nonlinear. We can't apply a transformation to linearize it. We must estimate the parameters using nonlinear regression. In nonlinear regression, just as in linear regression, we choose values for the parameters so that the sum of squared residuals is a minimum. There is not, however, a closed solution. We must solve for the values iteratively. There are several algorithms for the estimation of nonlinear models. See Fox (1984) and Draper & Smith (1981).

7.5
Fitting the Logistic Population-Growth Model

As an example of fitting a nonlinear equation, we will consider a model for population growth. Population growth is often modeled using a logistic population growth model of the form

$$Y_i = C/(1 + e_i^{A+B}) + E$$

where Y_i is the population size at time T_i. Although the model often fits the observed data reasonably well, the assumptions of independent error and constant variance may be violated, since with time series data errors are not independent and the size of the error may be dependent on the magnitude of the population. Since the logistic population growth model is not transformable to a linear model, we will have to use nonlinear regression to estimate the parameters.

Figure 7.5a contains a listing of decennial populations of the United States from 1790 to 1960 as found in Fox (1984). Figure 7.5b is a plot of the same data. For the nonlinear regression we will use the variable X, which is the number of years since 1790, as the independent variable. This should prevent possible computational difficulties arising from large data values (see Section 7.4).

Figure 7.5a Decennial population of the United States

```
DATA LIST / POP 1-6(3).
COMPUTE YEAR=1780+10*$CASENUM.
COMPUTE X=$CASENUM-1.
FORMATS X(F3) YEAR(F4).
BEGIN DATA.
data records
END DATA.
LIST.

   POP YEAR   X

  3.895 1790  0
  5.267 1800  1
  7.182 1810  2
  9.566 1820  3
 12.834 1830  4
 16.985 1840  5
 23.069 1850  6
 31.278 1860  7
 38.416 1870  8
 49.924 1880  9
 62.692 1890 10
 75.734 1900 11
 91.812 1910 12
109.806 1920 13
122.775 1930 14
131.669 1940 15
150.697 1950 16
178.464 1960 17
```

Figure 7.5b Plot of decennial population of the United States

```
PLOT PLOT=POP WITH YEAR.
```

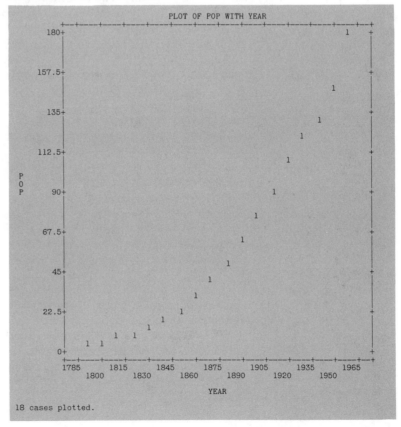

B

Statistics Guide

In order to start the nonlinear estimation algorithm, we must have initial values for the parameters. Unfortunately, the results of nonlinear estimation often depend on having good starting values for the parameters. There are several ways for obtaining starting values (see Sections 7.9–7.11).

For this example, we can obtain starting values by making some simple assumptions. In the logistic growth model the parameter C represents the asymptote. We'll arbitrarily choose an asymptote which is not too far from the largest observed value. Let's take an asymptote of 200, since the largest observed value for the population is 178.

Using the value of 200 for C, we can estimate a value for A based on the observed population at time 0:

$$3.895 = 200 / (1 + e^A)$$

So,

$$A = \ln (200/3.895 - 1) = 3.9$$

To estimate a value for B, we can use the population at time 1, and our estimates of C and A. This gives us

$$5.267 = 200/(1 + e^{B+3.9})$$

from which

$$B = \ln(200/5.27 - 1) - 3.9 = -.29$$

We use these values as initial values in the nonlinear regression routine.

7.6
Estimating the Parameters

Figure 7.6a shows the residual sums of squares and parameter estimates at each iteration. At step 1, the parameter estimates are the starting values which we have supplied. At the major iterations, which are identified with integer numbers, the derivatives are evaluated and the direction of the search determined. At the minor iterations, the distance is established. As the note at the end of the table indicates, iteration stops when the relative change in residual sums of squares between iteration is less than or equal to the convergence criterion.

Figure 7.6a Parameter estimates for nonlinear regression

```
MODEL PROGRAM A=3.9 B=-.3 C=200.
COMPUTE PRED=C/(1+EXP(A+B*X)).
NLR POP WITH X /SAVE PRED RESID(RESID).
```

Iteration	Residual SS	A	B	C
1	969.6898219	3.90000000	-.30000000	200.000000
1.1	240.3756732	3.87148503	-.27852484	237.513991
2	240.3756732	3.87148503	-.27852484	237.513991
2.1	186.5020615	3.89003377	-.27910189	243.721558
3	186.5020615	3.89003377	-.27910189	243.721558
3.1	186.4972404	3.88880285	-.27886478	243.975465
4	186.4972404	3.88880285	-.27886478	243.975465
4.1	186.4972278	3.88885122	-.27886164	243.985983
5	186.4972278	3.88885122	-.27886164	243.985983
5.1	186.4972277	3.88884856	-.27886059	243.987297

```
Run stopped after 10 model evaluations and 5 derivative evaluations.
Iterations have been stopped because the relative reduction between successive
residual sums of squares is at most SSCON = 1.000E-08
```

Summary statistics for the nonlinear regression are shown in Figure 7.6b. For a nonlinear model the usual tests which are used for linear models are not appropriate. In this situation the residual mean square is not an unbiased estimate of the error variance, even if the model is correct. For practical purposes we can still compare the residual variance with an estimate of the total variance, but the usual F statistic cannot be used for testing hypotheses.

The entry in Figure 7.6b labeled **Uncorrected Total** is the sum of the squared values of the dependent variable. The entry labeled **Corrected Total** is the sum of squared deviations about the mean. The **Regression** sum of squares is the sum of the squared predicted values. The entry labeled **R squared** is the coefficient of determination. It may be interpreted as the proportion of the total variation of the dependent variable about its mean that is explained by the fitted model. For nonlinear models, its value can be negative if the selected model fits worse than the mean. (For discussion of this statistic, see Kvalseth, 1985). Figure 7.6c is a plot of the observed and predicted values for the model. It appears from the R^2 value of 0.99650 that the model fits the observed values well.

Figure 7.6b Summary statistics for nonlinear regression

```
Nonlinear Regression Summary Statistics     Dependent Variable POP

  Source                DF  Sum of Squares  Mean Square

  Regression             3   123053.53112   41017.84371
  Residual              15      186.49723      12.43315
  Uncorrected Total     18   123240.02834

  (Corrected Total)     17    53293.92477

  R squared = 1 - Residual SS / Corrected SS =      .99650
```

Figure 7.6c Observed and predicted values for nonlinear model

```
VARIABLE LABELS POP 'Observed value' PRED 'Predicted'.
PLOT FORMAT=OVERLAY /SYMBOLS 'OP' /PLOT POP PRED WITH YEAR.
```

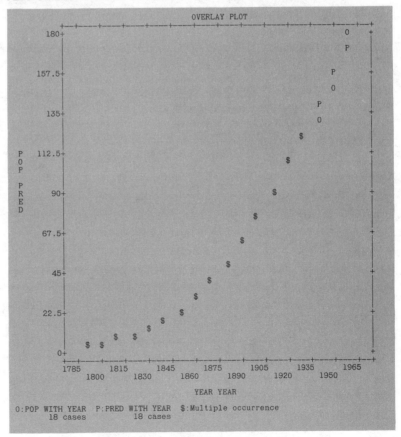

7.7
Approximate Confidence Intervals for the Parameters

In the case of nonlinear regression, it is not possible to obtain exact confidence intervals for each of the parameters. Instead, we must rely on asymptotic (large sample) approximations. Figure 7.7a shows the estimated parameters, standard errors, and asymptotic 95% confidence intervals. The asymptotic correlation matrix of the parameter estimates is shown in Figure 7.7b. If there are very large positive or negative values for the correlation coefficients, it is possible that the model is overparameterized. That is, a model with fewer parameters may fit the observed data as well. This does not necessarily mean that the model is inappropriate; it may mean that the amount of data is not sufficient to estimate all of the parameters.

Figure 7.7a Estimated parameters and confidence intervals

Parameter	Estimate	Asymptotic Std. Error	Asymptotic 95 % Confidence Interval Lower	Upper
A	3.888848558	.093704405	3.689122348	4.088574768
B	-.278860587	.015593951	-.312098307	-.245622868
C	243.98729731	17.967400515	205.69068964	282.28390497

Figure 7.7b Asymptotic correlation matrix of parameter estimates

Asymptotic Correlation Matrix of the Parameter Estimates

	A	B	C
A	1.0000	-.7244	-.3762
B	-.7244	1.0000	.9042
C	-.3762	.9042	1.0000

7.8
Examining the Residuals

The SPSS/PC+ NLR procedure allows you to save predicted values and residuals that can be used for exploring the goodness of fit of the model. Figure 7.8 is a plot of residuals against the observed values of the independent variable. You will note that the errors appear to be correlated and that the variance of the residuals increases with time.

Figure 7.8 Plot of residuals with observed values

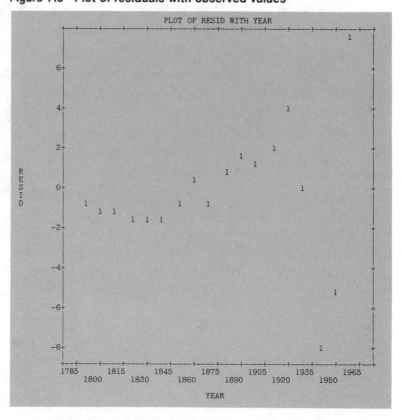

To compute asymptotic standard errors of the predicted values and statistics used for outlier detection and influential case analysis, you can use the REGRESSION procedure, using the residuals from NLR as the dependent variable and the derivatives (see Section 7.22) as the independent variables.

7.9
Estimating Starting Values

As previously indicated, you must specify initial values for all parameters. Good initial values are important and may provide a better solution in fewer iterations. In addition, computational difficulties can sometimes be avoided by a good choice of initial values. Poor initial values can result in nonconvergence, a local rather than global solution, or a physically impossible solution.

There are a number of ways to determine initial values for nonlinear models. Milliken (1987) and Draper & Smith (1981) describe several approaches, which are summarized in the following sections. Generally, a combination of techniques will be most useful. If you don't have starting values, don't just set them all to 0. Use values in the neighborhood of what you expect.

7.10
Linearize the Model

If you ignore the error term, sometimes a linear form of the model can be derived. Linear regression can then be used to obtain initial values. For example, consider the model

$$Y = e^{A+BX} + E$$

If we ignore the error term, we obtain the model

$$\ln Y = A + BX.$$

We can use linear regression to estimate A and B and use these values as starting values in nonlinear regression.

7.11
Use Properties of the Nonlinear Model

Sometimes we know the values of the dependent variable for certain combinations of parameter values. For example, if in the model

$$Y = e^{A+BX}$$

we know that when X is 0, Y is 2, we would select the natural log of 2 as a starting value for A. Examination of an equation at its maximum, minimum, and when all the independent variables approach 0 or infinity may help in selection of initial values.

7.12
Solve a System of Equations

By taking as many data points as you have parameters, you can solve a simultaneous system of equations. For example, in the previous model we could solve the equations

$$\ln Y_1 = A + BX_1$$
$$\ln Y_2 = A + BX_2$$

Then

$$\ln Y_1 - \ln Y_2 = BX_1 - BX_2 \quad B = \ln Y_1 - \ln Y_2 / (X_1 -$$

and

$$A = \ln Y_1 - BX_1$$

7.13
Computational Problems

Computationally, nonlinear regression problems can be difficult to solve. Models that require exponentiation or powers of large data values may cause underflows or overflows. (An overflow is caused by a number that is too large for the computer to handle, while an underflow is caused by a number that is too small for the computer to handle.) Sometimes the program may continue, especially if only a few data points caused the problem, and produce a reasonable solution. If this is not the case, you must eliminate the cause of the problem. If your data values are large, for example years, you can subtract the smallest year from all of the values. That's what was done with the population example. Instead of using the actual years we used years since 1790. You must, however, consider the effect of rescaling on the parameter values. Many nonlinear models are not scale invariant. You can also consider rescaling the parameter values.

If the program fails to arrive at a solution, that is, if it doesn't converge, you might consider choosing different starting values. If you haven't supplied derivatives, try including them. You can also change the criterion used for convergence.

You can also use the CNLR procedure to try to solve problems that are causing difficulties in NLR. CNLR uses a sequential quadratic programming algorithm, while NLR uses a Levenberg-Marquardt algorithm. For a particular problem, one algorithm may perform better than the other.

7.14
RUNNING PROCECURE NLR

Procedure NLR is used to estimate parameter values and goodness-of-fit statistics for models which are not linear in their parameters. The program estimates the values of the parameters for the model and, optionally, computes and saves predicted values, residuals, and derivatives. Final parameter estimates can be saved on a system file and used in subsequent analyses.

7.15
Introduction

To run NLR you must specify the model to be fit and initial values for the parameter estimates. Optionally, you may specify derivatives and criteria for terminating iteration.

NLR commands fall into three categories:

- *Model specification.* The MODEL PROGRAM command is used to specify the model to be fit and initial parameter estimates.
- *Derivatives specification.* The optional DERIVATIVES command is used to specify the derivatives with respect to each parameter. If derivatives are provided by the user, computational time is reduced, and sometimes a better solution is possible.
- *Regression specification.* The NLR command is used to specify the dependent and independent variables for the nonlinear regression, criteria for termination of iteration, as well as optional output to be displayed and/or saved.

7.16
A Simple Example

To run the NLR procedure you must use the MODEL PROGRAM to provide the initial parameter estimates and a transformation statement to define the model. You must also include the NLR command to provide the regression specifications.

For example, if you wish to estimate the parameters of the logistic model

$$Y = C / (1 + e^{A + BX})$$

with starting values of a=4, b=−.4, and c=200, specify

```
MODEL PROGRAM A=4 B=-.4 C=200.
COMPUTE PRED=C/(1 + EXP (A + B * X)).
NLR Y WITH X.
```

- The MODEL PROGRAM command assigns starting values to the three parameters (A, B, and C) to be estimated.
- The COMPUTE command gives the nonlinear function to be fit.
- The NLR command displays the default nonlinear regression statistics. Y is the dependent variable, since it precedes the keyword WITH. The independent variable is X. Both X and Y are variables on your active file. By default the procedure assumes that the variable name assigned to the model to be estimated is PRED. If you use a different name you will have to indicate this on the NLR command (see Section 7.21).

7.17
MODEL PROGRAM Command

The first step in estimating a nonlinear regression model is to determine which model you wish to fit. Any nonlinear model can be estimated with this program. There is no "default" model; you must specify the equation which best describes your data. The equation is specified in the MODEL PROGRAM.

The model program serves two purposes:

- Assignment of variable names and initial values to the parameters.
- Specification of the equation using the transformation language.

For example, consider the following equation, which is the sum of two exponentials:

$$Y = Ae^{BX} + Ce^{DX}$$

The equation has four parameters *(A, B, C,* and *D)* which must be estimated from the data. The data in this case consist of values for the independent variable, *X* and the dependent variable, *Y.* To estimate the model using NLR, you must assign variable names and starting values to each of the parameters. Any acceptable SPSS/PC+ variable name can be used for a parameter. To assign the variable names A, B, C, and D to the parameters and starting values of 10, 0, 5, and 0, specify:

```
MODEL PROGRAM  A=10 B=0 C=5 D=0.
```

You must specify each parameter individually on the MODEL PROGRAM command; you cannot use the TO keyword.

To specify the equation to be fit, you must use the SPSS/PC+ transformation commands described in the *SPSS/PC+ V2.0 Base Manual.* Since your specified equation is used to calculate predicted values for the dependent variable, based on the parameter estimates and the values of the independent variables, by default the program assumes that the variable name PRED is assigned to the result of the transformation. If you use a different variable name, you must supply it on the NLR command (see Section 7.21).

For example, you can use the following MODEL PROGRAM to assign starting values and names to the four parameters A, B, C, and D, and to define the model to be fit as the sum of two exponentials:

```
MODEL PROGRAM A=10 B=0 C=5 D=0.
COMPUTE PRED= A*EXP(B*X) + C*EXP(D*X).
```

All of the variables created in the MODEL PROGRAM are temporary. They will not be automatically saved on the active file. In the model program you can assign variable names and formats to any of the temporary variables which you create.

In a MODEL PROGRAM you can use all of the capabilities of the transformation language. For example, the following commands specify a segmented model in which join points are to be estimated. The form of the model is different for different ranges of the independent variable.

```
MODEL PROGRAM B0=14 B1=.01 K1=25 K2=55.
IF (X LE K1) PRED=B0.
IF (X GT K1 AND X LE K2) PRED=B0 + B1*(X-K1)*(X-K1).
IF (X GT K2) PRED=B0+B1*((K2-K1)*(K2-K1)+K2*(X-K2)).
```

7.18
DERIVATIVES Command

Nonlinear estimation is iterative and requires determination of direction and step size at each iteration based on the values of the derivatives with respect to each of the parameters. You can either supply some or all of the derivatives using the DERIVATIVES command or you can allow the program to numerically estimate the derivatives. If you supply the derivatives, computational time is reduced. In some situations, if you supply derivatives, the solution may actually be better.

The derivatives program consists of the DERIVATIVES command, followed by COMPUTE statements for each of the derivatives. The DERIVATIVES command must follow the model program. To name the derivatives, attach the prefix D. to each parameter name. For example, the derivative name for the parameter named PARM1 must be D.PARM1. The following derivatives program can be used to specify derivatives for the previously described sum of two exponentials model:

```
DERIVATIVES.
COMPUTE D.A = EXP (B * X).
COMPUTE D.B = A * EXP (B * X) * X.
COMPUTE D.C = EXP (D * X).
COMPUTE D.D = C * EXP (D * X) * X.
```

The previous program can also be written as:

```
DERIVATIVES.
COMPUTE D.A = EXP (B * X).
COMPUTE D.B = A * X * D.A.
COMPUTE D.C = EXP (D * X).
COMPUTE D.D = C* X * D.C.
```

You need not supply all of the derivatives. Those which are not supplied will be numerically estimated by the program. During the first iteration of the nonlinear estimation procedure, derivatives calculated in the DERIVATIVES program are compared with numerically calculated derivatives. This serves as a check on the values you supply. See the CKDER keyword on the CRITERIA subcommand in the Command Reference for options for controlling this check.

7.19
NLR Command

Once the model, and optionally the derivatives, have been specified, use the NLR command to provide information about the dependent and independent variables to be used in the regression. The NLR command must follow the last command within the derivatives program, if you've included a derivatives program. Otherwise, the NLR command must follow the last command within the model program.

On the NLR command you can use optional subcommands to request output which is not displayed by default, to identify the name of the function if it has not been named PRED, to save variables on the active file, or to modify the criteria used by the estimation algorithm.

7.20
Regression Variables

After the command NLR, give the name of the observed dependent variable. You can specify only one numeric variable as the dependent variable. After the keyword WITH, specify all of the independent variables. For example, in the command

```
NLR Y WITH X.
```

the observed dependent variable is named Y and the independent variable is named X.

Include among the independent variables any variables on your *active* file which you have used in the model program and derivatives program. Do not list variables you have created in the model or derivatives programs; just list the variables from the active file you have used to create the model and derivatives. For example, in the following session, X is the only variable which must be included in the list. It is the only variable from the active file used in the model and derivatives programs. All of the other variables are temporary variables created for the nonlinear task.

```
DATA LIST FREE / Y X
BEGIN DATA
data records
END DATA
MODEL PROGRAM A=10 B=0 C=5 D=0.
COMPUTE PRED = A*EXP(B*X) + C*EXP(D*X).
DERIVATIVES.
COMPUTE D.A = EXP (B * X).
COMPUTE D.B = A * EXP(B*X) * X.
COMPUTE D.C = EXP (D * X).
COMPUTE D.D = C * EXP(D*X) * X.
NLR Y WITH X.
```

7.21
PRED Subcommand

The PRED subcommand is used to identify the variable, created in the MODEL PROGRAM, which defines the model to be fit. By default, the variable is assumed to be named PRED. If you wish to use a name other than this, supply the name on the PRED subcommand. For example,

```
MODEL PROGRAM A=10 B=0 C=5 D=0
COMPUTE VALUE=A*EXP(B*X) + C*EXP(D*X)
NLR Y WITH X/PRED=VALUE
```

indicates that the variable VALUE is used to define the model.

7.22
Saving Predicted Values, Residuals, and Derivatives

By default, none of the variables created in the MODEL program are saved on the active file. If you wish to save predicted values for the dependent variable, residuals, or derivatives, use the SAVE subcommand. The following keywords can be specified on the SAVE subcommand:

PRED *Predicted values.* The variable name you used to define the model in the MODEL PROGRAM is the name assigned to the predicted values.

RESID(varname) *Residuals.* The variable name for the residuals is specified in parentheses after the keyword RESID. If a variable name is not specified, the name RESID will be used. If the residual cannot be computed, it is assigned the system missing value.

DERIVATIVES *The derivatives for each parameter.* Derivative names are created by adding D. to the parameter names. Derivatives are saved for all parameters.

For example,

```
NLR Y WITH X/SAVE PRED RESID.
```

saves two new variables on the active file. The variable PRED contains predicted values; the variable RESID contains residuals.

7.23
CRITERIA Subcommand

The CRITERIA subcommand controls the values of the five cutoff points used to stop iterative calculations in NLR. You can specify as many as you want of the following keywords. Those you don't specify retain their default values.

ITER n *Maximum number of iterations allowed.* The default is 100 iterations per parameter.

SSCON n *Convergence criterion for the sum of squares.* If successive iterations fail to reduce the sum of squares by this proportion, the procedure stops. The default is $1E-8$. Specify 0 to disable this criterion.

PCON n *Convergence criterion for the parameter values.* If successive iterations fail to change any of the parameter values by this proportion, the procedure stops. The default is $1E-8$. Specify 0 to disable this criterion.

RCON n   *Convergence criterion for the correlation between the residuals and the derivatives.* If the largest value for the correlation between the residuals and the derivatives becomes this small, the procedure stops because it lacks the information it needs to estimate a direction for its next move. This criterion is often referred to as a *gradient convergence criterion.* The default is 1E−8. Specify 0 to disable this criterion.

CKDER n   *Critical value for derivative checking.* If any score falls below the CKDER value on the first iteration, NLR terminates and issues an error message. Specify a number between 0 and 1; the default is 0.5. Specify 0 to disable this criterion.

In the following commands, CRITERIA changes two of the five iteration cutoff values, ITER and SSCON, and leaves the remaining three, PCON, RCON, or CKDER, at their default values.

```
MODEL PROGRAM A=.5 B=1.6.
COMPUTE PRED=A*SPEED**B.
NLR STOP WITH SPEED /CRITERIA=ITER(80) SSCON=(.000001).
```

7.24
Writing Parameter Estimates to a System File

You can save on a system file final parameter estimates, the residual sum of squares, and the number of cases used in the analysis. Use the keyword OUTFILE followed by a filename. The resulting file has one case. The names for the parameters are those used in the model program, the name SSE is used for the sum of squared residuals, and the name NCASES for the unweighted number of cases in the analysis.

The following command will create the file NLR.SYS.

```
NLR Y with X/OUTFILE=NLR.SYS.
```

7.25
Reading Parameter Estimates from a System File

The subcommand FILE indicates that initial estimates of parameter are on a system file saved in a previous NLR run. When starting values are read from a system file, the model program need list only the names of the variables on the system file, in any order. For example,

```
MODEL PROGRAM A B C.
...
NLR Y WITH X/FILE=ESTIM.SYS.
```

reads the initial values for parameters A, B, and C from the file ESTIM.SYS. If for certain parameters you want to specify a starting value which differs from the value on the system file, or you wish to include additional parameters and their starting values, list starting values only for new parameters or those you want changed.

7.26
Case Weights

If a WEIGHT command is being used, NLR uses case weights to calculate the residual sum of squares and derivatives. The degrees of freedom in the ANOVA table are based on unweighted cases. When the model program is first executed for each case, the value of the weight variable is that on the active file. The weight value can be changed by computing a new value in the model program. NLR uses the weight variable's value after each execution of the model program. For example, the following series of commands

```
COMPUTE WT=1.
WEIGHT BY WT.
MODEL PROGRAM
B0=2.3 B1=1.6 B2=.014
COMPUTE PRED=B0 +B1x1+B2X2
COMPUTE Z=(Y-PRED)/1.63
COMPUTE WT=EXP(-.3*ABS(Z)).
NLR Y WITH X1 X2.
```

can be used to perform a robust regression via iteratively reweighted least squares.

The weight for each case is a function of the scaled residuals, where 1.63 is the estimate of scale obtained from a preliminary linear least squares regression. (Note that the model in this case is linear. We are using NLR to obtain iteratively reweighted least squares.)

Contents_____

8 Probit Analysis: Procedure PROBIT

How much insecticide does it take to kill a pest? How low does a sale price have to be to induce a consumer to buy a product? In both of these situations we are concerned with evaluating the potency of a stimulus. In the first example, the stimulus is the amount of insecticide; in the second it is the sale price of an object. The response we are interested in is all-or-none. An insect is either dead or alive, a sale made or not. Since all insects and shoppers do not respond in the same way, that is, they have different tolerances for insecticides and sale prices, the problem must be formulated in terms of the proportion responding at each level of the stimulus.

Different mathematical models can be used to express the relationship between the proportion responding and the "dose" of one or more stimuli. In this chapter we will consider two commonly used models—the probit response model and the logit response model. We will assume that we have one or more stimuli of interest and that each stimulus can have several doses. We expose different groups of individuals to the desired combinations of stimuli. For each combination we record the number of individuals exposed and the number who respond.

8.1
PROBIT AND LOGIT RESPONSE MODELS

In probit and logit models, instead of regressing the actual proportion responding on the values of the stimuli, we transform the proportion responding using either a probit or logit transformation.

For a probit transformation we replace each of the observed proportions with the value of the standard normal curve below which the observed proportion of the area is found. To avoid negative numbers, the constant 5 is usually added. For example, if half (0.5) of the subjects respond at a particular dose, the corresponding probit value is 0, since half of the area in a standard normal falls below a Z score of 0. When the constant 5 is added, the transformed value for the proportion is 5. If the observed proportion is 0.95, the corresponding probit value is 1.64. Addition of the constant value of 5 makes this 6.64.

If the logit transformation is used, the observed proportion P is replaced by

$$\frac{ln(P/(1-P))}{2} + 5 \qquad \text{Equation 8.1a}$$

The quantity $ln(P/(1-P))$ is called a *logit*. Division by 2 and addition of the constant 5 is done to keep the values positive and to keep the two types of transformations on a similar scale. If the observed proportion is 0.5, the logit-transformed value is $0 + 5$, the same as the probit-transformed value. Similarly, if the observed proportion is 0.95, the logit-transformed value is 6.47 $(1.47 + 5)$. This differs somewhat from the corresponding probit value of 6.64. (In most situations, analyses based on logits and probits give very similar results.)

The regression model for the transformed response can be written as

$$Transformed(P_i) = A + BX_i \qquad \text{Equation 8.1b}$$

where P_i is the observed proportion responding at dose X_i. (Usually, the log of the dose is used instead of the actual dose.) If there is more than one stimulus variable, terms are added to the model for each of the stimuli. The PROBIT procedure estimates the regression coefficients using the method of maximum likelihood.

8.2
An Example

Finney (1971) presents data showing the effect of a series of doses of rotenone (an insecticide) when sprayed on Macrosiphoniella sanborni (some obscure insects). Table 8.2 contains the concentration, the number of insects tested at each dose, the proportion dying, and the probit transformation (probit + 5) of each of the observed proportions.

Table 8.2   Effects of rotenone

Concentration	Number observed	Number dead	Proportion dead	Probit + 5
10.2	50	44	0.88	6.18
7.7	49	42	0.86	6.08
5.1	46	24	0.52	5.05
3.8	48	16	0.33	4.56
2.6	50	6	0.12	3.82

Figure 8.2a is a plot of the observed probits against the logs of the concentrations. The vertical scale is adjusted by a SET LENGTH command. You can see that the relationship between the two variables is linear. If the relationship did not appear linear, the concentrations would have to be transformed in some other way in order to achieve linearity. If a suitable transformation could not be found, fitting a straight line would not be a reasonable strategy for modeling the data.

Figure 8.2a   Plot of observed probits against logs of concentrations

PROBIT DIED OF TOTAL WITH DOSE.

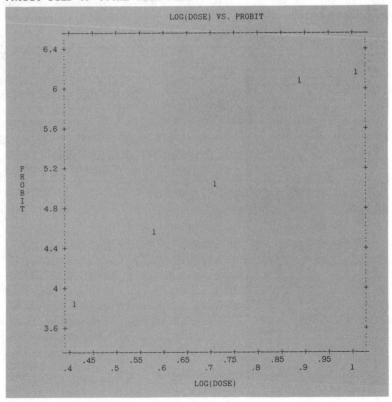

The parameter estimates and standard errors for this example are shown in Figure 8.2b. The regression equation is

Probit P_i + 5 = 2.14 + 4.17(log concentration i)

Equation 8.2a

Figure 8.2b   Parameter estimates and standard errors

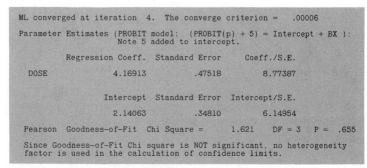

```
ML converged at iteration  4.  The converge criterion =   .00006

Parameter Estimates (PROBIT model:  (PROBIT(p) + 5) = Intercept + BX ):
                Note 5 added to intercept.

          Regression Coeff.  Standard Error   Coeff./S.E.
   DOSE          4.16913          .47518         8.77387


              Intercept  Standard Error  Intercept/S.E.
               2.14063        .34810        6.14954

Pearson  Goodness-of-Fit  Chi Square =     1.621   DF = 3   P =  .655

Since Goodness-of-Fit Chi square is NOT significant, no heterogeneity
factor is used in the calculation of confidence limits.
```

To see how well this model fits, consider Figure 8.2c, which contains observed and expected frequencies, residuals, and the predicted probability of a response for each of the log concentrations.

Figure 8.2c   Statistics for each concentration

```
Observed and Expected Frequencies

          Number of    Observed    Expected
    DOSE  Subjects   Responses   Responses   Residual    Prob
    1.01     50.0       44.0       45.586     -1.586     .91172
     .89     49.0       42.0       39.330      2.670     .80266
     .71     46.0       24.0       24.845      -.845     .54011
     .58     48.0       16.0       15.816       .184     .32951
     .41     50.0        6.0        6.253      -.253     .12507
```

You can see that the model appears to fit the data reasonably well. A goodness-of-fit test for the model, based on the residuals, is shown in Figure 8.2b. The chi-square goodness-of-fit test is calculated as

$$\frac{\Sigma (residual_i)^2}{n_i \widehat{P_i}(1 - \widehat{P_i})}$$

Equation 8.2b

where n_i is the number of subjects exposed to dose i and $\widehat{P_i}$ is the predicted proportion responding at dose i. The degrees of freedom are equal to the number of doses minus the number of estimated parameters. In this example we have five doses and two estimated parameters, so there are three degrees of freedom for the chi-square statistic. Since the observed significance level for the chi-square statistic is large, 0.655, there is no reason to doubt the model.

When the significance level of the chi-square statistic is small, several explanations are possible. It may be that the relationship between the concentration and the probit is not linear. Or it may be that the relationship is linear but the spread of the observed points about the regression line is unequal. That is, the data are heterogenous. If this is the case, a correction must be applied to the estimated variances for each concentration group (see Section 8.3).

**8.3
Confidence Intervals for
Expected Dosages**

Often you want to know what the concentration of an agent must be in order to achieve a certain proportion of response. For example, you may want to know what the concentration would have to be in order to kill half of the insects. This is known as the *median lethal dose*. It can be obtained from the previous regression equation by solving for the concentration that corresponds to an untransformed probit value of 0. For this example,

log median lethal dose = (5 − 2.14)/4.17
median lethal dose = 4.85

Equation 8.3

Confidence intervals can be constructed for the median lethal dose as well as for the dose required to achieve any response. The PROBIT procedure calculates 95% intervals for the concentrations required to achieve various levels of response. The values for this example are shown in Figure 8.3. To produce the confidence intervals for LOG(DOSE), set the width to 132 before running PROBIT.

Figure 8.3 Confidence intervals

```
Confidence Limits for Effective DOSE

                              95% Confidence Limits
     Prob        DOSE          Lower        Upper

      .01       1.34230        .90022      1.74018
      .02       1.56040       1.09066      1.97195
      .03       1.71680       1.23155      2.13530
      .04       1.84471       1.34918      2.26742
      .05       1.95574       1.45293      2.38120
      .06       2.05550       1.54733      2.48279
      .07       2.14715       1.63499      2.57565
      .08       2.23268       1.71755      2.66195
      .09       2.31341       1.79612      2.74315
      .10       2.39030       1.87148      2.82027
      .15       2.73682       2.21676      3.16607
      .20       3.04771       2.53270      3.47551
      .25       3.34243       2.83557      3.77006
      .30       3.63130       3.13372      4.06173
      .35       3.92122       3.43229      4.35924
      .40       4.21771       3.73491      4.67036
      .45       4.52588       4.04453      5.00302
      .50       4.85114       4.36404      5.36612
      .55       5.19978       4.69688      5.77015
      .60       5.57970       5.04782      6.22821
      .65       6.00159       5.42392      6.75754
      .70       6.48075       5.83595      7.38267
      .75       7.04086       6.30085      8.14158
      .80       7.72171       6.84694      9.09908
      .85       8.59886       7.52717     10.38067
      .90       9.84542       8.46059     12.28061
      .91      10.17267       8.70045     12.79297
      .92      10.54051       8.96786     13.37516
      .93      10.96035       9.27040     14.04743
      .94      11.44904       9.61924     14.84000
      .95      12.03304      10.03181     15.80075
      .96      12.75734      10.53755     17.01193
      .97      13.70780      11.19215     18.63257
      .98      15.08177      12.12235     21.03424
      .99      17.53224      13.74102     25.47613
```

The column labeled **Prob** is the proportion responding. The column labeled **DOSE** is the estimated dosage required to achieve this proportion. The 95% confidence limits for the dose are shown in the next two columns. If the chi-square goodness-of-fit test has a significance level less than 0.15 (the program default), a heterogeneity correction is automatically included in the computation of the intervals (Finney, 1971).

8.4
Comparing Several Groups

In the previous example, only one stimulus at several doses was studied. If you want to compare several different stimuli, each measured at several doses, additional statistics may prove useful. Consider the inclusion of two additional insecticides in the previously described problem. Besides rotenone at five concentrations, we also have five concentrations of deguelin and four concentrations of a mixture of the two.

Figure 8.4a is a plot of the observed probits against the logs of the concentrations for each of the three groups separately.

Figure 8.4a   Plot of observed probits against logs of concentrations

PROBIT DIED OF TOTAL WITH DOSE **BY AGENT**(1,3).

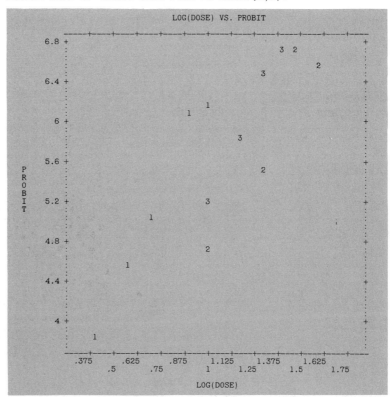

You can see that there appears to be a linear relationship between the two variables for all three groups. One of the questions of interest is whether all three lines are parallel. If so, it would make sense to estimate a common slope for them. Figure 8.4b contains the estimate of the common slope, separate intercept estimates for each of the groups, and a test of parallelism.

Figure 8.4b   Intercept estimates and test of parallelism

PROBIT DIED OF TOTAL WITH DOSE BY AGENT(1,3)
  /**PRINT=PARALL**.

```
ML converged at iteration  5.  The converge criterion =   .00002

Parameter Estimates (PROBIT model:  (PROBIT(p) + 5) = Intercept + BX ):
                 Note 5 added to intercept.

            Regression Coeff.   Standard Error      Coeff./S.E.

  DOSE            3.90634            .30694           12.72689


            Intercept   Standard Error   Intercept/S.E.   AGENT

            2.32658          .23538          9.88429    Rotenone
             .63428          .40789          1.55502    Deguelin
            1.28848          .37510          3.43502    Mixture

Pearson  Goodness-of-Fit  Chi Square =      7.471   DF = 10   P =  .680
         PARALLELISM TEST CHI SQUARE =      1.162   DF = 2   P = .559

Since Goodness-of-Fit Chi square is NOT significant, no heterogeneity
factor is used in the calculation of confidence limits.
```

The observed significance level for the test of parallelism is large, 0.559, so there is no reason to reject the hypothesis that all three lines are parallel. Thus, the equation for rotenone is estimated to be

$$Probit(P_i) + 5 = 2.33 + 3.91\ log(X_i)$$

Equation 8.4a

The equation for deguelin is

$Probit(P_i) + 5 = 0.63 + 3.91 \log(X_i)$ **Equation 8.4b**

and for the mixture is

$Probit(P_i) + 5 = 1.29 + 3.91 \log(X_i)$ **Equation 8.4c**

8.5
Comparing Relative Potencies of the Agents

The relative potency of two stimuli is defined as the ratio of two doses that are equally effective. In the case of parallel regression lines, there is a constant relative potency at all levels of response. For example, consider Figure 8.5a, which shows some of the doses needed to achieve a particular response for each of the three agents.

Figure 8.5a   Expected doses

```
Confidence Limits for Effective DOSE

 AGENT      1  rotenone

                              95% Confidence Limits
 Prob          DOSE          Lower          Upper

  .25        3.24874        2.82735        3.65220
  .30        3.54925        3.11784        3.97001
  .35        3.85248        3.40979        4.29394
  .40        4.16413        3.70782        4.63099
  .45        4.48964        4.01620        4.98815
  .50        4.83482        4.33941        5.37309
  .55        5.20653        4.68269        5.79508
  .60        5.61352        5.05273        6.26601
  .65        6.06764        5.45860        6.80215
  .70        6.58603        5.91348        7.42714
  .75        7.19524        6.43776        8.17788

Confidence Limits for Effective DOSE

 AGENT      2  deguelin

                              95% Confidence Limits
 Prob          DOSE          Lower          Upper
  .25        8.80914        7.23248       10.33786
  .30        9.62399        7.99105       11.21567
  .35       10.44622        8.75940       12.10296
  .40       11.29129        9.55065       13.01798
  .45       12.17391       10.37721       13.97841
  .50       13.10988       11.25236       15.00357
  .55       14.11781       12.19163       16.11673
  .60       15.22139       13.21459       17.34789
  .65       16.45275       14.34756       18.73840
  .70       17.85839       15.62830       20.34868
  .75       19.51032       17.11478       22.27345

Confidence Limits for Effective DOSE

 AGENT      3  mixture

                              95% Confidence Limits
 Prob          DOSE          Lower          Upper

  .25        5.99048        4.82657        7.12145
  .30        6.54461        5.33634        7.72101
  .35        7.10375        5.85372        8.32574
  .40        7.67842        6.38768        8.94792
  .45        8.27863        6.94681        9.59935
  .50        8.91512        7.54035       10.29285
  .55        9.60054        8.17919       11.04376
  .60       10.35101        8.87710       11.87185
  .65       11.18838        9.65257       12.80433
  .70       12.14425       10.53211       13.88102
  .75       13.26761       11.55635       15.16446
```

For rotenone the expected dosage to kill half of the insects is 4.83, for deguelin it is 13.11, and for the mixture is 8.91. The relative potency for rotenone compared to deguelin is 4.83/13.11, or 0.37, for rotenone compared to the mixture it is 0.54, and for deguelin compared to the mixture it is 1.47. These relative potencies and their confidence intervals are shown in Figure 8.5b.

Figure 8.5b Relative potencies and their confidence intervals

PROBIT DIED OF TOTAL WITH DOSE BY AGENT(1,3).

```
Estimates of Relative Median Potency

                            95% Confidence Limits
     AGENT        Estimate      Lower        Upper

     1 VS.  2        .3688      .23328       .52112
     1 VS.  3        .5423      .38072       .71260
     2 VS.  3       1.4705     1.20532      1.85160
```

If a confidence interval does not include the value of 1, we have reason to suspect the hypothesis that the two agents are equally potent.

8.6
Estimating the Natural Response Rate

In some situations the response of interest is expected to occur even if the stimulus is not present. For example, if the organism of interest has a very short life span, you would expect to observe deaths even without the agent. In such situations, you must adjust the observed proportions to reflect deaths due to the agent alone.

If the natural response rate is known, it can be entered into the PROBIT procedure. It can also be estimated from the data, provided that data for a dose of 0 are entered together with the other doses. If the natural response rate is estimated from the data, an additional degree of freedom must be subtracted from the chi-square goodness-of-fit degrees of freedom.

8.7
More than One Stimulus Variable

If several stimuli are evaluated simultaneously, an additional term is added to the regression model for each stimulus. Regression coefficients and standard errors are displayed for each stimulus. In the case of several stimuli, relative potencies and confidence intervals for the doses needed to achieve a particular response cannot be calculated in the usual fashion, since you need to consider various combinations of the levels of the stimuli.

8.8
Unaggregated Data

The PROBIT procedure is designed for situations in which several groups of subjects are exposed to different levels of stimuli. For each stimulus level, the data must contain counts of the totals exposed and the totals responding. You may need to use the AGGREGATE procedure to obtain the required summary counts. If you want to fit a logistic regression model when you do not have groups of subjects at each of several stimulus levels, you can use the LOGISTIC REGRESSION procedure, which contains many additional diagnostics.

8.9
RUNNING PROCEDURE PROBIT

The PROBIT procedure performs either probit or logit analysis with a dichotomous dependent variable. It is designed for use with aggregated data, where each case gives the number of responses and the number of total observations for a specific level of the predictor variable(s) and for a specific value of a grouping variable, if there is one. To use PROBIT with unaggregated data, where each case represents a single observation, you must use the AGGREGATE command (see Section 8.12).

8.10
Variable Specification

The PROBIT command requires at least three variable specifications: a variable indicating the number of cases exhibiting a response to a stimulus, the keyword OF followed by a variable representing the number of cases to which the stimulus was applied, and the keyword WITH followed by a variable containing the level of the stimulus. For example, the command

PROBIT R OF N WITH DOSE.

B

Statistics Guide

specifies that the variable N indicates how many observations received the stimulus, R indicates how many of them exhibited the response, and DOSE indicates the stimulus level shared by the N observations. The values of N and R must be positive, and N must be greater than R for each case. The command

```
PROBIT DIED OF TOTAL WITH DOSE.
```

produces a default analysis using the probit response model, with a base-10 logarithmic transformation of DOSE. This command produces the probit plot in Figure 8.2a, the parameter estimates in Figure 8.2b, the expected and observed frequencies in Figure 8.2c, and the confidence intervals in Figure 8.3.

You can name more than one predictor variable after the keyword WITH, as in:

```
PROBIT DIED OF TOTAL WITH DOSE AGE WEIGHT.
```

8.11
Using a Grouping Variable

To indicate a grouping variable in your data, use the keyword BY followed by the name of the grouping variable and a range of values in parentheses. You can specify the grouping variable either before or after the predictor variable, but you can specify only one grouping variable, as in:

```
PROBIT DIED OF TOTAL WITH DOSE BY AGENT(1,3).
```

With this command, each case corresponds to a group of observations at a specific level of DOSE in one of the three groups defined by AGENT. The default output includes fiducial confidence intervals for each group, a chi-square goodness-of-fit test, and relative median potencies for all pairs of groups. This command produces the output in Figures 8.4a, 8.5a, and 8.5b.

8.12
Using Case-by-Case Data

When your data file contains individual observations, you should aggregate it before using PROBIT, if possible. First recode the response variable for individual cases to 0 (no response) or 1 (response), if necessary, and then use commands modeled after these:

```
AGGREGATE OUTFILE=* /BREAK=AGENT DOSE /
   N=N(RESPONSE) /R=SUM(RESPONSE).
PROBIT R OF N WITH DOSE BY AGENT(1,3).
```

The aggregate variable N contains the number of nonmissing observations of the original response variable, and the aggregate variable R contains the number of observations that responded to the stimulus (code 1 for variable RESPONSE).

When it is not possible to aggregate your data, you can still use PROBIT. The response variable should again be coded 0 or 1. Then you must compute a variable equal to the constant 1 to indicate that each case represents a single observation.

```
COMPUTE N=1.
PROBIT R OF N WITH DOSE BY AGENT(1,3).
```

When you use unaggregated data in PROBIT, the goodness-of-fit tests will be based on the number of individual cases, not the number of levels of the stimuli.

8.13
MODEL Subcommand

The MODEL subcommand indicates which response model should be used to transform the response probabilities (see Section 8.1). Specify one of the following:

PROBIT *Probit response model.* This is the default.
LOGIT *Logit response model.*
BOTH *Both response models.*

8.14
NATRES Subcommand

Use the NATRES subcommand to indicate that there is a natural response rate even in the absence of the stimulus. There are two methods for indicating the natural response rate.

If you have data indicating the response rate at 0 level of the stimulus, enter the NATRES subcommand without any additional specifications, as in:

```
PROBIT R OF N WITH DOSE /NATRES.
```

Assuming that the data contain a case for which DOSE is 0, PROBIT estimates the natural response rate based on the fact that R of the N observations represented by that case showed the response in the absence of any stimulus.

If you know the natural response rate, you do not need to supply data with a 0 stimulus level. Simply indicate the natural response rate on the NATRES subcommand, as in:

```
PROBIT R OF N WITH DOSE /NATRES=0.1.
```

PROBIT adjusts its estimates for the fact that the response occurs 10% of the time even if DOSE is 0.

8.15
PRINT Subcommand

Use the PRINT subcommand to control statistical output. After PRINT, enter one or more of the following keywords:

FREQ   *Observed and predicted frequencies for each case.*

CI   *Fiducial confidence intervals for models with a single predictor variable. If you specify a grouping variable, PROBIT displays a table of confidence intervals for each group. The confidence intervals are calculated with a heterogeneity factor if the goodness-of-fit test is significant (see Section 8.17).*

RMP   *Relative median potency. This is available only when a grouping variable is used.*

PARALL   *Parallelism test for regression lines across categories of the grouping variable, if any.*

ALL   *All of the above that are applicable.*

DEFAULT   *FREQ, CI, and when a grouping variable is used, RMP.*

NONE   *Only the PROBIT plot (for a single-predictor model), the parameter estimates, and the covariances.*

For example, the command

```
PROBIT DIED OF TOTAL WITH DOSE BY AGENT(1,3)
  /PRINT=PARALL.
```

produces the parallelism test in Figure 8.4b.

If you use the PRINT subcommand, only the statistical output you specifically request will be displayed.

8.16
LOG Subcommand

You can use the LOG subcommand to control the logarithmic transformations that are normally applied to predictor variables in a PROBIT model. By default, the base-10 logarithms of all predictors are used to estimate the model. You can specify another base for the logarithmic transformation on the LOG subcommand:

base   *Base for the log transformation. If you specify LOG without any additional specifications, base is assumed to be e (approximately 2.718).*

NONE   *No logarithmic transformation. To transform some, but not all, of the predictors, use COMPUTE statements to carry out the transformations and specify LOG=NONE on the PROBIT command.*

8.17
CRITERIA Subcommand

The CRITERIA subcommand lets you control two parameters of the iterative parameter-estimation algorithm, plus the significance level for the goodness-of-fit test.

CONVERGE(eps)   *The convergence criterion for predicted values.* The default for *eps* is 0.001.

ITERATE(n)   *The maximum number of iterations.* The default *n* is 20.

P(p)   *Significance level for the test of heterogeneity.* By default, significance levels below 0.15 cause PROBIT to include a heterogeneity factor in its calculations of the confidence intervals.

8.18
MISSING Subcommand

PROBIT always excludes cases with system-missing values for any variable in the analysis. You can control the inclusion of cases with user-missing values by specifying one of the following after the MISSING subcommand:

LISTWISE   *Exclude cases with any system-missing or user-missing values.* This is the default.

INCLUDE   *Include cases with user-missing values.*

Contents

9 Survival Analysis: Procedure SURVIVAL

How long do marriages last? How long do people work for a company? How long do patients with a particular cancer live? To answer these questions you must evaluate the interval between two events—marriage and divorce, hire and departure, diagnosis and death. Solution of the problem is complicated by the fact that the event of interest (divorce, termination, and death) may not occur for all people during the period in which they are observed, and the actual period of observation may not be the same for all people. That is, not everyone gets divorced or quits their job, and not everyone gets married or starts a job on the same day.

These complicating factors eliminate the possibility of doing something simple like calculating the average time between the two events. In this chapter we will consider special statistical techniques for looking at the interval between two events when the second event does not necessarily happen to everyone and when people are observed for different periods of time.

9.1
THE FOLLOW-UP LIFE TABLE

A statistical technique useful for these types of data is called a *follow-up life table*. (The technique was first applied to the analysis of survival data, from which the term life table originates.) The basic idea of the life table is to subdivide the period of observation after a starting point, such as beginning work at a company, into smaller time intervals, say single years. For each interval, all people who have been observed at least that long are used to calculate the probability of an event, such as leaving the company, occurring in that interval. The probabilities estimated from each of the intervals are then used to estimate the overall probability of the event occurring at different time points. All available data are used for the computations.

9.2
A Personnel Example

As an example of life table techniques, consider the following problem. As personnel director of a small company you are asked to prepare a report on the longevity of employees in your company. You have available in the corporate database information on the date that employees started employment, and the last date they worked. You know that it is wrong to look at just the average time on the job for people who left. It doesn't tell you anything about the length of employment for people who are still employed. For example, if your only departures were 10 people who left during their first year with the company, an average employment time based only on them would be highly misleading. You need a way to use information from both the people who left and those who are still with the company.

The employment times for people who are still with the company are known as *censored* observations, since you don't know exactly how long these people will work for the company. You do know, however, that their employment time will be at least as long as the time they have already been at the company. People who have already left the company are uncensored, since you know their employment times exactly.

9.3
Organizing the Data

As a first step in analyzing the data you must construct a summary table like that shown in Table 9.3. Each row of the table corresponds to a time interval of one year. (You can choose any interval length you want. For a rapid-turnover company you might want to consider monthly intervals; for a company with minimal turnover you might want to consider intervals of several years.) The first interval corresponds to a time period of less than one year, the second interval to a time period of one year or more but less than two, and so on. The starting point of each interval is shown in the column labeled **Start of Interval**.

For each interval you count the number of people who left within that interval (**Left**). Similarly, you count the number of people who have worked that long and are still working for the company. For them this is the latest information available. For each interval you can also count the number of people who were observed in each of the intervals. That is, you can count how many people worked at least one year, at least two years, and so on.

Table 9.3 Summary table

Start of interval (years)	Left	Current employees working this long	Employees working at least this long	At risk
0 -	2	2	100	99
1 -	1	2	96	95
2 -	7	16	93	85
3 -	6	15	70	62
4 -	5	12	49	43
5 -	5	10	32	27
6 -	4	9	17	12.5
7 -	1	1	4	3.5
8 -	0	2	2	1.0
TOTAL	31	69		

For example, from Table 9.3 you see that you have information for 100 people, of whom 31 have left the company and 69 are still with the company. You see that 2 people left the company during their first year and 2 current employees have been employed for less than one year. Since 4 people have been observed for one year or less, all of the rest, 96 people, have worked for one or more years. (This is the entry in the second to the last column for the interval that starts at 1.)

9.4
Calculating Probabilities

Based on the data shown in Table 9.3 you can calculate some useful summary statistics to describe the longevity of the employees. These statistics will make maximum use of the available information by estimating a series of probabilities, each based on as much data as possible.

The first probability you want to estimate is the probability that an employee quits during the first year of employment. You have observations on 100 employees, 2 of whom quit during the first year. Initially, you may think that the estimate of the probability of leaving in the first year should be 2 out of 100. However, such a calculation does not take into account the fact that you have on staff 2 employees who have not yet completed their first year. They haven't been observed for the entire interval. You can assume, for simplicity, that they have been observed, on average, for half of the length of the interval. Thus, each is considered as contributing only half of an observation. So for the first interval, instead of having observations for 100 people, we have observations for 99 $(100 - (0.5 \times 2))$. The column labeled **At risk** in Table 9.3 shows the number of observations for each interval when the number is adjusted for the current employees who are assumed to be observed for half of the interval.

The probability of an employee leaving during the first year, using the number in the **At risk** column as the denominator, is 2/99, or 0.0202. The probability of staying until the end of the first interval is 1 minus the probability of leaving. For the first interval it is 0.9798.

The next probability you must estimate is that of an employee leaving during the second year, assuming that the employee did not leave during the first year. All employees who have been employed at least one year contribute information to this calculation. From Table 9.3 you see that 1 employee out of 95 at risk left during the second year. The probability of leaving during the second year, given that an employee made it through the first, is then 1/95, which is 0.0105. The probability of staying to the end of the second year, if the employee made it to the beginning of the second year, is 0.9895.

From these two probabilities (the probability of making it through the first year, and the probability of making it through the second year given that an employee has made it through the first) you can estimate the probability that the employee will make it to the end of the second year of employment. The formula is:

$$P(second) = P(first) \times P(second\ given\ first) \qquad \text{Equation 9.4}$$

For this example, the probability of surviving to the end of the second year is 0.9798×0.9895, or 0.9695. This is the cumulative probability of surviving to the end of the second interval.

9.5
The Life Table

Figure 9.5 is the life table computed by the SURVIVAL procedure for the personnel data. The contents of the columns of the life table are as follows:

Interval Start Time. The beginning value for the each interval. Each interval extends from its start time up to the start time of the next interval.

Number Entering This Interval. The number of cases that have survived to the beginning of the current interval.

Number Withdrawn during This Interval. The number of cases that entered the interval whose follow-up ends somewhere in the interval. These are censored cases. That is, these are cases for whom the event of interest has not occurred at the time of last contact.

Number Exposed to Risk. This is calculated as the number of cases entering the interval minus one half of those withdrawn during the interval.

Number of Terminal Events. The number of cases for whom the event of interest occurs within the interval.

Proportion of Terminal Events. An estimate of the probability of the event of interest occurring in an interval for a case that has made it to the beginning of that interval. It is computed as the number of terminal events divided by the number exposed to risk.

Proportion Surviving. The proportion surviving is 1 minus the proportion of terminal events.

Cumulative Proportion Surviving at End. This is an estimate of the probability of surviving to the end of an interval. It is computed as the product of the proportion surviving this interval and the proportion surviving all previous intervals.

Probability Density. The probability density is an estimate of the probability per unit time of experiencing an event in the interval.

Hazard Rate. The hazard rate is an estimate of the probability per unit time that an individual who has survived to the beginning of an interval will experience an event in that interval.

Standard Error of the Cumulative Proportion Surviving. This is an estimate of the variability of the estimate of the cumulative proportion surviving.

Standard Error of the Probability Density. This is an estimate of the variability of the estimated probability density.

Standard Error of the Hazard Rate. This is an estimate of the variability of the estimated hazard rate.

Figure 9.5   Life table

```
COMPUTE LENGTH=
  (YRMODA (LSTYR, LSTMO, LSTDAY) - YRMODA (HIRYR, HIRMO, HIRDAY))/365.
SURVIVAL TABLES=LENGTH
  /INTERVAL=THRU 10 BY 1
  /STATUS=EMPLOY(0).
```

```
LIFE TABLE
    SURVIVAL VARIABLE   LENGTH

           NUMBER  NUMBER  NUMBER  NUMBER                       CUMUL                        SE OF   SE OF
           ENTRNG  WDRAWN  EXPOSD    OF    PROPN   PROPN  PROPN          PROBA-          CUMUL   PROB-
    INTVL   THIS   DURING   TO     TERMNL  TERMI-  SURVI-  SURV   BILITY  HAZARD  SURV-   ABILTY  SE OF
    START   INTVL  INTVL   RISK   EVENTS  NATING   VING   AT END  DENSTY   RATE   IVING    DENS   HAZRD
    TIME                                                                                          RATE

     0.0   100.0    2.0    99.0     2.0   0.0202  0.9798  0.9798  0.0202  0.0204  0.014   0.014   0.014
     1.0    96.0    2.0    95.0     1.0   0.0105  0.9895  0.9695  0.0103  0.0106  0.017   0.010   0.011
     2.0    93.0   16.0    85.0     7.0   0.0824  0.9176  0.8896  0.0798  0.0859  0.033   0.029   0.032
     3.0    70.0   15.0    62.5     6.0   0.0960  0.9040  0.8042  0.0854  0.1008  0.045   0.033   0.041
     4.0    49.0   12.0    43.0     5.0   0.1163  0.8837  0.7107  0.0935  0.1235  0.056   0.040   0.055
     5.0    32.0   10.0    27.0     5.0   0.1852  0.8148  0.5791  0.1316  0.2041  0.070   0.054   0.091
     6.0    17.0    9.0    12.5     4.0   0.3200  0.6800  0.3938  0.1853  0.3810  0.090   0.080   0.187
     7.0     4.0    1.0     3.5     1.0   0.2857  0.7143  0.2813  0.1125  0.3333  0.115   0.099   0.329
     8.0     2.0    2.0     1.0     0.0   0.0000  1.0000  0.2813  0.0000  0.0000  0.115   0.000   0.000

THE MEDIAN SURVIVAL TIME FOR THESE DATA IS   6.43
```

9.6
Median Survival Time

An estimate of the median survival time is displayed below the life table. The median survival time is the time point at which the value of the cumulative survival function is 0.5. That is, it is the time point by which half of the cases are expected to experience the event. Linear interpolation is used to calculate this value. If the cumulative proportion surviving at the end of the last interval is greater than 0.5, the start time of the last interval is flagged with a plus sign ($+$) to indicate that the median time exceeds the start value of the last interval.

From Figure 9.5 you see that the median survival time for the personnel data is 6.43 years. This means that half of the people have left the company after 6.43 years. At six years almost 58% of the employees remain. At seven years only 39% remain.

9.7
Assumptions Needed to Use the Life Table

The basic assumption underlying life table calculations is that survival experience does not change during the course of the study. For example, if the employment possibilities or work conditions change during the period of the study, it makes no sense to combine all of the cases into a single life table. To use a life table you must assume that a person hired today will behave the same way as a person who was hired five years ago. You must also assume that observations that are censored do not differ from those that are not censored. These are critical assumptions that determine whether life table analysis is an appropriate technique.

9.8
Lost to Follow-up

In the personnel example we had information available for all employees in the company. We knew who left and when. This is not always the case. If you are studying the survival experience of patients who have undergone a particular therapeutic procedure, you may have two different types of censored observations. You will have patients whose length of survival is not known because they are still alive. You may also have patients with whom you have lost contact and all you know is that they were alive at some date in the past. If patients with whom you have lost contact differ from patients who remain in contact, the results of a life table analysis will be misleading.

Consider the situation in which patients with whom you have lost contact are healthier than patients who remain in contact. By assuming that patients who are lost to follow-up behave the same way as patients who are not, the life table will underestimate the survival experience of the group. Similarly, if sicker patients lose contact, the life table will overestimate the proportion surviving at various time points. It cannot be emphasized too strongly that no statistical procedure can atone for problems associated with incomplete follow-up.

9.9
Plotting Survival Functions

The survival functions displayed in the life table can also be plotted. This allows you to better examine the functions. It also allows you to compare the functions for several groups. For example, Figure 9.9 is a plot of the cumulative percentage surviving when the employees from Figure 9.5 are subdivided into two groups, clerical and professional. You see that clerical employees have shorter employment times than professional employees.

Figure 9.9   Plot of surviving clerical employees against professionals

```
SURVIVAL TABLES=LENGTH BY TYPE(1,2)
   /INTERVAL=THRU 10 BY 1
   /STATUS=EMPLOY(0)
   /PLOTS (SURVIVAL).
```

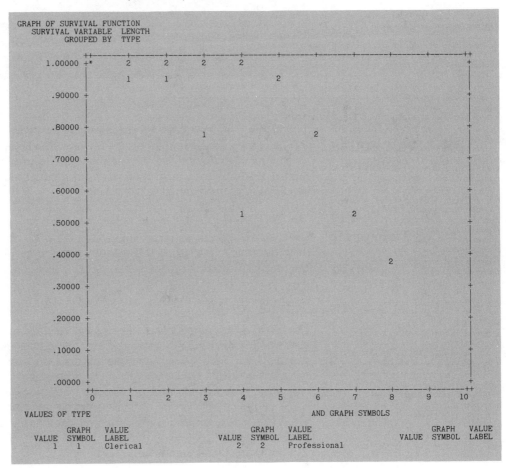

9.10
Comparing Survival Functions

If two or more groups in your study can be considered as samples from some larger population, you may want to test the null hypothesis that the survival distributions are the same for the subgroups. The statistic available in SURVIVAL is calculated according to the algorithm of Lee & Desu (1972).

As shown in Figure 9.10, the number of censored and uncensored cases, as well as an average score, are displayed for each group. The average score is calculated by comparing each case to all others and incrementing the score for a case by 1 if the case has a longer survival time than another case and decrementing it by 1 if the case has a shorter survival time (see Lee & Desu, 1972).

In Figure 9.10 the observed significance level for the test that all groups come from the same distribution is less than 0.00005, leading you to reject the null hypothesis that the groups do not differ.

Figure 9.10   Comparing subgroups

```
SURVIVAL TABLES=LENGTH BY TYPE(1,2)
  /INTERVAL=THRU 10 BY 1
  /STATUS=EMPLOY(0)
  /COMPARE.
```

```
COMPARISON OF SURVIVAL EXPERIENCE USING THE LEE-DESU STATISTIC
     SURVIVAL VARIABLE   LENGTH
          GROUPED BY   TYPE

  OVERALL COMPARISON   STATISTIC      26.786  D.F.     1   PROB.  0.0000

  GROUP  LABEL                  TOTAL N   UNCEN      CEN  PCT CEN  MEAN SCORE

      1  Clerical                   54      19       35    64.81    -15.444
      2  Professional               46      12       34    73.91     18.130
```

9.11
RUNNING PROCEDURE SURVIVAL

SURVIVAL requires a TABLES subcommand for naming a survival variable, an INTERVALS subcommand for setting the period to be examined, and a STATUS subcommand for identifying the variable that indicates the survival status. The remaining subcommands are optional and can appear in any order, but they must be placed after the required subcommands.

9.12
TABLES Subcommand

Use the TABLES subcommand to list the survival variables and control variables that you want to include in the analysis. For example, the following command produces Figure 9.5:

```
SURVIVAL TABLES=LENGTH
  /INTERVALS=THRU 10 BY 1
  /STATUS=EMPLOY(0).
```

Use the BY keyword to separate the survival variables from the first-order control variables. Use a second BY keyword to separate the first- and second-order control variable lists. Each control variable must be followed by a value range in parentheses. These values must be integers separated by a comma or a blank. Noninteger values in the data are truncated, and cases are assigned to subgroups based on the integer portion of their values on the variable. To specify only one value for a control variable, use the same value for the minimum and maximum, as in GROUP(1,1).

For example, the command

```
SURVIVAL TABLES=TIME BY GROUP(1,3) BY SEX(1,2)
  /INTERVALS=THRU 60 BY 12
  /STATUS=CENSOR(1).
```

produces a separate life table for each combination of GROUP and SEX, for a total of six life tables.

9.13
INTERVALS Subcommand

The survival variables are measured in units of time such as days, weeks, months, or years. The INTERVALS subcommand determines the period of time to be examined and how the time will be grouped for the analysis.

The INTERVALS subcommand has two required keyword specifications:

- The keyword THRU indicates the period of time to be examined. For example, if your data are recorded in yearly intervals, a specification of THRU 10 indicates a time period of 0 through 10 years.
- The keyword BY specifies the time intervals for the analysis. For example, if your data are recorded in monthly intervals, but you are only concerned with yearly changes, the specification BY 12 groups the monthly data into yearly intervals.

Even if your data are already recorded in the intervals you want to use, you must specify both THRU and BY, as in:

```
SURVIVAL TABLES=LENGTH
  /INTERVALS=THRU 10 BY 1
  /STATUS=EMPLOY(0).
```

which produces Figure 9.5.

You can divide the period into intervals of varying lengths with multiple THRU and BY keywords, as in:

```
SURVIVAL TABLES=LENGTH
  /INTERVALS=THRU 10 BY 1 THRU 20 BY 2
  /STATUS=EMPLOY(0).
```

The first interval always begins at 0. Subsequent intervals begin after the value specified on the preceding THRU keyword. So the second THRU specification above applies to values greater than 10 and less than or equal to 20. THRU values must be specified in ascending order, without any overlap in ranges.

Only one INTERVALS subcommand can be used in a SURVIVAL command. The interval specifications apply to all the survival variables listed on the TABLES subcommand.

9.14
STATUS Subcommand

For each survival variable listed on the TABLES subcommand, you must provide a variable that indicates the survival status of each case. The codes on these status variables distinguish between cases for which the terminal event has occurred and those that either survived to the end of the study or were dropped for some reason.

On the STATUS subcommand, specify a status variable with a value or value range enclosed in parentheses, optionally followed by the keyword FOR and the name of one or more of the survival variables. The value range identifies the codes that indicate the terminal event has taken place. For example,

```
SURVIVAL TABLES=LENGTH
  /INTERVALS=THRU 10 BY 1
  /STATUS=EMPLOY(0).
```

specifies that a code of 0 on EMPLOY means the terminal event for the survival variable LENGTH has occurred.

All observations that do not have a code in the value range are classified as censored cases. Only one status variable can be listed on a STATUS subcommand. Use separate STATUS subcommands for each of the survival variables or, if appropriate, list more than one survival variable after the FOR keyword. If the FOR keyword is not specified, the status variable specification applies to any of the survival variables not named on another STATUS subcommand.

9.15
PRINT Subcommand

By default, SURVIVAL displays life tables with its output. If you are interested only in the plots and subgroup comparisons available in SURVIVAL, use the PRINT subcommand to suppress the display of the life tables.

TABLE   *Display the life tables.* This is the default.

NOTABLE   *Suppress the display of the life tables.* Only plots and comparisons are displayed. If you specify PRINT=NOTABLE and you do not include either a PLOTS or COMPARE subcommand, no output is generated and SPSS/PC+ displays an error message.

9.16
PLOTS Subcommand

You can request plots of the three survival functions. There are five keywords available with the PLOTS subcommand:

(ALL)   *Produce all available function plots.* ALL is used if PLOTS is specified without any additional keyword specifications.

(LOGSURV) *Produce a plot of the cumulative survival distribution on a logarithmic scale.*

(SURVIVAL) *Plot the cumulative survival distribution on a linear scale.*

(HAZARD)   *Plot the hazard function.*

(DENSITY)   *Plot the density function.*

The specifications on PLOT should be enclosed in parentheses, as in:

```
SURVIVAL TABLES=LENGTH BY TYPE(1,2)
   /INTERVAL=THRU 10 BY 1
   /STATUS=EMPLOY
   /PLOTS (SURVIVAL).
```

which produces Figure 9.9.

You can specify more than one type of plot on the same PLOTS subcommand, as in:

```
/PLOTS (SURVIVAL HAZARD).
```

By default, each function requested is plotted for each survival variable listed on the TABLES subcommand. Optionally, you can limit the plots to specific variables by specifying an equals sign followed by a variable list, as in:

```
/PLOTS (SURVIVAL HAZARD)=LENGTH.
```

You can use the TO keyword to imply consecutive variables. The order of variables is determined by their order on the TABLES subcommand, not their order on the active system file.

9.17
COMPARE Subcommand

To compare the survival of subgroups defined by the control variables, use the COMPARE subcommand. COMPARE with no variable list produces a default set of comparisons using the TABLES variable list. At least one survival and one first-order control variable must be specified to make comparisons possible. For example, the command

```
SURVIVAL TABLES=LENGTH BY TYPE(1,2)
   /INTERVALS=THRU 10 BY 1
   /STATUS=EMPLOY(0)
   /COMPARE.
```

produces Figure 9.10.

9.18
CALCULATE Subcommand

The CALCULATE subcommand calculates survival comparisons for subgroups of cases. The default keyword is EXACT, for exact comparisons. Optionally, you can obtain pairwise comparisons or approximate comparisons. You can also produce only comparisons with no life tables or plots.

The following keywords are available:

EXACT   *Exact comparisons.* This is the default.

PAIRWISE   *Pairwise comparisons.* Comparisons of each possible pair of values of every first-order control variable are produced along with the overall comparison.

CONDITIONAL   *Approximate comparisons if memory is insufficient.*

APPROXIMATE   *Approximate comparisons only.*

COMPARE   *Comparisons only.* Survival tables specified on the TABLES subcommand are not computed and requests for plots are ignored. This allows all available workspace to be used for comparisons. You cannot use the WRITE subcommand when this specification is in effect.

9.19
Approximate Comparisons

Data can be entered into SURVIVAL on either an individual or an interval-level basis. Whether individual or aggregated data are used affects the outcome of SURVIVAL comparisons. With individual data, you can obtain exact comparisons. For exact comparisons, survival scores are calculated on the basis of the survival experience of each observation. While this method is the most accurate, it requires all data to be in memory simultaneously. Thus, exact comparisons may be impractical for large samples. There are also situations in which individual data are not available and data aggregated by interval must be used. (See Section 9.20 for a discussion of entering aggregated data.)

Keyword APPROXIMATE on the CALCULATE subcommand requests approximate comparisons. Keyword CONDITIONAL produces approximate comparisons only if there is insufficient memory available for exact comparisons. The approximate comparison approach assumes that all events—termination, withdrawal, and so forth—occur at the midpoint of the interval. Under EXACT comparisons, some of these midpoint ties can be resolved. However, if interval widths are not too great, the difference between EXACT and approximate comparisons should be small.

9.20
Entering Aggregated Data

When data are recorded for the entire sample at set points in time instead of on an individual basis, it is necessary to enter aggregated data for SURVIVAL analysis. When aggregated data are used, two records are entered for each interval, one for censored cases and one for uncensored cases. The number of cases included on each record is used as the weight factor (see *SPSS/PC+ Base Manual* for a discussion of the WEIGHT command). If control variables are used, there must be a pair of records (one for censored and one for uncensored cases) for each value of the control variable in each interval. These records must contain the value of the control variable and the number of cases that belong in the particular category as well as values for survival time and status.

For example, the commands

```
DATA LIST FREE /SURVEVAR  STATVAR  SEX  CASES.
BEGIN DATA
1 1 1 0
1 2 1 1
1 1 2 2
1 2 2 1
2 1 1 1
2 2 1 2
2 1 2 1
2 2 2 3
...
END DATA.
VALUE LABELS  STATVAR 1 'DECEASED' 2 'ALIVE'
  /SEX 1 'FEMALE' 2 'MALE'.
WEIGHT BY CASES.
SURVIVAL TABLES=SURVEVAR BY SEX (1,2)
  /INTERVALS=THRU 10 BY 1
  /STATUS=STATVAR (1).
```

B

Statistics Guide

read in aggregated data and perform a SURVIVAL analysis using a control variable with two values. The first data record has a code of 1 on the status variable STATVAR, indicating it is an uncensored case, and a code of 1 on SEX, the control variable. The number of cases for this subset is 0, the value of the variable CASES. CASES is not used in SURVIVAL but is the weight variable. In this example, each interval requires four records to provide all the data for each SURVEVAR interval.

9.21
MISSING Subcommand

The MISSING subcommand controls missing-value treatments. The default keyword on MISSING is GROUPWISE, which excludes cases with missing values on a variable from any calculation involving that variable. The MISSING subcommand can also exclude cases listwise. With either groupwise or listwise treatment of system-missing values, you can include user-missing values in the analysis.

With any missing-value treatment, negative values on the survival variables are automatically treated as missing data. In addition, cases outside the value range on a control variable are excluded.

GROUPWISE *Exclude missing values groupwise.* Cases with missing values on a variable are excluded from any calculation involving that variable. This is the default.

LISTWISE *Exclude missing values listwise.* Cases missing on any variables named are excluded from the analysis.

INCLUDE *Include cases with user-missing values.* Cases with user-missing values are included in the analysis.

You can specify INCLUDE with GROUPWISE or LISTWISE, as in:

    /MISSING=LISTWISE INCLUDE.

This command excludes cases with system-missing values on a listwise basis. Cases with user-missing values are included.

9.22
WRITE Subcommand

The optional WRITE subcommand writes data in the survival tables to an output file. This file can be used for further analyses or to produce graphic displays. You can specify one of the following keywords:

NONE *Do not write survival tables to resulting file.* This is the default if the WRITE subcommand is not specified.

TABLES *Write out survival table data records.* All survival table statistics are written to a file. This is the default when you specify the WRITE subcommand without additional specifications.

BOTH *Write out survival table data and label records.* Variable names, variable labels, and value labels are written out along with the survival table statistics.

When you specify the WRITE subcommand with SURVIVAL, the data are written to the resulting file. The default resulting file is SPSS.PRC. Before running the SURVIVAL command, you can change the name of the resulting file by running SET /RESULTS 'filename'. The SURVIVAL data overwrite any previous contents of the resulting file.

Bibliography

Agresti, A. 1984. *Analysis of ordinal categorical data.* New York: John Wiley & Sons.

Atkinson, A.C. 1980. A note on the generalized information criterion for choice of a model. *Biometrika* 67:413-418.

Andrews, D. F., R. Gnanadesikan, and J. L. Warner. 1973. Methods for assessing multivariate normality. In *Multivariate analysis III,* ed. P. R. Krishnaiah. New York: Academic Press.

Bacon, L. 1980. Unpublished data.

Barnard, R. M. 1973. Field-dependent independence and selected motor abilities. Ph.D. dissertation, School of Education, New York University.

Benedetti, J. K., and M. B. Brown. 1978. Strategies for the selection of log-linear models. *Biometrics* 34: 680–686.

Bishop, Y. M. M., S. E. Feinberg, and P. W. Holland. 1975. *Discrete multivariate analysis: Theory and practice.* Cambridge: MIT Press.

Bock, R. D. 1975. *Multivariate statistical methods in behavioral research.* New York: McGraw-Hill.

Brown, B. W., Jr. 1980. Prediction analyses for binary data. In *Biostatistics Casebook,* ed. R. G. Miller, B. Efron, B. W. Brown, and L. E. Moses. New York: John Wiley & Sons.

Cohen, J. 1977. *Statistical power analysis for the behavioral sciences.* New York: Academic Press.

Consumer Reports. 1983. Beer. *Consumer Reports* (July): 342–348.

Dillon, W. R., and M. Goldstein. 1984. *Multivariate analysis: Methods and applications.* New York: John Wiley & Sons.

Draper, N. R., and H. Smith. 1981. *Applied regression analysis.* New York: John Wiley & Sons.

Duncan, O. D. 1966. Path analysis: Sociological examples. *American Journal of Sociology* 72: 1–16.

Everitt, B. S. 1977. *The analysis of contingency tables.* London: Chapman & Hall.

——. 1978. *Graphical techniques for multivariate data.* New York: North-Holland.

Eysenck, M. W. 1977. *Human memory: Theory, research and individual differences.* New York: Pergamon Press.

Fienberg, S. E. 1977. *The analysis of cross-classified categorical data.* Cambridge: MIT Press.

Finn, J. D. 1974. *A general model for multivariate analysis.* New York: Holt, Rinehart & Winston.

Finney, D. J. 1971. *Probit analysis.* Cambridge: Cambridge University Press.

Fox, J. 1984. *Linear statistical models and related methods.* New York: John Wiley & Sons.

Gilbert, E. S. 1968. On discrimination using qualitative variables. *Journal of the American Statistical Association* 63: 1399–1412.

Gill, P. E., W. Murray, M. A. Saunders, and M. H. Wright. 1984. Procedures for optimization problems with a mixture of bounds and general linear constraints. *ACM Transactions on Mathematical Software* 10(3): 282–296.

Goldstein, M., and W. R. Dillon. 1978. *Discrete discriminant analysis.* New York: John Wiley & Sons.

Goodman, L. A. 1964. Simple methods of analyzing three-factor interaction in contingency tables. *Journal of the American Statistical Association* 59: 319–352.

——. 1984. *The analysis of cross-classified data having ordered categories.* Cambridge: Harvard University Press.

Greenhouse, S. W., and S. Geisser. 1959. On methods in analysis of profile data. *Psychometrika* 24: 95–112.

Haberman, S. J. 1978. *Analysis of qualitative data,* vol. 1. New York: Academic Press.

——. 1979. *Analysis of qualitative data,* vol. 2. New York: Academic Press.

——. 1982. Analysis of dispersion of multinomial responses. *Journal of the American Statistical Association* 77: 568–580.

Hand, D. J. 1981. *Discrimination and classification.* New York: John Wiley & Sons.

B

Statistics Guide

Hauck, W. W., and A. Donner. 1977. Wald's test as applied to hypotheses in logit analysis. *Journal of the American Statistical Association* 72: 851–853.

Hinds, M. A., and G. A. Milliken. 1982. Statistical methods to use nonlinear models to compare silage treatments. Unpublished paper.

Hosmer, D. W., and S. Lemeshow. 1989. *Applied logistic regression.* New York: John Wiley & Sons.

Huberty, C. J. 1972. Multivariate indices of strength of association. *Multivariate Behavioral Research* 7: 523–526.

Huynh, H., and L. S. Feldt. 1976. Estimation of the Box correction for degrees of freedom from sample data in randomized block and split-plot designs. *Journal of Educational Statistics* 1: 69–82.

Kennedy, J. J. 1970. The eta coefficient in complex anova designs. *Educational and Psychological Measurement* 30: 885–889.

Kvalseth, T. O. 1985. Cautionary note about R squared. *The American Statistician* 39(4): 279–285.

Lachenbruch, P. A. 1975. *Discriminant analysis.* New York: Hafner Press.

Lee, E., and M. Desu. 1972. A computer program for comparing k samples with right-censored data. *Computer Programs in Biomedicine* 2: 315–321.

Lee, E. T. 1980. *Statistical methods for survival data analysis.* Belmont, Calif.: Lifetime Learning Publications.

McCullagh, P., and J. A. Nelder. 1983. *Generalized linear models.* London: Chapman & Hall.

Milliken, G. A. 1987. A tutorial on nonlinear modeling with an application from pharmacokinetics. Unpublished manuscript.

Morrison, D. F. 1967. *Multivariate statistical methods.* New York: McGraw-Hill.

Muller, K. E., and B. L. Peterson. 1984. Practical methods for computing power in testing the multivariate general linear hypothesis. *Computational Statistics and Data Analysis* 2: 143–158.

Neter, J., W. Wasserman, and R. Kutner. 1985. *Applied linear statistical models,* 2nd ed. Homewood, Ill.: Richard D. Irwin Inc.

O'Brien, R. G. 1983. General Scheffe tests and optimum subeffects for linear models. Paper presented at the annual meeting of the American Statistical Association, August, 1983.

Olsen, C. L. 1976. On choosing a test statistic in multivariate analysis of variance. *Psychological Bulletin* 83: 579–586.

Overall, J. E., and C. Klett. 1972. *Applied multivariate analysis.* New York: McGraw-Hill.

Searle, S. R. 1971. *Linear models.* New York: John Wiley & Sons.

Snedecor, G. W., and W. G. Cochran. 1967. *Statistical methods.* Ames: Iowa State University Press.

Tatsuoka, M. M. 1971. *Multivariate analysis.* New York: John Wiley & Sons.

Van Vliet, P. K. J., and J. M. Gupta. 1973. THAM v. sodium bicarbonate in idiopathic respiratory distress syndrome. *Archives of Disease in Childhood* 48: 249–255.

Wahl, P. W., and R. A. Kronmal. 1977. Discriminant functions when covariances are unequal and sample sizes are moderate. *Biometrics* 33: 479–484.

Winer, B. J. 1971. *Statistical principles in experimental design.* New York: McGraw-Hill.

Witkin, H. A., et al. 1954. *Personality through perception.* New York: Harper & Brothers.

Command Reference

Contents

DSCRIMINANT

```
DSCRIMINANT GROUPS=varname(min,max) /VARIABLES=varlist

[/SELECT=varname(value)] [/ANALYSIS=varlist(level)[varlist...]]

[/METHOD={DIRECT  }] [/TOLERANCE={0.001}] [/MAXSTEPS={2v}]
         {WILKS   }              {t    }            {m }
         {MAHAL   }
         {MAXMINF }
         {MINRESID}
         {RAO     }

[/FIN={1.0}] [/FOUT={1.0}] [/PIN={1.0}] [/POUT={1.0}] [/VIN={0 }]
      {fi }        {fo }        {pi }         {po }        {vi}

[/FUNCTIONS={g-1,100.0,1.0}] [/PRIORS={EQUAL     }]
            {nf , cp ,sig}           {SIZE      }
                                     {value list}

[/SAVE=[CLASS varname] [PROBS rootname] [SCORES rootname]]

[/ANALYSIS=...]

[/OPTIONS=option numbers]

[/STATISTICS={statistic numbers}]
             {ALL               }
```

Options:

1 Include missing values
4 Suppress step output
5 Suppress summary table
6 Varimax rotation of function matrix
7 Varimax rotation of structure matrix

8 Include cases with missing values during classification
9 Classify only unselected cases
10 Classify only unclassified cases
11 Use individual covariance matrices for classification

Statistics:

1 Group means
2 Group standard deviations
3 Pooled within-groups covariance matrix
4 Pooled within-groups correlation matrix
5 Matrix of pairwise F ratios
6 Univariate F ratios
7 Box's M

8 Group covariance matrices
9 Total covariance matrix
10 Territorial map
11 Unstandardized function coefficients
12 Classification function coefficients
13 Classification results table
14 Casewise materials
15 Combined plot
16 Separate plot

Example:

```
DSCRIMINANT GROUPS=OUTCOME (1,4)
  /VARIABLES=VAR1 TO VAR7
  /SAVE CLASS=PREDOUT.
```

Overview

Procedure DSCRIMINANT performs discriminant analysis and allows great flexibility in the method used and in the output displayed. Linear discriminant analysis is a technique in which one finds the best possible linear combination of variables to predict which of several groups or categories will contain cases. This combination can then be used to classify cases whose group membership is unknown. The grouping variable must be categorical, and the independent (predictor) variables must be interval or dichotomous, since they will be used in a regression-type equation.

C

Command Reference

Defaults By default, DSCRIMINANT enters all variables simultaneously into the discriminating equation (the DIRECT method) provided that they are not so highly correlated that collinearity problems arise. Default output consists of counts of cases in the groups, the method used and associated parameters, and a summary of results including eigenvalues, standardized discriminant function coefficients, and within-groups correlations between the discriminant functions and the predictor variables.

Tailoring **Variable Selection Method.** In addition to the direct entry method, you can specify any of several stepwise methods for entering variables into the discriminant analysis, based on different statistical criteria. You can also specify the numerical parameters for these methods.

Case Selection. You can select a subset of cases for analysis within the DSCRIMINANT command.

Prior Probabilities. You can specify prior probabilities for membership in the different groups. These are used in classifying cases but not in the analysis leading to the discriminant functions.

Discriminant Statistics. You can add new variables to the active file containing the predicted group membership, the probabilities of membership in each of the groups, and the scores on the discriminant functions.

Classification Options. You can request that DSCRIMINANT classify only those cases that were not selected for inclusion in the discriminant analysis, or only those cases whose code on the grouping variable fell outside the range analyzed. In addition, you can classify cases on the basis of the separate-group covariance matrices rather than the pooled within-groups covariance matrix.

Statistical Display. You can request any of a variety of statistics. You can rotate the pattern or structure matrices. You can compare actual with predicted group membership using a classification results table or any of several types of plots or histograms. In addition, you can display the discriminant scores and the actual and predicted group membership for each case.

Missing Values. You can include user-defined missing values in the analysis. During the classification phase, you can substitute means for missing values so that cases with missing data will be classified.

Syntax
- The only required subcommands are GROUPS and VARIABLES.
- The GROUPS, VARIABLES, and SELECT subcommands must precede any other subcommands and may be entered in any order.
- An ANALYSIS subcommand specifies the predictor variables to be used in a single analysis. The variables must first have been named on the VARIABLES subcommand.
- All other subcommands may be entered in any order and apply only to the preceding ANALYSIS subcommand. If any of these subcommands are entered before the first ANALYSIS subcommand or if there is no ANALYSIS subcommand, the entire set of variables named on VARIABLES is analyzed as requested.
- Optional output is controlled by the OPTIONS and STATISTICS subcommands.
- Subcommands are separated by slashes.

Operations
- DSCRIMINANT causes the data to be read.
- The procedure first determines one or more discriminant functions that best distinguish between the groups.
- Using these functions, the procedure then classifies cases into the group predicted by the predictor variables.
- If more than one ANALYSIS command is supplied, these steps are repeated for each requested group of variables.

Limitations
- Only one each of the GROUPS, VARIABLES, and SELECT subcommands may be used.
- The number of predictor variables that may be used is limited by available memory.
- A maximum of 10 ANALYSIS subcommands may be entered.
- Pairwise deletion of missing data is not available.

Example
```
DSCRIMINANT GROUPS=OUTCOME (1,4)
  /VARIABLES=VAR1 TO VAR7
  /STATISTICS=3 8 9 11
  /SAVE CLASS=PREDOUT.
```
- Only cases for which the grouping variable GROUPS has values 1, 2, 3, or 4 will be used in computing the discriminant functions.
- The variables on the active file between and including VAR1 and VAR7 will be used to compute the discriminant functions and to classify cases.
- In addition to the default output, the STATISTICS subcommand requests the display of the pooled within-groups covariance matrix, the group and total covariance matrices, and the unstandardized discriminant function coefficients.
- Predicted group membership will be saved in the variable PREDOUT, which will be added to the active file if it does not already exist.

The Analysis Phase

DSCRIMINANT first calculates the discriminant function(s) that best distinguish the groups you have specified. This process is called the analysis phase. It is followed by the classification phase (see below).

GROUPS Subcommand

The GROUPS subcommand specifies the name of the grouping variable, which defines the categories or groups among which the discriminant function should distinguish. Along with the variable name, you must specify a range of categories. The discriminant analysis will attempt to predict membership in the categories of this variable.
- The GROUPS subcommand is required and may be used only once.
- The specification consists of a variable name followed by a range of values in parentheses.
- You can specify only one grouping variable, and its values must be integers.
- Empty groups are ignored and do not affect calculations. For example, if there are no cases in Group 2, the value range (1,5) will define only four groups.
- Cases with values outside the value range or with missing values are ignored during the analysis phase but will be classified during the classification phase.

VARIABLES Subcommand

The VARIABLES subcommand identifies the predictor variables, which are used to classify cases into the groups defined on the GROUPS subcommand. The list of variables follows the usual SPSS/PC+ conventions for variable lists.
- The VARIABLES subcommand is required and may be used only once. Use the ANALYSIS subcommand to obtain multiple analyses.
- Only numeric variables may be used.
- Variables should be suitable for use in a regression-type equation: either measured at the interval level, or dichotomous.

ANALYSIS Subcommand

Use the ANALYSIS subcommand to request several different discriminant analyses using the same grouping variable, or to control the order in which variables are entered into a stepwise analysis.
- The ANALYSIS subcommand is optional. By default all variables on the VARIABLES subcommand are included in the analysis.
- The variables named on ANALYSIS must first be specified on the VARIABLES subcommand.

• The keyword ALL includes all variables on the VARIABLES subcommand.

• If you use the TO convention to specify a list of variables on an ANALYSIS subcommand, it refers to the order of variables on the VARIABLES subcommand, which is not necessarily that in the active file.

Example
```
DSCRIMINANT GROUPS=SUCCESS(0,1)
  /VARIABLES=VAR10 TO VAR15, AGE, VAR5
  /ANALYSIS=VAR15 TO VAR5
  /ANALYSIS=ALL.
```

• The first ANALYSIS will use variables VAR15, AGE, and VAR5 to discriminate between cases where SUCCESS=0 and the cases where SUCCESS=1.

• The second ANALYSIS will use all variables on the VARIABLES subcommand.

Inclusion Levels. When you specify a stepwise method (any method other than the default METHOD=DIRECT), you can control the order in which variables are considered for entry or removal by specifying *inclusion levels* on the ANALYSIS subcommand. By default, all variables in the analysis are entered according to the criterion requested on the METHOD subcommand.

• An inclusion level is an integer between 0 and 99, specified in parentheses after a variable or list of variables on an ANALYSIS subcommand.

• The default inclusion level is 1.

• Variables with higher inclusion levels are considered for entry before variables with lower inclusion levels.

• Variables with even inclusion levels are entered as a group.

• Variables with odd inclusion levels are entered individually, according to the stepwise method specified on the METHOD subcommand.

• Only variables with an inclusion level of 1 are considered for removal. To make a variable with a higher inclusion level eligible for removal, name it twice on the ANALYSIS subcommand, first specifying the desired inclusion level and then an inclusion level of 1.

• Variables with an inclusion level of 0 are never entered. However, the statistical criterion for entry is computed and displayed.

• Variables which fail the TOLERANCE criterion are not entered regardless of their inclusion level.

The following are some common methods of entering variables along with the ANALYSIS subcommand and inclusion levels that could be used to achieve them. These examples assume that one of the stepwise methods is specified on the METHOD subcommand (otherwise, inclusion levels have no effect).

• *Direct.* ANALYSIS=ALL(2) forces all variables into the equation. (This is the default and can be requested with METHOD=DIRECT or simply by omitting the METHOD and ANALYSIS subcommands.)

• *Stepwise.* ANALYSIS=ALL(1) yields a stepwise solution in which variables are entered and removed in stepwise fashion. (This is the default when anything other than DIRECT is specified on the METHOD subcommand.)

• *Forward.* ANALYSIS=ALL(3) enters variables into the equation stepwise, but does not ever remove variables.

• *Backward.* ANALYSIS=ALL(2) ALL(1) forces all variables into the equation and then allows them to be removed stepwise if they satisfy the criterion for removal.

Example
```
DSCRIMINANT GROUPS=SUCCESS(0,1)
  /VARIABLES=A, B, C, D, E
  /ANALYSIS=A TO C (2) D, E (1)
  /METHOD=WILKS.
```

• A, B, and C are entered into the analysis first, assuming that they pass the tolerance criterion. Since their inclusion level is even, they are entered together.

• D and E are then entered stepwise. Whichever of the two minimizes the overall value of Wilks' lambda is entered first.

• After entering D and E, SPSS/PC+ checks whether the partial F for either one justifies removal from the equation (see the discussion under FOUT and POUT).

Example
```
DSCRIMINANT GROUPS=SUCCESS(0,1)
   /VARIABLES=A, B, C, D, E
   /ANALYSIS=A TO C (2) D, E (1).
```

- Since no stepwise method is specified, inclusion levels have no effect and all variables are entered into the model at once.

SELECT Subcommand

With the SELECT subcommand, you can limit the discriminant analysis to cases with a specified value on any one variable.

- Only one SELECT subcommand is allowed. It may follow the GROUPS and VARIABLES subcommands but must precede any other subcommands.
- Specifications for the SELECT subcommand consist of a variable name and a single value in parentheses. Multiple variables or values are not permitted.
- The selection variable need not have been named on the GROUPS (or VARIABLES) subcommand.
- Only cases with the specified value on the selection variable are used in the analysis phase.
- By default, all cases will be classified whether selected or not. You can use Option 9 to classify only the unselected cases.
- When you use the SELECT subcommand, classification statistics are reported separately for selected and unselected cases, unless you use Option 9 to restrict classification.

Example
```
DSC GRO=APPROVAL(1,5)
   /VAR=Q1 TO Q10
   /SEL=COMPLETE(1)
   /OPT=9.
```

- This example uses three-letter truncation of keywords.
- Using only the cases where variable COMPLETE = 1, DSCRIMINANT will form a discriminant function out of Q1 TO Q10 that discriminates between the categories 1 to 5 of the grouping variable APPROVAL.
- Because Option 9 is requested, the discriminant function will be used to classify only the unselected cases, namely the cases for which COMPLETE does not equal 1.

METHOD Subcommand

Use the METHOD subcommand to select any of six methods for entering variables into the analysis phase.

- A variable will never be entered into the analysis if it does not pass the tolerance criterion specified on the TOLERANCE subcommand (or the default).
- A METHOD subcommand applies to the *preceding* ANALYSIS subcommand or to an analysis using all predictor variables if no ANALYSIS subcommand has been specified.
- Only one METHOD command may be entered per ANALYSIS.

Any one of the following methods may be entered on the METHOD subcommand:

DIRECT   *All variables passing the tolerance criteria are entered simultaneously. This is the default method.*

WILKS   *The variable that minimizes the overall Wilks' lambda is entered.*

MAHAL   *The variable that maximizes the Mahalanobis' distance between the two closest groups is entered.*

MAXMINF   *The variable that maximizes the smallest F ratio between pairs of groups is entered.*

MINRESID   *The variable that minimizes the sum of the unexplained variation for all pairs of groups is entered.*

RAO   *The variable that produces the largest increase in Rao's V is entered.*

Statistical Criteria for Entry or Removal

In addition to naming a method for variable selection on the METHOD subcommand, you can specify a number of optional subcommands to set other parameters controlling the selection algorithm.

- These subcommands must follow the METHOD subcommand to which they apply and may be entered in any order.
- All of these subcommands except TOLERANCE apply only to the stepwise methods. Therefore, the METHOD subcommand is not required when you specify TOLERANCE.

TOLERANCE Subcommand

The tolerance of a variable that is a candidate for inclusion in the analysis is the proportion of its within-group variance that is not accounted for by other variables currently in the analysis. A variable with very low tolerance is nearly a linear function of the other variables; its inclusion in the analysis would make the calculations unstable. The TOLERANCE subcommand specifies the minimum tolerance a variable can have and still be entered into the analysis.

- The default tolerance is 0.001.
- You can specify any decimal value between 0 and 1 as the minimum tolerance.

FIN Subcommand

FIN specifies the minimum partial F value a variable must have to enter the analysis.

- The default is FIN=1.
- You can set FIN to any nonnegative number.
- PIN overrides FIN if both are specified.
- FIN is ignored if the METHOD subcommand is omitted or if METHOD specifies DIRECT.

PIN Subcommand

PIN specifies the minimum probability of F a variable must have to enter the analysis. Since the probability of F depends upon the degrees of freedom and the variables in the equation, it can change at each step. Use the PIN subcommmand to keep the minimum F's at a minimum significance level.

- If the PIN subcommand is omitted, the value of FIN is used.
- You can set PIN to any decimal value between 0 and 1.
- If PIN is specified, FIN is ignored.
- PIN is ignored if the METHOD subcommand is omitted or if METHOD specifies DIRECT.

FOUT Subcommand

As additional variables are entered into the analysis, the partial F for variables already in the equation changes. FOUT is the maximum partial F a variable can have before it is removed from the analysis.

- The default is FOUT=1.0.
- You can set FOUT to any nonnegative number. However, FOUT should be less than FIN if FIN is also specified.
- To be removed, variables must also have an inclusion level of 1 (the default).
- POUT overrides FOUT if both are specified.
- FOUT is ignored if the METHOD subcommand is omitted or if METHOD specifies DIRECT.

POUT Subcommand

POUT is the maximum probability of F a variable can have before it is removed from the analysis.

- By default, a variable is removed if its partial F falls below the FOUT specification.
- You can set POUT to any decimal value between 0 and 1. However, POUT should be greater than PIN if PIN is also specified.
- To be removed, variables must also have an inclusion level of 1 (the default).
- POUT overrides FOUT if both are specified.
- POUT is ignored if the METHOD subcommand is omitted or if METHOD specifies DIRECT.

VIN Subcommand

The VIN subcommand specifies the minimum Rao's V a variable must have to enter the analysis. When you use METHOD=RAO, variables satisfying one of the other criteria for entering the equation may actually cause a decrease in Rao's V for the equation. The default VIN prevents this, but does not prevent variables which provide no additional separation between groups from being added.

- The default is VIN=0.
- You can specify any value for VIN.
- VIN should be used only when you have specified METHOD=RAO. Otherwise, it is ignored.

MAXSTEPS Subcommand

By default, the maximum number of steps allowed in a stepwise analysis is the number of variables with inclusion levels greater than 1 plus twice the number of variables with inclusion levels equal to 1. This is the maximum number of steps possible without a loop in which a variable is repeatedly cycled in and out. Use the MAXSTEPS subcommand to decrease the maximum number of steps allowed.

- MAXSTEPS applies only to the stepwise methods.
- MAXSTEPS should be specified after the METHOD subcommand to which it applies.
- The format is MAX=n, where n is the maximum number of steps desired.

FUNCTIONS Subcommand

By default, DSCRIMINANT computes the maximum number of functions that are mathematically possible. This is either the number of groups minus 1 or the number of predictor variables, whichever is less. Use the FUNCTIONS subcommand to set more restrictive criteria for the extraction of functions.
The FUNCTIONS subcommand has three parameters:

nf *Maximum number of functions.* The default is the number of groups minus one or the number of predictor variables, whichever is less.

cp *Cumulative percentage of eigenvalues.* The default is 100%.

sig *Significance level of function.* The default is 1.0.

- You can restrict the number of functions with only one parameter at a time.
- The parameters must always be specified in the following order: *nf*, *cp*, *sig*. Thus, if you specify *cp*, you must explicitly specify the default for *nf*. If you specify *sig*, you must specify defaults for *nf* and *cp*. Since *nf* is first, it can be specified without *cp* and *sig*.
- If more than one nondefault restriction is specified on the FUNCTIONS subcommand, SPSS/PC+ uses the first one encountered.

Example

```
DSCRIMINANT  GROUPS=CLASS(1,5)
   /VARIABLES=SCORE1 TO SCORE20
   /FUNCTIONS=4,100,.80.
```

- The first two specifications on the FUNCTIONS subcommand are defaults: the default for *nf* is 4 (5, the number of groups, minus 1), and the default for *cp* is always 100.
- The third specification tells DSCRIMINANT to use fewer than four discriminant functions if the significance level of a function is greater than 0.80.

Statistical Display for the Analysis Phase

By default, the following statistics are produced during the analysis phase:

- *Summary table.* A table showing the action taken at every step (for stepwise methods only).
- *Summary statistics.* Eigenvalues, percentage of variance, cumulative percentage of variance, canonical correlations, Wilks' lambda, chi-square, degrees of freedom, and significance of chi-square are reported for the functions. (Summary statistics can be suppressed with Option 5.)

C

Command Reference

- *Step statistics.* Wilks' lambda, equivalent F, degrees of freedom, and significance of F are reported for each step. Tolerance, F-to-remove, and the stepping criterion value are reported for each variable in the equation. Tolerance, minimum tolerance, F-to-enter, and the stepping criterion value are reported for each variable not in the equation. (Step statistics can be suppressed with Option 4.)

- *Final statistics.* Standardized canonical discriminant function coefficients, the structure matrix of discriminant functions and all variables named in the analysis (whether they were entered into the equation or not), and functions evaluated at group means, are reported following the last step. (These statistics cannot be suppressed.)

In addition, you can request the following optional statistics on the STATISTICS subcommand:

Statistic 1 *Means.* Statistic 1 displays overall and group means for all variables named on the ANALYSIS subcommand.

Statistic 2 *Standard deviations.* Statistic 2 displays overall and group standard deviations for all variables named on the ANALYSIS subcommand.

Statistic 3 *Pooled within-groups covariance matrix.*

Statistic 4 *Pooled within-groups correlation matrix.*

Statistic 5 *Matrix of pairwise* F *ratios.* Statistic 5 displays the F ratio for each pair of groups. This F is the significance test for the Mahalanobis' distance between groups. This statistic is available only with the stepwise methods.

Statistic 6 *Univariate* F *ratios.* Statistic 6 displays F for each variable. This is a one-way analysis of variance test for equality of group means on a single predictor variable.

Statistic 7 *Box's* M *test.* This is a test for equality of group covariance matrices.

Statistic 8 *Group covariance matrices.*

Statistic 9 *Total covariance matrix.*

Statistic 11 *Unstandardized canonical discriminant functions.*

Statistic 12 *Classification function coefficients.* Although DSCRIMINANT does not directly use the Fisher linear discriminant functions to classify cases, you can use these coefficients to classify other samples.

Rotation Options

The pattern and structure matrices displayed during the analysis phase may be rotated to facilitate interpretation of results. To obtain a VARIMAX rotation, specify either Option 6 or 7 on the associated OPTIONS command.

Option 6 *Rotate pattern matrix.*

Option 7 *Rotate structure matrix.*

Neither Option 6 nor Option 7 affects the classification of cases since the rotation is orthogonal.

Display Format

Two options are available to reduce the amount of output produced during stepwise analysis:

Option 4 *Suppress display of step-by-step output.*

Option 5 *Suppress display of the summary table.*

These two options affect only display output, not the computation of intermediate results.

The Classification Phase

Once DSCRIMINANT has completed the analysis phase, you can use the results to classify your cases. DSCRIMINANT provides a variety of statistics for evaluating the ability of a particular model to classify cases, along with several subcommands and options to control the classification phase.

PRIORS Subcommand By default, DSCRIMINANT assumes equal probabilities for group membership when classifying cases. You can provide different prior probabilities with the PRIORS subcommand.

Any one of the following can be specified on PRIORS:

EQUAL *Equal prior probabilities.* This is the default specification.

SIZE *Proportion of the cases analyzed that fall into each group.* If 50% of the cases included in the analysis fall into the first group, 25% in the second, and 25% in the third, the prior probabilities are 0.5, 0.25, and 0.25, respectively. Group size is determined after cases with missing values for the predictor variables are deleted.

Value list *User-specified prior probabilities.* A list of probabilities summing to 1.0 is specified.

- Prior probabilities are used only during classification.
- If you provide unequal prior probabilities, DSCRIMINANT adjusts the classification coefficients to reflect this prior knowledge.
- If adjacent groups have the same prior probability, you can use the notation $n*c$ in the value list to indicate that n adjacent groups have the same prior probability c.
- The value list must name or imply as many prior probabilities as groups.
- You can specify a prior probability of 0. No cases are classified into such a group.
- If the sum of the prior probabilities is not 1, SPSS/PC+ rescales the probabilities to sum to 1 and issues a warning.

Example
```
DSCRIMINANT  GROUPS=TYPE(1,5)
   /VARIABLES=A TO H
   /PRIORS=4*.15,.4.
```

- The PRIORS subcommand establishes prior probabilities of 0.15 for the first four groups and 0.4 for the fifth group.

Example Specifying a list of prior probabilities is often used to produce classification coefficients for samples with known group membership. For example, if you have five groups, the value list might look like the following:
```
DSCRIMINANT  GROUPS=TYPE(1,5)
   /VARIABLES=A TO H
   /PRIORS = .25 .2 .3 .1 .15.
```

Classification Options Three options relating to the classification phase may be requested on the OPTIONS subcommand.

Option 9 *Classify only unselected cases.* If you use the SELECT subcommand, DSCRIMINANT will by default classify all cases with valid data for the predictor variables. Option 9 suppresses the classification phase for cases selected for the analysis, classifying only the unselected cases.

Option 10 *Classify only unclassified cases.* The analysis phase includes only cases with values for the grouping variable within the range specified. With Option 10 you can suppress classification of cases used to derive the discriminant functions. Only cases with missing or out-of-range values on the grouping variable will be classified.

Option 11 *Use individual-group covariance matrices of the discriminant functions for classification.* By default, DSCRIMINANT uses the pooled with-in-groups covariance matrix to classify cases. If you specify Option 11, it will instead use the individual-group covariance matrices.

Display Output You can request a classification results table and three types of plots to help you examine the effectiveness of the discriminant analysis. You can also display discriminant scores and related information for each case. Consult the Statistics Guide (Part B) and Examples (Part D) in this manual for examples of this output.

Statistic 10   *Territorial map.* A territorial map uses the first two discriminant functions as its axes and displays the boundaries between the territories predicted to fall into each group. It is not available for an analysis producing a single discriminant function. Only the first two discriminant functions can be used as axes. Group centroids are plotted as asterisks. Individual cases are not plotted on this map.

Statistic 13   *Classification results table.* This table reports the proportion of cases that are classified correctly and enables you to judge whether cases are systematically misclassified. If you include a SELECT subcommand, two tables are produced—one for selected cases and one for unselected cases.

Statistic 14   *Casewise classification information.* Statistic 14 displays the following information for each case classified: case sequence number; number of missing values in the case; value on SELECT variable, if any; actual group; highest group classification (G); the probability of a case which is in group G being that far from the group centroid ($P(D|G)$); the probability of a case with these discriminant scores being in group G ($P(G|D)$); the second-highest group classification and its $P(G|D)$; and the discriminant scores.

Statistic 15   *All-groups plot.* Cases in all groups are plotted on a single scatter plot, using the first two discriminant functions as axes. The plotting symbol for each case is the group number. Group centroids are plotted as asterisks. If the analysis yields only one discriminant function, a stacked histogram is plotted instead.

Statistic 16   *Separate-groups plots.* Cases in each group are plotted separately on plots that are otherwise the same as those produced by Statistic 15. If the analysis yields only one discriminant function, a histogram is plotted for each group.

Missing Values

By default, cases missing on any of the predictor variables named on the VARIABLES subcommand are used during neither phase. Cases out-of-range or missing on the grouping variable are not used during the analysis phase but are classified in the classification phase.

Two options are available for cases which are missing on the predictor variables:

Option 1   *Include missing values.* User-missing values are treated as valid values. Only the system-missing value is excluded.

Option 8   *Substitute means for missing values during classification.* Cases with missing values are not used during analysis. Cases with missing values on the classification variables are classified, using the mean as a substitute for the missing data.

SAVE Subcommand

The SAVE subcommand allows you to add much of the casewise information produced by Statistic 14 to the active file and to specify new variable names for this information. The following keywords may be specified on the SAVE subcommand:

CLASS   *Save a variable containing the predicted group membership.* Specify a name for this variable after the keyword CLASS.

SCORES   *Save the discriminant scores.* One score is saved for each discriminant function derived. Specify a *rootname* up to seven characters long after the SCORES keyword. DSCRIMINANT will use the rootname to form new variable names for the discriminant scores.

PROBS   *Save each case's probabilities of membership in each group.* As many variables are added to each case as there are groups. Specify a *rootname* up to seven characters long after the PROBS keyword. DSCRIMINANT will use the rootname to generate variable names for the new variables.

- Request only the keywords for the results you want saved.
- SAVE applies to the previous ANALYSIS subcommand (or to an analysis of all variables if no ANALYSIS subcommand precedes SAVE).
- To save casewise results from more than one analysis, enter a SAVE command after each, using different rootnames.
- You can specify the keywords CLASS, SCORES, and PROBS in any order, but the new variables are always added to the end of the active file in the following order: first class, then discriminant scores, then probabilities.
- Appropriate variable labels are generated automatically for the new variables.
- The CLASS variable will use the value labels (if any) from the GROUP variable specified for the analysis.

Example
```
DSCRIMINANT GROUPS = WORLD(1,3)
   /VARIABLES = FOOD TO FSALES
   /SAVE CLASS=PRDCLASS SCORES=SCORE PROBS=PRB.
```

- With three groups, the following variables are added to each case:

Name	Description
PRDCLASS	Predicted group
SCORE1	Discriminant score for Function 1
SCORE2	Discriminant score for Function 2
PRB1	Probability of being in Group 1
PRB2	Probability of being in Group 2
PRB3	Probability of being in Group 3

HILOGLINEAR

```
HILOGLINEAR {varlist} (min,max) [varlist (min,max)...]
            {ALL    }

[/METHOD=BACKWARD]

[/MAXORDER=k]

[/CRITERIA=[CONVERGE({0.25**})] [ITERATE({20**})]
                     {n     }            {n   }

          [P({0.05**})] [MAXSTEPS({10**})] [DEFAULT**]]
             {prob   }            {n   }

[/CWEIGHT={varname }]
          {(matrix)}

[/PRINT=[DEFAULT**] [FREQ**] [RESID**] [ESTIM**]
        [NONE] [ASSOCIATION] [ALL]]

[/PLOT=[{DEFAULT}] [RESID] [NORMPLOT] [NONE**]]
        {ALL    }

[/MISSING={LISTWISE**} {INCLUDE}]
          {DEFAULT**  }

[/DESIGN=[effectname effectname*effectname ...]]
[/DESIGN=...]
```

**Default if subcommand is omitted.

Example:

```
HILOGLINEAR AVAR(1,2) BVAR(1,2) CVAR(1,3) DVAR(1,3)
  /DESIGN=AVAR*BVAR*CVAR, DVAR.
```

Overview

HILOGLINEAR fits hierarchical log-linear models to multidimensional contingency tables using iterative proportional-fitting algorithms. HILOGLINEAR also estimates parameters for saturated models. These techniques are described in Everitt (1977), Bishop, Feinberg & Holland (1975), and Goodman (1978).

Defaults

By default, HILOGLINEAR estimates a saturated model for all variables in the analysis. The default display includes raw and expected cell counts, raw and standardized residuals, and parameter estimates. A case that has a missing value for any variable in the analysis is omitted.

Tailoring

Design Specification. You can request automatic model selection using backward elimination with the METHOD subcommand. You can also specify any hierarchical design and request multiple designs using the DESIGN subcommand.

Design Control. You can control the criteria used in the iterative proportional-fitting and model-selection routines with the CRITERIA subcommand. You can also limit the order of effects in the model with MAXORDER and specify structural zeros for cells in the tables you analyze with CWEIGHT.

Display and Plots. With the PRINT subcommand, you can limit the display for a design or include partial associations or tests for orders of effects for saturated models. You can request residuals plots or normal probability plots of residuals with the PLOT subcommand.

Missing Values. You can control the handling of user-missing values with the MISSING subcommand.

Syntax
- The minimum specification is a variable list with at least two variables followed by their minimum and maximum values.
- The variable list must be specified first.
- The DESIGN subcommand is optional. If no DESIGN subcommand is specified or DESIGN is not the last subcommand, a default model is estimated.
- The METHOD, PRINT, PLOT, CRITERIA, MAXORDER, and CWEIGHT subcommands should be placed before the designs to which they apply. Other than this, they can appear in any order.
- You can specify multiple PRINT, PLOT, CRITERIA, MAXORDER, and CWEIGHT subcommands. The last of each type specified is in effect for subsequent designs.
- The PRINT, PLOT, CRITERIA, MAXORDER and CWEIGHT subcommands remain in effect until they are overridden by new subcommands.
- You can specify multiple METHOD subcommands, but each one affects only the next design.
- The MISSING subcommand can be specified only once and can be placed anywhere after the variable list.
- Subcommands must be separated by slashes.

Operations
- HILOGLINEAR causes the data to be read.
- HILOGLINEAR builds a contingency table using all variables on the variable list. The table contains a cell for each possible combination of values within the ranges specified for each of the variables.
- HILOGLINEAR assumes there is a category for every integer value in the range of each variable. Empty categories waste space and can cause computational problems. If there are empty categories, you should use the RECODE command to create consecutive integer values for categories.
- Cases with values outside the range specified for any variable are excluded.
- If the last subcommand is not a DESIGN subcommand, HILOGLINEAR displays a warning and generates the default model. This is the saturated model unless MAXORDER is specified. This model is in addition to any that are explicitly requested.
- Only hierarchical log-linear models can be specified.
- If the model is not saturated (for example, when MAXORDER is less than the number of factors), only a goodness-of-fit and the observed and expected frequencies are given.
- The display uses the WIDTH defined on SET. If the defined width is less than 132, some portions of the display may be deleted.

Limitations
- Maximum 10 factors.
- Maximum 1 variable list.
- Maximum 1 MISSING subcommand.

Example
```
HILOGLINEAR AVAR(1,2) BVAR(1,2) CVAR(1,3) DVAR(1,3)
    /DESIGN=AVAR*BVAR*CVAR, DVAR.
```
- This example builds a $2 \times 2 \times 3 \times 3$ contingency table for analysis.
- The DESIGN subcommand specifies the generating class for a hierarchical model. This model consists of main effects for all four variables, two-way interactions among AVAR, BVAR, and CVAR, and the three-way interaction term AVAR by BVAR by CVAR.

Variable List
The required variable list specifies the variables in the analysis.

- Variables must have integer values. If a variable has a fractional value, the fractional portion is truncated.

- Keyword ALL can be used to refer to all user-defined variables in the active file. If ALL is specified, all variables must have the same range.
- A range must be specified for each variable, with the minimum and maximum values separated by a comma and enclosed in parentheses.
- If the same range applies to several variables, the range can be specified once after the last variable to which it applies.
- The variable list must precede all other subcommands.

METHOD Subcommand

By default, HILOGLINEAR tests the model specified on the DESIGN subcommand (or the default model) and does not perform any model selection. All variables are entered and none are removed. Use the METHOD subcommand to specify automatic model selection using backward elimination for the next design specified.

- You must specify the keyword BACKWARD on the METHOD subcommand.
- The METHOD subcommand affects only the next design.

BACKWARD *Backward elimination.* Perform backward elimination of terms in the model. All terms are entered. Those that do not meet the P criteria specified on the CRITERIA subcommand (or the default P) are removed.

MAXORDER Subcommand

The MAXORDER subcommand controls the maximum order of terms in the model estimated for subsequent designs. If MAXORDER is specified, HILOG-LINEAR will test a model only with terms of that order or less.

- MAXORDER specifies the highest-order term that will be considered from the next design. MAXORDER can thus be used to abbreviate computations for the BACKWARD method.
- If the integer on MAXORDER is less than the number of factors, parameter estimates and measures of partial association are not available. Only goodness-of-fit and the observed and expected frequencies are displayed.

Example

```
HILOGLINEAR VARA VARB VARC(1 2)
/MAXORDER=2
/DESIGN=VARA*VARB*VARC
/DESIGN=VARA VARB VARC.
```

- This example builds a $2 \times 2 \times 2$ contingency table for VARA, VARB, and VARC.
- The MAXORDER subcommand restricts the terms in the model specified on the first DESIGN subcommand to two-way interactions or less.
- The MAXORDER subcommand has no effect on the second DESIGN subcommand, since the design requested considers only main effects.

CRITERIA Subcommand

Use the CRITERIA subcommand to change the values of constants in the iterative proportional-fitting and model-selection routines for subsequent designs.

- The default criteria are in effect if the CRITERIA subcommand is omitted (see below).
- You cannot specify the CRITERIA subcommand without any keywords.
- Specify each criteria keyword followed by a criterion value in parentheses.
- Only those criteria specifically altered are changed.
- You can specify more than one keyword on CRITERIA, and they can be in any order.

The following criteria can be specified:

CONVERGE(n) *Convergence criterion.* The default is 0.25. Iterations stop when the change in fitted frequencies is less than the specified value.

ITERATE(n) *Maximum number of iterations.* The default is 20.

P(prob) *Probability of chi-square for model.* P is in effect only when method BACKWARD is specified. The default is 0.05.

MAXSTEPS(n) *Maximum number of steps.* MAXSTEPS is in effect only when method BACKWARD is specified. The default is 10.

DEFAULT *Default criteria.* Use DEFAULT to restore defaults changed by a previous CRITERIA subcommand.

CWEIGHT Subcommand

The CWEIGHT subcommand specifies cell weights for a model. CWEIGHT is typically used to specify structural zeros in the table.

- You can specify the name of a variable whose values are cell weights or provide a matrix of cell weights enclosed in parentheses.
- You must specify a weight for every cell in the contingency table, where the number of cells equals the product of the number of values of all variables.
- Cell weights are indexed by the values of the variables in the order in which they are specified on the variable list. The index values of the rightmost variable change the most quickly.
- A variable named on CWEIGHT must be numeric.
- You can use the notation $n*cw$ to indicate that cell weight cw is repeated n times in the matrix.
- CWEIGHT does not weight aggregated input data.
- CWEIGHT is ignored with saturated models.

Example
```
HILOGLINEAR AVAR(1,2) BVAR(1,2) CVAR(1,3)
   /CWEIGHT=CELLWGT
   /DESIGN AVAR*BVAR, BVAR*CVAR, AVAR*CVAR.
```

- This example weights a cell by the value of the variable CELLWGT when a case containing the frequency for that cell is read.

Example
```
HILOGLINEAR DVAR(1,3) EVAR(1,3)
   /CWEIGHT=(0 1 1  1 0 1  1 1 0)
   /DESIGN=DVAR, EVAR.
```

```
HILOGLINEAR DVAR(1,3) EVAR(1,3)
   /CWEIGHT=(0 3*1 0 3*1 0)
   /DESIGN=DVAR,EVAR.
```

- These two equivalent HILOGLINEAR commands set the diagonal cells in the model to structural zeros. This type of model is known as a quasi-independence model.
- Because both DVAR and EVAR have three values, weights must be specified for nine cells.
- The first HILOGLINEAR command specifies cell weights explicitly.
- The second HILOGLINEAR command uses the $n*cw$ notation to indicate that the cell weight is repeated.
- The first cell weight is applied to the cell in which DVAR is 1 and EVAR is 1; the second weight is applied to the cell in which DVAR is 1 and EVAR is 2, and so forth.

C

Command Reference

Example
```
TITLE AMERICAN BLADDER NUT SEPARABILITY  HARRIS(1910).
SUBTITLE AN INCOMPLETE RECTANGULAR TABLE.
DATA LIST FREE / LOCULAR RADIAL FREQ.
WEIGHT BY FREQ.
BEGIN DATA.
1 1 462
1 2 130
1 3 2
1 4 1
2 1 103
2 2 35
2 3 1
2 4 0
3 5 614
3 6 138
3 7 21
3 8 14
3 9 1
4 5 443
4 6 95
4 7 22
4 8 8
4 9 5
END DATA.
HILOGLINEAR LOCULAR (1,4) RADIAL (1,9)
  /CWEIGHT=(4*1 5*0   4*1 5*0   4*0 5*1   4*0 5*1)
  /DESIGN LOCULAR RADIAL.
```

- This example uses aggregated table data as input.
- The DATA LIST command defines three variables. The values of LOCULAR and RADIAL index the levels of those variables, so that each case defines a cell in the table. The values of FREQ are the cell frequencies.
- The WEIGHT command weights each case (cell) by the value of the variable FREQ. Since each case represents a cell, the cell frequency will have the value of FREQ for that case.
- The BEGIN DATA and END DATA commands enclose the lines of data.
- The HILOGLINEAR variable list specifies two variables. LOCULAR has values 1, 2, 3, and 4. RADIAL has integer values 1 through 4.
- The CWEIGHT subcommand identifies a block rectangular pattern of cells that are logically empty. There is one weight specified for each cell of the 36-cell table.
- The DESIGN subcommand specifies only main effects for LOCULAR and RADIAL. Lack of fit for this model indicates an interaction of the two variables.
- Since there is no PRINT or PLOT subcommand, HILOGLINEAR produces the default output for an unsaturated model.

PRINT Subcommand

The PRINT subcommand controls the display produced for the following designs.

- If the PRINT subcommand is omitted or included with no specifications, the default display is produced.
- If any keywords are specified on PRINT, only output specifically requested is displayed.

The following can be specified on PRINT:

FREQ
Frequencies. Display observed and expected cell frequencies. If the defined width is wide enough, HILOGLINEAR also displays cell percentages.

RESID
Residuals. Display raw and standardized residuals.

ESTIM
Parameter estimates for a saturated model. ESTIM is included in the default display for saturated models. ESTIM is not available for unsaturated models (including when MAXORDER is less than the number of factors).

ASSOCIATION
Partial associations of effects for a saturated model. ASSOCIA-TION is not available for unsaturated models (including when MAXORDER is less than the number of factors). This option is computationally expensive for tables with many factors.

DEFAULT   *Default display.* DEFAULT includes FREQ and RESID for all models and ESTIM for saturated models. This is the default if PRINT is omitted or included without any specifications.

ALL   *All available displays.*

NONE   *Design information and goodness-of-fit statistics only.* This option overrides all other specifications on the PRINT subcommand.

PLOT Subcommand

Use the optional PLOT subcommand to request residuals plots for the following designs.

- No plots are displayed for saturated models.
- If the PLOT subcommand is omitted, no plots are produced.
- If PLOT is included without specifications, standardized residuals and normal probability plots are produced.
- Plots use the box characters specified on the BOXSTRING subcommand of the SET command (see *SPSS/PC+ Base Manual*).

RESID   *Standardized residuals by observed and expected counts.*

NORMPLOT   *Normal probability plots of adjusted residuals.*

NONE   *No plots.* Specify NONE to suppress plots requested on a previous PLOT subcommand. This is the default if the PLOT subcommand is omitted.

DEFAULT   *Default plots.* DEFAULT includes RESID and NORMPLOT. This is the default when PLOT is specified without keywords.

ALL   *All available plots.*

MISSING Subcommand

By default, a case with missing values for any variable named on the variable list is omitted from the analysis. Use the MISSING subcommand to change the treatment of cases with user-missing values.

- The MISSING subcommand can be named only once and can be placed anywhere following the variable list.
- The MISSING subcommand cannot be used without specifications.
- A case with a system-missing value for any variable named on the variable list is always excluded from the analysis.

The following specifications are available for MISSING:

LISTWISE   *Delete cases with missing values listwise.* This is the default if the subcommand is omitted. You can also request listwise deletion with keyword DEFAULT.

INCLUDE   *Include user-missing values as valid.* Only cases with system-missing values are deleted.

DESIGN Subcommand

The default model is a saturated model that includes all variables in the variable list. A saturated model contains all main effects and interactions for those variables. Use the DESIGN subcommand to specify a different generating class for the model. In a hierarchical model, higher-order interaction effects imply lower-order interaction and main effects. The highest-order effects to be estimated are the generating class.

- If the DESIGN subcommand is omitted or included without specifications, the default model is estimated.
- To specify a design, list the the highest-order terms, using variable names and asterisks (*) to indicate interaction effects.
- Higher-order interaction terms specified on DESIGN imply all lower-order interaction and main effect terms. AVAR*BVAR*CVAR implies the three-way interaction AVAR by BVAR by CVAR, two-way interactions AVAR by BVAR, AVAR by CVAR, and BVAR by CVAR, and main effects for AVAR, BVAR, and CVAR.

- One model is estimated for each DESIGN subcommand.
- If the last subcommand on HILOGLINEAR is not DESIGN, the default model will be estimated in addition to models explicitly requested.
- Only hierarchical log-linear models can be specified.
- If the model is not saturated (for example, when MAXORDER is less than the number of factors), only a goodness-of-fit and the observed and expected frequencies are given.
- The display uses the WIDTH defined on SET. If the defined width is less than 132, some portions of the display may be deleted.

References   Bishop, Y., S. Fienberg, and P. Holland. 1975. *Discrete multivariate analysis: Theory and practice.* Cambridge: MIT Press.
Everitt, B. S. 1977. *The analysis of contingency tables.* New York: Halsted Press.
Goodman, L. A. 1978. *Analyzing qualitative/categorical data.* Cambridge: Abt Books.

LOGISTIC REGRESSION

```
LOGISTIC REGRESSION [VARIABLES=] dependent var [WITH ind.varlist]
   [BY var [BY var] ... ]

[/CATEGORICAL= var1, var2, ... ]

                                       {DEVIATION [(refcat)]     }
                                       {SIMPLE [(refcat)]        }
                                       {DIFFERENCE               }
[/CONTRAST (categorical var)={HELMERT                  }]
                                       {REPEATED                 }
                                       {POLYNOMIAL[({1,2,3...})]}
                                       {            {metric  }   }
                                       {SPECIAL (matrix)         }
                                       {INDICATOR [(refcat)]     }

[/METHOD={ENTER**                } [{ALL**                        }]
         {FSTEP [({WALD**})]}    {varlist [varname BY varname]}
                 {LR    }
         {BSTEP [({WALD**})]}
                 {LR    }

[/SELECT={ALL**                }]
         {varname relation value}

[/{NOORIGIN**}]
  {ORIGIN   }

[/ID = [variable]]

[/PRINT=[ALL] [SUMMARY] [CORR] [DEFAULT**] [ITER [({1**})]]]
                                                   {n  }

[/CRITERIA=[BCON ({0.001**})]]
                  {value  }

         [ITERATE({20**})] [LCON({0.01**})]
                  {n  }           {value }

         [PIN({0.05**})] [POUT({0.10**})] [EPS({.00000001**})]
              {value }         {value }        {value        }

[/CLASSPLOT]

[/MISSING={EXCLUDE **}]
          {INCLUDE  }

[/CASEWISE=[tempvarlist]  [OUTLIER({2**  })]]
                                   {value}

[/SAVE=tempvar[(newname)] tempvar[(newname)]...]

[/EXTERNAL]
```

**Default if the subcommand or keyword is omitted.

Temporary variables for logistic regression analysis are: PRED, PGROUP, RESID, DEV, LRESID, SRESID, ZRESID, LEVER, COOK, DFBETA.

Example:

```
LOGISTIC REGRESSION PROMOTED WITH AGE, JOBTIME, JOBRATE.
```

Overview   LOGISTIC REGRESSION regresses a dichotomous dependent variable on a set of independent variables (Aldrich & Nelson, 1984; Fox, 1984). Categorical independent variables can be replaced by sets of contrast variables, each set entering and leaving the model as a unit.

Options   **Processing of Independent Variables.** You can specify which of the independent variables are categorical in nature (the CATEGORICAL subcommand). Treatment of categorical independent variables is controlled by the CONTRAST subcommand. Five methods are available for entering independent variables into the model (the METHOD subcommand). Interaction terms can be entered into the model by using the keyword BY between variable names.

C

Command Reference

Selecting Cases. The SELECT subcommand defines subsets of cases to be used in estimating a model.

Regression through the Origin. The inclusion or exclusion of a constant term from a model is determined by the ORIGIN or NOORIGIN subcommands.

Specifying Termination and Model-Building Criteria. The CRITERIA subcommand provides additional control over computations.

Adding New Variables to the Active System File. You can save the residuals, predicted values, and diagnostics generated by LOGISTIC REGRESSION in the active system file.

Output. You can display optional output (the PRINT subcommand), request analysis of residuals (the CASEWISE subcommand), and specify a variable whose values or value labels identify cases (the ID subcommand). You can request plots of the actual and predicted values for each case (the CLASSPLOT subcommand).

Basic Specification

- The basic specification after the procedure name is VARIABLES followed by the name of a single dichotomous dependent variable. Following the dependent variable, you can specify WITH and a list of independent variables. The list of independent variables is optional if the independent variables are listed on a METHOD subcommand. The keyword TO cannot be used in any variable list.

- The default output includes goodness-of-fit tests for the model and a classification table for the predicted and observed group memberships. The regression coefficient, standard error of the regression coefficient, Wald statistic and its significance level, and a multiple correlation coefficient adjusted for the number of parameters (Harrell, 1986) are displayed for each variable in the equation.

Subcommand Order

- Subcommands can be named in any order.

- The ordering of METHOD subcommands determines the order in which models are estimated. Different sequences may result in different models.

Syntax Rules

- Only one dependent variable can be specified for each LOGISTIC REGRESSION.

- Any number of independent variables can be listed. The dependent variable cannot appear on this list.

- The independent variable list is required if any of the METHOD subcommands are used without a variable list or if the METHOD subcommand is not used.

- If you specify keyword WITH on the VARIABLES subcommand, all independent variables must be listed.

- If keyword WITH is used on the VARIABLES subcommand, interaction terms do not have to be specified on the variable list, but the individual variables comprising the interactions must be listed.

Operations

- Multiple METHOD subcommands are allowed.

- Independent variables specified by CATEGORICAL are replaced by sets of contrast variables. In stepwise analyses, the set of contrast variables associated with a categorical variable is entered or removed from the model as a block.

- Independent variables are screened to detect and eliminate redundancies.

- If the linearly dependent variable is one of a set of contrast variables, the set will be reduced by the redundant variable or variables. A warning will be issued, and the reduced set will be used.

- For the forward stepwise method, redundancy checking is done when a variable is to be entered into the model.

- When backward stepwise or direct entry methods are requested, all variables for each method subcommand are checked for redundancy before that analysis begins.

Limitations
- The dependent variable must be dichotomous for each split file group. Specifying a dependent variable with more or less than two non-missing values per split file group will result in an error.

Example   LOGISTIC REGRESSION PASS WITH GPA, MAT, GRE.

- PASS is specified as the dependent variable.
- GPA, MAT, and GRE are specified as independent variables.
- LOGISTIC REGRESSION produces the default output for the logistic regression of PASS on GPA, MAT, and GRE.

VARIABLES Subcommand

VARIABLES specifies the dependent variable and, optionally, all independent variables in the model. The dependent variable appears first in the list and is separated from the independent variables by keyword WITH.

- One VARIABLES subcommand is allowed for each LOGISTIC REGRESSION procedure.
- The dependent variable must be dichotomous. That is, it must have exactly two values other than system-missing and user-missing values for each split file group.
- The dependent variable may be a string variable if its two values can be differentiated by their first eight characters.
- You can indicate an interaction term on the variable list by using keyword BY to separate the individual variables.
- If all METHOD subcommands are accompanied by independent variable lists, keyword WITH and the list of independent variables may be omitted.
- If keyword WITH is used, all independent variables must be specified. For interaction terms, only the individual variable names that make up the interaction (e.g., X1, X2) need to be specified; specifying the actual interaction term (e.g., X1 BY X2) on the VARIABLES subcommand is optional if you specify it on a METHOD subcommand.

Example   LOGISTIC REGRESSION PROMOTED WITH AGE,JOBTIME,JOBRATE,
             AGE BY JOBTIME

- PROMOTED is specified as the dependent variable.
- AGE, JOBTIME, JOBRATE, and the interaction AGE BY JOBTIME are specified as the independent variables.
- Since no METHOD is specified, all three single independent variables and the interaction are entered into the model.
- LOGISTIC REGRESSION produces the default output.

CATEGORICAL Subcommand

CATEGORICAL identifies independent variables that are nominal or ordinal. Variables that are declared to be categorical are automatically transformed to a set of contrast variables (see CONTRAST Subcommand). If a variable coded as 0-1 is declared as categorical, by default its coding scheme will be changed to deviation contrasts.

- Independent variables not specified on CATEGORICAL are assumed to be at least interval level.
- Variables specified on CATEGORICAL must also appear after WITH keyword on the VARIABLES subcommand. If there is no WITH keyword and list, variables specified on CATEGORICAL must also appear after the METHOD subcommand.
- Variables specified on CATEGORICAL are replaced by sets of contrast variables. If the categorical variable has N distinct values, there will be N-1 contrast variables generated. The set of contrast variables associated with a categorical variable are entered or removed from the model together.
- If any one of the variables in an interaction term is specified on CATEGORICAL, the interaction term is replaced by contrast variables.

• String variables may be specified on CATEGORICAL. Only the first eight characters of each value of a string variable is used in distinguishing between values. Thus, if two values of a string variable are identical for the first eight characters, the values are treated as though they were the same value.

Example

```
LOGISTIC REGRESSION PASS WITH GPA, GRE, MAT, CLASS, TEACHER
   /CATEGORICAL=CLASS,TEACHER.
```

• The dichotomous dependent variable PASS is regressed on the interval-level independent variables GPA, GRE, and MAT and the categorical variables CLASS and TEACHER.

CONTRAST Subcommand

CONTRAST specifies the type of contrast used for categorical independent variables. The interpretation of the regression coefficients for categorical variables depends on the contrasts used. The default is DEVIATION. The categorical independent variable is specified in parentheses following CONTRAST. The closing parenthesis is followed by one of the CONTRAST keywords.

• If the categorical variable has N values, there will be N-1 rows in the contrast matrix. Each contrast matrix is treated as a set of independent variables in the analysis.

• Only one categorical independent variable can be specified per CONTRAST subcommand, but multiple CONTRAST subcommands can be specified.

The following contrast types are available. See Finn (1974) and Kirk (1982) for further information on a specific type.

DEVIATION(refcat) *Deviations from the overall effect.* This is the default. The effect for each category of the independent variable except one is compared to the overall effect. Refcat is the category for which parameter estimates are not displayed (they must be calculated from the others). By default, refcat is the last category. To omit a category other than the last, specify the sequence number of the omitted category (which is not necessarily the same as its value) in parentheses after the DEVIATION keyword.

SIMPLE(refcat) *Each category of the independent variable except the last is compared to the last category.* To use a category other than the last as the omitted reference category, specify its sequence number (which is not necessarily the same as its value) in parentheses following the keyword SIMPLE.

DIFFERENCE *Difference or reverse Helmert contrasts.* The effects for each category of the independent variable except the first are compared to the mean effect of the previous categories.

HELMERT *Helmert contrasts.* The effects for each category of the independent variable except the last is compared to the mean effects of subsequent categories.

POLYNOMIAL(metric) *Polynomial contrasts.* The first degree of freedom contains the linear effect across the categories of the independent variable; the second contains the quadratic effect; and so on. By default, the categories are assumed to be equally spaced; unequal spacing can be specified by entering a metric consisting of one integer for each category of the independent variable in parentheses after the keyword POLYNOMIAL. For example, CONTRAST (STIMULUS) = POLYNOMIAL(1,2,4) indicates that the three levels of STIMULUS are actually in the proportion 1:2:4. The default metric is always $(1,2,...,k)$, where k categories are involved. Only the relative differences between the terms of the metric matter: (1,2,4) is the same metric as (2,3,5) or (20,30,50), because in each instance the difference between the second and third numbers is twice the difference between the first and second.

REPEATED   *Comparison of adjacent categories.* Each category of the independent variable except the first is compared to the previous category.

SPECIAL(matrix)   *A user-defined contrast.* After this keyword a matrix is entered in parentheses with $k-1$ rows and k columns (where k is the number of categories of the independent variable). The rows of the contrast matrix contain the special contrasts indicating the desired comparisons between categories. If the special contrasts are linear combinations of each other, LOGISTIC REGRESSION reports the linear dependency and stops processing. If k rows are entered, the first row is discarded and only the last $k-1$ rows are used as the contrast matrix in the analysis.

INDICATOR(refcat) *Indicator variables.* Contrasts indicate the presence or absence of category membership. By default, refcat is the last category (represented in the contrast matrix as a row of zeros). To omit a category other than the last, specify the sequence number of the omitted category (which is not necessarily the same as its value) in parentheses after keyword INDICATOR.

Example
```
LOGISTIC REGRESSION PASS WITH GRE, CLASS
  /CATEGORICAL=CLASS
  /CONTRAST(CLASS)=HELMERT.
```

• A logistic regression analysis of the dependent variable PASS is performed on the interval-level independent variable GRE and the categorical independent variable CLASS.

• PASS is a dichotomous variable representing course pass/fail status and CLASS identifies whether a student is in one of three classrooms. A HELMERT-type contrast is requested.

Example
```
LOGISTIC REGRESSION PASS WITH GRE, CLASS
  /CATEGORICAL=CLASS
  /CONTRAST(CLASS)=SPECIAL(2 −1 −1
                          0  1 −1).
```

• In this example, the comparisons are specified using keyword SPECIAL.

METHOD Subcommand

METHOD indicates how the independent variables enter the model. The specification is METHOD followed by a single method keyword. Keyword METHOD can be omitted. Optionally, specify the independent variables and interactions for which the method is to be used. Use keyword BY between variable names of an interaction term.

• If no variable list is specified or if keyword ALL is used, all the independent variables following keyword WITH in the VARIABLES subcommand are eligible for inclusion in the model.

• If no METHOD subcommand is specified, the default method is ENTER.

• Variables specified on CATEGORICAL are replaced by sets of contrast variables. The set of contrast variables associated with a categorical variable are entered or removed from the model together.

• Any number of METHOD subcommands can appear in a LOGISTIC REGRESSION procedure. METHOD subcommands are processed in the order in which they are specified. Each method starts with the results from the previous method. If BSTEP is used, all remaining eligible variables are entered at the first step. All variables are then eligible for entry and removal unless they have been excluded from the METHOD variable list.

• The beginning model for the first METHOD subcommand is either the constant variable (by default or if NOORIGIN is specified) or an empty model (if ORIGIN is specified).

The available METHOD keywords are:

ENTER   *Forced entry.* All variables are entered in a single step. This is the default.

FSTEP   *Forward stepwise.* The independent variables specified in the variable list are tested for entry into the model one by one, based on the significance level of the score statistic. The variable with the smallest significance less than PIN is entered into the model. Additionally, variables that are already in the model at each step are tested for possible removal, based on either the significance of the WALD (default) or likelihood ratio (LR) criterion. The variable with the largest probability greater than the specified POUT value is removed and the model reestimated. Variables in the model are then again evaluated for removal. Once no more variables satisfy the removal criterion, variables not in the model are evaluated for entry.

BSTEP   *Backward stepwise.* On the first step, all variables specified on the BSTEP variable list are entered into the model. The variable with the largest significance level greater than POUT for the Wald (default) or LR statistic is then removed. The model is reestimated without the variable, and again the variable with the largest significance level greater than POUT is removed. This continues until no more variables meet removal criteria. Variables not in the model are then considered for entry based on the PIN criteria. After each entry, variables are again considered for removal. Model building stops when no more variables meet entry and removal criteria, or when one variable meets both PIN and POUT criteria.

- METHOD keywords FSTEP and BSTEP can be followed by an additional keyword in parentheses to indicate which statistic should be used to determine whether a variable is to be removed.

- Keyword WALD indicates that removal of a variable is based on the significance of the Wald statistic. This is the default.

- Keyword LR (likelihood ratio) indicates that the criterion for removal is the significance of the change in the log likelihood when the variable is removed from the model.

- If LR is specified, the model must be reestimated without each of the variables in the model. This can substantially increase computational time. However, the likelihood ratio statistic is better than the Wald statistic for deciding which variables are to be removed.

Example

```
LOGISTIC REGRESSION PROMOTED WITH AGE,JOB-
TIME,JOBRATE,RACE,SEX,AGENCY
 /CATEGORICAL RACE,SEX,AGENCY
 /METHOD ENTER AGE, JOBTIME
 /METHOD BSTEP (LR) RACE,SEX,JOBRATE,AGENCY.
```

- AGE, JOBTIME, JOBRATE, RACE, SEX, and AGENCY are specified as independent variables. RACE, SEX, and AGENCY are specified as categorical independent variables.

- The first METHOD subcommand enters AGE and JOBTIME into the model.

- Variables in the model at the termination of the first METHOD subcommand are included in the model at the beginning of the second METHOD subcommand.

- The second METHOD subcommand adds the variables SEX, RACE, JOB-RATE, and AGENCY to the previous model.

- Backward stepwise logistic regression analysis is then done with only the variables in the BSTEP variable list tested for removal using the *LR* statistic.

- The procedure continues until all variables from the BSTEP variable list have been removed or the removal of a variable will not result in a decrease in the log likelihood with a probability larger than POUT.

SELECT Subcommand

By default, all cases on the active system file are considered for inclusion in LOGISTIC REGRESSION. Use the optional SELECT subcommand to include a subset of cases in the analysis.

- The specification is either a logical expression or keyword ALL. ALL is the default. The format for SELECT is:

  `/SELECT=varname relation value`

- Variables named on VARIABLES, CATEGORICAL, or METHOD subcommands cannot appear on SELECT.

- In the logical expression on SELECT, the relation can be EQ, NE, LT, LE, GT, or GE. The variable must be numeric and the value can be any number.

- Only cases for which the logical expression on SELECT is true are included in calculations. All other cases, including those with missing values for the variable named on SELECT, are unselected.

- Diagnostic statistics and classification statistics are reported for both selected and unselected cases.

- Cases deleted from the active system file with the SELECT IF or SAMPLE commands are not included among either the selected or unselected cases.

Example

```
LOGISTIC REGRESSION VARIABLES=GRADE WITH GPA,TUCE,PSI
  /SELECT SEX EQ 1 /CASEWISE=RESID.
```

- Only cases with the value 1 for SEX are included in the logistic regression analysis.

- Residual values generated by CASEWISE are displayed for both selected and unselected cases.

ORIGIN and NOORIGIN Subcommands

ORIGIN and NOORIGIN control whether or not the constant is included. NOORIGIN (the default) includes a constant term (intercept) in all equations. ORIGIN suppresses the constant term and requests regression through the origin. (NOCONST can be used as an alias for ORIGIN.)

- The only specification is either ORIGIN or NOORIGIN.

- ORIGIN or NOORIGIN can be specified only once per LOGISTIC REGRESSION procedure, and they affect all METHOD subcommands.

Example

```
LOGISTIC REGRESSION VARIABLES=PASS WITH GPA,GRE,MAT /ORIGIN.
```

- ORIGIN suppresses the automatic generation of a constant term.

ID Subcommand

ID specifies a variable whose values or value labels identify the casewise listing. By default, cases are labeled by their case number.

- The only specification is the name of a single variable that exists on the active system file. If multiple variables are specified, only the first is used.

- Only the first eight characters of a string variable are used to label cases.

- Only the first eight characters of the value label are used to label cases. If the variable has no value labels, the values are used.

PRINT Subcommand

PRINT controls the display of optional output. The minimum specification is a single keyword. If PRINT is omitted, DEFAULT output (defined below) is displayed.

- The minimum specification is PRINT followed by a single keyword.

- If PRINT is used, only the requested output is displayed.

DEFAULT   *Classification tables and statistics for the variables in and not in the equation at each step.* Tables and statistics are displayed for each split file and METHOD subcommand.

SUMMARY   *Summary information.* Same output as DEFAULT, except that the output for each step is not displayed.

CORR   *Correlation matrix of parameter estimates for the variables in the model.*

ITER(value) *Iterations at which parameter estimates are to be displayed.* The value in parentheses controls the spacing of iteration reports. If the value is *n*, the parameter estimates are displayed for every *n*th iteration starting at 0. If ITER is used but no value is supplied, intermediate estimates are displayed at each iteration.

ALL *All available output.*

Example
```
LOGISTIC REGRESSION VARIABLES=PASS WITH GPA,GRE,MAT
  /METHOD FSTEP
  /PRINT CORR SUMMARY ITER(2).
```

- A forward stepwise logistic regression analysis of PASS on GPA, GRE, and MAT is specified.
- PRINT CORR causes the correlation matrix of parameter estimates for the variables in the model to be displayed.
- SUMMARY suppresses the output display for each step. Results are displayed for the final model only.
- ITER specifies that parameter estimates are to be displayed at every second iteration.

CRITERIA Subcommand

The optional CRITERIA subcommand controls the statistical criteria used in building the logistic regression models. The way in which these criteria are used depends on the method specified on the METHOD subcommand. The default criteria are noted in the description of each keyword below. Iterations will stop if the criteria for BCON, LCON, or ITERATE are satisfied.

BCON(value) *Change in parameter estimates to terminate iteration.* Iteration terminates when the parameters change by less than this value. The default is 0.001. To eliminate this criterion, specify a value of 0.

ITERATE *Maximum number of iterations.* The default is 20.

LCON(value) *Percent change in the log likelihood ratio for termination of iterations.* If the log likelihood decreases by less than this, iteration terminates. The default is 0.01%. To eliminate this criterion, specify a value of 0.

PIN(value) *Probability of score statistic for variable entry.* The default is 0.05. The larger the specified probability, the easier it is for a variable to enter the model.

POUT(value) *Probability of Wald or LR statistic to remove a variable.* The default is 0.1. The larger the specified probability, the easier it is for a variable to remain in the model.

EPS(value) *Epsilon value used for redundancy checking.* The specified value must be less than or equal to 0.05 and greater than or equal to 10^{-12}. The default is 0.00000001. Larger values make it harder for variables to pass the redundancy check; i.e., they are more likely to be removed from the analysis.

Example
```
LOGISTIC REGRESSION PROMOTED WITH AGE,JOBTIME,RACE
  /CATEGORICAL RACE
  /METHOD BSTEP
  /CRITERIA BCON(0.01) ITERATE(10) PIN(0.01) POUT(0.05).
```

- A backward stepwise logistic regression analysis is performed for the dependent variable PROMOTED and the independent variables AGE, JOBTIME, and RACE.
- CRITERIA alters four of the statistical criteria that control the building of a model.
- BCON specifies that if the change in the absolute value of all of the B estimates is less than 0.01, the iterative estimation process should stop. Larger values lower the number of iterations required. Notice that the ITER and LCON criteria remain unchanged and that if either of them is met before BCON, iterations will terminate. (LCON can be set to 0 if only BCON and ITER are to be used.)

- ITERATE specifies that the maximum number of iterations is 10.
- POUT requires that the probability of the statistic used to test whether a variable should remain in the model be smaller than 0.05. This is more stringent than the default value of 0.1.
- PIN requires that the probability of the score statistic used to test whether a variable should be included be smaller than 0.01. This makes it more difficult for variables to be included in the model than with the default PIN value.

CLASSPLOT Subcommand

The optional CLASSPLOT subcommand generates a classification plot of the actual and predicted values of the dichotomous dependent variable at each step.

- Keyword CLASSPLOT is the only specification.
- If CLASSPLOT is not specified, plots are not generated.

Example

```
LOGISTIC REGRESSION PROMOTED WITH JOBTIME RACE
  /CATEGORICAL RACE
  /CLASSPLOT.
```

- A logistic regression model is constructed for the dichotomous dependent variable PROMOTED and the independent variables JOBTIME and RACE.
- CLASSPLOT produces a classification plot for the dependent variable PROMOTED. The vertical axis of the plot is the frequency of the variable PROMOTED. The horizontal axis is the predicted probability of membership in the second of the two levels of PROMOTED.

CASEWISE Subcommand

CASEWISE produces a casewise listing of the values of the temporary variables created by LOGISTIC REGRESSION.

- The minimum specification is CASEWISE. This produces a listing of PRED, PGROUP, RESID, and ZRESID.
- The following keywords are available for specifying temporary variables (see Fox, 1984). If a list of variable names is given, only those names are displayed.

PRED   *Predicted probability.* For each case, the predicted probability of having the second of the two values of the dichotomous dependent variable.

PGROUP   *Predicted group.* The group to which a case is assigned based on the predicted probability.

RESID   *Difference between observed and predicted probability.*

DEV   *Deviance values.* For each case, a log-likelihood-ratio statistic is computed which measures how well the model fits the data.

LRESID   *Logit residual.* Residual divided by the product of PRED and 1-PRED.

SRESID   *Studentized residual.*

ZRESID   *Normalized residual.* Residual divided by the square root of the product of PRED and 1-PRED.

LEVER   *Leverage value.* A measure of the relative influence of each observation on the model's fit.

COOK   *Analog of Cook's influence statistic.*

DFBETA   *Difference in beta.* The difference in the estimated coefficients for each independent variable if the case is omitted.

The following keyword is available for restricting the cases to be displayed, based on the absolute value of SRESID.

OUTLIER (value)   *Cases with absolute values of SRESID greater than or equal to the specified value are displayed.* If OUTLIER is specified with no value, cases with absolute values of SRESID greater than or equal to 2 are displayed.

Example
```
LOGISTIC REGRESSION PROMOTED WITH JOBTIME, RACE, SEX
  /CATEGORICAL SEX
  /METHOD ENTER
  /CASEWISE SRESID LEVER DFBETA.
```

• CASEWISE produces a casewise listing of the temporary variables SRESID, LEVER, and DFBETA. There will be four values of DFBETA, one corresponding to the constant and one corresponding to each of the independent variables in the model.

MISSING Subcommand

MISSING controls the processing of missing values. The default is EXCLUDE.

EXCLUDE   *Listwise deletion of all cases with missing values.* A case is omitted from the analysis if any of the variables specified in the procedure have user- or system-missing values for that case. If a case has a missing value on the dependent variable and nonmissing values on all independent variables, predicted values are calculated for that case.

INCLUDE   *Include user-missing values in the analysis.*

SAVE Subcommand

SAVE saves the temporary variables created by LOGISTIC REGRESSION. To specify variable names for the new variables, assign the new names in parentheses following each temporary variable name. If new variable names are not specified, LOGISTIC REGRESSION generates default names.

• Assigned variable names must be unique on the active system file. Scratch or system variable names cannot be used (that is, the variable names cannot begin with # or $).

• A temporary variable can only be saved once on the same SAVE subcommand.

Example
```
LOGISTIC REGRESSION PROMOTED WITH JOBTIME AGE
  /SAVE PRED (PREDPRO) DFBETA (DF).
```

• A logistic regression analysis of PROMOTED on the independent variables JOBTIME and AGE is performed.

• SAVE adds four variables to the active system file. Variable PREDPRO contains the predicted value from the specified model for each case, and variables DF0, DF1, and DF2 contain the DFBETA values for each case for the constant and the independent variables JOBTIME and AGE, respectively.

EXTERNAL Subcommand

EXTERNAL indicates that the data for each split file group should be held in an external scratch file during processing. This can help conserve memory resources when running complex analyses or analyses with large data sets.

• Keyword EXTERNAL is the only specification.

• Specifying EXTERNAL may result in slightly longer processing time.

• If EXTERNAL is not specified, all data are held internally and no scratch file is written.

References

Aldrich, J. H., and F. D. Nelson. 1984. *Linear probability, logit, and probit models.* Beverly Hills, Calif.: Sage Publications.

Finn, J. D. 1974. *A general model for multivariate analysis.* New York: Holt, Rinehart & Winston.

Fox, J. 1984. *Linear statistical models and related methods: With applications to social research.* New York: John Wiley & Sons.

Harrell, F. E. 1986. The LOGIST procedure. *SUGI Supplemental Library User's Guide* 5: 269–293.

Kirk, R. E. 1982. *Experimental design,* 2d ed. Monterey, Calif.: Brooks/Cole Publishing Company.

LOGLINEAR

```
LOGLINEAR varlist(min,max)...[BY] varlist(min,max)

        [WITH covariate varlist]

[/MISSING={LISTWISE**}] [INCLUDE]
          {DEFAULT }

[/WIDTH={132}]
        { 72}

[/CWEIGHT={varname }] [/CWEIGHT=(matrix)...]
          {(matrix)}

[/GRESID={varlist }]  [/GRESID=...]
         {(matrix)}

[/PRINT={DEFAULT**}] [/NOPRINT={ESTIM** }]
        {FREQ**   }           {COR**   }
        {RESID**  }           {DESIGN**}
        {DESIGN   }           {RESID   }
        {ESTIM    }           {FREQ    }
        {COR      }           {DEFAULT }
        {ALL      }           {ALL     }
        {NONE     }

[/PLOT={DEFAULT }]
       {RESID   }
       {NORMPROB}
       {NONE**  }

                           {DEVIATION [(refcat)]     }
                           {DIFFERENCE               }
                           {HELMERT                  }
[/CONTRAST (varname)={SIMPLE [(refcat)]         }]...[/CONTRAST...]
                           {REPEATED                 }
                           {POLYNOMIAL [({1,2,3,...})]}
                           {            {metric    } }
                           {[BASIS]  SPECIAL(matrix) }

[/CRITERIA=[CONVERGE({0.001**})] [ITERATE({20**})] [DELTA({0.5**})]
                     {eps    }            {n   }           {d     }

        [DEFAULT]]

[/DESIGN=effect effect... effect BY effect...] [/DESIGN...]
```

**Default if the subcommand is omitted.
Example
```
LOGLINEAR JOBSAT (1,2) ZODIAC (1,12) /DESIGN=JOBSAT.
```

OVERVIEW   The LOGLINEAR procedure is a general procedure that does model fitting, hypothesis testing, and parameter estimation for any model that has categorical variables as its major components. As such, LOGLINEAR subsumes a variety of related techniques, including general models of multi-way contingency tables, logit models, logistic regression on category variables, and quasi-independence models. LOGLINEAR models cell frequencies using the multinomial response model and produces maximum likelihood estimates of parameters by means of the Newton-Raphson algorithm (Haberman, 1978). For hierarchical models, HILOGLINEAR, which uses an iterative proportional fitting algorithm, is more efficient, but cannot produce parameters for unsaturated models, permit specifying contrasts for parameters, or display a correlation matrix of the parameters.

Options   **Model Specification.** Models are specified with the DESIGN subcommand. Logit models may be specified by using the keyword BY. One or more continuous variables can be added to the model as a cell covariate by placing them at the end of the variables specification list preceded by the keyword WITH. This option models cell means for the continuous variable rather than case-by-case measurements. Specific combinations of the subcommands CWEIGHT and GRESID can produce any type of contrast desired for a factor as well as linear combinations of observed and expected cell frequencies and adjusted residuals. **Output.** Default output can be suppressed and additional statistics produced with the PRINT and NOPRINT subcommands. The design matrix, parameter estimates, standard errors, standardized values, confidence intervals, and the correlation matrix of parameter estimates can be displayed. The PLOT subcommand can provide plots of the adjusted residuals against observed and expected counts, and normal and detrended normal plots of the adjusted residuals.

Basic Specifications

The minimum specification is two or more categorical variables that define a crosstabulation followed by their minimum and maximum values in parentheses and one or more DESIGN subcommands for an unsaturated model. In response, LOGLINEAR produces a loglinear model for a multi-dimensional table including the factors or effects, their levels and any labels; observed and expected frequencies and percentages for each factor and code; residuals, standardized residuals, and adjusted residuals; two goodness-of-fit statistics (the likelihood ratio chi-square and Pearson's chi-square); estimates of the parameters with accompanying Z-values, and 95% confidence intervals. For logit models, LOGLINEAR displays an analysis of dispersion, along with two measures of association: entropy and concentration.

Subcommand Order

- The variables specification must come first.
- All subcommands can be used more than once and, with the exception of the DESIGN subcommand, are carried from model to model unless explicitly overridden.
- The subcommands that affect a DESIGN subcommand should be placed before the DESIGN subcommand.
- If subcommands are placed after the last DESIGN subcommand, LOGLINEAR generates the saturated model.

Example

```
LOGLINEAR JOBSAT (1,2) ZODIAC (1,12) /DESIGN=JOBSAT, ZODIAC.
```

- The LOGLINEAR variable list specifies two categorical variables, JOBSAT and ZODIAC. JOBSAT can take the values 1 and 2. ZODIAC has values 1 through 12.
- DESIGN tests the hypothesis that JOBSAT and ZODIAC are independent.

Variable List

The variable list specifies the variables to be included in the model and their minimum and maximum values.

- Cases with values outside the range specified for each variable that defines the cells of the crosstabulation are excluded from the analysis. Noninteger values within the range are truncated for purposes of building the table.
- If several variables have the same range, the specification can follow the last variable in the list with that range.
- Logit models require that the dependent variable lead the list and be followed with the keyword BY. This variable must also be categorical.
- Cell covariates must be preceded by the keyword WITH and are continuous level variables, needing no value range specification. A variable cannot be named as both a categorical variable and a cell covariate.

Example

```
LOGLINEAR GSLEVEL (4,8) EDUC (1,4) SEX (1,2)
    /DESIGN=GSLEVEL EDUC SEX.
```

- GSLEVEL is a categorical variable with values 4, 5, 6, 7, and 8. EDUC is a categorical variable with values 1 through 4. SEX has two values: 1 and 2.
- DESIGN will test the hypothesis that GSLEVEL, SEX, and EDUC are independent.

Example

```
LOGLINEAR GSLEVEL (4,8) BY EDUC (1,4) SEX (1,2)
    /DESIGN=GSLEVEL, GSLEVEL BY EDUC, GSLEVEL BY SEX.
```

- GSLEVEL is a categorical variable with values 4, 5, 6, 7, and 8. EDUC is a categorical variable with values 1 through 4. SEX has two values: 1 and 2.

• The structure of the variable list specifies a logit model in which GSLEVEL is the dependent variable, and EDUC and SEX are independent variables.

• DESIGN specifies a model that can be used to test that there is no joint effect of SEX and EDUC on GSLEVEL.

DESIGN Subcommand

The DESIGN subcommand specifies the model or models to be fit. Omitting the DESIGN subcommand or using DESIGN with no specifications produces the saturated model.

• One or more DESIGN subcommands may be specified in a LOGLINEAR command.

• Each DESIGN subcommand specifies one model.

• Simple effects models are obtained by naming variables listed on the variables specification.

• Interactions are specified by using the keyword BY.

• Single-degree-of-freedom partitions can be specified in parentheses following the variable name.

• While an interaction between a cell covariate and an independent variable can be specified, an interaction between two cell covariates cannot.

Example
```
COMPUTE X=MONTH.
LOGLINEAR MONTH (1,12) WITH X
   /DESIGN X.
```

• The variable specification identifies MONTH as a categorical variable with values 1 through 12. WITH identifies X as a covariate.

• The DESIGN tests the linear effect of MONTH.

CWEIGHT Subcommand

The CWEIGHT subcommand is used to specify cell weights for a model. By default, cell weights are equal to 1. There are two alternative specifications.

• A numeric variable can be specified on the CWEIGHT subcommand. Only one SPSS/PC+ variable may be specified as a cell weight variable.

• Alternatively, CWEIGHT can specify a matrix of weights enclosed in parentheses. The matrix must contain the same number of elements as the product of the levels of the categorical variables. An asterisk can be used to signify repetitions of the same value.

• If weights are specified for a multiple-factor model, the index value of the rightmost factor increments most rapidly.

• If a matrix of weights is specified on the CWEIGHT subcommand, more than one CWEIGHT subcommand with different weighting matrices may be used for the same LOGLINEAR command. The CWEIGHT specification remains in effect until explicitly overridden with another CWEIGHT subcommand.

• If more than one CWEIGHT subcommand is specified, they must all contain matrices of weights.

Examples
```
COMPUTE  CWT=1.
IF (HUSED EQ WIFED) CWT=0.
LOGLINEAR HUSED WIFED(1,4) WITH DISTANCE
   /CWEIGHT=CWT
   /DESIGN=HUSED WIFED DISTANCE.
```

• COMPUTE initially assigns CWT the value of 1 for all cases.

• IF assigns CWT the value 0 when HUSED equals WIFED.

• CWEIGHT imposes structural zeros on the diagonal of the symmetric crosstabulation table.

```
LOGLINEAR  HUSED WIFED(1,4) WITH DISTANCE
   /CWEIGHT=(0, 4*1, 0, 4*1, 0, 4*1, 0)
   /DESIGN=HUSED WIFED DISTANCE
   /CWEIGHT=(16*1)
   /DESIGN=HUSED WIFED DISTANCE.
```

• The first CWEIGHT matrix specifies the same values as in the first example.

• By using the matrix rather than CWEIGHT specified with a variable name, a different CWEIGHT subcommand can be used for the second model.

C

Command Reference

GRESID Subcommand

The GRESID subcommand (Generalized Residual) calculates linear combinations of observed cell frequencies, expected cell frequencies, and adjusted residuals. Just as with the CWEIGHT subcommand, a variable or variables or a matrix whose contents are coefficients of the desired linear combinations can be specified.

- The rules of the matrix specification are identical to the rules for CWEIGHT.
- Multiple GRESID subcommands using matrix specification can be used for one LOGLINEAR command, but only one GRESID subcommand can have a variable name.
- If the matrix is chosen, it must contain as many elements as the number of cells implied by the variables specification.

Example

```
LOGLINEAR  MONTH(1,18) WITH Z
with
  /GRESID=(6*1,12*0)
  /GRESID=(6*0,6*1,6*0)
  /GRESID=(12*0,6*1)
  /DESIGN=Z.
```

- The first GRESID subcommand combines the first six months into a single effect. The second GRESID subcommand combines the second six months, and the third GRESID subcommand combines the last six months.
- For each effect, LOGLINEAR displays the observed and expected count, the residual, the standardized residual, and the adjusted residual.

PRINT and NOPRINT Subcommands

The PRINT subcommand requests statistics and display not produced by default, and the NOPRINT subcommand suppresses the display of results.

- The absence of either subcommand results in the default output.
- The following keywords can be used on both the PRINT and NOPRINT subcommands. Multiple PRINT and NOPRINT subcommands can be specified.

FREQ   *Observed and expected cell frequencies and percentages.* This is displayed by default.

RESID   *Raw, standardized, and adjusted residuals.* This is displayed by default.

DESIGN *The design matrix of the model, showing the contrasts used.*

ESTIM   *The parameter estimates of the model.* If you do not specify a design on the DESIGN subcommand, LOGLINEAR generates a saturated model and displays the parameter estimates for the saturated model. LOGLINEAR does not display parameter estimates or correlation matrices of parameter estimates if any sampling zero cells exist in the expected table after DELTA is added. Parameter estimates and a correlation matrix are displayed when structural zeros are present.

COR   *The correlation matrix of the parameter estimates.*

ALL   *All available output.*

DEFAULT *FREQ and RESID.* ESTIM is also displayed by default if the DESIGN subcommand is not used.

NONE   *The design information and goodness-of-fit statistics only.* This option overrides all other specifications on the PRINT subcommand. The NONE option applies only to the PRINT subcommand.

Example

```
LOGLINEAR A(1,2) B(1,2)
  /PRINT=ESTIM
  /NOPRINT=DEFAULT
  /DESIGN=A,B,A BY B
  /PRINT=ALL
  /DESIGN=A,B.
```

- The first design is the saturated model. Since it fits the data exactly, there is no need to see the frequencies and residuals. The parameter estimates are displayed by PRINT=ESTIM.
- The frequencies and residuals output is suppressed by NOPRINT=DEFAULT.

• The second design is the main effects model, which tests the hypothesis of no interaction. The PRINT subcommand displays all available display output for this model.

PLOT Subcommand

The PLOT subcommand produces optional plots. None are displayed by default.

• Multiple PLOT subcommands can be used on one LOGLINEAR command.
• The specifications are cumulative.

The following keywords are available:

RESID   *Plots of adjusted residuals against observed and expected counts.*
NORMPROB   *Normal and detrended normal plots of the adjusted residuals.*
NONE   *No plots.*
DEFAULT   *RESID and NORMPROB.*

Example

```
LOGLINEAR  RESPONSE(1,2) BY TIME(1,4)
   /CONTRAST(TIME)=SPECIAL(4*1, 7 14 27 51, 8*1)
   /PLOT=DEFAULT
   /DESIGN=RESPONSE TIME(1) BY RESPONSE
   /PLOT=NONE
   /DESIGN.
```

• RESID and NORMPROB plots are displayed for the first design.
• No plots are displayed for the second design.

CONTRAST Subcommand

The CONTRAST subcommand indicates the type of contrast desired for a factor, where a factor is any categorical dependent or independent variable. The default contrast is DEVIATION for each factor.

• In LOGLINEAR, contrasts do not have to sum to 0 or be orthogonal.
• The design matrix used for the contrasts can be displayed by specifying the DESIGN keyword on the PRINT subcommand.
• Only one contrast is in effect for each factor for a DESIGN subcommand.
• Separate CONTRAST subcommands must be used for each factor for which contrasts are specified.
• A contrast specification remains in effect for subsequent designs until explicitly overridden with another CONTRAST subcommand.
• Another use of the CONTRAST subcommand is for fitting linear logit models. The BASIS keyword is not appropriate for such models.
• In a logistic regression model a CONTRAST is used to transform the independent variable into a metric variable. Again, BASIS is not appropriate.

The following contrasts are available:

DEVIATION(refcat)   *Deviations from the overall effect.* DEVIATION is the default contrast if the CONTRAST subcommand is not used. Refcat is the category for which parameter estimates are not displayed (they must be obtained as the negative of the sum of the others). By default, refcat is the last category of the variable.

DIFFERENCE   *Levels of a factor with the average effect of previous levels of a factor.* Also known as *reverse Helmert* contrasts.

HELMERT   *Levels of a factor with the average effect of subsequent levels of a factor.*

SIMPLE(refcat)   *Each level of a factor to the last level.* By default, LOGLINEAR uses the last category of the factor variable as the reference category. Optionally, any value can be specified as the reference category enclosed in parentheses after the keyword SIMPLE.

REPEATED	*Adjacent comparisons across levels of a factor.*
POLYNOMIAL(metric)	*Orthogonal polynomial contrasts.* The default is equal spacing. Optionally, the coefficients of the linear polynomial can be specified in parentheses, indicating the spacing between levels of the treatment measured by the given factor.
[BASIS]SPECIAL(matrix)	*User-defined contrast.* As many elements as the number of categories squared must be specified. If BASIS is specified before SPECIAL, a basis matrix is generated for the special contrast, which makes the coefficient of the contrast equal to the special matrix. Otherwise, the matrix specified is the basis matrix.

Examples

```
LOGLINEAR  A(1,4) BY B(1,4)
 /CONTRAST(B)=POLYNOMIAL
 /DESIGN=A A BY B(1)
 /CONTRAST(B)=SIMPLE
 /DESIGN=A A BY B(1).
```

• The first CONTRAST subcommand requests polynomial contrasts of B for the first design.

• The second CONTRAST subcommand requests the SIMPLE contrast of B, with the last category (value 4) used as the reference category for the second DESIGN subcommand.

```
OLOGLINEAR RESPONSE(1,2) BY YEAR(0,20)
 /PRINT=DEFAULT ESTIM
 /CONTRAST(YEAR)=SPECIAL(21*1, -10, -9, -8, -7, -6, -5, -4,
                        -3, -2, -1, 0, 1, 2, 3, 4, 5, 6, 7,
                        8, 9, 10, 399*1)
 /DESIGN=RESPONSE RESPONSE BY YEAR(1).
```

• YEAR measures years of education and ranges from 0 to 20. Therefore, allowing for the constant effect, YEAR has 20 estimable parameters associated with it.

• The SPECIAL contrast specifies the constant—that is, 21*1—and the linear effect of YEAR—that is, -10 to 10. The other 399 1's fill out the 21*21 matrix.

CRITERIA Subcommand

The CRITERIA subcommand specifies the values of some constants in the Newton-Raphson algorithm. Defaults or specifications remain in effect until overridden with another CRITERIA subcommand. The following keywords are available:

CONVERGE(eps)	*Convergence criterion.* Specify a value for the convergence criterion. The default is 0.001.
ITERATION(n)	*Maximum number of iterations.* Specify the maximum number of iterations for the algorithm. The default number is 20.
DELTA(d)	*Cell delta value.* The value of delta is added to each cell frequency for the first iteration. For saturated models, it remains in the cell. The default value is 0.5. LOGLINEAR does not display parameter estimates or correlation matrices of parameter estimates if any sampling zero cells exist in the expected table after DELTA is added. Parameter estimates and correlation matrices can be displayed in the presence of structural zeros.
DEFAULT	*Default values are used.* You can use DEFAULT to reset the parameters to the default.

Example

```
LOGLINEAR  DPREF(2,3) BY RACE ORIGIN CAMP(1,2)
 /CRITERIA=ITERATION(50) CONVERGE(.0001).
```

• ITERATION increases the maximum number of iterations to 50.

• CONVERGE lowers the convergence criterion to 0.0001.

WIDTH Subcommand

The default display uses the width specified on SET. The WIDTH subcommand specifies a different display width.

- Only one width can be in effect at a time and it controls all display.
- The WIDTH subcommand can be placed anywhere after the variables specification.
- With some width settings, the frequencies table displays fewer statistics and has fewer decimal places when narrow format is in effect. Observed and expected percentages might be omitted.

Example

```
LOGLINEAR  DPREF(2,3) RACE CAMP(1,2)
   /WIDTH=72.
```

- WIDTH sets the display width to 72 columns.

MISSING Subcommand

The MISSING subcommand controls missing values. Its default keyword is LISTWISE, which deletes cases with missing values on any variable listed on the variables specification.

- If INCLUDE is specified, user-missing values must also be included in the value range specification.

LISTWISE   *Delete cases with missing values listwise.* This is the default; it is made explicit by specifying the keyword DEFAULT.

INCLUDE   *Include user-missing values as valid.*

Example

```
MISSING VALUES A(0)
LOGLINEAR A(0,2) B(1,2) /MISSING=INCLUDE
   /DESIGN=B.
```

- Even though 0 was specified as missing, it is treated as a non-missing category of A in this analysis.

References

Haberman, S. J. 1978. *Analysis of qualitative data: Introductory topics,* vol 1. New York: Academic Press.

——. 1979. *Analysis of qualitative data: New developments,* vol 2. New York: Academic Press.

MANOVA: Overview

```
MANOVA dependent varlist [BY factor list (min,max) [factor list...]

                         [WITH covariate list]]

[/WSFACTORS=name (levels) [name...]]

[/READ[=SUMMARY]]

[/TRANSFORM [(varlist[/varlist])]=[ORTHONORM] [{DEVIATIONS (refcat) }]]
                                               {DIFFERENCE          }
                                [{CONTRAST}] {HELMERT              }
                                 {BASIS   } {SIMPLE (refcat)      }
                                             {REPEATED             }
                                             {POLYNOMIAL[(metric)] }
                                             {SPECIAL (matrix)     }

[/WSDESIGN=effect effect...]

[/MEASURE=newname newname...]

[/RENAME={newname} {newname}...]
         {*      } {*      }

[/MISSING=[LISTWISE] [INCLUDE]]

          {[CELLINFO ([MEANS**] [SSCP] [COV] [COR] [ALL])]            }

          {[HOMOGENEITY ([BARTLETT**] [COCHRAN**] [BOXM**] [ALL])]    }

          {[DESIGN ([ONEWAY] [OVERALL**] [DECOMP] [BIAS] [SOLUTION])]}

[/{PRINT  }={[ERROR ([SSCP] [COV**] [COR**] [STDDEV])]                }]
  {NOPRINT}
          {[SIGNIF ([MULTIV**] [EIGEN] [DIMENR] [UNIV**] [HYPOTH]     }
          {        [STEPDOWN] [{AVERF }] [BRIEF] [SINGLEDF] [ALL])]    }
          {                    {AVONLY}                               }

          {[PARAMETERS ([ESTIM**] [ORTHO] [COR] [NEGSUM] [ALL])]      }

          {[TRANSFORM]                                                }

[/PLOT=[CELLPLOTS] [STEMLEAF] [ZCORR]
       [NORMAL] [BOXPLOTS] [SIZE{(width,height)}]]
                                {(40,15)        }

[/PCOMPS[=[COR**] [NCOMP(n)] [MINEIGEN(eigencut)]
         [COV] [ROTATE(rottype)]         ]]

[/OMEANS[=[VARIABLES(varlist)] [TABLES ({factor name    })]]]
                                        {factor BY factor}
                                        {CONSTANT        }

[/PMEANS[=[VARIABLES(varlist)] [TABLES ({factor name    })]]]
                                        {factor BY factor}
               [ERROR(errorno)] [PLOT]  {CONSTANT        }

[/DISCRIM[=[ROTATE(rottype)] [ALPHA(alpha)] [ALL]]]
           [RAW**] [STAN**] [ESTIM**] [COR**]

[/RESIDUALS[=[CASEWISE**] [ERROR(errorno)] [PLOT] ]]

[/METHOD=[MODELTYPE ({MEANS       })]
                    {OBSERVATIONS}
```

```
              [ESTIMATION ({QR      } {NOLASTRES} {NOBALANCED} {CONSTANT  })]
                          {CHOLESKY} {LASTRES  } {BALANCED  } {NOCONSTANT}

              [SSTYPE ({UNIQUE    })]]
                      {SEQUENTIAL}

[/WRITE[=SUMMARY]]

[/ANALYSIS [({CONDITIONAL  })]=dependent varlist
            {UNCONDITIONAL}   [WITH covariate varlist]
                              [/dependent varlist...]]

[/PARTITION (factorname)[=({1,1...  })]]
                          {df,df...}

                              {DEVIATION [(refcat)]      }
                              {SIMPLE [(refcat)]         }
                              {DIFFERENCE                }
[/CONTRAST (factorname)={HELMERT                    }]
                              {REPEATED                  }
                              {POLYNOMIAL[({1,2,3...})]}
                              {           {metric  }     }
                              {SPECIAL (matrix)          }

         {WITHIN            }    {W }
[/ERROR={RESIDUAL          } or {R }]
         {WITHIN + RESIDUAL}    {WR}
         {n                }

         {[CONSTANT...]                                                    }
         {[effect effect...]                                               }
         {[effects BY effects...]                                          }
         {[POOL (varlist)...]                                              }
[/DESIGN={[effects {WITHIN} effects...]                                    }]
         {         {W     }                                                }
         {[effect + effect...]                                             }
         {[factor (level)... [WITHIN factor (partition)...]]               }
         {[MUPLUS...]                                                      }
         {[MWITHIN...]                                                     }
         {[{term-to-be-tested} {AGAINST} {WITHIN  }    {W } ]              }
         {[{term=n          } {VS     } {RESIDUAL} or {R }                }
         {                                 {WR      }    {RW}              }
         {                                 {n       }                      }
```

**Defaults if subcommands are entered without specifications. In repeated measures, SIGNIF(AVERF), not SIGNIF(MULTIV), is printed by default.

Example 1: Analysis of Variance

```
MANOVA RESULT BY TREATMNT(1,4) GROUP(1,2).
```

Example 2: Analysis of Covariance

```
MANOVA RESULT BY TREATMNT(1,4) GROUP(1,2) WITH RAINFALL.
```

Example 3: Repeated-Measures Analysis

```
MANOVA SCORE1 TO SCORE4 BY CLASS(1,2)
  /WSFACTORS=MONTH(4).
```

Example 4: Parallelism Test with Crossed Factors

```
MANOVA YIELD BY PLOT(1,4) TYPEFERT(1,3) WITH FERT
  /ANALYSIS YIELD
  /METHOD SSTYPE(SEQUENTIAL)
  /DESIGN FERT, PLOT, TYPEFERT,
    FERT BY PLOT + FERT BY TYPEFERT
    + FERT BY PLOT BY TYPEFERT.
```

C

Command Reference

Overview   MANOVA (multivariate analysis of variance) is a generalized analysis of variance and covariance procedure. You can use MANOVA to analyze a wide variety of univariate and multivariate designs, including analysis of repeated measures. MANOVA is *not* restricted to multivariate analysis of variance. Some univariate designs, such as those involving mixed models, partitioned effects, nested factors, or factor-by-covariate interactions, can only be analyzed in SPSS/PC+ by this procedure.

To simplify the presentation, reference material on MANOVA is divided into three sections: *univariate* designs with one dependent variable; *multivariate* designs with several interrelated dependent variables; and *repeated-measures* designs in which the dependent variables represent the same types of measurements taken at more than one time.

If you are unfamiliar with the models, assumptions, and statistics used in MANOVA, consult the Statistics Guide in Part B of this manual.

The full syntax diagram for MANOVA is presented here. The MANOVA sections that follow include partial syntax diagrams showing the subcommands and specifications discussed in that section. Individually, those diagrams are incomplete. Subcommands listed for univariate designs are available for any analysis, and subcommands listed for multivariate designs can be used in any multivariate analysis, including repeated measures.

MANOVA was designed and programmed by Philip Burns of Northwestern University.

MANOVA: Univariate

```
MANOVA dependent var [BY factor list (min,max) [factor list...]
                              [WITH covariate list]    ]

[/MISSING={LISTWISE}
          {INCLUDE }

                  {[CELLINFO ([MEANS**] [SSCP] [COV] [COR] [ALL])]        }

                  {[HOMOGENEITY ([BARTLETT**] [COCHRAN**] [ALL])]         }

[/{PRINT  }={[DESIGN ([ONEWAY] [OVERALL**] [DECOMP] [BIAS] [SOLUTION])] }
  {NOPRINT}
                  {[PARAMETERS ([ESTIM**] [ORTHO] [COR] [NEGSUM] [ALL])]  }

                  {[SIGNIF(SINGLEDF)]                                      }

[/PLOT=[CELLPLOTS] [STEMLEAF] [NORMAL] [BOXPLOTS] ]
       [SIZE{(width,height)}]
            {(40,15)        }

[/OMEANS[=[VARIABLES(varlist)] [TABLES ({factor name   })]]]
                                        {factor BY factor}
                                        {CONSTANT        }

[/PMEANS[=[VARIABLES(varlist)] [TABLES ({factor name   })]]]
                                        {factor BY factor}
              [ERROR(errorno)] [PLOT]   {CONSTANT        }

[/RESIDUALS=[CASEWISE**] [ERROR(errorno)] [PLOT] ]

[/METHOD=[MODELTYPE ({MEANS       })]
                    {OBSERVATIONS}

          [ESTIMATION ({QR      } {NOLASTRES} {NOBALANCED} {CONSTANT  })]
                      {CHOLESKY} {LASTRES  } {BALANCED  } {NOCONSTANT}

          [SSTYPE ({UNIQUE    })]]
                  {SEQUENTIAL}

[/READ[=SUMMARY]]   [/WRITE[=SUMMARY]]

[/ANALYSIS=dependent var [WITH covariate list]]

[/PARTITION (factorname)[=({1,1...  })]]
                          {df,df...}

                          {DEVIATION [(refcat)]        }
                          {SIMPLE [(refcat)]           }
                          {DIFFERENCE                  }
[/CONTRAST (factorname)={HELMERT                       }]
                          {REPEATED                    }
                          {POLYNOMIAL[({1,2,3...})]}
                          {           {metric }  }
                          {SPECIAL (matrix)            }

        {WITHIN            }   {W }
[/ERROR={RESIDUAL          } or {R }]
        {WITHIN + RESIDUAL}   {WR}
        {n                 }

        {[CONSTANT...]                                      }
        {[effect effect...]                                 }
        {[POOL (varlist)...]                                }
        {[effects BY effects...]                            }
[/DESIGN={[effects {WITHIN} effects...]                     }]
        {        {W     }                                   }
        {[effect + effect...]                               }
        {[factor (level)... [WITHIN factor (partition)...]] }
        {[CONPLUS...]                                       }
        {[MWITHIN...]                                       }
        {[{term-to-be-tested} {AGAINST} {WITHIN  }   {W }] }
        {[{term=n           } {VS     } {RESIDUAL} or {R }  }
        {                                {WR      }   {RW}  }
        {                                {n       }         }
```

**Defaults if subcommands are entered without specifications.

Example:
```
MANOVA YIELD BY SEED(1,4) FERT(1,3) WITH RAIN
  /PRINT=CELLINFO(MEANS COV) PARAMETERS(ESTIM)
  /DESIGN.
```

Overview

MANOVA is the most powerful of the analysis of variance procedures in SPSS/PC+ and can be used for both univariate and multivariate designs. Only MANOVA allows you to

- Specify nesting of effects.
- Specify individual error terms for effects in mixed model analyses.
- Estimate covariate-by-factor interactions to test the assumption of homogeneity of regression lines.
- Obtain parameter estimates for a variety of contrast types, including irregularly spaced polynomial contrasts with multiple factors.
- Test user-specified special contrasts with multiple factors.
- Partition effects in models.
- Pool effects in models.

This section describes the use of MANOVA for univariate analyses. However, the subcommands described here can be used in any type of analysis with MANOVA. See MANOVA: Multivariate and MANOVA: Repeated Measures for additional subcommands used for those types of analysis. If you are unfamiliar with the models, assumptions, and statistics used in MANOVA, consult the Statistics Guide in Part B of this manual.

Defaults

If you do not specify a DESIGN subcommand, MANOVA will use a full factorial model, which includes all main effects and all possible interactions among factors. Estimation is performed, by default, using the cell-means model and UNIQUE (regression-type) sums of squares, adjusting each effect for all other effects in the model. Factors are tested using *deviation* contrasts to determine if their categories significantly differ from the mean. Default output for a univariate design consists of the number of cases processed, the effects included (explicitly or implicitly) in the model, and an analysis of variance table.

Tailoring

Design Specification. You can specify which terms to include in the design. This allows you to estimate a model other than the full factorial model, incorporate factor-by-covariate interactions, indicate nesting of effects, and indicate specific error terms for each effect in mixed models.

Contrast Types. You can specify contrasts other than the default deviation contrasts.

Parameter Estimation. You can request parameter estimates for the model. You can also control the manner in which the model is estimated by requesting the observations model rather than the cell means model; by specifying sequential decomposition of the sums of squares; and by choosing among alternative methods of parameter estimation.

Optional Output. You can choose from a wide variety of optional output. Output appropriate to univariate designs includes cell means, design or other matrices, parameter estimates, tests for homogeneity of variance across cells, tables of observed and/or predicted means, and various plots useful in checking assumptions.

Matrix Materials. You can write matrices of intermediate results to the resulting file, and you can read such matrices to perform further analyses.

Syntax

MANOVA begins with a variable list identifying the dependent variable, the factors (if any), and the covariates (if any). This is followed by a slash and any optional subcommands.

- Subcommands are separated from one another by slashes.
- Most subcommands include additional specifications, which can be separated by spaces or commas. Some of these specifications, in turn, have parenthetical subspecifications.
- For many analyses, the MANOVA variable list and the DESIGN subcommand are the only specifications needed. If a full factorial design is desired, the DESIGN subcommand can be omitted.

• The DESIGN subcommand triggers the estimation of a specific model. An analysis of one model is produced for each DESIGN subcommand.

• All other subcommands apply only to designs that *follow* them. If you do not enter a DESIGN subcommand or if you enter any subcommand after the last DESIGN subcommand, MANOVA will use a full factorial model for the last DESIGN.

• MANOVA subcommands other than DESIGN remain in effect for all subsequent models unless replaced.

• The MISSING subcommand can only be specified once.

• The following keywords cannot be used as factor names: BY, CONSTANT, WITHIN, W, MUPLUS, AGAINST, VS, MWITHIN, or POOL.

Limitations

• Memory requirements depend primarily on the number of cells in the design. For the default saturated model, this equals the product of the number of levels or categories in each factor.

• MANOVA does not calculate covariate-by-covariate interaction terms. You must calculate these using the COMPUTE statement before invoking MANOVA.

Example

```
MANOVA YIELD BY SEED(1,4) FERT(1,3) WITH RAINFALL
   /PRINT=CELLINFO(MEANS) PARAMETERS(ESTIM)
   /DESIGN.
```

• YIELD is the dependent variable; SEED (with values 1, 2, 3, and 4) and FERT (with values 1, 2, and 3) are factors; RAINFALL is a covariate.

• The means of the dependent variable for each cell are requested with PRINT = CELLINFO(MEANS).

• The parameter estimates have been requested with PRINT = PARA-METERS(ESTIM).

• The default design, a full factorial model, will be estimated. This statement could have been omitted, or could have been specified in full as DESIGN = SEED, FERT, SEED BY FERT.

MANOVA Variable List

The variable list specifies all variables that will be used in any subsequent analyses.

• The dependent variable must be the first specification on MANOVA.

• The names of the factors follow the dependent variable. Use the keyword BY to separate the dependent variable from the factors.

• Factors must have adjacent integer values, and you must supply the minimum and maximum values in parentheses after the factor name(s).

• Enter the covariates, if any, following the factors and their ranges. Use the keyword WITH to separate covariates from factors (if any) and the dependent variable.

• MANOVA will remove the linear effect of the covariates from your dependent variable before performing analysis of variance.

Example

```
MANOVA DEPENDNT BY FACTOR1 (1,3) FACTOR2, FACTOR3 (1,2).
```

• In this example, three factors are specified.

• FACTOR1 has values 1, 2, and 3, while FACTOR2 and FACTOR3 have values 1 and 2.

DESIGN Subcommand

The DESIGN subcommand specifies the effects included in a specific model. It must be the last subcommand entered for any model.

The *cells* in a design are defined by all of the possible combinations of levels of the factors in that design. The number of cells equals the product of the number of levels of all the factors. A design is *balanced* if each cell contains the same number of cases.

- The specifications on the DESIGN subcommand consist of a list of terms to be included in the model, separated by spaces or commas.
- The default design, which may be specified with a DESIGN subcommand with no specifications, is a saturated model containing all main effects and all orders of factor-by-factor interaction.
- If no DESIGN subcommand is entered or if any other subcommand is entered after the last DESIGN subcommand, a default (saturated) design is estimated.
- To include a term for the main effect of a factor, enter the name of the factor on the DESIGN statement.
- To include a term for an interaction between factors, specify FACT1 BY FACT2, where FACT1 and FACT2 are the names of the factors involved in the interaction.
- Terms are entered into the model in the order you list them on the DESIGN subcommand. This order affects the significance tests if you have specified METHOD = SSTYPE(SEQUENTIAL) to partition the sums of squares in a hierarchical fashion.
- You can specify other types of terms in the model, as described in the following sections.

Example
```
MANOVA Y BY A(1,2) B(1,2) C(1,3)
  /DESIGN
  /DESIGN A, B, C
  /DESIGN A, B, C, A BY B, A BY C.
```

- The first DESIGN subcommand produces the default full factorial design, with all main effects and interactions for factors A, B, and C.
- The second DESIGN subcommand produces an analysis with main effects only for A, B, and C.
- The third DESIGN subcommand produces an analysis with main effects and the interactions between A and the other two factors. The interaction between B and C is not in the design, nor is the interaction between all three factors.

Example
```
MANOVA Y BY A(1,3) WITH X
  /DESIGN.
```

- The linear effect of the covariate X is removed from the dependent variable Y before any other effects are estimated.
- The default full factorial design in this case is simply the factor A.

Nesting Effects (WITHIN Keyword)

The effects of a factor are nested within those of another factor if the levels of the nested factor are substantively different within each level of the second factor. In the example at the beginning of this section, the two factors were type of seed (SEED) and type of fertilizer (FERT). If different fertilizers were used for each type of seed, the effects of FERT would be nested within the effects of SEED.

- Indicate a nested effect with the keyword WITHIN; for example, FERT WITHIN SEED.
- An effect can be nested within an interaction term; for example, FERT WITHIN SEED BY PLOT. Here the levels of FERT are considered distinct for each combination of levels of SEED and PLOT.
- A factor may be nested within one specific level of another factor by indicating the level in parentheses. The term FERT WITHIN SEED(2) indicates that the levels of FERT are defined only within the second level of SEED.

MWITHIN Keyword

A term of the form MWITHIN factor (level) tests whether the dependent variable is 0 within the specified level of the factor.

- MWITHIN is followed by the name of a factor and, in parentheses, the number of one of its levels.
- The level is indicated by ordinal position, not value. If you have specified TIME(3,6) on the MANOVA variable list, the term MWITHIN TIME(1) refers to the first level of TIME, which is the level associated with the value 3.
- You can form an interaction with an MWITHIN term. For example, the term GROUP BY MWITHIN TIME(1) tests whether the means of the dependent variable are significantly different for different levels of GROUP, *within only the first level of TIME.* This allows you to estimate "simple effects."

Pooled Effects   Different effects can be "pooled" for the purpose of significance testing.

- To pool effects, connect them with a plus sign; for example, FERT + FERT BY SEED. A single test will be made for the combined effect of FERT and the FERT by SEED interaction.
- The keyword BY is evaluated before effects are pooled together. Syntactically, A + B BY C is evaluated as A + (B BY C). Parentheses are not allowed in this context. To get the equivalent of (A + B) BY C, specify A BY C + B BY C.

MUPLUS Keyword   If a term is preceded by keyword MUPLUS, the constant term (MU) in the model is combined with that term. The normal use of this specification is to obtain parameter estimates that represent weighted means for the levels of some factor. For example, the term MUPLUS SEED represents the constant, or overall mean, plus the effect for each level of SEED. The significance of such effects is usually uninteresting, but the parameter estimates represent the weighted means for each level of SEED, adjusted for any covariates in the model.

- MUPLUS cannot appear more than once on a given DESIGN subcommand.
- MUPLUS (factor) is the only way to get standard errors for the predicted means for each level of that factor. The predicted means themselves can be obtained with the PMEANS subcommand.
- Parameter estimates are not displayed by default; you must explicitly request them on the PRINT subcommand.

Partitioned Effects   To identify individual degrees of freedom or partitions of the degrees of freedom associated with an effect, enter a number in parentheses on the DESIGN subcommand.

- If you specify the PARTITION subcommand, the number refers to a partition.
- If you do not use the PARTITION subcommand, the number refers to a single degree of freedom associated with the effect. For example, if SEED is a factor with four levels, you can treat its three degrees of freedom as independent effects by naming them SEED(1), SEED(2), and SEED(3) on the DESIGN subcommand.
- The number in parentheses always refers to an individual degree of freedom for a factor if that factor follows keyword WITHIN or MWITHIN, regardless of how or whether you have partitioned the degrees of freedom.
- Partitions can include more than one degree of freedom provided that you use the PARTITION subcommand. If the first partition of SEED includes two degrees of freedom, the term SEED(1) on a DESIGN subcommand tests both degrees of freedom.
- A factor has one fewer degrees of freedom than it has levels or values.

**Effects of Continuous
Variables**   Usually you name factors but not covariates on the DESIGN subcommand. The linear effects of covariates are removed from the dependent variable before the design is tested. However, the design can include variables measured at the interval level and originally named as covariates or as additional dependent variables.

- Continuous variables on a DESIGN subcommand must be named as dependents or covariates on the MANOVA variable list.
- Before you can name a continuous variable on a DESIGN subcommand, you must supply an ANALYSIS subcommand that does *not* name the variable. This excludes it from the analysis as a dependent variable or covariate and makes it eligible for inclusion on DESIGN.
- More than one continuous variable can be pooled into a single effect (provided that they are all excluded on an ANALYSIS subcommand) with the keyword POOL(varlist). For a single continuous variable, POOL(VAR) is equivalent to VAR.
- The TO convention in the variable list for POOL refers to the order of continuous variables (dependent variables and covariates) on the original MANOVA variable list, which is not necessarily their order on the active file. This is the *only* allowable use of the keyword TO on a DESIGN subcommand.

C

Command Reference

• You can specify interaction terms between factors and continuous variables. If FAC is a factor and COV is a covariate that has been omitted from an ANALYSIS subcommand, FAC BY COV is a valid term on a DESIGN statement.

• You cannot specify an interaction between two continuous variables. Use the COMPUTE command to create a variable representing the interaction prior to MANOVA.

Example   This example tests whether the regression line of the dependent variable Y on the two variables X1 and X2 has the same slope across all the categories of the factors AGE and TREATMNT.

```
MANOVA Y BY AGE(1,5) TREATMNT(1,3) WITH X1, X2
    /ANALYSIS = Y
    /METHOD = SSTYPE(SEQUENTIAL)
    /DESIGN = POOL(X1,X2),
              AGE, TREATMNT, AGE BY TREATMNT,
              POOL(X1,X2) BY AGE + POOL(X1,X2) BY TREATMNT
                  + POOL(X1,X2) BY AGE BY TREATMNT.
```

• The ANALYSIS subcommand excludes X1 and X2 from the standard treatment of covariates, so that they can be used in the design.

• The METHOD subcommand requests a sequential (or hierarchical) decomposition of the sums of squares.

• The DESIGN subcommand includes five terms. POOL(X1,X2), the overall regression of the dependent variable on X1 and X2, is entered first, followed by the two factors and their interaction.

• The last term is the test for equal regressions. It consists of three factor-by-continuous-variable interactions pooled together. POOL(X1,X2) BY AGE is the interaction between AGE and the combined effect of the continuous variables X1 and X2. It is combined with similar interactions between TREATMNT and the continuous variables and between the AGE BY TREATMNT interaction and the continuous variables.

• If the last term is not statistically significant, there is no evidence that the regression of Y on X1 and X2 is different across any combination of the categories of AGE and TREATMNT.

Error Terms for Individual Effects   The "error" sum of squares against which terms in the design are tested is specified on the ERROR subcommand. For any particular term on a DESIGN subcommand, you can specify a different error term to be used in the analysis of variance.

• To test a term against only the within-cells sum of squares, specify the term followed by VS WITHIN on the DESIGN subcommand. For example, GROUP VS WITHIN tests the effect of the factor GROUP against only the within-cells sum of squares. For most analyses this is the default error term.

• To test a term against only the residual sum of squares (the sum of squares for all terms not included in your DESIGN), specify the term followed by VS RESIDUAL.

• To test against the combined within-cells and residual sums of squares, specify the term followed by VS WITHIN+RESIDUAL.

• To test against any other sum of squares in the analysis of variance, include a term corresponding to the desired sum of squares in the design and assign it to a number between 1 and 10. You can then test against the number of the error term. It is often convenient to test against the term before you define it. This is perfectly acceptable, so long as you define the error term on the same DESIGN subcommand.

Example
```
MANOVA DEP BY A, B, C (1,3)
    /DESIGN=A VS 1,
            B WITHIN A = 1 VS 2,
            C WITHIN B WITHIN A = 2 VS WITHIN.
```

• In this example the factors A, B, and C are completely nested; levels of C occur within levels of B, which occur within levels of A. Each factor is tested against everything within it.

- A, the outermost factor, is tested against the B WITHIN A sum of squares, to see if it contributes anything beyond the effects of B within each of its levels. The B WITHIN A sum of squares is defined as "error term" number 1.
- B nested within A, in turn, is tested against "error term" number 2, which is defined as the C WITHIN B WITHIN A sum of squares.
- Finally, C nested within B nested within A is tested against the within-cells sum of squares.

User-defined error terms are specified "on the fly" by simply inserting = n after a term. Keywords used in building a design term, such as BY or WITHIN, are evaluated first. For example, error term number 2 in the above example consists of the entire term C WITHIN B WITHIN A. An error-term *number,* but not an error-term *definition,* can follow the keyword VS.

CONSTANT Keyword   By default, the constant term is included as the first term in the model.

- If you have specified NOCONSTANT on the METHOD subcommand, a constant term will not be included in any design unless you request it with the CONSTANT keyword on DESIGN.
- You can specify an error term for the constant.
- A factor named CONSTANT will not be recognized on the DESIGN subcommand.

ERROR Subcommand

The ERROR subcommand allows you to specify or change the error term used to test all effects for which you do not explicitly specify an error term on DESIGN. The ERROR subcommand affects all terms in all subsequent designs, except terms for which you explicitly provide an error term.

WITHIN   *Terms in the model are tested against the within-cells sum of squares.* This is the default unless there is no variance within cells or unless the observations model is used (see the MODELTYPE parameter under METHOD Subcommand).

RESIDUAL   *Terms in the model are tested against the residual sum of squares.* This includes all terms not named on the DESIGN statement.

WITHIN+RESIDUAL   *Terms are tested against the pooled within-cells and residual sum of squares.* This is the default for designs processed using the observations model.

error number   *Terms are tested against a numbered error term.* The error term must be defined on each DESIGN subcommand (see the discussion of error terms under DESIGN Subcommand).

- If you specify ERROR=WITHIN+RESIDUAL and one of the components does not exist, MANOVA uses the other component alone.
- If you specify your own error term by number, you must define a term with that number on each DESIGN subcommand. If a design does not have an error term with the specified number, MANOVA does not carry out significance tests. It will, however, display hypothesis sums of squares and, if requested, parameter estimates.

Example
```
MANOVA DEP BY A(1,2) B(1,4)
  /ERROR = 1
  /DESIGN = A, B, A BY B = 1 VS WITHIN
  /DESIGN = A, B.
```

- The ERROR subcommand defines error term 1 as the default error term.
- In the first design, A by B is defined as error term 1 and is therefore used to test the A and B effects. The A by B effect itself is explicitly tested against the within-cells error.
- In the second design, no term is defined as error term 1, so no significance tests are carried out. Hypothesis sums of squares are displayed for A and B.

**CONTRAST
Subcommand**

Use the CONTRAST subcommand to specify the type of contrast desired among the levels of a factor. For a factor with k levels or values, the contrast type determines the meaning of its $(k-1)$ degrees of freedom.

- Specify the factor name in parentheses following the subcommand CON-TRAST.

- You can specify only one factor per CONTRAST subcommand, but you can enter multiple CONTRAST subcommands.

- After closing the parentheses, enter an equals sign followed by one of the CONTRAST keywords.

- To obtain significance levels for individual degrees of freedom for the specified contrast, enter the factor name followed by a number in parentheses on the DESIGN subcommand. The number refers to a partition of the factor's degrees of freedom. If you do not use the PARTITION subcommand, each degree of freedom is a distinct partition.

Example

```
MANOVA DEP BY FAC(1,5)
  /CONTRAST(FAC)=DIFFERENCE
  /PRINT=PARAM(ESTIM)
  /DESIGN=FAC(1) FAC(2) FAC(3) FAC(4).
```

- The factor FAC has five categories and therefore four degrees of freedom.

- The CONTRAST subcommand requests DIFFERENCE contrasts, which compare each level (except the first) with the mean of the previous levels.

- Each of the four degrees of freedom is tested individually on the DESIGN subcommand.

- Parameter estimates for each degree of freedom will be displayed.

Orthogonal contrasts are particularly useful. In a balanced design, contrasts are orthogonal if the sum of the coefficients in each contrast row is 0 and if for any pair of contrast rows, the products of corresponding coefficients sum to 0. Difference, Helmert, and polynomial contrasts always meet these criteria in balanced designs.

The available contrast types are

DEVIATION　*Deviations from the grand mean.* This is the default. Each level of the factor except one is compared to the grand mean. One category (by default the last) must be omitted so that the effects will be independent of one another. To omit a category other than the last, specify the number of the omitted category (which is not necessarily the same as its *value*) in parentheses after the DEVIA-TION keyword. For example,

```
MANOVA A BY B(2,4)
  /CONTRAST(B)=DEVIATION(1)
```

omits the first category, in which B has the value 2. Deviation contrasts are not orthogonal.

DIFFERENCE　*Difference or reverse Helmert contrasts.* Each level of the factor except the first is compared to the mean of the previous levels. In a balanced design, difference contrasts are orthogonal.

HELMERT　*Helmert contrasts.* Each level of the factor except the last is compared to the mean of subsequent levels. In a balanced design, Helmert contrasts are orthogonal.

SIMPLE　*Each level of the factor except the last is compared to the last level.* To use a category other than the last as the omitted reference category, specify its number (which is not necessarily the same as its *value*) in parentheses following the keyword SIMPLE. For example,

```
MANOVA A BY B(2,4)
  /CONTRAST(B)=SIMPLE(1)
```

compares the other levels to the first level of B, in which B has the value 2. Simple contrasts are not orthogonal.

POLYNOMIAL   *Polynomial contrasts.* The first degree of freedom contains the linear effect across the levels of the factor; the second contains the quadratic effect; and so on. In a balanced design, polynomial contrasts are orthogonal. By default, the levels are assumed to be equally spaced; you can specify unequal spacing by entering a *metric* consisting of one integer for each *level* of the factor in parentheses after the keyword POLYNOMIAL. For example, CONTRAST(STIMULUS) = POLYNOMIAL(1,2,4) indicates that the three levels of STIMULUS are actually in the proportion 1:2:4. The default metric is always $(1,2,...,k)$, where k variables are involved. Only the relative differences between the terms of the metric matter: (1,2,4) is the same metric as (2,3,5) or (20,30,50), because in each instance the difference between the second and third numbers is twice the difference between the first and second.

REPEATED   *Comparison of adjacent levels.* Each level of the factor except the first is compared to the previous level. Repeated contrasts are not orthogonal.

SPECIAL   *A user-defined contrast.* After this keyword enter a square matrix in parentheses with as many rows and columns as there are levels in the factor. The first row represents the mean effect of the factor and is generally a vector of *1*'s. It represents a set of weights indicating how to collapse over the categories of this factor in estimating parameters for *other* factors. The other rows of the contrast matrix contain the special contrasts indicating the desired comparisons between levels of the factor. If the special contrasts are linear combinations of each other, MANOVA reports the linear dependency and stops processing.

PARTITION Subcommand

The PARTITION subcommand subdivides the degrees of freedom associated with a factor. This permits you to test the significance of the effect of a specific contrast or group of contrasts of the factor instead of the overall effect of all contrasts of the factor.

• Specify the factor name in parentheses following the PARTITION subcommand.

• After closing the parentheses, you can enter an equals sign followed by a parenthetical list of integers indicating the degrees of freedom for each partition or subdivision.

• If you omit the list specifying degrees of freedom, MANOVA partitions the factor into single degrees of freedom.

• Each value in the partition list must be a positive integer and the sum of the values cannot exceed the degrees of freedom for the factor.

• The degrees of freedom available for a factor are one less than the number of levels of the factor.

• The meaning of each degree of freedom depends upon the contrast type for the factor. For example, with deviation contrasts (the default), each degree of freedom represents the deviation of the dependent variable in one level of the factor from its grand mean over all levels. With polynomial contrasts, the degrees of freedom represent the linear effect, the quadratic effect, and so on.

• If your list does not account for all the degrees of freedom, MANOVA adds one final partition containing the remaining degrees of freedom.

• You can use a repetition factor of the form $n*$ to specify a series of partitions with the same number of degrees of freedom. PARTITION(TREATMNT) = (3*2,1) builds three partitions with two degrees of freedom each followed by a fourth partition with a single degree of freedom. If any degrees of freedom remain, they will be placed in a fifth partition.

• Include the effect of a specific partition of a factor in your design with a number in parentheses on the DESIGN subcommand (see example below).

• If you want the default single-degree-of-freedom partition, you can omit the PARTITION subcommand and simply enter the appropriate term on the DESIGN subcommand.

Example
```
MANOVA OUTCOME BY TREATMNT(1,12)
   /PARTITION(TREATMNT) = (3,2,6)
   /DESIGN TREATMNT(2).
```

- The factor TREATMNT has twelve categories and therefore eleven degrees of freedom.
- The PARTITION subcommand divides the effect of TREATMNT into three partitions, containing respectively 3, 2, and 6 degrees of freedom. The specification (3,2) would have produced the same division, since MANOVA would have supplied a final partition to contain the remaining six degrees of freedom.
- The DESIGN subcommand specifies a model in which only the second partition of TREATMNT is tested. This partition contains the fourth and fifth degrees of freedom.
- Since the default contrast type is DEVIATION (see the CONTRAST subcommand), this second partition represents the deviation of the fourth and fifth levels of TREATMNT from the grand mean.

ANALYSIS Subcommand

The ANALYSIS subcommand allows you to work with a subset of the continuous variables (dependent variable and covariates) you have named on the MANOVA variable list. In univariate analysis of variance, you can use the ANALYSIS subcommand to allow factor-by-covariate interaction terms in your model (see DESIGN Subcommand). You can also use it to switch the roles of the dependent variable and a covariate.

- In general, the ANALYSIS subcommand gives you complete control over which continuous variables are dependent variables, which are covariates, and which are to be neither.
- ANALYSIS specifications are like the MANOVA variables specification except that factors are not named. Enter the dependent variable and, if there are covariates, the keyword WITH and the covariates.
- Only variables listed as dependent variables or covariates on the MANOVA variables specification can be entered on an ANALYSIS subcommand.
- In a univariate analysis of variance, the most important use of ANALYSIS is to *omit* covariates altogether from the analysis list, thereby making them available for inclusion on DESIGN (see examples below and under DESIGN Subcommand).
- For more information on the ANALYSIS subcommand, refer to MANOVA: Multivariate.

Example
```
MANOVA DEP BY FACTOR(1,3) WITH COV
   /ANALYSIS DEP
   /DESIGN FACTOR, COV, FACTOR BY COV.
```

- COV, a continuous variable, is included on the MANOVA variable list as a covariate.
- COV is not mentioned on the ANALYSIS subcommand, so it will not be included in the model as a dependent variable or covariate. It can, therefore, be explicitly included on the DESIGN subcommand.
- The DESIGN subcommand includes the main effects of FACTOR and COV, and the FACTOR by COV interaction.

PRINT and NOPRINT Subcommands

Use the PRINT and NOPRINT subcommands to control the display of optional output. (Additional output can be obtained on the PCOMPS, DISCRIM, OMEANS, PMEANS, PLOT, and RESIDUALS subcommands.) PRINT specifications appropriate for univariate MANOVA are described below. For information on PRINT specifications appropriate for other MANOVA models, see MANOVA: Multivariate, and MANOVA: Repeated Measures.

- Specifications on PRINT subcommand remain in effect for all subsequent designs.
- Some PRINT output, such as CELLINFO, applies to the entire MANOVA procedure and is displayed only once.

• You can "turn off" optional output that you request on the PRINT subcommand by entering a NOPRINT subcommand with the specifications originally used on the PRINT subcommand.

• Some optional output greatly increases the processing time. Request only the output you want to see.

CELLINFO   *Basic information about each cell in the design.*

PARAMETERS   *Parameter estimates.*

HOMOGENEITY *Tests for homogeneity of variance.*

DESIGN   *Design information.*

ERROR   *Error standard deviations* (in univariate analysis).

CELLINFO Keyword   Use the CELLINFO keyword on PRINT to request any of the following.

• Enclose CELLINFO specifications in parentheses after the CELLINFO keyword.

• Since output from CELLINFO is displayed once before the analysis of any particular design, specify CELLINFO only once.

MEANS   *Cell means, standard deviations, and counts for the dependent variable and covariates.* Confidence intervals for the cell means are displayed if you have SET WIDTH WIDE.

SSCP   *Within-cell sum-of-squares and cross-products matrices for the dependent variable and covariates.*

COV   *Within-cell variance-covariance matrices for the dependent variable and covariates.*

COR   *Within-cell correlation matrices, with standard deviations on the diagonal, for the dependent variable and covariates.*

• When you specify SSCP, COV, or COR, the cells are numbered for identification, beginning with Cell 1.

• The levels vary most rapidly for the factor named last on the MANOVA variables specification.

• Empty cells are neither displayed nor numbered.

• A table showing the levels of each factor corresponding to each cell number is displayed at the beginning of MANOVA output.

Example
```
MANOVA DEP BY A(1,4) B(1,2) WITH COV
  /PRINT=CELLINFO(MEANS COV)
  /DESIGN.
```

• For each combination of levels of A and B, MANOVA displays separately the means and standard deviations of DEP and COV. Beginning with Cell 1, it will then display the variance-covariance matrix of DEP and COV within each non-empty cell.

• A table of cell numbers will be displayed to show the factor levels corresponding to each cell.

• The keyword COV, as a parameter of CELLINFO, is not confused with the variable COV.

PARAMETERS Keyword   The PARAMETERS keyword displays information relating to the estimated size of the effects in the model.

• Specify any of the following in parentheses on PARAMETERS.

• There is no default specification for PARAMETERS.

ESTIM   *The estimated parameters themselves, along with their standard errors, t-tests, and confidence intervals. Only nonredundant parameters are displayed.*

NEGSUM   *The negative of the sum of parameters for each effect.* For main effects this equals the parameter for the omitted (redundant) contrast. NEGSUM is displayed along with the parameter estimates.

ORTHO   *The orthogonal estimates of parameters used to produce the sums of squares.*

COR   *Covariances and correlations among the parameter estimates.*

C

Command Reference

SIGNIF Keyword   The SIGNIF keyword requests special significance tests, most of which apply to multivariate designs (see MANOVA: Multivariate). The following specification is useful in univariate applications of MANOVA:

SINGLEDF *Significance tests for the single degrees of freedom making up each effect* for ANOVA tables in univariate designs. When orthogonal contrasts are being applied, these degrees of freedom correspond to the degrees of freedom in the contrast. This output is therefore particularly useful for orthogonal contrasts. You can always see the exact linear combinations being tested by requesting the solution matrix with PRINT = DESIGN(SOLUTION).

Example
```
MANOVA DEP BY FAC(1,5)
  /CONTRAST(FAC)=POLY
  /PRINT=SIGNIF(SINGLEDF) DESIGN(SOLUTION)
  /DESIGN.
```

• POLYNOMIAL contrasts are applied to FAC, testing the linear, quadratic, cubic, and quartic components of its five levels. POLYNOMIAL contrasts are orthogonal in balanced designs.

• The SINGLEDF specification on PRINT=SIGNIF requests significance tests for each of these four components.

• The SOLUTION matrix is also requested to verify the linear combinations tested with SIGNIF(SINGLEDF).

HOMOGENEITY Keyword   The HOMOGENEITY keyword requests tests for the homogeneity of variance of the dependent variable and covariates across the cells of the design. Enter one or more of the following specifications in parentheses:

BARTLETT *Bartlett-Box* F *test.*

COCHRAN *Cochran's* C.

DESIGN Keyword   You can request the following by entering one or more of the specifications in parentheses following the keyword DESIGN. See Bock (1975) for discussion of these matrices.

ONEWAY *The one-way basis matrix (not the contrast matrix) for each factor.*

OVERALL *The overall reduced-model basis (design) matrix (not the contrast matrix).*

DECOMP *The QR/CHOLESKY decomposition of the design.*

BIAS *Contamination coefficients displaying the bias present in the design.*

SOLUTION *Coefficients of the linear combinations of the cell means used in significance testing.* These are *not* the coefficients used in estimating parameters, unless the parameters are orthogonal.

• The DECOMP and BIAS matrices can provide valuable information on the confounding of the effects and the estimability of the chosen contrasts. If two effects are confounded, the entry corresponding to them in the BIAS matrix will be nonzero; if they are orthogonal, the entry will be 0. This is particularly useful in designs with unpatterned empty cells.

• The SOLUTION matrix shows the exact linear combination of cell means used to test effects and can be useful in interpreting those tests.

ERROR Keyword   Generally, the ERROR keyword on PRINT produces error matrices. In univariate analyses, the only valid specification for ERROR is STDDEV.

STDDEV *The error standard deviation.* Normally this is the within-cells standard deviation of the dependent variable. If you specify multiple error terms on DESIGN (a mixed model), this specification will display the standard deviation of each.

OMEANS Subcommand

The OMEANS (observed means) subcommand displays tables of the means of continuous variables for levels or combinations of levels of the factors.

- Use keywords VARIABLES and TABLES to indicate which observed means you want to display.
- With no specifications, the OMEANS subcommand is equivalent to PRINT = CELLINFO(MEANS).
- OMEANS displays confidence intervals for the cell means if you have SET WIDTH WIDE.
- Since output from OMEANS is displayed once before the analysis of any particular design, this subcommand should be specified only once.

VARIABLES *The continuous variables for which you want means.* Specify the variables in parentheses after the VARIABLES keyword. You can request means for the dependent variable or any covariates. If you omit the VARIABLES keyword, observed means are displayed for the dependent variable and all covariates. If you enter the VARIABLES keyword, you must also enter the TABLES keyword discussed below.

TABLES *The factors for which you want the observed means displayed.* List the factors, or combinations of factors separated with BY, in parentheses. Observed means are displayed for each level, or combination of levels, of the factors named (see example below). Both weighted means (based on all cases) and unweighted means (where all cells are weighted equally regardless of the number of cases they contain) are displayed. If you enter the keyword CONSTANT, the grand mean is displayed.

Example
```
MANOVA DEP BY A(1,3) B(1,2)
 /OMEANS=TABLES(A,B)
 /DESIGN.
```

- Since there is no VARIABLES specification in the OMEANS subcommand, observed means are displayed for all continuous variables. DEP is the only dependent variable here, and there are no covariates.
- The TABLES specification in the OMEANS subcommand requests tables of observed means for each of the three categories of A (collapsing over B) and for both categories of B (collapsing over A).
- MANOVA displays both weighted means, in which all cases count equally, and unweighted means, in which all cells count equally.

PMEANS Subcommand

The PMEANS (predicted means) subcommand displays a table of the predicted cell means of the dependent variable, both adjusted for the effect of covariates in the cell and unadjusted for covariates. For comparison, it also displays the observed cell means.

- Output from PMEANS can be computationally expensive.
- PMEANS without any additional specifications displays a table showing for each cell the observed mean of the dependent variable, the predicted mean adjusted for the effect of covariates in that cell (ADJ. MEAN), the predicted mean unadjusted for covariates (EST. MEAN), and the raw and standardized residuals from the estimated means.
- Cells are numbered in output from PMEANS so that the levels vary most rapidly on the factor named last in the MANOVA variables specification (as in output from PRINT=CELLINFO). A table showing the levels of each factor corresponding to each cell number is displayed at the beginning of the MANOVA output.
- Predicted means are suppressed if the last term is being calculated by subtraction because of METHOD = ESTIM(LASTRES).
- Predicted means are also suppressed for any design in which the MUPLUS keyword appears.
- Covariates are not predicted.

C

Command Reference

The following keywords are available to modify the output of the PMEANS subcommand:

VARIABLES *The dependent variables for which you want tables of predicted means.* Used in multivariate MANOVA. If you enter the VARIABLES keyword, you must also enter the TABLES keyword.

TABLES *Additional tables showing adjusted predicted means for specified factors or combinations of factors.* Enter the names of factors or combinations of factors in parentheses after this keyword. For each factor or combination, MANOVA displays the predicted means (adjusted for covariates) collapsed over all other factors.

ERROR *The error term used in standardizing the residuals, when more than one error term is specified.* MANOVA normally uses the default error term (see ERROR Subcommand) to standardize the residuals for PMEANS. When the DESIGN subcommand specifies more than one error term, you must specify which is to be used in standardizing PMEANS residuals by entering the ERROR keyword on a PMEANS subcommand and the desired error term in parentheses. Specify either WITHIN, RESIDUAL, WITHIN + RESIDUAL, or an error number you define for a term on the DESIGN subcommand.

PLOT *A plot of the predicted means for each cell.* The SIZE keyword on the PLOT subcommand controls the size of this plot.

• No predicted means will be produced for a design with multiple error terms unless you use the ERROR keyword on the PMEANS subcommand to indicate which term should be used in standardizing the residuals.

• If you specify a defined error number on the ERROR keyword for PMEANS, no predicted means will be produced for designs in which you do not define that error term.

Example
```
MANOVA DEP BY A(1,4) B(1,3)
   /PMEANS TABLES(A, B, A BY B)
   /DESIGN = A, B.
```

• The PMEANS subcommand displays the default table of observed and predicted (both adjusted for covariates and unadjusted) means for DEP and raw and standardized residuals in each of the twelve cells in the model.

• The TABLES specification on PMEANS displays tables of predicted means for A (collapsing over B), for B (collapsing over A), and all combinations of A and B.

• Since A and B are the only factors in the model, the means for A by B in the TABLES specification come from every cell in the model. They are identical to the adjusted predicted means in the default PMEANS table, which always includes all nonempty cells.

• Predicted means for A by B can be requested in the TABLES specification, even though the A by B effect is not in the design.

Example
```
MANOVA DEP BY A B C(1,3)
   /PMEANS ERROR(1)
   /DESIGN A VS 1, B WITHIN A = 1, C.
```

• Two error terms are used in this design: the B within A sum of squares, which is defined as error term 1 (to test the A effect), and the usual within-cells sum of squares (to test B within a itself as well as the C effect).

• Consequently, the PMEANS subcommand *requires* an ERROR specification. If the keyword ERROR is omitted from the PMEANS subcommand, MANOVA does not display the means.

• Since there is no TABLES keyword on the PMEANS subcommand, the default table of predicted means for each cell is produced.

PLOT Subcommand

MANOVA can display a variety of plots useful in checking the assumptions needed in the analysis. Plots are produced only once in the MANOVA procedure, regardless of how many DESIGN subcommands you enter. Use the following keywords on the PLOT subcommand to request plots:

CELLPLOTS *Cell statistics, including a plot of cell means vs. cell variances, a plot of cell means vs. cell standard deviations, and a histogram of cell means.* Plots are produced for each continuous variable (dependent or covariate) named on the MANOVA variable list. The first two plots aid in detecting heteroscedasticity (nonhomogeneous variances) and in determining an appropriate data transformation if one is needed. The third plot gives distributional information for the cell means.

BOXPLOTS *Boxplots.* Plots are displayed for each continuous variable (dependent or covariate) named on the MANOVA variable list. Boxplots provide a simple graphical means of comparing the cells in terms of mean location and spread. The data must be stored in memory for these plots; if there is not enough memory, boxplots are not produced and a warning message is issued.

NORMAL *Normal and detrended normal plots.* Plots are produced for each continuous variable (dependent or covariate) named on the MANOVA variable list. MANOVA ranks the scores and then plots the ranks against the expected normal deviate, or detrended expected normal deviate, for that rank. These plots aid in detecting non-normality and outlying observations. All data must be held in memory to compute ranks. If not enough memory is available, MANOVA displays a warning and skips the plots.

STEMLEAF *A stem-and-leaf display.* Plots are produced for each continuous variable (dependent or covariate) named on the MANOVA variable list. This display details the distribution of each continuous variable as a whole, not for each cell. The plots are not produced if there is insufficient memory.

• An additional plot available on the PLOT subcommand, ZCORR, is described in under MANOVA: Multivariate.

• You can request other plots on the PMEANS and RESIDUALS subcommands.

The following keyword is available on the plot subcommand to control the size of these plots.

SIZE *The dimensions of MANOVA plots.* Includes plots specified on the PMEANS and RESIDUALS subcommands. The default size is 40 horizontal spaces by 15 vertical lines. If you enter SIZE(80,20) on the PLOT subcommand, plots will be 80 horizontal spaces by 20 vertical lines. Large plots require more memory.

RESIDUALS Subcommand

Use the RESIDUALS subcommand to display and plot casewise values and residuals for your models.

• In a saturated design (the default), there are no residuals. Unless you specify a design with residual error, the RESIDUALS subcommand produces no output.

• In designs with multiple error terms, you must specify the ERROR keyword, as described below, on the RESIDUALS subcommand.

• If a designated error term does not exist for a given design, no predicted values or residuals are calculated.

• If you specify RESIDUALS without any specifications, CASEWISE output is displayed.

C

Command Reference

The following keywords are available.

CASEWISE *A case-by-case listing of the observed, predicted, residual, and stand-ardized residual values for each dependent variable.*

PLOT *A plot of observed values, predicted values, and case numbers vs. the standardized residuals, plus normal and detrended normal probability plots for the standardized residuals (5 plots in all).* Keyword SIZE on the PLOT subcommand controls the size of these plots.

ERROR *The error term that will be used to calculate the standardized residuals that you display or plot in a model containing multiple error terms.* Specify WITHIN, RESIDUAL, or WITHIN + RESIDUAL in parentheses after the keyword ERROR, or specify the number of an error term defined on the DESIGN subcommand. When the same error term is used in testing all effects, that is the term used to calculate residuals. See ERROR Subcommand for the specification of a default error term.

METHOD Subcommand

Use the METHOD subcommand to control computational aspects of your MANOVA analysis. You can specify any or all of three keywords:

SSTYPE *The method of partitioning sums of squares.*

MODELTYPE *The model for parameter estimation.*

ESTIMATION *How parameters are to be estimated.*

SSTYPE Keyword

MANOVA offers two different methods of partitioning the sums of squares. Specify either one in parentheses following keyword SSTYPE.

UNIQUE *Regression approach.* Each term is corrected for every other term in the model. With this approach, sums of squares for various components of the model do not add up to the total sum of squares unless the design is balanced. SSTYPE(UNIQUE) is the default.

SEQUENTIAL *Hierarchical decomposition of the sums of squares.* Each term is adjusted only for the terms that precede it in the DESIGN statement. This is an orthogonal decomposition, and the sums of squares in the model add up to the total sum of squares.

MODELTYPE Keyword

This keyword specifies the model for parameter estimation. You can specify either of the following in parentheses after the keyword MODELTYPE:

MEANS *The cell means model.* This model requires significantly less processing time and is the default unless you specify continuous variables on the DESIGN subcommand.

OBSERVATIONS *The observations model.* This more costly model is used by default when you specify one or more continuous variables on the DESIGN subcommand.

ESTIMATION Keyword

Four different aspects of parameter estimation are controlled by keyword ESTIMATION. You can enter one choice from each of the following pairs of alternatives in parentheses after ESTIMATION. In each case, the default is listed first.

QR
CHOLESKY QR uses Householder transformations to effect a QR (orthogonal) decomposition of the design matrix. This method bypasses the normal equations and the inaccuracies that can result from creating the cross-products matrix, and it generally results in extremely accurate parameter estimates. The CHOLESKY method is computationally less expensive but sometimes less accurate.

NOBALANCED
BALANCED By default, MANOVA assumes that your design is not balanced. If you are analyzing a balanced, orthogonal design, specifying the BALANCED keyword can result in substantial savings in processing time. Use BALANCED only if 1) all cell sizes are equal; 2)

you are using the cell-means model; and 3) the contrast type for each factor is orthogonal. If you specify balanced processing but your design does not conform to these requirements, MANOVA reverts to the more general unbalanced processing mode. If you have specified METHOD = ESTIMATION(BALANCED), you can revert to unbalanced estimation in a later design with METHOD = ESTIMATION(NOBALANCED).

NOLASTRES
LASTRES

By default, MANOVA explicitly calculates all effects in the design. You can sometimes save processing time by suppressing the calculation of the last effect in the model with the LASTRES keyword. Do this only if 1) you have specified SSTYPE(SEQUENTIAL) in a METHOD subcommand; 2) you do not want parameter estimates for the last effect in the model (you can get a significance test for this effect); and 3) the last effect in the model does not contain any continuous variables. With LASTRES, the sum of squares for the last effect in the DESIGN statement is calculated as the residual sum of squares, by subtraction from the total sum of squares. This is particularly economical when the last effect is a high-order interaction term, a common situation. If you have specified LASTRES, you can revert to normal direct estimation with METHOD = ESTI-MATION(NOLASTRES).

CONSTANT

CONSTANT requests that all models include a constant (grand mean) term, even if none is explicitly specified on the DESIGN subcommand. NOCONSTANT excludes constant terms from models that do not include the keyword CONSTANT on the DESIGN subcommand. If you have specified ESTIMATION (NOCONSTANT), you can revert to the default on later models by entering ESTIMATION (CONSTANT).

NOCONSTANT PLACE THIS UNDER CONSTANT ABOVE

Example

```
MANOVA DEP BY A B C (1,4)
  /METHOD=SSTYPE(SEQUENTIAL) ESTIMATION(CHOLESKY BALANCED
LASTRES)
   /DESIGN
   /METHOD=ESTIMATION(NOLASTRES)
   /PRINT=PARAM(ESTIM)
   /DESIGN=A, B, C, A BY B, A BY C, B BY C.
```

• For the first design, a fully saturated model, the METHOD options are chosen to reduce processing costs as much as possible.

• Results will not be satisfactory unless the conditions detailed above are met.

• Parameter estimates are not requested for the first design, so it does not matter that estimates for the last effect are unavailable.

• The second METHOD subcommand turns off LASTRES so that in subsequent designs all terms are estimated directly. Other parameters from the first METHOD subcommand remain in effect.

• The PRINT subcommand requests parameter estimates for subsequent designs.

• The second DESIGN omits the third-order interaction. If no METHOD subcommand had been entered to restore NOLASTRES, the final term (B by C) would have been estimated by subtraction and no parameter estimates would have been possible.

MISSING Subcommand

By default, cases with missing values for any of the variables on the MANOVA variable list are excluded from the analysis. The MISSING subcommand allows you to include cases with user-missing values. Available specifications are

LISTWISE *Cases with missing values for any variable named on the MANOVA variable list are excluded from the analysis.* This is the default.

INCLUDE *User-missing values are treated as valid.* For factors, you must include the missing-value codes within the range specified on the MANOVA variable list. It may be necessary to recode these values so that they will be adjacent to the other factor values. System-missing values may not be included in the analysis.

- The same missing-value treatment is used to process all designs in a single execution of MANOVA.
- If you enter more than one MISSING subcommand, the last one entered will be in effect for the entire procedure, including for designs specified before the MISSING subcommand.
- Pairwise deletion of missing data is not available in MANOVA.

WRITE Subcommand

MANOVA allows you to write intermediate results to the resulting file and then read them back into a later run for further analysis. This can significantly reduce processing time when you are analyzing large numbers of cases or variables.

- The WRITE subcommand writes matrix materials to the resulting file (by default, SPSS.PRC) in a format that can be read in by the MANOVA READ subcommand.
- WRITE requires no specifications.
- Six types of records are written to the resulting file.

The formats of the output records are as follows:

Type 1 *Design information.* Four 10-character fields containing, respectively, the number of nonempty cells, the number of observations, the number of factors, and the number of continuous variables (dependent variables and covariates).

Type 2 *Factor codes for cells.* For each nonempty cell, a Type 2 record lists the value of each factor. These values are written in 8-character fields. Each Type 2 record is followed by the corresponding Type 3 records.

Type 3 *Cell means for continuous variables.* Each number occupies 16 characters. Means for continuous variables are written in the order variables were named on the MANOVA variables specification.

Type 4 *Cell n's.* Following the pairs of Type 2 and 3 records, MANOVA writes out case counts for all cells on Type 4 records, using 10 characters per count.

Type 5 *Within-cell error correlation matrix for continuous variables.* The matrix is written in lower-triangular form, with ones on the diagonal and correlations in F10.6 format. The order of variables is that on the MANOVA variables specification.

Type 6 *Within-cell standard deviations for continuous variables.* Standard deviations are written in the order variables were named on the MANOVA variables specification.

READ Subcommand

The READ subcommand reads matrix materials formatted as described for the WRITE subcommand. Starting an analysis with these intermediate results can significantly reduce processing time.

- READ requires no specifications.
- READ must be used with a DATA LIST MATRIX command, as shown in the example below.
- Since a matrix, rather than a case file, must be active when you use the READ subcommand, residuals analysis cannot be performed. You cannot use the RESIDUALS subcommand with READ.
- The only plot that can be obtained with matrix input is ZCORR.
- You cannot specify continuous variables or factor-by-covariate interactions on the DESIGN subcommand when using matrix input.
- The homogeneity-of-variance tests specified by PRINT = HOMOGENEITY are not available with matrix input.

Example   When using the READ subcommand in MANOVA, you must precede the MANOVA command by a DATA LIST of this form:

```
DATA LIST MATRIX FILE='filename.ext' / varlist .
```

- You do not need to use the same names that were used when the matrix materials were written.

- The order in which you list variables on DATA LIST MATRIX does not matter, except in determining the order of variables on the active file created by MANOVA.

- The active file created by MANOVA when it reads these matrix materials cannot be used by any procedure other than MANOVA.

Example
```
GET FILE='MYFILE.SYS'.
SET RESULTS 'MANOVA.MAT'.
MANOVA V1 V2 V3 V4 BY SEX(1,2) CLASS(1,3)
   /WRITE
   /DESIGN SEX CLASS.

DATA LIST MATRIX FILE='MANOVA.MAT'
   /X1 TO X4 SEX CLASS.

MANOVA X1 X2 X3 X4 BY SEX(1,2) CLASS(1,3)
   /READ
   /ANALYSIS X1 WITH X2 X3
   /PRINT=PARAM(ESTIM)
   /DESIGN=SEX, CLASS, SEX BY CLASS.
```

- The SET RESULTS command specifies that matrix materials should be written to the file MANOVA.MAT.

- In the first MANOVA procedure, the WRITE subcommand sends formatted matrix materials to MANOVA.MAT. These materials describe the four continuous variables V1 TO V4 in the six cells defined by SEX and CLASS.

- The DATA LIST MATRIX command names the MANOVA.MAT file and assigns names to the variables. The names X1 TO X4 will now be used for the variables originally known as V1 TO V4. The order in which variables are named on DATA LIST MATRIX does not matter.

- The second MANOVA command uses the new names. The variables specification defines four continuous variables and two factors. The number and order of continuous variables, the number and order of factors, and the levels of each factor must be the same as those in the MANOVA command that wrote the matrix materials. The names of the six variables must be chosen from among the names on the DATA LIST MATRIX command.

- The ANALYSIS subcommand redefines X2 and X3 as covariates and omits X4 entirely from the analysis.

- The DESIGN subcommand specifies a different design than the one in the original analysis.

- Any analysis using these four continuous variables and two factors can be performed. However, the RESIDUALS subcommand, most plots, the homogeneity-of-variance tests, and continuous variables on the DESIGN subcommand cannot be specified.

References   Bock, R. D. 1975. *Multivariate statistical methods in behavioral research.* New York: McGraw-Hill.

C

Command Reference

MANOVA: Multivariate

```
MANOVA dependent varlist [BY factor list (min,max) [factor list...]

                          [WITH covariate varlist]]

[/TRANSFORM [(varlist [/varlist])]=[ORTHONORM] [{DEVIATIONS (refcat) }]]
                                                 {DIFFERENCE          }
                                    [{CONTRAST}] {HELMERT             }
                                     {BASIS   }  {SIMPLE (refcat)     }
                                                 {REPEATED            }
                                                 {POLYNOMIAL [(metric)]}
                                                 {SPECIAL (matrix)    }

[/RENAME={newname} {newname}...]
         {*      } {*      }

          {[HOMOGENEITY ([BOXM**])]                                       }
          {                                                               }
[/{PRINT }={[ERROR ([SSCP] [COV**] [COR**] [STDDEV])]                     }]
  {NOPRINT} {                                                             }
          {[SIGNIF [([MULTIV] [EIGEN] [DIMENR] [UNIV] [HYPOTH]            }
          {         [STEPDOWN] [{AVERF }] [BRIEF] [SINGLEDF])]            }
          {                     {AVONLY}                                  }
          {[TRANSFORM]                                                    }

[/PCOMPS=[COR**] [NCOMP(n)] [MINEIGEN(eigencut)] ]
         [COV] [ROTATE(rottype)]

[/PLOT=[ZCORR]]

[/DISCRIM[=[RAW**] [STAN**] [ESTIM**] [COR**] [ALL]]]
          [ROTATE(rottype)] [ALPHA(alpha)]

[/ANALYSIS [({CONDITIONAL  })]=dependent varlist
            {UNCONDITIONAL}
                             [WITH covariate varlist]
                             [/dependent varlist...]
```

**Defaults if subcommands are entered without specifications. In repeated measures, SIGNIF(AVERF) is printed by default instead of SIGNIF(UNIV).

Example:

```
MANOVA SCORE1 TO SCORE4 BY METHOD(1,3).
```

Overview

This section discusses the subcommands that are used in *multivariate* analysis of variance and covariance designs with several interrelated dependent variables. It does not contain information on all subcommands you will need to specify the design. For subcommands not covered here, refer to MANOVA: Univariate.

Syntax

- Multivariate syntax for MANOVA is identical to univariate syntax, except that two or more dependent variables are named before the keyword BY in the MANOVA variables specification.

- Several subcommands are available in multivariate analysis that do not apply to univariate analysis. Additional keywords for some subcommands are also available.

- If you enter one of the multivariate specifications in a univariate analysis, MANOVA will ignore it.

MANOVA Variable List

The basic syntax for the MANOVA variables specification in multivariate designs is

```
MANOVA dependent varlist BY factors(range) WITH covariates
```

- Multivariate MANOVA calculates statistical tests that are valid for analyses of dependent variables that are correlated with one another.

- If the dependent variables are uncorrelated, *univariate* significance tests (also available in MANOVA) have greater statistical power.

ANALYSIS Subcommand

The ANALYSIS subcommand is discussed in MANOVA: Univariate as a means of obtaining factor-by-covariate interaction terms. In multivariate analyses it is considerably more useful.

- The ANALYSIS subcommand specifies a subset of the continuous variables (dependent variables and covariates) listed on the MANOVA variable list and completely *redefines* which variables are dependent and which are covariates.

- All variables named on an ANALYSIS subcommand must have been named on the MANOVA variable list. It does not matter whether they were named as dependent variables or as covariates.

- Factors cannot be named on an ANALYSIS subcommand.

- After the keyword ANALYSIS, specify the names of one or more dependent variables and, optionally, the keyword WITH followed by one or more covariates.

- An ANALYSIS specification remains in effect for all designs until you enter another ANALYSIS subcommand.

- Continuous variables named on the MANOVA variable list but *omitted* from the ANALYSIS subcommand currently in effect can be specified on the DESIGN subcommand.

- You can use an ANALYSIS subcommand to request analyses of several groups of variables, provided that the groups do not overlap. Separate the groups of variables with slashes and enclose the entire ANALYSIS specification in parentheses.

When you specify multiple analyses on a single subcommand, you can specify keyword CONDITIONAL in parentheses after the subcommand but before the equals sign.

- If you specify CONDITIONAL on an ANALYSIS subcommand, the variables in an analysis group will be used as covariates in subsequent analysis groups.

- The default is to process each list of variables separately, without regard to other lists. The keyword UNCONDITIONAL can be used to request this treatment explicitly.

- CONDITIONAL analysis is not carried over from one ANALYSIS subcommand to another.

Example

```
MANOVA A B C BY FAC(1,4) WITH D, E
   /ANALYSIS = (A, B / C / D WITH E)
   /DESIGN.
```

- The first analysis uses A and B as dependent variables and no covariates.

- The second analysis uses C as a dependent variable and no covariates.

- The third analysis uses D as the dependent variable and E as a covariate.

Example

You can share one or more covariates among all the ANALYSIS groups by "factoring them out" from the parentheses, as in the following:

```
MANOVA A, B, C, D, E BY FAC(1,4) WITH F G
   /ANALYSIS = (A, B / C / D WITH E) WITH F G
   /DESIGN.
```

- The first analysis uses A and B with F and G as covariates.

- The second analysis uses C with F and G as covariates.

- The third analysis uses D with E, F, and G as covariates.

- Factoring out F and G is the only way to use them as covariates in all three analyses, since no variable can be named more than once on an ANALYSIS subcommand.

Example

```
MANOVA A B C BY FAC(1,3)
   /ANALYSIS(CONDITIONAL) = (A WITH B / C)
   /DESIGN.
```

- In the first analysis, A is the dependent variable, B is a covariate, and C is not used.

- In the second analysis, C is the dependent variable, and both A and B are covariates.

TRANSFORM Subcommand

The TRANSFORM subcommand performs linear transformations of some or all of the continuous variables (dependent variables and covariates).

• Transformations apply to all subsequent designs unless replaced by another TRANSFORM subcommand.

• TRANSFORM subcommands are not cumulative. Only the transformation specified most recently is in effect at any time. You can restore the original variables in later designs by requesting TRANSFORM=SPECIAL with an identity matrix.

• You should *not* use TRANSFORM when you use the WSFACTORS subcommand to request repeated measures analysis; a transformation is automatically performed in repeated measures analysis (see MANOVA: Repeated Measures).

• Transformations are in effect only for the duration of the MANOVA procedure. After the procedure is complete, the original variables remain on the active file.

• The transformation matrix is not displayed by default. Use PRINT= TRANSFORM to see the matrix generated by the TRANSFORM subcommand.

• If you do not use the RENAME subcommand with TRANSFORM, the continuous variables listed in the MANOVA variables specification are renamed temporarily (for the duration of the procedure) as T1, T2, etc. Explicit use of RENAME is recommended.

• Subsequent references to transformed variables must use the new names. The only exception is when you supply a VARIABLES specification on the OMEANS subcommand after using TRANSFORM. In this case, specify the original names. OMEANS displays observed means of original variables.

Specifications on the TRANSFORM subcommand include an optional list of variables to be transformed; optional keywords to describe how to generate a transformation matrix from the specified contrasts; and a required keyword specifying the transformation contrasts.

Variable Lists

• By default, MANOVA applies the transformation you request to all continuous variables (dependent variables and covariates) *together*.

• You can enter a variable list in parentheses following the TRANSFORM keyword; if you do, only the listed variables are transformed.

• You can enter multiple variable lists, separated by slashes, within a single set of parentheses. Each list must have the same number of variables, and the lists must not overlap. The transformation is applied separately to the variables in each list.

• In designs with covariates it is usually inappropriate to transform them together with the dependent variables. Transform only the dependent variables, or, in some designs, apply the same transformation to the dependent variables and the covariates.

Optional Keywords

• You can enter the optional keywords CONTRAST, BASIS, and ORTHONORM following the subcommand TRANSFORM, the variable list(s), if any, and an equals sign. CONTRAST and BASIS are alternatives; ORTHONORM can be requested along with either CONTRAST or BASIS.

• By default, the transformation matrix is generated directly from the contrast matrix of the given type (see CONTRAST Subcommand under MANOVA: Univariate). You can request this method explicitly with keyword CONTRAST.

• If you enter keyword BASIS, the transformation matrix is generated from the one-way basis matrix corresponding to the specified contrast. This only makes a difference if the transformation contrasts are not orthogonal.

• Keyword ORTHONORM requests that the transformation matrix be orthonormalized by rows before use. MANOVA eliminates redundant rows. Orthonormalization is not done by default.

• ORTHONORM is independent of the CONTRAST/BASIS choice; you can enter it before or after either of those keywords.

Transformation Methods   You must enter one of the keywords listed below on the TRANSFORM subcommand to indicate the type of transformation contrasts you want. There is no default.

• The transformation keyword (and its specifications, if any) must follow all other specifications on the TRANSFORM subcommand.

Note that these are identical to the keywords available for the CONTRAST subcommand (see MANOVA: Univariate). However, in univariate designs, they are applied to the different *levels* of a factor. Here they are applied to the *continuous variables* in the analysis. This reflects the fact that the different dependent variables in a multivariate MANOVA setup can often be thought of as corresponding to different levels of some factor.

DEVIATION   *Deviations from the mean of the variables being transformed.* The first transformed variable is the mean of all variables in the transformation. Other transformed variables represent deviations of individual variables from the mean. One of the original variables (by default the last) is omitted as redundant. To omit a variable other than the last, specify the number of the variable to be omitted in parentheses after the DEVIATION keyword. For example, TRANSFORM (A B C) = DEVIATION(1) omits A and creates variables representing the mean, the deviation of B from the mean, and the deviation of C from the mean. A deviation transformation is not orthogonal.

DIFFERENCE   *Difference or reverse Helmert transformation.* The first transformed variable is the mean of the original variables. Each of the original variables except the first is then transformed by subtracting the mean of those (original) variables which precede it. A difference transformation is orthogonal.

HELMERT   *Helmert transformation.* The first transformed variable is the mean of the original variables. Each of the original variables except the last is then transformed by subtracting the mean of those (original) variables that follow it. A Helmert transformation is orthogonal.

SIMPLE   *Each original variable, except the last, is compared to the last of the original variables.* To use a variable other than the last as the omitted reference variable, specify its number in parentheses following the keyword SIMPLE. For example, TRANSFORM(A B C) = SIMPLE(2) specifies the second variable, B, as the reference variable. The three transformed variables represent the mean of A, B, and C; the difference between A and B; and the difference between C and B. A simple transformation is not orthogonal.

POLYNOMIAL   *Orthogonal polynomial transformation.* The first transformed variable represents the mean of the original variables. Other transformed variables represent the linear, quadratic, and higher-degree components. By default, values of the original variables are assumed to represent equally spaced points. You can specify unequal spacing by entering a *metric* consisting of one integer for each variable in parentheses after the keyword POLYNOMIAL. For example, TRANSFORM(RESP1 RESP2 RESP3) = POLYNOMIAL(1,2,4) might indicate that three response variables correspond to levels of some stimulus that are in the proportion 1:2:4. The default metric is always $(1,2,...,k)$, where k variables are involved. Only the relative differences between the terms of the metric matter: (1,2,4) is the same metric as (2,3,5) or (20,30,50), because in each instance the difference between the second and third numbers is twice the difference between the first and second.

> **REPEATED** *Comparison of adjacent variables.* The first transformed variable is the mean of the original variables. Each additional transformed variable is the difference between one of the original variables and the original variable that followed it. Such transformed variables are often called *difference scores.* A repeated transformation is not orthogonal.
>
> **SPECIAL** *A user-defined transformation.* After keyword SPECIAL, enter a square matrix in parentheses with as many rows and columns as there are variables to transform. MANOVA multiplies this matrix by the vector of original variables to obtain the transformed variables (see the following examples).

Example

```
MANOVA X1 TO X3 BY A(1,4)
    /TRANSFORM(X1 X2 X3) = SPECIAL( 1  1 -1,
                                    2  0  1,
                                    1  0 -1 )
    /DESIGN.
```

- The given matrix will be multiplied by the three continuous variables (considered as a column vector) to yield the transformed variables. The first transformed variable will therefore equal $X1 + X2 - X3$, the second will equal $2X1 + X3$, and the third will equal $X1 - X3$.

- The variable list is optional in this example, since all three interval-level variables are transformed.

- You do not need to enter the matrix one row at a time, as shown here. TRANSFORM = SPECIAL(1 1 −1 2 0 1 1 0 −1) is fully equivalent.

- You can specify a repetition factor, followed by an asterisk, to indicate multiple consecutive elements of a SPECIAL transformation matrix. TRANSFORM = SPECIAL (2*1 −1 2 0 2*1 0 −1) is equivalent to the above matrix.

Example

```
MANOVA X1 TO X3, Y1 TO Y3 BY A(1,4)
    /TRANSFORM(X1 X2 X3/Y1 Y2 Y3) = SPECIAL( 1  1 -1
                                             2  0  1
                                             1  0 -1 )
    /DESIGN.
```

- Here the same transformation as in the previous example is applied to X1, X2, X3, and also to Y1, Y2, Y3.

RENAME Subcommand

Use the RENAME subcommand to assign new names to transformed variables. Renaming variables after a transformation is strongly recommended. If you transform but do not rename the variables, the names T1, T2, ..., Tn are used as names for the transformed variables.

- Follow the RENAME subcommand with a list of new variable names.

- You must enter a new name for each dependent variable and covariate on the MANOVA variables specification.

- Enter the new names in the order the original variables appeared in the MANOVA variables specification.

- To retain the original name for one or more of the interval variables, you can either enter an asterisk or reenter the old name as the new name.

- References to dependent variables and covariates on subcommands following RENAME *must* use the new names. The original names will not be recognized within the MANOVA procedure. The only exception is the OMEANS subcommand, which displays observed means of the original (untransformed) variables. Use the original names on OMEANS.

- The new names exist only during the MANOVA procedure that created them. They do not remain in the active file after the procedure is complete.

Example

```
MANOVA A, B, C, V4, V5 BY TREATMNT(1,3)
    /TRANSFORM(A, B, C) = REPEATED
    /RENAME = MEANABC, AMINUSB, BMINUSC, *, *
    /DESIGN.
```

- The REPEATED transformation produces three transformed variables, which are then assigned mnemonic names MEANABC, AMINUSB, and BMINUSC.

- V4 and V5 retain their original names.

Example   MANOVA WT1, WT2, WT3, WT4 BY TREATMNT(1,3) WITH COV
                   /TRANSFORM (WT1 TO WT4) = POLYNOMIAL
                   /RENAME = MEAN, LINEAR, QUAD, CUBIC, *
                   /ANALYSIS = MEAN, LINEAR, QUAD WITH COV
                   /DESIGN.

- After the polynomial transformation of the four WT variables, RENAME assigns appropriate names to the various trends.

- Even though only four variables were transformed, the RENAME subcommand applies to all five continuous variables. An asterisk is required to retain the original name for COV.

- The ANALYSIS subcommand following RENAME refers to the interval variables by their new names. A reference to WT1, for example, would produce a syntax error.

PRINT and NOPRINT Subcommands

All of the PRINT specifications described under MANOVA: Univariate are available in multivariate analyses. The following additional output can also be requested. To suppress any optional output, specify the appropriate keyword on NOPRINT.

ERROR   *Error matrices.* Three types of matrices are available (see below).

SIGNIF   *Significance tests.*

TRANSFORM *Transformation matrix.* Available if you have transformed the dependent variables with the TRANSFORM subcommand.

HOMOGENEITY *A test for multivariate homogeneity of variance, BOXM, is available.*

ERROR Keyword

In multivariate analysis, error terms consist of entire matrices, not single values. You can display any of the following error matrices on a PRINT subcommand by requesting them in parentheses following the keyword ERROR. If you enter PRINT=ERROR without further specifications, COV and COR are displayed.

SSCP *Error sums-of-squares and cross-products matrix.*

COV   *Error variance-covariance matrix.*

COR   *Error correlation matrix with standard deviations on the diagonal.* This also displays the determinant of the matrix and Bartlett's test of sphericity, a test of whether the error correlation matrix is significantly different from an identity matrix.

SIGNIF Keyword

You can request any of the optional output listed below by entering the appropriate specification in parentheses after the SIGNIF keyword on the PRINT subcommand. Further specifications for SIGNIF are described under MANOVA: Repeated Measures.

- By default, MANOVA displays the output corresponding to MULTIV and UNIV for a multivariate analysis not involving repeated measures.

- If you enter any specification for SIGNIF on the PRINT subcommand, the default output is suppressed and MANOVA displays only what you have explicitly requested.

MULTIV   *Multivariate F tests for group differences.* This is displayed by default.

EIGEN   *Eigenvalues of the $S_h S_e^{-1}$ matrix.* This matrix is the product of the hypothesis sums-of-squares and cross-products (SSCP) matrix and the inverse of the error SSCP matrix.

DIMENR   *A dimension-reduction analysis.*

UNIV   *Univariate F tests.* This is displayed by default, except in repeated measures analysis. If the dependent variables are uncorrelated, univariate tests have greater statistical power.

HYPOTH   *The hypothesis SSCP matrix.*

STEPDOWN *Roy-Bargmann stepdown F tests.*

BRIEF   *Abbreviated multivariate output.* This is similar to a univariate analysis of variance table but with Wilks' multivariate *F* approximation (lambda) replacing the univariate *F*. BRIEF overrides any of the SIGNIF specifications listed above.

The SINGLEDF keyword described under MANOVA: Univariate does not apply to analysis of variance tables in multivariate designs, except for the averaged *F*-tests described in MANOVA: Repeated Measures.

TRANSFORM Keyword

PRINT = TRANSFORM displays the transposed transformation matrix in use for each subsequent design. This matrix is helpful in interpreting a multivariate analysis in which you have transformed the interval-level variables with either TRANSFORM or WSFACTORS.

• The matrix displayed by this option is the *transpose* of the transformation matrix.

• Original variables correspond to the rows of the matrix, and transformed variables to the columns.

• A transformed variable is a linear combination of the original variables, using the coefficients displayed in the column corresponding to that transformed variable.

HOMOGENEITY Keyword

In addition to the BARTLETT and COCHRAN specifications described under MANOVA: Univariate, the following test for homogeneity is available for multivariate analyses.

BOXM   *Box's* M *statistic.*

PLOT Subcommand

In addition to the plots described under MANOVA: Univariate, the following is available for multivariate analyses:

ZCORR   *A half-normal plot of the within-cells correlations among the dependent variables.* MANOVA first transforms the correlations using Fisher's Z transformation. If errors for the dependent variables are uncorrelated, the plotted points should lie close to a straight line.

PCOMPS Subcommand

The PCOMPS subcommand requests a principal components analysis of each error sum-of-squares and cross-product matrix in a multivariate analysis. You can display the principal components of the error correlation matrix, the error variance-covariance matrix, or both. These principal components are corrected for differences due to the factors and covariates in the MANOVA analysis. They tend to be more useful than principal components extracted from the raw correlation or covariance matrix when there are significant group differences between the levels of the factors or when a significant amount of error variance is accounted for by the covariates. You can specify any of the keywords listed below on PCOMPS.

• You must specify either COR or COV (or both). Otherwise, MANOVA will not produce any principal components.

COR   *Principal components analysis of the error correlation matrix.*

COV   *Principal components analysis of the error variance-covariance matrix.*

ROTATE   *Rotate the principal components solution.* By default, no rotation is performed. Specify a rotation type (either VARIMAX, EQUAMAX, QUARTIMAX, or NOROTATE) in parentheses after keyword RO-TATE. Specify PCOMPS = ROTATE (NOROTATE) to cancel a rotation specified for a previous design.

NCOMP   *The number of principal components to rotate.* Specify a number in parentheses. The default is the number of dependent variables.

MINEIGEN   *The minimum eigenvalue for principal component extraction.* Specify a cutoff value in parentheses. Components with eigenvalues below the cutoff will not be retained in the solution. The default is 0: all components (or the number specified on NCOMP) are extracted.

- Both NCOMP and MINEIGEN limit the number of components that are rotated.

- If the number specified on NCOMP is less than two, two components are rotated (provided that at least two components have eigenvalues greater than any value specified on MINEIGEN).

- Principal components analysis is computationally expensive if the number of dependent variables is large.

DISCRIM Subcommand

The DISCRIM subcommand produces a canonical discriminant analysis for each effect in a design. (For covariates, DISCRIM produces a canonical correlation analysis.) These analyses aid in the interpretation of multivariate effects. You can request the following statistics by entering the appropriate keywords after the subcommand DISCRIM:

RAW   *Raw discriminant function coefficients.*

STAN   *Standardized discriminant function coefficients.*

ESTIM   *Effect estimates in discriminant function space.*

COR   *Correlations between the dependent variables and the canonical variables defined by the discriminant functions.*

ROTATE   *Rotation of the matrix of correlations between dependent and canonical variables.* Specify VARIMAX, EQUAMAX, or QUARTIMAX in parentheses after this keyword.

ALPHA   *Set the significance level required before a canonical variable is extracted.* The default is 0.25. To change the default, specify a decimal number between 0 and 1 in parentheses after ALPHA.

- The correlations between dependent variables and canonical discriminant functions are not rotated unless at least two discriminant functions are significant at the level defined by ALPHA.

- If you set ALPHA to 1.0, all discriminant functions are reported (and rotated, if you so request).

- If you set ALPHA to 0, no discriminant functions are reported.

MANOVA: Repeated Measures

```
MANOVA dependent varlist [BY factor list (min,max)
    [factor list...] [WITH covariate list]]

/WSFACTORS=name (levels) [name...]

[/MEASURE=newname newname...]

[/WSDESIGN=effect effect...]

[/{PRINT  }=[SIGNIF({AVERF }) (MULTIV)] ]
  {NOPRINT}            {AVONLY}
```

Example:

```
MANOVA Y1 TO Y4 BY GROUP(1,2)
    /WSFACTORS=YEAR(4).
```

Overview

This section discusses the subcommands that are used in *repeated measures* designs on MANOVA, in which the dependent variables represent measurements of the same variable (or variables) at different times. This section does not contain information on all subcommands you will need to specify the design. For some subcommands not covered here, such as DESIGN and PRINT, refer to MANOVA: Univariate. For information on optional output and the multivariate significance tests available, refer to MANOVA: Multivariate.

- In a simple repeated-measures analysis, all dependent variables represent different measurements of the same variable for different values (or levels) of a *within-subjects factor*. Between-subjects factors and covariates can also be included in the model, just as in analyses not involving repeated measures.

- A within-subjects factor is simply a factor that distinguishes measurements made on the same subject or case, rather than distinguishing different subjects or cases.

- MANOVA permits more complex analyses, in which the dependent variables represent levels of two or more within-subjects factors.

- MANOVA also permits analyses in which the dependent variables represent measurements of several variables for the different levels of the within-subjects factors. These are known as *doubly multivariate* designs.

- A repeated-measures analysis includes a within-subjects design describing the model to be tested with the within-subjects factors, as well as the usual between-subjects design describing the effects to be tested with between-subjects factors. The default for both types of design is a full factorial model.

- MANOVA always performs an orthonormal transformation of the dependent variables in a repeated-measures analysis. By default, MANOVA renames them as T1, T2, and so forth.

Defaults

Whenever you enter the WSFACTORS command, MANOVA performs special repeated-measures processing. Default output includes SIGNIF(AVERF) but not SIGNIF(UNIV). In addition, for any within-subjects effect involving more than one transformed variable, the Mauchly test of sphericity is displayed to test the assumption that the covariance matrix of the transformed variables is constant on the diagonal and 0 off the diagonal. The Greenhouse-Geiser epsilon and the Huynh-Feldt epsilon are also displayed for use in correcting the significance tests in the event that the assumption of sphericity is violated. These tests are discussed in Part B: Statistics Guide.

Syntax

- The WSFACTORS (within-subject factors), WSDESIGN (within-subjects design), and MEASURE subcommands are used only in repeated-measures analysis.

- WSFACTORS is required for any repeated-measures analysis. A default WSDESIGN consisting of all main effects and interactions among within-subjects factors is used if you do not enter a WSDESIGN subcommand. The MEASURE subcommand is used for *doubly multivariate* designs, in which the dependent variables represent repeated measurements of more than one variable.

- WSFACTORS must be the first subcommand you enter, following the list of dependent variables, factors, and covariates on the MANOVA variables specification.

- The WSFACTORS subcommand automatically triggers special repeated-measures analysis and implies a full factorial within-subjects design (unless you specify the WSDESIGN subcommand).

- Do not use the TRANSFORM subcommand with the WSFACTORS subcommand, since WSFACTORS automatically causes an orthonormal transformation of the dependent variables.

- The WSFACTORS subcommand determines how the dependent variables on the MANOVA variable list will be interpreted.

- The number of cells in the within-subjects design is the product of the number of levels for each within-subjects factor.

- The number of dependent variables on the MANOVA variable list must be a multiple of the number of cells in the within-subjects design. If there are six cells in the within-subjects design, each group of six dependent variables represents a single variable that has been measured in each of the six cells.

- Normally, the number of dependent variables should equal the number of cells in the within-subjects design multiplied by the number of variables named on the MEASURE subcommand (if one is used). If you have more groups of dependent variables than are accounted for by the MEASURE subcommand, MANOVA will choose variable names to label the output, which may therefore be difficult to interpret.

- If you use covariates in a repeated-measures analysis, there must be one covariate for each cell in the within-subjects design. Normally the covariates should be identical copies of one another (you can create these with the COMPUTE command).

Example

```
MANOVA Y1 TO Y4 BY GROUP(1,2)
  /WSFACTORS=YEAR(4)
  /CONTRAST(YEAR)=POLYNOMIAL
  /RENAME=CONST, LINEAR, QUAD, CUBIC
  /PRINT=TRANSFORM PARAM(ESTIM)
  /WSDESIGN=YEAR
  /DESIGN=GROUP.
```

- The WSFACTORS subcommand immediately follows the MANOVA variable list and specifies a repeated-measures analysis in which the four dependent variables represent a single variable measured at four levels of the within-subjects factor. The within-subjects factor is called YEAR for the duration of the MANOVA procedure.

- The CONTRAST subcommand requests polynomial contrasts for the levels of YEAR. Since the four variables Y1, Y2, Y3, Y4 in the active file represent the four levels of YEAR, the effect is to perform an orthonormal polynomial transformation of these variables.

- The RENAME subcommand assigns names to the dependent variables to reflect the transformation.

- The PRINT subcommand requests that the transformation matrix and the parameter estimates be displayed.

- The WSDESIGN subcommand specifies a within-subjects design that includes only the effect of the YEAR within-subjects factor. Since YEAR is the only within-subjects factor specified, this is the default design and WSDESIGN could have been omitted.

- The DESIGN subcommand specifies a between-subjects design that includes only the effect of the GROUP between-subjects factor. This subcommand could have been omitted.

C

Command Reference

Example

```
COMPUTE SES1 = SES.
COMPUTE SES2 = SES.
COMPUTE SES3 = SES.
COMPUTE SES4 = SES.
MANOVA SCORE1 TO SCORE4 BY METHOD(1,2) WITH SES1 TO SES4
  /WSFACTORS=SEMESTER(4)
  /CONTRAST(SEMESTER)=DIFFERENCE
  /RENAME=MEAN,DIF2 TO DIF4,*,*,*,*.
```

- The four dependent variables represent a score measured four times (corresponding to the four levels of SEMESTER).

- The four COMPUTE commands create four copies of the constant covariate SES so that there will be one covariate for each of the within-subjects cells.

- The RENAME subcommand supplies names for the difference transformation of the within-subjects factor SEMESTER. Since the MANOVA variables specification includes eight continuous variables, eight names are specified. The four asterisks indicate that the existing names are kept for the covariates.

- Covariates are transformed in the same way as the dependent variables. However, since these covariates are identical, the orthonormal transformation does not affect them.

WSFACTORS Subcommand

The WSFACTORS subcommand names the within-subjects factors and specifies the number of levels for each.

- For repeated-measures designs, WSFACTORS must be the first subcommand after the MANOVA variable list.

- Only one WSFACTORS subcommand is permitted per execution of MANOVA.

- Names for the within-subjects factors are specified on the WSFACTORS subcommand. Factor names must not duplicate any of the dependent variables, factors, or covariates named on the MANOVA variable list.

- If there is more than one within-subjects factor, they must be named in the order corresponding to the order of the dependent variables on the MANOVA variable list. MANOVA varies the levels of the last-named WSFACTOR most rapidly when assigning dependent variables to within-subjects cells (see example below).

- Levels of the factors must be represented in the data by the dependent variables named on the MANOVA variable list.

- Enter a number in parentheses after each factor to indicate how many levels the factor has. If two or more adjacent factors have the same number of levels, you can enter the number of levels in parentheses after all of them.

- You enter only the number of levels for WSFACTORs, not a range of values.

Example

```
MANOVA X1Y1 X1Y2 X2Y1 X2Y2 X3Y1 X3Y2 BY TREATMNT(1,5) GROUP(1,2)
  /WSFACTORS=X(3) Y(2)
  /DESIGN.
```

- The MANOVA variable list names six dependent variables and two between-subjects factors, TREATMNT and GROUP.

- The WSFACTORS subcommand identifies two within-subjects factors whose levels distinguish the six dependent variables. X has three levels and Y has two. Thus, there are $3 * 2 = 6$ cells in the within-subjects design, corresponding to the six dependent variables.

- Variable X1Y1 corresponds to levels 1,1 of the two WSFACTORS; variable X1Y2 corresponds to levels 1,2; X2Y1 to levels 2,1; and so on up to X3Y2, which corresponds to levels 3,2. The first within-subjects factor named, X, varies most slowly, and the last within-subjects factor named, Y, varies most rapidly in the list of dependent variables.

- Since there is no WSDESIGN subcommand, the within-subjects design will include all main effects and interactions: X, Y, and X by Y.

- Likewise, the between-subjects design includes all main effects and interactions: TREATMNT, GROUP, TREATMNT by GROUP.

- In addition, repeated-measures analysis *always* includes interactions between the within-subjects factors and the between-subjects factors. There are three such interactions for each of the three within-subjects effects.

WSDESIGN
Subcommand

The WSDESIGN subcommand specifies the design for within-subjects factors. Its specifications are like those of the DESIGN subcommand, but it uses the within-subjects factors rather than the between-subjects factors.

- The default WSDESIGN is a full factorial design, which includes all main effects and all interactions for within-subjects factors. The default is in effect whenever a design is processed without a preceding WSDESIGN or when the preceding WSDESIGN subcommand has no specifications.

- A WSDESIGN specification can include main effects for WS factors; factor-BY-factor interactions among WS factors; nested terms (term WITHIN term) involving WS factors and their interactions; terms using the MWITHIN keyword; and combinations of the above pooled together with the plus sign.

- A WSDESIGN specification can *not* include between-subjects factors or terms based on them; interval-level variables; the MUPLUS or CONSTANT keywords; or error-term definitions or references.

- The WSDESIGN specification applies to all subsequent between-subjects designs until another WSDESIGN subcommand is encountered.

Example

```
MANOVA JANLO,JANHI,FEBLO,FEBHI,MARLO,MARHI BY SEX(1,2)
  /WSFACTORS MONTH(3) STIMULUS(2)
  /WSDESIGN MONTH, STIMULUS
  /DESIGN SEX
  /WSDESIGN.
```

- There are six dependent variables, corresponding to three months and two different levels of stimulus.

- The dependent variables are named on the MANOVA variable list in such an order that the level of stimulus varies more rapidly than the month. Thus, STIMULUS is named last on the WSFACTORS subcommand.

- The first WSDESIGN subcommand specifies only the main effects for within-subjects factors. There is no MONTH by STIMULUS interaction term.

- The second WSDESIGN subcommand has no specifications and therefore invokes the default within-subjects design, which includes the main effects and their interaction.

- Since the last subcommand is not DESIGN, MANOVA generates a full factorial design at the end. In this example there is only one between-subjects factor, SEX, so the last design is identical to the one specified by DESIGN =SEX. The last design, however, will include the MONTH BY STIMULUS within-subjects interaction. It will *automatically* include the interaction between SEX and MONTH BY STIMULUS; you do not need to specify, and indeed cannot specify, such interactions between elements of the within-subjects and the between-subjects designs.

PRINT Subcommand

Two additional specifications on the PRINT subcommand are useful in repeated-measures analysis: SIGNIF (AVERF) and SIGNIF (AVONLY).

- SIGNIF (AVERF) and SIGNIF (AVONLY) are mutually exclusive.

- When you request repeated-measures analysis with the WSFACTORS subcommand, the default display includes SIGNIF(AVERF) but does not include the usual SIGNIF(UNIV).

- The averaged *F* tests are appropriate in repeated measures because the dependent variables that are averaged actually represent the same variable at different times. When the analysis is not *doubly multivariate,* as discussed below, you can specify PRINT = SIGNIF (AVERF UNIV) to obtain significance tests for each degree of freedom, just as in univariate MANOVA.

SIGNIF(AVERF)   *An averaged* F *test* for use with repeated measures. This is the default display in repeated measures analysis. The averaged *F* test in the multivariate setup for repeated measures is equivalent to the univariate (or split-plot or mixed-model) approach to repeated measures.

SIGNIF(AVONLY)   *Only the averaged* F *test* for repeated measures. AVONLY produces the same output as AVERF and suppresses all other PRINT=SIGNIF output.

C

Command Reference

**MEASURE
Subcommand**

In a *doubly multivariate* analysis, the dependent variables represent multiple variables measured under the different levels of the within-subjects factors. Use the MEASURE subcommand to assign names to the variables that you have measured for the different levels of within-subjects factors.

- Specifications on MEASURE consist of a list of one or more variable names to be used in labeling the output of PRINT=SIGNIF(HYPOTH AVERF) and PRINT=SIGNIF(UNIV).

- The number of dependent variables on the DESIGN subcommand should equal the product of the number of cells in the within-subjects design and the number of names on the MEASURE subcommand.

- If you do not enter a MEASURE subcommand and there are more dependent variables than cells in the within-subjects design, MANOVA assigns names (normally MEAS.1, MEAS.2, etc.) to the different measures.

- All of the dependent variables corresponding to each measure should be listed together and ordered so that the within-subjects factor named last on the WSFACTORS subcommand varies most rapidly.

Example

```
MANOVA TEMP1 TO TEMP6, WEIGHT1 TO WEIGHT6 BY GROUP(1,2)
  /WSFACTORS=DAY(3) AMPM(2)
  /MEASURE=TEMP WEIGHT
  /WSDESIGN=DAY, AMPM, DAY BY AMPM
  /PRINT=SIGNIF(HYPOTH AVERF)
  /DESIGN.
```

- There are twelve dependent variables: six temperatures and six weights, corresponding to morning and afternoon measurements on three days.

- The WSFACTORS subcommand identifies the two factors (DAY and AMPM) that distinguish the temperature and weight measurements for each subject. These factors define six within-subjects cells.

- The MEASURE subcommand indicates that the first group of six dependent variables correspond to TEMP and the second group of six dependent variables correspond to WEIGHT.

- These labels, TEMP and WEIGHT, are used on the output requested by PRINT = SIGNIF (HYPOTH AVERF).

- The WSDESIGN subcommand requests a full factorial within-subjects model. Since this is the default, WSDESIGN could have been omitted.

**CONTRAST
Subcommand for
WSFACTORS**

The levels of a within-subjects factor are represented by different dependent variables. Therefore, contrasts between levels of such a factor compare these dependent variables. Specifying the type of contrast amounts to specifying a transformation to be performed on the dependent variables.

- An orthonormal transformation is automatically performed on the dependent variables in a repeated-measures analysis.

- To specify the type of orthonormal transformation, use the CONTRAST subcommand for the within-subjects factors.

- Regardless of the contrast type you specify, the transformation matrix is orthonormalized before use.

- If you do not specify a contrast type for within-subjects factors, the default contrast type (deviation) is orthonormalized and used to form a transformation matrix. Parameter estimates based on this transformation are not particularly suited to repeated-measures analysis. The contrast types that are intrinsically orthogonal are recommended for within-subjects factors. These are difference, Helmert, and polynomial.

- When you implicitly request a transformation of the dependent variables with CONTRAST for within-subjects factors, the same transformation is applied to any covariates in the analysis. There must be as many covariates as dependent variables. Normally the covariates are identical copies of one another, in which case the orthonormal transformation does not have any effect.

- You can display the transpose of the transformation matrix generated by your within-subjects contrast by using the TRANSFORM keyword on the PRINT subcommand.

Example
```
MANOVA SCORE1 SCORE2 SCORE3 BY GROUP(1,4)
  /WSFACTORS=ROUND(3)
  /CONTRAST(ROUND)=DIFFERENCE
  /CONTRAST(GROUP)=DEVIATION
  /PRINT=TRANSFORM PARAM(ESTIM).
```

- This analysis has one between-subjects factor, GROUP, with levels 1, 2, 3, and 4, and one within-subjects factor, ROUND, with three levels that are represented by the three dependent variables.

- The first CONTRAST subcommand specifies difference contrasts for ROUND, the within-subjects factor. Since this subcommand applies to the within-subjects analysis, it must precede the CONTRAST subcommand for GROUP.

- There is no WSDESIGN subcommand, so a default full factorial within-subjects design is assumed. This could also have been specified as WSDESIGN= ROUND, or simply WSDESIGN.

- The second CONTRAST subcommand specifies deviation contrasts for GROUP, the between-subjects factor. This subcommand could have been omitted since deviation contrasts are the default.

- The PRINT subcommand requests the display of the transformation matrix generated by the within-subjects contrast and the parameter estimates for the model.

- There is no DESIGN subcommand, so a default full factorial between-subjects design is assumed. This could also have been specified as DESIGN = GROUP, or simply DESIGN.

Example
```
COMPUTE COV2=COV.
COMPUTE COV3=COV.
COMPUTE COV4=COV.
MANOVA DEP1 DEP2 DEP3 DEP4 BY FAC(1,2) WITH COV COV2 COV3 COV4
  /WSFACTOR=MONTH(4)
  /CONTRAST(MONTH)=POLYNOMIAL
  /RENAME=CONST,LINEAR,QUAD, CUBIC,*,*,*,*
  /PRINT=TRANSFORM PARAM(ESTIM)
  /DESIGN.
```

- Since there are four dependent variables, four copies of the covariate are needed. Three COMPUTE commands create the extra copies.

- The MANOVA variable list names four dependent variables representing the levels of the within-subjects factor MONTH; a single between-subjects factor with two categories; and the four copies of the covariate.

- The CONTRAST subcommand specifies an orthonormalized polynomial transformation of the dependent variables. This transformation will also be applied, separately, to the covariates.

- The PRINT subcommand requests the display of the transformation matrix and the parameter estimates.

RENAME Subcommand

Since any repeated-measures analysis involves a transformation of the dependent variables, it is *always* a good idea to rename the dependent variables. Choose appropriate names depending on the type of contrast specified for within-subjects factors. This is easier to do if you are using one of the orthogonal contrasts; the most reliable way to assign new names is to inspect the transformation matrix.

Example
```
MANOVA LOW1 LOW2 LOW3 HI1 HI2 HI3
  /WSFACTORS=LEVEL(2) TRIAL(3)
  /CONTRAST(TRIAL)=DIFFERENCE
  /RENAME=CONST LEVELDIF TRIAL2 TRIAL3 HITRIAL2 HITRIAL3
  /PRINT=TRANSFORM
  /DESIGN.
```

- This analysis has two within-subjects factors and no between-subjects factors.

- Difference contrasts are requested for TRIAL, which has three levels.

- Since all orthonormal contrasts are equivalent for a factor with two levels, there is no point in specifying a contrast type for LEVEL.

- New names are assigned to the transformed variables based on the transformation matrix, which was displayed in a previous trial. These names correspond to the meaning of the transformed variables: the mean or constant, the average difference between levels, the average effect of Trial 2 compared to 1, the average effect of Trial 3 compared to 1 and 2, and the two interactions between LEVEL and TRIAL.

Transformation matrix

	CONST	LEVELDIF	TRIAL2	TRIAL3	HITRIAL2	HITRIAL3
LOW1	0.408	0.408	−0.500	−0.289	−0.500	−0.289
LOW2	0.408	0.408	0.500	−0.289	0.500	−0.289
LOW3	0.408	0.408	0.000	0.577	0.000	0.577
HI1	0.408	−0.408	−0.500	−0.289	0.500	0.289
HI2	0.408	−0.408	0.500	−0.289	−0.500	0.289
HI3	0.408	−0.408	0.000	0.577	0.000	−0.577

NLR

```
MODEL PROGRAM varname=value [varname=value ...
transformation commands]

[DERIVATIVES
 transformation commands]

NLR depvar WITH varlist

 [/OUTFILE=file]    [/FILE=file]

 [/PRED=varname]

 [/SAVE [PRED] [RESID [(varname)]] [DERIVATIVES]]

 [/CRITERIA=[ITER {100**}] [CKDER {0.5**}]]
                  {n    }         {n    }

    [SSCON {1E-8**}]  [PCON {1E-8**}]  [RCON {1E-8**}]]
           {n     }        {n     }          {n     }
```

**Default if subcommand is omitted.
Example

```
MODEL PROGRAM A=.5 B=1.6.
COMPUTE PRED=A*SPEED**B.
DERIVATIVES.
COMPUTE D.A=SPEED**B.
COMPUTE D.B=A*LN(SPEED)*SPEED**B.
NLR STOP WITH SPEED.
```

Overview

NLR (Nonlinear Regression) estimates parameter values and regression statistics for models that are not linear in their parameters. NLR uses a Levenberg-Marquardt algorithm to solve unconstrained models. For constrained problems, use CNLR (Constrained NonLinear Regression), which is available in SPSS for OS/2, Macintosh, CMS, and other systems. It is a more general procedure and uses a sequential quadratic programming algorithm.

Options

Any number of transformation commands can follow the MODEL PROGRAM command in order to define complex models. Derivatives can be supplied with the optional DERIVATIVES command followed by transformation commands. The SAVE subcommand can add predicted values, residuals, and derivatives to the active file. With the OUTFILE subcommand, final parameter estimates can be saved on a system file and used in subsequent analyses with the FILE subcommand. The iteration process can be controlled in several ways by the CRITERIA subcommand.

Basic Specification

The minimum specification requires three commands. MODEL PROGRAM specifies the initial parameter estimates. It must be followed by a COMPUTE command that generates a variable PRED to define the model. The NLR command specifies the dependent variable followed by the keyword WITH and the independent variables.

For each iteration, the residual sum of squares and estimated values of the model parameters will be displayed. Statistics generated include regression and residual sums of squares and mean squares, corrected and uncorrected total sums of squares, R squared, parameter estimates with their asymptotic standard errors and 95% confidence intervals, and an asymptotic correlation matrix of the parameter estimates.

Command Order

• The MODEL PROGRAM command must precede the NLR command and be followed by one or more transformation commands. The transformations in the MODEL PROGRAM block must follow any permanent transformations in a program because the SPSS system variables created by the MODEL PROGRAM transformations do not become a part of the active file.

• The optional DERIVATIVES command must follow the MODEL PROGRAM and its block of transformation commands. DERIVATIVES is followed by its own set of transformation commands, each of which calculates a derivative for

C

Command Reference

one of the parameters. DERIVATIVES and its transformation statements must precede the NLR command.

- The NLR command must follow the block of transformations for a MODEL PROGRAM command or a DERIVATIVES command if it is given.

- NLR subcommands may appear in any order.

Syntax Rules   **MODEL PROGRAM Command.** The MODEL PROGRAM command is required. Unless the parameter starting values are read from an existing system file with the FILE subcommand, each parameter must be assigned a value in the MODEL PROGRAM command. The MODEL PROGRAM command must be followed by one or more transformation commands, including at least one command that uses the parameters and the independent variables (or preceding transformations of these) to calculate the predicted value of the dependent variable. This predicted value defines the nonlinear model. There is no default model.

- Any acceptable SPSS/PC+ variable name can be used for a parameter in the MODEL PROGRAM command.

- Each parameter must be individually specified on the MODEL PROGRAM command. The TO keyword is not allowed.

- If the required COMPUTE command that defines the model in the MODEL PROGRAM block of transformation statements does not create a variable named PRED, a PRED subcommand must be used with the NLR command that follows. Variable labels can be assigned to the predicted values variable and its write format can be changed in the MODEL PROGRAM transformation commands. Missing values should not, however, be specified.

- The MODEL PROGRAM block of transformation statements can contain any kind of computational command (such as COMPUTE, IF, RECODE, or COUNT) in the transformation language. It cannot contain input commands (such as DATA LIST, GET, JOIN MATCH, or JOIN ADD).

- Transformations in the MODEL PROGRAM section are used only by NLR, and do not affect the active file.

DERIVATIVES Command. The DERIVATIVES command is optional and can be used to supply some or all of the derivatives of the model. DERIVATIVES is followed by a block of transformation statements for computing the derivatives. This set of statements can contain any kind of computational command (such as COMPUTE, IF, RECODE, or COUNT) in the transformation language and in the output command WRITE. It cannot contain input commands (such as DATA LIST, GET, JOIN MATCH, or JOIN ADD).

- To name the derivatives, specify the prefix D. before each parameter name.

- Once a derivative has been calculated by a transformation, the variable for that derivative can be used in subsequent transformations.

- If the DERIVATIVES command is not used, NLR numerically estimates derivatives for all the parameters. Providing derivatives reduces computational time and, in some situations, may result in a better solution.

- Transformations in the DERIVATIVES command are used only by NLR, and do not affect the active file.

NLR Command. The NLR command is required. Its minimum specification is a dependent variable followed by the keyword WITH and a list of independent variables.

- Only a single numeric dependent variable may be specified. This variable must be in the active file and cannot be a variable generated by MODEL PROGRAM or DERIVATIVES.

- The variable list of independent variables is required and must include every variable from the active file used in the MODEL PROGRAM and DERIVATIVES transformation commands. The TO convention may be used in specifying this list.

Limitations   • No more than 100 variables can be named in the independent variable list on the NLR command.

Cautions   • The derivatives supplied in the DERIVATIVES transformations must be correct. On the first iteration, NLR always checks any derivatives calculated on the DERIVATIVES command and compares them with numerically calculated derivatives. For each comparison, it computes an agreement score. A score of 1 indicates agreement to machine precision; a score of 0 indicates definite disagreement. If any score is below 1, NLR displays a table to show the worst (lowest) score for each derivative. If a score is less than 1, either an incorrect derivative was supplied or there are numerical problems in estimating the derivative. Highly correlated parameters may cause disagreement even when a correct derivative is supplied. If the agreement score is not 1, DERIVATIVES calculations should be checked. The smaller the score, the more likely it is that the derivative (or the model) is incorrectly specified. If any score falls below 0.5, the procedure stops. (This cutoff value can be changed with CHKDER on the CRITERIA subcommand.)

• If case weighting is in effect, NLR uses case weights when calculating the residual sum of squares and derivatives. The degrees of freedom in the ANOVA table are based on unweighted cases. When the model program is first invoked for each case, the weight variable's value is set equal to its value in the active file. The model program may recalculate that value. For example, to effect a robust estimation, the model program may recalculate the weight variable value as an inverse function of the residual magnitude. NLR uses the weight variable's value *after* the model program executes.

• The selection of good initial values for the parameters selected in the MODEL PROGRAM is very important to the operation of NLR. The selection of poor initial values can result in no solution, a local rather than a general solution, or a physically impossible solution. (Information on selecting initial values can be found in Part B of this manual.)

Missing Values   Cases with missing values for any of the dependent or independent variables named on the NLR command are excluded.

• Predicted values, but not residuals, can be calculated for cases with missing values on the dependent variable.

• NLR ignores cases that have missing, negative, or zero weights. The procedure displays a warning message if it encounters any negative or zero weights at any time during its execution.

• An error message that the predicted value and some or all of the derivatives are missing for every case may be the result of omitting a variable used in the MODEL PROGRAM or the DERIVATIVES command from the independent variable list on the NLR command.

Example
```
MODEL PROGRAM A=.5 B=1.6.
COMPUTE PRED=A*SPEED**B.
DERIVATIVES.
COMPUTE D.A=SPEED**B.
COMPUTE D.B=A*LN(SPEED)*SPEED**B.
NLR STOP WITH SPEED.
```

• MODEL PROGRAM assigns values to the model parameters A and B.

• COMPUTE generates the variable PRED that is used to define the nonlinear model using parameters A and B and the variable SPEED from the active file. Because this variable is named PRED, the PRED subcommand is not required on NLR.

• DERIVATIVES indicates that calculations for derivatives are being supplied.

• The two COMPUTE statements in the DERIVATIVES transformations list calculate the derivatives for the parameters A and B. If either one had been omitted, NLR would have calculated it numerically.

• NLR declares the dependent variable STOP and one independent variable SPEED from the active file.

OUTFILE Subcommand

OUTFILE stores final parameter estimates for use in a subsequent session. The only specification on OUTFILE is the target system file. Some or all of the values from this system file can be read into an NLR procedure by using the FILE subcommand. The system file created by the OUTFILE subcommand stores the following variables:

- All the parameter variables named on the MODEL PROGRAM command.
- The sum of squared residuals (named SSE).
- The number of cases on which the analysis was based (named NCASES).
- If variables named SSE or NCASES are created in the model, an error will result.

The SSE and NCASES variables have no labels or missing values. The print and write format for SSE is F10.8. The print and write format for NCASES is F8.0.

Example

```
MODEL PROGRAM A=.5 B=1.6.
COMPUTE PRED=A*SPEED**B.
NLR STOP WITH SPEED /OUTFILE='PARAM.SYS'.
```

- OUTFILE generates a system file containing one case for four variables: A and B, SSE, and NCASES.

FILE Subcommand

FILE reads starting values for the parameters from a system file created by an OUTFILE subcommand from a previous NLR procedure. The only specification on FILE is the system file that contains the starting values. When starting values are read from a file, they do not need to be specified on the MODEL PROGRAM command. The MODEL PROGRAM command simply names the parameter variables that correspond to the variables in the system file.

- The parameters do not have to be named in the order they occur in the system file, and all the variables contained in the file need not be named.
- Some new parameters may be specified for the model on the MODEL PROGRAM while others are read from the designated system file.
- To read starting values from a system file and then replace those system file values with the final results from NLR, specify the same file on the FILE and OUTFILE subcommands. The input file is read completely before anything is written on the output file.

Example

```
MODEL PROGRAM A B C=1 D=3.
COMPUTE PRED=A*SPEED**B + C*SPEED**D.
NLR STOP WITH SPEED /FILE=PARAM /OUTFILE=PARAM.
```

- MODEL PROGRAM names four of the parameters used to calculate PRED but assigns values to only C and D. The values of A and B are read from the existing system file PARAM.
- After NLR computes the final estimates of the four parameters, OUTFILE writes over the old input file. If in addition to these new final estimates the former starting values of A and B are still desired, different system files can be specified on the FILE and OUTFILE subcommands.

PRED Subcommand

PRED identifies the predicted values variable for NLR. Its only specification is a variable name, which must be identical to the variable name used to calculate predicted values in the MODEL PROGRAM command. If the variable that defines the nonlinear model in the MODEL PROGRAM block of transformation is not named PRED, the PRED subcommand is required.

Example

```
MODEL PROGRAM A=.5 B=1.6.
COMPUTE PSTOP=A*SPEED**B.
NLR STOP WITH SPEED /PRED=PSTOP.
```

- COMPUTE in the MODEL PROGRAM transformation command list creates a variable named PSTOP to temporarily store the predicted values for the dependent variable STOP.
- PRED identifies PSTOP as the model to be used for the NLR procedure.

SAVE Subcommand   SAVE is used to save the temporary variables for the predicted values, residuals, and derivatives created by the MODEL PROGRAM and DERIVATIVES commands to the active file. The minimum specification is SAVE and a single keyword. If the active file already contains a variable with the same name as one of the variables generated by SAVE, an error message results and NLR will not be run. The following keywords are available and can be used in any combination. Although the keywords may be specified in any order on the SAVE subcommand, the new variables are always appended to the active file in the order in which the keywords creating them appear on the keyword list.

PRED   *Save the predicted values.* The variable's name, label, and formats are those specified for it in the MODEL PROGRAM transformation list.

RESID [(varname)]   *Save the residuals variable.* By default, the name of the variable is the keyword name RESID. Any keyword that begins with RES may be substituted. Optionally, a name for the variable can be specified in parentheses. The residuals variable has the same print and write format as the predicted variable created by MODEL PROGRAM. It has no variable label and no values defined as missing. It is system-missing for any case in which either the dependent variable is missing or the predicted value cannot be computed.

DERIVATIVES   *Save the derivative variables.* The derivative variable names are created by adding the prefix D. to the first six characters of the parameter names. Derivative variables use the print and write formats of the predicted variable and have no value labels or defined missing values. Derivative variables are saved in the same order as the parameters named on the MODEL PROGRAM command. Derivatives are saved for all parameters, whether or not the derivative was supplied by the DERIVATIVES command.

Asymptotic standard errors of predicted values and residuals, and special residuals used for outlier detection and influential case analysis are not provided by the NLR procedure. However, the asymptotically correct values for all these statistics can be calculated using the SAVE subcommand with NLR and then using the REGRESSION procedure. In REGRESSION, the NLR residuals are used as the dependent variable and the derivatives of the model parameters as independent variables. Casewise plots, standard errors of prediction, partial regression plots, and other diagnostics of the regression are valid for the nonlinear model.

Example   MODEL PROGRAM A=.5 B=1.6.
COMPUTE PSTOP=A*SPEED**B.
NLR STOP WITH SPEED /PRED=PSTOP
  /SAVE=RESID(RSTOP) DERIVATIVES PRED.
REGRESSION VARIABLES=RSTOP D.A D.B
  /DEPENDENT=RSTOP /ENTER D.A D.B /RESIDUALS.

• SAVE adds four new variables to the active file: PSTOP, RSTOP, D.A, and D.B, in that order.

• RESID creates the residuals variable RSTOP.

• DERIVATIVES creates the derivative variables D.A and D.B.

• Since the PRED subcommand is used to identify PSTOP as the predicted variable in the nonlinear model, PRED adds the variable PSTOP to the active file.

• The subcommand RESIDUALS for REGRESSION produces the default analysis of residuals.

C

Command Reference

CRITERIA Subcommand

CRITERIA controls the values of the five cutoff points used to stop the iterative calculations in NLR. The minimum specification is the subcommand and any number of the keywords with an appropriate value. Each keyword's value can be specified in parentheses, after an equals sign, or after a space or comma.

ITER n   *Maximum number of iterations allowed.* Any positive integer can be specified for *n*. The default is 100 iterations per parameter. If the search for a solution stops because this limit is exceeded, NLR issues a warning message.

SSCON n   *Convergence criterion for the sum of squares.* Any non-negative number can be specified for *n*. The default is 1E−8. If successive iterations fail to reduce the sum of squares by this proportion, the procedure stops. Specifying n=0 disables this criterion.

PCON n   *Convergence criterion for the parameter values.* Specify any non-negative number for *n*. The default is 1E−8. If successive iterations fail to change any of the parameter values by this proportion, the procedure stops. Specifying 0 disables this criterion.

RCON n   *Convergence criterion for the correlation between the residuals and the derivatives.* Any non-negative number can be specified for *n*. The default is 1E−8. If the largest value for the correlation between the residuals and the derivatives becomes this small, the procedure stops because it lacks the information it needs to estimate a direction for its next move. This criterion is often referred to as a gradient convergence criterion. Specifying 0 disables this criterion.

CKDER n   *Critical value for derivative checking.* A number between 0 and 1 must be specified for n; the default is 0.5. If any score falls below the CKDER value on the first iteration, NLR terminates and issues an error message. Specifying 0 disables this criterion.

Example

```
MODEL PROGRAM A=.5 B=1.6.
COMPUTE PRED=A*SPEED**B.
NLR STOP WITH SPEED /CRITERIA=ITER(80) SSCON=.000001.
```

• CRITERIA changes two of the five iteration cutoff values, ITER and SSCON, and leaves the remaining three, PCON, RCON, or CKDER, at their default values.

References

Draper, N. R., and H. Smith. 1981. *Applied regression analysis,* 2nd ed. New York: John Wiley & Sons.

Gill, P. E., W. Murray, M. A. Saunders, and M. H. Wright. 1984. Procedures for optimization problems with a mixture of bounds and general linear constraints. *ACM Transactions on Mathematical Software* 10(3)(September): 282–296.

Hinds, M.A., and G. A. Milliken. 1982. Statistical methods to use nonlinear models to compare silage treatments. Unpublished paper.

Kvalseth, T. O. 1985. Cautionary note about R squared. *American Statistical Association* 39(4)(Pt.1): 279–285.

PROBIT

```
PROBIT response count varname OF observation count varname

      WITH varlist [BY varname(min,max)]

[/MISSING={LISTWISE**}]  [/MODEL={PROBIT**}]  [/LOG[={10**  }]]
         {INCLUDE  }            {LOGIT   }          {2.718*}
         {DEFAULT  }            {BOTH    }          {base  }
                                                    {NONE  }


[/CRITERIA=[CONVERGE({0.001**})]  [ITERATE({20**})]  [P({0.15**})]]
                    {eps   }               {n  }       {p    }


[/NATRES[=c]]

[/PRINT=[ALL]  [CI**]  [FREQ**]  [RMP**]  [PARALL]  [NONE]  [DEFAULT]]
```

**Default if the subcommand is omitted.
*Default if the subcommand is included and the specification omitted.

Example:
```
PROBIT   R OF N BY ROOT(1,2) WITH X
   /MODEL = BOTH.
```

Overview

PROBIT can be used to estimate the effects of one or more independent variables on a dichotomous dependent variable (such as dead or alive, employed or unemployed, product purchased or not). The program is designed for dose-response analyses and related models, but PROBIT can also estimate logistic regression models.

Options

Specifying the Model. You can specify a PROBIT or LOGIT response model, or both, for the observed response proportions. See MODEL Subcommand.

Transform Predictors. You can specify the base of the log transformation applied to all predictors. You can also request no log transformation of the predictors. See LOG Subcommand.

Natural Response Rates. You can instruct PROBIT to estimate the natural response rate (threshold) of the model, or you can supply a known natural response rate to be used in the solution. See NATRES Subcommand.

Algorithm Control Parameters. You can specify values of algorithm control parameters such as the limit on iterations. See CRITERIA Subcommand.

Statistics. By default, PROBIT calculates frequencies, fiducial confidence intervals, and the relative median potency. It also produces a plot of the observed probits or logits against the values of a single independent variable. Optionally, you can obtain a test of the parallelism of regression lines for different levels of the grouping variable. You can suppress any or all of these statistics. See PRINT Subcommand.

Basic Specification

• The basic specification is the response count variable, keyword OF, the observation count variable, keyword WITH, and at least one independent variable. PROBIT calculates maximum likelihood estimates for the parameters of the requested response model. The procedure automatically displays estimates of the regression coefficient and intercept terms, their standard errors, a covariance matrix of parameter estimates, and a Pearson chi-square goodness-of-fit test of the model.

Subcommand Order

• The variable specification must be first.
• Subcommands can be named in any order.

Command Reference

Syntax Rules
- The variables must include a response count, an observation count, and at least one predictor. A categorical grouping variable is optional.
- All subcommands are optional and each can appear only once.
- Generally, data should not be entered for individual observations. PROBIT expects predictor values, response counts, and total number of observations as the input case.
- If the data are available only in case-by-case form, first use AGGREGATE to compute the required response and observation counts.

Operations
- The transformed response variable is predicted as a linear function of other variables.
- PROBIT always adds 5 to the intercept to make the new values uniformly positive (or nearly so), as in Finney (1971).
- PROBIT always divides the logit by 2 (and adds 5 to the intercept) to produce values similar to those derived from the probit transformation.
- If individual cases are entered in the data, PROBIT skips the plot of transformed response proportions and predictor values.
- If individual cases are entered, the degrees of freedom for the chi-square goodness-of-fit statistic are based on the individual cases.

Limitations
- Only one prediction model can be tested in a single PROBIT procedure, although both probit and logit response models can be requested for that prediction.
- Confidence limits, the plot of transformed response proportions and predictor values, and computation of relative median potency are necessarily limited to single-predictor models.

Example
```
PROBIT  R OF N BY ROOT(1,2) WITH X
    /MODEL = BOTH.
```
- This example specifies that both the probit and logit response models be applied to the response frequency R, given N total observations and the predictor X.
- By default, the predictor is log transformed.

Example

To produce collapsed input cases procedure AGGREGATE can be used. For a dose-response model (from Finney, 1971), a researcher tests four different preparations at varying doses and observes whether each subject responds. The data are individually recorded for each subject, with 1 indicating a response and 0 indicating no response. The data recorded for each subject can be summarized by cases representing all subjects who received the same preparation at the same dose.

```
TITLE  'AGGREGATING CASE-BY-CASE DATA'.

DATA LIST FREE/PREPARTN DOSE RESPONSE.
BEGIN DATA
     1.00     1.50      .00
      ...
     4.00    20.00     1.00
END DATA.
AGGREGATE OUTFILE=*
    /BREAK=PREPARTN DOSE
    /SUBJECTS=N(RESPONSE)
    /NRESP=SUM(RESPONSE).
PROBIT NRESP OF SUBJECTS BY PREPARTN(1,4) WITH DOSE.
```

- AGGREGATE computes summary cases for observations having the same values for the group and predictor variables, PREPARTN and DOSE.
- The number of cases having a nonmissing response is recorded in the aggregated variable SUBJECTS.
- Because RESPONSE is coded as 0 for no response and 1 for a response, the SUM of the values gives the number of observations with a response.

- PROBIT requests a default analysis.
- The parameter estimates for this analysis are the same as those calculated for individual cases in the next example. The chi-square test, however, is based on the number of dosages.

Example

```
TITLE  'USING DATA IN CASE-BY-CASE FORM'.

DATA LIST FREE / PREPARTN DOSE RESPONSE.
BEGIN DATA
1 1.5 0
...
4 20.0 1
END DATA.
COMPUTE SUBJECT = 1.
PROBIT RESPONSE OF SUBJECT BY PREPARTN(1,4) WITH DOSE.
```

- This dose-response model (using the same data from Finney, 1971) illustrates case-by-case analysis. The number of observations is always 1 and is stored in variable SUBJECT.
- PROBIT warns that the data are in case-by-case form and that the plot is therefore skipped.
- Degrees of freedom for the goodness-of-fit test are based on individual cases, not dosage groups.
- PROBIT displays predicted and observed frequencies for all individual input cases unless the output is suppressed on PRINT.

Variable Specification

The PROBIT variable specification identifies the variables for response count, observation count, groups, and predictors. The variable specification is required.

- The variable specification must be first. The specification shows the response count variable, followed by keyword OF, then the observation count variable.
- If the value of the response count variable exceeds that of the observation count variable, a procedure error occurs and PROBIT is not executed.
- One or more continuous predictors must be specified following keyword WITH. The number of predictors is limited only by available workspace.
- To specify a categorical grouping variable, name the variable after keyword BY, and, in parentheses after the variable name, specify a range to indicate the minimum and maximum values. Each integer value in the specified range defines a group. Only one variable can be specified; it must be numeric and can contain only integer values.
- Cases with values for the grouping variable that are outside the specified range are excluded from the analysis.
- Keywords BY and WITH can appear in either order. However, both must follow the response and observation count variables.
- OF is not a reserved word and can be used as a variable name.

Example

```
PROBIT R OF N WITH X.
```

- The number of observations having the measured response appears in variable R, and the total number of observations is in N. The predictor is X.

Example

```
PROBIT  R OF N BY ROOT(1,2) WITH X.
PROBIT  R OF N WITH X BY ROOT(1,2).
```

- Because BY and WITH can be used in either order, these two commands are equivalent. Each command specifies X as a continuous variable and ROOT as a categorical grouping variable used to predict response rates.
- Groups are identified by the levels of variable ROOT, which may be 1 or 2.
- For each combination of predictor and grouping variables, the variable R contains the number of observations with the response of interest, and N contains the total number of observations.

MODEL Subcommand

MODEL specifies the form of the dichotomous response model.

The response models can be thought of as transformations (T) of response rates, which are proportions or probabilities (p). The transformations, whether logit or probit, add 5 to make the new values uniformly positive (or nearly so), as in Finney (1971). For the probit response model, the program uses

$$T(p) = PROBIT(p) + 5$$

A probit is the inverse of the cumulative standard normal distribution function. Thus, for any proportion, the probit transformation returns the value below which that proportion of standard normal deviates is found. Hence:

$$T(0.025) = PROBIT(0.025) + 5 = -1.96 + 5 = 3.04$$
$$T(0.400) = PROBIT(0.400) + 5 = -0.25 + 5 = 4.75$$
$$T(0.500) = PROBIT(0.500) + 5 = 0.00 + 5 = 5.00$$
$$T(0.950) = PROBIT(0.950) + 5 = 1.64 + 5 = 6.64$$

A logit is simply the natural log of the odds ratio, $p/(1 - p)$. In the PROBIT procedure, the response function is given as

$$T(p) = \log_e(p/(1 - p)/2 + 5)$$

The simple logit is scaled by 2 to produce values similar to those derived from the probit transformation. Hence:

$$T(0.025) = LOGIT(0.025)/2 + 5 = -1.83 + 5 = 3.17$$
$$T(0.400) = LOGIT(0.400)/2 + 5 = -0.20 + 5 = 4.80$$
$$T(0.500) = LOGIT(0.500)/2 + 5 = 0.00 + 5 = 5.00$$
$$T(0.950) = LOGIT(0.950)/2 + 5 = 1.47 + 5 = 6.47$$

- If subgroups and multiple predictor variables are defined, PROBIT estimates a separate intercept (a_i) for each subgroup and a regression coefficient (b_j) for each predictor.

PROBIT   *Probit response model.* This is the default.

LOGIT   *Logit response model.*

BOTH   *Both probit and logit response models.* PROBIT displays all the output for the logit model, followed by the output for the probit model.

LOG Subcommand

LOG specifies the base of the logarithmic transformation of the predictor variables or suppresses the default log transformation.

- LOG applies to all predictors.
- To transform only selected predictors, use COMPUTE commands before the PROBIT procedure. Then specify NONE on LOG.
- If LOG is omitted, a logarithm base of 10 is used.
- If LOG is used without a specification, a logarithm base of 2.718 is used.

10   *Logarithm base of 10.* This is the default if the LOG subcommand is omitted.

2.718   *The natural logarithmic base,* e. This is the default if LOG is specified without an explicit base.

base   *Logarithm base other than defaults.* To specify any other base, indicate its numeric value following the equals sign on LOG.

NONE   *No transformation of the predictors.*

Example

```
PROBIT R OF N BY ROOT (1,2) WITH X
  /LOG = 2.
```

- LOG specifies a base 2 logarithmic transformation.

CRITERIA Subcommand

Use CRITERIA to specify the values of PROBIT algorithm-control parameters. Specify any or all of the keywords below. Defaults remain in effect for parameters that are not changed.

CONVERGE(eps)   *Criterion for convergence of predicted values.* Specify the cutoff value of the convergence criterion for the iterative estimation algorithm. The default value is 0.001.

ITERATE(n) *Iteration limit.* Specify the maximum number of iterations. The default is 20.

P(p) *Heterogeneity criterion probability.* Specify the cutoff value for the significance of the goodness-of-fit test. The default is 0.15. The cutoff value determines whether a heterogeneity factor is included in calculations of confidence levels for effective levels of a predictor. If the significance of chi-square is greater than the cutoff, the heterogeneity factor is not included.

NATRES Subcommand

Use NATRES in either of two ways: to instruct PROBIT to estimate the natural (or threshold) response rate of the model, or to supply a known natural response rate to be used in the solution.

- To instruct PROBIT to estimate the natural response rate of the model, a control level must be provided. Indicate the control level by giving a 0 value to any of the predictor variables.

- To supply a known natural response rate as a constraint on the model solution, specify a constant on NATRES. The value of the constant must be between 0 and 1 but cannot be equal to 0 or 1.

Example
```
DATA LIST FREE / SOLUTION DOSE NOBSN NRESP.
BEGIN DATA
1   5  100 20
1  10   80 30
1   0  100 10
. . .
END DATA.
PROBIT NRESP OF NOBSN BY SOLUTION(1,4) WITH DOSE
  /NATRES.
```

- This example reads four variables and requests a default analysis with an estimate of the natural response rate.

- The predictor variable, DOSE, has a value of 0 for the third case.

- The response count (10) and the observation count (100) for this case establish the initial estimate of the control level for the analysis.

Example
```
DATA LIST FREE / SOLUTION DOSE NOBSN NRESP.
BEGIN DATA
1   5  100 20
1  10   80 30
. . .
END DATA.
PROBIT NRESP OF NOBSN BY SOLUTION(1,4) WITH DOSE
  /NATRES = 0.10.
```

- This example reads four variables and requests an analysis in which the natural response rate is set to 0.10. No control level is included in the data.

PRINT Subcommand

Use PRINT to control the statistics calculated by PROBIT.

- By default, FREQ, CI, and RMP are calculated.

- If PRINT is used, the requested statistics are calculated in addition to the plot and parameter estimates.

DEFAULT *FREQ, CI, and RMP.* This is the default.

ALL *All available output.* This is the same as requesting FREQ, CI, RMP, and PARALL.

FREQ *Frequencies.* Display a table of observed and predicted frequencies with their residual values. If observations are entered on a case-by-case basis, this listing can be quite lengthy.

CI *Fiducial confidence intervals.* Print Finney's (1971) fiducial confidence intervals for the levels of the predictor needed to produce each proportion of responses. PROBIT displays this default output for single-predictor models only. If a categorical grouping variable is specified, PROBIT produces a table of confidence intervals for each group. If the Pearson chi-square goodness-of-fit test is significant (p < 0.15 by default), PROBIT uses a heterogeneity factor to calculate the limits.

RMP   *Relative median potency.* Display the relative median potency (RMP) of each pair of groups defined by the grouping variable. PROBIT displays this default output for single-predictor models only. For any pair of groups, the RMP is the ratio of the *stimulus tolerances* in those groups. Stimulus tolerance is the value of the predictor necessary to produce a 50% response rate. If the derived model for one predictor and two groups estimates that a predictor value of 21 produces a 50% response rate in the first group, and a predictor value of 15 produces a 50% response rate in the second group, the relative median potency would be $21/15 = 1.40$. In biological assay analyses, RMP measures the comparative strength of preparations.

PARALL   *Parallelism test.* Produce a test of the parallelism of regression lines for different levels of the grouping variable. This test displays a chi-square value and its associated probability. It requires an additional pass through the data and, thus, additional processing time.

NONE   *No conditional displayed output.* This option can be used to override any other specification on the PRINT subcommand for PROBIT. With NONE, only the unconditional output is displayed: the PROBIT case and model information, the PROBIT plot (for a single-predictor model), and the parameter estimates and covariances for the PROBIT model.

MISSING Subcommand

MISSING controls the missing-value treatment. Cases containing system-missing values for any variable in the analysis are always deleted. In the output, PROBIT indicates how many cases it rejected because of missing data. This number is included with the *DATA information* displayed at the beginning of the output.

LISTWISE   *Delete cases with missing values listwise.* PROBIT deletes cases having a missing value for any variable. This is the default, and you can make it explicit by using the keyword DEFAULT.

INCLUDE   *Include user-missing values.* PROBIT treats user-missing values as valid.

SURVIVAL

```
SURVIVAL TABLES=survival varlist

                    [BY independent varlist (min,max)...]

                    [BY control varlist (min,max)...]

    /INTERVALS=THRU n BY a [THRU m BY b ...]

    /STATUS=status variable({min,max}) FOR {ALL            }
                           {value }     {survival varlist}
    [/STATUS=...]

    [/PLOTS({ALL**   })={ALL**           } BY {ALL**               }
            {LOGSURV }  {survival varlist}   {independent varlist}
            {SURVIVAL}
            {HAZARD  }  BY {ALL**        }]
            {DENSITY }     {control varlist}

    [/PRINT={TABLE**}]
            {NOTABLE}

    [/COMPARE={ALL**           } BY {ALL**               }
              {survival varlist}   {independent varlist}

              BY {ALL**        }]
                 {control varlist}

    [/CALCULATE=[{EXACT**     }] [PAIRWISE] [COMPARE]
                 {CONDITIONAL}
                 {APPROXIMATE}

    [/MISSING={GROUPWISE**} [INCLUDE]]
              {LISTWISE   }

    [/WRITE[={NONE**}]]
            {TABLES}
            {BOTH  }
```

**Default if the subcommand is omitted.

Example:
```
SURVIVAL TABLES=MOSFREE BY TREATMNT(1,3)
  /STATUS = PRISON (1) FOR MOSFREE
  /INTERVAL=THRU 24 BY 3.
```

Overview

SURVIVAL produces life tables, plots, and related statistics for examining the length of time between two events (Berkson & Gage, 1950). Cases can be classified into groups, and separate analyses and comparisons can be obtained for each group. The time interval between two dates can be calculated with the SPSS/PC+ date conversion function YRMODA.

Options

Life Tables. You can list the variables to be used in the analysis, including any control variables (see TABLES Subcommand). You can also suppress display of the life tables in the output (see PRINT Subcommand).

Intervals. SURVIVAL reports the percentage alive at various times after the initial event. You can select the time points for reporting with the INTERVALS subcommand.

Survival Status. To determine whether the terminal event has occurred for a particular observation, SURVIVAL checks the value of a status variable. See STATUS Subcommand.

Plots. You can plot the survival functions for all cases or separately for various subgroups. See PLOTS Subcommand.

Comparisons. When control variables are listed on TABLES, you can compare groups based on the Lee & Desu (1972) *D* statistic (see COMPARE Subcommand). Pairwise comparisons are available, as are approximate comparisons for aggregated data (see CALCULATE Subcommand).

Writing a File. You can write the life tables, including the labeling information, to a file for use with other programs, or with a graphics device that produces high-quality graphics. See WRITE Subcommand.

Basic Specification

The basic specification requires three subcommands: TABLES, INTERVALS, and STATUS.

- TABLES: Identify at least one survival variable from the active system file. Optionally, use keyword BY to specify control variables.
- INTERVALS: To divide the time period into equal intervals, specify THRU followed by a constant which defines the termination point for the analysis. Then specify BY and a constant which defines the length of each interval.
- STATUS: For each variable, name a variable that indicates whether the terminal event occurred. In parentheses after the variable name, specify the value(s) that indicate that the terminal event occurred.

The basic specification displays one or more life tables, depending on the number of survival and control variables specified.

Subcommand Order

- TABLES must be first.
- Remaining subcommands can be named in any order.

Limitations

- Maximum 20 survival variables.
- Maximum 100 control variables on the first- and second-order control variable lists combined.
- Maximum 20 THRU . . . BY . . . specifications on INTERVALS.
- Maximum 35 values can appear on a plot.

Example

```
SURVIVAL TABLES=MOSFREE BY TREATMNT(1,3)
 /STATUS = PRISON (1) FOR MOSFREE
 /INTERVALS = THRU 24 BY 3.
```

- Survival analysis is used to examine the length of time between release from prison and return to prison for prisoners in three treatment programs. The variable MOSFREE is the length of time in months to reentry. The variable TREATMNT indicates the treatment group for each case.
- A value of 1 on the STATUS variable PRISON indicates a terminal outcome. That is, cases coded as 1 have returned to prison. Cases with other nonnegative values for PRISON have not returned. Such cases are called *censored* since we don't know their final outcome.
- Life tables are produced for each of the three subgroups. INTERVALS specifies that the survival experience be described every three months for the first two years.

Example

The data in this example are from a study of 647 cancer patients. The variables are

- TREATMNT—the type of treatment received.
- ONSETMO, ONSETYR—month and year cancer was discovered.
- RECURSIT—indicates whether a recurrence took place.
- RECURMO, RECURYR—month and year of recurrence.
- OUTCOME—status of patient at end of study: alive or dead.
- DEATHMO, DEATHYR—month and year of death, or, for those who are still presumed alive, the date of last contact.

Using these date variables and the YRMODA function, the number of months from onset to recurrence and from onset to death or last contact are calculated. These new variables become the survival variables with TREATMNT as the single control variable. The SPSS/PC+ commands are

```
SET WIDTH=132.
DATA LIST   FILE = SURVDATA/ 1 TREATMNT 15 ONSETMO 19-20
                ONSETYR 21-22 RECURSIT 48 RECURMO 49-50 RECURYR 51-52
                OUTCOME 56 DEATHMO 57-58 DEATHYR 59-60.
COMMENT    TRANSFORM ALL DATES TO DAYS FROM AN ARBITRARY TIME
POINT.
COMPUTE    ONSDATE=YRMODA(ONSETYR,ONSETMO,15).
COMPUTE    RECDATE=YRMODA(RECURYR,RECURMO,15).
COMPUTE    DEATHDT=YRMODA(DEATHYR,DEATHMO,15).

COMMENT    NOW COMPUTE ELAPSED TIME IN MONTHS FROM DIAGNOSIS TO
                LAST CONTACT OR DEATH.
COMPUTE    ONSSURV = (DEATHDT-ONSDATE)/30.

COMMENT    COMPUTE TIME TO RECURRENCE.
IF   RECURSIT EQ O RECSURV = ONSSURV.
IF   RECURSIT NE O RECSURV = (RECDATE-ONSDATE)/30.

VARIABLE LABELS   TREATMNT 'PATIENT TREATMENT'
                ONSSURV 'MONTHS FROM ONSET TO DEATH'
                RECSURV 'MONTHS FROM ONSET TO RECURRENCE'.
VALUE LABELS   TREATMNT 1 'TREATMENT A' 2 'TREATMENT B'
                3 'TREATMENT C'.
SURVIVAL   TABLES = ONSSURV,RECSURV BY TREATMNT(1,3)
   /STATUS = RECURSIT(1,9) FOR RECSURV
   /STATUS = OUTCOME(3,4) FOR ONSSURV
   /INTERVALS = THRU 50 BY 5 THRU 100 BY 10
   /PLOTS /COMPARE /CALCULATE=CONDITIONAL PAIRWISE.
```

- The SET command sets the page width to 132.

- The onset, recurrence, and death dates are transformed to days from a starting date using the YRMODA function in the COMPUTE command. The constant 15 is used as the day argument for YRMODA since only month and year were recorded, not the actual day.

- ONSSURV, the first survival variable, is the number of months between the date of death (or survival) and the date the cancer was discovered (ONSDATE). The number of days between the two events is divided by 30 to convert it from days to months.

- RECSURV, the second survival variable, is calculated conditionally using the IF command. For cases with RECURSIT values of 0, indicating no recurrence took place, the length of time to recurrence is equal to the length of time from diagnosis to last contact or death.

- The TABLES subcommand in SURVIVAL specifies two survival variables, ONSSURV and RECSURV, and one control variable, TREATMNT.

- The status variable for RECSURV is RECURSIT, with codes 1 THRU 9 indicating that the termination event, recurrence, took place. OUTCOME is the status variable for ONSSURV with codes 3 and 4 indicating death.

- The INTERVALS subcommand requests reporting at five-month intervals for the first 50 months, and at ten-month intervals for the remaining 50 months.

- The default plots are requested using PLOTS.

- COMPARE with no specifications requests comparisons for all variables.

- Keyword CONDITIONAL on the CALCULATE subcommand requests approximate comparisons if memory is insufficient for exact comparisons. Keyword PAIRWISE requests that all pairs of treatments be compared.

TABLES Subcommand

TABLES identifies the survival variables and control variables to be included in the analysis.

- The minimum specification is one or more survival variables.

- To specify one or more first-order control variables, use keyword BY followed by the control variable(s).

- Separate life tables are generated for each combination of values of the first-order and second-order controls.

- Each control variable must be followed by a value range in parentheses. These values must be integers separated by a comma or a blank. Noninteger values in the data are truncated and the case is assigned to a subgroup based on the integer portion of its value on the variable. To specify only one value for a control variable, use the same value for the minimum and maximum.

- Use a second BY keyword to separate first- and second-order control variable lists. As with first-order control variables, second-order control variables must be followed by a value range in parentheses.

- To generate life tables for all cases combined, as well as for control variables, use COMPUTE to create a variable that has the same value for all cases. With this variable as a control, tables for the entire set of cases, as well as for the control variables, will be produced.

Example
```
SURVIVAL TABLES = MOSFREE BY TREATMNT(1,3) BY RACE(1,2)
  /STATUS = PRISON(1)
  /INTERVAL=THRU 24 BY 3.
```

- MOSFREE is the survival variable, and TREATMNT is the first-order control variable. The second BY defines RACE as a second-order control group having a value of 1 or 2.

- Keyword FOR is omitted on STATUS, since it applies to all survival variables on the TABLES subcommand (in this case, just MOSFREE).

- Six life tables are produced, one for each pair of values for the two control variables. Each is accompanied by its respective median survival time.

INTERVALS Subcommand

INTERVALS determines the period of time to be examined and how the time will be grouped for the analysis. Only one INTERVALS subcommand can be used in a SURVIVAL command. The interval specifications apply to all the survival variables listed on TABLES.

- Specify THRU, the final value, BY, and the grouping increment. SURVIVAL always uses 0 as the starting point for the first interval. You do not specify the 0. The INTERVALS specification must begin with keyword THRU.

- The final interval includes any observations that exceed the range specified with keyword THRU.

- The grouping increment, which follows keyword BY, is in the same units as the survival variable.

- The period to be examined can be divided into intervals of varying lengths by repeating the THRU and BY keywords. The period must be divided in ascending order. If the time period is not a multiple of the increment, the endpoint of the period is adjusted upward to the next even multiple of the BY value.

- When the period is divided into intervals of varying lengths by repeating the THRU and BY specifications, the adjustment of one period to produce even intervals changes the starting point of subsequent periods. If the upward adjustment of one period completely overlaps the next period, no adjustment is made and the procedure terminates with an error.

Example
```
SURVIVAL TABLES = MOSFREE BY TREATMNT(1,3)
  /STATUS = PRISON(1) FOR MOSFREE
  /INTERVALS=THRU 12 BY 1 THRU 24 BY 3.
```

- MOSFREE (months free) is the survival variable, and TREATMNT is the first-order control variable. A terminal event for MOSFREE is coded with a value of 1 for PRISON.

- INTERVALS produces life tables computed from 0 to 12 months at one-month intervals and from 13 to 24 months at three-month intervals.

Example
```
/INTERVALS = THRU 50 BY 6
```

- The value following BY (6) does not divide evenly into the period to which it applies (50). Thus, the endpoint of the period is adjusted upward to the next even multiple of the BY value, resulting in a period of 54 with 9 intervals of 6 units each.

Example   /INTERVALS = THRU 50 BY 6 THRU 100 BY 10 THRU 200 BY 20

- The period is divided into intervals of varying lengths by repeating the THRU and BY specifications. The adjustment of one period to produce even intervals changes the starting point of subsequent periods. Thus, the INTERVALS specification is automatically readjusted to result in a first period through 54 by 6, a second period through 104 by 10, and a third period through 204 by 20.

STATUS Subcommand

To determine whether the terminal event has occurred for a particular observation, SURVIVAL checks the value of a status variable. STATUS lists the status variable associated with each survival variable and the codes which indicate that a terminal event occurred.

- Specify a status variable followed by a value range enclosed in parentheses. The value range identifies the codes that indicate that the terminal event has taken place. All cases with non-negative times that do not have a code in the value range are classified as censored cases, which are cases for whom the terminal event has not yet occurred. If the status variable does not apply to all the survival variables, specify FOR and the name of the survival variable(s) to which the status variable applies.

- Each survival variable on TABLES must have an associated status variable identified by a STATUS subcommand.

- Only one status variable can be listed on each STATUS subcommand. To specify multiple status variables, use multiple STATUS subcommands.

- If FOR is omitted on the STATUS specification, the status variable specification applies to all of the survival variables not named on another STATUS subcommand.

- If more than one STATUS subcommand omits keyword FOR, the final STATUS subcommand without FOR applies to all survival variables not specified by FOR in other STATUS subcommands. No warning is displayed.

Example   SURVIVAL ONSSURV BY TREATMNT (1,3)
     /INTERVALS = THRU 50 BY 5, THRU 100 BY 10
     /STATUS= OUTCOME (3,4) FOR ONSSURV.

- STATUS specifies that a code of 3 or 4 on OUTCOME means that the terminal event for the survival variable ONSSURV occurred.

Example   SURVIVAL TABLES = NOARREST MOSFREE BY TREATMNT(1,3)
     /STATUS = ARREST (1) FOR NOARREST
     /STATUS = PRISON (1)
     /INTERVAL=THRU 24 BY 3.

- STATUS defines the terminal event for NOARREST as a value of 1 for ARREST. Any other value for ARREST is considered censored.

- The second STATUS subcommand defines the value of 1 for PRISON as the terminal event. Keyword FOR is omitted. Thus, the status variable specification applies to MOSFREE, which is the only survival variable not named on another STATUS subcommand.

- Separate life tables are produced for each of the survival variables for each of the three values of TREATMNT.

PLOTS Subcommand

PLOTS produces plots of the cumulative survival distribution, the hazard function, and the probability density function. PLOTS can only plot the survival functions generated by the TABLES subcommand; PLOTS cannot eliminate control variables.

- The minimum specification, the subcommand PLOT, produces all available plots for each survival variable. Points on each plot are identified by values of the first-order control variables. If second-order controls are used, a separate plot is generated for every value of the second-order control variables.

- To request specific plots, specify, in parentheses following PLOTS, any combination of the keywords defined below.

C

Command Reference

• Optionally, generate plots for only a subset of the requested life tables. Use the same syntax as used on TABLES for specifying survival and control variables, omitting the value ranges. Each survival variable named on PLOTS must have as many control levels as were specified for that variable on TABLES; however, only one control variable need be specified for each level. If a required control level is omitted on the PLOTS specification, the default BY ALL is used for that level. Keyword ALL can be used to refer to an entire set of survival or control variables.

• To determine the number of plots that will be produced, multiply the number of functions plotted by the number of survival variables times the number of first-order controls times the number of distinct values represented in all of the second-order controls.

ALL   *Plot all available functions.* ALL is the default if PLOTS is used without specifications.

LOGSURV *Plot the cumulative survival distribution on a logarithmic scale.*

SURVIVAL *Plot the cumulative survival distribution on a linear scale.*

HAZARD   *Plot the hazard function.*

DENSITY *Plot the density function.*

Example

```
SURVIVAL TABLES = NOARREST MOSFREE BY TREATMNT(1,3)
 /STATUS = ARREST (1) FOR NOARREST
 /STATUS = PRISON (1) FOR MOSFREE
 /INTERVALS = THRU 24 BY 3
 /PLOTS (SURVIVAL,HAZARD) = MOSFREE.
```

• NOARREST with status variable ARREST and MOSFREE with status variable PRISON are the survival variables, and TREATMNT, the first-order control variable.

• Separate life tables are produced for each of the survival variables for each of the three values of TREATMNT.

• PLOTS produces plots of the cumulative survival distribution and the hazard rate for MOSFREE for the three values of TREATMNT, even though TREATMNT is not included on the PLOTS specification. Since plots are requested only for the survival variable MOSFREE, no plots are generated for variable NOARREST.

PRINT Subcommand

By default, SURVIVAL displays life tables. PRINT can be used to suppress the display of the life tables.

TABLE   *Display the life tables.* This is the default.

NOTABLE *Suppress the display of the life tables.* Only plots and comparisons are displayed. The WRITE subcommand, used to write the life tables to a file, can be used when NOTABLES is in effect.

Example

```
SURVIVAL TABLES = MOSFREE BY TREATMNT(1,3)
 /STATUS = PRISON (1) FOR MOSFREE
 /INTERVALS = THRU 24 BY 3
 /PLOTS (ALL)
 /PRINT = NOTABLE.
```

• MOSFREE with status variable PRISON is the survival variable, and TREATMNT, the first-order control variable.

• PLOTS produces all four available function plots for MOSFREE, controlling for the three categories of TREATMNT.

• PRINT NOTABLE suppresses the display of life tables.

COMPARE Subcommand

COMPARE compares the survival experience of subgroups defined by the control variables. At least one first-order control variable is required for calculating comparisons.

• The minimum specification, the subcommand keyword, produces comparisons using the TABLES variable list.

- Alternatively, specify the survival and control variables for the comparisons. Use the same syntax as used on TABLES for specifying survival and control variables, omitting the value ranges. Only variables that appear on TABLES can be listed on COMPARE, and their role as survival, first-order, and second-order control variables cannot be altered. Keyword TO can be used to refer to a group of variables and keyword ALL can be used to refer to an entire set of survival or control variables.

- By default, COMPARE calculates exact comparisons between subgroups. Use the CALCULATE subcommand to obtain pairwise comparisons or approximate comparisons.

Example
```
SURVIVAL TABLES = MOSFREE BY TREATMNT(1,3)
    /STATUS = PRISON (1) FOR MOSFREE
    /INTERVAL = THRU 24 BY 3
    /COMPARE.
```

- MOSFREE is the survival variable, and TREATMNT, the first-order control variable. Life tables are produced for each of the values of TREATMNT.

- COMPARE computes a test statistic, degrees of freedom, and observed significance level for the hypothesis that the three survival curves based on the values of TREATMNT are identical. (See Lee & Desu, 1972.)

Example
```
SURVIVAL TABLES=ONSSURV,RECSURV BY TREATMNT(1,3)
    /STATUS = RECURSIT(1,9) FOR RECSURV
    /STATUS = STATUS(3,4) FOR ONSSURV
    /INTERVAL=THRU 50 BY 5 THRU 100 BY 10
    /COMPARE=ONSSURV BY TREATMNT.
```

- COMPARE requests a comparison of ONSSURV by TREATMNT. No comparison is made of RECSURV by TREATMNT.

CALCULATE Subcommand

CALCULATE controls the comparisons of survival for subgroups specified on the COMPARE subcommand. If CALCULATE is specified, the COMPARE subcommand must also be specified.

- The minimum specification is a single keyword. EXACT is the default.

- Only one of the keywords EXACT, APPROXIMATE, and CONDITIONAL can be selected. If APPROXIMATE is used with either EXACT or CONDITIONAL, APPROXIMATE is in effect. If EXACT is used with CONDITIONAL, CONDITIONAL is in effect.

- PAIRWISE and COMPARE can be used for EXACT, APPROXIMATE, or CONDITIONAL comparisons.

- If CALCULATE is used without the COMPARE subcommand, CALCULATE is ignored. However, if CALCULATE=COMPARE is specified and the COMPARE subcommand is omitted, SPSS/PC+ generates an error message.

- Data can be entered into SURVIVAL for each individual case or aggregated for all cases in an interval. The way in which data are entered affects the way in which the statistic for comparing groups can be calculated. With individual data, you can obtain exact comparisons based on the survival experience of each observation. While this method is the most accurate, it requires that all of the data be in memory simultaneously. Thus, exact comparisons may be impractical for large samples. There are also situations in which individual data are not available and data aggregated by interval must be used. See Entering Aggregated Data, below.

EXACT   *Calculate exact comparisons.* This is the default.

APPROXIMATE   *Calculate approximate comparisons only.* Approximate comparisons are appropriate for aggregated data. The approximate comparison approach assumes that all events occur at the midpoint of the interval. Under EXACT comparisons, some of these midpoint ties can be resolved. However, if interval widths are not too great, the difference between EXACT and APPROXIMATE comparisons should be small.

CONDITIONAL   *Calculate approximate comparisons if memory is insufficient.* Approximate comparisons are produced only if there is insufficient memory available for exact comparisons.

PAIRWISE   *Perform pairwise comparisons.* Comparisons of all pairs of values of the first-order control variable are produced along with the overall comparison.

COMPARE   *Produce comparisons only.* Survival tables specified on TABLES are not computed and requests for plots are ignored. This allows all available workspace to be used for comparisons. The WRITE subcommand cannot be used when this specification is in effect.

Examples

```
SURVIVAL TABLES = MOSFREE BY TREATMNT(1,3)
   /STATUS = PRISON (1) FOR MOSFREE
   /INTERVAL = THRU 24 BY 3
   /COMPARE /CALCULATE = PAIRWISE.
```

• MOSFREE with status PRISON is the survival variable, and TREATMNT, the first-order control variable. Life tables are produced for each of the values of TREATMNT.

• CALCULATE=PAIRWISE computes test statistics, degrees of freedom, and observed significance levels for each pair of values of TREATMNT, as well as for an overall comparison of survival across all three TREATMNT subgroups. Hence TREATMNT group 1 is compared with TREATMNT group 2, group 1 with group 3, and group 2 with group 3. All comparisons are exact comparisons.

Example

```
SURVIVAL TABLES = MOSFREE BY TREATMNT(1,3)
   /STATUS = PRISON (1) FOR MOSFREE
   /INTERVAL = THRU 24 BY 3
   /COMPARE /CALCULATE = APPROXIMATE COMPARE.
```

• CALCULATE=APPROXIMATE computes the D statistic, degrees of freedom, and probability for the overall comparison of survival across all three TREATMNT subgroups using the approximate method.

• Because keyword COMPARE is specified on CALCULATE, survival tables are not computed.

Entering Aggregated Data

When aggregated survival information is available, the number of censored and uncensored cases at each time point must be entered. Two records are entered for each interval, one for censored cases and one for uncensored cases. The number of cases included on each record is used as the weight factor. If control variables are used, there must be a pair of records (one for censored and one for uncensored cases) for each value of the control variable in each interval. These records must contain the value of the control variable and the number of cases that belong in the particular category as well as values for survival time and status.

Example

```
DATA LIST   / SURVEVAR 1-2 STATVAR 4 SEX 6 COUNT 8.
VALUE LABELS   STATVAR 1 'DECEASED' 2 'ALIVE'
               /SEX 1 'FEMALE' 2 'MALE'.
BEGIN DATA
  1 1 1 6
  1 1 1 1
  1 2 2 2
  1 1 2 1
  2 2 1 1
  2 1 1 2
  2 2 2 1
  2 1 2 3
     ...
END DATA.
WEIGHT   COUNT.
SURVIVAL   TABLES = SURVEVAR BY SEX (1,2)
   /INTERVALS = THRU 10 BY 1
   /STATUS = STATVAR (1) FOR SURVEVAR.
```

• This example reads aggregated data and performs a SURVIVAL analysis when a control variable with two values is used.

• The first data record has a code of 1 on the status variable STATVAR, indicating it is an uncensored case, and a code of 1 on SEX, the control variable. The number of cases for this interval is 6, the value of the variable COUNT. Intervals with weights of 0 do not have to be included.

• COUNT is not used in SURVIVAL but is the weight variable. In this example, each interval requires four records to provide all the data for each SURVEVAR interval.

MISSING Subcommand

MISSING controls missing value treatments. The default is GROUPWISE, which excludes cases with missing values on a variable from any calculation involving that variable.

- Negative values on the survival variables are automatically treated as missing data. In addition, cases outside the value range on a control variable are excluded.

- GROUPWISE and LISTWISE are mutually exclusive. However, each can be used with INCLUDE.

GROUPWISE   *Exclude missing values groupwise.* Cases with missing values on a variable are excluded from any calculation involving that variable. This is the default.

LISTWISE   *Exclude missing values listwise.* Cases missing on any variables named on TABLES are excluded from the analysis.

INCLUDE   *Include missing values.* User-missing values are included in the analysis.

WRITE Subcommand

WRITE writes data in the survival tables to a resulting file. This file can be used for further analyses or to produce graphics displays.

- The only specification is a single keyword. WRITE without a specification is equivalent to WRITE=TABLES.

- When WRITE is used, the data are written to the file specified on the /RESULTS subcommand of the SET command. If you have not specified a resulting file, the data are written to the default resulting file, SPSS.PRC. The data from this subcommand overwrite any existing contents of whichever resulting file is current.

NONE   *Do not write survival tables.* This is the default when WRITE is omitted.

TABLES   *Write out survival table data records.* All survival table statistics are written to a file.

BOTH   *Write out survival table data and label records.* Variable names, variable labels, and value labels are written out along with the survival table statistics.

Format

WRITE writes five types of records to a procedure file. Keyword TABLES writes record types 30, 31, and 40. Keyword BOTH writes record types 10, 20, 30, 31, and 40. Record type 10, produced only by keyword BOTH, is formatted as follows:

Columns	Content	Format
1–2	Record type (10)	F2.0
3–7	Table number	F5.0
8–15	Name of survival variable	A8
16–55	Variable label of survival variable	A40
56	Number of BY's (0, 1, or 2)	F1.0
57–60	Number of rows in current survival table	F4.0

The number (0, 1, or 2) in column 56 specifies the number of orders of control variables (none, first-order, or first- and second-order controls) that have been applied to the life table. Columns 57–60 specify the number of rows in the life table. This number is the number of intervals in the analysis that show subjects entering; intervals in which no subjects enter are not noted in the life tables. One type 10 record is produced for each life table.

Record type 20, also produced by keyword BOTH, is formatted as follows:

Columns	Content	Format
1–2	Record type (20)	F2.0
3–7	Table number	F5.0
8–15	Name of control variable	A8
16–55	Variable label of control variable	A40
56–60	Value of control variable	F5.0
61–80	Value label for this value	A20

C

Command Reference

One type 20 record is produced for each control variable on each life table. If only first-order controls have been placed on the survival analysis, one type 20 record will be produced for each table; if second-order controls have also been applied, two type 20 records will be produced per table.

Record type 30, and its continuation 31, produced by both keywords TABLES and BOTH, are formatted as follows:

Columns	Content	Format
1–2	Record type (30)	F2.0
3–7	Table number	F5.0
8–13	Beginning of interval	F6.2
14–21	Number entering interval	F8.2
22–29	Number withdrawn in interval	F8.2
30–37	Number exposed to risk	F8.2
38–45	Number of terminal events	F8.2

Columns	Content	Format
1–2	Record type (31)	F2.0
3–7	Table number	F5.0
8–15	Proportion terminating	F8.6
16–23	Proportion surviving	F8.6
24–31	Cumulative proportion surviving	F8.6
32–38	Probability density	F8.6
40–47	Hazard rate	F8.6
48–54	S.E. of cumulative proportion surviving	F7.4
55–61	S.E. of probability density	F7.4
62–68	S.E. of hazard rate	F7.4

Each pair of type 30 and 31 records contains the information from one line of the life table. As many type 30 and 31 record pairs are output for a table as it has lines (this number is noted in columns 57–60 of the type 10 record for the table).

Record type 40, produced by both keywords TABLES and BOTH, is formatted as follows:

Columns	Content	Format
1–2	Record type (40)	F2.0

Type 40 records indicate the completion of the series of records for one life table.

Record Order   The SURVIVAL output file contains records for each of the life tables specified on the TABLES subcommand. All records for a given table are produced together in sequence.

The records for the life tables are produced in the same order as the tables themselves. All life tables for the first survival variable are written first. The values of the first- and second-order control variables rotate, with the values of the first-order controls changing most rapidly.

Example
```
PROCEDURE OUTPUT OUTFILE = SURVTBL.
SURVIVAL TABLES = MOSFREE BY TREATMNT(1,3)
  /STATUS = PRISON (1) FOR MOSFREE
  /INTERVAL = THRU 24 BY 3
  /WRITE = BOTH.
```

• SURVIVAL performs an analysis of MOSFREE with PRISON as the variable determining termination status. WRITE and the keyword BOTH generate a procedure file called SURVTBL, containing both life tables, variable names and labels, and value labels, stored as record types 10, 20, 30, 31, and 40.

References   Berkson, J., and R. Gage. 1950. Calculation of survival rates for cancer. *Proceedings of the Mayo Clinic* 25: 270.

Lee, E., and M. Desu. 1972. A computer program for comparing *k* samples with right-censored data. *Computer Programs in Biomedicine* 2: 315–321.

Examples

Contents_____

Examples

DSCRIMINANT

This example analyzes 1979 prices and earnings in 45 cities around the world, compiled by the Union Bank of Switzerland. The variables are

- FOOD—the average net cost of 39 different food and beverage items in the city, expressed as a percentage above or below that of Zurich, where Zurich equals 100%.
- SERVICE—the average cost of 28 different goods and services in the city, expressed as a percentage above or below that of Zurich, where Zurich equals 100%.
- BUS, MECHANIC, CONSTRUC, COOK, MANAGER, FSALES—the average gross annual earnings of municipal bus drivers, automobile mechanics, construction workers, cooks, managers, and female sales workers, working from five to ten years in their respective occupations. Each variable is expressed as a percentage above or below that of Zurich, where Zurich equals 100%.
- WORLD—economic development status of the country in which the city is located, divided into three groups: economically advanced nations, such as the United States and most European nations; nations that are members of the Organization for Petroleum Exporting Countries (OPEC); and nations that are economically underdeveloped. The groups are labeled **1ST WORLD, PETRO WORLD,** and **3RD WORLD,** respectively.

There are two objectives to this analysis. First, we discriminate between cities in different categories by examining their wage and price structures. Secondly, we predict a city's economic class category from coefficients calculated using wages and prices as predictors. The data are in an external file named ADSC.DAT.

The SPSS/PC+ commands in the command file named on the INCLUDE command are

```
DATA LIST FREE FILE='ADSC.DAT'
 /WORLD FOOD SERVICE BUS MECHANIC CONSTRUC
  COOK MANAGER FSALES.
MISSING VALUE ALL (0).
VALUE LABELS WORLD 1 '1ST WORLD' 2 'PETRO WORLD' 3 '3RD WORLD'.
DSCRIMINANT GROUPS=WORLD(1,3)
 /VARIABLES=FOOD SERVICE BUS MECHANIC CONSTRUC COOK MANAGER FSALES
 /PRIORS=SIZE
 /SAVE=CLASS=PRDCLAS SCORES=DISCSCR
 /STATISTICS=11 13.
FINISH.
```

- The DATA LIST command names the file that contains the data and assigns variable names. The FREE keyword indicates that the data are in freefield format.
- The MISSING VALUE command assigns 0 as a user-missing value to all the variables.
- The VALUE LABELS command assigns descriptive labels to the values of variable WORLD.
- The DSCRIMINANT command requests a three-group discriminant analysis. The variable WORLD named on the GROUPS subcommand defines the groups.
- The variables FOOD, SERVICE, BUS, MECHANIC, CONSTRUC, COOK, MANAGER, and FSALES, named on the VARIABLES subcommand, are used as predictor variables during the analysis phase.
- The PRIORS subcommand tells SPSS/PC+ that during the classification phase, prior probabilities are equal to the known size of the groups (Figure A).
- The SAVE subcommand saves three variables on the active file: the predicted group for each of the classified cases (variable PRDCLAS) and the two discriminant scores (variables DISCSCR1 and DISCSCR2). The saved variables are shown in Figure B.

• The STATISTICS subcommand requests the display of the unstandardized discriminant functions (Figure C) and the classification results table (Figure D).

The display is shown in Figures A through D. The exact appearance of printed display depends on the characters available on your printer.

A Prior probabilities

```
Prior Probabilities
    Group     Prior     Label
        1     0.58140   1ST WORLD
        2     0.13953   PETRO WORLD
        3     0.27907   3RD WORLD
    Total     1.00000
```

B The saved variables

```
These new variables will be created:
    Name      Label
    _____  _____
    PRDCLAS   ---- PREDICTED GROUP FOR ANALYSIS     1
    DISCSCR1  ---- FUNCTION    1 FOR ANALYSIS       1
    DISCSCR2  ---- FUNCTION    2 FOR ANALYSIS       1
```

C Discriminant coefficients

```
Unstandardized Canonical Discriminant Function Coefficients

                  FUNC 1          FUNC 2
FOOD          -.7133619D-02    .6194062D-01
SERVICE        .8472984D-02   -.5365943D-01
BUS            .5255502D-01   -.2000084D-01
MECHANIC       .2805062D-01    .1326366D-01
CONSTRUC      -.4256104D-02   -.7536312D-02
COOK          -.1677760D-01    .2545888D-01
MANAGER       -.2570614D-01   -.2155895D-01
FSALES         .1637516D-01    .1486991D-01
(constant)   -1.852548       -.9620797
```

D Classification results

```
Classification Results -

                         No. of    Predicted Group Membership
        Actual Group     Cases         1         2         3

Group        1            25           24         1         0
1ST WORLD                             96.0%      4.0%      0.0%

Group        2             6            0         5         1
PETRO WORLD                            0.0%     83.3%     16.7%

Group        3            12            1         0        11
3RD WORLD                              8.3%      0.0%     91.7%

Percent of "grouped" cases correctly classified:  93.02%

Classification Processing Summary
        45 Cases were processed.
         0 Cases were excluded for missing or out-of-range group codes.
         2 Cases had at least one missing discriminating variable.
        43 Cases were used for printed output.
        45 Cases were written into the active file.
```

HILOGLINEAR   In this example we will consider a market research analysis of laundry detergent preferences. Consumers in the survey prefer either Brand M or Brand X detergent. This analysis examines the relationship among brand preference and three other variables. The variables are

- BRANDPRF—preference for either BRAND M or BRAND X detergent.
- WATSOFT—water softness.
- PREVUSE—previous use of BRAND M.
- TEMP—washing temperature.

The data are in an external file named AHILOG.DAT. The SPSS/PC+ commands in the command file named on the INCLUDE command are

```
TITLE DETERGENT PREFERENCES RIES & SMITH(1963).
DATA LIST FREE FILE='AHILOG.DAT'
  / WATSOFT BRANDPRF PREVUSE TEMP FREQ.
VARIABLE LABELS WATSOFT  'WATER SOFTNESS'
                BRANDPRF 'BRAND PREFERENCE'
                PREVUSE  'PREVIOUS USE OF M'
                TEMP     'WATER TEMPERATURE'
                FREQ     'NUMBER IN CONDITION'.
VALUE LABELS WATSOFT 1 'SOFT' 2 'MEDIUM' 3 'HARD' /
             BRANDPRF 1 'BRAND X' 2 'BRAND M' /
             PREVUSE 1 'YES' 2 'NO' /
             TEMP 1 'HIGH' 2 'LOW'.
WEIGHT BY FREQ.
HILOGLINEAR WATSOFT (1,3) BRANDPRF PREVUSE TEMP (1,2)
  /PRINT=ALL
  /PLOT=DEFAULT
  /METHOD=BACKWARD
  /CRITERIA=MAXSTEPS(24)
  /DESIGN.
FINISH.
```

- The TITLE command puts the title **DETERGENT PREFERENCES RIES & SMITH (1963)** at the top of each page of output for this session.
- DATA LIST names the file that contains the data and defines the variables. Keyword FREE indicates that the data are in freefield format.
- The VARIABLE LABELS and VALUE LABELS commands complete the variable definition.
- The WEIGHT command weights the observations by FREQ, the variable containing the number of observations for each combination of values.
- HILOGLINEAR specifies four variables. The variable WATSOFT has three levels and the other three variables each have two.
- The PRINT subcommand requests all available displays: observed, expected, and residual values (display not shown); the result of the iterative proportional fitting algorithm and tests of effects for the saturated model and for each order (Figure A); measures of partial association for effects (Figure B); and parameter estimates (Figure C).
- The PLOT subcommand requests the default plots: residuals against observed and expected values, and a normal probability plot (partial display in Figure F).
- The METHOD subcommand requests backward elimination. The CRITERIA subcommand specifies a maximum of 24 steps, and the DESIGN subcommand successively eliminates terms from the default saturated model (partial display in Figure D). The observed and expected frequencies for the final model are also displayed (Figure E).

Portions of the display are shown in Figures A through F. The exact appearance of printed display depends on the characters available on your printer.

A Tests of effects for the saturated model and for each order

```
Tests that K-way and higher order effects are zero.

     K     DF   L.R. Chisq    Prob   Pearson Chisq    Prob   Iteration

     4      2        .738   .6915            .738   .6915          3
     3      9       9.846   .3631           9.871   .3611          3
     2     18      42.926   .0008          43.902   .0006          2
     1     23     118.626   .0000         115.714   .0000          0
Tests that K-way effects are zero.

     K     DF   L.R. Chisq    Prob   Pearson Chisq    Prob   Iteration

     1      5      75.701   .0000          71.812   .0000          0
     2      9      33.080   .0001          34.031   .0001          0
     3      7       9.108   .2450           9.133   .2433          0
     4      2        .738   .6915            .738   .6915          0
```

B Partial associations

```
Tests of PARTIAL associations.

Effect Name                            DF   Partial Chisq    Prob   Iter

WATSOFT*BRANDPRF*PREVUSE                 2           4.571   .1017      3
WATSOFT*BRANDPRF*TEMP                    2            .162   .9223      3
WATSOFT*PREVUSE*TEMP                     2           1.377   .5022      3
BRANDPRF*PREVUSE*TEMP                    1           2.222   .1361      3
WATSOFT*BRANDPRF                         2            .216   .8977      3
WATSOFT*PREVUSE                          2           1.005   .6051      3
BRANDPRF*PREVUSE                         1          19.892   .0000      3
WATSOFT*TEMP                             2           6.095   .0475      3
BRANDPRF*TEMP                            1           3.738   .0532      3
PREVUSE*TEMP                             1            .740   .3898      3
WATSOFT                                  2            .502   .7780      2
BRANDPRF                                 1            .064   .7996      2
PREVUSE                                  1           1.922   .1656      2
TEMP                                     1          73.211   .0000      2
```

C Partial display of parameter estimates for saturated model

```
Estimates for Parameters.

WATSOFT*BRANDPRF*PREVUSE*TEMP

Parameter      Coeff.      Std. Err.     Z-Value Lower 95 CI Upper 95 CI

     1     -.0086293293      .04833       -.17856     -.10335      .08609
     2     -.0296475092      .04734       -.62629     -.12243      .06313

WATSOFT*BRANDPRF*PREVUSE

Parameter      Coeff.      Std. Err.     Z-Value Lower 95 CI Upper 95 CI

     1      .0925171313      .04833      1.91437     -.00221      .18724
     2     -.0318024179      .04734       -.67182     -.12458      .06098

WATSOFT*BRANDPRF*TEMP

Parameter      Coeff.      Std. Err.     Z-Value Lower 95 CI Upper 95 CI

     1     -.0203612840      .04833       -.42132     -.11508      .07436
     2      .0048119005      .04734       .10165     -.08797      .09759

WATSOFT*PREVUSE*TEMP

Parameter      Coeff.      Std. Err.     Z-Value Lower 95 CI Upper 95 CI

     1     -.0474552194      .04833       -.98194     -.14218      .04727
     2      .0488797573      .04734      1.03257     -.04390      .14166

BRANDPRF*PREVUSE*TEMP

Parameter      Coeff.      Std. Err.     Z-Value Lower 95 CI Upper 95 CI

     1     -.0504586672      .03363     -1.50056     -.11637      .01545
```

D Partial display of final statistics

```
Backward Elimination for DESIGN 1 with generating class

   WATSOFT*BRANDPRF*PREVUSE*TEMP

Likelihood ratio chi square =       0.0        DF = 0  P = 1.000



Step 8

  The best model has generating class

       WATSOFT*TEMP
       BRANDPRF*TEMP
       BRANDPRF*PREVUSE

 Likelihood ratio chi square =    11.88633   DF = 14 P =  .615


If Deleted Simple Effect is                  DF  L.R. Chisq Change   Prob  Iter

 WATSOFT*TEMP                                  2                6.098  .0474    2
 BRANDPRF*TEMP                                 1                4.361  .0368    2
 BRANDPRF*PREVUSE                              1               20.578  .0000    2
Step 9

  The best model has generating class

       WATSOFT*TEMP
       BRANDPRF*TEMP
       BRANDPRF*PREVUSE

 Likelihood ratio chi square =    11.88633    DF = 14  P =  .615
The final model has generating class

       WATSOFT*TEMP
       BRANDPRF*TEMP
       BRANDPRF*PREVUSE

The Iterative Proportional Fitting converged at iteration 0.
```

E Observed and expected frequencies for selected model

```
Observed, Expected Frequencies and Residuals.
     Factor            Code        OBS count  EXP count  Residual  Std Resid


WATSOFT          SOFT
 BRANDPRF          BRAND X
  PREVUSE           YES
   TEMP              HIGH          19.0       19.5       -.52       -.12
   TEMP              LOW           57.0       47.8       9.15       1.32
  PREVUSE           NO
   TEMP              HIGH          29.0       28.4        .61        .11
   TEMP              LOW           63.0       69.6      -6.58       -.79
 BRANDPRF          BRAND M
  PREVUSE           YES
   TEMP              HIGH          29.0       30.8      -1.85       -.33
   TEMP              LOW           49.0       57.5      -8.52      -1.12
  PREVUSE           NO
   TEMP              HIGH          27.0       25.2       1.76        .35
   TEMP              LOW           53.0       47.1       5.94        .87

WATSOFT          MEDIUM
 BRANDPRF          BRAND X
  PREVUSE           YES
   TEMP              HIGH          23.0       23.7       -.65       -.13
   TEMP              LOW           47.0       47.0        .01        .00
  PREVUSE           NO
   TEMP              HIGH          33.0       34.4      -1.40       -.24
   TEMP              LOW           66.0       68.3      -2.32       -.28
 BRANDPRF          BRAND M
  PREVUSE           YES
   TEMP              HIGH          47.0       37.4       9.63       1.57
   TEMP              LOW           55.0       56.5      -1.48       -.20
  PREVUSE           NO
   TEMP              HIGH          23.0       30.6      -7.58      -1.37
   TEMP              LOW           50.0       46.2       3.79        .56

WATSOFT          HARD
 BRANDPRF          BRAND X
  PREVUSE           YES
   TEMP              HIGH          24.0       26.1      -2.09       -.41
   TEMP              LOW           37.0       42.9      -5.89       -.90
  PREVUSE           NO
   TEMP              HIGH          42.0       37.9       4.06        .66
   TEMP              LOW           68.0       62.4       5.63        .71
 BRANDPRF          BRAND M
  PREVUSE           YES
   TEMP              HIGH          43.0       41.2       1.77        .28
   TEMP              LOW           52.0       51.6        .44        .06
  PREVUSE           NO
   TEMP              HIGH          30.0       33.7      -3.73       -.64
   TEMP              LOW           42.0       42.2       -.18       -.03
Goodness-of-fit test statistics

   Likelihood ratio chi square =    11.88633    DF = 14  P =  .615
            Pearson chi square =    11.91780    DF = 14  P =  .613
```

F HILOGLINEAR residuals plots

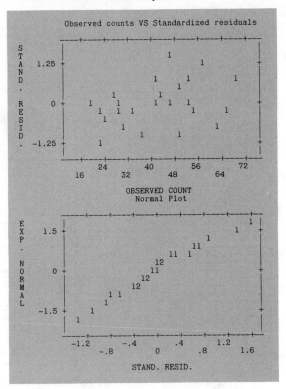

LOGISTIC REGRESSION

This example illustrates the use of logistic regression to predict students' grades in a class. The data are from Sage paperback #45 (Aldrich & Nelson, 1984). The variables are

- GPA — entering grade point average.
- TUCE — score on the pretest.
- PSI — teaching method, coded as 0 if the traditional method was used and 1 if the new PSI method was used.
- GRADE — coded as 1 if the student received an A, 0 otherwise. This is the dependent variable.
- INITIAL — student's initials used for identification purposes.

The SPSS/PC+ commands are:

```
SET WIDTH 80.
TITLE     'A DICHOTOMOUS DEPENDENT VARIABLE'.
SUBTITLE 'LOGISTIC REGRESSION'.
* THE DATA COME FROM THE SAGE PAPERBACK #45 BY ALDRICH AND NELSON.
DATA LIST FILE=ALDNEL /
    GPA 1-4(2) TUCE 6-7 PSI 9 GRADE 11 INITIAL 13-14(A).
VARIABLES LABELS
    GPA 'ENTERING GRADE POINT AVERAGE'
    TUCE 'PRETEST SCORE'
    PSI 'TEACHING METHOD'
    GRADE 'FINAL GRADE'.
VALUE LABELS PSI 1 'PSI USED' 0 'OTHER   METHOD' /
    GRADE 1 'A' 0 'NOT A'.
COMPUTE ID=$CASENUM.
LOGISTIC REGRESSION GRADE WITH GPA TUCE PSI /CLASSPLOT
  /METHOD=ENTER GPA /METHOD=FSTEP(LR) TUCE PSI
  /PRINT=ITER(2) /ID=INITIAL
  /CASEWISE=PGROUP PRED RESID /SAVE=DFBETA.
PLOT PLOT DFB1_1 WITH ID BY GRADE.
```

- The DATA LIST command defines the variables. The VALUE LABELS and VARIABLE LABELS commands provide additional descriptive information for the variables.
- The COMPUTE command creates a sequential case number which is an additional identifier for each case. It will be used for plots.
- The LOGISTIC REGRESSION command identifies GRADE as the dependent variable and GPA, TUCE, and PSI as the independent variables. The CATEGORICAL subcommand is not used for the variable PSI since PSI is already an indicator (0,1) variable.
- The PRINT subcommand requests that parameter estimates be displayed at every second iteration. By default, intermediate estimates are not displayed.
- The ID subcommand instructs that the casewise plot be labeled with the values of the variable INITIAL.
- The first METHOD subcommand enters the GPA variable into an equation which already contains the constant. (The constant can be suppressed with the ORIGIN subcommand.) Figure 1 contains the output when GPA is entered into the model.
- The second METHOD subcommand requests forward stepwise variable selection using the likelihood ratio as the criterion for variable removal. Only the variables TUCE and PSI are eligible for entry and removal. The variable GPA is already in the model and cannot be removed during the stepwise algorithm since it is not included in the list of variables for FSTEP. If the variable list for FSTEP is not given, all independent variables are eligible for entry and removal.
- Figure 2 shows statistics for variables in the equation and those not in the equation when PSI is selected for entry into the model. It also shows the log likelihood for the model if PSI were removed. The message at the bottom of Figure 2 indicates that no additional variables meet the default entry and removal p-values, so model building terminates.
- The CLASSPLOT subcommand requests a plot of the estimated probabilities of receiving an A. Cases are identified on the plot by the first letter of the value label for the dependent variable. The plot when PSI is entered into the model containing the constant and GPA is shown in Figure 3.

- The SAVE subcommand requests that the change in coefficients when a case is eliminated from the analysis be saved. Three new variables named by default DFB0_1 to DFB2_1 are saved. The first variable corresponds to the constant, the second to GPA, and the third to PSI. Output from this step is shown in Figure 4.

- The CASEWISE subcommand requests the casewise plot shown in Figure 5. The variables PGroup (the predicted group membership), Pred (the predicted probability of receiving an A), and Resid (the difference between the observed probability and that predicted by the model) are listed for all of the cases. Cases are identified by their value of INITIAL. Misclassified cases are marked with asterisks.

- The PLOT command requests a plot of the change in the coefficient for GPA when each case is removed from the analysis against the sequence number for each case. This plot is shown in Figure 6. Note the large change for the last case. (Each point is identified by the group to which it belongs.)

Figure 1

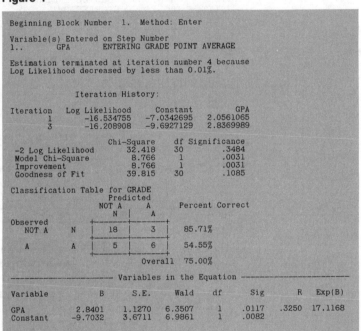

```
Beginning Block Number  1.  Method: Enter

Variable(s) Entered on Step Number
1..      GPA        ENTERING GRADE POINT AVERAGE

Estimation terminated at iteration number 4 because
Log Likelihood decreased by less than 0.01%.


               Iteration History:

Iteration  Log Likelihood      Constant          GPA
   1          -16.534755      -7.0342695     2.0561065
   3          -16.208908      -9.6927129     2.8369989

                     Chi-Square      df Significance
-2 Log Likelihood      32.418        30      .3484
Model Chi-Square        8.766         1      .0031
Improvement             8.766         1      .0031
Goodness of Fit        39.815        30      .1085

Classification Table for GRADE
                    Predicted
              NOT A      A        Percent Correct
                N   |    A
Observed
  NOT A    N   | 18  |    3  |      85.71%
                                 
  A        A   |  5  |    6  |      54.55%
                                 
                   Overall  75.00%

-------------- Variables in the Equation --------------

Variable        B       S.E.     Wald     df     Sig       R     Exp(B)

GPA          2.8401    1.1270    6.3507    1    .0117    .3250   17.1168
Constant    -9.7032    3.6711    6.9861    1    .0082
```

Figure 2

```
-------------------- Variables in the Equation --------------------

Variable        B       S.E.     Wald     df     Sig       R     Exp(B)

GPA          3.0631    1.2228    6.2751    1    .0122    .3631   21.3948
PSI          2.3376    1.0408    5.0449    1    .0247    .3065   10.3565
Constant   -11.6007    4.2127    7.5830    1    .0059

--------------- Variables not in the Equation ---------------
Residual Chi Square      .459 with      1 df      Sig =  .4980

Variable       Score     df      Sig       R

TUCE           .4592      1     .4980    .0000

--------------- Model if Term Removed ---------------

Term       Log                           Significance
Removed    Likelihood   -2 Log LR    df  of Log LR

PSI        -16.209        6.165        1      .0130

No variables can be removed.

No variables can be added.
```

Figure 3

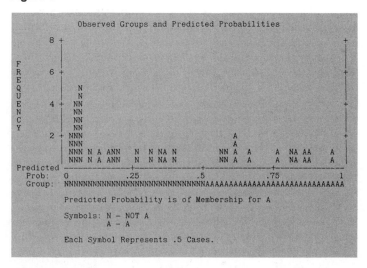

```
              Observed Groups and Predicted Probabilities
     8 +                                                                    +
F
R    6 +                                                                    +
E
Q        N
U        N
E    4 + NN                                                                 +
N        NN
C        NN
Y        NN
     2 + NNN                                  A                             +
         NNN                                  A
         NNN N A ANN   N  N NA N        NN A  A    A  NA AA   A
         NNN N A ANN   N  N NA N        NN A  A    A  NA AA   A
Predicted ----------------------+----------------+-----------------------
   Prob:  0          .25          .5          .75                        1
  Group:  NNNNNNNNNNNNNNNNNNNNNNNNNNNNNNNNNAAAAAAAAAAAAAAAAAAAAAAAAAAAAAAAA

          Predicted Probability is of Membership for A

          Symbols: N - NOT A
                   A - A

          Each Symbol Represents .5 Cases.
```

Figure 4

```
3 new variables have been created.
   Name          Contents

   DFB0_1        Dfbeta for the constant
   DFB1_1        Dfbeta for GPA
   DFB2_1        Dfbeta for PSI
```

Figure 5

ID	Observed GRADE		PGroup	Pred	Resid
am	S N		N	.0307	-.0307
cd	S N		N	.0602	-.0602
ez	S N		N	.1746	-.1746
rt	S N		N	.0656	-.0656
mk	S A		A	.6574	.3426
or	S N		N	.0552	-.0552
fs	S N		N	.0412	-.0412
rn	S N		N	.0568	-.0568
an	S N		N	.0895	-.0895
ds	S A		A	.6003	.3997
kb	S N		N	.0281	-.0281
rp	S N		N	.1929	-.1929
bz	S N		N	.3396	-.3396
ak	S A	**	N	.1659	.8341
cl	S N		N	.3126	-.3126
ws	S N		N	.0389	-.0389
ms	S N		N	.0400	-.0400
dh	S N		N	.0506	-.0506
ae	S N	**	A	.5730	-.5730
pp	S A		A	.6026	.3974
nn	S N		N	.0496	-.0496
oy	S A		A	.8612	.1388
ap	S N		N	.3988	-.3988
fu	S N	**	A	.8159	-.8159
hk	S A		A	.8293	.1707
rt	S A	**	N	.3556	.6444
mz	S A		A	.7542	.2458
gg	S N		N	.2527	-.2527
hi	S A		A	.8718	.1282
ln	S A		A	.9521	.0479
dp	S N	**	A	.5579	-.5579
ss	S A	**	N	.1254	.8746

```
S=Selected U=Unselected cases
** = Misclassified cases
```

Figure 6

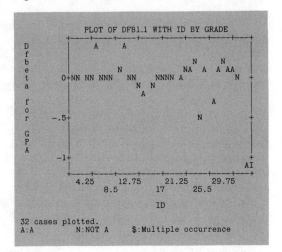

LOGLINEAR   You can use LOGLINEAR to analyze many types of designs for categorical variables. Combinations of variable specifications, CWEIGHT, CONTRAST, GRESID, and DESIGN subcommands can produce general log-linear models, logit models, quasi-independence models, logistic regressions on category variables, and others. The following examples, although not exhaustive, demonstrate some of the types of models you can analyze. These examples have been obtained from books and articles on the analysis of categorical data. The examples use the WEIGHT command to replicate the published tables.

Example 1: Logit Model   The logit model is a special case of the general log-linear model in which one or more variables are treated as dependent, and the rest are used as independent variables. Typically, logit models use dichotomous variables. This example uses dichotomous variables to analyze data from *The American Soldier* (Stouffer et al., 1948). The researchers interviewed soldiers in training camps. The variables used in this example are

- PREF—preference for training camps, where 1=stay in the same camp, 2=move to a northern camp, 3=move to a southern camp, 4=move—but undecided about location, and 5=undecided.
- RACE—race of soldier, where 1=black and 2=white.
- ORIGIN, CAMP—geographic origin and geographic location of camp, where 1=north and 2=south.
- FREQ—actual cell count obtained from the published table.

In this example, we transform the preference variable into the dichotomy north vs. south. Typically, the first step in fitting a logit model is to use a saturated model and remove nonsignificant effects. This example fits only the significant effects in the interest of parsimony. The SPSS/PC+ commands are

```
SET WIDTH=130.
TITLE "Stouffer's American Soldier".
DATA LIST FREE / RACE  ORIGIN  CAMP  PREF  FREQ.
BEGIN DATA
1 1 1 1 196
1 1 1 2 191
1 1 1 3  36
1 1 1 4  41
1 1 1 5  52
2 2 2 1 481
 ...
2 2 2 2  91
2 2 2 3 389
2 2 2 4  91
2 2 2 5  91
END DATA.
WEIGHT BY FREQ.
VARIABLE LABELS RACE 'RACE OF RESPONDENT'
   ORIGIN 'GEOGRAPHICAL ORIGIN'
   CAMP 'PRESENT CAMP'
   PREF 'PREFENCE FOR LOCATION'.
VALUE LABELS RACE 1 'BLACK' 2 'WHITE' /
   ORIGIN 1 'NORTH' 2 'SOUTH' /
   CAMP 1 'NORTH' 2 'SOUTH' /
   PREF 1 'STAY' 2 'GO NORTH' 3 'GO SOUTH'
   4 'MOVE UNDECIDED' 5 'UNDECIDED'.

* COLLAPSE CATEGORIES 1, 2, AND 3 INTO A DICHOTOMY.
COMPUTE DPREF=PREF.
IF (CAMP=1 AND PREF=1) DPREF=2.
IF (CAMP=2 AND PREF=1) DPREF=3.

VARIABLE LABELS DPREF 'PREFERENCE FOR LOCATION'.
VALUE LABELS DPREF 2 'NORTH' 3 'SOUTH'.

LOGLINEAR DPREF(2,3) BY RACE ORIGIN CAMP(1,2)
   /PRINT=DEFAULT ESTIM
   /DESIGN=DPREF, DPREF BY RACE, DPREF BY ORIGIN, DPREF BY CAMP,
      DPREF BY ORIGIN BY CAMP.
```

- The SET WIDTH command uses a wide format to permit listing of all the statistics, including percentages.
- The DATA LIST command reads the data with a FREE format.
- Variable FREQ is the actual cell count obtained from the published table. The WEIGHT command weights each case (which represents a cell) back to the sample size.
- The COMPUTE and IF statements transform the first three category preference values into a dichotomy.
- The LOGLINEAR command specifies one design. The DESIGN subcommand specifies the dependent variable, as well as interactions involving the dependent variable. Note that this design is not the saturated model. When you specify a logit model with the keyword BY and do not use a DESIGN subcommand, LOGLINEAR implicitly includes all the effects and interactions of independent factors. See Haberman (1979) for more details.
- The PRINT subcommand displays the frequencies and residuals table as well as the estimates for the parameters.

Figures 1 and 2 contain portions of the display for this example. Figure 1 shows the final model fit. The chi-square statistics show a good fit, and all of the adjusted residuals are less than 1.

Figure 1 Model fit

```
Observed, Expected Frequencies and Residuals

    Factor          Code          OBS. count & PCT.    EXP. count & PCT.    Residual   Std. Resid.   Adj. Resid.


DPREF           NORTH
 RACE           BLACK
  ORIGIN         NORTH
   CAMP           NORTH         387.00 (91.49)       390.64 (92.35)       -3.6431      -.1843        -.7714
   CAMP           SOUTH         876.00 (77.80)       879.35 (78.09)       -3.3479      -.1129        -.4178
  ORIGIN         SOUTH
   CAMP           NORTH         383.00 (58.65)       376.80 (57.70)        6.2000       .3194         .9994
   CAMP           SOUTH         381.00 (18.20)       380.21 (18.17)         .7909       .0406         .1131
 RACE           WHITE
  ORIGIN         NORTH
   CAMP           NORTH         955.00 (85.50)       951.36 (85.17)        3.6431       .1181         .7714
   CAMP           SOUTH         874.00 (63.15)       870.65 (62.91)        3.3479       .1135         .4178
  ORIGIN         SOUTH
   CAMP           NORTH         104.00 (37.14)       110.20 (39.36)       -6.2000      -.5906        -.9994
   CAMP           SOUTH          91.00 ( 9.47)        91.79 ( 9.55)        -.7909      -.0825        -.1131

DPREF           SOUTH
 RACE           BLACK
  ORIGIN         NORTH
   CAMP           NORTH          36.00 ( 8.51)        32.36 ( 7.65)        3.6431       .6405         .7714
   CAMP           SOUTH         250.00 (22.20)       246.65 (21.91)        3.3479       .2132         .4178
  ORIGIN         SOUTH
   CAMP           NORTH         270.00 (41.35)       276.20 (42.30)       -6.2000      -.3731        -.9994
   CAMP           SOUTH        1712.00 (81.80)      1712.79 (81.83)        -.7909      -.0191        -.1131
 RACE           WHITE
  ORIGIN         NORTH
   CAMP           NORTH         162.00 (14.50)       165.64 (14.83)       -3.6431      -.2831        -.7714
   CAMP           SOUTH         510.00 (36.85)       513.35 (37.09)       -3.3479      -.1478        -.4178
  ORIGIN         SOUTH
   CAMP           NORTH         176.00 (62.86)       169.80 (60.64)        6.2000       .4758         .9994
   CAMP           SOUTH         870.00 (90.53)       869.21 (90.45)         .7909       .0268         .1131

- - - - - - - - - - - - - - - - - - - - - - - - - - - - - - - - - - - - - - - - - - - - - - - - - - -


Goodness-of-Fit test statistics

   Likelihood Ratio Chi Square =     1.44756    DF = 3   P =   .694
              Pearson Chi Square =     1.45707    DF = 3   P =   .692
```

Figure 2 shows the parameter estimates for the final model. To obtain regression-like coefficients, multiply the estimates by 2 (see Haberman, 1978).

Figure 2 Parameter estimates

```
Estimates for Parameters
 DPREF

  Parameter         Coeff.        Std. Err.       Z-Value     Lower 95 CI     Upper 95 CI

       1        .1352217166         .01518        8.90608         .10546          .16498
 DPREF BY RACE

  Parameter         Coeff.        Std. Err.       Z-Value     Lower 95 CI     Upper 95 CI

       2        .1857281674         .01557       11.93145         .15522          .21624
 DPREF BY ORIGIN

  Parameter         Coeff.        Std. Err.       Z-Value     Lower 95 CI     Upper 95 CI

       3        .6195921388         .01687       36.72886         .58653          .65266
 DPREF BY CAMP

  Parameter         Coeff.        Std. Err.       Z-Value     Lower 95 CI     Upper 95 CI

       4        .3794390119         .01534       24.73658         .34937          .40950
 DPREF BY ORIGIN BY CAMP

  Parameter         Coeff.        Std. Err.       Z-Value     Lower 95 CI     Upper 95 CI

       5       -.0744977447         .01521       -4.89942        -.10430         -.04470
```

Use these coefficients to obtain log-odds coefficients; use their anti-log to translate the model into odds rather than log odds. Table 1 shows the model coefficients.

Table 1 Model coefficients

Effect	Coefficient	Coefficient*2	Antilog
DPREF	0.135	0.270	1.311
DPREF BY RACE	0.186	0.371	1.450
DPREF BY ORIGIN	0.620	1.239	3.452
DPREF BY CAMP	0.379	0.759	2.136
DPREF BY ORIGIN BY CAMP	−0.074	−0.149	0.862

The regression-like model implied by the coefficients is

$$\ln(F_{ijk1}/F_{ijk2}) = B + B(A)_i + B(B)_j + B(C)_k + B(BC)_{jk}$$

where F is an expected frequency, and

B equals	0.270
$B(A)_i$ equals	0.371 for $i = 1$
	−0.371 for $i = 2$
$B(B)_j$ equals	1.239 for $j = 1$
	−1.239 for $j = 2$
$B(C)_k$ equals	0.759 for $k = 1$
	−0.759 for $k = 2$
$B(BC)_{jk}$ equals	−0.149 for $j = k$
	0.149 for j ne k.

To evaluate the model in terms of odds rather than log odds, use an analogous multiplicative model, with the antilogs shown in Table 1 as coefficients. That is,

$$(F_{ijk}1/F_{ijk2})=T * T(A)_i * T(B)_j * T(C)_k * T(BC)_{jk}$$

where

T equals	1.311	
$T(A)_i$ equals	1.450	for i =1
	1/1.450	for i =2
$T(B)_j$ equals	3.452	for j =1
	1/3.452	for j =2
$T(C)_k$ equals	2.136	for k =1
	1/2.136	for k =2
$T(BC)_{jk}$ equals	0.862	for j =k
	1/1.862	for j ne k.

For example, consider someone whose race is black, who is originally from the north, and who is presently located in a northern camp. For this individual, i=j=k=1 because of the coding of the variable indicated at the beginning of this example. This person's observed odds of preferring northern versus southern camp location is 10.75 (91.49/8.51) from Figure 1. The expected odds given the model are 12.072 (92.35/7.65) from Figure 1. The model decomposes these expected odds into components (see Table 1)

$$12.072=(1.311)(1.450)(3.452)(2.136)(0.862)$$

where the effects are interpretable.

- 1.311 is the mean or overall effect.
- 1.450 is the race effect indicating the net effect of being black versus white on preference of camp location. Other things equal, blacks prefer northern camp locations by 1.450 to 1.
- 3.452 is the net effect of region of origin on present preference. Other things equal, someone originally from the north prefers a northern camp location by 3.452 to 1.
- 2.136 is the net effect of present location on camp preference. Other things equal, someone presently located in the north states a northern preference over twice as often as they state a southern preference.
- 0.862 is the interaction effect between region of origin and present camp location. The effect is negative; this means that the effect of being a northerner in a northern camp is less positive than is indicated by combining the main effect of being a northerner with the main effect of being in a northern camp.

Example 2: A General Log-linear Model

The general log-linear model has all dependent variables. This example uses the same data analyzed as the logit model in the first example. The general log-linear model treats all variables as jointly dependent. The following LOGLINEAR command is used to request this model:

```
LOGLINEAR DPREF(2,3) RACE ORIGIN CAMP(1,2)
  /PRINT=DEFAULT ESTIM
  /DESIGN=DPREF, RACE, ORIGIN, CAMP,
   DPREF BY RACE, DPREF BY ORIGIN, DPREF BY CAMP,
   RACE BY CAMP, RACE BY ORIGIN, ORIGIN BY CAMP,
   RACE BY ORIGIN BY CAMP,
   DPREF BY ORIGIN BY CAMP.
```

The LOGLINEAR command for the general log-linear model does not use the keyword BY in the first line. In this model, the DESIGN subcommand uses all the variables as main effects or as part of an interaction term. Compare this with the logit model shown in the first example, which uses the dependent variable and interactions involving the dependent variable.

Figures 3 and 4 are the display produced by this example. Figure 3 shows that expected frequencies are identical to the logit model in the first example (Figure 1). However, observed and expected cell percentages differ. In the logit model, cell percentages sum to 100 across categories of the dependent variable within each combination of independent variable values. In other words, cell percentages in the logit model are comparable to row or column percentages in crosstabulation. In the general model, they sum to 100 across all categories and are comparable to total percentages in a crosstabulation.

Figure 3 Log-linear model fit for Example 2

```
Observed, Expected Frequencies and Residuals

    Factor          Code        OBS. count & PCT.   EXP. count & PCT.   Residual   Std. Resid.   Adj. Resid.

DPREF          NORTH
  RACE           BLACK
    ORIGIN         NORTH
      CAMP           NORTH        387.00 ( 4.82)      390.64 ( 4.86)     -3.6431      -.1843        -.7714
      CAMP           SOUTH        876.00 (10.90)      879.35 (10.94)     -3.3479      -.1129        -.4178
    ORIGIN         SOUTH
      CAMP           NORTH        383.00 ( 4.77)      376.80 ( 4.69)      6.2000       .3194         .9994
      CAMP           SOUTH        381.00 ( 4.74)      380.21 ( 4.73)       .7909       .0406         .1131
  RACE           WHITE
    ORIGIN         NORTH
      CAMP           NORTH        955.00 (11.88)      951.36 (11.84)      3.6431       .1181         .7714
      CAMP           SOUTH        874.00 (10.87)      870.65 (10.83)      3.3479       .1135         .4178
    ORIGIN         SOUTH
      CAMP           NORTH        104.00 ( 1.29)      110.20 ( 1.37)     -6.2000      -.5906        -.9994
      CAMP           SOUTH         91.00 ( 1.13)       91.79 ( 1.14)      -.7909      -.0825        -.1131
DPREF          SOUTH
  RACE           BLACK
    ORIGIN         NORTH
      CAMP           NORTH         36.00 (  .45)       32.36 (  .40)      3.6431       .6405         .7714
      CAMP           SOUTH        250.00 ( 3.11)      246.65 ( 3.07)      3.3479       .2132         .4178
    ORIGIN         SOUTH
      CAMP           NORTH        270.00 ( 3.36)      276.20 ( 3.44)     -6.2000      -.3731        -.9994
      CAMP           SOUTH       1712.00 (21.30)     1712.79 (21.31)      -.7909      -.0191        -.1131
  RACE           WHITE
    ORIGIN         NORTH
      CAMP           NORTH        162.00 ( 2.02)      165.64 ( 2.06)     -3.6431      -.2831        -.7714
      CAMP           SOUTH        510.00 ( 6.35)      513.35 ( 6.39)     -3.3479      -.1478        -.4178
    ORIGIN         SOUTH
      CAMP           NORTH        176.00 ( 2.19)      169.80 ( 2.11)      6.2000       .4758         .9994
      CAMP           SOUTH        870.00 (10.82)      869.21 (10.82)       .7909       .0268         .1131

- - - - - - - - - - - - - - - - - - - - - - - - - - - - - - - - - - - - - - - - - - - - - - - - - - -


Goodness-of-Fit test statistics

    Likelihood Ratio Chi Square =    1.44756    DF = 3  P =  .694
              Pearson Chi Square =    1.45707    DF = 3  P =  .692
```

Figure 4 Parameter estimates for Example 2

```
Estimates for Parameters
 DPREF

  Parameter        Coeff.        Std. Err.        Z-Value      Lower 95 CI      Upper 95 CI
      1         .1352217166        .01518         8.90608         .10546          .16498

 RACE

  Parameter        Coeff.        Std. Err.        Z-Value      Lower 95 CI      Upper 95 CI
      2         .0355803941        .01363         2.61113         .00887          .06229

 ORIGIN

  Parameter        Coeff.        Std. Err.        Z-Value      Lower 95 CI      Upper 95 CI
      3         .0403904261        .01614         2.50201         .00875          .07203

 CAMP

  Parameter        Coeff.        Std. Err.        Z-Value      Lower 95 CI      Upper 95 CI
      4        -.4480592813        .01614       -27.76919        -.47968         -.41643

 DPREF BY RACE

  Parameter        Coeff.        Std. Err.        Z-Value      Lower 95 CI      Upper 95 CI
      5         .1857281674        .01557        11.93145         .15522          .21624

 DPREF BY ORIGIN

  Parameter        Coeff.        Std. Err.        Z-Value      Lower 95 CI      Upper 95 CI
      6         .6195921388        .01687        36.72886         .58653          .65266

 DPREF BY CAMP

  Parameter        Coeff.        Std. Err.        Z-Value      Lower 95 CI      Upper 95 CI
      7         .3794390119        .01534        24.73658         .34937          .40950

 RACE BY CAMP

  Parameter        Coeff.        Std. Err.        Z-Value      Lower 95 CI      Upper 95 CI
      8        -.1364780340        .01413        -9.65595        -.16418         -.10878

 RACE BY ORIGIN

  Parameter        Coeff.        Std. Err.        Z-Value      Lower 95 CI      Upper 95 CI
      9        -.4413477997        .01591       -27.73754        -.47253         -.41016

 ORIGIN BY CAMP

  Parameter        Coeff.        Std. Err.        Z-Value      Lower 95 CI      Upper 95 CI
     10        -.0375668525        .01632        -2.30190        -.06955         -.00558

 RACE BY ORIGIN BY CAMP

  Parameter        Coeff.        Std. Err.        Z-Value      Lower 95 CI      Upper 95 CI
     11        -.0885302170        .01359        -6.51497        -.11516         -.06190

 DPREF BY ORIGIN BY CAMP

  Parameter        Coeff.        Std. Err.        Z-Value      Lower 95 CI      Upper 95 CI
     12        -.0744977447        .01521        -4.89942        -.10430         -.04470
```

Compare Figure 4 with Figure 2 in the first example. Note that identical results are produced for effects in common in the two models.

Example 3: A Multinomial Logit Model

The first two examples analyze Stouffer's data with "preference for location" transformed into a dichotomy. Example 3 uses the original five-category preference variable to demonstrate the multinomial logit model. This example uses orthogonal special contrasts to make desired comparisons among the categories of the dependent variable. The LOGLINEAR command is as follows:

```
LOGLINEAR PREF(1,5) BY RACE ORIGIN CAMP(1,2)
  /PRINT=DEFAULT ESTIM
  /CONTRAST(PREF)=SPECIAL(5*1,1 1 1 1 -4,3 -1 -1 -1 0,
    0 1 1 -2 0,0 1 -1 0 0)
  /DESIGN=PREF, PREF BY RACE, PREF BY ORIGIN, PREF BY CAMP,
    PREF BY RACE BY ORIGIN, PREF BY RACE BY CAMP,
    PREF BY ORIGIN BY CAMP, PREF BY RACE BY ORIGIN BY CAMP.
```

Figure 5 is the display of the parameter estimates for Example 3. This example fits the saturated model. If no DESIGN subcommand had been specified, the saturated model would have also included effects that are redundant when a logit model is specified. Parameter estimates for a multinomial model can be more interpretable when you specify special contrasts as in this example. The CONTRAST subcommand contrasts the movers and stayers vs. the undecided, the movers vs. the stayers, the decided vs. the undecided, and northern vs. southern camps.

Figure 5 Parameter estimates for Example 3

```
Estimates for Parameters
PREF

Parameter        Coeff.       Std. Err.      Z-Value    Lower 95 CI    Upper 95 CI

         1     .1234825883       .00807      15.29520        .10766        .13931
         2     .0724662120       .00826       8.77654        .05628        .08865
         3     .2043174993       .01408      14.51506        .17673        .23191
         4     .1282571558       .02068       6.20092        .08772        .16880


PREF BY RACE

Parameter        Coeff.       Std. Err.      Z-Value    Lower 95 CI    Upper 95 CI

         5    -.0051416644       .00807       -.63687       -.02097        .01068
         6    -.0063669961       .00826       -.77112       -.02255        .00982
         7     .0062485789       .01408        .44391       -.02134        .03384
         8     .0960361288       .02068       4.64311        .05550        .13658

PREF BY ORIGIN

Parameter        Coeff.       Std. Err.      Z-Value    Lower 95 CI    Upper 95 CI

         9    -.0021584482       .00807       -.26736       -.01798        .01367
        10    -.0586990400       .00826      -7.10917       -.07488       -.04252
        11    -.0025353715       .01408       -.18012       -.03012        .02505
        12     .6555140380       .02068      31.69248        .61497        .69605

PREF BY CAMP

Parameter        Coeff.       Std. Err.      Z-Value    Lower 95 CI    Upper 95 CI

        13    -.0191848042       .00807      -2.37633       -.03501       -.00336
        14     .0320805342       .00826       3.88534        .01590        .04826
        15     .0038808442       .01408        .27570       -.02371        .03147
        16    -.0156364228       .02068       -.75598       -.05618        .02490

PREF BY RACE BY ORIGIN

Parameter        Coeff.       Std. Err.      Z-Value    Lower 95 CI    Upper 95 CI

        17    -.0033156723       .00807       -.41070       -.01914        .01251
        18    -.0237329647       .00826      -2.87435       -.03992       -.00755
        19     .0611636379       .01408       4.34517        .03357        .08875
        20    -.0516750973       .02068      -2.49836       -.09221       -.01114

PREF BY RACE BY CAMP

Parameter        Coeff.       Std. Err.      Z-Value    Lower 95 CI    Upper 95 CI

        21     .0030208725       .00807        .37418       -.01280        .01884
        22     .1027873616       .00826      12.44880        .08660        .11897
        23    -.0189810333       .01408      -1.34845       -.04657        .00861
        24     .0076967580       .02068        .37212       -.03284        .04824

PREF BY ORIGIN BY CAMP

Parameter        Coeff.       Std. Err.      Z-Value    Lower 95 CI    Upper 95 CI

        25     .0049220965       .00807        .60968       -.01090        .02075
        26     .1316990028       .00826      15.95036        .11552        .14788
        27    -.0090552616       .01408       -.64330       -.03664        .01853
        28    -.0320161528       .02068      -1.54790       -.07256        .00852

PREF BY RACE BY ORIGIN BY CAMP

Parameter        Coeff.       Std. Err.      Z-Value    Lower 95 CI    Upper 95 CI

        29    -.0008598058       .00807       -.10650       -.01668        .01496
        30     .0217737066       .00826       2.63706        .00559        .03796
        31    -.0115700249       .01408       -.82195       -.03916        .01602
        32     .0406113662       .02068       1.96346        .00007        .08115
```

MANOVA

The following examples demonstrate some of the more commonly used MANOVA models.

Example 1: Analysis of Covariance Designs

You can test different models with MANOVA through correct use of syntax. This example shows how to use MANOVA for analysis of variance and covariance. The example comes from Winer (1971).

The variables are

- A—a factor that represents three methods of training.
- X—a covariate that is a score on an aptitude test.
- Y—a dependent variable that contains the scores on an achievement test on material covered in the training course. The test is given to the subjects after the training is complete.

The data are in an external file named AMAN.DAT. The SPSS/PC+ commands in the command file named on the INCLUDE command are

```
SET WIDTH=WIDE.
DATA LIST FILE='AMAN.DAT' / A 1 X Y 2-5.
MANOVA Y BY A(1,3)
  /PRINT=PARAM(ESTIM)
  /DESIGN.
MANOVA Y BY A(1,3) WITH X
  /PMEANS=VARIABLES(Y)
  /PRINT=PARAM(ESTIM)
  /DESIGN
  /ANALYSIS=Y
  /METHOD=SSTYPE(SEQUENTIAL)
  /DESIGN=X, A, A BY X
  /DESIGN=X WITHIN A, A.
FINISH.
```

- The SET command sets the display width to 132 characters.
- The DATA LIST command reads variables A, X, and Y from the data included in the file AMAN.DAT.
- The first MANOVA command specifies the first analysis—a one-way analysis of variance—using the default DESIGN subcommand. The PRINT subcommand requests that parameter estimates be included in the display.
- The second MANOVA command specifies the second through fourth analyses. The second is an analysis of covariance using the default DESIGN subcommand. The default analysis fits covariates, factors, and factor-by-factor interactions if you specify more than one factor, and assumes homogeneous slopes.
- The PMEANS subcommand displays predicted means for the second through fourth models. The PRINT subcommand requests that parameter estimates be included in the display.
- The third analysis tests the assumption of homogeneous slopes. If the A by X interaction is significant, you must reject the hypothesis of parallel slopes. The ANALYSIS subcommand specifies the dependent variable. The METHOD subcommand asks for sequential sums of squares. The DESIGN subcommand specifies effects, including the factor-by-covariate interaction.
- The fourth analysis fits separate regression coefficients in each group of the factor. As in the third analysis, the ANALYSIS subcommand specifies the dependent variable for the analysis. The WITHIN keyword on the DESIGN subcommand fits separate regression models within each of the three groups of Factor A.

Portions of the display output are shown in Figures A through E. The exact appearance of printed display depends on the characters available on your printer.

- Figure A shows the display for the first analysis, including an analysis of variance table.
- Figure B shows the display for the second analysis, which includes the covariate X. MANOVA displays the analysis of variance table and regression statistics associated with X.

- Figure C shows the table of predicted means for the second analysis requested with the PMEANS subcommand. MANOVA displays the observed means, the adjusted means (which are adjusted for the covariate), and the estimated means (which are the cell means estimated with knowledge of A, not adjusted for the covariate).
- Figure D shows the analysis of variance table for the third analysis. Since the A by X interaction is not significant, the hypothesis of parallel slopes is not rejected. That is, we can assume that the effect of change in X on Y is the same across levels of A.
- Finally, Figure E shows the analysis of variance table for the fourth analysis. The X within A effect is the joint effect of the separate regressions. Since the third analysis shows the factor-by-covariate interaction is not significant, the second analysis (not the fourth) is the preferred solution.

A Results for first analysis

```
Tests of Significance for Y using UNIQUE sums of squares
Source of Variation          SS       DF       MS          F   Sig of F

WITHIN CELLS               26.86      18      1.49
CONSTANT                  817.19       1    817.19      547.69     .000
A                          36.95       2     18.48       12.38     .000

- - - - - - - - - -
Estimates for Y
CONSTANT

 Parameter      Coeff.   Std. Err.    t-Value    Sig. t  Lower -95% CL- Upper

        1     6.23809524    .26655    23.40281     0.0     5.67809     6.79810

A

 Parameter      Coeff.   Std. Err.    t-Value    Sig. t  Lower -95% CL- Upper

        2    -1.8095238    .37696     -4.80027     .000    -2.60149    -1.01755
        3     1.33333333    .37696     3.53704     .002      .54136     2.12530
```

B Results for second analysis

```
Tests of Significance for Y using UNIQUE sums of squares
Source of Variation          SS     DF       MS          F   Sig of F

WITHIN CELLS               10.30     17      .61
REGRESSION                 16.56      1    16.56        27.32     .000
CONSTANT                   58.05      1    58.05        95.80     .000
A                          16.93      2     8.47        13.97     .000

- - - - - - - - -
Estimates for Y adjusted for 1 covariate
CONSTANT

 Parameter      Coeff.   Std. Err.    t-Value    Sig. t  Lower -95% CL- Upper

        1     4.18639456    .42772     9.78766     .000     3.28398     5.08881

A

 Parameter      Coeff.   Std. Err.    t-Value    Sig. t  Lower -95% CL- Upper

        2    -1.3496599    .25584     -5.27535     .000    -1.88944     -.80988
        3     .838095238    .25825     3.24530     .005      .29324     1.38295

- - - - - - - - -
Regression analysis for WITHIN CELLS error term
Dependent variable .. Y

COVARIATE            B          Beta     Std. Err.      t-Value    Sig. of t   Lower -95%   CL- Upper

X          .7428571429    .7851199742      .14213      5.22671        .000       .44300      1.04272
```

C Adjusted means for second analysis

```
Adjusted and Estimated Means
Variable .. Y
CELL        Obs. Mean  Adj. Mean   Est. Mean  Raw Resid. Std. Resid.

    1         4.429      4.888       4.429       0.0        0.0
    2         7.571      7.076       7.571       0.0        0.0
    3         6.714      6.750       6.714       0.0        0.0
```

D Results for third analysis

```
Tests of Significance for Y using SEQUENTIAL Sums of Squares
Source of Variation            SS      DF       MS         F  Sig of F

WITHIN+RESIDUAL               9.63     15      .64
CONSTANT                    817.19      1   817.19   1272.24    .000
X                            36.58      1    36.58     56.94    .000
A                            16.93      2     8.47     13.18    .000
A BY X                         .67      2      .33       .52    .605
```

E Results for fourth analysis

```
Tests of Significance for Y using SEQUENTIAL Sums of Squares
Source of Variation            SS      DF       MS         F  Sig of F

WITHIN+RESIDUAL               9.63     15      .64
CONSTANT                    817.19      1   817.19   1272.24    .000
X WITHIN A                   47.48      3    15.83     24.64    .000
A                             6.69      2     3.35      5.21    .019
```

Example 2: Multivariate Multiple Regression and Canonical Correlation

MANOVA produces multivariate results, individual regression results, and analysis of residuals, although residual analysis is not as extensive as in REGRESSION. Since there is no canonical correlation procedure in SPSS/PC+, MANOVA can be used for canonical correlation analysis.

This example uses MANOVA for multivariate multiple regression and canonical correlation analysis. The data for this example come from Finn (1974) and were obtained from tests administered to 60 eleventh-grade students in a western New York metropolitan school.

The dependent variables are

• SYNTH—a measurement of achievement.

• EVAL—another measurement of achievement.

There are three types of independent variables. The first is

• INTEL—general intelligence as measured by a standard test.

For the second type of independent variables, there are three measures of creativity:

• CONOBV—consequences obvious, which involves the ability of the subject to list direct consequences of a given hypothetical event.

• CONRMT—consequences remote, which involves identifying more remote or original consequences of similar situations.

• JOB—possible jobs, which involves the ability to list a quantity of occupations that might be represented by a given emblem or symbol.

The third type of independent variable is a set of multiplicative interactions of the three creativity measures with intelligence to assess whether creativity has a greater effect on the achievement of individuals having high intelligence than on individuals of low intelligence. These variables are created using the SPSS/PC+ transformation language. For all independent variables, standardized scores are used. The data are in an external file named AMAN.DAT.

The SPSS/PC+ commands in the command file named on the INCLUDE command are

```
SET WIDTH=WIDE.
DATA LIST FILE='AMAN.DAT' /
    SYNTH 1 EVAL 3 CONOBV 5-8(1) CONRMT 9-12(1)
    JOB 14-17(1) INTEL 19-23(1).
MISSING VALUE SYNTH TO INTEL(9.9).
DESCRIPTIVES INTEL CONOBV CONRMT JOB
    /OPTIONS=3 5.
COMPUTE CI1=ZCONOBV*ZINTEL.
COMPUTE CI2=ZCONRMT*ZINTEL.
COMPUTE CI3=ZJOB*ZINTEL.
MANOVA  SYNTH EVAL WITH ZINTEL ZCONOBV ZCONRMT ZJOB CI1 CI2 CI3
    /PRINT=ERROR(SSCP COV COR)
           SIGNIF(HYPOTH STEPDOWN DIMENR EIGEN)
    /DISCRIM=RAW,STAN,ESTIM,COR,ALPHA(1.0)
    /RESIDUALS=CASEWISE PLOT
    /DESIGN.
FINISH.
```

- The SET command sets the display width to 132 characters.

- The DATA LIST command names the file containing the data and defines six variables.

- The MISSING VALUE command declares the value 9.9 as user-missing for all the variables read from the data file.

- Option 3 on the DESCRIPTIVES procedure computes standardized scores for the intelligence and creativity measures. The new variables—ZINTEL, ZCONOBV, ZCONRMT, and ZJOB—are automatically added to the active file. Option 5 on DESCRIPTIVES specifies listwise deletion of missing values for the calculation.

- The COMPUTE commands compute three interaction variables—CI1, CI2, and CI3—from the standardized variables created with DESCRIPTIVES.

- The MANOVA specification names SYNTH and EVAL as joint dependent variables and specifies seven covariates—ZINTEL, ZCONOBV, ZCONRMT, ZJOB, CI1, CI2, and CI3.

- The PRINT subcommand requests several displays. The ERROR keyword prints the error sums-of-squares and cross-products (SSCP) matrix, the error variance-covariance matrix, and the error correlation matrix with standard deviations on the diagonal (Figure A).

- The SIGNIF keyword has four specifications. HYPOTH prints the hypothesis SSCP matrix (Figure A). STEPDOWN prints the Roy-Bargmann stepdown F tests for the dependent variables. DIMENR prints the dimension reduction analysis, and EIGEN prints the eigenvalues and canonical correlations (Figure B).

- The DISCRIM subcommand requests a canonical analysis. The results correspond to canonical correlation analysis, since a set of continuous dependent variables is related to a set of continuous independent variables. The RAW keyword prints canonical function coefficients; the STAN keyword prints standardized canonical function coefficients; the ESTIM keyword produces effect estimates in canonical function space; the COR keyword prints correlations between the original variables and the canonical variables defined by the canonical functions; and the ALPHA keyword sets a generous cutoff value (1.0) for the significance of the canonical functions in the analysis, thereby ensuring that MANOVA calculates all possible canonical functions. Two is the maximum possible in this analysis (Figures C and D).

- The RESIDUALS subcommand with keyword CASEWISE prints four casewise results for each dependent variable: the observed value of the dependent variable, the predicted value of the dependent variable, the residual value, and the standardized residual, where standardization consists of dividing the residual by the error standard deviation (Figure F).

D

Examples

- The PLOT keyword on the RESIDUALS subcommand produces plots of the observed values, predicted values, and case number against standardized residuals, as well as normal and detrended normal probability plots for the standardized residuals (Figures G through I).
- Finally, the DESIGN subcommand specifies the model, which in this example is the default full factorial model.

Portions of the output are shown in Figures A through I. The exact appearance of printed display depends on the characters available on your printer.

- Figure A shows within-cells statistical results. The correlation of 0.380 is the partial correlation of SYNTH and EVAL, taking into account the independent variable set. The two standard deviations are adjusted. The Bartlett test of sphericity leads to rejection of the hypothesis that the partial correlation between SYNTH and EVAL is zero. Figure A also shows the adjusted variance-covariance matrix, the error SSCP matrix, and the hypothesis SSCP matrix for the regression effect.
- Figure B shows the default display and the stepdown display. Both the multivariate and univariate test results indicate that the predictor set has a statistically significant impact on the dependent variables. While two dimensions are fit, it appears that one dimension will suffice. Of the two eigenvalues, the first eigenvalue has most of the variance associated with it, while the second eigenvalue has relatively little variability associated with it. Likewise, the first canonical correlation is moderately sized, while the second canonical correlation is negligible in magnitude. Provided that you accept the order of the criterion variables—SYNTH, then EVAL—the stepdown F tests show that after taking SYNTH into account, EVAL does not contribute to the association with the predictors.
- Figure C shows canonical results for the two dependent variables. Recall that only the first canonical function is statistically significant. Correlations between the dependent variables and the first canonical variable are of similar magnitude. The part of the figure labeled **Variance explained by canonical variables of DEPENDENT variables** provides a *redundancy analysis* (Cooley & Lohnes, 1971).
- Figure D shows the analogous canonical results for the covariates. The correlations between covariates and the first canonical variable load most heavily on intelligence.
- Figure E shows the default display of the regression results for the two dependent variables.
- Figure F shows a portion of the casewise results for the synthesis variable produced by RESIDUALS=CASEWISE.
- Figure G shows two plots. The plot of observed versus predicted values for SYNTH reflects the multiple R for the model. The plot of observed values versus residuals shows how residuals vary in sign and magnitude across values of the dependent variable.
- Figure H shows two plots: the plot of predicted values versus residuals, and the plot of case number versus residuals. The latter plot is useful when there is some meaning to the order of cases in your file.
- Finally, Figure I shows the normal and detrended normal plots of the residuals.

A Within-cells results and hypothesis SSCP

```
Adjusted WITHIN CELLS Correlations with Std. Devs. on Diagonal

                    SYNTH          EVAL

SYNTH              1.370
EVAL                .380         1.513


- - - - - - - - -
Statistics for ADJUSTED WITHIN CELLS correlations

Determinant =                          .85577
Bartlett test of sphericity =      7.86554 with 1 D. F.
Significance =                         .005

F(max) criterion =                 1.21806 with (2,52) D. F.


- - - - - - - - -
Adjusted WITHIN CELLS Variances and Covariances

                    SYNTH          EVAL

SYNTH              1.878
EVAL                .787         2.288


- - - - - - - - -
Adjusted WITHIN CELLS Sum-of-Squares and Cross-Products

                    SYNTH          EVAL

SYNTH             97.669
EVAL              40.937        118.967


- - - - - - - - -
Adjusted Hypothesis Sum-of-Squares and Cross-Products

                    SYNTH          EVAL

SYNTH             81.181
EVAL              69.413         67.216
```

B Test results and dimensionality statistics

```
EFFECT .. WITHIN CELLS Regression
Multivariate Tests of Significance (S = 2, M = 2 , N = 24 1/2)

Test Name        Value   Approx. F Hypoth. DF   Error DF  Sig. of F

Pillais          .55946    2.88501      14.00     104.00      .001
Hotellings      1.05995    3.78553      14.00     100.00      .000
Wilks            .47077    3.33286      14.00     102.00      .000
Roys             .49886


- - - - - - - -
Eigenvalues and Canonical Correlations

Root No.    Eigenvalue      Pct.    Cum. Pct.  Canon Cor.   Sq. Cor

     1           .995      93.914     93.914       .706       .499
     2           .065       6.086    100.000       .246       .061


- - - - - - - -
Dimension Reduction Analysis

Roots        Wilks L.      F Hypoth. DF   Error DF  Sig. of F

1 TO 2        .47077    3.33286     14.00     102.00      .000
2 TO 2        .93940     .55910      6.00      52.00      .761


- - - - - - - -
Univariate F-tests with (7,52) D. F.

Variable   Sq. Mul. R    Mul. R  Adj. R-sq.   Hypoth. MS   Error MS          F   Sig. of F

SYNTH         .45390    .67372     .38039     11.59727    1.87825    6.17450      .000
EVAL          .36102    .60085     .27500      9.60230    2.28783    4.19712      .001


- - - - - - - -
Roy-Bargman Stepdown F - tests

Variable   Hypoth. MS   Error MS StepDown F Hypoth. DF   Error DF  Sig. of F

SYNTH       11.59727    1.87825    6.17450          7         52      .000
EVAL         2.32700    1.99625    1.16569          7         51      .339
```

C Canonical results for dependent variables

```
Raw canonical coefficients for DEPENDENT variables
        Function No.

Variable            1           2

SYNTH             .404        -.597
EVAL              .226         .670

- - - - - - - - -
Standardized canonical coefficients for DEPENDENT variables
        Function No.

Variable            1           2

SYNTH             .704       -1.040
EVAL              .402        1.189

- - - - - - - - -
Correlations between DEPENDENT and canonical variables
        Function No.

Variable            1           2

SYNTH             .947        -.320
EVAL              .828         .561

- - - - - - - - -
Variance explained by canonical variables of DEPENDENT variables

CAN. VAR.   Pct Var DE Cum Pct DE Pct Var CO Cum Pct CO

    1         79.146      79.146     39.482     39.482
    2         20.854     100.000      1.264     40.746
```

D Canonical results for the covariates

```
Raw canonical coefficients for COVARIATES
        Function No.

COVARIATE           1           2

ZINTEL            .848        -.103
ZCONOBV           .265         .230
ZCONRMT           .193         .472
ZJOB             -.064        -.279
CI1              -.014        1.035
CI2              -.076        -.324
CI3               .207        -.047

- - - - - - - - -
Standardized canonical coefficients for COVARIATES
        CAN. VAR.

COVARIATE           1           2

ZINTEL            .848        -.103
ZCONOBV           .265         .230
ZCONRMT           .193         .472
ZJOB             -.064        -.279
CI1              -.012         .887
CI2              -.101        -.431
CI3               .217        -.049

- - - - - - - - -
Correlations between COVARIATES and canonical variables
        CAN. VAR.

Covariate           1           2

ZINTEL            .946        -.091
ZCONOBV           .303        -.061
ZCONRMT           .562         .418
ZJOB              .578        -.127
CI1               .180         .868
CI2               .494        -.010
CI3               .449         .063

- - - - - - - - -
Variance explained by canonical variables of the COVARIATES

CAN. VAR.   Pct Var DE Cum Pct DE Pct Var CO Cum Pct CO

    1         15.074      15.074     30.217     30.217
    2           .832      15.906     13.728     43.945
```

E Regression results

```
Regression analysis for WITHIN CELLS error term
Dependent variable .. SYNTH

COVARIATE          B         Beta    Std. Err.    t-Value    Sig. of t  Lower -95%  CL- Upper

ZINTEL         1.00235      .57571      .217        4.617       .000        .567       1.438
ZCONOBV         .27761      .15945      .236        1.178       .244       -.195        .750
ZCONRMT         .16002      .09191      .238         .672       .504       -.318        .638
ZJOB           -.03625     -.02082      .267        -.136       .892       -.571        .499
CI1            -.15800     -.07779      .236        -.670       .506       -.631        .315
CI2            -.04376     -.03348      .215        -.204       .839       -.475        .387
CI3             .24763      .14904      .252         .982       .331       -.259        .754

Dependent variable .. EVAL

COVARIATE          B         Beta    Std. Err.    t-Value    Sig. of `t  Lower -95%  CL- Upper

ZINTEL          .85582      .48177      .240        3.571       .001        .375       1.337
ZCONOBV         .33193      .18686      .260        1.277       .207       -.190        .854
ZCONRMT         .31633      .17807      .263        1.204       .234       -.211        .843
ZJOB           -.13500     -.07600      .294        -.459       .648       -.726        .456
CI1             .23964      .11563      .260         .921       .362       -.283        .762
CI2            -.15804     -.11852      .237        -.667       .508       -.634        .317
CI3             .20367      .12014      .278         .732       .468       -.355        .762
```

F Casewise output

```
Observed and Predicted Values for Each Case
Dependent Variable.. SYNTH

Case No.    Observed   Predicted Raw Resid. Std Resid.

     1        5.000      2.824      2.176      1.588
     2        0.0        1.905     -1.905     -1.390
     4        4.000      3.648       .352       .257
     5        1.000      2.030     -1.030      -.752
     6        7.000      4.210      2.790      2.036
     7        1.000      1.950      -.950      -.694
     8        2.000      2.036      -.036      -.027
     9        1.000      1.763      -.763      -.557
    10        4.000      3.861       .139       .102
     .          .          .          .          .
     .          .          .          .          .
```

G Observed values vs. predicted values and residuals

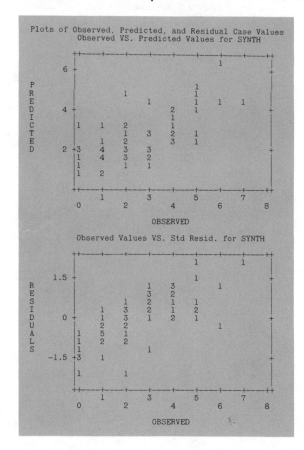

H Residuals vs. predicted values and case number

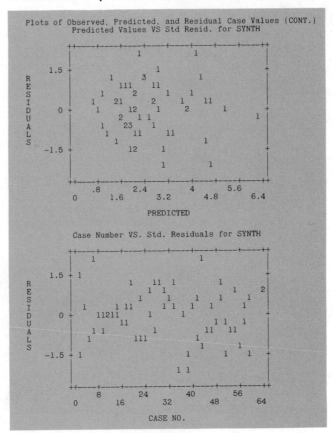

I Normal and detrended normal probability plots

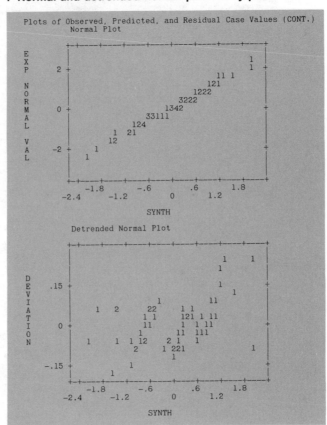

Example 3: Repeated Measures

This example is a repeated measures design using data from an experiment that studies the effects of four drugs on reaction time to a series of tasks (Winer, 1971). The subjects are trained in the tasks prior to the experiment so that the learning of the tasks does not confound the analysis. The experimenter observes each subject under each drug, and the order of administration of drugs is randomized. Since there are only five subjects in the analysis, the data are included inline.

The SPSS/PC+ commands in the command file named on the INCLUDE command are

```
SET WIDTH=WIDE.
DATA LIST FREE/ DRUG1 DRUG2 DRUG3 DRUG4.
BEGIN DATA.
 30 28 16 34
 14 18 10 22
 24 20 18 30
 38 34 20 44
 26 28 14 30
END DATA.
MANOVA DRUG1 TO DRUG4
  /WSFACTORS=TRIAL(4)
  /CONTRAST(TRIAL)=SPECIAL(4*1, 1,-1,0,0,
                          1,1,0,-2, 1,1,-3,1)
  /PRINT=CELLINFO(MEANS)
   TRANSFORM
   SIGNIF(UNIV)
  /DESIGN.
FINISH.
```

- The SET command sets the width of the display to 132 characters.
- The DATA LIST command defines four variables that will be read in freefield format from the command file.
- The BEGIN DATA—END DATA commands surround the inline data.
- The MANOVA specification names DRUG1 to DRUG4 as four joint dependent variables. There are no between-subjects factors or covariates in the analysis.
- The WSFACTORS subcommand defines TRIAL as a within-subjects factor. The 4 in parentheses after the factor name indicates there are four drugs.
- The CONTRAST subcommand specifies a special set of contrasts for comparisons of the means across scores. The within-subjects factor requires *orthogonal* contrasts, which include difference, Helmert, and polynomial contrasts. If you do not specify orthogonal contrasts for the within-subjects factor, MANOVA takes your specified contrasts and orthonormalizes them.
- The first row of the special matrix is always the contrast for the overall mean and is typically a set of 1's. The remaining rows of the matrix contain the special contrasts signifying the desired comparisons between levels of the factor. After inspection of the four means, the following comparisons are specified: (1) the mean of DRUG1 versus the mean of DRUG2; (2) the means of DRUG1 and DRUG2 versus the mean of DRUG4; and (3) the means of DRUG1, DRUG2, and DRUG4 versus DRUG3.
- The PRINT subcommand has three specifications. CELLINFO prints the means (Figure A). TRANSFORM prints the orthonormalized transformation matrix, which directly reflects the contrasts on the within-subjects factor (Figure B). SIGNIF(UNIV) prints the univariate F tests (Figure G).
- The DESIGN subcommand specifies the model for the between-subjects factor. Since there is no between-subjects factor in this model, the DESIGN subcommand simply triggers the analysis.

Portions of the display output are shown in Figures A through H.

- Figure A shows the cell means and standard deviations. Inspection of the cell means provides a rationale for the special contrast used in the analysis. Notice that the means for DRUG1 and DRUG2 have the smallest difference. Then, the mean for DRUG4 has a smaller difference from these two than does the mean for DRUG3. Finally, the mean for DRUG3 is most different from the others. Note: If the width is not set wide (132 characters), the confidence intervals are not included in the display.

D

Examples

- Figure B shows the within-subjects design. The orthonormalized transformation matrix shows the contrasts on the means. The original contrasts on the CONTRAST subcommand are orthogonal. MANOVA normalizes the contrasts so that the sum of squares of any column of the matrix is 1.
- Figure C shows the beginning of the default display for multivariate repeated measures analysis. A message indicating that the variables are transformed is also displayed.
- Figure D shows the test of significance for the between-subjects effect, which in this example is just the overall constant.
- Figure E shows the next cycle of the analysis, which is the test for the trial within-subjects effect. MANOVA jointly tests the three transformed variables, making this a multivariate test.
- Figure F shows Mauchly's test of sphericity, which is printed by default. This tests the hypothesis that the covariance matrix of the transformed variables has a constant variance on the diagonal and zeros off the diagonal.
- Figure G shows the multivariate tests of significance of the trial within-subjects effect. The multivariate tests are significant at the 0.05 level. The univariate F tests, the result of specifying SIGNIF(UNIV), reveal more detailed aspects of the pattern. Recall that the T2 effect after transformation—the contrast between the means of DRUG1 and DRUG2—is the first contrast of interest. The F statistic for this effect is not significant, which leads to the conclusion that these two drugs do not produce differences in reaction time. On the other hand, the transformed T3 and T4 effects are significant at the 0.01 level.
- Finally, Figure H shows the averaged test of significance for the drug effect; these are the *univariate approach* statistics. There are twelve error degrees of freedom for this test, while there are two error degrees of freedom for the multivariate tests. Given the error correlation results above, the averaged test is appropriate. The observed level of significance of this test is less than 0.0005, so the averaged F test corroborates the multivariate test results.

A Cell means and standard deviations

```
Cell Means and Standard Deviations
Variable .. DRUG1
                                        Mean  Std. Dev.      N   95 percent Conf. Interval

For entire sample                     26.400      8.764      5      15.519     37.281

- - - - - - - - - -
Variable .. DRUG2
                                        Mean  Std. Dev.      N   95 percent Conf. Interval

For entire sample                     25.600      6.542      5      17.477     33.723

- - - - - - - - - -
Variable .. DRUG3
                                        Mean  Std. Dev.      N   95 percent Conf. Interval

For entire sample                     15.600      3.847      5      10.823     20.377

- - - - - - - - - -
Variable .. DRUG4
                                        Mean  Std. Dev.      N   95 percent Conf. Interval

For entire sample                     32.000      8.000      5      22.067     41.933
```

B Within-subjects design

```
Orthonormalized Transformation Matrix (Transposed)

                 T1        T2        T3        T4

DRUG1         .50000    .70711    .40825    .28868
DRUG2         .50000   -.70711    .40825    .28868
DRUG3         .50000    0.0       0.0      -.86603
DRUG4         .50000    0.0      -.81650    .28868
```

C Constant within-subjects effect

```
Order of Variables for Analysis

  Variates     Covariates

  T1

  1 Dependent Variable
  0 Covariates

 _ _ _ _ _ _ _ _ _ _
Note..  TRANSFORMED variables are in the variates column.
        These TRANSFORMED variables correspond to the
        Between-subject effects.
```

D Analysis of variance for CONSTANT

```
Tests of Between-Subjects Effects.

Tests of Significance for T1 using UNIQUE sums of squares
Source of Variation          SS       DF       MS        F  Sig of F

WITHIN CELLS              680.80       4   170.20
CONSTANT                12400.20       1 12400.20     72.86     .001
```

E Trial within-subjects effect

```
Order of Variables for Analysis

  Variates     Covariates

   T2
   T3
   T4

  3 Dependent Variables
  0 Covariates

 _ _ _ _ _ _ _ _ _ _
Note..  TRANSFORMED variables are in the variates column.
        These TRANSFORMED variables correspond to the
        'TRIAL' WITHIN-SUBJECT effect.
```

F Error correlation statistics

```
Tests involving 'TRIAL' Within-Subject Effect.


Mauchly sphericity test, W =        .18650
Chi-square approx. =                4.57156 with 5 D. F.
Significance =                      .470

Greenhouse-Geisser Epsilon =        .60487
Huynh-Feldt Epsilon =              1.00000
Lower-bound Epsilon =               .33333
```

G Multivariate tests of significance

```
EFFECT .. TRIAL
Multivariate Tests of Significance (S = 1, M = 1/2, N = 0)

Test Name        Value   Approx. F Hypoth. DF   Error DF  Sig. of F

Pillais         .97707   28.41231       3.00       2.00      .034
Hotellings    42.61846   28.41231       3.00       2.00      .034
Wilks           .02293   28.41231       3.00       2.00      .034
Roys            .97707

 - - - - - - - - - -
Univariate F-tests with (1,4) D. F.

Variable   Hypoth. SS   Error SS Hypoth. MS   Error MS         F  Sig. of F

T2            1.60000   26.40000    1.60000    6.60000    .24242      .648
T3          120.00000   12.00000  120.00000    3.00000  40.00000      .003
T4          576.60000   74.40000  576.60000   18.60000  31.00000      .005
```

H Averaged test of significance

```
AVERAGED Tests of Significance for DRUG using UNIQUE sums of squares
Source of Variation           SS      DF        MS         F  Sig of F

WITHIN CELLS              112.80      12      9.40
TRIAL                     698.20       3    232.73     24.76      .000
```

References Cooley, W. W., and P. R. Lohnes. 1971. *Multivariate data analysis.* New York: John Wiley & Sons.

Finn, J. D. 1974. *A general model for multivariate analysis.* New York: Holt, Rinehart & Winston.

Winer, B.J. 1971. *Statistical principles in experimental design.* New York: McGraw-Hill.

NLR   The following example shows how to use NLR to do nonlinear estimation. The example includes a method for obtaining good initial estimates for NLR.

A Basic Nonlinear Model   Draper and Smith (1981) pose the following exercise. Under adiabatic conditions, the wind speed Y is given by the nonlinear model

$$Y = a \ln(bX + c) + e$$

where

X = the nominal height of the anemometer
a = friction velocity
b = 1 + (zero point displacement)/(roughness length)
c = 1/(roughness length)

The data are as follows:

```
   X       Y

  40    490.2
  80    585.3
 160    673.7
 320    759.2
 640    837.5
```

To arrive at good initial values, consider the model without the error term:

$$Y = a \ln(bX + c)$$

Simple algebraic manipulation transforms the model into linear form. First, divide both sides by a:

$$Y/a = \ln(bX + c)$$

Then, use the EXP function, which is the inverse of the natural logarithm:

$$\exp(Y/a) = bX + c$$

The model is now in linear form. The dependent variable, exp(Y/a), should be regressed on X to obtain estimates of b and c. To determine the value to use for a, you need to consider the magnitudes of the Y values. Recall that the transcendental number e is 2.7183 to four decimal places. Thus, e raised to the Y power, represented as exp(Y), will be outside the bounds of machine storage if Y is at all large, as is the case here. Considering the scale of the Y variable, we decide to set a equal to 100 initially. If you choose naive initial values for a, b, and c, chances are you will get NLR off to a bad start. Having gone through the above exercise, however, we can confidently supply initial values to NLR.

The following SPSS/PC+ commands show how to arrive at initial estimates for NLR:

```
TITLE 'NLRDS7--EXAMPLE G'.
DATA LIST / X 1-3 Y 5-9(1).
BEGIN DATA
 40 490.2
 80 585.3
160 673.7
320 759.2
640 837.5
END DATA.

PLOT PLOT=Y WITH X.
* LET A=100 SO THAT EXP DOESN'T PRODUCE TOO LARGE NUMBERS.
COMPUTE EY=EXP(Y/100).
REGRESSION VAR=EY,X/DEP=EY/ENTER.
```

Figure 1 shows the plot of the Y versus X association. The relationship is nonlinear.

Figure 1 The functional form

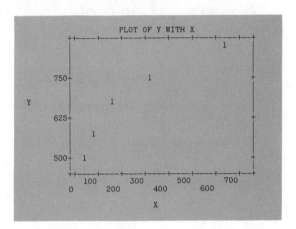

Figure 2 shows the regression used to get initial values for *b* and *c*.

Figure 2 Regression results

```
Multiple R              .99940
R Square                .99879
Adjusted R Square       .99839
Standard Error        69.22830

Analysis of Variance
                      DF        Sum of Squares       Mean Square
Regression             1      11886580.22650      11886580.22650
Residual               3         14377.67112         4792.55704

F =    2480.21675      Signif F =   .0000


------------------ Variables in the Equation ------------------

Variable            B          SE B         Beta        T    Sig T

X            7.065892      .141880      .999396   49.802   .0000
(Constant) -223.259958   46.867778                -4.764   .0176
```

Recall that we set *a* to 100. The initial values for *b* and *c* are 7.06 and -223, respectively. The following commands show how to use NLR to estimate the model.

```
MODEL PROGRAM
   A=100 B=7.06 C=-223.26.
COMPUTE PRED=A*LN(B*X+C).
NLR Y WITH X/PRED=PRED/SAVE PRED.
PLOT
   FORMAT=OVERLAY
   /PLOT=PRED WITH X;Y WITH X.
```

Figure 3 shows the iteration history from NLR. NLR takes some time to get to a final solution, but an inspection of values as they change across iterations reveals that nothing is awry.

Figure 3 Iteration history

```
Iteration   Residual SS        A            B          C

   1        7512.661160   100.000000   7.00000000   -223.26000
   1.1      2968.843479   106.979248   2.90124411    -26.228854
   2        2968.843479   106.979248   2.90124411    -26.228854
   2.1       212.6078278  115.135547   2.19272905    -21.406742
   3         212.6078278  115.135547   2.19272905    -21.406742
   3.1         7.153975767 115.150187  2.30716419    -22.017236
   4           7.153975767 115.150187  2.30716419    -22.017236
   4.1         7.013265991 115.147029  2.31062136    -22.028261
   5           7.013265991 115.147029  2.31062136    -22.028261
   5.1         7.013265848 115.146868  2.31064676    -22.028795
   6           7.013265848 115.146868  2.31064676    -22.028795
   6.1         7.013265848 115.146864  2.31064731    -22.028808

Run stopped after 12 model evaluations and 6 derivative evaluations.
Iterations have been stopped because the relative reduction between
successive residual sums of squares is at most SSCON = 1.000E-08
```

Figure 4 shows the remaining NLR results. The ANOVA for the regression shows that the fit of the final solution is very good. Using 5 data points to estimate a 3-parameter model is a highly parameterized situation. This is reflected in the high correlations of the estimates. The standard error of the c coefficient is relatively large. This dovetails with the iteration history shown in Figure 3, wherein NLR began with an initial value of -223 and ended up with a final value of -22.

Figure 4 NLR results

```
-Nonlinear Regression Summary Statistics      Dependent Variable Y
 Source                 DF  Sum of Squares  Mean Square
 Regression              3  2314527.69673   771509.23224
 Residual                2        7.01327        3.50663
 Uncorrected Total       5  2314534.71000
 (Corrected Total)       4    75525.34800
 R squared = 1 - Residual SS / Corrected SS =      .99991
                                           Asymptotic 95 %
                            Asymptotic   Confidence Interval
 Parameter    Estimate     Std. Error   Lower        Upper

 A         115.14686755   2.040555902 106.36706413 123.92667097
 B           2.310646755    .280311739   1.104562687   3.516730823
 C         -22.02879484   6.409417887 -49.60629420   5.548704532
 Asymptotic Correlation Matrix of the Parameter Estimates
                  A          B          C

 A            1.0000      -.9963      .9666
 B            -.9963      1.0000     -.9802
 C             .9666      -.9802     1.0000
```

Figure 5 shows a plot of PRED versus X superimposed on a value of Y versus X. The fit is very good.

Figure 5 The fitted function

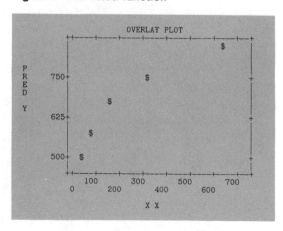

PROBIT

You can use PROBIT for a variety of dichotomous response models. The example shown here illustrates one of the most common applications: a dose-response model.

Dose-Response Model

The following shows the use of the PROBIT procedure to analyze an example from Finney (1971).

```
TITLE    "PROBIT ANALYSIS. DATA FROM 'PROBIT' BY FINNEY P.132".
DATA LIST / ROOT 1 X 3-7 N 9-11 R 13-15.
BEGIN DATA
1 148.0 142 142
1 100.0 127 126
1  48.0 128 115
1  12.0 126  58
2  62.0 125 125
2  46.0 117 115
2  31.0 127 114
2  14.8  51  40
2   3.8 132  37
2   0.0 129  21
END DATA.
PROBIT  R OF N BY ROOT(1,2) WITH X
  /MODEL = BOTH
  /NATRES
  /PRINT = ALL.
```

- The TITLE command sets up a title for the run.
- The DATA LIST command reads the variables ROOT, X, N, and R from the data included in the command file.
- The PROBIT command specifies that the number of responses is in variable R and the number of observations is in N. The response rate will be predicted from variable X. Two groups are defined by variable ROOT.
- The MODEL subcommand specifies both probit and logit response models.
- The NATRES subcommand requests an estimate of the natural response rate (or threshold) for each model. This specification requires that a control level be entered with the data.
- The PRINT subcommand requests all available output.
- The first data case shows 142 responses for the 142 observations with an X of 148.0 in the first group. The second-to-last case shows 37 responses for the 132 observations with an X of 3.8 in the second group. The last case has a value of 0.0 for predictor X, so the response rate used as the control level is 21 out of 129.

Figure 1 shows the case and model information displayed by PROBIT. When both models are estimated, all output for the logit model is displayed before that for the probit model. Selected output from the logit model and all the output from the probit model are shown in Figures 1 through 9.

Figure 1 PROBIT case and model information

```
DATA  Information

        9 unweighted cases accepted.
        0 cases rejected because of out-of-range group values.
        0 cases rejected because of missing data.
        0 Cases rejected because LOG-transform can't be done.


Group Information

        ROOT      Level  N of Cases   Label
                    1          4        1
                    2          5        2


MODEL Information

        BOTH Probit and Logit models are requested.


Natural Response rate to be estimated

        The number of  subjects in the CONTROL group   129.0
        The number of responses in the CONTROL group    21.0
```

Figure 2 shows the parameter estimates from the logit model. Figure 3 shows these estimates from the probit model. The number of iterations required to reach the convergence criterion and the final value for the criterion are displayed first. The default cutoff values for these terms are 20 iterations and a convergence criterion of 0.001. If the convergence criterion had failed to reach the cutoff value in the allotted iterations, PROBIT would have displayed an appropriate message and the estimates from the iterations that were completed.

Figure 2 Parameter estimates and covariances for logit model

```
ML converged at iteration  6.  The converge criterion =    .00095

Parameter Estimates (LOGIT model:  (LOG(p/(1-p))/2 + 5) = Intercept + BX ):
                      Note 5 added to intercept and logit divided by 2.

           Regression Coeff.  Standard Error     Coeff./S.E.

    X              2.45569           .19850         12.37135


           Intercept  Standard Error  Intercept/S.E.  ROOT

             2.02382         .30064        6.73182       1
             2.59473         .28483        9.10988       2

Estimate of Natural Response Rate = .172976  with  S.E. =    .03147

Pearson  Goodness-of-Fit  Chi Square =      8.966   DF = 6   P = .176
         PARALLELISM TEST CHI SQUARE =       .048   DF = 1   P = .826

Since Goodness-of-Fit Chi square is NOT significant, no heterogeneity
factor is used in the calculation of confidence limits.
- - - - - - - - - - - - - - - - - - - - - - - - - - - - - - - - - -
Covariance(below) and Correlation(above) Matrices of Parameter Estimates

                    X    NAT RESP

X              .03940    .42344
NAT RESP       .00264    .00099
```

Figure 3 Parameter estimates and covariances for probit model

```
ML converged at iteration  6.  The converge criterion =    .00063

Parameter Estimates (PROBIT model:  (PROBIT(p) + 5) = Intercept + BX ):
                      Note 5 added to intercept.

           Regression Coeff.  Standard Error     Coeff./S.E.

    X              2.78382           .20654         13.47809


           Intercept  Standard Error  Intercept/S.E.  ROOT

             1.59842         .33212        4.81282       1
             2.26158         .30366        7.44765       2

Estimate of Natural Response Rate = .168731  with  S.E. =    .03177

Pearson  Goodness-of-Fit  Chi Square =      5.933   DF = 6   P = .431
         PARALLELISM TEST CHI SQUARE =       .050   DF = 1   P = .823

Since Goodness-of-Fit Chi square is NOT significant, no heterogeneity
factor is used in the calculation of confidence limits.
- - - - - - - - - - - - - - - - - - - - - - - - - - - - - - - - - -
Covariance(below) and Correlation(above) Matrices of Parameter Estimates

                    X    NAT RESP

X              .04266    .46719
NAT RESP       .00307    .00101
```

Next, PROBIT displays parameter estimates with their standard errors (see Figures 2 and 3). Three kinds of parameters are estimated: a regression coefficient, group intercepts, and a natural response rate. Probit and logit models produced similar estimates. The regression coefficient for X is positive and large relative to its standard error. PROBIT produces separate intercept estimates for each group. Because no value labels are defined for ROOT, the actual values of the variable are used to label the subgroup intercepts. The second group has the greater response rate. Finally, PROBIT produces the estimate of the threshold or natural response rate.

Following the parameter estimates, PROBIT reports two chi-square statistics and their associated probabilities. The goodness-of-fit test displays by default. It tests whether residuals are distributed homogeneously about the regression line. If this test is significant, PROBIT uses a heterogeneity factor to calculate confidence limits. A large chi-square can indicate that a different response model or predictor transformation is required. In this example, the probit model has the better fit. The PRINT subcommand requests all output, which includes the parallelism chi-square. This test indicates whether regression slopes differ between subgroups. Since the test is not significant, the regression slopes are treated as equivalent.

PROBIT estimated more than one parameter (excluding intercepts), so it automatically displays their covariance/correlation matrix. The diagonal entries (variances) simply equal the squares of the standard errors. The off-diagonal correlation and covariance terms indicate how much the estimate of the natural response rate depends on the estimate of the coefficient for X, and vice versa. Here, the two estimates are moderately correlated. In multiple predictor models, this matrix is useful for examining multicollinearity.

Figures 4 and 5 show the observed and predicted frequencies from logit and probit models. PROBIT displays one row for each input case. The first column labels each case with the value of the grouping variable, **ROOT**. The second column shows the values for the predictor, **X**. PROBIT can display values for no more than six predictors when WIDTH is set to 132 columns, even though all predictors are used in the calculations. The procedure displays the number of observations and the number of responses in the next two columns. The following two columns contain the number of responses predicted by the response model (**Expected Responses**) and the differences between the observed number of responses and those predicted (**Residual**). The probit response model in this example has smaller residual values than the logit, indicating a better fit to the data. The final column (**Prob**) contains the predicted probability (or proportion) of responses for the predictor and group values in each row.

Figure 4 Observed and predicted frequencies for logit model

```
Observed and Expected Frequencies


                       Number of    Observed     Expected
                          X          Subjects    Responses   Responses    Residual      Prob
    ROOT
      1        2.17       142.0       142.0       140.728      1.272      .99105
      1        2.00       127.0       126.0       124.406      1.594      .97958
      1        1.68       128.0       115.0       116.388     -1.388      .90928
      1        1.08       126.0        58.0        43.158     14.842      .34252

      2        1.79       125.0       125.0       122.735      2.265      .98188
      2        1.66       117.0       115.0       113.057      1.943      .96630
      2        1.49       127.0       114.0       117.491     -3.491      .92512
      2        1.17        51.0        40.0        36.644      3.356      .71850
      2         .58       132.0        37.0        16.255     20.745      .12314
```

Figure 5 Observed and predicted frequencies for probit model

```
Observed and Expected Frequencies

                        Number of    Observed    Expected
   ROOT            X    Subjects    Responses    Responses    Residual    Prob
      1          2.17     142.0        142.0       141.411       .589      .99586
      1          2.00     127.0        126.0       125.075       .925      .98485
      1          1.68     128.0        115.0       115.136      -.136      .89950
      1          1.08     126.0         58.0        43.540     14.460      .34556

      2          1.79     125.0        125.0       123.477      1.523      .98782
      2          1.66     117.0        115.0       113.566      1.434      .97065
      2          1.49     127.0        114.0       116.994     -2.994      .92121
      2          1.17      51.0         40.0        35.611      4.389      .69825
      2           .58     132.0         37.0        17.215     19.785      .13042
```

Figure 6 displays the plot of probit-transformed response proportions against log-transformed values of the predictor, X. The plotting character (1 or 2) is the number of the group in which the observation appears. Because output width is restricted to 80, the plot appears in compact form. In this plot, the relation of the variables appears linear, and the response rate appears greater in the second group.

Figure 6 PROBIT plot for single-predictor probit model

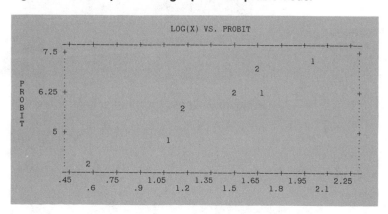

Figures 7 and 8 present the confidence intervals for estimated effects of the predictor, X. For each group, PROBIT displays a table of estimated values for X to produce selected response rates from 0.01 to 0.99. Ninety-five percent fiducial confidence intervals are provided for these estimates (Finney, 1971). If the chi-square test had been significant, PROBIT would have used a heterogeneity factor to calculate the limits. The stimulus tolerance (the predictor estimate for a response rate of 0.50) is 16.66914 in the first group and 9.63145 in the second. If an output width of 132 is in effect, PROBIT also displays effective levels and confidence limits for the log-transformed predictor.

Figure 7 Confidence intervals for effects by group in probit model

```
Confidence Limits for Effective X


ROOT          1            1

                                95% Confidence Limits
Prob          X            Lower           Upper

.01        2.43358      1.49073          3.54170
.02        3.04907      1.93470          4.32588
.03        3.51801      2.28205          4.91252
.04        3.91772      2.58346          5.40658
.05        4.27613      2.85742          5.84556
.06        4.60690      3.11310          6.24774
.07        4.91792      3.35578          6.62356
.08        5.21417      3.58886          6.97966
.09        5.49906      3.81465          7.32052
.10        5.77505      4.03482          7.64936
.15        7.07305      5.08714          9.18084
.20        8.30973      6.11123         10.62212
.25        9.54166      7.14783         12.04574
.30       10.80286      8.22256         13.49459
.35       12.11989      9.35637         15.00163
.40       13.51780     10.56970         16.59764
.45       15.02357     11.88506         18.31571
.50       16.66914     13.32937         20.19508
.55       18.49495     14.93677         22.28584
.60       20.55513     16.75274         24.65563
.65       22.92596     18.84086         27.40086
.70       25.72100     21.29482         30.66690
.75       29.12076     24.26177         34.68812
.80       33.43794     27.99319         39.87663
.85       39.28436     32.97398         47.05260
.90       48.11392     40.33718         58.20447
.91       50.52866     42.31938         61.31623
.92       53.28948     44.57022         64.90463
.93       56.49958     47.16756         69.11657
.94       60.31388     50.22764         74.17419
.95       64.97940     53.93463         80.43461
.96       70.92392     58.60509         88.52216
.97       78.98231     64.85142         99.66931
.98       91.12942     74.10611        116.83393
.99      114.17771     91.23085        150.43809
```

Figure 8 Confidence intervals for effects by group in probit model

```
Confidence Limits for Effective X


ROOT          2            2

                                95% Confidence Limits
Prob          X            Lower           Upper

.01        1.40612       .83171          2.10009
.02        1.76176      1.07972          2.56433
.03        2.03271      1.27386          2.91142
.04        2.26367      1.44239          3.20359
.05        2.47075      1.59564          3.46308
.06        2.66188      1.73871          3.70072
.07        2.84158      1.87455          3.92270
.08        3.01275      2.00506          4.13295
.09        3.17737      2.13153          4.33413
.10        3.33683      2.25489          4.52814
.15        4.08682      2.84506          5.43077
.20        4.80137      3.42031          6.27872
.25        5.51318      4.00355          7.11474
.30        6.24190      4.60933          7.96390
.35        7.00289      5.24966          8.84530
.40        7.81060      5.93636          9.77656
.45        8.68064      6.68260         10.77649
.50        9.63145      7.50419         11.86722
.55       10.68641      8.42131         13.07685
.60       11.87678      9.46096         14.44321
.65       13.24665     10.66101         16.02005
.70       14.86163     12.07738         17.88828
.75       16.82601     13.79805         20.17822
.80       19.32048     15.97345         23.11903
.85       22.69855     18.89332         27.16715
.90       27.80029     23.23350         33.43063
.91       29.19553     24.40516         35.17470
.92       30.79073     25.73678         37.18464
.93       32.64553     27.27463         39.54249
.94       34.84944     29.08777         42.37235
.95       37.54519     31.28554         45.87376
.96       40.97994     34.05583         50.39566
.97       45.63608     37.76201         56.62695
.98       52.65470     43.25369         66.22123
.99       65.97204     53.41329         85.00561
```

You can compute the relative median potency (RMP) as the ratio of the stimulus tolerances in the two groups. The tolerances (from Figures 7 and 8, for Prob = 0.50) are 16.66914 and 9.63145, which have a ratio of 1.73070. The RMP and its confidence limits appear in Figure 9. The confidence limits do not include 1, so the difference is significant.

Figure 9 Estimates of relative median potency (RMP) from probit model

```
Estimates of Relative Median Potency


                            95% Confidence Limits
    ROOT        Estimate    Lower        Upper

   1 VS.  2      1.7307    1.34843      2.30803
```

SURVIVAL The data in this example are from a study of 647 cancer patients. The variables are

- TREATMNT—the type of treatment received.
- ONSETMO, ONSETYR—month and year cancer was discovered.
- RECURSIT—indicates whether a recurrence took place.
- RECURMO, RECURYR—month and year of recurrence.
- OUTCOME—status of patient at end of study, alive or dead.
- DEATHMO, DEATHYR—month and year of death, or, for those who survived, the date the study ended.

Using these date variables and the YRMODA function, the number of months from onset to recurrence and from onset to death or survival are calculated. These new variables become the survival variables, with TREATMNT as the single control variable. The SPSS commands are

```
SET WIDTH=130.
DATA LIST   FILE = SURVDATA/ 1 TREATMNT 15 ONSETMO 19-20
            ONSETYR 21-22 RECURSIT 48 RECURMO 49-50 RECURYR 51-52
            OUTCOME 56 DEATHMO 57-58 DEATHYR 59-60.
COMMENT   TRANSFORM ALL DATES TO RUNNING CALENDAR DAYS.
COMPUTE   ONSDATE=YRMODA(ONSETYR,ONSETMO,15).
COMPUTE   RECDATE=YRMODA(RECURYR,RECURMO,15).
COMPUTE   DEATHDT=YRMODA(DEATHYR,DEATHMO,15).

COMMENT   NOW COMPUTE SURVIVAL VARIABLES.
COMPUTE   ONSSURV = (DEATHDT-ONSDATE)/30.
IF   RECURSIT EQ 0 RECSURV = ONSSURV.
IF   RECURSIT NE 0 RECSURV = (RECDATE-ONSDATE)/30.

VARIABLE LABELS   TREATMNT 'PATIENT TREATMENT'
                  ONSSURV 'MONTHS FROM ONSET TO DEATH'
                  RECSURV 'MONTHS FROM ONSET TO RECURRENCE'.
VALUE LABELS   TREATMNT 1 'TREATMENT A' 2 'TREATMENT B'
               3 'TREATMENT C'.
SURVIVAL   TABLES = ONSSURV,RECSURV BY TREATMNT(1,3)
  /STATUS = RECURSIT(1,9) FOR RECSURV
  /STATUS = OUTCOME(3,4) FOR ONSSURV
  /INTERVALS = THRU 50 BY 5 THRU 100 BY 10
  /PLOTS /COMPARE /CALCULATE=CONDITIONAL PAIRWISE.
```

- The SET command sets the page width to 130.
- The onset, recurrence, and death dates are transformed to running days using the YRMODA function in the COMPUTE command. The constant 15 is used as the day argument for YRMODA since only month and year were recorded, not the actual day.
- ONSSURV, the first survival variable, is calculated by taking the difference between the date of death (or survival) and the date the cancer was discovered (ONSDATE). The difference is divided by 30 to convert it from days to months.
- RECSURV, the second survival variable, is calculated conditionally using the IF command. For cases with RECURSIT values of 0, indicating no recurrence took place, RECSURV is set equal to ONSSURV.
- The TABLES subcommand in SURVIVAL specifies two survival variables, ONSSURV and RECSURV, and one control variable, TREATMNT. The life table for ONSSURV is shown in Figure 1.
- The status variable for RECSURV is RECURSIT with codes 1–9, indicating that the termination event, recurrence, took place. OUTCOME is the status variable for ONSSURV with codes 3 and 4 signaling the terminal event, death.
- The INTERVALS subcommand groups the first 50 months into 5-month intervals and the remaining 50 months into 10-month intervals.
- The default plots are requested using PLOTS. Figure 2 contains the plot of the survival function for ONSSURV.
- COMPARE with no specifications requests all comparisons. The subgroup comparisons for ONSSURV are shown in Figure 3.
- Keyword CONDITIONAL on the CALCULATE subcommand requests approximate comparisons if memory is insufficient for exact comparisons. Keyword PAIRWISE requests the pairwise output.

Figure 1 Life table

```
LIFE TABLE
    SURVIVAL VARIABLE   ONSSURV    MONTHS FROM ONSET TO DEATH
                 FOR    TREATMNT   PATIENT TREATMENT                                  =     1  TREATMENT A

             NUMBER  NUMBER  NUMBER  NUMBER                    CUMUL                            SE OF   SE OF
     INTVL   ENTRNG  WDRAWN  EXPOSD    OF    PROPN    PROPN     PROPN    PROBA-            SE OF  CUMUL   PROB-   SE OF
     START    THIS   DURING    TO    TERMNL  TERMI-   SURVI-    SURV    BILITY   HAZARD   CUMUL   SURV-   ABILTY  HAZRD
     TIME    INTVL   INTVL    RISK   EVENTS  NATING   VING     AT END   DENSTY    RATE   IVING    DENS    RATE

       0.0   501.0    0.0    501.0     3.0  0.0060   0.9940   0.9940   0.0012   0.0012   0.003   0.001   0.001
       5.0   498.0    1.0    497.5    16.0  0.0322   0.9678   0.9620   0.0064   0.0065   0.009   0.002   0.002
      10.0   481.0    1.0    480.5    26.0  0.0541   0.9459   0.9100   0.0104   0.0111   0.013   0.002   0.002
      15.0   454.0    0.0    454.0    17.0  0.0374   0.9626   0.8759   0.0068   0.0076   0.015   0.002   0.002
      20.0   437.0    0.0    437.0    23.0  0.0526   0.9474   0.8298   0.0092   0.0108   0.017   0.002   0.002
      25.0   414.0    1.0    413.5    25.0  0.0605   0.9395   0.7796   0.0100   0.0125   0.019   0.002   0.002
      30.0   388.0    1.0    387.5    22.0  0.0568   0.9432   0.7354   0.0089   0.0117   0.020   0.002   0.002
      35.0   365.0    1.0    364.5    24.0  0.0658   0.9342   0.6870   0.0097   0.0136   0.021   0.002   0.003
      40.0   340.0    0.0    340.0    24.0  0.0706   0.9294   0.6385   0.0097   0.0146   0.022   0.002   0.003
      45.0   316.0    1.0    315.5    14.0  0.0444   0.9556   0.6101   0.0057   0.0091   0.022   0.001   0.002
      50.0   301.0    1.0    300.5    34.0  0.1131   0.8869   0.5411   0.0069   0.0120   0.022   0.001   0.002
      60.0   266.0    0.0    266.0    22.0  0.0827   0.9173   0.4963   0.0045   0.0086   0.022   0.001   0.002
      70.0   244.0    2.0    243.0    15.0  0.0617   0.9383   0.4657   0.0031   0.0064   0.022   0.001   0.002
      80.0   227.0    3.0    225.5    24.0  0.1064   0.8936   0.4161   0.0050   0.0112   0.022   0.001   0.002
      90.0   200.0    2.0    199.0    18.0  0.0905   0.9095   0.3785   0.0038   0.0095   0.022   0.001   0.002
     100.0+  180.0  104.0    128.0    76.0  0.5938   0.4063   0.1538     **       **    0.019     **      **

**     THESE CALCULATIONS FOR THE LAST INTERVAL ARE MEANINGLESS.

THE MEDIAN SURVIVAL TIME FOR THESE DATA IS  69.18
```

Figure 2 Plot output for survival function

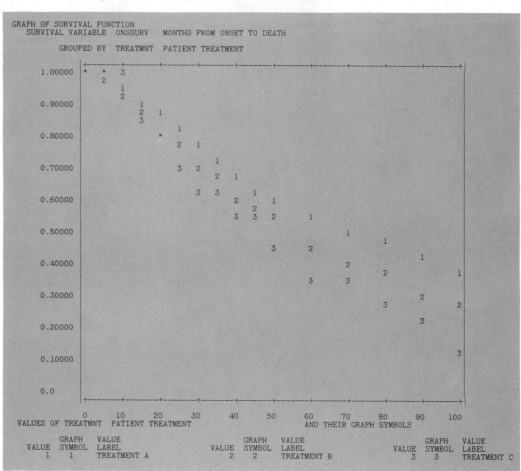

Figure 3 Subgroup comparisons

```
COMPARISON OF SURVIVAL EXPERIENCE USING THE LEE-DESU STATISTIC
   SURVIVAL VARIABLE   ONSSURV    MONTHS FROM ONSET TO DEATH
        GROUPED BY   TREATMNT   PATIENT TREATMENT

OVERALL COMPARISON     STATISTIC        9.001  D.F.      2   PROB.   0.0111

GROUP   LABEL                  TOTAL N   UNCEN     CEN  PCT CEN  MEAN SCORE

    1   TREATMENT A               501     383     118    23.55      20.042
    2   TREATMENT B                97      82      15    15.46     -67.412
    3   TREATMENT C                26      24       2     7.69    -134.69
```

Figure 4 Pairwise comparisons

```
COMPARISON OF SURVIVAL EXPERIENCE USING THE LEE-DESU STATISTIC
   SURVIVAL VARIABLE   ONSSURV    MONTHS FROM ONSET TO DEATH
        GROUPED BY   TREATMNT   PATIENT TREATMENT

OVERALL COMPARISON     STATISTIC        9.001  D.F.      2   PROB.   0.0111

GROUP   LABEL                  TOTAL N   UNCEN     CEN  PCT CEN  MEAN SCORE

    1   TREATMENT A               501     383     118    23.55      20.042
    2   TREATMENT B                97      82      15    15.46     -67.412
    3   TREATMENT C                26      24       2     7.69    -134.69

PAIRWISE COMPARISON    STATISTIC        5.042  D.F.      1   PROB.   0.0247

GROUP   LABEL                  TOTAL N   UNCEN     CEN  PCT CEN  MEAN SCORE

    1   TREATMENT A               501     383     118    23.55      13.603
    2   TREATMENT B                97      82      15    15.46     -70.258

PAIRWISE COMPARISON    STATISTIC        4.768  D.F.      1   PROB.   0.0290

GROUP   LABEL                  TOTAL N   UNCEN     CEN  PCT CEN  MEAN SCORE

    1   TREATMENT A               501     383     118    23.55       6.4391
    3   TREATMENT C                26      24       2     7.69    -124.08

PAIRWISE COMPARISON    STATISTIC        0.766  D.F.      1   PROB.   0.3814

GROUP   LABEL                  TOTAL N   UNCEN     CEN  PCT CEN  MEAN SCORE

    2   TREATMENT B                97      82      15    15.46       2.8454
    3   TREATMENT C                26      24       2     7.69     -10.615
```

Index

Index

SPSS/PC+
Advanced Statistics™
4.0
Reference Card

This card provides a convenient reference to SPSS/PC+ Advanced Statistics™ 4.0. It is arranged by command in alphabetic order. The format diagrams for procedure and nonprocedure commands are constructed according to the following conventions:

Square brackets enclose optional specifications not necessary to the correct completion of the command.

Braces enclose alternative specifications. One of these specifications must be entered in order to complete the specifications correctly. The brackets and braces themselves should not be coded.

Ellipses indicate the possibility of repeating an element in the specifications or the entire cycle of specifications.

Uppercase elements must be entered as they appear in the diagrams.

Lowercase elements describe information to be filled in by the user.

Boldface entries denote defaults. Two asterisks (**) indicate that a specification is a default when its associated subcommand is not specified.

■ DISCRIMINANT

```
DSCRIMINANT GROUPS=varname(min,max) /VARIABLES=varlist
   [/SELECT=varname(value)] [/ANALYSIS=varlist(level) [varlist...]]
   [/METHOD={DIRECT  }] [/TOLERANCE={0.001}] [/MAXSTEPS={2v}]
             {WILKS   }              {t    }              {m }
             {MAHAL   }
             {MAXMINF }
             {MINRESID}
             {RAO     }
   [/FIN={1.0}] [/FOUT={1.0}] [/PIN={1.0}] [/POUT={1.0}] [/VIN={0 }]
         {fi }         {fo }        {pi }         {po }        {vi}
   [/FUNCTIONS={g-1,100.0,1.0}] [/PRIORS={EQUAL     }]
               {nf , cp ,sig}           {SIZE      }
                                        {value list}
   [/SAVE=[CLASS varname] [PROBS rootname] [SCORES rootname]]
   [/ANALYSIS=...]
   [/OPTIONS=option numbers]
   [/STATISTICS={statistic numbers}]
                {ALL              }
```

Options:

1	Include missing values	8	Include cases with missing values during classification
4	Suppress step output		
5	Suppress summary table	9	Classify only unselected cases
6	Varimax rotation of function matrix	10	Classify only unclassified cases
7	Varimax rotation of structure matrix	11	Use individual covariance matrices for classification

Statistics:

1	Group means	8	Group covariance matrices
2	Group standard deviations	9	Total covariance matrix
3	Pooled within-groups covariance matrix	10	Territorial map
4	Pooled within-groups correlation matrix	11	Unstandardized function coefficients
5	Matrix of pairwise F ratios	12	Classification function coefficients
6	Univariate F ratios	13	Classification results table
7	Box's M	14	Casewise materials
		15	Combined plot
		16	Separate plot

■ HILOGLINEAR

```
HILOGLINEAR {varlist} (min,max) [varlist (min,max)...]
            {ALL    }
   [/METHOD=BACKWARD]
   [/MAXORDER=k]
   [/CRITERIA=[CONVERGE({0.25**})] [ITERATE({20**})]
                       {n     }            {n   }
         [P({0.05**})] [MAXSTEPS({10**})] [DEFAULT**]]
            {prob   }            {n   }
   [/CWEIGHT={varname }]
             {(matrix)}
   [/PRINT=[DEFAULT**] [FREQ**] [RESID**] [ESTIM**]
           [NONE] [ASSOCIATION] [ALL]]
   [/PLOT=[{DEFAULT}] [RESID] [NORMPLOT] [NONE**]]
          {ALL    }
   [/MISSING={LISTWISE**} {INCLUDE}]
             {DEFAULT**  }
   [/DESIGN=[effectname effectname*effectname ...]]
   [/DESIGN=...]
```

**Default if subcommand is omitted.

■ LOGISTIC REGRESSION

```
LOGISTIC REGRESSION [VARIABLES=] dependent var [WITH ind. varlist]
   [BY var [BY var] ... ]

   [/CATEGORICAL= var1, var2, ... ]

                               {DEVIATION [(refcat)]      }
                               {SIMPLE [(refcat)]         }
                               {DIFFERENCE                }
   [/CONTRAST (categorical var)={HELMERT                   }]
                               {REPEATED                  }
                               {POLYNOMIAL[({1,2,3...})]] }
                               {           {metric   }    }
                               {SPECIAL (matrix)          }
                               {INDICATOR [(refcat)]      }

   [/METHOD={ENTER**                } [{ALL**                           }]
            {FSTEP [({WALD**})])]}    {varlist [varname BY varname]}
            {       {LR    }     }
            {BSTEP [({WALD**})])]}
            {       {LR    }     }

   [/SELECT={ALL**                   }]
            {varname relation value}

   [/{NOORIGIN**}]
     {ORIGIN   }

   [/ID = [variable]]

   [/PRINT=[ALL] [SUMMARY] [CORR] [DEFAULT**] [ITER [({1**})]]]]
                                                     {n  }

   [/CRITERIA=[BCON ({0.001**})]]
                    {value  }

            [ITERATE({20**})] [LCON({0.01**})]
                    {n   }          {value }

            [PIN({0.05**})] [POUT({0.10**})] [EPS({.00000001**})]
                {value }          {value }        {value      }

   [/CLASSPLOT]

   [/MISSING={EXCLUDE **}]
             {INCLUDE  }

   [/CASEWISE=[tempvarlist]  [OUTLIER({2**   })]]
                                     {value}

   [/SAVE=tempvar[(newname)] tempvar[(newname)]...]

   [/EXTERNAL]
```

**Default if the subcommand or keyword is omitted.

Temporary variables for logistic regression analysis are: PRED, PGROUP, RESID, DEV, LRESID, SRESID, ZRESID, LEVER, COOK, DFBETA.

LOGLINEAR

```
LOGLINEAR varlist(min,max)...[BY] varlist(min,max)

        [WITH covariate varlist]

[/MISSING={LISTWISE**}] [INCLUDE]
         {DEFAULT  }

[/WIDTH={132}]
        { 72}

[/CWEIGHT={varname }] [/CWEIGHT=(matrix)...]
         {(matrix)}

[/GRESID={varlist }] [/GRESID=...]
         {(matrix)}

[/PRINT={DEFAULT**}] [/NOPRINT={ESTIM**  }]
        {FREQ**    }          {COR**    }
        {RESID**   }          {DESIGN** }
        {DESIGN    }          {RESID    }
        {ESTIM     }          {FREQ     }
        {COR       }          {DEFAULT  }
        {ALL       }          {ALL      }
        {NONE      }

[/PLOT={DEFAULT }]
       {RESID   }
       {NORMPROB}
       {NONE**  }

                     {DEVIATION [(refcat)]}
                     {DIFFERENCE          }
                     {HELMERT             }
[/CONTRAST (varname)={SIMPLE [(refcat)]   }]...[/CONTRAST...]
                     {REPEATED            }
                     {POLYNOMIAL [({1,2,3,...})]}
                     {                {metric}  }
                     {[BASIS]  SPECIAL(matrix)  }

[/CRITERIA=[CONVERGE({0.001**})]] [ITERATE({20**})] [DELTA({0.5**})]
                    {eps    }             {n  }          {d     }

            [DEFAULT]]

[/DESIGN=effect effect... effect BY effect...] [/DESIGN...]
**Default if the subcommand is omitted.
```

MANOVA

```
MANOVA dependent varlist [BY factor list (min,max) [factor list...]
                         [WITH covariate list]]
[/WSFACTORS=name (levels) [name...]]
[/READ[=SUMMARY]]
[/TRANSFORM ((varlist[/varlist]))]=[ORTHONORM] [{DEVIATIONS (refcat) }]]
                                               {DIFFERENCE          }
                                   [{CONTRAST}] {HELMERT             }
                                   {BASIS   }  {SIMPLE (refcat)      }
                                               {REPEATED             }
                                               {POLYNOMIAL[(metric)] }
                                               {SPECIAL (matrix)     }

[/WSDESIGN=effect effect...]
[/MEASURE=newname newname...]
[/RENAME={newname} {newname}...]
         {*      } {*      }
[/MISSING=[LISTWISE] [INCLUDE]]

              [CELLINFO ([MEANS**] [SSCP] [COV] [COR] [ALL])]

              [HOMOGENEITY ([BARTLETT**] [COCHRAN**] [BOXM**] [ALL])]

              [DESIGN ([ONEWAY] [OVERALL**] [DECOMP] [BIAS] [SOLUTION])]

[/{PRINT  }={[ERROR ([SSCP] [COV**] [COR**] [STDDEV])]                  }]
  {NOPRINT}
              [SIGNIF ([MULTIV**] [EIGEN] [DIMENR] [UNIV**] [HYPOTH]
                       [STEPDOWN] [{AVERF }] [BRIEF] [SINGLEDF] [ALL])]
                                  {AVONLY}

              [PARAMETERS ([ESTIM**] [ORTHO] [COR] [NEGSUM] [ALL])]

              [TRANSFORM]

[/PLOT=[CELLPLOTS] [STEMLEAF] [ZCORR]
       [NORMAL] [BOXPLOTS] [SIZE({width,height})]]
                                 {(40,15)     }
[/PCOMPS=[[COR**] [NCOMP(n)] [MINEIGEN(eigencut)]
         [COV] [ROTATE(rottype)]               ]]
[/OMEANS=[VARIABLES(varlist)] [TABLES ({factor name    })]]]
                                      {factor BY factor}
                                      {CONSTANT        }
[/PMEANS=[VARIABLES(varlist)] [TABLES ({factor name    })]]]
                                      {factor BY factor}
         [ERROR(errorno)] [PLOT]     {CONSTANT        }
[/DISCRIM=[ROTATE(rottype)] [ALPHA(alpha)] [ALL]]
          [RAW**] [STAN**] [ESTIM**] [COR**]
[/RESIDUALS=[CASEWISE**] [ERROR(errorno)] [PLOT]]
[/METHOD=[MODELTYPE ({MEANS       })]
                    {OBSERVATIONS}
         [ESTIMATION ({QR      } {NOLASTRES} {NOBALANCED} {CONSTANT  })]
                     {CHOLESKY} {LASTRES  } {BALANCED  } {NOCONSTANT}
         [SSTYPE ({UNIQUE    })]]
                 {SEQUENTIAL}
[/WRITE[=SUMMARY]]
[/ANALYSIS [({CONDITIONAL  })]=dependent varlist
            {UNCONDITIONAL}  [WITH covariate varlist]
                             [/dependent varlist...]]
```

LOGLINEAR (continued, right column)

```
[/PARTITION (factorname)[=({1,1... })]]
                          {df,df...}
                                   {DEVIATION [(refcat)]        }
                                   {SIMPLE [(refcat)]           }
                                   {DIFFERENCE                  }
[/CONTRAST (factorname)={HELMERT                     }]
                                   {REPEATED                    }
                                   {POLYNOMIAL[({1,2,3...})]    }
                                   {           {metric}         }
                                   {SPECIAL (matrix)            }
           {WITHIN            }        {W }
[/ERROR={RESIDUAL          } or {R }]
           {WITHIN + RESIDUAL }        {WR}
           {n                 }

            {[CONSTANT...]                                          }
            {[effect effect...]                                     }
            {[effects BY effects...]                                }
            {[POOL (varlist)...]                                    }
[/DESIGN={[effects {WITHIN} effects...]                          }]
            {        {W    }                                        }
            {[effect + effect...]                                   }
            {[factor (level)... [WITHIN factor (partition)...]]     }
            {[MUPLUS...]                                            }
            {[MWITHIN...]                                           }
            {[{term-to-be-tested} {AGAINST} {WITHIN   } {W } ]      }
            {[{term=n          } {VS     } {RESIDUAL } or {R } ]    }
            {                              {WR       }    {RW}      }
            {                              {n        }              }

**Defaults if subcommands are entered without specifications. In repeated
measures, SIGNIF(AVERF), not SIGNIF(MULTIV), is printed by default.
```

NLR

```
MODEL PROGRAM varname=value [varname=value ...
transformation commands]
[DERIVATIVES
transformation commands]
NLR depvar WITH varlist

[/OUTFILE=file]    [/FILE=file]

[/PRED=varname]

[/SAVE [PRED] [RESID [(varname)] [DERIVATIVES]]

[/CRITERIA=[ITER {100**}] [CKDER {0.5**}]]
                 {n   }          {n    }

   [SSCON {1E-8**}]  [PCON {1E-8**}]  [RCON {1E-8**}]]
         {n     }          {n     }          {n     }
**Default if subcommand is omitted.
```

PROBIT

```
PROBIT response count varname OF observation count varname
       WITH varlist [BY varname(min,max)]
[/MISSING={LISTWISE**}] [/MODEL={PROBIT**}] [/LOG[={10**  }]]
          {INCLUDE  }          {LOGIT   }         {2.718*}
          {DEFAULT  }          {BOTH    }         {base  }
                                                  {NONE  }

[/CRITERIA=[CONVERGE({0.001**})] [ITERATE({20**})] [P({0.15**})]]
                    {eps    }             {n  }       {p     }
[/NATRES[=c]]
[/PRINT=[ALL] [CI**] [FREQ**] [RMP**] [PARALL] [NONE] [DEFAULT]]
**Default if the subcommand is omitted.
*Default if the subcommand is included and the specification omitted.
```

SURVIVAL

```
SURVIVAL TABLES=survival varlist
               [BY independent varlist (min,max)...]
               [BY control varlist (min,max)...]
   /INTERVALS=THRU n BY a [THRU m BY b ...]
   /STATUS=status variable({min,max}) FOR {ALL             }
                           {value  }      {survival varlist}
[/STATUS=...]
[/PLOTS({ALL** })={ALL**           } BY {ALL**               }
        {LOGSURV} {survival varlist}    {independent varlist}
        {SURVIVAL}
        {HAZARD }         BY {ALL**           }]
        {DENSITY}            {control varlist}
[/PRINT={TABLE**}]
        {NOTABLE}
[/COMPARE={ALL**           } BY {ALL**               }
          {survival varlist}    {independent varlist}
          BY {ALL**           }]
             {control varlist}
[/CALCULATE=[{EXACT**    }] [PAIRWISE] [COMPARE]]
             {CONDITIONAL}
             {APPROXIMATE}
[/MISSING={GROUPWISE**}  [INCLUDE]]
          {LISTWISE  }
[/WRITE={NONE**}]
        {TABLES}
        {BOTH  }
**Default if the subcommand is omitted.
```